Understanding Human Differences

Multicultural Education for a Diverse America

Kent L. Koppelman
Professor Emeritus, University of Wisconsin-La Crosse

 Pearson

Director and Publisher: Kevin Davis
Portfolio Manager: Rebecca Fox-Gieg
Managing Content Producer: Megan Moffo
Content Producer: Faraz Sharique Ali
Portfolio Management Assistant: Maria Feliberty and Casey Coriell
Digital Development Editor: Krista (Slavicek) McMurray
Executive Product Marketing Manager: Christopher Barry
Executive Field Marketing Manager: Krista Clark
Procurement Specialist: Carol Melville
Cover Design: Pearson CSC, Jerilyn Bockorick
Cover Art: Agsandrew/Shutterstock
Media Producer: Autumn Benson
Full Service Vendor: Pearson CSC
Full Service Project Management: Pearson CSC, Gowri Duraiswamy
Editorial Project Manager: Pearson CSC, Jennylyn Rosiento
Printer-Binder: LSC Communications
Cover Printer: LSC Communications
Text Font: Palatino LT Pro

Library of Congress Cataloging-in-Publication Data

Names: Koppelman, Kent L., author.
Title: Understanding human differences : multicultural education for a
   diverse America / Kent L. Koppelman, Professor Emeritus, University of
   Wisconsin, La Crosse
Description: Sixth edition. | Boston : Pearson Education, 2018.
Identifiers: LCCN 2018041226 | ISBN 9780135196731 | ISBN 0135196736
Subjects: LCSH: Multicultural education—United States. |
   Discrimination—United States.
Classification: LCC LB1050 .R477 2019 | DDC 370.117—dc23 LC
record available at https://lccn.loc.gov/2018041226

ISBN 10:   0-13-519673-6
ISBN 13: 978-0-13-519673-1

Dedicated to
Burt Altman and Dick Rasmussen,
who demonstrated the meaning of the word good
to precede the nouns colleague, mentor, friend,
and human being.

Preface

Why Do We Need to Understand Diversity?

Americans live in the most racially, ethnically, and socially diverse country on earth. Yet too often we live, work, and play as if our own social, gender, or religious group is the only one that matters. To enjoy the advantages of our national diversity, it is necessary that Americans seek as many facts and consider as many issues as possible to enhance their ability to interact effectively with individuals from diverse groups. This text is not a collection of essays providing multiple perspectives on diversity—there are many books that already do that; instead, this text uses research to examine problems, perceptions, misperceptions, and the potential benefits of the diversity that exists in the United States. Understanding diversity is obviously a prerequisite for becoming an individual who values the diversity in American society.

If we are to value and respect the diversity represented by different groups in the United States, we can begin by learning how to value and respect opinions that differ from our own. It is not necessary to agree with everything a person might say, but it is necessary that when we disagree, we are able to express disagreement based upon a consideration of all available information and within a context of mutual respect.

The issues this text addresses are not new: Human beings have struggled with them in one form or another for centuries, as illustrated by the quotations from individuals of different eras that appear in each chapter. The quotations are not placed randomly in the text, but near a section of text that relates to each one. For example, near the section in Chapter 2 addressing the confusion about positive prejudices and explaining why prejudices are always negative, the quotation by Charles Lamb suggests that prejudices involve "likings and dislikings." Because Lamb was a respected writer of his era, his confusion about some prejudices being positive was not based on a lack of education or intellectual ability but instead illustrates how ancient this misperception is.

Since the first edition of *Understanding Human Differences* was published, the rights of various minority groups in the United States have become common topics for debate. The issue of *transgender soldiers* being able to serve openly in the U.S. military has become a controversy affecting the military, the president, and members of Congress. Students used to come to diversity classes oblivious of the issues, but that is less likely now, even though many diversity topics are still misunderstood.

New to This Edition

Two specific goals for this edition were (1) to include content that had not been addressed in previous editions, such as how American Indians are portrayed in K–12 curricula, research on the positive impact of immigrants on urban economies, the consequences for people with a disability of low wages paid to health care workers, and the reaction to the proposed travel ban against Muslims, and (2) to expand the coverage of critical issues such as new developments affecting income inequality, the incarceration of people of color and the school-to-prison pipeline, the ongoing struggle for civil rights for LGBT people, the economic and social consequences of closing urban schools, and the principles and successful practices of restorative justice programs in K–12 schools. Diversity issues are not static as new factors impact ongoing issues and as new issues emerge. It is important for all of us to try to be as knowledgeable as we can to participate in the discussions and debates on these issues.

As with any new edition, care has been taken to update statistics and sources and to find more current examples of issues, and this edition has expanded the number of examples pertaining to issues in K–12 schools. With regard to specific additions of content, the sixth edition of *Understanding Human Differences* includes the following:

- Update of racial profiling, especially police officers killing unarmed black men (Ch. 2 and 8)

- Impact of the 2016 election on student expressions of prejudice in K-12 schools (Ch. 3)

- Additional content on increased fears of undocumented workers about deportation (Ch. 4)

- New content on need for K-12 schools to prepare immigrant youth for college (Ch. 4)

- Added content on Religious Freedom Restoration Act and arguments for teaching about religion in K–12 public schools (Ch. 6)

- Expanded coverage of economic issues increasingly affecting elderly and young Americans (Ch. 9)

- Expanded coverage of health care issues for low-income families and for people with a disability (Ch. 9 and 12)

- Expanded information on influence of cultural body images on males (Ch. 10)

- Examination of arguments from opponents of same-sex marriage (Ch. 11)

- Added content on implications for people with a disability of low-wages paid to home care workers (Ch. 12)

- Update on Common Core State Standards and the political opposition (Ch. 13)

- Updated information on corporate efforts to promote diversity (Ch. 14)

- New information on gender issues in the military such as the Marine Corps sexist web site scandal (Ch. 14)

e-Text Enhancements

This text is available as an enhanced Pearson e-Text with the following features:

- **Application Exercises,** brand new to this edition, are tied to video and appear in every chapter. Students will be given a video to watch that ties into chapter concepts and theories, and a few short answer questions to respond to, and then, upon submission of their answers, they will be provided with author-written feedback. Application Exercises allow readers to take their understanding of chapter topics one step further with deeper analysis.

- **Video Examples** are available throughout the sixth edition. About three Video Examples are included in most chapters. In these videos, students will listen to experts, watch footage of diverse classrooms, listen to teachers and students from diverse classrooms, and watch videos that challenge biased behaviors and attitudes. Videos are accompanied by reflective questions.

- **Self-Check Quizzes** align with learning outcomes and appear as a link at the end of every major section within a chapter in the e-text edition. Using multiple choice questions, the quizzes allow readers to test their knowledge of the concepts, research, strategies, and practices discussed in each section.

Students should benefit from exploring all of these issues because each is relevant to today's society as well as the future society that they may influence. The first step in problem solving is to understand why a problem exists and how it is perpetuated; with that understanding, a person or a community, a state or a nation can implement solutions to address root causes of persistent problems. Consistent with this text's first five editions, the additional content offers information to enable students to understand problems or issues in society in order to find solutions, or in some

cases to describe solutions that have been proposed or implemented.

These features are only available in the Pearson e-Text, available exclusively from www.pearsonhighered.com/etextbooks or by ordering the Pearson e-Text plus print (ISBN 0135166926) or the Pearson eText Access Code Card (ISBN 0135170699).

Organization/The Conceptual Framework for this Text

Understanding human differences is an ongoing challenge. Initially, scholars focused on *individual attitudes and behaviors*; later, they described the influence of *cultural expectations* in shaping individual attitudes. Finally, scholars addressed *institutional policies and practices* in which either discrimination was intentional against minority groups or it was an unintentional outcome. Vega (1978) describes a conceptual framework incorporating these three elements to understand human differences and the oppression of minority groups by dominant groups. This conceptual framework provides the basis for the organization of this text as we examine individual attitudes and actions, the evolution of cultural biases, and the establishment of discriminatory institutional practices (see Figure F.1).

To understand human differences, Vega's conceptual framework allows us to analyze American cultural, individual, and institutional behaviors. In exploring culture, the objective is to describe *cultural norms and standards*. What images are associated with the ideal? Any culture

Figure F.1 A Conceptual Framework for the Study of Intergroup Relations

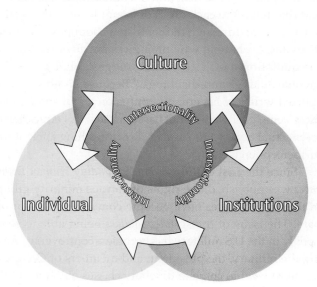

associates particular images with the ideal woman, the ideal man, and the ideal family. For many Americans, those images are primarily White middle-class people living in a nuclear family. Norms and standards are powerful determinants of individual expectations and behaviors, represented by the arrow pointing from culture to individual. Once we understand norms and standards, we can begin to understand what is meant by *cultural biases*. In a multicultural society, cultural biases can be detrimental to minority groups whose norms or standards do not conform to those of the dominant culture.

The influence of culture on individuals is powerful, as can be seen in the analysis of *individual beliefs, attitudes, values, opinions, actions, and inactions*; sometimes what a person chooses *not* to do reveals as much as his or her actions. Although individuals are influenced by their cultural norms and standards, the Vega conceptual framework portrays that arrow as double headed, meaning that when significant numbers of individuals accept cultural norms, express their agreement, and behave in accordance with them, the cultural norms and standards are reinforced. Any analysis of individual behavior must include the influence of prejudice on an individual's choices.

Finally, it is critical to analyze *institutional practices, policies*, and *standard operating procedures* that are influenced by cultural norms and standards as well as by individual attitudes and behavior. To the extent that they reflect cultural norms and standards as well as individual attitudes and behaviors, institutions also reinforce them. To relate institutions to human differences, the analysis must focus on discrimination, identifying both ways in which the institution intentionally discriminates against certain groups and ways in which the institution unintentionally advantages certain groups and disadvantages others. In the late 1980s, the term "intersectionality" was coined to address the social reality of overlapping identities based on factors such as race, gender, sexual orientation and social class and the unique forms of oppression occurring as a consequence of individuals having multiple social identities. The term was intended to expand our understanding of the complexity of oppression and the need for anti-oppressive awareness and activity to go beyond the rigid, established categories (Robertson, 2017). This term is being included in the Vega conceptual framework for the 6th edition of this textbook in recognition of its usefulness in understanding how multiple identities influence oppression. Although the Vega conceptual framework describes the intricate relationship among the three areas—cultural, individual, and institutional—chapter narratives of necessity deal with each discretely. Readers are asked to keep in mind the double-headed arrows signifying that all three areas are interlocked to create the following relationships:

1. Cultural norms and standards influence and are reinforced by individual attitudes and behaviors and institutional policies and procedures.

2. Individual attitudes and behaviors influence and are reinforced by cultural norms and standards and by institutional policies and procedures.

3. Institutional policies and procedures influence and are reinforced by cultural norms and standards and individual attitudes and beliefs.

The four sections of this text that relate to the conceptual framework are as follows.

- Section 1 focuses on the *individual* by exploring personal values, interpersonal communication, and the way an individual develops negative attitudes toward other people based on perceptions of group identity (leading to bias, stereotypes, prejudice, and negative behavior toward members of these groups).

- Section 2 focuses on *culture* by examining the pattern of historical responses in American society toward immigration and the increased racial and religious diversity that has always been a consequence of this immigration. The final chapter of this section describes how those who are pluralism advocates are engaged in efforts to reject this historical pattern of discrimination, but as the following section illustrates, discrimination remains a problem in our society.

- Section 3 describes interrelationships among culture, individuals, and institutions to produce discrimination based on race, gender, social class, sexual orientation, and disability, with institutional issues being a major focus of this section.

- Section 4 addresses changes that have been implemented to reduce levels of individual prejudice and institutional discrimination, focusing on major institutions in our society such as K–12 schools, higher education, business, the media, and the military; their pluralistic policies and practices are designed to benefit from the diversity that exists in our society. This conceptual framework helps us to appreciate not only the changes that are occurring but also the ongoing issues that illustrate how much further we have to go.

Before concluding this explanation of Vega's conceptual framework, consider this example to illustrate how interreliant culture is with individual and institutional behaviors. Although many forms of family exist in the United States, our cultural bias is for the nuclear family (the norm). Influenced by this cultural bias, Americans tend to form nuclear families. Even when people with a cultural tradition of extended families immigrate to the United States, they tend to form nuclear families within a few generations, sometimes reversing convention with older adult parents receiving care in nursing homes rather than at home.

American institutions have encouraged the formation of nuclear families because they are more able to relocate in an age in which mobility of workers is highly desirable. In an analysis of discrimination, problems may emerge for minority subcultures that value extended families if they maintain that value rather than adjust to the cultural norm. As this example illustrates, Vega's conceptual framework helps clarify the complexity of intergroup relations by describing the related factors involved in the oppression of minority groups by a dominant group.

Inquiry Approach/ Discussion Exercises

Chapter narratives in this text are presented in an inquiry format. After a brief introduction, each chapter consists of related questions with responses based on research from a variety of disciplines and on author expertise. As references illustrate, information for this text has been collected from studies in a broad array of behavioral sciences, including education, psychology, sociology, anthropology, history, science, and literature. Although sources cited are from relatively recent publications, some older sources are also included either because they are still highly regarded in the field or simply because an author expressed a conclusion replicated by other research but not stated with as much clarity.

Discussion Exercises

To reinforce the inquiry approach, exercises for group discussion are provided at the end of each chapter to examine serious ethical questions. Based on specific issues, activities encourage readers to reflect on and discuss aspects of issues that involve ethical or moral dilemmas. The exercises are not designed to manipulate readers into finding a "politically correct" solution; rather, they enable students to hear the variety of responses from others and appreciate the complexity of individual, institutional, and cultural issues in America today.

The Intent of This Text

The information provided in this text is intended to challenge readers to think and talk about issues that each of us must consider as citizens in a multicultural society; this text is not necessarily intended to change reader values but to challenge attitudes based on incomplete or erroneous information (see Chapter 1 for a description of the difference

between *values* and *attitudes*). Diversity brings benefits as well as challenges, but the surest way to enjoy the benefits is to meet the challenges with a firm foundation of knowledge and insight that is based on research from all behavioral sciences. Once students have read this text, the primary goal will be realized if they have gained a better understanding of the issues addressed. Whether or not that is accompanied by changes in attitudes is up to each individual; and there is an Attitude Inventory in the Instructor's Manual that accompanies this text. Your instructor may ask for your cooperation in taking this inventory before, during, or on completion of the course.

The intent of this text is to clarify our understanding of human differences and the role they play in interpersonal and intergroup relations. The Vega conceptual framework allows us to recognize how the interlocking circles of cultural biases, individual attitudes and actions, and institutional policies and practices have produced inequities that continue to polarize and all too often prevent Americans from achieving ideals first expressed over two centuries ago when dreamers imagined a radical new concept: a nation where each person would be given the freedom to be whoever he or she wanted to be.

Support Materials for Instructors

The following resources are available for instructors to download on www.pearsonhighered.com/educators. Instructors enter the author or title of this text, select this particular edition of the text, and then click on the "resources" tab to log in and download textbook supplements.

Instructor's Resource Manual and Test Bank (0135170567)

The Instructor's Resource Manual and Test Bank includes a wealth of interesting ideas and activities designed to help instructors teach the course. Each chapter contains learning outcomes and a comprehensive test bank containing multiple choice questions, discussion questions, exercises, and suggested readings. There is also an Attitude Inventory and instructions for its potential use.

PowerPoint™ Slides (0135170575)

Designed for teachers using the text, the PowerPoint™ Presentation consists of a series of slides that can be shown as is or used to make handouts. The presentation highlights key concepts and major topics for each chapter.

Acknowledgments

I want to thank Tess Cameron for her assistance in revising Chapter 10 on sexism, and Alison Leonard for assisting with resources for the e-text. I am also grateful to Robin DiAngelo for her contributions to individual and cultural racism in Chapter 8. I also want to extend a special thanks to Jan Koppelman for her assistance on numerous aspects of revising this text and improving both content and illustrations. I am grateful to my editor, Rebecca Fox-Gieg, for her advice and assistance. Thanks also to the reviewers for this edition: E. Jean Swindle, Unversity of Alabama; Kelly Jennings-Towle, University of Central Florida; Mary Frances Mattson, Georgia State University.

Brief Contents

Contents

SECTION 2

Cultural Foundations of Oppression in the United States

SECTION 3
Contemporary Dilemmas for Intergroup Relations

Chapter 1
Understanding Ourselves and Others: Clarifying Values and Language

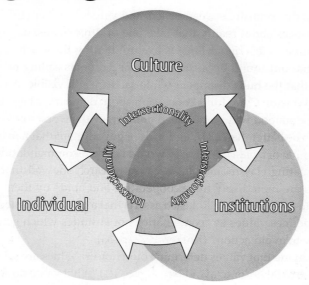

 ## Learning Outcomes

After reading this chapter you will know and be able to:

1.1 Explain how Americans learn their beliefs and values, and the role of these beliefs and values in shaping behavior.

1.2 Provide meaningful definitions and distinctions for two sets of related terms: (1) *bias, stereotype, prejudice, bigotry*, and *discrimination*, and (2) *race, ethnicity, nationality*, and *minority group*.

> "I have striven not to laugh at human actions, not to weep at them, nor to hate them, but to understand them."
>
> — BARUCH SPINOZA (1632–1677)

If we take Spinoza's quote seriously, we need to understand all kinds of diversity—including opinions, appearances, values, and beliefs—as well as the categories of race, ethnicity, social class, gender, sexual orientation, and disability. Because America is not only a diverse society but also a democratic one, we have the freedom to choose our perceptions, assumptions, and behaviors. The study of human diversity obviously requires an examination of social groups that encounter discrimination. However, in addition to focusing on the sociocultural differences among groups, we must also acknowledge the importance of individual differences. Each of us wants to be recognized as an individual. Our experiences are affected by multiple factors, including whether we are White or an individual of color; female or male; from a low-, middle-, or upper-income family; or from a rural, suburban, or urban home. Each individual's opinion offers a unique perspective that only the individual expressing it can fully understand. The task for us as listeners is to understand as best as we can the beliefs and values articulated by the individuals we encounter.

The Role of Beliefs and Values in Human Differences

How do scholars distinguish between beliefs and values? Kniker (1977) suggests that **beliefs** are inferences about reality that take one of three forms: descriptive, evaluative, or prescriptive. A *descriptive belief* is exemplified by those who argued that the world was not flat but round because they observed boats sailing off to the horizon and recognized that the hulls disappear while sails are still visible. An *evaluative belief* is illustrated by Winston Churchill's conclusion about democracy based on his reading of history: He understood why some called democracy the worst form of government, but he found it to be better than all other forms of government that had been attempted thus far. An example of a *prescriptive belief* would be the recommendation that students take a role in creating classroom rules because research showed that students who help create rules are more likely to be cooperative and abide by them. All beliefs are predispositions to types of action. Rokeach asserts that a cluster of related beliefs creates an **attitude**; he defines **values** as "combinations of attitudes which generate action or deliberate choice to avoid action" (Kniker, 1977, p. 33).

Rokeach is saying that values determine our choices: Values are the foundation for actions we choose to take—or to avoid (see Figure 1.1). What value do Americans place on wealth? For some, money and possessions are the primary measures of success. They admire others who are rich and successful, and they define their own worth by their income and wealth. For others, money is not a priority. Their main concern is to make enough money to support a comfortable lifestyle, however they choose to define it. There are also people who believe the biblical caution that love of money is "the root of all evil" and refuse to let wealth play an important role in their choices. Their behavior is a reflection of their values. While serving as vice president to John Adams, Thomas Jefferson was once turned away from a prominent hotel because his clothes were soiled and he had no servants with him. After the proprietor was told whom he had refused, he sent word to Jefferson, offering him any room in the hotel. Having been accepted into another hotel, Jefferson sent a reply politely refusing the offer of a room, noting that if the hotel proprietor did not have a room for a "dirty farmer," then he must not have a room for the vice president either (Botkin, 1957).

What is the relationship between values and behaviors?

America has a history of social commentary on the role of values in people's lives, and scholars engage in research examining the relationship between expressed values and behavior. Searching for consistent patterns in values research is challenging. However, one theme from social critics has been repeatedly supported by research and case study: There is a consistent inconsistency between what we say we value and our actual behavior (Aronson, 2012; Lefkowitz, 1997; Myrdal, 1944; Terry, Hogg, & Duck, 1999).

Figure 1.1 The Relationship of Values, Beliefs, Attitudes, and Choices

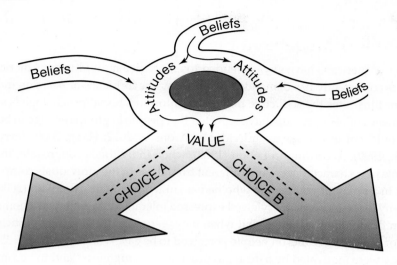

The tendency for Americans to say we believe in a certain value and then engage in contradictory behavior is a curious and yet consistent pattern. Contradictory behavior by human beings has been criticized and even ridiculed by essayists, novelists, and observers of American society. In 1938, the Carnegie Foundation invited Swedish social economist Gunnar Myrdal to the United States to conduct a study on the "American Negro Problem." Myrdal (1944) went far beyond a study of racial relations: He attempted to identify and understand the core values of American society.

In his analysis of Myrdal's research, Risberg (1978) identified nine values that Americans perceived as defining their culture:

1. Worth and dignity of the individual
2. Equality
3. Inalienable rights to life, liberty, property, and the pursuit of happiness
4. Rights to freedom of speech, press, religion, assembly, and private association
5. Consent of the governed
6. Majority rule
7. Rule of law
8. Due process of law
9. Community and national welfare. (pp. 5–6)

These identified core values seem to be accurate, especially if we compare American culture to other cultures. For example, many nations around the world put great emphasis on the collective good, but in the United States we tend to focus on personal worth and to reward individual achievements. Expectations of equality and of having "inalienable rights" are expressed in founding documents such as the Declaration of Independence, and our various freedoms are guaranteed by the Bill of Rights to the U.S. Constitution. Our representative form of democracy is based on the assumption that local, state, and national governments will be elected by the majority, with an expectation that they will rule with the consent of the governed for the welfare of the community, state, and nation. Finally, being ruled by laws and being given a chance to resolve issues by making our case in court (due process) was established to protect our citizens from the whims of the wealthy and powerful (a reaction to oppressive behavior from aristocrats and monarchs in the past). These values have historically defined America as a society, and they represent beliefs that all Americans share.

Despite the consensus about them, Myrdal observed that all of the values were regularly contradicted by American behavior. He provided examples from his observations, primarily based on race relations, to illustrate his conclusion.

What inconsistencies exist between American values and American behaviors?

Although Americans have always tended to emphasize individuality, American society quite consistently has demanded conformity. The influence of peers on individual behavior illustrates the seductive power of conformity. Social psychologists studying the influence of peer pressure have reported that people in groups engage in behaviors they would not undertake as individuals (Aronson, 2012; Haag, 2000; Terry, Hogg, & Duck, 1999). According to LeBon (1968), when individuals congregate, the group "presents new characteristics very different from those of the individuals composing it" (p. 27). In a study of young men who had assaulted gay males, Franklin (2000) found that many of the men she interviewed expressed tolerant attitudes toward homosexuality even though they admitted that when they were with friends, they participated in verbal or physical assaults on people perceived to be gay. When questioned, 35 percent said they were motivated by a desire to prove their "toughness" and to become closer to the friends who engaged in antigay behavior.

"The primal principle of democracy is the worth and dignity of the individual."
— EDWARD BELLAMY (1850–1898)

Contradictory behavior also is illustrated in the belief that Americans value equality. The Declaration of Independence proclaims that the United States is founded on the belief that "all men are created equal," and yet the man who wrote that statement owned slaves. During World War II, boxing champions Joe Louis and Sugar Ray Robinson signed up for military service. At a bus stop in Alabama, a military policeman insisted that the two "colored soldiers" move to the rear of the station. When they refused, they were arrested. After an officer had reprimanded them, Louis responded, "Sir, I'm a soldier like any other American soldier. I don't want to be pushed to the back because I'm a Negro" (Mead, 1985, p. 231). Despite the gains made from the 1964 Civil Rights Act, the United States has still not achieved the goal of racial equality.

This nation also was founded on the rule of law and the belief in a justice system that would be fair to everyone, yet people with wealth and status are able to circumvent this ideal. One of many examples challenging this belief occurred in Texas in 2013. A mother and daughter tried to assist a woman whose car had stalled on the side of a highway, and a youth pastor also stopped to help. Suddenly a pickup veered off the road, smashing into the cars and killing the four people. Two people in the back of the pickup were also injured; one had a brain injury that deprived him of the ability to move or talk. The teenage driver, Ethan Couch, had a blood alcohol level of 0.24, three times the legal limit. When the case came to trial, the boy's wealthy father hired an expensive legal defense team. A psychologist testified that Ethan was a victim of "affluenza," describing his misbehavior as a result of having wealthy, privileged parents who never set limits for him. After the trial, the judge insisted that the "affluenza" claim had no influence on her ruling; however, as punishment for killing four innocent people and injuring two others, Ethan Couch was sentenced to no jail time and only 10 days' probation. In response to outrage over this light punishment, the judge modified her sentence to order Couch to a residential treatment facility. The judge did not indicate what length of time the teenager would be required to stay there (Ford, 2014). In contrast to Ethan Couch, there are a lot of poor people in prison today because they could not afford to hire the skilled lawyers available to wealthy clients who are more likely to be successful in getting desired outcomes in court.

Even when wealthy people are convicted and incarcerated, they may have a very different experience than the average individual. Since the 1990s, certain Southern California city jails and prisons have provided upscale cells for affluent prisoners. For $45 to $175 a day, incarcerated people can have luxuries such as an iPod, a cell phone, an exercise bike, DVDs, or a computer. They may also request a private cell, have their meals catered, or be placed in a work release program depending on what they can afford. In contrast, jail conditions in Los Angeles County offer a compelling reason to avoid them. A *Michigan Law Review* article described the fate of 21,000 inmates who were each housed with three other prisoners in filthy cells (originally built for two people); 85 percent of these inmates were pretrial detainees, and most were arrested on nonviolent charges. In 2007, over 2000 prisoners in the Pasadena jail paid about $234,000 for what some have called "incarceration vacations" (Clark, 2014). Other states are copying the practices of California city jails and state prisons, and these luxury jail cells illustrate that our justice system does not dispense punishment equally.

What Myrdal observed and reported in the 1940s continues to be true: As individuals and as a society, Americans behave inconsistently, engaging in actions that contradict expressed values. Myrdal's observations reinforced what American social critics had been saying for years and what research and case studies have documented. These observations require some explanation, and it seems logical to begin by examining how people choose their values.

> "The law, in its majestic equality, forbids the rich as well as the poor to sleep under bridges, to beg in the streets, and to steal bread."
>
> — ANATOLE FRANCE (1844–1924)

Are values individually chosen, or are we taught to accept certain values?

The way American values are taught plays a major role in our acceptance of them. Individuals, subcultures, and institutions are involved in teaching values; parents, teachers, peers, clergy, relatives, and youth counselors are just a few examples. By studying how individuals and organizations in America teach values to children and youth, Raths, Harmin, and Simon (1978) identified seven traditional approaches.

The first way to teach values is to (1) *set an example*. Parents and teachers are supposed to be role models for children and youth. Young people are also told to emulate various individuals—from historical leaders to contemporary athletes—whose achievements are attributed to practicing certain values. In similar fashion, schools and other organizations use (2) *rules and regulations* to promote certain behaviors in children and youth (and adults) that represent important values. Learning punctuality is considered important enough that teachers send children to the principal's office for a tardy pass if they are late for class. This example is especially interesting because the child securing the tardy pass from the principal is kept away from the classroom for additional time while the other children engage in some kind of learning activity, which is supposedly the primary purpose for requiring students to attend school.

Another approach is to (3) *persuade or convince* others to accept certain values. Respectful discussions with reasonable arguments can be an effective means of convincing someone that the values being espoused are appropriate for living a good life. Related to this is (4) an *appeal to conscience* in which a parent or teacher may challenge a child or youth who seems to advocate an inappropriate value or belief. This approach is illustrated when a teacher responds to a student making an inappropriate comment by saying, "You don't really believe that, do you?" The point of such questions is not to give the student a chance to explain or defend what he or she said but to produce a subtle and insistent form of moral pressure intended to coerce the student into rejecting an unacceptable point of view.

Parents often teach values by offering (5) *limited choices*. By limiting choices, parents intend to manipulate children into making acceptable decisions. If a mother values cooperation and tells her children that family members should share in household duties, what can she do if one of her children refuses? She asks one child to wash dishes twice a week, but the child hates to wash dishes and refuses. The mother might say, "Either you agree to wash dishes twice a week, or you will not be allowed to play with your friends after school." The child is restricted to two options in the hope that he or she will choose to do the dishes, reinforcing the mother's original objective of wanting her children to learn the value of sharing domestic responsibilities.

Organizations have employed the approach of (6) *inspiring people* to embrace certain values, often by sponsoring a "retreat" with inspirational or motivational speakers or a social function where the combination of speakers, films, and activities is designed to have emotional or spiritual impact. Although religious groups employ this approach, corporations sponsor such events to inspire employees to work harder to achieve personal or group goals and, in doing so, contribute to the achievement of organizational goals.

Some religious groups and secular organizations emphasize (7) *religious or cultural dogma* to teach values. To accept beliefs without questioning them is to be **dogmatic**. If a Christian with dogmatic beliefs were questioned, he or she might say, "That's what the Bible says," or, similarly, a dogmatic Muslim might say, "This is what it says in the Qu'ran," even though for centuries people have interpreted the teachings of Jesus and Muhammad in different ways. Even early Christians held widely divergent views on the meanings of the life and words of Jesus (Pagels, 2006). Dogmatic beliefs stifle debate by emphasizing tradition: "This is what we have always believed."

Dogmatic beliefs also can be found in a secular context. When someone questions a value based on cultural beliefs, a dogmatic response might be "We've always done it this way." The appeal to tradition in opposing change has been employed in such controversies as using Native American mascots for school sports teams and including the Confederate flag in the official flags of some southern states. Only in 2003 did Georgia change its state flag to remove the Confederate symbol, and in 2015, South Carolina finally removed the Confederate flag from its statehouse grounds after a White supremacist murdered nine Black people in a church.

Understanding how values are taught provides some insight in answering the question about why people consistently behave in ways that contradict their expressed values. Each of the seven traditional approaches to teaching values seems to be based on a common assumption, and that assumption might explain the inconsistencies.

> "When people are free to do as they please they usually imitate each other."
>
> — ERIC HOFFER (1902–1983)

How does the way values are taught explain the inconsistency between values and behavior?

What do the seven traditional approaches to teaching values have in common? They are all based on an assumption that certain prescribed values should be taught and that the individuals being instructed should accept them. The individual teaching values—the teacher, parent, Scout leader, minister, priest, rabbi, imam, or employer—knows which values are appropriate. The goal is to persuade the student, child, parishioner, or worker to accept those values. In actuality, each approach is a form of **indoctrination**, where the intent is to dictate cultural values that must be accepted rather than assist people in deciding what is right and wrong (see Figure 1.2).

This assumption shared by all seven traditional approaches to teaching values in America caused Raths et al. (1978) to question whether all approaches were primarily successful in convincing people to *say* the right thing, yet not *do* the right thing. If this is true, there are important implications for how values should be taught. It is neither ethical nor prudent to teach values that are advocated but not practiced in our everyday lives. This teaches hypocrisy, not values. If the goal of teaching is to help learners understand what they genuinely believe and choose values to incorporate into their behavior, then those who teach must recognize the limitations of coercing children and youth to feign acceptance of prescribed values. For Americans to behave consistently with our expressed values, we must demonstrate authentic commitment to them.

Why should anyone be concerned about inconsistencies between values and behavior?

If we understand our values and consistently act on them, it is more likely that our choices will reflect our highest ideals. We are constantly confronted with ethical dilemmas that challenge our values and require us to make moral choices. A *New York Times* reporter

Figure 1.2 "The First Thanksgiving"

Often found in public school textbooks, illustrations such as this one suggest that Native Americans and colonists had a peaceful, harmonious relationship, but the reality was one of consistent conflict as Indians were pushed off their lands and forced to move westward.

SOURCE: "The First Thanksgiving," painting by Jean Leon Gerome Ferris (1863–1930). Library of Congress Prints and Photographs Division [Jean Leon Gerome Ferris/LC-USZ62-1234].

interviewed a national sales manager for Wachovia who was living in an upper-middle-class suburb of Atlanta—a homogeneous community where everyone was of the same race and social class, and residents even shared similar opinions on a variety of issues. At his corporate worksite, the manager said the importance of diversity was emphasized: "At work, diversity is one of the biggest things we work on" (Kilborn, 2005, p. 157). Yet in his private life, the manager admitted that he and his suburban neighbors were "never challenged" to learn about other groups, so they did not. The contrast between what happens at work and what takes place at home reveals an inconsistency that could call into question the sincerity of the manager's commitment to diversity. Another example is that many people assume that well-educated White people harbor fewer prejudices than poorly educated White people, but studies have found that highly educated White people are not more likely to support proposed policies to address racial inequality than White people who are less well educated (Wodtke, 2012). In contrast, there is the example of Bono, lead singer for the rock group U2, who has used his position and wealth to lobby for human rights. Accepting an NAACP Image Award in 2007 for his work on poverty issues and the AIDS crisis in Africa, Bono identified Martin Luther King Jr. as someone who inspired him, and he went on to say:

> The poor are where God lives. God is in the slums, in the cardboard boxes where the poor play house. God is where the opportunity is lost and lives are shattered. God is with the mother who has infected her child with a virus that will take both their lives. God is under the rubble in the cries we hear during wartime. God, my friends, is with the poor. God is with us if we are with them. This is not a burden. This is an adventure. (Gamber, 2007, p. 37)

Should parents rather than schools teach values to children?

The question of who should teach values is a rhetorical one. Both parents and schools in America are expected to contribute to the development of children's value systems.

We constantly encounter people who reveal their values in everyday words and actions. Teachers model their values regardless of whether they consciously choose to do so. The question is not whether values should be taught but how they should be taught.

Of the many approaches Kniker (1977) identified for teaching values, the most effective allow children and youth opportunity for discussion and debate, employing activities that stimulate them to think about their beliefs, hear other perspectives, and consider what effect different decisions could have for others as well as themselves. Discussing values, related behaviors, and possible consequences exposes young people to perspectives of others; evaluating arguments about values from their peers can help them decide which ones seem more attractive, compelling, and meaningful. In the process, they learn not only what values are important to them but also how to accept people with values different from their own.

As adults we do not tend to make decisions about values at a particular point in time and then never change our minds. Our values are based on beliefs and attitudes that change frequently, resulting in an ongoing process in which decisions are made and reevaluated throughout our lives. Culture, geographical location, parents, and life experiences influence each individual's decisions. Each individual must determine what he or she believes is best, and the cumulative decisions individuals make influence the evolution of our society (Bellah, Madsen, Sullivan, Swidler, & Tipton, 1991; Lappe, 1989; Zinn, 1990). School classrooms are part of this journey. Teachers must present students with moral dilemmas and trust that when our children and youth are given the freedom to choose, they will be capable of making ethical decisions.

> "Consciously we teach what we know; unconsciously we teach who we are."
>
> — DON HAMACHEK (CONTEMPORARY)

What problems can interfere with making ethical decisions?

One of the main problems in making ethical decisions about human differences is confusion concerning the language employed to address those differences. Many essential words or phrases are either unfamiliar terms or common expressions with a history of misuse. Confused language often reflects the discomfort people feel toward sensitive issues. For example, the word *racism* did not appear in most English dictionaries until the 1960s. As the civil rights movement gained momentum and attracted considerable attention from the media and people across America, we could no longer avoid using the term. Similarly, the word *sexism* did not appear in dictionaries until the early 1970s, as the women's movement became increasingly successful at bringing issues concerning the treatment of women to public attention (Miller & Swift, 2000).

Using inaccurate or ambiguous language creates problems when we are addressing sensitive, uncomfortable issues. To be coherent and meaningful in our discussion of human differences, we must clarify our vocabulary and agree to specific appropriate meanings for significant words and concepts.

Application Exercise 1.1

In this video, a class discusses values. Think about the values being expressed by both the students and the teachers. Review the video and complete the activity.

✓ Self-Check 1.1 Complete this self-check quiz to check your understanding of the traditional ways values have been taught in the United States, what all of these approaches have in common, and how this common factor contributes to the phenomenon of Americans consistently engaging in actions inconsistent with American values.

Defining Terms Related to Human Differences

One would expect that consultation with any scholarly authority would provide definitions for a term such as *prejudice*, but the scholarly world is not free from confusion. Some textbooks have defined *prejudice* as a prejudgment that could be either positive or negative; this definition confuses prejudice with *bias*, a feeling in favor of—or opposed to—anything or anyone. *Stereotypes* always refer to people and also can be positive or negative. As with stereotypes, prejudice always refers to people, but prejudice is always negative.

This chapter includes a series of definitions intended to clarify terms referring to human differences. Definitions throughout the text are based on the work of scholars from various fields in the behavioral sciences, including racial and ethnic studies, women's studies, education, sociology, and anthropology. Unless cited, definitions reflect a distillation of common themes identified in several scholarly sources (Andrzejewski, 1996; Feagin & Feagin, 2010; Herdt, 1997; Levin & Levin, 1982; Schaefer, 2015; Simpson & Yinger, 1985). The following series of definitions makes distinctions and indicates relationships between the terms.

> **Bias** A preference or inclination, favorable or unfavorable, that inhibits impartial judgment.
>
> **Stereotype** A positive or negative trait or traits ascribed to a certain group and to most members of that group.
>
> **Prejudice** A negative attitude toward a group and individuals perceived to be members of that group; being predisposed to behave negatively toward members of a group.
>
> **Bigotry** Extreme negative attitudes leading to hatred of a group and individuals regarded as members of the group.
>
> **Discrimination** Actions or practices carried out by a member or members of dominant groups or their representatives that have a differential and negative impact on a member or members of subordinate groups.

Notice that each of the first four terms just listed represents attitudes of greater intensity than the previous one. Regarding bias and stereotypes, attitudes can be either positive or negative and can influence an individual's perceptions of an individual or group. Having a *bias* related to a group creates an inclination to favor or dislike an individual from that group. (See Table 1.1.) *Stereotyping* a group indicates an expectation that most members of the group will behave in certain positive or negative ways. No positive option exists for prejudice or bigotry because of the greater intensity of these attitudes. *Prejudices* are negative attitudes based on a prejudgment of a group; *bigotry* involves hatred and represents a harsher form of prejudgment against an individual or group. Note that whereas bias, stereotype, prejudice, and bigotry relate to attitudes, discrimination refers to actions taken that demonstrate negative attitudes. An individual can have a bias, stereotype, or prejudice, or even be a bigot and still not engage in any kind of negative or positive behavior. Unless an individual's attitudes are publicly expressed, others may not be aware of them. Discrimination can be seen and documented, and it can cause physical and emotional harm.

How do negative attitudes develop?

We learn various biases, stereotypes, and prejudices as we grow up. We can be biased in favor of or against certain kinds of foods, categories of books, styles of clothing, or types of personalities. Bias can affect decisions about what we eat, read, or wear; it can influence our choice of friends. A stereotype assumes that individuals possess certain human traits simply because they are members of a particular group. Some traits are regarded as positive—such as Black people have rhythm, Asian people are good in math—and other traits are viewed as negative—certain groups are lazy, shiftless, dishonest, or violent. Although negative stereotypes are regarded as unacceptable, many people accept positive stereotypes. The problem with positive stereotypes is that they cause us to have specific expectations for individuals and groups even though we have little or no evidence for these assumptions. A positive stereotype may sabotage the process of forming a realistic and accurate perception of an individual, as is illustrated in the following example.

Table 1.1 Examples of Bias

The following selection comes from a list of 27 biases:

1. **Family Bias:** Believing information from family members without seeking evidence to support the accuracy of their information.
2. **Attractiveness Bias:** Believing information provided by attractive people.
3. **Confirmation Bias:** Believing information that reinforces beliefs already held and ignoring information that contradicts these beliefs.
4. **Self-Serving Bias:** Believing information that is beneficial to self-interest and goals.
5. **In-Group Bias:** Believing information from people who are members of our group (e.g., friends, co-workers, racial or ethnic group, etc.).
6. **Expectancy Bias:** Tending to pursue information and draw conclusions that reinforce our beliefs when looking for information (or even conducting research).
7. **Pleasure Bias:** Assuming that pleasant experiences offer greater insights for strengthening our beliefs than unpleasant experiences.
8. **Perceptual Bias:** Assuming that our own perceptions and experience of reality reveal objective truths to confirm our beliefs.
9. **Perseverance Bias:** Perpetuating our beliefs even after encountering information that contradicts those beliefs.
10. **Uncertainty Bias:** Choosing to believe or disbelieve information rather than remain uncertain because people tend to be uncomfortable with ambiguity.

SOURCE: Adapted from Newburg and Waldman (2006), *Why We Believe What We Believe*. Free Press.

During a coffee break at a Midwestern university, three Asian American women employed by a student services office reminisced about their undergraduate days. They complained about how difficult math classes had been and laughed as they recalled some of their coping strategies. The student services director, an African American, walked into the room, overheard what they were saying, and interrupted their discussion to chastise them for "putting yourselves down." He said they should stop. He also said he was disappointed in them and departed.

After the director left, the three women initially were too surprised to speak. Once they started talking, they realized they were angry because his comments suggested that he assumed they all had good math skills and were not being honest when discussing their lack of math ability. The women had thought the director viewed them as individuals, and they were angry and hurt when they realized that he had allowed a stereotype to distort his perception of them. They were especially upset because they had not expected an individual of color to believe in a stereotype—even a positive one about the math abilities of Asian people—but apparently he did.

One of the ways that positive or negative stereotypes are reinforced is a result of **confirmation bias**. Newberg and Waldman (2006) describe *confirmation bias* as the tendency to accept information reinforcing your beliefs while ignoring information contradicting those beliefs. It is a bias with a long history in human attitudes and behavior. In 1620, philosopher Francis Bacon observed: "the human understanding, once it has adopted an opinion, collects any instances that confirm it, and though the contrary instances may be more numerous and weightier, it either does not notice them or else rejects them, in order that the opinion will remain unshaken" (Mlodinow, 2008, p. 189).

How does confirmation bias influence people, and can it be overcome?

Confirmation bias not only causes people to look for evidence that reinforces their views, it also causes them to interpret ambiguous information in a way that strengthens their preconceived notions. The latter is especially disturbing since accurate information about most issues is likely to have some degree of ambiguity that should stimulate critical thinking and perhaps lead to new insights. Instead, confirmation bias pushes people along well-worn paths, diminishing their ability to think critically and solve problems effectively. Kolbert (2017) cites a Stanford study in which some participants supported the death penalty and some did not. All participants were given a packet of research in which half of the packet supported the death penalty as a deterrent to crime and half refuted this claim. Participants were instructed on the weaknesses of each study, but in the end, participants who had held opinions about the death penalty prior to being given the research said that reading these studies had reinforced their views. This outcome is especially disturbing because we hope that reason is used to make good judgments and not simply reinforce biases that lead to a greater polarization.

Kolbert (2017) also reported on a study asking participants for their views on social issues such as favoring a single-payer health-care system, rating how strongly they agreed or disagreed. Afterward they were asked to explain in detail how they would implement proposals related to each issue. This proved difficult, and when asked again to rate their views, they tended to rate themselves as less intense than before. In another study with positive implications, participants were given a bogus personality test and then half were randomly identified as "open-minded" or "closed-minded." Almost all of the participants accepted these identifications as accurate. They were then given two controversial issues and asked to comment on both. The students identified as "closed-minded" typically articulated one point of view on each issue, whereas the "open-minded" participants tended to make comments that reflected both sides of the issues. By using learning activities that promote being "open-minded," teachers could help students to take account of confirmation bias. Both studies support the approach of science teachers who ask students to question their assumptions, beliefs, and theories, an approach that could be used in other disciplines. Mlodinow (2008) recommends that teachers ask students to engage in research to find evidence that contradicts their views as well as search for supportive evidence. Aronson (2012) described a study suggesting how confirmation bias could be used to achieve a positive outcome. Participants were given a bogus personality test, and half were randomly identified as either "open-minded" or "closed-minded." Almost all of the participants accepted these identifications as accurate. They were then given two controversial issues and asked to comment on both. The students identified as "closed-minded" articulated one point of view on each issue, whereas the "open-minded" participants tended to make comments that reflected both sides of the issues. This suggests that if schools and other institutions engage students in learning activities designed to promote being "open-minded," students could be taught to be aware of and take into account the influence of confirmation bias. Mlodinow (2008) recommends that we also teach students to search just as actively for information that contradicts their views as they do for evidence that supports them. Teaching science offers an opportunity to reinforce an open-minded approach because scientists are taught to question their assumptions, beliefs, and theories; this approach could be used in other disciplines as well.

If the influence of confirmation bias is reduced, the power and pervasiveness of stereotypes should also be diminished. On the other hand, negative attitudes reinforced by confirmation bias can strengthen prejudices, which are always negative, and may result in negative behavior. If an individual engages in negative actions toward a group, this usually reinforces his or her negative attitudes about that group. If left unchallenged, prejudice can transform an individual into a bigot whose hatred of others could even lead to violence. Prejudice and bigotry toward others are usually based on human differences such as race, ethnicity, or nationality.

Video Example 1.1

This video explores the challenges of cultural bias. When the speaker talks about the biases of children and teachers, consider the kinds of bias from Table 1.1 that she might be referring to. Thinking about the various kinds of bias that both children and teachers may exhibit in schools, what are some ways in which teachers can model appropriate behavior that limits that kind of bias?

What are the differences among race, ethnicity, and nationality?

Race is not a scientific concept but a social reality dictated by the color of someone's skin, even though skin color as a basis for human categorization is absurd. African Americans are identified as black, yet the skin color for many African Americans is more accurately described as brown. White is an inaccurate description of skin color for White Americans. At an elementary school in Minneapolis, young children created a poster with the title "The Human Rainbow." The first band of their rainbow was colored with a light brown crayon, making a very pale brown band, and each band above it was a slightly darker shade of brown until the outer band, which was colored in such a dark brown color that it almost looked black. The children had created a realistic way of representing and understanding the effect of melanin on the color of human skin.

The concept of race is both easy and difficult to discuss. Most Americans believe they know the meaning of the term, yet there is no specific set of racial categories that is acceptable to the scientific community. In 1758, Carolus Linnaeus proposed the first racial classifications based largely on human geographical origins, but as Gould (2002) pointed out, J. F. Blumenbach has usually been credited as the originator of racial categories. It was Blumenbach who created the term *Caucasian*, and his taxonomy established a racial hierarchy with White people on top. This would be the foundation for much "scientific" theory and research in the eighteenth and early nineteenth centuries. In the 1930s, scientists such as anthropologist Franz Boas challenged theories describing a hierarchy of races (Gosset, 1997). In 1937, American historian Jacques Barzun bluntly denounced the spuriousness of race as a legitimate scientific concept:

> [Racial classifications] come and go and return, for the urge to divide mankind into fixed types and races is evidently endless. Each attempt only illustrates anew how race-groupings have been shaped not by nature but by the mode of thought or the stage of mechanical efficiency that mankind valued at the moment. The history of these attempts confirms . . . that race-theories occur in the minds of men for an ulterior purpose. (1965, p. 196)

The series of paintings on "Caste" from the Spanish colonial era (see Figure 1.3) supports Barzun's point about the historical effort to find ways to divide and label human beings. Current research on the human genome emphasizes human similarities rather than differences. According to this research, every woman living today has the mitochondrial DNA of a single woman who lived approximately 150,000 years ago, and every man living today has the Y chromosome of a single man who lived approximately 59,000 years ago (Wade, 2006). Scientists involved in this research report that 85 percent of human genetic variation occurs within groups, and only 15 percent of human genetic variation occurs between groups. And yet, as Olson (2002) acknowledges, "societies have built elaborate systems of privilege and control around these miniscule genetic differences" (p. 69).

"In claiming the unity of the human race we resist the unsavory assumption of higher and lower races."

— ALEXANDER VON HUMBOLDT (1769–1859)

Although race is based on perceptions of physical differences, **ethnicity** is based on cultural differences (Jones, 1997). Ethnicity refers to the historic origins of an individual's family. For immigrants to the United States, ethnicity identifies their country of origin or that from which their ancestors came—Poland, Mexico, China, Italy, Cuba, Ethiopia, Russia, or Iran, for example. For those whose ancestors emigrated from different countries of origin, ethnicity can represent a choice about personal identity based on culture. As Dalton (2008) explains it,

> [Ethnicity] describes that aspect of our heritage that provides us with a mother tongue and that shapes our values, our worldview, our family structure, our rituals, the foods we eat, our mating behavior, our music—in short, much of our daily lives. (p. 16)

Most Americans identify more than one ethnic group as part of their heritage, and for that reason ethnicity may have little meaning because of a lack of strong cultural identification with one of those groups. Some of us with multiple ethnic heritages may claim a stronger cultural affinity with one of the groups. An individual may be a mixture of Irish, German, and Swedish ancestry and yet, perhaps because her surname is Irish or because Irish traditions were more strongly promoted in her family, she identifies most strongly with being Irish (Banks, 1994).

Figure 1.3 Eighteenth-century Paintings of "Castas"

A series of Mexican paintings from the eighteenth century identifies categories of people (such as Indian, Spanish, or African) and names the children of mixed marriages. For example, the child of a Spanish and African couple is a Mulatto, and the child of a Spanish and Mulatto couple is a Morisco. In these three paintings, the artist illustrates how descendants of a Spanish and Indian couple can regain status as a White individual. The child of the Spanish and Indian couple is a Mestizo, the child of a Spanish and Mestizo couple is a Castiza, and the child of a Spanish and Castiza couple is considered Spanish.

SOURCE: De Espanol, y India, na ce Mestiza (190.1996.1), De Espanol, y Mestiza, Castiza (190.1996.3), and De Espanol, y Castiza, Espanol (1990.1996.2), c. 1775, Francisco Clapera, Frederick and Jan Mayer Collection, Denver Art Museum.

For Native Americans, ethnicity generally refers to tribal affiliation: Apache, Kwakiutl, Cherokee, Seminole, Mohawk, Hopi, or Lakota. For most African Americans, ethnic identity was obliterated by the experience of slavery, making it practically impossible to trace an individual's heritage to a specific tribal group such as Hausa, Ibo, or Tsutsi. The introduction of the term "African American" in the 1980s was intended to provide an "ethnic" label for Black people as distinct from race (Dalton, 2008). Because of the unique preservation of his oral family history, Alex Haley (1976) was able to reconnect with his ethnic group as described in the book *Roots*.

Nationality refers to the nation in which an individual has citizenship. To ask people about their nationality is to ask where they reside or what nation is identified on their passport. People curious about someone's ethnic heritage often ask, "What is your nationality?" instead of "What is your ethnic background?" Being asked about your nationality may be considered quite insulting because it implies that the questioner does not perceive you as American but as belonging to another country (see Figure 1.4). What do the terms *race, ethnicity*, and *nationality* have in common? They each refer to people considered to represent minority groups in the United States.

What are minority groups and why are they called minority groups?

The term **minority group** does not necessarily indicate anything about the *number* of people in the group; however, it does imply something about their power. Minority group members possess limited power compared to members of a dominant group. It is possible for a minority group to be larger than a dominant group because it is the group's lack of power that defines it. When the White minority held power in South Africa, Black South Africans were the majority in terms of numbers, but they were considered a minority group because they lacked power under the racist system of

Figure 1.4 Nationalities of Ethnic Immigrants to America

These pie graphs show the nationality of immigrants since the early 1800s and illustrate the dramatic change that has occurred in recent years.

SOURCE: Schaefer, R. T. *Racial and Ethnic Groups*, 14th Edition. Copyright © 2015, p. 92. Reprinted and Electronically reproduced by permission of Pearson Education, Inc., Upper Saddle River, NJ.

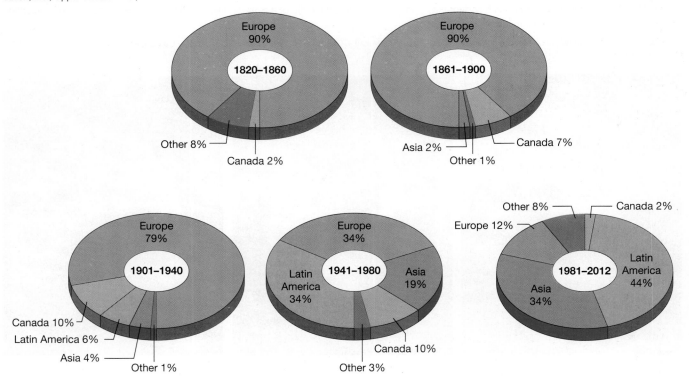

apartheid. Women in the United States are included as a minority in affirmative action plans and equity proposals even though numerically they are the majority because historically they have not held as much power as have men.

An individual in a minority group must overcome obstacles—handicapping conditions—related to her or his group identification based on such factors as race, ethnicity, gender, sexual orientation, socioeconomic status, religion, or disability. Some people refer to minority groups and diversity as if the two terms are synonymous, but **diversity** refers to the presence of human beings with perceived or actual differences based on a variety of human characteristics. Diversity exists both in classrooms having no minorities and in classrooms where all students are African American; too often, these differences can result in some children being stigmatized and marginalized by other children. The concept of diversity includes minority groups as well as groups identified according to differences based on age, marital status, parental status, educational status, geographic location, physical characteristics, and other factors that influence individual personality and behavior.

How have minority groups been perceived by the majority?

The majority group has created derogatory names for members of minority groups. When a dominant group has the power to label a subordinate group, others will consistently associate that label with individuals from the subordinate group. The power to label results in the power to define the people in a group, not only for the dominant group, but sometimes for the members of the labeled group as well. In recognition of the power of such labels, many groups have engaged in efforts to label themselves in a positive way. In the 1960s, many in the group that the majority had labeled *colored people* or *Negroes* rejected the majority group's names and chose to call themselves *Blacks*. This was accompanied by calls for "Black power" and claims that "Black is beautiful." Many Black people continue to prefer that designation because they believe it makes a positive contribution to an individual's sense of identity. Since the 1980s, *African American* has also become a popular choice among Black people and others as a positive label for this group.

When a majority group has the power to label and define those belonging to a minority group, they also can control subordinate group members, obviously by limiting their opportunities, but sometimes in more subtle ways as well. Macedo and Bartoleme (2001) compare the term *migrant*, which most often labels Latinos seeking economic opportunity in the United States, with the term *settlers*, which is used to designate English and other Europeans immigrating to America to improve their economic opportunities. Reactions to the two terms are significantly different, even though both terms describe people engaged in a similar quest.

How have labels been used to define and control subordinate groups?

The idea that the power to label equals the power to define, which equals the power to control, was illustrated by the 2012 media coverage of the shooting in a movie theater at Aurora, Colorado, where James Holmes killed 12 people and wounded 70 others. The media reported on the shooter's history of mental illness (i.e., schizophrenia), but the coverage never mentioned that such violent acts were unusual for the 46 percent of American adults diagnosed with some form of mental illness at some point in their lives (Friedman, 2008). Instead, the media too often resorts to labels. After the Sandy Hook mass shooting, where Adam Lanza killed 20 children and 6 adults with a semi-automatic gun, two respected media outlets reported on the speculation that he had a mental illness, specifically with *undiagnosed* schizophrenia. After Dylan Roof murdered eight African Americans at their Bible study class, several newspaper accounts suggested that he had a mental illness, but his website included racial slurs, guns, and violent content. Studies show that one of the consequences when people read accounts of shootings by an individual with a mental illness is they react more negatively to people with mental illness (Metzl & MacLeish, 2015).

Media portrayal of mental illness in movies and television programs tends to focus on people with severe problems rather than problems that can be controlled by therapy and medications. Characters with mental illness on prime time television programs were 10 to 20 times more likely to be shown engaged in violent behavior than happens in reality (Fawcett, 2015). From 1995 to 2015, people with mental illness were responsible for only 4 percent of individual acts of violence, a conclusion reported by multiple studies. During that same 20-year period, a study of a random sample of over 400 news accounts related to mental illness reported disproportionate news coverage of people with mental health problems engaging in acts of violence, especially mass shootings. Only 7 percent of news stories during this period described the successful treatment of an individual with mental illness (McGinty, Kennedy-Hendricks, Choksy, & Barry, 2015). A recent study reported that media portrayals of people with a mental illness are still largely stereotypical, ranging from describing them as behaving childishly to the other extreme of viewing them as violent people. In 2013, the Associated Press revised its Stylebook to assist journalists in avoiding such stereotyped portrayals (Fawcett, 2015).

Labels related to mental illness are official, formal, bureaucratic terms; others are informal and societal—terms used or heard by people in everyday life. The existence of **derisive labels**—terms reflecting a sense of contempt or ridicule based on factors such as race, class, disability, sexual orientation, and gender—and their variety suggest the extent to which prejudices exist. Wessler (2001) described the observations of elementary educators who have heard children using such labels, especially during recess, where children may feel they have more freedom to express themselves. Stephan (1999) insists that reducing prejudice requires that teachers help children become aware of the tendency to attach negative labels to others. After all, such words can be heard on the playgrounds of America, and some, for example, the word *squaw*, even show up in instructional materials such as maps, textbooks, or activities.

One theory of the origin of the word *squaw* is that it derives from a French word meaning vagina and was used by early French trappers to indicate that they wanted sex, usually followed by an offer to pay or barter something (Chavers, 1997). Other linguists claim that squaw has a more neutral origin, merely referring to a woman, but as Green (1975) demonstrated, its use has been consistently negative. The word *squaw* can still be found in elementary school materials and in names for lakes and other geographic sites around the United States.

Because they objected to the term, high school students in Minnesota successfully lobbied the state legislature to change the names of state geographical sites containing the word *squaw*, yet at least one White community in Minnesota, Squaw Lake, refused to change. Chavers (1977) reports that students have lobbied other state legislatures to delete *squaw* in geographic sites or town names because the word is offensive and insulting to Native American women.

The power of labels was the focus of a study that asked participants to supervise groups whose task was to make a collective decision on various issues (Zimbardo, 2007). The "supervisor" listened to the group's conversation from an adjacent room and was asked to evaluate the group's decision-making process using criteria provided that was supposed to describe good decision making. If the group made a bad decision, the supervisor was supposed to give them an electric shock ranging from a mild shock at level 1 to the maximum level of 10. No one was actually shocked, but supervisors heard a recording that simulated people being shocked.

The researcher was interested in how supervisors would be affected by overhearing labels ascribed to a group. The participants "overheard" the researcher talking to his assistant over the intercom, describing the group that the participant was asked to supervise as an "animalistic, rotten bunch" or as a "perceptive, thoughtful group"; another group was not labeled either positively or negatively. Supervisors tended to give minimal shocks to all groups after the first trial, but as the experiment went on and groups continued to make bad decisions, the "punishments" chosen for the groups began to diverge. Supervisors tended to shock the group labeled *animalistic* with more intensity, and they increased the shock level on subsequent decision-making exercises, whereas they gave those teams labeled positively the smallest amount of shock, with the neutral group falling in between. The study suggested that labels can enhance or diminish the human qualities we ascribe to others, and when human qualities are diminished, our concerns about not harming an individual or group may also be diminished.

What is the impact of labels on individuals who are labeled?

Wright (1998) believes that young children are only minimally aware of skin color and are often unaware of race. Asked what color she was, a 3-year-old Black girl wearing a pink-and-blue dress responded, "I'm pink and blue. What color are you?" At about the age of 4, children begin to understand that skin color is permanent, yet they do not regard it as negative. At 5 years of age, children are likely to become more interested in differences of skin color and may ask teachers many questions; they also begin to be aware of race and societal attitudes about racial differences. Early childhood educators can be proactive in promoting positive racial awareness. In one study, a multicultural curriculum was implemented to a class of preschool students who tended to develop a more favorable attitude toward children of ethnicities other than their own (Gellini, Pereda, Cordero, & Suarez-Morales, 2016). Such interventions could reduce negative behaviors such as name calling that teachers often confront on playgrounds and in their classrooms.

Racist name calling usually involves blatant, ugly words that carry harshly negative connotations. What impact does it have on a child to hear such words? Some members of a subordinate group may believe and internalize myths, stereotypes, and prejudices expressed about their group. Even for those who do not internalize the negative messages, being called derisive names, especially by other children, has an impact. Anthropologist Jamake Highwater, who identified as a Native American, recalled the impact of the derisive terms he heard as a child:

> At first, the words had no meaning to me. Even when I was told their meaning, I couldn't easily grasp why they were supposed to be shameful. . . . [They] were whispered in the classroom and remorselessly shouted when adults were not around. On the playground. In the locker room. In the darkness of the balcony at Saturday movie matinees. Those were the words that filled my childhood. . . . They were words that aroused a sense of power and self-aggrandizement for those who shouted them; they brought shame and humiliation in those at whom they were shouted. (Highwater, 1997, pp. 24–25)

Highwater believes that *derisives*, derogatory terms, damage individuals in the dominant group as well as those in minority groups because derisive language creates boundaries. Derisive terms define the oppressor as superior and the oppressed as inferior. Herbst (1997) agrees that such terms create suspicion, fear, and contempt in members of dominant groups and arouse frustration and anger in individuals from minority groups. Some groups have tried to take over certain words, to "own" them and reshape them to make them less hurtful. For example, gay men and lesbians, especially young people, use the word *queer* as a generic term for the gay community, and courses in queer studies are taught in colleges in an attempt to change formal, bureaucratic language (James, 2013).

How are negative bureaucratic terms as harmful as social derisive terms?

When we think of derisive terms, we usually think of informal, social labels. Derisive terms for social class, such as *hillbilly* or *redneck*, often have a regional origin but may become widespread, as in *White trash*, a term that evolved into a variety of forms, including *trailer park trash*. Yet some argue that the most harmful derisive terms for low-income people come from formal sources such as government reports and scholarly studies; these terms include *culturally deprived, culturally disadvantaged, welfare households*, and *inner-city residents*. What images do such terms suggest? Derisive bureaucratic terms are powerful purveyors of negative images primarily because they have the sanction of authority behind them.

In addition to negative images, derisive bureaucratic terms send a negative message. Being labeled *culturally deprived* represents a form of blaming the victim. What group are we talking about? What do they lack? The term *cultural deprivation* suggests that poor people lack an ability to appreciate arts and humanities; it does not acknowledge the reality that they are economically deprived and need financial assistance for such things as job training, employment, and better health care. Using such a label implies that a deficiency in cultural qualities or values is the cause of their problems.

People without disabilities have used many negative terms in reference to people with a disability (Brown, 2016). Linton (1998) explained that when adults refer to someone as a "retard" or children tell "moron" jokes, they are asserting a claim to normalcy by rejecting those who have a disability. Negative labels are also used in a bureaucratic setting, as illustrated by the term "handicapped." Since the 1950s, people with disabilities have objected to the term *handicapped* and have been largely successful in having it removed. Phrases such as *the retarded* or *the disabled* are also derisive bureaucratic terms because they isolate one adjective for an individual with a disability and make it a noun to label the group. According to Charlton (1998), people with disabilities object to being labeled with such adjectives because "their humanity is stripped away and the individual is obliterated, only to be left with the condition—disability" (p. 54).

To understand what Charlton means, imagine someone who is bold and energetic, impish yet compassionate, and now add *disabled* to the description. If the last adjective is singled out and made a noun, that word defines the individual. This is how a term like *the disabled* distorts and diminishes people with a disability. People without disabilities in America have viewed people with disabilities as unable to care for themselves and institutionalized them, justifying this by claiming that it was "for their own good." The history of institutionalizing people with disabilities illustrates the power of labels to control the quality of life for a labeled group.

How has our society responded to social problems experienced by minority groups?

Ryan (1976) described two radically different approaches involved in addressing social problems. The **exceptionalistic perspective** focuses on individuals; it perceives all problems as local, unique, exclusive, and unpredictable. Because problems are viewed as a consequence of individual defect, accident, or unfortunate circumstance, proposed remedies must be tailored to fit each individual case that is an "exception" to the general situation. A criticism of this approach is that it treats only symptoms of problems and not causes; exceptionalistic remedies have been derided as "Band-Aid solutions" that alleviate but do not solve problems.

Ryan describes an alternative approach, a **universalistic perspective** that views social problems as systemic, originating in flaws in the fundamental social structures within a community or a society. Because social structures are inevitably imperfect and inequitable, the problems that emerge are predictable and preventable because they do not stem from a situation unique to one individual but rather from conditions common to many. The universalistic perspective emphasizes engaging in research to collect and analyze data and to identify patterns that predict certain outcomes. Once patterns and root causes are identified, appropriate solutions can be created and implemented through public action, institutional policy, or legislation. Research takes time, so the universalistic approach has been criticized because it does not address the immediate consequences of particular problems or assist people who are currently suffering.

To illustrate the difference between exceptionalistic and universalistic perspectives, Ryan describes two responses to the problem of smallpox. An exceptionalistic approach would be to provide smallpox victims with medical care to help them recover; a universalistic approach would first demand legislation to fund inoculation of the population to prevent the disease from spreading. The contrast is similar to a metaphor from Kilbourne (1999) about bodies floating down a river and ambulances being called to rescue the drowning people. Although rescuing people from the river is important, it is also important to send someone upstream to investigate why people are falling in (p. 30).

These metaphors illustrate a need for both approaches. While people are engaged in studying problems, help must be provided to those who are suffering right now. If everyone goes upstream to discover why people are falling into the river, no one is

---

"One may no more live in the world without picking up the moral prejudices of the world than one will be able to go to Hell without perspiring."

— H. L. MENCKEN (1880–1956)

Video Example 1.2

In what ways does this video demonstrate how people without disabilities stereotype and diminish those with a disability? How do those with a disability challenge those stereotypes and offer suggestions for more appropriate and respectful behavior?

https://www.youtube.com/watch?v=Gv1aDEFlXq8&list=UUrd8W0u23ND2XxxjqHq5-aA

left to save those who are drowning; if everyone stays downstream to rescue drowning people, the cause of the problem will never be found. Neither perspective can be neglected in the efforts employed to solve social problems.

 Self-Check 1.2 Complete this self-check quiz to check your understanding of the definitions and distinctions for the two sets of related terms: (1) *bias, stereotype, prejudice, bigotry*, and *discrimination*, and (2) *race, ethnicity, nationality*, and *minority group*.

Afterword

The chapter began by discussing diversity and individuality. Holding differing values is part of both diversity and individuality. The values we choose are influenced by our membership in groups defined by such factors as race, ethnicity, gender, and social class; however, the ultimate decision to embrace certain values is up to the individual. Almost everyone holds some values similar to those of their parents, and almost everyone holds some values different from those of their parents. We share some values with friends, yet we hold some values that are different, too. Values, and the attitudes and beliefs that determine them, are part of the landscape of human differences. But beliefs and attitudes change as we learn more information that helps us to understand and appreciate diversity.

Language is the primary tool we use to pursue understanding. When we use language that labels a group of people, we create misunderstanding. It is important to observe and evaluate the behaviors of others, but we will never understand them without interacting with them or reading what they have written. Confusing or ambiguous language is like a smudge on the lens of a microscope; it prevents us from having a clear understanding of our subject. This chapter has tried to clarify some confusing terms so that our view is not distorted as we begin our study of human differences.

When Jewish author Isaac Bashevis Singer was asked if he believed people had free will, he replied, "Of course we have free will, we have no choice." As citizens of a democracy, we have many choices. As human beings living in a diverse society surrounded by a multitude of global cultures, trying to understand human differences would seem to be a necessary choice. For every reader who has already made that choice, this text offers insights and information to enhance your understanding. For readers who have not made that choice, this text may help to create an understanding of why the choice is necessary. But it is still each individual's choice to make; as Singer said, we have no choice about that.

"Freedom is the right to choose; the right to create for yourself the alternatives of choice. Without the possibility of choice and the exercise of choice, human beings are not human but instruments, things."

— ARCHIBALD MACLEISH (1892–1982)

Summary

- Scholars have defined nine major values of American culture, yet Americans have historically behaved inconsistently with regard to these values. Values have usually been taught in one or more of seven traditional approaches, but all of them involve indoctrination, which contributes to these inconsistencies in American behavior.

- There are two sets of terms that are often muddled together, creating confusion: (1) There is an increasing intensity of negative attitudes in the terms *bias, stereotype, prejudice*, and *bigotry*, but *discrimination* is the only term that involves actions; (2) *ethnicity* relates to cultural heritage, *nationality* has to do with country of origin, and *minority group* involves limitations on a group's power, but *race* is an unscientific concept based on observed or assumed physical attributes.

Terms and Definitions

Attitude A cluster of particular related beliefs, values, and opinions

Beliefs Inferences an individual makes about reality that take one of three forms: descriptive, evaluative, or prescriptive

Bias A preference or inclination, favorable or unfavorable, that inhibits impartial judgment

Bigotry Extreme negative attitudes leading to hatred of a group and individuals regarded as members of the group

Confirmation bias Believing information that reinforces beliefs already held and ignoring information that contradicts these beliefs

Derisive labels Names that reflect attitudes of contempt or ridicule for individuals in the group being named

Discrimination Actions or practices carried out by a member or members of dominant groups or their representatives that have a differential and negative impact on a member or members of subordinate groups

Diversity The presence of human beings with perceived or actual differences based on a variety of human characteristics

Dogmatic To accept beliefs you have been taught without questioning them

Ethnicity Identification of an individual according to national origin and/or distinctive cultural patterns

Exceptionalistic perspective Views social problems as private, local, unique, exclusive, and unpredictable, a

consequence of individual defect, accident, or unfortunate circumstance, which requires that all proposed remedies be tailored to fit each individual case

Indoctrination Instruction whose purpose is to force the learner to accept a set of values or beliefs, to adopt a particular ideology or perspective

Minority group A subordinate group whose members have significantly less power to control their own lives than do members of a dominant, or majority, group

Nationality Refers to the nation in which an individual has citizenship status

Prejudice A negative attitude toward a group and individuals perceived to be members of that group; being predisposed to behave negatively toward members of a group

Race A social concept with no scientific basis that categorizes people according to obvious physical differences such as skin color

Stereotype A positive or negative trait or traits ascribed to a certain group and to most members of that group

Universalistic perspective Views social problems as public, national, general, inclusive, and predictable; a consequence of imperfect and inequitable social arrangements that require research to identify their patterns and causes so that remedial institutional action can be taken to eliminate these problems and prevent them from reoccurring

Values Combinations of attitudes that generate action or the deliberate choice to avoid action

Discussion Exercises

Discussion exercises are provided in which groups of three to five students can delve deeper into the content presented in the chapter.

Clarification Exercise—My Values: What I Believe

Directions: Share your responses to the following questions:

1. How would you describe the way your parents raised you? If you choose to have children, will you raise them the same way your parents raised you? Explain.

2. Do you value experiences over possessions? Upon graduating from college, what if a wealthy relative offered to pay for a trip anywhere in the world or to

give you an expensive gift (e.g., a new car) that you have wanted for a long time? Which option would you choose, and why would you choose that option?

3. An eccentric multimillionaire approaches you and says he wants to give you money. He will either give you $100,000 to spend on yourself any way you want, or he will give you $1 million if you will anonymously distribute it to strangers. If you choose the first option,

what would you spend the money on? If you choose the second option, on what basis would you give money to strangers (i.e., what would be your criteria)?

4. Can you think of anything that has happened to you that was beyond your control and had an impact on your life? What was that event, and how did it change you? Given that such events happen to most people, how much control do you think you (or anyone else) have over the course of your life?

5. After getting married, you and your spouse have your first child. Even as a toddler, your child shows signs of incredible intelligence, and it becomes clear that you will be raising a child much more intelligent than you are. How would you feel about that? When your second child is born, it soon becomes clear that this child has health problems and learning difficulties. How would you feel about raising that child?

6. It is early in your career, and you have a job you really enjoy, working with people you really like, that pays enough for you to maintain a middle-class lifestyle.

You are offered a job that will not be as enjoyable, and you will be competing with your co-workers, but the salary is twice what you currently make and may go even higher. Would you keep the job you enjoy or take the job with the higher salary? Explain.

7. You are walking to your car in a parking lot, and a stranger comes up and asks for a dollar to catch a bus home, explaining that he has lost his wallet. Would you give him the money? Explain. The next day a rather unkempt stranger approaches you in that same parking lot and says he has lost his job and his home and is living on the streets; then he asks you for a dollar for food. Would you give him the money? Explain.

8. When America enters the next (twenty-second) century, do you think our nation will be a better place to live than it is today or worse? Explain.

Selected and adapted from Gregory Stock, *The Book of Questions* (1987) and *The Kid's Book of Questions* (1988) (New York, NY: Workman Publishing).

Intergroup Exercise—A Mutual Support Dilemma

Directions: Examine the case situation explained below. Discuss it with the members of your assigned group. Respond to each of the questions. Then explain your group position to the class.

The Story of Mary and Luke: A Mutual Support Dilemma

Mary and Luke were married during their senior year in college. After their graduation, Mary took a secretarial job in the registrar's office of the university where Luke was attending graduate school. Mary worked for five years while Luke completed his doctoral degree. Their first and only child was born during the second of the five years, and Mary missed only two months of work at that time.

Luke has now been offered an assistant professorship at a prominent eastern school and is eager to accept it. Mary has applied to and been accepted into graduate school at the University of Chicago. She is eager to accept the assistantship she has been offered.

Mary argues that Luke should give her the chance for an education now that he has completed his. She also reminds him that he has been offered a job at the Chicago Junior College. Luke says that he intends to take the job in the east and that Mary can find someplace out there to go to school. If Mary refuses to follow him, Luke promises to file for a divorce and seek custody of their 3-year-old daughter.

Questions for discussion:

1. What would you do if you were Mary?
2. What advice do you have for Luke?
3. How could this situation be handled so that neither Mary nor Luke loses?
4. Does your group agree that either Mary or Luke loses?

Chapter 2
Understanding Prejudice and Its Causes

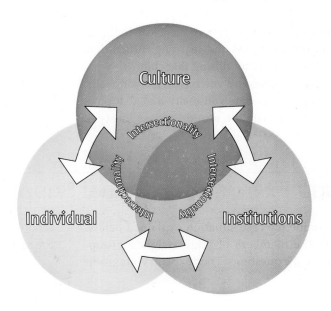

Learning Outcomes

After reading this chapter you will know and be able to:

2.1 Describe confusion regarding the term *prejudice*, and provide examples of how prejudice is reflected in language and media.

2.2 Understand how denial, avoidance, and victim blaming perpetuate prejudice, and identify examples of these rationalizations in written or spoken language.

2.3 Describe how frustration, threat to self-esteem, uncertainty, and competition foster the development of individual prejudice and how that prejudice can lead to discriminatory behavior; also discuss how discrimination occurs in the absence of prejudice.

"No one has ever been born a Negro hater, a Jew hater, or any other kind of hater. Nature refuses to be involved in such suicidal practices."

—HARRY BRIDGES (1900–1990)

No credible studies have concluded that prejudice is part of human nature, that it is an innate outcome of being human. In fact, Hauser (2006) cited a study reporting that during their first hours of life, babies will cry if they hear other babies crying. One developmental psychologist explained this phenomenon as a "rudimentary form of empathy" (p. 193). The evidence supports the claim that prejudice, as Bridges suggests, must be learned. It is also important to remember that prejudice is an attitude, not an action. Whether you are looking at definitions in a dictionary or reading scholarly writing, you will inevitably encounter puzzling uses of the term *prejudice*. Some people describe prejudice as a hatred of others, but hatred is bigotry. Based on their study of world cultures, anthropologists have argued that people everywhere in the world have prejudices, yet they do not claim that hatred—or bigotry—is widespread.

Confusion, not clarification, is caused by a definition suggesting that prejudice is synonymous with bigotry. Such a definition may cause many of us to deny that we are prejudiced: A bigot hates, and we are certain we don't hate anyone. In addition, we deny the pervasiveness of prejudice because we don't observe widespread hatred in the world; thus confusing prejudice with bigotry creates misunderstanding about the nature and extent of prejudice.

Conceptions and Misconceptions of Prejudice

We confuse prejudice with bias, stereotypes, and bigotry. As defined in Chapter 1, *bias* is a mildly positive or negative feeling about someone or something; and to *stereotype* is to associate positive or negative traits with a group of people. **Prejudice** is a stronger feeling, but it is always negative, and it always refers to a group of people. Prejudice predisposes us to behave negatively toward certain people because of a group to which they belong. And when prejudice reaches the intensity of hatred, it becomes bigotry. Even educated people, including linguists and other scholars, have contributed to misconceptions regarding prejudice.

What are examples of misconceptions about prejudice?

Some dictionaries define *prejudice* as the process of forming opinions without looking at relevant facts, yet people with prejudices may examine relevant facts and simply interpret them to confirm their prejudices. Other definitions describe prejudice as being irrational, implying that those we acknowledge as rational could not possibly be prejudiced. The problem here is that rational people also hold prejudices; we know this from reading what they wrote. Aristotle claimed that a woman was an inferior man. Abraham Lincoln believed Black people were intellectually inferior to White people. Carroll (2001) quoted Martin Luther warning German Christians, "Do not doubt that next to the devil you have no enemy more cruel, more venomous and virulent, than a true Jew" (p. 368). However, their prejudices did not deter any of these men from achieving significant improvements in human rights.

It is easy to view ancient racist or sexist attitudes as patently absurd and to denounce them, yet often we do not acknowledge current widespread prejudices that future generations may find just as incongruous. In fifty or one hundred years, what will people think about today's programs for the poor in the United States? Or how people with disabilities were so often isolated or ignored? Or how gay men and lesbians were condemned by so many people?

How widespread is prejudice?

Although this text focuses on attitudes in the United States, prejudices are not limited to one country or one race. People living in nations around the world possess negative attitudes toward others within their own borders or close to them. Prejudices have been ignored, promoted, or tolerated but rarely challenged. When prejudice has been challenged, the case often has become a cause célèbre, as when Emile Zola published "J'accuse," an essay denouncing anti-Semitism in France's prosecution of Alfred Dreyfus for treason (Bredin, 2008). Persistence of prejudice was illustrated by Jean-Paul Sartre's 1945 description of French anti-Semitic attitudes as Jewish people returned to France following World War II, even though French people were aware of the existence of Nazi concentration camps and of the genocide against the Jews. Today, migrants continue to leave their homes for economic reasons or to escape violence and persecution of their group, and demographers predict that diversity is going to increase significantly in the populations of most nations around the world.

> "There are, in every age, new errors to be rectified, and new prejudices to be opposed."
>
> — SAMUEL JOHNSON (1709–1784)

More than twenty years ago, scholars such as Gioseffi (1993) described a growing global economy, arguing that it required functional and respectful relationships among nations, and that prejudice was a destructive force. Since 2011, the Syrian civil war has significantly increased the numbers of immigrants, with over half going to Europe. This migration seems to be causing a change in European attitudes as immigrants are being increasingly viewed as a burden on society by 50 percent of people in France and Poland and nearly 70 percent of Greeks and Italians (Krogstad, 2015). In the United States only 41 percent of the people view immigrants as a burden, but this negative attitude seems to be increasing, causing social justice advocates to criticize the media for promoting prejudicial attitudes with negative portrayals of racial and ethnic groups. Language is an important source for understanding a culture because analyzing language reveals a culture's assumptions, beliefs, values, and priorities, as well as examples of prejudice. Some countries are now addressing their historic prejudices by changing or eliminating media images and language that have promoted negative attitudes, especially toward racial or ethnic groups.

How are prejudices reflected in American media?

To understand how prejudices are transmitted in our culture, we need only observe some of the prevalent images of racial or cultural groups in our everyday lives. Look for magazine advertisements that depict Native Americans, Asian Americans, or Hispanic Americans. Why is it that most advertisements seem to use African American models to reflect diversity? If people of color are included in advertisements, why are they often featured in ways that reflect historic stereotypes? Native Americans are almost never portrayed as part of contemporary society but instead as nineteenth-century warriors; Asian Americans are often shown working at computers or in math-related professions; Mexican Americans are presented as gardeners or servants. Problems of omission and stereotyping affect other groups as well: People with disabilities are invisible; blue-collar workers are usually stereotyped, if they appear at all; and women appear frequently in advertisements as sex objects to sell products. Still, we typically don't recognize such advertisements as stereotypes because these images are so familiar that they seem not to be stereotypes at all but rather to portray reality. This is one reason so many White Americans do not understand why Native Americans are offended by the use of Indian mascots for sports teams. (See Figure 2.1.)

Media portrayals of Muslim Americans represent the most recent example of pervasive stereotyping. Although anti-Muslim attitudes in the United States have a long history, Ansari (2004) insists that ever since the 1979 Iranian hostage crisis, the media has focused on activities of militant Muslims. In a 2015 poll, 55 percent of Americans said they had an "unfavorable" view of Islam, and 40 percent supported the proposal that the federal government should establish a national registry of Muslims (Chalabi, 2015).

Figure 2.1 Cultural Images

The cartoonist is illustrating some of the stereotypes in our culture that shape how non-Indians think about "Indians."

SOURCE: John Branch, *San Antonio Express-News*.

In one national survey, 40 percent of White Americans said they believed Muslims sanction and support terrorism, and 40 percent of African Americans shared that belief (Sue, 2015). In a 2016 Pew Research Center survey, about half of Americans believed that a significant percentage of Muslims harbor anti-American attitudes (Lipka, 2017). Chalabi (2015) says the lack of familiarity between White and Muslim Americans contributes to negative attitudes, citing a study that found that only 13 percent of non-Muslims had been inside a mosque, and only 26 percent of them had Muslim co-workers. Media portrayals of Muslims are another factor. In a panel discussion at Duke University, veteran journalists acknowledged the role of the media in promoting a strong association between Muslims and violence (Ballentine, 2017).

Although the media bears some responsibility for reinforcing stereotypes, many Americans may not recognize portrayals of certain groups as stereotypical because of the prejudices embedded in our language.

> "You can tell the ideals of a nation by its advertisements."
> — NORMAN DOUGLAS (1868–1952)

What examples of prejudice exist in our language?

One pattern observed in the English language has been called the **black/white syndrome**. Scholars report that this language pattern emerged in English long before the British knew that people described as Black were living in Africa (Moore, 2006). Although the pattern likely originated in biblical language referring to Satan, evil, and hell as black or dark, it has been argued that a consistently negative pattern for references to *black* affected British perceptions of Africans and that negative connotations for blackness were readily applied to all dark-skinned people they encountered. A negative pattern for *black* has persisted in the English language, as can be seen in familiar phrases: black deed, black day, black-hearted, black mass, black magic, the Black Death, black thoughts, black looks, and blacklist. Such words and phrases illustrate the point made by linguist Skuttnab-Kangas (2000), "Dominant groups keep a monopoly of defining others, and it is their labels we see in dictionaries" (p. 154).

Skuttnab-Kangas also argues that labeling others includes "the power to define oneself" by not having to accept the definitions others have for your group. It should not be surprising that references to *white* in the English language follow a consistently positive pattern: telling little white lies, having a white wedding, cheering white knights (in shining armor), indicating approval by saying "that's really white of you," and even engaging in white-collar crime (perceived as less harmful than other crimes). Some authors such as Robert Frost and Herman Melville have exploited the pervasive black/white pattern by deliberately using *white* as a negative term, invoking images of sterility, death, or evil to shock readers with unexpected associations.

Sometimes prejudice is not just black and white but is instead a shade of gray, as in the expression, "Where there's a will there's a way." At first glance this expression seems nothing more than an attempt to encourage children and youth to try hard, but it has another meaning: If all that it takes to be successful is to have the will to succeed, then those people who are not successful are at fault for their failure because they just didn't "try" hard enough. This belief leads to blaming the victim, providing an ethical escape for middle-class people. After all, if they were successful because they worked hard, then someone who is poor must not have worked hard enough, perhaps because they are lazy or incompetent.

Such stereotypes for "the poor" reinforce the conclusion that poor people are responsible for their poverty and thus the rest of us are under no obligation to help them. Other stereotypes may be revealed in expressions. When people negotiate with the seller on the price of a product, they might say, "I Jewed him down," alluding to an old stereotype. Parents and teachers have been overheard telling children to stop behaving "like a bunch of wild Indians." Teenagers who say, "That's so gay" do not intend it as a compliment. Boys are still ridiculed by comments such as "he throws like a girl" or "he's a sissy." Children are no longer limited to the term *sissy*. Today, even elementary children can be heard calling one another a *faggot*. They may not be certain what the word means, but they know it is a negative term (Wessler, 2001).

Some people tell sexist, racist, and ethnic jokes that clearly reveal their prejudices. When others complain that these jokes aren't funny, they are likely to be told they don't have a sense of humor: "It was a joke!" Just a joke. Although people are more careful today about telling racist jokes, sexist jokes are frequently told at work and in school. Perhaps the numerous examples of sexist words and phrases in our language make it easier to express sexist attitudes publicly.

How does gender prejudice in our language promote sexist attitudes?

Unlike many other languages, English does not have a neutral pronoun that includes both men and women, so the word *he* is used to refer to someone of indeterminate gender. *Man* has traditionally been used in words or phrases where the referent could be female (even though there are neutral nouns such as *human* and *people*). Some people continue to insist that *man* is generic when used in words such as *businessman, chairman, congressman, fireman, layman, mailman, policeman, salesman, spokesman,* and *statesman,* but studies over the past twenty years have concluded that generic language invoked mental images of men.

For example, in a study reported by Miller and Swift (2000) involving 500 junior high students, one group of students received instructions to draw pictures of "early man" engaged in various activities and to give each individual drawn a name (so researchers could be certain that a man or woman was the subject of the drawing). The majority of students of both sexes tended to draw only men for every activity identified except the one representing infant care, and even for that activity, 49 percent of boys drew an image of a man. A second group of students was instructed to draw pictures of "early people" engaged in the same activities and to give each human figure drawn a name; once again, the majority of the humans drawn by both sexes were men. It is possible that the phrase *early people* sounded strange and that many students translated

Application Exercise 2.1

In this video, two teachers discuss culturally responsive teaching. Pay attention to what they discuss about how misconceptions and prejudices form and how racism is perpetuated in daily life. Think about the strategies that the teachers recommend for combating prejudice and how racial injustice in America is positioned in relationship to White America. Review the video and complete the activity.

it as "cave men" and drew pictures of men. The third group of students was asked to draw pictures of "early men and early women," once again giving names to human figures. Only in this group did the figures drawn by students include a significant number of images of women, but even with these instructions, some students of both sexes drew only men.

What sexist terms for men could be considered derisive?

Although a plethora of derisive terms exist for women, derisive language for men often sends a mixed message. It may be intended as an insult to call a man a *prick* or a *bastard*, but it can also be interpreted as being envious of a man's power. Men may feel that they have to be tough, ruthless, and relentless if they are going to be successful in a "dog eat dog world"; such language could be regarded as a compliment to a man's prowess, his masculinity.

In American English, unambiguously derisive terms for men often accuse a man of being feminine. No little boy wants to be called a *sissy*; no man wants to be called a *wimp* or a *pussy*. Although a man may not like being called a name that implies he acts like a woman, according to Baker (1981), it is even more insulting to be called a name suggesting that a woman controls him, that he's *pussy whipped*. Men often use such language in a joking manner, but the message is serious.

That it is an insult for a man to be compared to a woman was illustrated by an incident at a summer festival. A man and his son were setting up a dunking booth. Three young men came up and volunteered to be dunked. The man said he had all the volunteers he needed. Animated by alcohol, the three of them badgered the man for several minutes before they gave up. As they walked away, the man at the booth said, "Goodbye, girls!" One of the young men turned around and shouted, "What the f*** did you call me?" He came storming back clearly intending to engage in violence for this insult, even though the father's young son stood next to him.

A group of mothers and daughters standing nearby in a line for face painting had observed this confrontation. One mother shouted sarcastically, "Oh, what a terrible thing to be called!" The young man looked angrily at the group of women, and other mothers shouted similar comments. The young man's face betrayed his confusion. His body had swelled up with anger, but now it seemed to deflate. His expression became almost sheepish as he approached the man at the dunking booth; he was still angry but not to the point of engaging in violence. A security officer arrived and escorted the young man away. Considering the hostility aroused by such a flippant remark, you have to wonder about the attitudes men are being taught concerning women. Is it possible for a man to hate the idea of being called a woman and not subconsciously hate women as well?

Aren't some prejudices positive?

Some people misuse the term *prejudice* by saying they are prejudiced *for* something, but they are misusing the word because prejudice is always a negative attitude. A milder attitude of liking or disliking anything or anyone is a bias. The concept of prejudice involves learning to fear and mistrust other groups of people and to strengthen negative attitudes we have been taught about them. Once we learn to be prejudiced against a certain group, we tend to behave in negative ways toward others who appear to be members of that group. Negative behavior is *discrimination*: We no longer merely hold a negative attitude—we have acted on that attitude. To prevent such negative consequences of prejudice, it is necessary to unlearn whatever prejudices we have been taught, but that is more difficult than it sounds because there are powerful factors motivating people to persist in maintaining their prejudices.

▶ **Video Example 2.1**
In this video, people are asked to act out activities "like a girl." Pay attention to the ways in which young people perpetuate sexism through their interpretations. How do they discuss the sexism reproduced through language and actions when confronted with the realization that they are perpetuating negative stereotypes?

https://www.youtube.com/watch?v=XjJQBjWYDTs

"I am, in plainer words, a bundle of prejudices—made up of likings and dislikings."
— CHARLES LAMB (1775–1834)

> ✓ **Self-Check 2.1** Complete this self-check quiz to check your understanding of the confusion regarding the term *prejudice* and of how prejudice is reflected in language and media.

The Perpetuation of Prejudice

People want to be successful and often will try to promote their own self-interests. When members of one group believe that individuals from another group are becoming more successful than they are, they may become angry at those individuals—even hostile toward the entire group—and rationalize that an advantage other than talent or skill is responsible for that individual's or group's success. Resentment stemming from economic competition for good jobs with high salaries and status fosters prejudice. Because humans are intelligent enough to identify these various causes of prejudice, it seems logical to assume that people should be able to recognize that they have prejudices and attempt to eliminate them.

How are prejudices perpetuated?

A major factor in the perpetuation of prejudice is the tendency to rationalize prejudices and the negative behaviors prejudices promote. As Gioseffi (1993) noted, this not only affects individuals but also is an international phenomenon: "Just as individuals will rationalize their hostile behaviors . . . so nations do also" (p. xvii). Vega (1978) described rationalizations as taking three forms: (1) denial, (2) victim-blaming, and (3) avoidance. To unlearn our prejudices and develop effective ways of confronting prejudices expressed by others, we need to recognize these rationalizations so we can respond appropriately when they are expressed.

Denial rationalizations. In making **denial rationalizations**, an individual refuses to recognize that there are problems in our society resulting from prejudices and discrimination. Such claims are astonishing in their ignorance, yet they continue to be made. In response to assertions of racism, the most common denial rationalization is the *reverse discrimination* argument claiming that women and minorities receive the best jobs because of affirmative action programs. Is there any truth to this claim?

According to the Bureau of Labor Statistics, people of color today represent 36 percent of American workers, and White people account for 64 percent; since women comprise about 50 percent of all White workers, White men are only about 32 percent of the workforce (Burns, Barton, & Kerby, 2012). One study defined the best jobs in terms of annual earnings placing them in the top 25 percent of all workers. Historically, 85–90 percent of this group has been White workers, but since 2000, the White share has declined to 70 percent, still twice as high as their presence in the workforce. Despite this change, among the professional, managerial and other occupations regarded as being the most desirable, White people are still the dominant group, and even when people of color are found in these jobs, they tend to be paid less (Alba, 2016). Further, Woodruff (2013) reported that the income for White households in the United States was almost $30,000 higher than the incomes for Black or Latino households. Claims that White men are unfairly discriminated against as a result of affirmative action policies appear to be inaccurate (see Table 2.1).

The most common denial rationalization related to sexism is the "natural" argument, which denies gender discrimination, claiming that it is natural for women to do some things better than men, and for men to do some things better than women. This denial rationalization is offered as an explanation for why men and women have historically held certain types of jobs. The argument does not explain the difference between the skills of a tailor (predominantly men) compared to a seamstress (predominantly women) to justify the differences in their compensations. Nor does it explain

Table 2.1 Annual Incomes of Full-Time Workers in the United States

Race/Gender	Median Weekly Earnings	
	2014	2017
White men	$897 (100 percent)	$977 (100 percent)
Black men	$680 (75.8 percent)	$722 (73.9 percent)
Hispanic men	$616 (68.7 percent)	$692 (70.8 percent)
White men	$734 (81.8 percent)	$790 (80.8 percent)
Black men	$611 (68.1 percent)	$645 (66.0 percent)
Hispanic men	$548 (61.1 percent)	$596 (61.0 percent)

SOURCE: Adapted from U.S. Bureau of Labor Statistics, 2017.

why construction workers (mostly men) should be compensated at a greater rate than college-educated social workers (mostly women). Historically, women have been paid less than men for doing the same work, and occupations dominated by women still receive lower wages than occupations dominated by men (U.S. Bureau of Labor Statistics, 2013). This is the reality, but denial rationalizations have little to do with reality.

The most subtle denial rationalization is personal denial illustrated by the man who says, "How can I be sexist? I love women! I married a woman. I have daughters." This seems a reasonable statement: A man who denies he has gender prejudices does not appear to be denying the existence of widespread prejudice against women—but the statement actually does imply a more sweeping denial. Psychologically, most people feel they are normal, average people. If an individual denies being prejudiced, he is actually denying that most other normal, average people are prejudiced as well. The real meaning of such a statement is that the speaker does not believe prejudice and discrimination are serious problems in society. If the individual making this denial rationalization argues this point, she might resort to victim-blaming responses because the two are closely related.

Victim-blaming rationalizations. Ryan (1976) was one of the first scholars to identify **victim-blaming rationalizations**, in which individuals reject the idea that prejudice and discrimination are problems in society, even while they admit that problems exist. The problems they identify, however, are typically deficiencies or flaws in members of minority groups. Victim blamers focus on the group being harmed by societal prejudices and insist that the group is the problem, not the society. Victim blamers urge individuals to stop being so sensitive or so pushy, to work harder, and to quit complaining. Group members are told they are responsible for whatever problems they must overcome. Ironically, victim blamers often do not hold themselves responsible for their own failures. In a study of college students who took an intelligence test, participants tended to explain the poor performance of others as an indication of inferior intellectual ability, but if *they* performed poorly, they were more likely to view the results as a consequence of the level of difficulty of the test (Aronson, 2008).

Victim blaming often occurs among people who want to believe in a just world. In one study, participants observed two people working equally hard at a task. By a random decision, researchers gave one of the workers a significant reward when the task was completed; the other worker received nothing. When asked to rate how hard the two people had worked, the participants tended to describe the individual who received nothing as not working as hard as the individual receiving the reward. Aronson (2008) concluded his analysis of this study by suggesting that "we find it frightening to think about living in a world where people, through no fault of their own, can be deprived of what they deserve or need" (p. 323).

People who engage in victim-blaming rationalizations often go beyond blame to propose solutions. By defining the problem as a deficiency existing in the victimized

"Prejudice blinds, ignorance retards, indifference deafens, hate amputates. In this way do some people disable their souls."
— MARY ROBINSON (1944–)

group, every solution proposed by a victim blamer involves how the victim needs to resolve the problem. The rest of us need do nothing. Rape is increasing on college campuses? That's a woman's problem, so what women need to do is to wear less provocative clothing, avoid going out late at night, and learn to defend themselves by taking martial arts classes or carrying pepper spray. What to do about the rapist isn't addressed. Because victim blamers offer solutions, it is easy to confuse victim blaming with some avoidance rationalizations.

Avoidance rationalizations. Unlike people who employ denial and victim-blaming rationalizations, those who promote **avoidance rationalizations** recognize the problems in society as stemming from prejudice and discrimination. This is a significant departure from the previous rationalizations. Even though an individual making avoidance rationalizations admits there are problems, he will not address them and will rationalize a reason to avoid them. Ways to avoid confronting issues include offering a solution that (1) addresses only part of a problem or (2) is a false solution that does not address the problem at all.

If college administrators decide to confront prejudice by requiring students to take an ethnic studies course, that requirement will address a small part of the problems caused by prejudice and discrimination. Learning more about ethnic groups is a good idea, but if colleges are serious about actively opposing prejudice and improving intergroup relations, administration and faculty must recruit diverse students, hire diverse faculty, and promote cultural diversity through workshops and seminars both on campus and in the community.

An example of a false solution that does not address problems of sexism is the proposal that "sexism would just disappear if we didn't pay so much attention to it." Problems created by sexism did not suddenly appear, and they won't disappear unless people engage in actions to confront, challenge, and change sexist attitudes, policies, and laws. The only way any society can solve problems and improve conditions is to analyze a problem, create appropriate solutions, implement the solutions that seem most likely to be effective, and, after time passes, assess the impact of these solutions.

Another form of avoidance rationalization involves making an argument that distracts attention from the issue or question being discussed. Imagine a group of people discussing efforts that could be made to increase social justice in our society. Suddenly someone says, "You're being too idealistic. We are never going to solve this problem because we're never going to have a utopia." The speaker was not arguing for the creation of a utopia, a perfect society, but for ways to improve society. By making the reasonable statement that utopias are not possible, the speaker has shifted the focus of the conversation to a different topic that avoids the issue. It is not realistic to believe that it is possible to create a perfect society, but it is possible—in fact, essential—to believe that any society can be improved.

Another example of a distracting argument: In a discussion about the need for child-care centers at a work site, someone says, "I support the idea, but it takes time; it's not going to happen overnight." This is a reasonable response, except what has been achieved if the discussion ends with that comment? To implement any solution successfully, it is necessary to clarify what is entailed: What needs to be done? Who will do what? Which actions should be taken next month? What can we expect in the next 6 months? Who will determine whether the solution is working, and how will progress be assessed? Saying a solution takes time may be true, but it is still necessary to discuss what must be done to implement it. Such a discussion avoids dealing with the problem or confronting your own prejudices. Problems are not solved by talk or the passage of time but by taking some kind of action.

Conservatives are often accused of engaging in denial and victim-blaming rationalizations. Their solutions tend to concentrate on perceived flaws in victims of prejudice rather than addressing the prejudice and discrimination that create many of these difficult circumstances. On the other hand, liberals are more likely to be criticized for engaging in avoidance rationalizations in which they acknowledge and express sympathy for the problems faced by oppressed groups but never do anything to address the causes of these problems. As long as significant numbers of individuals continue to employ such rationalizations, Americans are not likely to perceive or confront causes or consequences of the persistent inequities stemming from prejudices based on race, gender, and other human differences.

 Self-Check 2.2 Complete this self-check quiz to check your understanding of how denial, avoidance, and victim blaming perpetuate prejudice, and look at examples of these rationalizations found in written or spoken language.

Causes and Consequences of Prejudice and Discrimination

Considerable research has been conducted to address the question of how and why individuals become prejudiced. Some studies suggest that elitist attitudes foster prejudice. **Elitism** is the belief that the most able people succeed in society and form a natural aristocracy, whereas the least able enjoy the least success because they are flawed in some way or lack the necessary qualities to be successful. This condescending attitude promotes the belief that those in the lower levels of society deserve to be where they are and that successful people have earned their place in society. Unsuccessful people are often held responsible for their failure. Elitist attitudes are a major factor in studies based on social dominance theory (Duckitt & Sibley, 2007; Howard, 2006).

Other studies suggest a link between prejudice and attitudes about power. Some people express a **zero-sum** attitude, a highly competitive orientation toward power based on the assumption that the personal gains of one individual mean a loss for someone else; therefore, to share power is regarded as having less power. According to Levin and Levin (1982), an individual with a zero-sum orientation toward power tends to be an individual with strong prejudices. Some have even proposed that prejudice is innate, but there are no scientific studies to support that claim. To be as pervasive and persistent as it has been, prejudice must serve some purpose and offer some benefit to individuals or to society.

What are the major causes promoting the development of prejudice?

Having reviewed research concerning causes of prejudice, Levin and Levin (1982) identified four primary causes, and within these causes, functions of prejudice that sustain it. The four causes include (1) personal frustration, (2) uncertainty about an individual based on lack of knowledge or experience with the group to which the individual belongs, (3) threat to self-esteem, and (4) competition among individuals in our society to achieve their goals in relation to status, wealth, and power.

> "Everyone is a prisoner of his own experiences. No one can eliminate prejudices—just recognize them."
>
> — EDWARD R. MURROW (1908–1965)

How does frustration cause prejudice?

The frustration-aggression hypothesis maintains that as frustration builds, it leads to aggressive action. Frustration causes tension to increase until an individual chooses to act on the frustration to alleviate the tension. Jones (1997) and others have called this the "scapegoat phenomenon." The word **scapegoat** derives from an ancient Hebrew custom described in Leviticus 16:20–22, in which each year the Hebrew people reflected on their sins during days of atonement. At the end of that time, a spiritual leader would stand before them with a goat, lay his hands on the goat's head, and recite a list of the people's sins, transferring the sins of the people to the goat—which was then set free. In modern America, the term generally refers to blaming an individual or group for problems they did not cause.

When we take aggressive action—from verbal abuse to physical violence—we inevitably cause harm to others. Because most individuals define themselves as "good" according to some criteria, they will usually find a way to rationalize their actions as being good or at least justified. When Southerners lynched Black people in the late nineteenth and early twentieth centuries, they justified their actions by insisting that all Black people were lazy, lustful, or liars. Using the Kafkaesque reasoning that all Black people were guilty and therefore it didn't matter what crime a Black individual was accused of committing, they executed victims with no regard for whether that specific Black individual was guilty of a crime. Today some Americans use American Muslims as a scapegoat by assuming that they are terrorists or at least sympathetic to terrorists and acting aggressively against them by vandalizing mosques and verbally or even physically abusing them.

Finding a scapegoat does not necessarily solve problems, as illustrated in domestic abuse cases. When a man takes out his frustrations by abusing his partner, he has to justify his actions. It is common for men arrested for domestic abuse to claim that: "She made me do it," or "She kept nagging and wouldn't shut up." This not only depicts the man as a victim (the suffering husband) but also reinforces the stereotype of nagging wives, providing the husband with an excuse for assaulting the woman he once claimed to love. As violence escalates with each domestic abuse complaint from the same home, it is obvious that blaming a spouse or partner doesn't solve the problem; in fact, it may cause the abuser to become more violent toward those interfering with his actions.

Because of the high rates of injury and death to police officers responding to domestic abuse cases, many American cities, counties, and states require officers to file abuse charges directly, even over the objections of the one abused. Courts often mandate counseling for abusers to address and understand how gender prejudices and stereotypes created negative attitudes leading to abuse, and to teach abusive men effective, nonviolent strategies for managing anger. The role of gender stereotypes in contributing to domestic abuse illustrates another major cause of prejudice—uncertainty.

What do stereotypes have to do with uncertainty, and how do they cause prejudice?

Most of us only have knowledge of the groups to which we belong; often we do not know much about other groups. In the United States, schools have historically implemented curricula reflecting perspectives, contributions, and experiences of the dominant (White) group, and many of our neighborhoods still tend to be segregated by race or social class. The result is that people from different racial and ethnic groups have few opportunities to learn about one another. Because of our lack of accurate information, we may believe in stereotypes as a way to convince ourselves that we know about certain groups. (See Figure 2.2.) Our stereotypes can be reinforced by images or information contained in such media as advertisements, textbooks, and films.

For an example of ignorance promoting prejudice, how many Americans know that Muslims have been in the United States from colonial times because many slaves brought to America from West Africa were Muslim? The evidence is in the names that "read like a Who's Who of traditional Muslim names"—Bullaly (Bilali), Mahomet (Muhammad), Walley (Wali), and Sambo meant "second son" to Muslim Fulbe people (Abdo, 2006, p. 66). Although Americans tend to stereotype all Arabs as Muslims, the majority of Arabs immigrating to the United States in the late nineteenth century were Christians. Another stereotype is that Muslims have only lived in urban areas. How many Americans know that in the 1920s a small group of Muslims settled in Ross, South Dakota, and built the first mosque in the United States or that the oldest continuously functioning mosque is in Cedar Rapids, Iowa (Abdo, 2006)?

Figure 2.2 Learning about Stereotyping

This drawing has been used for research and in classrooms. One individual is shown this picture and whispers a description of the entire scene to another individual, who then whispers the description to another individual until each individual in the room has heard it. The last individual is asked to describe the scene to everyone. Typically, the individual describes a poorly dressed Black man with a weapon preparing to attack a well-dressed White man, thus illustrating the power of racial stereotypes.

Even if they don't know this history, how many Americans know that 27 percent of Muslim Americans own their own business (Wolfe, 2017)? How many know that Muslims tend to be well educated or that more undergraduate and graduate degrees have been earned by women (40 percent) than by men (35 percent) in the Muslim American community (Mogahed & Chouhoud, 2017)? About 50 percent of Muslim Americans today are immigrants, and they are doing what America expects of immigrants. But, unaware of this information, and surrounded by stereotypes and the media's focus on Islamic terrorists, how many Americans harbor negative views of both the Islamic faith and Muslims? According to a poll by the Pew Research Center (2013), 46 percent of Americans believed that the religion of Islam was no more likely to promote violence than any other religion, and yet 42 percent of Americans disagreed, believing that the Islamic faith encouraged violence more than other faiths.

People have long known that stereotypes skew an individual's perception of a group, but more recently scholars have reported that being aware of the stereotypes of your own group can adversely affect group members. This is called a **stereotype threat**, which Aronson (2012) defines as "the apprehension experienced by members of a minority group that they might behave in a manner that confirms an existing cultural stereotype" (p. 437). Such apprehensions can contribute to feelings of anxiety and poor performance.

Ariely (2008) described a study in which Asian American women were divided into two groups and administered the same math exam. Prior to receiving the exam, one group was asked numerous questions related to their gender, and the other group was asked numerous questions related to their race. The second group performed much better than the first group on the math test, suggesting that stereotypes about women being deficient in math and Asian people excelling at math may have influenced their performance. Other studies have reported similar results, including one study of White male engineering students who had almost perfect math scores on the SAT tests. These

White men were randomly divided into two groups, and prior to being given a challenging math test, one group was told that the test would measure their math abilities, whereas the other group was told that the purpose of the study was to understand why Asian people appear to be superior to all others in their math ability. The second group had much lower scores on the math exam than the first group (Aronson, 2008).

When an individual actually encounters individuals of a different race, ethnicity, or social class, selective perception of the behaviors of those individuals often reinforces stereotypes. Stephan (1999) reported on one study where participants were presented with equal amounts of positive and negative information about a group to which they belonged (in-group) and a group to which they did not belong (out-group). Participants tended to recall more positive information about the in-group and more negative information about the out-group. According to Stephan, negative attitudes in our memory tend to increase over time.

Selective perception was illustrated in another study in which two groups of participants viewed consecutive videos: The first video was of a fourth-grade girl playing with friends, and the second video was of the same girl taking an oral test in school in which she answered some difficult questions correctly but missed some easy questions. Although the second video was the same for both groups, the first video shown to one group was the girl playing in a low-income neighborhood, and the first video shown to the other group was the girl playing in a high-income neighborhood. After watching both videos, participants were asked to judge the girl's academic abilities. Those who saw her playing in the low-income neighborhood rated her academic ability lower than those who saw her playing in the more affluent neighborhood. Whether the participants focused more on the girl's correct or incorrect answers appears to have been influenced by the neighborhood in which they believed she lived and stereotypes associated with affluence and poverty (Aronson, 2008).

Researchers have also shown that becoming more knowledgeable about others helps people overcome stereotypical perceptions. In a psychiatric hospital with an all-White staff, clients acting violently were either taken to a "time-out room" or subjected to the harsher penalty of being put in a straitjacket and sedated. In the first month of a research study, both Black and White clients were admitted. Although the Black clients admitted were diagnosed as being less violent than the Whites, they were four times more likely to be put in a straitjacket and sedated by the staff if they became violent. The discrepancy in the White staff's use of restraints suggests that they believed in the stereotype that Black people were more prone to violence. As they became better acquainted with the clients, the staff responded to violent incidents with more equal use of restraints for both Black and White clients (Aronson, 2012). Stereotypes that portray a group as being prone to violence, lazy, or less intelligent can influence an individual's behavior; stereotypes can also play a part in an individual's self-esteem being threatened, which is another major cause of prejudice identified in research.

How does threat to self-esteem cause prejudice?

In the United States, people are encouraged to develop self-esteem by comparing themselves with others. We do so by grades in school, music contests, debates in speech, and athletic competitions. But what happens when positive self-esteem is achieved by developing feelings of superiority to someone else? Or when we achieve our sense of superiority by projecting our feelings of inferiority onto another individual or group? If we believe in the innate superiority of our group compared to other groups, then we believe we are better than anyone who is a member of the inferior group. If members of an inferior group become successful, their achievements threaten those whose self-esteem was based on feelings of group superiority, and that group's condescending attitude unconsciously turns into prejudice.

"Sometimes (prejudice) is like a hair across your cheek. You can't see it, you can't find it with your fingers, but you keep brushing at it because the feel of it is irritating."

— MARIAN ANDERSON (1897–1993)

People of color confront the issue of self-esteem based on race as a cause of prejudice when they encounter White people whose self-esteem is threatened by their achievements or success. Derrick Bell, the first African American to teach at Harvard University Law School, commented:

> You have to simultaneously function on a high level and try not to upset those whose racial equilibrium is thrown off when they recognize that you are not incompetent, not mediocre, and don't fit the long accepted notions about persons of color that serve as unrecognized but important components of their self-esteem. (Bell, 2002, pp. 66–67)

When we possess this kind of self-esteem, we are insecure and easily threatened. A study found that men felt insecure when their partners were successful, but this is not true for women. The researchers suggest that the reason could be based on men accepting gender stereotypes that men are smarter and more capable than women (Marcotte, 2013). Coleman (2007) argued that people who perceive others as inferior "are more likely to identify and maintain negative stereotypes about members of stigmatized groups" (p. 222).

Studies have long suggested that part of the self-esteem of many men derives just from being male. Similar attitudes appear among adults. In their research on self-esteem, Martinez and Dukes (1991) reported that men displayed higher self-esteem than did women, and that White men had the highest self-esteem of all groups. In Michigan, over a thousand children wrote essays about what their lives would be like if they were the opposite gender. Although almost half the girls found many positive things to say about being male, 95 percent of the boys could find nothing positive to say about being female (Sadker & Sadker, 1994). A recent cross-cultural study involving over a million participants analyzed the gender impact on self-esteem. The researchers found a gender gap in all cultures, but the gap was much wider in developed nations than in developing nations (Sliwa, 2017).

When men's self-esteem derives from perceiving their gender as superior, it is easily threatened by women's achievements. American men often rationalize female achievements by attributing women's success to reasons other than competence. Their rationalizations may be characterized by resentment or anger, which intensifies the prejudice that created the initial illusion of superiority. If a woman receives the promotion a man wanted, he might complain that she is "sleeping her way to the top." Because self-esteem based on a belief in gender superiority is an illusion, it is ultimately inadequate because the individual has done nothing to earn it. Fearing that an "inferior" individual might receive rewards the "superior" individual desires is related to the fourth primary cause of prejudice: competition for status, wealth, and power.

How does competition for status, wealth, and power cause prejudice?

There is evidence that competition fosters prejudicial attitudes. Jones (1997) described a study at a summer camp where Boy Scouts were given time to become acquainted and to develop friendships before being divided into two groups and housed in separate bunkhouses. The groups were divided so that approximately two thirds of each boy's friends were in the other bunkhouse. The two groups were encouraged to play a series of competitive games such as tug-of-war, football, and baseball. Boys who had liked each other began to intensely dislike each other and to engage in name calling. Although there was solidarity within groups, friendships that had been established with boys from the other group no longer existed. After competitive games were concluded, researchers brought the boys together, but animosity remained until the boys were given tasks that required them to cooperate with each other. Working together to achieve a common goal reduced the hostility and resulted in the boys again making friendships with individuals from the other group. From this study we can argue how important it is, in schools and at work sites, to promote collaborative efforts among students or workers from diverse groups so that they not only complete necessary tasks but also build better relationships. This may be one of the most effective ways to reduce both prejudice and the kinds of discriminatory practices that stem from prejudice such as racial profiling.

What is racial profiling?

Racial profiling occurs when authorities assume that members of certain racial or ethnic groups are more likely to engage in criminal activity. Approximately two-thirds of African Americans have experienced or know someone who has experienced police harassment or violence (Grossfeld, 2017). A national study found that Black young adults (18–29) were twice as likely to report being harassed by police as their White peers, and another study found that Black youth (15–19) were over 20 times more likely to be shot and killed by police as their White peers (Center for American Progress, 2016). It is not surprising that only about 10 percent of African Americans believe that police officers treat them as fairly as they treat other groups (Sue, 2015). For example, for years African Americans have complained about being disproportionately stopped by police for no reason, or for what police insisted was a "routine" traffic stop. Black people refer to this as being guilty of the crime of "Driving While Black" (DWB). But DWB is no longer the only form of racial profiling. Muslims have reported being similarly singled out by airport authorities for FWM ("Flying While Muslim"). A poll of American Muslims reported that 21 percent of them had been taken aside by airport security for further screening (Chalabi, 2015). Federal and state funding of anti-terrorism training for local police has contributed to racial profiling of Muslims. Stalcup and Craze (2011) observed specific trainers reinforcing anti-Muslim stereotypes and presenting false statements about Islamic beliefs, including the attribution of extremist beliefs to mainstream Muslims. Critics argue that racial profiling is not only discriminatory but also an ineffective approach to curbing terrorism; yet when Americans were asked about their attitudes toward Islam, a 2009 poll revealed that almost half of Americans had an "unfavorable opinion," and a 2010 Pew Research Center survey found 35 percent of Americans believing that Islam encouraged its followers to engage in violence, and attitudes seem to be getting worse. In 2010, 36 percent of Americans expressed a favorable opinion of American Muslims, but by 2014 only 27 percent had a favorable opinion (Siddiqui, 2014). In addition, the controversy over illegal immigration has led to racial profiling of Latinos by some law enforcement officials. This was exacerbated by Arizona's passage of a harsh immigration law that allows police officers to detain an individual on a suspicion of being an undocumented worker. With the passage of SB 1070, Latinos in Arizona can be forced to produce papers proving that they are U.S. citizens or legal immigrants, and without such papers they could be arrested and incarcerated. At a naturalization ceremony in the Rose Garden, President Obama warned that the Arizona law could potentially "undermine basic notions that we cherish as Americans, as well as the trust between police and our communities that is so crucial to keeping us safe" (Archibold, 2010, p. 1). Yet in a 2010 poll of more than a thousand Americans, 61 percent said they approved of the Arizona law. This approval spanned political parties with 49 percent of Democrats, 80 percent of Republicans, and 54 percent of Independents supporting the law (Tolev, 2010). Arizona's law should increase the pressure on federal lawmakers to pass some kind of immigration reform, but a divided Congress seems unwilling to address this critical issue. Meanwhile, Latino organizations and advocacy groups are monitoring police activities in Arizona to make sure that the rights of American citizens and legal immigrants are not abused by those charged with enforcing this law.

What other forms of discrimination are a consequence of prejudice?

Allport (1979) identified five negative behaviors caused by prejudice:

1. *Verbal abuse* against others that occurs among friends or results in name-calling directed at others from a particular group is a consequence of prejudice. Name-calling can escalate into the next form of negative behavior.

2. *Physical assaults* are a consequence of prejudice, sometimes occurring even when the victim is not a member of the despised group. When a large group of ethnic Hmong from Southeast Asia settled in a Wisconsin community of 50,000 people, some local citizens did not accept them. A Japanese foreign exchange student who attended a college in that community was severely beaten by a White man in the mistaken belief that his victim was Hmong. Another common example of violence based on misperceptions is heterosexual men who have been physically assaulted because they were perceived to be gay.

3. *Extreme violence* includes the desire to commit murder. Such behavior is now called a "hate crime." In 2015, the seventh White man was convicted (two White women were also convicted) of severely beating a Black man and then killing him by running over his defenseless body with a pickup truck (Amy, 2015). When homicidal rage spreads, it might lead to the extreme form of violence called **genocide**—the systematic and deliberate extermination of a nationality or a racial or ethnic group (Feagin & Feagin, 2008). An individual can play a passive role that still supports genocide. After World War II, most Germans (also Poles, Austrians, and others) claimed they didn't know that six million Jewish people were killed in concentration camps; persuasive evidence has been gathered to argue that they knew but were not concerned enough to do anything about it (Goldhagen, 2002). In contrast to confrontational negative behavior stemming from prejudice and bigotry, a more passive negative response to prejudice is to avoid members of other groups.

4. *Limited interactions* with people from racial or ethnic groups other than our own can result in discriminatory behaviors. Measuring attitudes about avoiding others was the focus of research by Bogardus; this study used a Social Distance Scale in which people encounter a list of racial, ethnic, and religious groups and are asked to rank them in order of preference (Schaefer, 2008). People consistently reveal a preference for those groups most like their own, and they have less regard for people from groups they perceive as least like themselves.

5. *Engage in or condone discrimination* in such areas as education, employment, and housing. To illustrate this behavior, consider how people choose what sort of neighborhood they want to live in. In the 1960s, when courts ordered urban school districts to desegregate, many school administrators responded by busing students to different schools, a controversial solution that caused massive movement of White families from urban neighborhoods to racially segregated suburbs, the **White flight** phenomenon (see Figure 2.3). Despite the passage of the 1968 National Fair Housing Act, studies have documented the preference of most White Americans to live in racially segregated neighborhoods (Farley, 2005). The problem of segregation goes beyond the concept of "fair housing." As Fowler (2012) noted, when urban neighborhoods are racially segregated, it creates other consequences related to criminal activity, pollution problems, and health issues.

Is prejudice the main cause of discrimination in society?

For years scholars believed that discrimination was caused by prejudice; therefore, the way to reduce discrimination was to reduce prejudice. Efforts were made in schools and through popular culture vehicles to address and reduce prejudice with what

Figure 2.3 Neighborhood Preference of White Respondents

In a study cited by Farley (2005), participants were shown diagrams of neighborhoods consisting of 15 homes with an X on the home in the center of the neighborhood indicating the participant's home. Each shaded home represented an African American family. White respondents were asked: How comfortable would they feel in each neighborhood? If they were uncomfortable, would they leave? Would they move to such a neighborhood? The percentage not willing to live in those neighborhoods where only a fifth or a third of homeowners were African Americans illustrates attitudes that produced White flight.

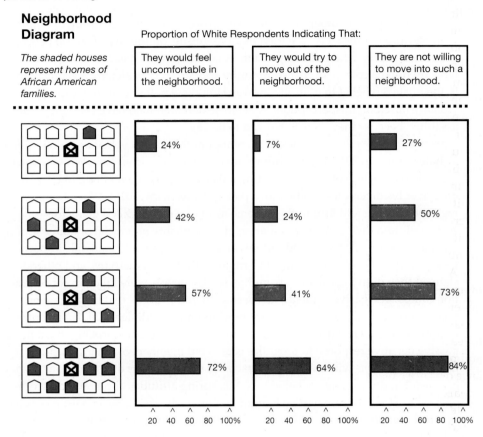

appear to be positive results. Since the 1960s, a number of studies have reported a significant decrease in racial prejudice among the American people (Pearson, Dovidio, & Gaertner, 2009); however, studies of discrimination have not reported a similar decline (Astor, 1997). A study by Fryer, Pager and Spenkuch (2014) found that White workers were still more likely to be hired than workers of color and that when people of color were hired they were typically offered lower rates of compensation. Over thirty years ago, Feagin and Feagin (1986) proposed alternative theories of discrimination that do not involve prejudice as the prime cause of discrimination. Two of their theories have been especially helpful to those trying to understand this seeming paradox: the interest theory and the institutionalized discrimination theory.

How does the interest theory explain discrimination?

The **interest theory** describes discrimination resulting from people protecting their power and privilege. Instead of being motivated by prejudice, people discriminate against individuals from subordinate groups because of self-interest. For example, White men may object to affirmative action programs not because of a prejudice against any group but rather from fear of policies that might reduce their opportunities to be hired, retained, or promoted. Homeowners might persuade neighbors not to sell their home to a family of color because they are worried about what will happen to property values. Discrimination is a function of protecting interests, a motivation that is addressed on a broader scale in the institutionalized discrimination theory.

How is discrimination explained by the institutionalized discrimination theory?

The **institutionalized discrimination theory** begins with an historic analysis outlining how privilege was created in the United States when the dominant group—White European men—exploited subordinate groups to assume control of America's resources: land from American Indians, unpaid labor by African slaves, and wages and property of wives. Furthermore, by gaining control over resources and exploiting them, certain White European men achieved positions that provided them access to technological advances and control of industrial developments in the United States. Once they attain a position of power, people will do whatever they can to maintain their advantage and stay in power, so it is this effort to maintain power, rather than prejudice, that drives their behavior. Proceeding from this historical framework, the institutionalized discrimination theory focuses on the present by engaging in an analysis to understand mechanisms and methods that lead to discrimination in institutional policies and practices. Similar to the interest theory, institutionalized discrimination theory is not concerned with prejudice (what U.S. courts have called "evil intent") but is based on the assumption that much discrimination today is unintentional.

An example of unintended discrimination was described to the author as part of an urban research project. Several urban women in leadership roles in their city government were interviewed, and one of them explained how a group of female department heads had solved a problem. At the end of a workday, the women tended to leave immediately because of family responsibilities such as picking up children and preparing meals. Male department heads tended to meet for a drink after work once or twice a week, and they often played golf together on weekends while women department heads spent that time with their families. At meetings in which they made decisions about funding for programs, female department heads were frustrated by their inability to be as effective as their male counterparts in supporting each other.

The women understood why the men had an advantage. Because of their social activities, male department heads knew more about one another's departments, so they could make informed arguments in support of one another's programs. To create a similar advantage for themselves, the women started meeting together one evening every month (child care provided) to talk about their programs and needs and to prepare for debates on funding priorities. As a result of their efforts, a greater amount of funding was distributed to departments headed by women (Koppelman, 1994).

This example provides a realistic basis for understanding the value of the institutionalized discrimination theory: The actions of the male department heads were not based on a prejudice against women; rather, the men were doing their job in accordance with historic practices that benefited their departments. The women understood that the solution was not to berate the men but rather to devise a strategy to offset advantages already established for male department heads. Even though informal institutional procedures favored the men, the women found a way to "play the game" more effectively. Discriminatory actions can still be a direct result of prejudice on the part of people making decisions, but causes for discrimination are more likely to stem from reasons far more subtle and complex. Although prejudices may not play as significant a role in discrimination as we once thought they did, they still contribute to many problems in our society, and we should continue to do what we can to reduce individual prejudices.

What can schools do to reduce prejudice?

The 2016 Presidential campaign was controversial because some candidates expressed negative stereotypes toward Muslims, Mexican Americans, and immigrants in general. During that fall, teachers struggled with the issue of how to address these prejudices. Some Americans used social media to joke about the campaign, but Mexican Americans and Muslim students were not laughing. They were hearing one candidate for president in particular disparage Mexicans and denounce Muslims as terrorists. Donald Trump also promised to end birthright citizenship and demonized Black and brown people living in Chicago, threatening to "send in the feds" to deal with gun violence (Michie, 2017). In this era of unarmed Black men being killed by police officers, that was not a reassuring promise. In response to the campaign rhetoric, a Chicago student asked his teacher, "If Donald Trump wins and my mom gets deported, can I come live with you and your family?" (Michie, 2017).

In fall 2016, the Southern Poverty Law Center (SPLC) surveyed about 2000 K–12 teachers to ascertain if negative language from the campaign was having any impact on students. Teachers reported that they had observed an alarming amount of fear and anxiety among the children in their classrooms and that it had intensified racial and ethnic tension. Over one-third of teachers reported an increase in students expressing anti-Muslim and anti-immigrant sentiments. During an Indiana basketball game where the opposing team consisted primarily of Latinos, White students chanted: "Build a wall" (Costello, 2016). At a school with diverse students, White girls came to a school assembly waving a Confederate flag. At another school White students taunted Hispanic students, saying they were going to be deported, and White students pulled hijabs from the heads of Muslim girls. At another school male students grabbed girls' crotches as they joked about Donald Trump's videotaped comments on sexually harassing women (Editors of Rethinking Schools, 2016–2017). Further, many teachers believed that the overt hostility Trump expressed during the campaign toward immigrants, especially Mexicans, contributed to an increase in bullying behavior. Over two-thirds of teachers said they had observed an increase of intimidating behaviors toward students who were immigrants, children of immigrants, or Muslims (Costello, 2016).

In addition to student anxiety, teachers expressed frustration over how they should respond to the prejudices being promoted in this campaign. Historically, most teachers have been comfortable teaching about the issues and providing information about the candidates while maintaining a nonpartisan position, but given the anxiety the minority children were feeling during this presidential campaign, teachers were concerned that they needed to be more proactive. In a survey of elementary schools, about half of the teachers chose to address these issues, and at middle and high schools, an increasing number of teachers, most of them for the first time, decided to address the prejudice and hostility directed at minority groups in statements made by political candidates (Costello, 2016). In Richmond, California, students from five high schools asked teachers to work with them to organize a walkout where students would not have class but attend workshops on such topics as student rights, promoting demands for social justice, and creating political art. The walkout ended with a demonstration in downtown Richmond. Parents responded by thanking the teachers and administrators for creating a safe space for students to be active rather than passively ignoring the prejudice and bigotry of the 2016 presidential campaign (Editors of Rethinking Schools, 2016–2017).

More than two-thirds of teachers said students who were Muslim or immigrants had expressed at least some concern, if not outright fear, of what might happen to their families after the 2016 election, especially the possibility of deportation (Costello, 2016). Their concerns turned out to be well founded. By the end of his first week in office, President Trump had signed the executive order to begin erecting the wall on the U.S. border with Mexico. Former President Obama had prioritized that immigrants with criminal records be pursued for deportation, but on January 25, 2017, Trump issued an executive order directing immigration officials to pursue people who had simply been charged with a crime or who had improperly used public benefits, which could allow immigration agents to pursue families whose children receive free lunches at school. Since Trump's executive order, arrests have increased by almost one-third (Law, 2017).

The problem of bullying behavior has persisted, prompting some schools to more strictly enforce anti-bullying rules, but top-down approaches are often not effective. As an alternative, many schools have implemented talking circles and other interactive strategies to reinforce the perception of the school as a community of diverse people who are able to openly share their perspectives. One study had teachers assigning research projects where students worked collaboratively in diverse groups. When these projects were completed, students reported a more positive attitude to diverse students included in their groups, and these positive attitudes seemed to have a lasting effect (Donald, 2013). Teachers will need to continue monitoring students to ascertain their concerns and implement activities and strategies that address these concerns while helping all of their students come to a better understanding of prejudice and its causes.

Video Example 2.2

In this video, immigrant students discuss their experiences with culture shock and conflicts they encounter as a result of being immigrants. What kinds of conflicts, related to prejudice and discrimination, do they discuss? How might the strategies in schools to reduce prejudice that are discussed in the chapter help these students?

 Self-Check 2.3 Complete this self-check quiz to check your understanding of how frustration, threat to self-esteem, uncertainty, and competition foster the development of individual prejudice; how that prejudice can lead to discriminatory behavior; and how discrimination occurs in the absence of prejudice.

Afterword

If prejudice were part of human nature, people would be justified in feeling despair because the implication would be that human beings eventually will destroy each other. But no evidence supports the idea that prejudice is innate. Instead, studies have consistently concluded that prejudice is learned. The fact that prejudice is learned offers hope because anything that can be learned can be unlearned. In our schools, educators can confront negative attitudes both in the media and in our language to help students unlearn prejudices they have been taught and also understand why it is in everyone's best interest not to act on prejudices.

In their study of brain research, Newberg and Waldman (2006) found that people could "interrupt" prejudicial beliefs and stereotypes and generate new ideas, and that these new ideas "can alter the neural circuitry that governs how we behave and what we believe. Our beliefs . . . aren't necessarily static. They can change; we can change them" (p. 9).

Prejudice can be reduced by providing accurate information, promoting formal and informal learning, and establishing equitable workplace policies and practices. Prejudices can also be unlearned by friends challenging one another's negative attitudes. Even though some people may not be able to give up their prejudices, they do not have to act on them. It is not inevitable that our prejudices control us. When we can identify our prejudices and understand how we learned them, we can choose to limit their influence on our behavior. We can change these prejudices or at least make sure we can control them instead of letting them control us.

When we make positive choices, we affirm the basis for having hope for the future. Positive choices that individuals have made throughout history have resulted in genuine human progress. If our society is to benefit from its diversity, it will be because enough Americans have chosen to regard diversity as an asset and to confront their prejudices. Those who make such positive choices today will shape the nature of the society in which our children and their children must live.

Video Example 2.3

In this video, two teachers discuss how one of the teachers dealt with a racial blunder in which she made a cultural assumption about a student. How does this instance relate to the points discussed in the Chapter 2 Afterword? What lesson did the teacher learn through that instance?

"You don't make progress by standing on the sidelines, whimpering and complaining. You make progress by implementing ideas."

— SHIRLEY CHISHOLM (1924–2005)

Summary

- Prejudice has been misunderstood in a variety of ways, and these misunderstandings have been reinforced by biased portrayals of minorities in the media and patterns of bias in our language such as the black/white syndrome and the negative implications in common cultural sayings.

- Individuals can perpetuate their prejudice by denying that they harbor negative attitudes, claiming minority group members create the problems they complain about, or avoiding serious discussions of topics related to prejudice and discrimination.

- Although there are many causes of prejudice, scholars have identified frustration, threat to self-esteem, uncertainty, and competition as major factors fostering prejudice, and they have explained how prejudice may lead to negative behavior. Today, experts are also explaining how discrimination may be a consequence of causes other than prejudice.

Terms and Definitions

Avoidance rationalization A response to a social problem—such as injustice toward a minority group—that acknowledges the existence of a problem but avoids confronting the problem by offering partial or false solutions or by using arguments that do not address the situation, as in "Yes, but you should have seen how bad it was last year."

Black/white syndrome A pattern in the English language consisting of negative meanings for phrases, including the word *black* and positive meanings for phrases including the word *white*

Denial rationalization A response to a social problem—such as injustice toward a minority group—that does not acknowledge the existence of a problem but insists instead that no injustice has occurred, as in "That's not discrimination. Men have always been the boss; it's just the way things are meant to be."

Elitism The belief that the best people ascend to a place of superiority in society and represent a natural aristocracy, whereas those who are not successful are viewed as lacking the necessary qualities to be successful within society

Genocide The deliberate and systematic extermination of a particular nationality, or racial, ethnic, or minority group

Institutionalized discrimination theory Institutional policies and practices that have differential and negative effects on subordinate groups in a society

Interest theory People engaging or acquiescing in discriminatory actions based on a desire to protect their power or privilege

Prejudice A negative attitude toward a group and anyone perceived to be a member of that group; a predisposition to negative behavior toward members of a group

Racial profiling People in authority taking actions against members of racial or ethnic groups based on assumptions that these groups are more likely to engage in criminal activity

Scapegoat An individual or a group of people blamed for another individual's problems or difficulties; identifying a scapegoat is often employed to justify taking a negative action against that individual or group

Stereotype threat The apprehension experienced by members of a minority group that they might behave in a manner that confirms an existing cultural stereotype

Victim-blaming rationalization A response to a social problem—such as injustice toward a minority group—that identifies the problem as a deficiency in the minority group and not a societal problem, as in "If poor people want to escape poverty they just have to be willing to work harder."

White flight The migration of White families from an urban to a suburban location because of court rulings to desegregate urban schools

Zero sum An orientation toward power and resources based on assumptions of scarcity, as when struggling to achieve goals, one individual gains at the expense of another. The belief that sharing power means a reduction of power

Discussion Exercises

Clarification Exercise—Rationalizations: Victim-Blame, Denial, and Avoidance

Directions: This exercise provides everyday statements we might hear; each one is a specific kind of rationalization. Based on the text and on your group discussion, identify the statements below according to one of the three types of rationalizations. First, select which passages would most likely represent an avoidance of a problem. Then select those in which the speaker employs a denial rationalization—that the problem either does not exist or the speaker is suggesting, "That's just the way things are." Finally, locate victim-blaming statements in which a specific individual or group is being charged with its own downfall or problem.

Rationalizations for Our Prejudices

Directions: Decide whether the following statements represent a denial of the problem (**D**), a victim-blame that it is the speaker's problem (**D/VB**), or an avoidance of the problem (**A**).

_____ 1. Women and minorities are getting everything their way. They are taking away our jobs, and pretty soon they are going to take over everything.

_____ 2. What we have here, basically, is a failure to communicate. We must develop better programs in interpersonal communications to address this issue.

_____ 3. This is the way these people want to live. You can't change poor people; they can't help the way they are.

_____ 4. We must move with deliberation on these issues. Real change takes time. We have to educate people.

_____ 5. All those women on welfare have it made. All they do is stay home and make babies while the rest of us have to work and pay taxes to support them.

_____ 6. I can't figure out what to call all these people. Why can't we all just be human instead of Black, Chicano, Latino, Native American, or Asian American?

_____ 7. Indians are their own worst enemy. They should stop fighting among themselves and get together on whatever it is they really want.

_____ 8. If Black people want to make it in our society, they are going to have to get rid of those dreadlocks and other weird hairstyles, the baggy clothes and funny handshakes, and they better start speaking better English.

_____ 9. Yes, but in the old days, race and sex discrimination were much worse. And even today, women and minorities are much better off in this country than anywhere else in the world.

_____ 10. Women are just too sensitive about sexism. They need to look at these things less emotionally and much more rationally.

_____ 11. We need more programs in African American studies, Latino studies, Native American studies, and Asian American studies to learn about all the contributions these groups have made to our society.

_____ 12. Feminists are pushing too hard for the changes that they demand. They are hurting themselves more than they are helping.

_____ 13. I understand that some people face more difficulties than others, but this is a free country, and I believe that anybody who is willing to work hard enough can be successful.

Follow-Up: Select any two from each of the three categories—D, VB, and A—and rewrite them to be the fourth kind of statement—those without rationalization. Explain why you chose to rewrite them as you did.

Exercise—The Liver Transplant Problem

Background: Today, the only medical procedure available to save the lives of individuals who have diseases of the liver is an organ transplant. Unfortunately, there are not enough livers to take care of all cases now, and there will not be enough in the near future to save the lives of all those in need.

Your Role: The decision about which people can be saved must be made on criteria other than medical criteria. Your hospital has decided that the best way to select individuals for a transplant is by setting up a volunteer citizens panel to make the decisions. You are on the panel and receive a Profile Sheet of applicants for transplants (see the table). Doctors have screened all clients, and all have equal prognosis for medical success.

Problem: There is a liver available for one individual on the list. All those not served will die. The availability of other livers cannot be anticipated, although if other livers become available, additional individuals on the list could receive transplants.

Liver Transplant Recipient Profile Sheet

Code	Age	Race	Sex	Marital Status	Religious Affiliation	Children	Occupation
A	24	Black	M	Married	Muslim	None	Postal worker
B	45	White	M	Married	Atheist	2	Executive
C	39	Asian American	F	Divorced	Buddhist	None	Medical doctor
D	40	White	F	Married	Jew	3	Housewife
E	23	Black	M	Unmarried	Episcopal	None	PhD student
F	40	White	F	Unmarried	Pentecostal	9	Welfare mother
G	28	Native American	M	Unmarried	Native	3	Seasonal worker
H	30	Latina	F	Married	Catholic	7	Housewife
I	19	White	M	Unmarried	Baptist	None	Special student

Directions: Your panel must make a unanimous decision regarding the individual to be the liver recipient. A lottery violates institutional ethics and is not an acceptable strategy. As you deliberate, discuss your values and consider those of others related to the process being utilized and the criteria you propose:

1. The criteria you develop for choosing the recipient.
2. Why you believe that the individual you chose best fits your criteria.
3. How your panel arrives at a single selection of a recipient.

Please see below for more detailed notes about the recipients.

Notes about Recipients:
A. Devotes time to volunteer work for Black organizations
B. Possible candidate for U.S. Senate
C. College physician and feminist speaker
D. Active in local synagogue and charitable activities
E. Middle states chair of a gay rights task force
F. Advocate and organizer of welfare mothers
G. State chair, Indian Treaty Rights Organization
H. Blind and or individual with a disability
I. Individual with a cognitive disability

Chapter 3
Communication, Conflict, and Conflict Resolution

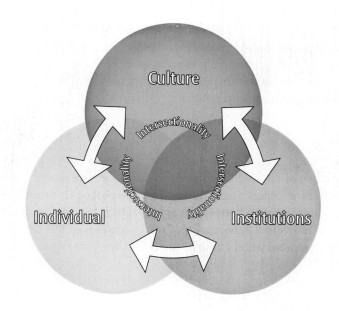

Culture
Intersectionality
Individual
Institutions
Intersectionality
Intersectionality

Learning Outcomes

After reading this chapter you will know and be able to:

3.1 Identify and explain five misconceptions about communication, and describe a communication model that explains how to resolve conflicts.

3.2 Discuss why certain values and skills are necessary for conflict resolution.

3.3 Explain a theory on the development of moral reasoning supported by research studies.

> "The meanings of words are not in the words; they are in us."
>
> — S. I. HAYAKAWA (1906–1992)

Communication seems simple. One individual talks, and other people listen to understand what the speaker is saying; when the first individual stops talking, another individual responds, perhaps to agree or disagree with the first speaker. Nothing seems complicated here, so why are there misunderstandings that so often lead to conflicts among individuals, groups, organizations, and nations? One answer was suggested in the 1960s film *Cool Hand Luke*, in which Paul Newman as Luke, an inmate, keeps breaking the warden's rules. As he prepares to punish Luke once again, the warden says, "What we have here is a failure to communicate." Actually it's not that Luke doesn't understand the rules; the problem is he doesn't respect the rules, so he violates them. By referring to a failure in communication, the warden means that Luke has not demonstrated that he understands he must conform to the rules.

Communication and Conflict

Communication is more than merely speaking, listening, and comprehending one another's words. Understanding the concept of communication requires some knowledge of the purpose served by communication and what attitudes support it. Spitzberg (2008) reported that we interact with other people 70 percent of the time we are awake. Communicating effectively is an asset in your personal and professional life, especially when conflicts occur, because conflict resolution can only happen if the people involved communicate effectively.

What is an appropriate definition of communication?

Although mass media is also a form of communication, when people talk about communication, they are more likely to be focused on interpersonal communication. Kougl (1997) offers a practical definition of **interpersonal communication**: "A dynamic process of interaction between people in which they assign meaning to each other's verbal and nonverbal behavior" (p. 7). Two features of this definition provide clues about how communication can lead to conflict: *assigning meaning* and *nonverbal behavior*.

How does assigning meaning lead to conflict?

We not only listen to words; we also make assumptions about what the other individual means. If our assumptions are accurate, there is no problem, but if they are not, the result is likely to be a misinterpretation of the message.

When interaction occurs between members of different groups, individuals may interpret the meaning of a statement in terms of the perceived influence of stereotypes or prejudices. An example of assigning meanings to statements that result in conflict occurred during a college ethnic studies class discussion of offensive words, phrases, and images based on ethnic and racial differences. An Asian American college student described his visit to a local middle school. As soon as he entered the building, he saw a few White male students put their fingers next to their eyes and pull their skin to create a "slant-eyed" look, and they began talking with a stereotypical Asian accent. The Asian American college student was appalled that these middle school students would taunt a visitor to their school with such blatant stereotypes, but another college student said this did not necessarily reflect their prejudice, just their immaturity. He argued that students at that age, especially boys, tend to be very insecure and they make fun of everyone and everything to get attention.

An American Indian student disagreed, saying that when he was in middle school and high school he heard a lot of students talking in terms of stereotypes. That was one of the reasons he was opposed to using Indians as mascots for sports teams because such images reinforced stereotypes of American Indians. A White woman in the class who was a nontraditional student said she didn't think there was anything wrong with Indian mascots because they had an Indian mascot at her high school, and she felt that it was used to honor Indian people. That led to the following dialogue among the White female (WF), American Indian (AI), and Asian American (AA) students:

AI: How am I supposed to be honored by an image like the Cleveland Indians mascot? These things are caricatures, cartoon figures! Even images that try to be respectable are just "noble savage" stereotypes that do not realistically depict real Indian people today . . . or at any time actually.

WF: Well, I suppose if you look at something long enough you can always find something to be offended about.

AA: Hold on, wait a minute! Are you saying that the problem is just in his head? That some people just make up stuff to be offended about but there's really nothing offensive there, nothing going on?

WF: No, no, I'm not saying that. I just meant that . . . like with the Indian mascots. . . I don't think anyone intends to offend anyone, but some people are offended.

AA: But you seem to be saying that the problem isn't real; that it's only a problem because of the way some Indian people look at this issue.

AI: Yeah, it sounds like you don't think Indian mascots are stereotypes, and if we would just stop saying they were, then there'd be no problem.

AA: Isn't that just another example of what we've talked about before? . . . You know, blaming the victim?

WF: But that's not what I'm saying!

AA: Maybe not, but that's what it sounds like. And if we keep talking like that, then no one will ever confront the stereotypes that kids have learned about Asian or Black people, Native Americans, or any other group. It's not about immaturity or good intentions. It's about what people are doing, you know, it's about certain behaviors that should be confronted, especially in schools, and how to go about doing that.

The White woman continued to defend her position, but she was frustrated that she could not seem to get the other students to understand what she was saying—yet they felt they understood her meaning all too well. They perceived that she was denying the problem of stereotypes affecting White people's perceptions of people of color; they also believed that she blamed people of color for being offended by things that were never meant to be offensive. The White woman wanted to emphasize intent, but the other two students were focused on the consequences for people of color no matter what was intended. From this example, it is easy to see how conflicts can arise from the meanings assigned to verbal statements. Regardless of what a speaker intended to say, people will make assumptions and interpretations about the meaning of that individual's statements. When the meaning assigned to a speaker's words becomes significantly different from what was intended, a conflict is likely to occur. Similarly, nonverbal communication can also lead to conflict based on an interpretation of the meaning of a nonverbal message.

How does nonverbal communication lead to conflict?

Hecht and DeVito (2008) define **nonverbal communication** as "all the messages other than words that people exchange" (p. 4). Estimates of how much meaning is taken from interpretations of nonverbal communication have been as high as 93 percent, although Burgoon (2002) estimated that 60 percent to 65 percent is more realistic. Although

Figure 3.1 Contempt or Anger?

According to Ekman (2003), expressions of contempt and disgust are often used to indicate hatred of another. Prior studies have indicated that expressions of hatred and anger are often confused. In these two photographs from Ekman's research, one expression represents contempt, and the other is anger. Try to identify the emotion represented in each facial expression. (For the answer, see the Ekman annotation in the References at the end of the text.)

SOURCE: Used by permission of Paul Ekman.

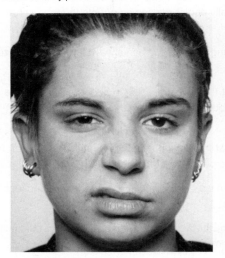 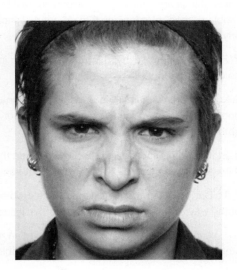

> "Communication is something so simple and so difficult that we can never put it into simple words."
>
> — T. S. MATTHEWS (1901–1991)

children don't tend to find as much meaning from nonverbal behavior as adults do, for a child to understand adults, the adults must be careful that their verbal messages are not contradicted by nonverbal messages, especially while giving discipline. Perhaps the child is teasing or taunting other children, so the adult says, "Teasing is bad. It hurts people's feelings. It may make them angry, and it certainly makes me angry. You must stop doing this, or no one will like you, and no one will want to play with you." The message is clear and provides good reasons, including self-interest, for the child to change his behavior. However, if this message is accompanied by angry looks, a loud voice, and gestures such as the adult pointing or jabbing a finger at the child, the good advice may get lost. The message the child gets is not that the behavior is bad but that "I'm bad" or "She hates me." (See Figure 3.1.)

Children receiving this message are not likely to change their behavior but to persist in it, either as a way of rebelling against the adult who has made this negative comment about them or as a self-fulfilling prophecy: "She says I'm bad so I might as well be bad." Being told that certain behavior is unacceptable implicitly offers a child the power to choose. Children may not think they can change who they are, but they know they can change their behavior. If they hear an adult make a negative judgment about who they are, they can do nothing about that. Conflicts arising from such misinterpretations of nonverbal messages also occur among adults.

The need to assign meaning and the influence of nonverbal messages address two misconceptions about communication: (1) that communication simply means telling people something and (2) that communication is a verbal process to transmit messages using only words. Teachers should seek constant feedback from students to ensure that the knowledge they impart is being understood. Postman and Weingartner (1987) described ineffective teachers taking an "inoculation approach" by communicating information as if they were inoculating students against ignorance. When test grades revealed that students didn't retain much information, the teachers' reaction was similar to that of a physician not understanding why a vaccine had no effect when she knows she injected it.

What are other misconceptions about communication?

Of the many misconceptions about communication identified by Stone, Singletary, and Richmond (1999), the following five examples are especially important to recognize:

> Communication is a natural human ability.
> Communication is a good thing and should be encouraged.
> Communication will solve all our problems.
> Communications can break down.
> Communication competence is equal to communication effectiveness. (pp. 56–61)

Communication is a natural human ability. In a longitudinal study of three communities in the Piedmont Plateau region of the Carolinas, Heath (2006) described the way children learned communication skills and how these skills varied depending on the way the children had been taught. Heath found that low-income White parents taught language to children by reading storybooks with a moral for each tale. Parental communication style was didactic and authoritarian; their children memorized Bible verses, learned strict rules for right and wrong, and were severely punished for lying. When the children went to school, they did well initially because the learning activities and communication styles of teachers were similar to what they had experienced at home. The children obeyed teachers, looked for a single meaning—the moral—of a story, and memorized material as required.

As the children from low-income White families progressed through elementary school, however, they encountered activities requiring critical thinking and creativity. They had trouble making up stories because it seemed like lying. They struggled to make sense of stories with multiple meanings and to identify and analyze different perspectives for strengths and weaknesses. Their life experiences had not prepared them for reading, thinking, and communicating at any level of complexity. As they approached middle school, their grades declined, as did their confidence. The majority never achieved academic competence in school, and some dropped out before finishing high school.

Heath described the language learning of Black children from low-income homes as a more creative process where children listened to adults tell stories that often had no particular moral point; these stories related what had happened at work or in the neighborhood or gossip about "crooked politicians . . . or wayward choir leaders" (p. 168). Adults often told stories with a basis in fact but with embellishment. When the stories got too far removed from reality, the teller was accused of "talkin' junk." In addition to telling stories, boys developed language skills to respond to teasing based on "feigned hostility, disrespect and aggressive behavior," while girls honed their language skills by making up songs when skipping rope (p. 85). Both boys and girls practiced telling stories and, like adults, embellished their stories with fictional details.

Black children from low-income homes came to school with highly creative communication skills, but they did not do well in the early elementary classes because they were not as adept at memorization or sticking to the facts. They saw many meanings to a story other than the simple moral the teacher wanted. As the students struggled with their assignments and growing feelings of inadequacy, they lost confidence in themselves as learners. When they finally encountered the more creative and complex learning activities later in elementary school, they were not successful because they had given up on the possibility of achievement.

Heath noted that for both Black and White people, children who succeeded in school at all levels were from middle-class homes where their parents had read to them and had asked for didactic meanings of stories but also encouraged engagement in creative and analytical activity. A parent might read a story and then ask, "Would you have liked to go fishing with Little Bear? What do you think you would have caught?" (p. 250). Middle-class children came to school with a range of communication and language skills: They were successful at memorization and didactic activities during early elementary years; they were also able to adjust to activities emphasizing creativity or critical thinking in later years. Heath's research demonstrated that learning to communicate is not a natural human ability but rather is a product of the cultural and social context one experiences as a child.

Communication is a good thing and should be encouraged. Communication is a tool, and tools can be employed for good or bad purposes. Hitler used oratorical skills to arouse feelings of Aryan superiority and to deepen the anti-Semitic prejudices of Germans into a hatred that condoned persecution and execution. Martin Luther King Jr. employed his oratorical skills to urge nonviolent resistance to oppression, warning his followers not to hate oppressors but to focus on the cause of justice. With any communication it is essential to ascertain the speaker's purpose and then determine whether that purpose is a good one. As Skuttnab-Kangas (2000) says, language is "a tool for domination (or) a tool for change and self-determination" (p. 134).

It is also important to recognize when additional communication is not necessary—when the time has come to take action. Martin Luther King Jr. deplored the "paralysis of analysis," in which people continue to talk about problems without ever doing anything to resolve them. Of course it is essential to be thoughtful before acting, taking time to consider alternatives and consequences before deciding on a course of action, but there comes a time when you must stop analyzing every possible outcome and take action. After taking action, it is important to consider the consequences to determine whether to continue or choose another tactic. It is what Freire (2000) meant by the term **praxis**—taking action to address injustice and then reflecting on the effectiveness of the actions taken as the individual or group continues their activities.

Communication will solve all our problems. Communication has the potential to solve problems, but it also has the potential to create them. In a speech to college students, poet Maya Angelou noted that whenever anyone asked, "Can I be brutally honest?" she always said no because she did not want to encourage anyone to do anything brutally. Whether information is accurate or inaccurate, truthful or distorted, if communication is delivered brutally, it will be hurtful, creating problems rather than solving them. We can communicate respectfully and honestly without being brutal.

Some people talk about problems with no intent of solving them. Berne (2004) described such interaction as playing "games." In the "Ain't It Awful" game, two people talk about a problem simply to affirm each other's perceptions, often at the expense of another. Imagine two teachers discussing a student. One describes Danny's misbehavior; the other responds with a similar story about something Danny did in her class, and they continue to exchange stories. The teachers are not trying to understand the boy's behavior to help him; instead, each is telling the other, "You and I are all right. Danny is the problem." When their conversation ends, both teachers walk away believing they are not to blame, nor are they obligated to do anything to help Danny.

Another game Berne has described is "Yes, but . . . ," where one individual comes to another asking for advice but actually wanting something else. For example, Luis is a teenager who is having problems with his parents. He goes to his best friend for advice. His friend suggests several strategies, and each time Luis says either (a) he tried that (or something similar) and it didn't work, or (b) he thought about doing that but explains why the suggestion wouldn't work. After the friend has exhausted all possible strategies he can think of, he may say something like, "Well, I don't know what else to tell you. I don't know what else you can do." At this point, Luis walks away saying, "That's okay." The friend may be frustrated that he could not help solve the problem, but for Luis, the point of the conversation was to hear that he had done everything he could, and there was nothing more for him to do. Both "Ain't It Awful" and "Yes, but . . ." involve a "solution" only in the sense that someone gets what she wants from the interaction, but the communication is not intended to solve the problem.

Communications can break down. Most of us have used this particular misconception about communication to justify ongoing conflicts. Rebellious teenagers say their parents don't understand them; husbands and wives complain that their partners don't appreciate them; workers may go on strike claiming that management isn't bargaining in good faith. In such cases we may rationalize that our conflict cannot be resolved because communication has broken down. When machines break, they stop; however, communication cannot break down because it never stops, even if people stop talking to each other. Their communication could be hearsay, or it could be nonverbal; it could consist of interpretations by one person about perceived decisions and actions of another.

Communication occurs because one individual wants or needs to know what the other is thinking about or doing; an individual may make decisions to do (or not do) something based on assumptions about someone else. For example, one individual may decide not to attend a holiday party so that a co-worker will know he is still angry with her, or he may decide to attend the party but not speak to or make eye contact with her. Communication can be verbal or nonverbal, ineffective or effective, but it does not stop. If verbal exchange ceases, communication in some other form—whether words or actions—will replace it.

Communication competence is equal to communication effectiveness. Except for those in teacher education, most college professors learn how to communicate from mentors or self-study. Many professors have acquired the skills to become good teachers, yet the misconception that communication competence equals communication effectiveness is often the basis for student complaints that they aren't learning because a professor is incompetent. Professors may have **communication competence** because they have the necessary knowledge and may even have published articles and books on their specialty, yet they may not display **communication effectiveness** because they lack the appropriate skills to communicate effectively in a classroom.

A major function of teacher education programs consists of preparing people to be effective at organizing and communicating information. Whether they are lecturing or using alternative means of delivering information, teachers must understand what studies have concluded about effective ways of helping people learn. To assess how effectively they deliver information, teachers must also evaluate how well students learn. Tests and other forms of assessment may measure student learning; more importantly, however, they reveal how effectively the teacher communicated.

How does effective communication occur?

Numerous excellent models have been developed that examine the communication process and analyze communication to ascertain why misunderstandings occur (Narula, 2006; Stone et al., 1999). The following model describes four factors involved in interpersonal communication. Each instance of an individual interacting with another is influenced by these four cumulative factors (see Figure 3.2).

A Circular Model of Communication

1. Attitudes toward people or groups
2. Observations and assumptions
3. Conclusions and judgments
4. Verbal and nonverbal action

First, the communication process is grounded in an individual's *attitudes toward people or groups*. All people develop a general attitude about their interactions with others. Some are trusting, others are suspicious; some are willing to share ideas, others are reserved; some are motivated by dominance and control, others function with an egalitarian view.

> "Information voids will be filled by rumors and speculation unless they are preempted by open, credible, and trustworthy communication."
>
> — JEAN KEFFLER (CONTEMPORARY)

Figure 3.2 The Circular Model of Communication

This model emphasizes the cognitive process that occurs prior to the actual verbal or nonverbal behavior from each individual involved in the interpersonal communication.

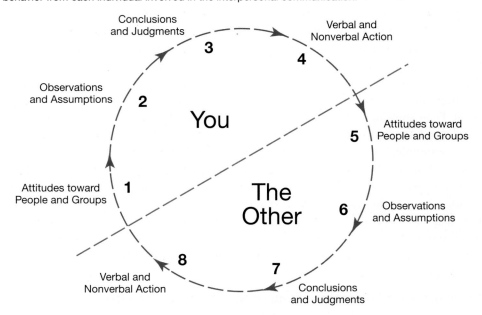

Our attitudes may change based on our relationship with the individuals involved in our interactions. Our interactions with family are different than they are with strangers. We communicate differently within same-gender groups than in mixed groups or with people of the opposite gender. Our behavior is different with others of our own race or ethnic group as opposed to being in mixed groups or with individuals from another race or ethnic group. Having prejudices or stereotypes about a particular minority group will certainly influence our interactions with a member of that group.

Second, our *observations and assumptions* about another individual shape the communication between us before anything is said. Our initial reaction may be friendly and accepting, aloof and suspicious, or even hostile and rejecting, depending on the appearance of the other individual and sometimes on which behaviors we choose to observe—a phenomenon known as **selective perception**. If an individual believes a stereotype about someone from a certain group, that stereotype is likely to be reinforced by selective perceptions.

How do our observations influence our assumptions? What if an individual were introduced to a long-haired young White man who was dressed in torn overalls and wore a red bandanna around his head? Based on observation, you might assume that the young man has rejected our materialistic society by imitating college students from the 1960s who questioned authority figures and rebelled against middle-class values, conformity, and the Vietnam War. These observations and assumptions are now taken to the next level.

The third step, *conclusions and judgments*, refers to the values and beliefs we employ to draw conclusions or to judge others. In the example of the young man with long hair, various people observing him and making reasonable assumptions could come to different conclusions. One individual may have been in college in the 1960s and remember it as an exciting time that had a profound influence on his life. His initial reaction may be a positive conclusion: "That young man reminds me of myself when I was his age." Conversely, someone who was taught to respect authority and appreciate the material comforts of our society and whose goal is to acquire those material comforts may make a negative judgment, perhaps generating additional assumptions about the young man smoking marijuana or using other illegal drugs. Prejudice and negative stereotypes lead to negative assumptions, which result in a negative judgment of another individual.

The fourth and final step in the process is *verbal and nonverbal action*. When individuals meet, one individual will say or do something to initiate interaction. Doing something might be as simple as smiling or frowning, making eye contact with the other, or looking away. Nonverbal behavior employing such body language can initiate communication just as much as words, often equally powerfully.

What does this communication model suggest about conflict resolution?

The most common response to conflict is to focus on the words or behavior (action) that initiated the conflict. For example, elementary teachers often witness conflict during recess in which one child insults or hurts another. Some teachers respond by making the perpetrator apologize: The problem was the child's action, so the teacher forces the child to take another action to offset the first. This response focuses on the symptoms of the conflict and not the cause, so it is not likely to result in a resolution. Because the child may not feel genuinely sorry, what is learned from such an apology is hypocrisy—being forced to say something that is not true.

Effective conflict resolution analyzes other factors to identify probable causes of the conflict. Most strategies for resolving conflicts are intended to get past surface meanings:

- Expressing "I" messages (Gordon, 2000)
- Engaging in transactional analysis (Harris, 2004)
- Using empathy to promote understanding (Rogers, 1995)
- Negotiating "win/win" strategies (Jandt, 1985)

This communication model (Figure 3.2) requires individuals to assess each other's attitudes, question their own assumptions, refrain from making judgments, and be aware of the messages in their nonverbal communication. Still, any approach may be ineffective if the people involved do not accept the value of the process or techniques that are employed.

Video Example 3.1
In this video, the student "conflict managers" work to resolve a conflict between two students on the playground. First, determine what strategies the student "conflict managers" utilize while communicating with the disputing students to solve this conflict. Why might or might not using "conflict managers" be an effective way to resolve conflicts?

How can attitudes toward people or groups create conflict?

When people involved in interpersonal communication identify themselves—or are identified by others—as part of a specific group (such as by race or ethnicity), individual attitudes can be significantly influenced. In a multicultural society such as the United States, it is probable that people, especially in urban areas, will interact with others who are of different races, ethnicities, nationalities, or religions (see Figure 3.3). The extent to which these differences will affect communication will depend on the level of cultural awareness that an individual has with regard to the diversity represented by these groups in our society.

What are the levels of cultural awareness?

Kimmel (2006) identified levels of cultural awareness:

Cultural chauvinism Belief that your culture is the best, superior to all other cultures; feeling no need to learn about other cultures.
Tolerance Awareness of cultural differences, recognition that differences stem from the country of origin for that individual (or his ancestors); no judgment of cultural differences as inferior, simply as different ways of thinking or behaving.
Minimalization Minimizing cultural differences by emphasizing a universality of human needs and behaviors as a means of creating a stronger sense of relationship or connectedness with culturally different people.
Understanding Recognizing that reality is shaped by culture and that each individual's reality is different from that of an individual from a different culture; having no judgment of different cultural realities; accepting and respecting cultural differences (cultural relativism).

Figure 3.3 United States: Present and Future

As ethnic diversity increases in the United States, being aware of cultural differences will become increasingly important.

SOURCE: Uncle Sam image, Library of Congress Prints and Photographs Division [LC-USZC4-2736]. Data from U.S. Census.

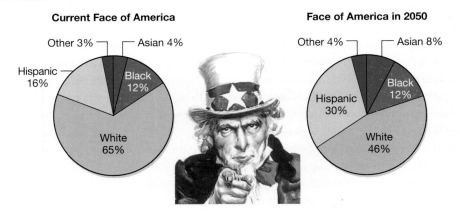

Communication conflicts occur readily between people at the cultural chauvinism level, and they also may occur at the tolerance and minimalization levels. Only when people understand cultural differences and practice cultural relativism is it likely that conflicts between people from different cultures can be avoided or resolved.

 Self-Check 3.1 Complete this self-check quiz to check your understanding of the five misconceptions about communication and the communication model that explains how to resolve conflicts.

Values and Skills Needed for Conflict Resolution

Differences in cultural norms can cause misunderstanding and conflict. In the United States, business executives usually engage in minimal personal conversation before discussing a proposal at a group meeting. In some other cultures, communication is commonly expected to focus first on personal matters—questions about the individual's health, family, or interests—before business is discussed. Varner and Beamer (2010) stressed how the global marketplace requires business executives to be knowledgeable about and employ appropriate communication strategies concerning use of direct speech, acceptable levels of informality, attitudes about time, and expressions of emotion in order to negotiate successfully with people from other cultures. Similar advantages have been reported from research in the United States where studies have found that competent implementation of diversity policies has resulted in greater worker productivity (Garbis, 2015).

What are some communication style differences that are based on culture?

In American culture, it has become acceptable to take a direct approach to conflict resolution, with each party openly expressing their concerns. In other global cultures, people are expected to show sensitivity to the feelings of others by taking an indirect

"The test of a first rate intelligence is the ability to hold two opposed ideas in the mind at the same time, and still retain the ability to function."

— F. SCOTT FITZGERALD (1896–1940)

approach to resolving conflicts. In some cultures, people tend to speak in a linear progression, going from one idea to the next, but in other cultures, people digress, often telling stories or anecdotes to illustrate their point. Cultures also reflect differences in nonverbal behavior. In Arab cultures, people tend to stand much closer in conversation than do Americans. In the United States, men greet one another with a firm handshake; in France, anything other than a quick handshake is considered rude; in Ecuador, greeting an individual without offering your hand is a sign of special respect. In the United States, the forefinger to thumb gesture means "okay"; in France, it signifies that something is worthless; and in Brazil, the gesture is considered obscene (Jandt, 2003).

Differences in communication styles have also been identified in subcultures in the United States. In his classic book on communication styles, Kochman (1981) described how Black and White children learn to express aggression. For most middle-class White people, aggressive language is viewed as a harbinger of aggressive behavior. "Fighting words" are words that may provoke a physical confrontation (Meltzoff, 2007). Most White children learn to repress aggressive feelings and maintain a calm demeanor even though they may be furious. If they begin using language aggressively, it is likely that a fight is imminent. For some Black men, however, words can be used aggressively without a conflict. Foster (1986) was the first to describe how urban Black male children may taunt one another in a playground game known by different names, including "sounding" or "playing the dozens." Situations may become intense and emotional; however, a fight will only occur if a child gives an obvious signal such as making a fist to indicate that he is angry.

The contrast between the reactions of Black and White people to aggressive language can lead to misunderstanding. Imagine two Black children still playing the insult game as they come back to their classroom after recess. The teacher tries to intervene, but the boys continue to insult each other. A Black teacher may recognize the childhood game and firmly tell them to stop, but a White teacher may perceive the boys as engaged in a hostile quarrel and order them to the principal's office. If the principal asks them why they were sent, they are likely to say they don't know. When the principal says their teacher saw them fighting, they will vigorously deny it, insisting that they were just teasing each other. Because the teacher has made this "false accusation," they might think she doesn't like them and become hostile to her in return.

Kochman (1981) describes another difference in communication styles concerning the conduct of arguments. White people are encouraged to present unbiased, objective arguments, but Black people tend to accept the existence of bias and are skeptical of claims of objectivity. Although White people have been taught to argue in a calm, dispassionate manner, people in many Black communities defend their beliefs passionately. In debates, Black people do not expect impersonal or dispassionate arguments, and they may distrust people who are not passionate. Expressing ideas passionately during an argument is regarded as a measure of sincerity (Sue, 2015). In White society, the norm in debating issues is to repress emotions because they are believed to interfere with keeping an open mind. For many White Americans, arguing passionately seems confrontational; they think it exacerbates conflict and makes consensus less likely.

The potential for misunderstanding about how arguments are conducted was revealed in a televised program showing academics discussing racial issues in which a White professor misperceived a Black professor based on his communication style. The Black professor was making an eloquent and passionate argument. The White professor sitting beside him appeared uncomfortable, yet displayed no emotion. As the Black professor paused before concluding, the White professor remarked in a defensive tone of voice but without facial expression, "Well, you don't have to be so angry." Startled by the interruption, the Black professor looked over at his White colleague and said, "Excuse me, you are mistaking intensity for anger."

> "Misunderstandings and inertia cause perhaps more to go wrong in this world than slyness and evil intent."
>
> — JOHANN WOLFGANG VON GOETHE
> (1749–1832)

Video Example 3.2

This video discusses how teachers can engage with cultural communication styles in the classroom. Pay attention to the kinds of cultural communication styles that are mentioned by Dr. Olmedo. First, what cultural communication styles are dominant in American schools? Can you think of other cultural communication styles not mentioned in the video that you might encounter in a school setting that differ from the most dominant communication styles practiced in American schools? How might teachers engage with these communication styles in ways that both respect the students and help them learn how to effectively communicate in the classroom? What can teachers learn from students' cultural communication styles that could help them more effectively facilitate respectful communication in their classrooms?

In describing communication style differences, the intent is not to find fault with any group or individual, nor is it to say that one communication style is better than the other. It is important to understand that communication styles are influenced by cultural heritage; we should not make assumptions about others based on their communication style. This is especially important for teachers. For example, in the dominant culture, the norm is for speakers to take turns talking, and in a classroom this is consistently illustrated as students quietly listen to other students or to the teacher, who may then ask questions to which students individually respond. In other cultures, communication tends to be active rather than passive, with people taking a participatory approach rather than "waiting their turn." If teachers understand this communication style difference, they are not likely to misperceive this behavior as an indication of disrespect (Rychly & Graves, 2012). In addition to understanding such communication style differences, teachers should work on becoming proficient in their ability to engage in alternate communication styles. Meanwhile, studies suggest that differences in communication styles can create misunderstandings based not only on cultural differences but on gender differences as well.

How does gender influence communication styles?

Communication differences based on gender are said to originate in variations in the way boys and girls are socialized. Traditionally, Americans have encouraged boys to be aggressive and girls to be nice; this has been documented in studies of children's play activities. American boys tend to play outdoors, typically in competitive games that require groups and involve aggressive behavior; they resolve disputes by engaging in debates in which everyone participates. In contrast, girls tend to play indoor types of games in small groups or with a friend; these games involve conversation and collaboration, and a quarrel will usually disrupt the game (Dow & Wood, 2006; Lau, 2014).

Gender differences persist even as children leave childhood behind. Some scholars believe that male aggressiveness in conversation is revealed in studies showing that men interrupt women more than women interrupt men (Dow & Wood, 2006), but Tannen (1994) argued that it is simplistic to say such behavior is always a dominance issue. Reviewing communication research on gender differences, Goman (2016) reported that women are more competent than men at giving and understanding nonverbal messages. Grumet (2008) found that women tend to have more eye contact than men and to pay more attention to their conversational partner.

Differences in degree of eye contact and face-to-face interaction often reflect differences in the way women and men express intimacy. Tannen (2007) described differences in men's and women's communication styles originating in childhood and continuing into adult years. In one study with participants ranging from children to young adults, two people of the same age and gender were taken to a room, seated in chairs placed side by side, and asked to talk about a serious topic. The younger boys had trouble with the task; they didn't move the chairs, did not make eye contact, and spent much of their time shifting restlessly and talking about not wanting to talk. Men of all ages would sit in the chairs in their original position with minimal face-to-face interaction. At all age levels, female partners either moved the chairs or positioned themselves to face each other; they began talking immediately on a serious topic as requested.

High school boys express intimacy through aggressive behavior. Pushing, shoving, even punching each other is an indication of a close friendship. As adults, men transform aggressive physical behavior into aggressive verbal behavior. For example, American men are careful about expressing disagreement with someone they don't know very well, but they bluntly disagree with and even use sarcasm with a close friend. It is a sign of intimacy and trust when men don't have to "pull their punches" with each other.

From childhood through adulthood, American women tend to express intimacy by engaging in face-to-face interactions and expressing concern for the other individual's feelings. For most, outright disagreement is regarded as a threat to intimacy and a lack of sensitivity or respect. When a woman disagrees with another woman, she will often begin by saying something positive or something they agree on, and then address the issue about which they disagree. The difference in men's and women's communication styles creates opportunities for misunderstanding. If a man and a woman have an intimate relationship and discuss an issue on which they disagree, he may make direct, honest comments because he feels so close to her, but she may interpret his harsh comments as insensitive, disrespectful, and even contemptuous of her opinions.

With such an emphasis on competition and aggression, boys become men who directly express wants, needs, or demands. With such an emphasis on cooperating, being nice, and caring about how others might feel, girls become women who are concerned about not imposing their wants or demands, preferring consensus. A man might attempt to convince someone to do what he wants, but a woman is more likely to ascertain whether the other individual is interested in doing what she wants to do. Tannen (2007) argues that this difference may be a basis for historic gender stereotypes that have contributed to misunderstandings and conflict: men perceiving women as devious and cunning, and women perceiving men as arrogant and intimidating.

How do gender differences in communication styles lead to misunderstanding and conflict?

Imagine a woman coming home from work, greeting her husband, and then remembering, "Oh, John, I meant to stop at the store and pick up a few things, but I am so tired I forgot to do it. This has been such a rotten day." She is indirectly asking him to go to the store for her, yet he may not get the message. Even if he tries to be sympathetic—"I'm sorry to hear that"—she will be upset if he doesn't offer to go to the store. If he wanted her to go to the store, he would ask her directly; he needs to understand that her socialization and her communication style does not allow her to make demands as he would.

In a similar example, after leaving early for a long trip, a couple has been driving all morning on the interstate, and it's almost noon. The wife sees a sign advertising a restaurant she likes at the next exit, points it out to her husband, and says, "Would you like to stop there and get something to eat?" He hears her comment not as an indirect request but as a genuine question. He wants to drive for another hour before stopping to eat, so he says no and drives on. When he realizes she is upset, they discuss the reason, and he criticizes her for not stating explicitly what she wanted. She thinks he should be able to understand that she did tell him in a manner that took account of his feelings. She believes that she has been sensitive, and he has not. He believes she was being dishonest while he was being straightforward with her.

The reason for identifying gender differences is not to blame men or women, nor to say that one communication style is better than another. It is important to recognize the diverse ways people communicate so that differences in communication styles do not result in conflict. Knowing the influence on communication style of such factors as gender or culture provides a basis for preventing misunderstandings. If people recognize problems as possibly stemming from a difference in communication styles, they can modify their interaction to communicate more effectively (Jandt, 2003; Prince, 2004).

What kinds of conflicts occur in K–12 schools?

Sometimes resolving conflicts seems hopeless. Groups have been in conflict for centuries, and some individuals take unresolved conflicts to their graves. Conflict resolution is not easy, and people approach conflict with apprehension. Because K–12

Video Example 3.3

In this video, three teachers and school staff discuss issues of communication, bullying, and gender. Pay attention to the assumptions and stereotypes that they reference related to gender and gender differences in communication. What are some of the ways that they recommend to promote healthy relationships and communication between students and with students? What are some of the ways in which they might also contribute to reproducing gender assumptions and stereotypes in how they approach communicating with students?

schools provide adult supervision for children and youth, we would expect to find less conflict there. Studies report that students usually identify schools as one of the places where they felt safest, even safer than their home, and yet conflicts do occur at school. Although only 4 percent of all public school students report being actually victimized in some way, 7 percent were threatened or injured by another student with a weapon, with twice as many female victims as male. Even teachers are not immune: slightly more secondary teachers were threatened than elementary teachers (8 percent compared to 7 percent), but 6 percent of elementary teachers were attacked compared to only 2 percent of secondary teachers (Robers, Kemp, Truman, & Snyder, 2013). One of the consequences of bullying is financial. As in many other states, California funds schools based not on enrollment but on per-pupil daily attendance. A 2016–2017 study of California K–12 schools found that students who had encountered bullying accounted for 630,000 absences during the school year, costing school districts more than $276 million. There is also a cost to families if a parent has to stay home from work or hires a caretaker or pays for a child to receive counseling (Moon, 2017).

For students who were threatened, racist verbal abuse remained at levels reported in previous years; students being called a hate-related term included 9 percent of Asian Americans, 10 percent of Latinos, 11 percent of African Americans, and 8 percent of White people. Students who reported seeing graffiti with hate language toward their group included 30 percent of Asian Americans, 29 percent of Latinos, 28 percent of African Americans, and 28 percent of Whites. On the positive side, from 1995 to 2011, K–12 students who said they feared that they might be physically attacked or harmed in some way at school decreased from 12 percent to 4 percent. Although these levels of threat and violence are still low, incidences of bullying occur at least on a weekly if not daily basis in public schools. Among adolescent students (ages 12–18), nearly 28 percent report being bullied at school, with slightly higher numbers for women than for men (Robers, Kemp, Truman, & Snyder, 2013). The bullying differs by gender, with women being called names, insulted, being the subject of rumors, or being intentionally excluded from activities, whereas boys were more likely to be pushed, shoved, tripped, or spit upon. Many schools still regard bullying as generic bad behavior and fail to recognize the bias implicit in a bully's choice of victims. These biases are based on race, gender, disability, religion, or sexual orientation (Moon, 2017).

Although bullying in public schools seems to be decreasing, it is still a concern, and now 9 percent of adolescent students report being cyberbullied. Cyberbullying occurs online and can appear on social media sites such as Facebook when students post derogatory information about another student or send harassing text messages. Women were victims three times as often as men. In response, most school districts have developed Acceptable Use Policies for technology in schools. For example, 93 percent of public schools have limited access to social networking websites for students using school computers, and 91 percent of public schools forbid the use of cell phones and text messaging devices in school (Robers, Kemp, Truman, & Snyder, 2013).

The ongoing problem of school shootings has forced school administrators to consider steps to keep students safe from violence, especially gun violence. Zero tolerance policies were first instituted in the 1990s to increase security, and they have largely focused on preventing weapons from being brought to school and reducing violence in schools.

What does "Zero Tolerance" mean, and has it been effective in schools?

Once they were implemented, **zero tolerance** programs evolved into a school discipline policy that punished "both nonviolent behaviors that are perceived to be disruptive and weapons and drug related infractions of school discipline codes" (Robbins, 2008, p. 5). In recent years, it has become increasingly obvious that "zero tolerance" programs have been a failure, not only as a policy to prevent conflict but also because their results appear to show a racial bias.

During the 2009–2010 school year, a nationwide study by the Department of Education reported that 24 percent of Black students and 12 percent of Latino students were suspended at least once compared to 7 percent of White students. Brownstein (2009) found that suspensions and expulsions nationally had nearly doubled since zero tolerance policies were implemented, and Stucki (2014) cited a 2008 study reporting students of color being disproportionately punished for engaging in the same kinds of misbehaviors as their White peers. Suspensions and expulsions often result in students dropping out of school, a major factor in what is being called the "school-to-prison pipeline" that especially affects Black men. Stucki (2014) cited a 2009 study reporting that almost 25 percent of Black male dropouts between the ages of 16 and 24 were incarcerated, compared to only 6.6 percent of White male dropouts. Based on his review of zero tolerance policies, Robbins (2008) concluded that they had failed to reduce conflict and make schools safer, but instead had produced "intolerance, alienation, exclusion and the denial of educational opportunity" (p. 17). These examples demonstrate that to be effective, conflict resolution programs must teach not only particular skills but also cultivate and reinforce certain values that are essential for conflict resolution.

What values and skills are necessary for conflict resolution to be effective?

Conflict offers opportunity for constructive change, if all parties are prepared to make concessions and to establish a context conducive to resolution. Deutsch (2006) identified values that participants must share if they want to resolve conflict: fallibility, equality, reciprocity, and nonviolence.

1. *Fallibility* refers to accepting the possibility of being wrong. In conflict, people are customarily presented with evidence and arguments. However, presenting evidence will not help resolve a conflict if participants refuse to acknowledge that their position could be wrong. In one court case, for example, during deliberations, the foreman of a jury said he believed the defendant was guilty and that he would not change his mind. Another jury member pointed out that such an attitude violated the jury process that requires discussing and debating evidence, listening to arguments with an open mind, and changing one's mind if justified by the weight of evidence or arguments. Although still believing the defendant guilty, the foreman admitted the jury member was right, and he agreed to listen with an open mind. Ultimately he changed his mind.

2. *Equality* refers to the belief that every human being, regardless of status, occupation, or wealth, deserves to be treated respectfully, with consideration for her values, beliefs, and behavior. It is an acknowledgment that every human life has value and that no one should be treated unjustly. In another jury trial, some members of the jury began to criticize the testimony of two overweight and casually dressed female witnesses, based on their appearance rather than on what they said. Another juror chastised them for their negative attitudes and argued that if the jury were to render a just verdict, they needed to focus on the evidence the women presented, not on how they looked. Other jurors agreed.

3. *Reciprocity* means that participants in a conflict must behave toward others with the same sense of fairness and attentiveness that they would want for themselves—a restatement of the golden rule that appears as an ethical principle in practically all cultures, or as modified by Confucius: "Do not do to others what you would not like yourself" (Waley, 1938, p. 162). Apparently Confucius believed one did not have to be good to others as long as no harm was done to them. Either way, the feeling of reciprocity is essential for participants in a conflict if they hope to negotiate a resolution to it.

"The man who strikes first admits that his ideas have given out."

— CHINESE PROVERB

4. To value *nonviolence* is to believe that the only genuine solutions are peaceful ones. As Deutsch explained in his fourth shared value, coercing others into accepting an imposed solution winds a long and tragic path through human history marked by brutality and blood, civil and global wars, leaving little evidence that solutions imposed by the strong on the weak are effective—or lasting—solutions.

In the context of the four shared values proposed by Deutsch, conflict need not be a destructive event; it can be a constructive opportunity. But to achieve a positive outcome from a conflict will depend on individuals having not only appropriate values but also the necessary skills to engage constructively in discussing issues with others when everyone is not in agreement.

Johnson, Johnson, and Tjosvold (2006) identified effective negotiation strategies to engage in what they termed **skilled disagreement**. These strategies are as follows:

1. All parties agree to emphasize rationality, seek the best possible answer based on the available evidence and arguments, and express willingness to change their position when it is justified by the evidence. This strategy is similar to what the jury member described in the fallibility anecdote.
2. Participants agree that criticizing an idea is not criticizing those who propose the idea—they acknowledge that their worth as human beings is separate from their ideas.
3. Participants must also make a conscious commitment to encourage others to contribute to the discussion and to listen thoughtfully to the contributions they make.
4. Participants agree to restate ideas to ensure that everyone understands the issue from all perspectives being presented.
5. Finally, participants are asked to remember that the problem and any recommended solution will affect everyone. They must not be focused on winning a debate but on arriving at a collaborative solution that everyone can support.

Application Exercise 3.1
This video discusses bullying in schools and providing clear expectations for behavior. Review the video and complete the activity.

These conflict resolution skills are not difficult to learn, and many educators say they can and should be taught in schools, even to young children. By teaching these skills, educators may foster the development of both cognitive and moral reasoning abilities.

 Self-Check 3.2 Complete this self-check quiz to check your understanding of why certain values and skills are necessary for conflict resolution.

Conflict Resolution and the Role of Moral Reasoning Theory

Although there are differing theories regarding the development of moral reasoning, William Perry began developing a theory in the 1960s that was supported by considerable research as an accurate description of moral reasoning engaged in by people of different ages, from different cultures or subcultures, and from both genders (Belenky, Clinchy, Goldberger, & Tarulle, 1997; Perry, 1999; Hall, 2013). Using this theory, teachers can provide students with moral dilemmas and controversial issues; then they can analyze student discussions and engage students with questions to challenge and strengthen their moral reasoning.

Perry's theory is based on the assumption that changes in moral reasoning are related to cognitive development: Increased cognitive ability allows individuals the possibility of increasing the complexity of their moral reasoning. Although there are nine developmental positions in Perry's continuum, as an introduction to the theory, it is sufficient to understand two major areas Perry has identified—**dualism**

Figure 3.4 A Continuum of Moral Reasoning

SOURCE: Perry, W. (1970). *Forms of Intellectual and Ethical Development in the College Years: A Scheme.* New York, NY: Holt, Rinehart & Winston.

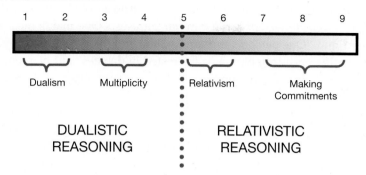

and **relativism**—and the mental shift that occurs within each: A dualistic thinker may transition into **multiplicity**, and a relativistic thinker may transition into the **commitment** level (see Figure 3.4).

Dualism. All human beings start out as dualistic thinkers when confronted with moral decisions; children tend to operate simplistically with absolute categories of right and wrong. In dualism, every moral issue is a question of either/or: Either it's right or it's wrong, it's true or it's false, it's good or it's bad. This is also called "black and white" thinking because there are no "shades of gray" for dualistic thinkers. To be dualistic is to believe that what is true must be regarded as an absolute truth: It has always been and will always be true. Newberg and Waldman (2006) say that brain research offers a biological explanation for dualistic thinking: "The brain tends to reduce cause-and-effect cognition into dualistic scenarios because they are an easy, neurologically efficient way to make sense of the world" (p. 88).

Believing in absolutes is challenged when an individual is confronted with problems that don't lend themselves to the either/or style of thinking. A popular moral dilemma exercise is to ask people what they would have done if they were hiding Jewish people in the early 1940s and Gestapo officers came to their home to ask if they knew the whereabouts of any Jews. For the individual who believes "honesty is the best policy," this is a difficult question to answer. Another problem with dualistic thinking is that the cognitive process of simplification and generalization inevitably leads to stereotyping others because the process does not consider individual differences. As studies have reported, the "'us-versus-them' mentality can be easily converted into racism" (Newberg & Waldman, 2006, p. 89). Complex issues that challenge dualistic thinking may not present themselves until a student enters high school or college, but when students confront such issues, they often feel compelled to move away from rigid dualistic thinking and engage in the kind of moral reasoning called *multiplicity*.

Multiplicity. The perspective of multiplicity recognizes the difficulty of knowing "the right answer" in every situation. When the right answer is not obvious, the only recourse is for the individual to examine various opinions or multiple perspectives without being certain which one is right. Each individual must consider the different perspectives and decide which one seems best. This is not satisfying for people at the multiplicity position because they are still influenced by dualistic thinking. They would prefer to know the answer or the truth in a given situation, and often complain that all we have are opinions. Because of the influence of dualistic thinking, people at a multiplicity position still believe the truth can be known and will be known some day, but for the moment, they reluctantly accept that they do not have the answer for a number of issues.

> "The question should never be who is right, but what is right."
> — GLENN GARDINER (CONTEMPORARY)

Relativism. When people move beyond multiplicity to relativism, they tend to exhibit a change in attitude from reluctantly accepting the existence of multiple perspectives to becoming intrigued by the idea that each individual must decide what is right. Relativism is based on the assumptions that there are no absolute truths, and that truth is relative, a concept reflected in the familiar phrases: "One man's meat is another man's poison" and "One person's treasure is another person's junk." The relativist is stimulated by differences of opinion, is interested in debates, and may enjoy playing the devil's advocate in a discussion by articulating arguments and ideas to defend a particular perspective without really believing in it.

Relativism requires an individual to be comfortable with ambiguity and not demand specific answers that are right for everyone. Many people are uncomfortable living in a world where they have to accept many points of view without regarding any of them as the right one. The difficulty of accepting such ambiguity causes some people to "retreat" (as Perry calls it) by resuming a dualistic thinking process. Other people who never progress beyond relativistic thinking sometimes adopt a cynical attitude toward life because relativistic thinking does not often result in becoming passionate about or personally invested in any issue or cause. However, some people who have also felt a sense of dissatisfaction with relativism's moral ambiguity have identified questions they wanted answered and are engaged deliberately in efforts to find their own answers.

Commitment. Relativistic thinkers who continue to develop their moral reasoning are attracted to the idea of making commitments to certain personal truths, ideals, or causes that seem to give meaning to their lives. Most people need to believe in something and to feel a sense of satisfaction that their belief enhances the quality of their lives. Commitments may include being active in a political party or joining a church, an advocacy group, or some other organization. A commitment may result in volunteer work or influence an individual's career decision. Whatever the choice, it is made from among many alternatives and the individual makes the commitment because it reflects his values.

Once people make commitments, they often become advocates for that particular cause or perspective. Because commitment is made in the context of relativistic thinking, people who reflect this perspective do not advocate like dualistic thinkers whose arguments are based on a sense of certainty. Relativistic thinkers may emphasize the sense of satisfaction they feel that their commitment provides a stronger sense of meaning and purpose in their lives, and they invite others to join them. In contrast, when dualistic thinkers advocate for truths they believe are absolute, they tend to view those who agree with them as right and those who disagree as wrong. There is no other option. When people at the commitment level argue on behalf of their commitments, they do not tend to judge those who agree or disagree. They recognize that it is an individual's obligation to make her own choices, and they respect the individual's right to choose. Someone at the commitment level does not reject relativism and its view of reality as ambiguous, but this individual does recognize the satisfaction that may be gained by making commitments to provide a sense of meaning and purpose to his life. Being able to respect individual choice is not only important for moral reasoning but also essential for engaging in successful conflict resolution.

With so much conflict occurring, how can conflicts be resolved?

As evidence mounted that zero tolerance was a failed strategy, schools began implementing conflict resolution programs, often including peer mediation, in an effort to give students the tools to resolve conflicts. Nation (2007) described a study of three elementary schools that implemented a peer-focused conflict resolution program and reported a dramatic reduction in the children's physically aggressive behaviors.

The Peaceful Kids program trained teachers and staff to teach and model conflict resolution skills to preschool children in Boston, Dallas, and Los Angeles (Coleman & Fisher-Yokida, 2008). After one year, program evaluations reported increased student self-control, increased cooperation among students, and significant decreases in student acts of aggression and student withdrawal behaviors.

Coleman and Fisher-Yokida (2008) described a project at a New York City high school that implemented cooperative learning strategies and conflict resolution training. After two years, the program evaluation reported improved relationships between students, an increased ability among students to handle conflicts effectively, and students feeling a greater sense of control over their lives. Further, students reported having higher self-esteem and improved academic performance. In Minnesota, schools have implemented a radically different strategy called "restorative justice." Reacting against the zero tolerance emphasis on punishing students, restorative justice emphasizes community and gives misbehaving students an opportunity to repair whatever harm they may have done in order to be accepted back into the community.

Restorative justice programs typically offer students opportunities to develop peer mediation techniques and provide empathy training; the goal is to replace the fear of retribution by having students develop strong interpersonal relationships and build a sense of community. Teachers play a critical role by paying attention to student conflicts. When teachers become aware that a conflict is developing or has developed, they send the individuals involved to students with peer mediation training to talk about the problem and generate solutions. Some of these schools are using what is called a "restorative circle," which is based on the Native American concept of a "talking circle." As students sit in a circle, a totem that identifies the individual who has a right to speak for the moment is passed around from speaker to speaker. These "talking circle" meetings are called periodically for various reasons, but they become especially critical when serious misbehavior occurs, such as a violent quarrel or the defacing or destruction of school property. In such serious cases, all members of the school community participate. The totem is given to individuals involved in the incident, and each individual explains how she has been affected. After everyone involved has spoken, the group collectively proposes a plan for the participants to carry out in order to resolve the conflict (Stucki, 2014).

In 1995, St. Paul became the first Minnesota school district to implement a restorative justice program in its schools, and the programs had an immediate effect. One elementary school saw violent misbehavior fall from seven incidents a day to less than two, and at the end of one school year, the number of high school students given out-of-school suspensions dropped from 110 to 65. The St. Paul program continued to be effective, and by 2001, 50 percent of all Minnesota school districts had implemented restorative justice programs. As impressive as the results have been, even advocates caution that restorative justice is not a panacea. Any program will be limited by the reality that schools cannot address poverty, domestic abuse, neglect, gangs, and other external causes of student misbehavior. Another obstacle is funding. Although it does not cost a lot to implement restorative justice programs, they are not free, and many schools are grappling with declining budgets. For a restorative justice approach to be effective, schools need to provide as much as $60,000 to train faculty, and they also require an adequate support staff, including assistant principals, counselors, and restorative justice coordinators. Despite these challenges, restorative justice continues to attract the attention of educators, and efforts have been made to establish such programs in Chicago, Denver, and in 21 Oakland public schools (Brown, 2013).

Some critics feel that a restorative justice approach will only work for students who attend middle-class schools, but advocates say that students who live in neighborhoods that frequently experience violence look to schools as the one place where they can feel safe. When restorative justice facilitates this outcome, students respond positively not only toward the school but to their fellow students. Advocates have examples to support their argument. Only one year after a restorative justice program was implemented in a low-income school in Philadelphia, serious examples of misbehavior decreased by 60 percent, suspensions declined from 200 to less than 40, and there was a 66 percent reduction in the number of students being arrested. As one advocate noted: "The students feel attached to one another and their school in a way they didn't before" (Stucki, 2014, p. 8). In addition to Philadelphia, Los Angeles, Denver, and San Francisco have implemented pilot programs to test the restorative justice approach.

 Self-Check 3.3 Complete this self-check quiz to check your understanding of conflict resolution and the role of moral reasoning theory.

Afterword

Even if we say exactly what we want to say, we can never assume that our meaning is heard and understood in the way we intend. When misunderstandings are not clarified at the time they occur, they can cause people to become antagonistic, thereby laying the foundation for an eventual conflict. In schools, some efforts to reduce conflict have been successful. In elementary classrooms, teachers must emphasize respect and nonviolence in their work with students. At middle and high schools, schools can empower students to intervene in conflicts by offering workshops and providing other opportunities to develop mediation skills. At all levels it is important for students to work in groups and to have other experiences (e.g., peer tutoring) where they become better acquainted because there is a reduction of conflict in schools when children and youth have more opportunities to get to know each other.

> "Wrongdoing can only be avoided if those who are not wronged feel the same indignation at it as those who are."
>
> — SOLON (640–558 BCE)

Conflict resolution is not easy, yet it's better than coping with unresolved conflict. It is in everyone's interest to embrace the values that make conflict resolution possible and to practice communication strategies necessary for engaging in skilled disagreement. Conflict—whether personal or global—is inevitable, but the resolution of conflicts is not. Teachers must challenge and enhance the moral reasoning abilities of children and youth, and all educators must be committed to the process of conflict resolution. The quality of individual lives and the quality of life for communities and for countries depends on the willingness of people to choose to resolve conflicts rather than hopelessly perpetuate them.

People must also recognize that there is no one best way to engage in moral reasoning. Hauser (2006) found that different moral systems have emerged in different cultures, and concluded: "I favor a pluralistic position, one that recognizes different moral systems, and sees adherence to a single system as oppressive" (p. 425). By respecting and being open to diverse moral systems, human beings can lay the foundation for resolving conflicts and strengthening relationships between individuals (and nations) representing diverse cultures.

Summary

- Because of the many misconceptions about communication, five representative examples are explained before examining a communication model that identifies key factors in the communication process. This model explains how communication conflicts are resolved.

- There are four values and five communication skills that communication scholars have identified as prerequisites for engaging successfully in conflict resolution.

- Perry's theory on the development of moral reasoning is supported by research studies and is based on individual cognitive development.

Terms and Definitions

Commitment Moral reasoning in a relativist context that recognizes the importance of becoming actively committed to certain personal truths to strengthen and deepen the meaningfulness of life experiences

Communication competence Having sufficient knowledge of a subject to communicate accurate information about that subject

Communication effectiveness Having the skills to communicate information in order to be easily understood

Cultural chauvinism An attitude that your culture is the best, superior to other cultures

Dualism Moral reasoning involving a belief in absolute truths and unambiguous categories of right and wrong behavior; also called "either/or reasoning"

Interpersonal communication A dynamic process of interaction between people in which they assign meaning to each other's verbal and nonverbal behavior (Kougl, 1997)

Minimalization An attitude about other cultures that reduces the importance of cultural differences and emphasizes the universality of human needs and behaviors to create a stronger sense of relationship with all people

Multiplicity Moral reasoning in a dualistic context recognizing that it isn't possible to know what is the right behavior in certain situations, in which case opinions from multiple perspectives must be examined; an individual can't be confident of the final decision in such instances because he can't be certain of having made the right choice

Nonverbal communication Those messages other than words that people exchange, also called "nonverbal behavior" or "nonverbal messaging"

Praxis Taking action to address injustice and then reflecting on the effectiveness of the actions taken as the individual or group continues their activities

Relativism Moral reasoning that rejects absolute truth and is based on the assumptions that all truth is relative and that determining the right behavior depends on the individual and the situation

Restorative justice Discipline programs emphasizing community and the need to repair any harm done so people can be accepted back into the community

Selective perception Paying attention to behaviors of another individual that reinforce our expectations for that individual

Skilled disagreement Strategies that have been proven effective in achieving a successful resolution to conflicts

Tolerance Awareness of cultural differences without judging cultures as superior or inferior

Understanding Recognizing that culture shapes individual reality, including acceptance of and respect for cultural differences

Zero tolerance A school discipline policy initially focused on preventing students from bringing weapons and drugs to school but later broadened to include punishments for "disruptive behavior"

Discussion Exercises

Exercise 1: Statements Illustrating Perry's Continuum

Directions: Conversations can be categorized according to Perry's concepts. Identify each of the following statements according to the four broad areas in Perry's continuum of moral development. You will find three examples from each area. Record your answers as (a) dualism, (b) multiplicity, (c) relativism, or (d) commitment.

Statements Illustrating Perry's Continuum

_____ 1. In areas where even the experts disagree, everyone has a right to his own opinion.

I mean, if answers aren't given, like in lots of things, then it has to be just anyone's opinion.

_____ 2. Understanding another point of view, especially a contrary one, helps me understand my own point of view. So trying to see through the other individual's eyes helps my own understanding of the issue.

_____ 3. I came here from a small town in the Midwest where everyone believed the same things and everyone is, like, Methodist and Republican.

But here, there are a variety of Protestants and Catholics and a Chinese guy who follows the teachings of Confucius. Some people even say they're atheists, but I don't think they really are.

_____ 4. I'm not sure how to make any decision at all. When you have the issues thrust at you and read about the people who pushed their thought to the absolute limit and see how that did not result in an all-encompassing answer . . . , you begin to have respect for how great their thought could be even though it did fall short.

_____ 5. The science lectures are all right. They sort of say the facts, but when you get to a humanities course, they are awful! The lecturer is just reading things into the book that were never meant to be there.

_____ 6. This place is full of bull. If you turn in a speech or a paper that is well written, whether it has one single fact in it or not is beside the point . . . So you sit down and write a paper in an hour, just because you know that whatever it is isn't going to make any difference to anyone.

_____ 7. I get frustrated in class when the teacher only looks at things from her point of view. There are other ideas to consider. What is important to me is trying to understand and evaluate ideas and to come up with my own. I dislike discussions in which everyone just voices an opinion without backing it up. What good are opinions unless you put them to the test?

_____ 8. When I have an idea about something, and it differs from the way another individual is thinking about it, I will usually try to look at it from that individual's point of view, see how they could say that, why they think they are right, why it makes sense.

_____ 9. In science you don't really want to say that something is true. We're dealing with a model and models are always simpler than the real world, which is more complex than anything we can create. We simplify so we can work with it. When we try to describe things, we leave out the truth because we are oversimplifying.

_____ 10. About the only thing I guess I would say to a prospective student is that if you come to this college, you had better do everything you are supposed to do and then you will be all right. That's just about all.

_____ 11. As soon as someone tells me his point of view, I immediately start arguing in my head the opposite point of view. When someone is saying something, I can't help turning it upside down.

_____ 12. I can't really say that one opinion is better than another. It depends on your beliefs. I am the type of person who would never tell someone that their opinion is wrong. If they have searched, well, even if they haven't searched, if they just believe it, that's cool for them.

Exercise 2: Words and Phrases That Hurt

Directions: Our conversations carry implications that reflect personal understanding, values, or beliefs. The 10 statements here contain implications that can offend others. Considering who the communicants are, why might the statements have been made in the first place? What are the implications in each? How does the context in which each is spoken make it offensive or hurtful?

1. A White individual to a Black individual: "We must have law and order."

2. In a discussion of inequitable school funding, a suburban parent to an inner city parent: "You can make your schools as good as ours."

3. A Korean American to a Black acquaintance: "You're different from most Black people."

4. A White employer announcing the intention of integrating the workplace: "Of course, we will make sure we only hire a qualified minority applicant."

5. In a discussion of racial discrimination in America, a Black individual to a Japanese American: "Asian people have done well in America; you shouldn't have anything to complain about."

6. A White individual to a Latino: "I don't understand what you people want."

7. A White individual to a Black individual: "Our old neighborhood used to be good when I was a kid, but it's gone downhill since it was integrated."

8. A Chinese American to a Black individual: "The death of Martin Luther King was a terrible loss to your race."

9. A Black Christian to a Jewish person: "Oh, you're Jewish? I didn't realize you were Jewish—you sure don't act like one."

10. A White individual to a Native American: "I think your people have made great progress."

Chapter 4
Immigration and Oppression: The Assault on Cultural and Language Diversity

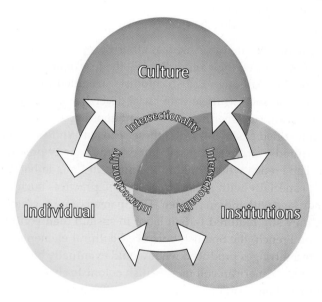

Learning Outcomes

After reading this chapter you will know and be able to:

4.1 Describe the origin of xenophobia in the British colonies and the United States and how it contributed to the Nativist attitudes toward immigrants of diverse nationalities.

4.2 Explain how negative attitudes toward immigrants evolved over time and what political actions were taken against immigrants.

4.3 Describe the actions of some individuals and organizations that reflect negative attitudes toward immigrants, explain how immigrants have contributed to the American economy, and debunk persisting myths about contemporary immigrants.

4.4 Explain attitudes toward the cultural and linguistic diversity of the United States, and describe which educational approaches have been most effective for learning English.

> "We are all citizens of one world; we are all of one blood. To hate someone because he was born in another country, because he speaks a different language or because he takes a different view on a subject, is a great folly."
>
> —JOHN COMENIUS (1592–1670)

This section of the text examines the history of oppression in the United States as experienced by immigrants who came to America in pursuit of the American dream. Immigrants encountered discomfort, rejection, and even persecution because they arrived as "foreigners" with different customs, traditions, attitudes, and beliefs. Immigrants of color also experienced oppression based on their race, and followers of certain religions have been oppressed for their beliefs. Andrzewjewski (1996) has provided a comprehensive definition of **oppression**:

> Oppression exists when any entity (society, organization, group, or individual) intentionally or unintentionally distributes resources inequitably, refuses to share power, imposes ethnocentric culture, and/or maintains unresponsive and inflexible institutions toward another entity for its supposed benefit and rationalizes its actions by blaming or ignoring the victim. (p. 56)

As British colonists settled in America, other Europeans quickly followed, and this ethnic diversity aroused their **xenophobia**—the fear of or prejudice against people from other nations. Although British colonists struggled to be tolerant of ethnic diversity, there was no such struggle with racial diversity. As Kammen (1972) noted, European colonists came to America with racist notions of primitive Africans and savage Indians that justified enslaving them; these seeds of White supremacy were sustained—and nurtured—on American soil. But ethnic diversity presented a challenge to be resolved. The French who settled to the north in Canada had readily adapted to Indian ways, especially with regard to economic practices such as trapping and through intermarriage with Indian women. The Spanish came as conquerors, but after their conquest, they still required Indian labor to sustain their control of conquered territory. Like the French, the Spanish borrowed cultural elements from conquered peoples, and intermarriages produced what would eventually be termed a new race: "La Raza." Yet in the American colonies, British colonists chose to retain their identity and to maintain their position as the dominant group; even today, Americans are still caught in an ongoing paradox of established immigrants fearing each wave of newcomers.

Those who settled the English-speaking colonies tended to emigrate in family groups. Although some immigrants came to seek their fortune and return home, most came to establish permanent settlements. The British came as subjects of the English king, prepared to create an English colony as an extension of Britain. Although settlers occasionally used information gained from Indians about such things as edible plants and food preparation, their goal was to recreate as much of the Old World as was possible in the New World.

The problem with recreating the Old World was that it was not possible to make the colonies into a new England. In addition to British colonists (English, Scottish, and Irish), significant numbers of Dutch, German, and French colonists arrived, as well as small groups from other European countries and adventurers from parts of the world other than Europe. Germans in particular were as adamant as the English about maintaining their cultural heritage. They lived together in communities, spoke to each other in German, posted signs in German, imported books from Germany, and founded schools where their children were taught in German.

By the beginning of the eighteenth century, British colonial leaders became so alarmed by German behavior that some called for restrictions or exclusions of Germans from further immigration. Benjamin Franklin believed it was necessary to Anglicize the Germans because of the size of their population. As their numbers continued to grow, he feared that the Germans would "shortly be so numerous as to Germanize us instead of us Anglifying them" (Feagin, 1997, p. 18). Although Franklin obviously shared the desire of British colonists to Anglicize the colonies, he also recognized positive attributes of German immigrants and the contributions they were making to colonial development: "All that seems necessary is to distribute them more equally, mix them with the English, and establish English schools where they are now too thick settled" (Brands, 2000, p. 219).

Franklin was concerned with Anglicizing Germans and all immigrants who were not from Britain and, therefore, unfamiliar with British customs and language. In 1749, he sponsored the establishment of a school that included no foreign language instruction. His desire to Anglicize foreign colonists was also reflected in the views of President George Washington: "The more homogeneous our citizens can be made . . . the greater will be our prospect of permanent union" (Kammen, 1972, p. 74). Perhaps the desire for a more homogeneous citizenry was the reason the New American Congress passed a law in 1790 that limited citizenship in the United States to immigrants who were "White." This early expression of xenophobia would lead to the growth of nativism in the United States.

> "Law is a reflection and source of prejudice. It both enforces and suggests forms of bias."
>
> — DIANE SCHULDER (1937–)

Causes of Xenophobia and Nativism in the United States

Assimilation refers to a process in which immigrants adopt cultural traits from their host country and are absorbed into society (see Figure 4.1). British colonists preferred a homogeneous population of immigrants who could be assimilated into a dominant Anglo culture, but immigrants from other countries often insisted on maintaining their own ethnic heritages. Their desires contributed to the development of xenophobia in

---

Figure 4.1 Assimilation Issues?

The cartoonist illustrates that assimilation has to do with power; there must be a dominant cultural group to demand that members of other groups assimilate to their cultural norms.

SOURCE: *The Denver Post.*

response to the constant infusion of ethnicities among immigrants to America. When established immigrants, who considered themselves "natives," felt threatened by the many non-British immigrants, organizations based on nativist concerns would appear. Feagin and Feagin (1996) define **nativism** as "an anti-immigrant ideology that advocates the protection of native inhabitants of a country from [new or potential] immigrants who are seen as threatening or dangerous" (p. 503). Nativists have been the primary group engaging in the oppression of immigrants.

Franklin's desire to Anglicize non-British immigrants and Washington's desire for a homogeneous population can be described as a benign form of nativism based on nationalistic concerns. Although nationalism represents one of the primary themes of nativist activities in the United States, two additional themes have characterized many nativist attitudes and actions: anti-Catholicism and anti-radicalism.

Why were Nativists anti-Catholic?

Although the religious beliefs of Benjamin Franklin, Thomas Jefferson, and other founders of the American republic were quite different from those of most Christians today, at its birth the United States was a nation strongly influenced by Protestant Christianity. The presence of Catholics had been tolerated throughout the colonial period, but by 1820, the 200,000 Catholics in the United States stimulated anti-Catholic sentiment, especially in urban areas. (See Figure 4.2.) By 1850, there were almost two million Catholics in the United States; the Irish alone constituted 42 percent of that foreign-born population (Fuchs, 1990).

During George Washington's presidency, immigrants were required to be U.S. residents for a minimum of five years to be eligible for citizenship. The Nationalization Act signed by President John Adams changed the requirement to 14 years of residency, but it was returned to five years after Thomas Jefferson became president. A nativist group calling itself "Native Americans" began forming in some of the larger cities; the party lobbied vigorously against immigrants becoming eligible for citizenship after five years. The Native American party insisted on a residency of 21 years before an immigrant

Figure 4.2 Anti-Catholic Attitudes

A major factor in the anti-Catholic sentiment was the fear that Catholics would try to convert Protestants, especially children. The cartoonist, Thomas Nast, made Catholic bishops into alligators coming to U.S. shores, reflecting such fears.

SOURCE: Library of Congress Prints and Photographs Division [Thomas Nast/LC-USZ6-790]

was eligible for citizenship. Their main concern was voting, arguing that immigrants coming from nations governed by monarchs were not prepared to be self-governing. Since an immigrant came with:

> all his foreign habits, prejudices and predilections . . . can it be believed that he can disburden himself so completely of these, and have so learned to fulfill the duties of a citizen of the United States, in the very short term of five years? (Myers, 1960, p. 111)

At first, the Native American party encouraged people to welcome immigrants, only opposing their eligibility for citizenship after five years, but by 1843, the movement had become hostile to continued immigration of both Irish and Catholics. In Philadelphia, the Native American party held a meeting in an Irish district of the city, initiating a confrontation between Protestants and Catholics; the violence that followed culminated in an angry mob setting fire to many buildings, and was reported in newspapers around the country. Federal troops were called in to restore order, which was no easy task, and peace prevailed for a little more than a month before mobs attacked a Catholic church and troops fired at the crowd to force them to disperse. Two more days of violence resulted in two soldiers being killed and 26 soldiers wounded.

Being confronted with such extreme violence was unusual, but American Catholics employed a number of strategies in response to anti-Catholic activities. To avoid having their children subjected to anti-Catholic sentiments in public schools, Catholics created their own privately funded K–12 schools nationwide, eventually establishing Catholic colleges and universities as well. To counter anti-Catholic rhetoric in mainstream and Protestant newspapers, Catholics published their own newspapers. Hennesey (1985) described how Bishop John Hughes submitted several anti-Catholic articles to a Protestant newspaper under the name of "Cranmer" and then publicly announced that he was the author and that the articles included lies and distortions that the editors had not bothered to question or confirm. In addition, several Catholic organizations were founded in the 1800s, including the Knights of Columbus, which engaged in political activism but also provided centers for recreational activities and chapels for meditation and prayer. By the 1920s, church leaders adopted a different strategy, encouraging Catholics to become involved with "general reform groups in society and not limit their exertions to narrowly conceived partisan issues" (Hennesey, 1985, p. 247).

Why were Nativists opposed to radical immigrants?

Both anti-Catholicism and prejudice against the Irish fueled the nativism movement that flourished briefly in the 1850s, but the other negative sentiment contributing to the success of nativism was anti-radicalism. Most immigrants admitted to the United States in the first decades of the nineteenth century were overwhelmingly impoverished European laborers with minimal skills and little education. Some were sponsored by American capitalists to be contract laborers who would be paid less than the wage native workers would accept. As new immigrant workers adapted to life in the United States, they came to realize how they were being exploited; many joined or helped create unions to demand better wages and benefits by engaging in strikes, marches, and protests. Nativists saw union actions as un-American, especially when the "foreigners" expressed socialist, anarchist, or other radical ideas. The antagonism toward what was regarded as radical activities by recent immigrants was clearly and frequently expressed on the editorial pages of urban newspapers (Higham, 1955):

> "Our National existence and . . . our National and social institutions are at stake."
> "These people are not Americans, but the very scum and offal of Europe."
> "Europe's human and inhuman rubbish." (p. 55)

The first quotation illustrates a nationalism often expressed by nativists; the other two quotations reveal hostility and a dehumanized view of perceived "radicals." The un-American implication in each statement is central to the nativist perspective. Nativist concerns at that time also had to do with the decreasing amount of land available for immigrants in the Midwest and West; as a result, immigrants increasingly settled in urban areas. Because many immigrants were moving from southern and eastern Europe, land reformer Henry George commented, "What, in a few years more, are we to do for a dumping ground? Will it make our difficulty the less that our human garbage can vote?" (Higham, 1955, p. 42). The issue of immigrants becoming eligible for citizenship and voting continued to fuel the xenophobia, and nativist political actions document a fear of the potential political power of incoming immigrants.

 Self-Check 4.1 Complete this self-check quiz to check your understanding of the origin of xenophobia in the British colonies and the United States, and how it contributed to the Nativist attitudes toward immigrants of diverse nationalities.

Nativism, Politics, and Social Change

The Native American party never gained political dominance, yet by the 1850s it had prepared the way for the rise of the "Know-Nothings," a somewhat secret movement whose members were told to respond to any question about the organization by saying that they knew nothing about it. Staunchly anti-immigrant and anti-Catholic, Know-Nothings were concerned with what they perceived as the growing political influence of Catholics; these fears were confirmed by President Franklin Pierce's appointment of a Catholic, James Campbell, to be the nation's attorney general.

How successful were the nativists in their political activities?

The Know-Nothings fielded candidates for the American Party, and in 1854 elected 9 governors, 8 (of 62) senators, and 104 (of 234) members of the House of Representatives (Myers, 1960). In the 1856 elections, Know-Nothing members used force and threats to keep immigrants from voting and encouraged election-day riots in Louisville, Kentucky, and St. Louis, Missouri. When the Whig Party refused to nominate Millard Fillmore for a second term as president, the American Party nominated him as their candidate. Despite the success of other American Party candidates, Fillmore received only eight electoral votes.

Reaction to the political success of the Know-Nothings was swift. In Congress a resolution was submitted, then voted down, condemning secret organizations and citing the Know-Nothings as a specific example. Political and religious leaders across the nation denounced the activities of the Know-Nothings, including the young political aspirant Abraham Lincoln, who wrote in a letter to a friend,

As a nation we began by declaring that "all men are created equal." We now practically read it, "all men are created equal except Negroes." When the Know-Nothings obtain control, it will read: "All men are created equal except Negroes, foreigners, and Catholics."

(MYERS, 1960, P. 146)

Why did nativists fail to form a major political party?

The political success of nativism in the 1850s was brief because the issue of slavery began to take precedence over anti-Catholic prejudice and fears, and it divided the Know-Nothings. By the end of the Civil War, the Know-Nothings and the American Party were no longer a political force, although the nativist fears that fueled their activity persisted as a major influence in the United States. As the American people debated the issue of slavery, American capitalists continued to sponsor importation of labor from overseas to keep wages low and profits high.

Throughout U.S. history, a significant percentage of Americans consisted of recent immigrants or children of immigrants who appreciated the opportunities in America and vigorously opposed attempts by nativists to restrict immigration. Meanwhile, there was constant pressure from society to promote the **Americanization** of immigrants, and public schools carried out societal expectations by encouraging immigrants to abandon their heritage and conform to American ways (Pai & Adler, 2006). Nativist attitudes in the United States continued to wax and wane, with xenophobia historically balanced by those who believed in America as a place for oppressed people to achieve freedom and fortune.

The demand for Americanization of immigrants intensified in the late 1800s as the majority of immigrants were *not* northern Europeans—they were Greeks, Italians, Slavs, and Jews—people who did not conform to the Anglo ideal. Because of an economic downturn in the 1890s, nativism experienced a renewed popularity with American people; then in the ebb and flow of xenophobia, nativist fears succumbed to a confidence inspired by the U.S. triumph in the Spanish-American War and by heroes such as Teddy Roosevelt. Although nativists never again succeeded in sponsoring an independent political party, events in the early twentieth century would establish the foundation for their greatest political triumphs.

What influenced twentieth-century nativist attitudes in America?

It seemed certain to most Americans that if the United States were going to become a dominant political and economic power in the world, immigrants would be needed in the labor market of its dynamic economy. But when World War I began, attitudes changed. Nativism surged again, driven by feelings of nationalism and anti-radicalism. German Americans were singled out for especially opprobrious treatment, and their loyalty to the United States was questioned. Rumors abounded that German Americans were spying for Germany.

Because German Americans insisted on maintaining their dual identity as Americans of German descent, influential people such as Teddy Roosevelt admonished them by denouncing all immigrants who claimed a dual identity. German Americans were surprised by such criticisms. From colonial times they had maintained their culture, language, and traditions through separate schools, organizations, and newspapers; these efforts had been tolerated by American society because of the German Americans' industriousness. At the start of World War I, however, nativist individuals and organizations attacked German Americans for keeping themselves separate and not assimilating to an Anglo ideal.

During World War I, surging patriotism intensified the demand that immigrants be Americanized quickly. Although this nationalism was a less abrasive form of nativism, it became more virulent when reinforced by anti-radical attitudes. Radical organizations were attacked as un-American, especially radical unions like the International Workers of the World, the "Wobblies." Nativists accused certain immigrants of espousing ideas that were disloyal to the country and demanded their deportation.

German Americans were not the only targets of anti-American accusations. **Anti-Semitism**—having prejudices, stereotypes, or engaging in discrimination against Jewish people—increased with the success of the Russian Revolution in 1917. Jewish people were associated not only with communism but also with international financiers who profited from the war. After World War I, nativists continued to complain that the Anglo ideal for America would disappear if diverse European ethnic groups continued to emigrate; however, most Americans seemed to believe that those who came would eventually assimilate into the dominant culture.

Video Example 4.1

In this video, students explore immigration through writing journal entries in the voices of immigrants. Pay attention to how the teacher frames the unit and engages with students. Do you feel that journaling is an effective strategy for teaching and learning about immigration? Why or why not?

"There is no room in this country for hyphenated Americans."
— THEODORE ROOSEVELT (1858–1919)

By the 1920s, a revised perspective was being expressed. In settlement houses such as Hull House in Chicago, people providing social services began to appreciate the diversity of the immigrants. Social activist Jane Addams, cofounder of Hull House, and University of Chicago philosopher John Dewey described the advantages of diverse cultures and the value of people maintaining their heritages while still learning, as Benjamin Franklin had recommended, the language and customs of American culture. Although resentment toward Germans slowly dissipated after the war, anti-Semitism persisted as part of a new development in xenophobic attitudes in the United States—the influence of racism.

How did racism affect nativist attitudes and actions?

In 1899, William Z. Ripley published a so-called scientific study identifying three European races: Teutonic, Alpine, and Mediterranean (Higham, 1955). Based on emerging theories about race, nativists argued that for U.S. citizenry to achieve unity, immigrants of the blue-eyed, blond-haired Teutonic type (also called "Nordic" or "Anglo Saxon") should be given preference. Senator Henry Cabot Lodge of Massachusetts called for an end to all further immigration, and Teddy Roosevelt chastised Anglo Saxon women in America for contributing to the possibility of "race suicide" by not producing as many children as immigrant women (Brodkin, 2002). In the aftermath of World War I, pessimism about diverse groups being able to assimilate into an Anglo Saxon American culture fueled racist sentiments expressed in widely read books such as Lothrop Stoddard's *The Rising Tide of Color*. (See Figure 4.3.)

Madison Grant (1916/1970) provided the most influential expression of this pessimism in *The Passing of the Great Race*. Grant rejected the idea that immigrants with other than Nordic heritage could achieve the Anglo Saxon ideal; thus the "Great Race" of Anglo Saxons was doomed to disappear in America. Claiming that his ideas were grounded in the emerging science of genetics, Grant concluded that intermarriage between races produced degraded offspring who would revert to lower qualities in

---

Figure 4.3 White Supremacy

This advertisement from a 1923 *Time* magazine warns its readers that the days of White supremacy may be numbered and urges White people who want to do something about it to read Stoddard's book, *The Rising Tide of Color*.

SOURCE: *Time* magazine.

Three books by LOTHROP STODDARD

The Revolt Against Civilization

"The reason why this book has attracted such an extraordinary amount of attention is not far to seek. It is, so far as we know, the first successful attempt to present a scientific explanation of the world-wide epidemic of unrest that broke out during the Great War and still rages in both hemispheres."—*Saturday Evening Post.* $2.50

The New World of Islam

This book is *true*—current events are bearing it out in startling fashion. "He has presented, in compact and readable form, what did not exist before in any language: a short, concise account of the modern Mohammedan world and its reaction to the invasion of the West."—*Atlantic Monthly.*   *With maps.* $3.00

The Rising Tide of Color

White world supremacy is in danger. The world-wide ascendancy of the white race, apparently so unshakable, is in reality threatened by the colored races. This is a startling book, one for the reader who is able to stand up against the impact of new ideas. It is a clear, sharp warning to the whites, and an appeal for white solidarity.   *With maps.* $3.00

© *Bachrach*

LOTHROP STODDARD

From early manhood he has prepared himself, by wide travel and extensive study, to qualify as a true expert on world affairs. His is the mind of a trained observer who has received the soundest scientific training.

their parents' genes. Referring to Ripley's European races, Grant stated, "The cross between any of the European races and a Jew is a Jew" (p. 16). Confirming Grant's assertion, the eugenics movement provided "scientific" evidence of the human degradation caused by miscegenation, and 30 states passed laws banning interracial marriage (Stubblefield, 2007). Many respected Americans such as automaker Henry Ford expressed beliefs consistent with Grant's theories, and Grant's popular book was translated into other languages. According to historians, the German translation became known as Adolf Hitler's "bible" (Aronson & Amatullah, 2016).

Nativists used the new racist concern for preserving the nation's Anglo Saxon heritage to sound the alarm about the numbers of immigrants from southern and eastern Europe—80 percent of all U.S. immigrants from 1900 to 1910. Nativists triumphed in 1924 with the passage of an immigration law establishing quotas for immigrants based on country of origin. The quotas ensured that immigrants from northern Europe would constitute the majority of U.S. immigrants; these guidelines remained largely unchanged for the next four decades. Although people of color were the primary targets of nativists, other groups were also affected by racist attitudes.

What groups were affected by the addition of racism to xenophobia?

This new racist form of nativism was directed not only against people of color but also against White people perceived as not being White enough, which often meant that they did not share the common prejudices of the White majority. This was especially observed in southern states. In 1898, debates at Louisiana's state constitutional convention focused on who would be denied the right to vote. Although Black people were the main targets, Italians were considered "as black as the blackest negro in existence" (Barrett & Roediger, 2002, p. 32). Because of such perceptions, some Italians were victims of violence in the nineteenth century. In Tallulah, Louisiana, five Sicilian immigrants owned businesses serving primarily Black customers. Local White people resented the immigrant storekeepers for treating Black people as equals. Before long, the locals fabricated a quarrel over a goat and lynched the five Sicilians (Higham, 1955).

The idea of perceiving Italians, Irish, or others as separate races based on their national origins seems strange today; yet most Americans of that era accepted this designation, just as they would finally accept the immigrants, many of whom also eventually developed anti-immigrant attitudes. In time, the idea of national origin defining separate races declined as skin color became the primary determinant of racial identity, and racism would prolong the oppression of people of color much beyond the period it was experienced by White ethnic groups. There were only minimal changes to the immigration law favoring White immigrants, but following World War II, this became one of the targets of a social movement challenging the nation to address problems of racism.

As the civil rights movement gained momentum, allegations of racism increased. President John Kennedy admitted to inequities in immigration policies based on the 1924 law. Attorney General Robert Kennedy stated the issue more bluntly, "As we are working to remove the vestiges of racism from our public life, we cannot maintain racism as the cornerstone of our immigration laws" (Eck, 2001, p. 7). In 1965, Congress eliminated the racially biased National Origins Quotas by passing the Immigration and Nationality Act. Since then, the numbers of immigrants of color have increased dramatically, and so has nativism. The influx of illegal immigrants has also stirred anti-immigrant sentiments and created controversy even though individual and corporate employers are often dependent on them (see Figure 4.4).

Figure 4.4 Contradictions in Anti-Immigrant Attitudes

The cartoon's satire is directed at Americans who fail to recognize our society's dependence on immigrant labor.

SOURCE: David Horsey © 2007. Tribune Media Services. Reprinted by permission.

 Self-Check 4.2 Complete this self-check quiz to check your understanding of how negative attitudes toward immigrants evolved over time and the political actions that were taken against immigrants.

The Paradox of Xenophobia and Nativism in a Nation of Immigrants

Daniels (2002) noted the absurdity among Americans to regard the people who first came to the United States as "colonists" or "settlers" and then to identify the people who came later as "immigrants." Part of being accepted involved the former immigrants expressing xenophobic sentiments against current immigrants. Although Americans have not consistently expressed such negative sentiments, author John Steinbeck (1966) observed the following pattern:

> We gave [immigrants] disparaging names: Micks, Sheenies, Krauts, Dagos, Wops . . . until [each group] became sound, solvent . . . whereupon each group joined the older boys and charged down on the newest ones . . . Having suffered, one would have thought they might have pity on the newcomer, but they did not (p. 15).

To support their anti-immigrant sentiments and actions, nativists would increasingly use the work of scholars and scientists within the growing ranks of the eugenics movement.

Table 4.1 World War I Army Mental Tests

Alpha and Beta Tests developed by psychologists Robert Yerkes, Louis Terman, and Henry Goddard assisted by Carl Campbell Brigham, Founder of Educational Testing Service (ETS).

These sample questions reveal how culturally biased and inappropriate the early tests of "intelligence" could be; yet such tests were used with immigrants to determine which ones were of acceptable intelligence and which were "feeble minded."

Sample questions:				
1.	Seven-up is played with:	rackets	cards	pins	dice
2.	The Merino is a kind of:	horse	sheep	goat	cow
3.	Christy Mathewson is famous as a:	writer	artist	baseball player	comedian
4.	"There's a reason" is an "ad" for a:	drink	revolver	flour	cleanser
5.	Soap is made by:	B. T. Babbitt	Smith & Wesson	W. L. Douglas	Swift & Co.
6.	The Brooklyn Nationals are called the:	Giants	Orioles	Superbas	Indians
7.	The most prominent industry of Minneapolis is:	flour	packing	autos	brewing
8.	The forward pass is used in:	tennis	hockey	football	golf
9.	The Pierce Arrow car is made in:	Buffalo	Detroit	Toledo	Flint

SOURCE: Owen, David. *None of the Above: The Truth Behind the SATs,* 1999, p. 176 and *History Matters* at: http://historymatters.gmu.edu/d/5293

How did the eugenics movement influence anti-immigrant attitudes?

British scientist Francis Galton coined the term **eugenics** as "the study of agencies under social control that may improve or repair the racial qualities of future generations, either physically or mentally" (Lynn, 2001, p. 4). American scholars endorsing the eugenics movement were concerned about the perceived degeneration of mental abilities among Americans. Many believed there was a racial component to the problem represented by immigrants, whom they regarded as the primary cause of this decline of intelligence in America. As Stubblefield (2007) noted, many scholars believed that "White people were 'civilization builders,' while members of other races supposedly lacked the ability to produce civilization" (p. 163). Scholarly support for the eugenics movement would decline precipitously after the Nazis tainted it with their emphasis on race purification and their implementation of genocidal practices.

Although the eugenics movement in the United States never attracted a majority of academics, some in the eugenics camp were influential scholars: Robert Yerkes of Harvard (president of the American Psychological Association), Lewis Terman of Stanford, and Edward Thorndike from Teachers College, Columbia University (Selden, 2006). Because of their academic interests, Yerkes, Terman, and Thorndike were responsible for developing early intelligence tests (see Table 4.1). When Henry Goddard implemented intelligence tests with the immigrants at Ellis Island, he reported that 80 percent were "feeble minded" (Brodkin, 2002).

Because some respected scholars supported it, the eugenics movement flourished from 1910 to 1940, shaping the content of biology textbooks, reinforcing popular views concerning White supremacy, and contributing to the growth of anti-immigrant attitudes. One legacy of the eugenics movement is the standardized testing that students still take today to measure academic achievement—but testing is not the only legacy of the eugenics movement.

Established in 1937 to promote eugenics policies, the Pioneer Fund advocated the forcible removal of "American Negroes" to Africa. The first Pioneer Fund President, Harry Laughlin, wrote the Model Eugenical Sterilization Law, adopted by 30 states in the United States and Nazi Germany. Laughlin proposed that Adolf Hitler be given honorary membership in the American Eugenics Society. The Pioneer Fund continues to support scholars working on race-based IQ theories as part of their ongoing support for eugenics research (Rendall, 2014), and it has also been a major funding source for the English Only movement (DeParle, 2011).

How is the english only movement an example of xenophobic behavior?

Nativists have always been critical of immigrants who maintain their native language. They lobbied for literacy tests to reduce immigration, but for almost two decades Congress rejected the idea. When Congress finally passed such legislation, both Democratic and Republican presidents vetoed these laws until 1917, when Congress passed this requirement over President Wilson's veto (Delgado, 1997). Nativist opposition to immigrants maintaining their native language was evident in their criticisms of German immigrants, and culminated during World War I with state and local laws that forbade public displays of signs with German words and banned the teaching of German in public schools. In some communities German textbooks were burned as an act of patriotism (Crawford, 2000). The percentage of students taking German in U.S. high schools went from 25 percent in 1915 to 0.6 percent by 1922 (Baron, 2000). Today, **English Only** advocates demand that English be declared the "official language" of the United States, and they are working on that goal using a state-by-state strategy. English Only supporters claim that their desire to establish English as the official language of the United States is simply a response to those immigrants who refuse to learn how to speak English (US English, 2014).

The problem with this claim is the lack of supporting evidence. English Only proponents point to the existence of dual language street signs, billboards, and government brochures and to bilingual instruction in schools. They believe that the use of non-English languages, especially in bilingual instruction, legitimizes these languages and elevates their status as well as the status of those who speak them. Yet studies do not indicate a threat to the widespread use of English since well over 90 percent of U.S. residents speak English fluently. Of the 55 million Americans who speak a language other than English at home, 51 million (92 percent) are fluent in English (Grosjean, 2012). Critics of English Only have argued that the real driving force behind this organization is clearly not the failure of immigrants to learn English but the prejudices of the group's leaders and supporters.

Baron (2000) argues that the history of such organizations "often masks racism and certainly fails to appreciate cultural difference" (p. 447). Crawford (2000) reported on an investigation of US English, a major English Only organization, that found evidence of their real agenda: "determination to resist racial and cultural diversity in the United States" (p. 23). Latino immigrants appear to be a main target. In a survey of financial supporters of U.S. English to ascertain the reason for their support, 42 percent of respondents agreed with the statement: "I wanted America to stand strong and not cave in to Hispanics who shouldn't be here" (p. 24). Such comments support criticism that English Only disguised xenophobic attitudes by saying they promote assimilation by encouraging immigrants to learn English. Reviewing efforts to pass English Only legislation, Baron (2000) concludes: "no matter how idealistic or patriotic its claims . . . (it has) a long history of nativism, racism, and religious bigotry" (p. 451).

Immigrants have always tended to learn English out of necessity for economic and social well-being. Today, about 20 percent of Americans speak a language other than English: fewer than 7 percent of Americans speak no English (Grosjean, 2012; Ryan, 2013). Despite these facts, the English Only movement has been successful; by 2014, 31 states had passed laws declaring English as the official language. In some states these laws are largely symbolic—no penalties are enforced, and teaching foreign languages or implementing and supporting bilingual programs are not prohibited—but other states have passed laws that prohibit their governments from printing materials in other languages.

Video Example 4.2

In this video, immigrant students discuss their experiences in American classrooms. In what ways have they encountered English Only and other xenophobic movements and behavior? What are some of the suggestions these students have for their teachers and peers for being more respectful and inclusive?

Spanish is the first language of the majority of immigrants, so English Only laws largely affect Latino immigrants, preventing many from being able to gain access to useful information. Such laws may also prevent legally eligible people from voting. Whether symbolic or harmful, English Only laws reflect the xenophobic attitudes of many Americans against recent immigrants, especially people of color who are not fluent or literate in English upon their arrival. It is no coincidence that activities of English Only advocates surged following the passage of the 1965 Immigration and Nationality Act; by eliminating national origins as a consideration, this reform radically changed the demographics of those immigrating to the United States.

What changes in immigration have occurred since the passage of the immigration and Nationality Act of 1965?

Prior to 1965, most U.S. immigrants were White and primarily European, but in the first three decades after this immigration reform was implemented, about 80 percent of immigrants were people of color coming from Central and South America, the Caribbean, and Asia (Roberts, 1997). Foreign-born immigrants now constitute about 13 percent of the U. S. population, and they account for 23 percent of all births. In the period between 2005 and 2050, the children of immigrants will represent 80 percent of the population growth in the United States (Kenny, 2015). From 1970 to 2000, more than 20 million immigrants became permanent U.S. residents, and 3 million achieved this status even though they had initially entered the country illegally (Chavez, 2009). There are over 40 million Latinos in the United States, representing 15 percent of the workforce, and they are expected to exceed 50 million people and constitute 18 percent of the workforce in 2018 (Pabst, 2011). Given such numbers, it should not be surprising that Latinos are beginning to have an increasing political influence in states where they are concentrated, such as Florida, Virginia, California, and Texas. Further, demographers predict that people of color, especially Latinos, will continue to be the majority of immigrants in the future. From 2010 to 2050, the population of the United States is expected to increase by almost 150 million, and 82 percent of this increase will be people of color who immigrated after 2005 and their descendants. By 2050, it appears likely that over half (53 percent) of Americans will be people of color (Meacham, 2009), and some Americans have reacted to such predictions with fear and anxiety, resulting in the perpetuation of nativist attitudes and activities.

What American nativist attitudes and actions are evident today?

A focal point for nativist activity is the 2000-mile border between the United States and Mexico. In 1990, the United States built a steel wall on the border near San Diego. Even though the wall proved ineffective at curbing illegal entry into the United States, nativists continued to lobby for additional fencing along the border. Since 2006, over 1000 miles of fencing has been built at a cost of $3.5–$6.5 million per mile, with maintenance costs expected to reach $60 billion by 2035 (Henderson, 2011). On January 25, 2017, newly elected President Donald Trump issued an executive order shifting federal funds to pay for further construction of the wall, but the order did not stipulate what existing funds would be used for this purpose. The Government Accountability Office has estimated that the cost of just a single-layer fence will likely be equal to if not higher than the cost for building the existing wall with an additional $4.2 million per mile for roads and collateral costs as well as the ongoing cost of maintaining a 2000 mile wall (Davis, Sanger, & Haberman, 2017). Critics challenge the efficacy of this plan for keeping out illegal immigrants since a wall cannot be built through the Rio Grande River, which flows along the border in many parts of Texas. The river's banks are a designated flood plain that is governed by international treaty. A 2017 Associated Press poll reported that 58 percent of Americans oppose expanding the existing wall, and some of the strongest opposition comes from ranchers and other landowners who will have to sell part of their land to the government in order to construct the wall (Lee, 2017).

To address concerns about terrorists infiltrating the immigrant population to gain entry into the United States, additional Border Patrol agents have been hired; yet a study reported that over a two-year period only 12 immigrants were charged with any terrorist activity (0.0015 percent of all immigrants), with six charges being dropped and one dismissed (Nevins, 2010). A more significant issue has been the high turnover rate for the Border Patrol, higher than police departments or other comparable law enforcement agencies (Browne, 2014). Nevins (2010) suggested that it is related to the nature of their work. Police officers pursue criminals and often provide assistance to citizens, but Border Patrol agents pursue unemployed people who are poor and need a job, and the people they arrest often include women and children.

The increased Border Patrol presence does not appear to have addressed the concerns about immigrants entering the United States illegally. Nevins (2010) cited a study acknowledging that it was more difficult to cross the U.S./Mexican border, but the study went on to note that two thirds of those seeking illegal entry were still successful, and of the one third who were caught, 92–97 percent of them persisted in their efforts to cross the border. As Schuck (2014) noted: "Border . . . enforcement, despite large and growing costs, have not prevented the illegal presence of an estimated ten to eleven million undocumented immigrants" (p. 243). Further, one of the major factors frustrating this effort to control the border is the North American Free Trade Agreement (NAFTA). Because of NAFTA, approximately 222,000 vehicles cross the border every day, and of necessity, Border Patrol agents allow much of that traffic to pass uninspected.

In 2013, a new immigration issue arose as the Border Patrol reported a significant increase in the number of unaccompanied children apprehended while illegally crossing the U.S./Mexican border—nearly 39,000, representing an increase of almost 60 percent from the previous year (Gordon, 2014). By the summer of 2014, the number of unaccompanied children illegally crossing the border increased even more. Approximately 74 percent of these children came from Central America—primarily from Guatemala, Honduras, and El Salvador—with most of the rest coming from Mexico. Other Central American nations also experienced increased numbers of migrants seeking asylum, including Panama, Nicaragua, and Costa Rica (Lind, 2014). These nations have their own problems with poverty, but their citizens were less likely to encounter violence, and that is a major factor behind this Central American migration.

Honduras and El Salvador have the highest murder rates in the world, with Guatemala not far behind in fifth place (Gordon, 2014). Gang wars in the three countries have created extremely dangerous conditions for all citizens but especially for those living in poverty and especially for their children. These children came to the border to seek **asylum** (a safe place; a shelter from danger). Some Americans insisted that these children and youth were illegal immigrants and should be deported immediately, but in 2002, Congress passed a law establishing a specific process for screening unaccompanied child migrants. Under this law, child migrants from Mexico could be returned right away, but not unaccompanied children from Central American nations. The process begins with an asylum officer interviewing the unaccompanied child, and any child not approved for asylum proceeds to immigration court for a deportation hearing. During this hearing, the court can decide if the child is qualified for some kind of status that requires humanitarian protection (Lind, 2014).

As tens of thousands of children came to the Mexican border, trying to escape the violence in their home countries by seeking entry to the United States, critics attacked the Obama Administration for not responding aggressively and effectively to this problem. The president noted that this surge of immigrants was a consequence of American immigration policies and a significant increase in violence in the past three years, especially in Guatemala, Honduras, and El Salvador. According to Cohn (2015), the Administration's solution was to engage in diplomacy with Mexico and the Central American nations and provide them with economic support. At the border, the top priority was to expedite the immigration review process. Within three months, the flow of immigrant children had dramatically decreased, and since there was no longer a crisis, the national media moved on to cover other stories. Such lack of coverage of a successful response to a crisis may be the reason that Americans' expressed faith in government has plummeted from a high of 77 percent in 1964 to a persistent finding today of between 15 percent and 25 percent (Cohn, 2015).

Latinos comprise the majority of immigrants, whether they are children or adults, so the anti-immigrant backlash is largely directed at them, especially in areas such as Southern California where the Mexican population is expected to increase by two thirds from 2000 to 2020. Scherer (2005) quotes one Southern Californian's reaction: "Migration from Mexico is the catalyst that's starting the demise of America" (p. 57). This is not an isolated opinion. According to a 2010 survey by the Pew Research Center, nearly half of Americans agreed with the statement that immigrants "threaten traditional American customs and values" and only 39 percent believed that immigrants "strengthen our country because of their hard work and talents" (Navarro, 2011, p. A18). Despite such negative attitudes, a number of U.S. communities have erected signs in English and Spanish announcing sites that are places to procure day laborers, and many Americans hire Latino immigrants at these sites for minimal compensation with no apparent concern about whether they are in the country legally. (See Figure 4.5.)

Anti-immigrant sentiment may be waning, according to recent polls. Blake (2014) reported that 46 percent of Americans believe immigrants should be welcomed, with 56 percent believing that immigration strengthens the United States, and more Americans recognize that immigrants contribute to our nation. Yet 41 percent of Americans call for less immigration, perhaps expressing their concern about undocumented workers. Because of nativist rhetoric, many Americans assume all undocumented workers entered the United States illegally, but at least 40 percent crossed the border legally with

Figure 4.5 Day Labor Site

An immigrant waits to be hired at a day labor pickup site in Santa Barbara, California, an upscale oceanside community. Note the city-posted sign sanctioning this site, and the portable toilets provided for day laborers who must wait here, sometimes for many hours, before being picked up for a job.

SOURCE: Kent Koppelman

a visa, were hired for a job, and then remained after their visa expired (Papademetriou, 2013). Employers often prefer to keep these workers, so they don't ask them if their visas have expired. Meanwhile, anti-immigrant invective may be contributing to an increase in violence against people perceived as immigrants, especially Latinos. In 2008, two White men from Brooklyn attacked two brothers from Ecuador because they were Latinos, yet both were legal immigrants. One of the brothers died. In 2010, a White man in Arizona shot and killed his Latino neighbor after they argued about the state's controversial new immigration law; the victim was a third generation American. In 2011, a group of men shouting anti-Mexican slurs attacked a Latino man at his home in Staten Island (Potok, 2011). A Bureau of Justice Statistics report found that hate crimes against Latinos tripled from 2011 to 2012 (Haglage, 2014).

The immigrant group that seems to garner the most support is known as "The Dreamers." The term refers to over 800,000 youth brought illegally to the United States during their childhood whose academic success has demonstrated that they have the ability to make a positive contribution to this society if they are allowed to stay. Most Americans who believe merit is the best basis for rewarding people agree that Dreamers have earned the right to stay, but neither Congress nor the White House have proposed legislation to address the issue, and late in 2017, President Trump announced his decision to order the Department of Homeland Security to cancel the program. In 2018, a federal judge ruled that the Trump administration must not only reinstate the program, allowing participants to renew their status, but also accept new applications (Robbins & Dickerson, 2018). The uncertainty about the fate of the program continues, but in the spring of 2018, the President announced that his administration was ending the temporary protected status for immigrants from nations such as Honduras and El Salvador. Even though many of these immigrants were accepted into various communities and have lived in the United States for many years, they were told to leave or face deportation. The decision has alarmed Dreamers who fear they may have to face a similar dilemma (Foley, 2018).

This anti-immigrant backlash is occurring even though deportations have nearly doubled from 2005 to 2010 (Navarro, 2011), causing lasting harm to many families. Nevins (2010) wrote of a father who was deported to Colombia as his 17-year-old son began his junior year in high school. The young man was so depressed over his father's absence that he committed suicide. When the father asked for permission to attend his son's funeral, the U.S. government denied his request. From 1998 to 2007, deportations separated over a million individuals from their families, including children who were American citizens by birth. Many of these families were forced to accept the separation of a spouse or parent because keeping the family together required "uprooting their children from a community and lifestyle that is all (the children) have ever known" (Nevins, 2010, p. 187). Responding to criticism, U.S. Immigration and Customs Enforcement (2014) began focusing on deporting individuals involved in criminal activity. In 2013, 82 percent of those living in the interior of the United States who were deported had been convicted of a crime, and 84 percent of those deported without a criminal conviction were caught at the border trying to enter the United States illegally.

Arizona provided a unique example of anti-immigrant sentiment by passing a bill outlawing the teaching of ethnic studies in schools. This law was primarily a response to the Tucson School District, which had developed courses on Mexican American studies, Native American studies, and African American studies. State Superintendent Tom Horne defended the bill, arguing that such classes were racially segregated and accusing the program of teaching antipathy toward White people and hatred of America. There was little evidence to support this criticism and more evidence to refute it. For example, one instructor taught a Luis Valdez poem that emphasized the concept of the Golden Rule, an ethical principle found in all major world religions. What critics called antipathy was in reality efforts by instructors to promote critical thinking as they explored literature and history (Carjuzaa, Baldwin, & Munson, 2015). Further, the course content was relevant and meaningful to the students, in part because it affirmed their cultural identities. Students did not reject American values because, as Mexican Americans, American values were as much a part of them as is true for all American students. What should have been the critical factor was the impressive academic success of Latino students, who constituted half of Tucson's student population. Latino students enrolled in Mexican American studies had higher test scores and were more likely to graduate from high school than Latino students not enrolled in the program. Yet Arizona's legislature passed the law, and the governor signed it.

The response by Arizona's legislature was not surprising given the history of Arizona schools teaching a Eurocentric curricula and state politicians consistently opposing multicultural issues, such as their 1986 vote against celebrating Martin Luther King Jr.'s birthday as a holiday and their 2000 vote to eliminate bilingual education. In January 2011, Arizona's new State Superintendent of Schools, John Huppenthal, ordered an audit of the ethnic studies courses at Tucson's schools to ensure they were in compliance with the new ethnic studies law. In June, the audit report concluded that these courses did not violate the state law, went on to praise the academic success promoted by the ethnic studies program, and recommended that these courses be retained in the high school's core curriculum. Ignoring the audit, Huppenthal declared that the Tucson School District was in violation of the new state law and might lose $15 million of state funding. As students registered for classes for the fall 2011 semester, there were reports that the counselors assisting students were discouraging them from enrolling in ethnic studies classes and that faculty teaching ethnic studies courses were being reassigned to teach other classes. Eleven Tucson teachers filed a lawsuit against the state, alleging that the ethnic studies law was unconstitutional. In September 2017, a federal judge ruled the law unconstitutional and clearly stated the motivation for the law as "the enactment and enforcement were motivated by racial animus" (Bloomekatz, 2017, 8). This ruling gives Tucson's Latino students hope that they will be able to revive their ethnic studies classes.

> "We must get rid of fear; we cannot act at all till then. A man's acts are slavish, not true but specious, his very thoughts are false, he thinks as a slave and coward, till he have got fear under his feet."
>
> — THOMAS CARLYLE (1795–1881)

Spanglish?

Many commonly used words in American English are direct or slightly modified borrowings from the Spanish language. Many place names come from Spanish, including cities such as San Diego, Los Angeles, San Francisco, and Santa Fe, and states such as Arizona, California, Colorado, Florida, Montana, and Nevada. This list includes just a few of the many Spanish contributions to American English: adios, adobe, amigo, bronco, burro, canyon, chili, cigar, coca, cola, coyote, guerrilla, hacienda, hombre, hurricane, lasso, loco, macho, mesquite, mosquito, padre, peon, pinto, plaza, poncho, ranch, rodeo, savvy, sombrero, vista.

Video Example 4.3
In this video, a social worker discusses working with immigrants who are fearful of family members getting "picked up by [immigration officers]." What are her concerns about how these fears affect the larger community? What does the mentor social worker recommend in response to these concerns? How do these issues relate to the current context of immigration in the United States?

Many Arizona legislators argued that Spanish-speaking immigrants were not learning English fast enough, were not assimilating to our culture, and were changing American culture from Anglo to Spanish. Although the Census Bureau reports that 78 percent of Hispanic Americans tend to speak Spanish even if they can speak English, 83 percent of Hispanic high school students spoke English fluently, a higher rate than for high school students whose parents spoke another language at home (Ryan, 2013). Although Latinos are more likely than other immigrants to maintain their native language, immigrant groups in the past, such as Germans, Italians, Chinese, Jews, and Japanese, established schools so their children would maintain their native language and culture. It is true that Latinos have changed American society, influencing music, entertainment, literature, business, scholarly activity, and even the English language (see the "Spanglish" box). Mexican cuisine can be found everywhere, and salsa recently surpassed ketchup as the most popular American condiment. Yet previous immigrant groups have also altered American culture by the influence of their native cuisine, language, and creativity. This has never meant that immigrants were not assimilating to American culture; all immigrant groups have always contributed to the American economy.

How do immigrants today contribute to the American economy?

Since undocumented workers are the focus of most anti-immigrant hostility, it may be useful to begin with the role they play in our economy. Of the estimated 11.2 million undocumented workers in the United States, one million work in restaurants; they also represent 58 percent of all farm workers and 15 percent of all construction workers (Dubose, 2013). Although they are only about 5.2 percent of the workforce, undocumented workers pay billions in sales taxes; in 2010 they paid over $1 billion in income taxes (Dubose, 2013). They pay state income taxes ranging from $2 million (Montana) to $3 billion (California), and 75 percent of undocumented workers pay into social security to fund benefits that they are not likely ever to receive (Soergel, 2016). Anti-immigrant leaders still insist that illegal immigrants are getting services such as welfare and health care that deplete resources of state and local governments, but this claim was debunked two decades ago by a University of California, Davis, study reporting that the majority of undocumented workers do not enroll in government assistance programs because (1) they are not adequately fluent in English, (2) they are not aware of such programs, and (3) they fear that they will be detained by authorities and deported (Ramos, 2002). With the anti-immigrant rhetoric of the 2016 presidential campaign and the election of Donald Trump, immigrant anxiety has intensified. Throughout the United States, undocumented parents are keeping their children home from school and not taking them to after-school programs at public libraries for fear someone will be suspicious of their immigration status and report them to Immigration and Custom Enforcement (ICE). Further, many of these parents no longer take their family out to restaurants, and they are staying off social media. Some schools have reached out to these children to assure them that they will be safe in school, but the families have been traumatized by fears that the new administration will come for their parents to deport them (Sanchez, 2017).

Shorris (2001) has argued that all immigrants, especially illegal immigrants, have contributed to the U.S. economy by taking: "the worst of jobs, the ugly work, the dangerous work, the backbreaking debilitating work, the jobs that even the jobless reject" (p. 272). These jobs range from cultivating and harvesting mushrooms in damp caves to doing fieldwork as contract laborers (digging onions, picking beans, or harvesting other fruits and vegetables) to working in manufacturing sweatshops for Third World wages. Despite complaints about illegal immigrants, it is questionable if Americans would be willing to pay the price, literally, if they were absent. (See Figure 4.4.)

One of the most significant ways that all immigrants have contributed to the U. S. economy can be observed in urban areas. As the twenty-first century began, scholars were making dire predictions that America's urban areas were likely to be enmeshed in a downward economic spiral, but except for a few cities such as Detroit, the majority of cities continued to thrive. One compelling argument to explain this phenomenon was the impact of immigrants on these metropolitan areas. By the turn of the century, cities with declining populations began to report increased numbers of immigrants. This increase in population was accompanied by an increase in vitality, especially in cities with the largest increase in the numbers of immigrants. A 2014 study found that immigration to New York City not only increased the population but also resulted in fewer vacant or abandoned buildings and revitalization of the local economy. This outcome is consistent with the "broken windows" theory from the early 1980s that said vacant or abandoned buildings were a sign of neighborhood decline or disorder and encouraged crime, but by occupying vacant housing, immigrants sent a different message about the vitality of these neighborhoods. In Chicago, many immigrants settled along the 26th Street corridor, which has evolved into an economically dynamic area that has benefited native-born people as well as immigrants (Sampson, 2015).

One of the myths associated with immigrants is that large concentrations of immigrant populations would result in more crime, but the crime rate is lower in areas with large immigrant populations. In urban areas in general, violent crimes such as murder have declined to the levels reported in the 1960s or earlier. Experts have argued that low crime rates for cities with high immigrant populations were not an accident but were a consequence of a "selection bias" that occurred because "most immigrants, Mexicans in particular, selectively migrate to the United States based on characteristics that predispose them to low crime, such as motivation to work and ambition" (Sampson, 2015, p. 23). In addition, recent immigrants born outside the United States are likely to be law-abiding to avoid the being deported. By 2015, there were 40 million foreign-born people living in the United States, and evidence suggests that their presence played a significant role in the decrease of urban crime rates. For example, in a Chicago study, researchers reported that first generation immigrants were 45 percent less likely to be involved in violent crime, and their rates of violence were significantly lower than either Black or White people (Sampson, 2015).

Studies show that these lower crime rates benefit native-born urban Americans as well. New York City was ranked as one of the safest cities in America, and in Los Angeles, increased immigration in the 1990s was accompanied by a 45 percent decline in number of homicides—and the same occurred in other cities with large Latino populations (e.g., Dallas, Chicago, San Jose, and Phoenix). Cities near the border that have a history of large immigrant populations (especially Latinos), such as San Diego and El Paso, have been low-crime areas for many years. As cities became safer, life expectancy rates were affected. From 1990 to 2010, the life-expectancy rate for Black men increased by 7.3 years, and the White male life expectancy increased by 3.8 years. In addition, the pregnancy rate for teenagers declined by 56 percent for Black females and 45 percent for White females. Finally, as the cities became more economically dynamic, poverty rates were reduced. From 2000 to 2010, poverty increased to a greater degree in the suburbs than in the cities (Sampson, 2015). Despite all of this evidence, anti-immigrant advocates have continued to argue that a concentrated immigrant population in urban areas leads to increased crime as well as other negative myths about immigrants.

What myths about immigrants do many Americans believe?

Myths about "foreigners" who legally or illegally enter the United States have fueled negative attitudes for decades. Many Americans have continued to express anti-immigrant sentiments openly, and immigrants and their children have been affected by these prejudices (Costello, 2015). Although most myths about immigration refer to all immigrants, some refer specifically to immigrants with refugee status. According to the United Nations, a **refugee** is an individual "unable or unwilling to return to his or her country because of a well-founded fear of persecution . . . based on race, religion, nationality, or membership in a particular social group or political party" (Pipher, 2002, p. 18). The following myths illustrate current nativist attitudes about immigrants and refugees.

MYTH #1: Immigrants arrive ignorant, penniless, and with very little formal education and immediately have to go on welfare.

The reality is that many immigrants were professionals in their country of origin—doctors, professors, and engineers. Although the figure varies each year, 33 percent of U.S. immigrants had a college degree in 2011 (Ji, & Batalova, 2013). Yet, those arriving with graduate degrees may have to take minimum wage jobs because professional organizations or institutions in the United States may not recognize their skills or degrees, forcing them to return to school to be certified or retrained in related fields. Despite issues of language and culture, the percentage of immigrants, including refugees, receiving welfare is approximately the same as for natives, and studies of modern immigrants to the United States document that they rarely become permanent recipients of public assistance (Fitz, Wolgin, & Oakford, 2013).

> "All the people like us are We.
> And everyone else is They."
>
> — RUDYARD KIPLING (1865–1936)

Immigrants pay rent and buy groceries and other products that help strengthen the economy. Most studies of the economic impact of immigrants report that they ultimately benefit local economies, even taking into account the services that may be required to assist them during their first few years in the country. With regard to undocumented immigrants, they are not eligible to receive most forms of public assistance beyond admitting their children to public schools or to the emergency room of a hospital, but they do pay taxes. As noted earlier, illegal undocumented immigrants contribute approximately $7 billion each year to Social Security, and since they can never claim this money, it will be used to fund the benefits of other workers in the Social Security system (Scherr, 2008).

MYTH #2: Immigrants cling to their culture, language, and traditions, and refuse to assimilate into the American "melting pot."

New immigrants have always maintained their cultural heritage, in part because their identity has been profoundly shaped by their native culture. When immigrant children become adults, they typically integrate their cultural heritage with American culture, producing a hybrid of traditions and values taken from both. As for learning English, it is not unusual to find that immigrants are multilingual when they arrive; often English is one of the languages they know. Baron (2000) observed that some Americans appear to equate bilingualism with a lack of patriotism, as can be heard on talk radio shows where callers have referred to "bilinguals" in a clearly derisive manner. It is ironic to see the ability to speak fluently in more than one language transformed into a racial slur.

Immigrants pay taxes, send children to schools, serve in the military, and are affected by local political decisions. Recent immigrants have demonstrated their desire to be actively engaged in our democratic society by participating in voter registration efforts and transporting voters to the polls for elections. Because the Constitution leaves the issue of voting qualifications up to the local government, some cities have responded by giving voting rights to immigrants who are not yet citizens. The assimilation of immigrants is further complicated by a backlog of individuals pursuing naturalization—the caseload has increased by twice as much in the last fifteen years. The recent dramatic increase in unaccompanied children illegally crossing the border (mentioned earlier) has made the backlog problem even worse (Becerra, 2014).

MYTH #3: The United States is taking more than its fair share of immigrants; other countries need to take more.

This myth promotes the belief that we have more immigrants that ever before, but in 1900, 34.5 percent of residents in the United States were first- or second-generation immigrants compared to 2012, when they constituted only 24.5 percent (Hanes, 2013). In terms of sheer numbers, it is true that the United States takes in more immigrants than any other country, and currently has 40 million foreign-born residents (including an estimated 11 million undocumented immigrants). First-generation immigrants constitute 12 percent of our population, but in many European countries, immigrants represent more than 10 percent. In Germany, this percentage is predicted to rise to 30 percent by 2030. In accepting immigrants as a percent of population, the United States ranks low in the world, with the list of countries accepting more immigrants including Canada, Australia, Germany, and Switzerland (Ozimek, 2012). The major difference between the United States and other countries is that more diverse groups are admitted to the United States.

People who express concerns about an excess of immigrants to the United States often refer specifically to Mexicans, but although 12 million immigrants have come from Mexico, 18.5 million have come from other nations (Hanes, 2013). Many Americans have demanded restrictions on Mexican immigration and more money for Border Patrol agents to keep out illegal immigrants. Although Mexican immigration has significantly decreased since the 2008 recession, those who come tend to stay. Beginning in the 1990s, increased border scrutiny resulted in a dramatic decline in the numbers of legal Mexican immigrants returning to Mexico for fear they would not be allowed reentry.

MYTH #4: The main problem with U.S. immigration is the large number of illegal immigrants getting into the country.

Illegal immigrants make up 20 percent of the immigrant population and about 2 percent of the U.S. population. Although most U.S. immigrants come from Mexico, since 2007 there has been a drastic reduction in the number of undocumented immigrants entering the United States and far fewer legal Mexican immigrants since 2010 (Papademetriou, 2013). The stereotype of illegal immigrants is that of Mexicans illegally crossing the border, but over 41 percent of illegal immigrants entered the United States legally, often recruited by employers, and only become illegal by remaining after their work visas have expired.

The United States has a visa waiver program for residents of 36 selected countries, mostly in Western Europe, whose citizens can come to America for up to 90 days if they buy a round-trip travel ticket. The Immigration and Naturalization Service (INS) reports that many people who come with such visas stay beyond the 90-day limit, becoming illegal immigrants (Seminara, 2013). These people overstaying their visas are coming from places like France, Sweden, and Italy, so why is it that Americans persist in believing the stereotype of "illegal immigrants" as Mexicans who sneak across the border?

MYTH #5: Illegal immigrants are responsible for increased crime, disease, and terrorism in the United States.

This allegation appeared in a 34-page booklet on illegal immigration published by the American Legion and disseminated to its nearly three million members

(Scherr, 2008). It included the false assertion that illegal immigrants infected more than 7000 Americans with leprosy, even though this myth had already been proven false through investigations by many sources, including the news program *60 Minutes*. The source of the claim that immigrants were bringing various diseases into the United States was an article written by a lawyer with a history of anti-immigrant attitudes and no medical expertise. According to Scherr (2008), there is no medical research reporting an increase in the numbers of Americans with diseases stemming from the presence of immigrants.

As for the myth about immigrants engaging in criminal acts, a *New York Times* article claimed that 21 percent of all crime in the United States was committed by undocumented workers; however, when the author of the article was confronted with evidence of errors in his interpretation of the data, he corrected his calculations and reduced his estimate to 6.1 percent (Wilson, 2008). In addition, estimates of criminal behavior often come from data about people in prisons; many immigrants are in prison for violating immigration laws, not for violent crimes. As Wilson (2008) reported, research on criminal activities over several decades has consistently concluded that: "Immigrants aren't a crime problem" (p. 21). Finally, with regard to the terrorism aspect of this myth, Scherr (2008) cited a Nixon Center study that found this allegation to be patently false, concluding that "not a single (terrorist) entered from Mexico" (p. 34).

MYTH #6: Immigrants are taking jobs away from Americans.

The total number of legal and unauthorized immigrants is slightly more than 17 percent of the American workforce, about 12 percent and 5 percent, respectively. Despite the widespread belief that both categories of immigrants are taking jobs away from American workers, a Pew Research Center report finds that immigrants are not the dominant group in any occupation but are spread out over a number of different occupations, and the jobs where their numbers are the largest are jobs with low wages and few or no benefits that most American don't want. For example, immigrants constitute about one-third of textile workers and one fifth of food preparation and servers. Immigrants also comprise about 45 percent of those working in private households in jobs ranging from a child's nanny to a housekeeper to a gardener, and almost half of these workers are unauthorized immigrants. Unauthorized immigrants tend to be found among a narrower range of occupations than legal immigrants, making up 60 percent of agricultural workers and 60 percent of employees (pedicurists, etc.) who provide personal appearance services (DeSilver, 2017).

For as long as there has been immigration, business owners have insisted that immigration is necessary to sustain U.S. economic growth. Kugler and Oakford (2013) cite research reporting that immigrants and native workers usually have different skills and compete for different jobs, and that as immigration increases, the number of jobs being moved overseas decreases, keeping manufacturing jobs in our economy. In addition, immigrant entrepreneurs increase American jobs. Partnership for a New American Economy (2013) reported that the number of Hispanic immigrants who became entrepreneurs increased by 71.5 percent from 2000 to 2010, and they had a significant impact on employment. In 2012, one in ten Mexican immigrants was an entrepreneur. These studies illustrate why immigrants are an asset to our economy; more Americans need to recognize the immediate and potential benefits of a culturally and linguistically diverse citizenry.

Self-Check 4.3 Complete this self-check quiz to check your understanding of how the actions of some individuals and organizations reflect negative attitudes toward immigrants, how immigrants have contributed to the American economy, and the debunking of persistent myths about contemporary immigrants.

Attitudes toward Cultural and Linguistic Diversity

Cultural and linguistic diversity have evolved in human societies around the world, and each manifestation of a distinctive culture and language illustrates the complexity and richness of human creativity. Although human beings occupy the same planet, each language demonstrates how diverse groups interpret and understand their world; the differences between languages reveal that despite our similarities, human beings tend to see that world in distinctive ways. The four languages spoken by the most people in our world are Mandarin Chinese (over 1 billion), English (1 billion), Spanish (500 million), and Hindustani (490 million), but over 200 languages today are spoken by more than a million people (KryssTal, 2010). These different worldviews provide a dynamic perspective on human beings accommodating to diverse environments.

Skutnabb-Kangas (2000) defines **linguistic diversity** as "the range of variation exhibited by human language" (p. 70), and she reports that there are between 6500 and 10,000 languages throughout the world, as well as a number of different sign language systems. A more precise estimate is impossible because so many languages are disappearing. In the United States alone there used to be more than 300 indigenous languages, but only 154 still remain, and many are becoming extinct. The Tuscarora were once part of the powerful alliance known as the Six Nations of the Iroquois Confederacy, but when 93-year-old Helen Sater died in a Canadian hospital, she was the last living person fluent in the Tuscarora language (Skutnabb-Kangas, 2000). Linguists have identified 43 indigenous languages that are on the verge of extinction, and they fear that only three of them will survive: Cree, Ojibway, and Inuktitut (Crawford, 2000). With over 300 indigenous languages already present and with the arrival of people speaking diverse European languages, the history of North America should be regarded as an ongoing chronicle of communities that were multilingual as well as multicultural. Even today, the reality of linguistic diversity in the United States can best be appreciated by visiting urban classrooms; yet Americans continue to be ambivalent about linguistic and cultural diversity.

Why should immigrants maintain their native language?

According to Ryan (2013), 21 percent of all K–12 students in the United States currently come from a home where a language other than English is spoken. Although more than two thirds of these students are Spanish-speaking, the following list includes other languages spoken by children in U.S. schools:

- Southeast Asia: Hmong, Khmer, Lao, and Vietnamese
- South Asia: Hindi, Punjabi, and Urdu
- Asia: Cantonese, Japanese, Korean, Mandarin, and Russian
- Europe: Armenian, French, Polish, Portuguese, and Serbo-Croatian
- Other: Arabic, Haitian Creole, Tagalog, and Navajo

Some Americans argue that immigrants and their children should not be encouraged to maintain fluency in their native languages but should focus on learning English and assimilating into American society. They often cite nations such as Canada, the former Yugoslavia, India, or the former Soviet Union to illustrate their concern that social disruptions can occur when groups within a nation maintain their cultural and linguistic heritage, but based on his review of history, Baron (2000) found that: "where multilingualism has produced civil strife . . . (it) invariably occurs when minority-language rights are suppressed" (p. 451). Some Americans also believe that it is normal for a nation's citizens to be monolingual, yet most individuals in the world today are either bilingual or multilingual. As we began the twenty-first century, Skutnabb-Kangas (2000) noted that those of us who were monolingual were the abnormal ones.

A primary motivation for maintaining your native language is to preserve your sense of identity and ability to function within a linguistic community. The parents that Olivera (2012) interviewed wanted their children to become bilingual and bicultural so that they could communicate with family members and participate in cultural celebrations in their community. In addition, an individual's identity is often grounded in religious faith. Skutnabb-Kangas (2000) has described the intimate relationship between language and religion, finding that people who have learned to pray in their native language have established their sense of connection to their God in a way that often makes it difficult for them to pray in their second language. Despite many reasons for maintaining a native language, most immigrants in the United States tend to learn English and cease to be fluent in their native language.

Why do immigrants tend to lose their native language?

In contrast to American fears concerning the failure of immigrants to learn English and assimilate into American culture, studies document a pattern of the loss of linguistic diversity in subsequent generations of immigrant families. Jody Vallejo, a sociology scholar who studies immigration, described the pattern of language loss: (1) the first-generation immigrants learn enough English to function in society but prefer to speak their native language, (2) the second generation becomes fluent in English and maintains fluency in speaking their native language, and (3) the third generation tends to only be fluent in English (Mejina, 2016). Rodriguez (2013) confirms Vallejo's description with a Pew study finding that third-generation Latino families are English-dominant, meaning that they listen to English-speaking television programs and music, and they think in English. Because of ongoing immigration, demographers predict that the number of Spanish speakers in the United States is likely to reach 40 million by 2020. Yet of all Latinos living in the United States at that date, it is predicted that only two-thirds of them will speak Spanish fluently, compared to three-quarters of Latinos today (Rodriguez, 2013). Paradoxically, while Latinos are losing fluency in Spanish, non-Latino parents are lobbying for bilingual education, especially dual immersion programs. Schools offering such programs introduce students to Spanish throughout their elementary school years with the goal of producing students who are fluent in both speaking and writing.

The United States is not the only nation whose immigrants lose their language. It is happening in other Western nations where the dominant group (speaking English or French or German) demands that immigrants abandon their own language and heritage and adopt the language and cultural traditions of the dominant group. This can be most clearly seen in the education of immigrant children. After describing this form of assimilation that demands cultural and language conformity, Skutnabb-Kangas (2000) concludes: "This is the preferred Western strategy in the education of ethnic minority children. It amounts to linguistic genocide" (p. 174). Some educators in the United States and elsewhere have been sensitive to this issue and have advocated a different approach.

What alternative pedagogical strategy have American educators proposed?

Beginning in the 1960s, numerous activist groups, including Chicano, Puerto Rican, Asian American, and Native American people, addressed educational issues such as segregation, inadequate resources, and the need for bilingual/bicultural programs (Bale, 2015). These grassroots groups were effective enough to get the attention of Congress, which passed the Bilingual Education Act in 1968, but even the advocates for this bill did not share the same rationale for supporting it as the activist groups. The bill's chief sponsor, Ralph Yarborough (D-Texas), offered this argument to his Senate colleagues:

> It is not the purpose of this bill to create pockets of different languages throughout the country. It is the main purpose of the bill to bring millions of school children into the mainstream of American life and make them literate in the national language of the country in which they live: namely, English (Crawford, 2000, p. 88).

Yarborough made this argument to convince his Senate colleagues that this bill would serve the needs of Mexican Americans like those in his district where adults with limited English skills tried to find jobs while their children struggled to learn English. He portrayed the Bilingual Education Act as an anti-poverty program for a constituency he believed largely had been overlooked in other "Great Society" programs. The politicians who passed this bill viewed bilingual education not as a way to achieve bilingualism but as a more effective means of encouraging assimilation. If students learned better by teaching them in Spanish, then some instruction could be delivered in Spanish so that students would not fall behind in their content learning. The assumption was that bilingual education was a transitional program that would temporarily maintain fluency in a native language until the student's English skills were sufficient to allow all instruction to be in English.

Many advocates for bilingual education disagreed with this interpretation, arguing that students had a right to maintain not only their native language but also their cultural heritage while they learned English and adapted to their new culture. These advocates, including students and parents, effectively challenged their local school districts to address their concerns, especially their desire for bilingual/bicultural education. These issues were dramatized in 1968 when thousands of Chicano/a students walked out of East Los Angeles schools and in 1969 when students in Crystal City, Texas, boycotted their schools. As Bale (2015) noted, "It was the conscious, ambitious, and collective actions of anti-racist activists that brought real change to schools for emergent bilingual youth" (p. 23). Unfortunately, the vision and commitment of these activists was not widely shared by other Americans or by Congressional leaders, and it wasn't long before critics began to attack the newly established bilingual education programs.

In the early 1970s, Massachusetts and several other states repealed their English Only laws and established programs for "transitional bilingual education," but before the end of the decade, the findings of a nationwide study disturbed many Americans when it reported that 86 percent of bilingual programs retained Spanish-speaking students after they had become fluent in English (Crawford, 2000). In 1978, Congress voted to allow federal funds to be used only for "transitional" bilingual education programs. Another study reported that half of bilingual teachers were not proficient in students' native languages, raising doubts about whether bilingual programs could produce students who were as fluent in English as they were in their native language. In 1980, a report by the President's Commission on Foreign Language and International Studies encouraged advocates for bilingual education by stating: "The melting pot tradition that denigrates immigrants' maintenance of their skills to speak their native tongue still lingers, and unfortunately causes linguistic minorities (in the U.S.) to be ignored as a potential asset" (Tse, 2001, p. 51).

Yet doubts continued to plague bilingual education programs, and early research did not diminish these doubts. By the end of the 1980s, Shorris (2001) described numerous conflicting studies that reported findings both supportive and critical of bilingual education. Increasingly, critics of bilingual education portrayed it as a language-maintenance program rather than as a way for children of immigrants to learn English and academic content more effectively. In the midst of this debate, the Reagan administration funded the implementation of English-only approaches for students learning English as a second language (Crawford, 2000).

As the controversy continued, it became obvious that this was not simply an educational debate, but that there were social and political aspects as well. Advocates for bilingual education were interested in more than language learning; they argued for the value of teaching diverse "viewpoints, histories, sociopolitical realities and languages, and to promote the intrinsic worth of diversity in general" (Gort, 2005, p. 34). Opponents were adamant that such goals went beyond the original mandate of helping non-English-speaking students to learn English, and they criticized bilingual programs for separating their students from their peers in the regular classes, isolating them from interactions with these students that might enable their assimilation into American society. Critics of bilingual education became increasingly successful in persuading Americans that bilingual education programs were not working.

By the 1990s, many Americans believed that bilingual education was more likely to promote students' maintenance of their native language and culture than it was to foster their learning English and assimilating into American society, even though ongoing research began to make a stronger case for the efficacy of bilingual education programs. Salas (2006) cited a number of studies finding that students whose first language was not English achieved more academic progress in English when they also had instruction in their first language. Salas also referred to a review of research on bilingual education programs concluding that students in these programs "do as well as or better on standardized tests than students in comparison groups of English-learners in English-only programs" (p. 34). Still, the five million English Language Learners (ELLs) in K–12 public schools today are unlikely to be enrolled in bilingual programs because the federal Bilingual Education Act was not renewed in 2002, and, despite research supporting bilingual education, federal policies continue to emphasize English-only educational programs for ELLs.

Have research studies identified effective approaches to ELL instruction?

English-only programs have often involved a total immersion approach in which only English is spoken in the classroom, yet advocates can produce no credible studies of support, usually offering anecdotal evidence. By contrast, there are numerous studies documenting the diverse outcomes achieved in bilingual education programs. According to the U. S. Department of Education, there were only 260 dual-language schools in 2000, but by 2017 there were over 2000 dual-language schools, and states like Texas, Utah, and North Carolina had passed laws promoting such schools. The increasing popularity of dual-language schools stems from the combination of scientific and pedagogical research, as studies that report on student academic achievement and neurological research clearly support this approach (Peterson, 2017). In 2006, the National Literacy Panel published its review of research on programs educating ELLs, and in that same year the Center for Research on Education, Diversity and Excellence published its review of these programs. Literacy expert Claude Goldenberg of Stanford University engaged in a meta-analysis of these two major reviews of literacy studies to determine what conclusions could be reached.

Goldenberg (2008) began by providing some demographic data: Of the five million ELLs in U.S. schools, 80 percent were Spanish-speaking. Approximately 60 percent of

ELLs received some form of English-only instruction. Test results revealed that ELLs tended to have low scores on measures of academic achievement, but there was no way of knowing if these scores reflected poor content knowledge or simply the limitations of the students' proficiency in English. Yet Goldenberg (2008) reported that one of the major findings emerging from both studies was that "Teaching students to read in their first language promotes higher levels of reading achievement in English" (p. 14). He also noted that this finding was consistent with four previous meta-analyses of research on ELLs and emphasized the historic significance of this finding: "No other area in educational research with which I am familiar can claim five independent meta-analyses based on experimental studies, much less five that converge on the same finding" (p. 15). Further, both research reviews reported that ELLs in bilingual education programs tended to develop sufficient literacy skills to be not only fluent in speaking two languages but also fluent in reading and writing in both languages.

For those students who achieve such fluency, educators should be encouraging them to enroll in college. Liou (2016) interviewed numerous immigrant students and found that all of them expressed a desire to enroll in a college, but not one had been encouraged by a teacher or guidance counselor to pursue this goal. Instead, studies have found that educators have low expectations for immigrant children, even when those children's parents have high expectations for them. A 2015 study found that immigrant students were the fastest growing population in America's K–12 public schools, yet they are being underserved, not because of any hostile attitudes but because educators tend to pity the immigrants as having limited options for their future (Liou, 2016). These immigrant children do face difficulties. Some were born in refugee camps and spent years without receiving any formal education. After arriving in the United States, often these children were crowded into apartments and took care of younger siblings. For that reason, when the immigrant children finally got the chance to attend school, many were grateful and prepared to work hard to improve their academic abilities. Instead of encouraging them, Liou (2016) reported teacher responses such as "They won't be able to make it. You're setting them up to fail," or "College isn't for everyone" (pp. 86–87). Advocates challenge teachers to have much higher expectations for immigrant students and to employ strategies that affirm student abilities and identities and provide these students with the support and mentoring that will promote their academic achievement.

Why should educators be advocates for bilingual programs?

As the global economy becomes increasingly important for our national economy, it is an advantage for any nation to have citizens fluent in one or more languages other than their native tongue. The U.S. government has understood this advantage for decades. Since 1946, when it was first established, the largest foreign language school in the United States has been the Defense Language Institute for military and government personnel. Tse (2001) probably had the Defense Language Institute in mind as she wrote the first of her three arguments describing the advantages of increasing the number of Americans who are bilingual or multilingual:

1. *Diplomacy/security*—having fluent speakers of the world's languages enables the United States to play a major role in global affairs and negotiate peaceful solutions to political conflicts. Bilingual Americans also strengthen our ability to gather credible intelligence with regard to issues affecting our national security.
2. *Economic*—because of globalization, businesses increasingly need employees who not only can speak another language but also can understand the culture in which the language is spoken. Businesses that are able to navigate the linguistic and cultural terrain will be able to establish better relations with trading partners around the world.

Application Exercise 4.1

This video depicts how educators can affirm the language that students bring to school. Review the video and complete the activity.

3. *Educational*—promoting bilingualism in our children and youth will increase the numbers of college students majoring in a language, and that will likely result in increasing the numbers of bilingual students choosing to enroll in teacher training courses. For many years now, it has often been difficult for K–12 schools to find teachers who are both fluent in another language and have teaching certification.

For all of these reasons, educators who are advocates for bilingualism may be more successful today if they renew their efforts to implement bilingual education programs in K–12 schools. There are various forms of bilingual education, but both students and parents have had high praise for the dual language approach (also known as two-way immersion). Dual language programs pair ELLs with students who want to learn another language in the same classroom. A bilingual teacher may provide instruction in two languages, and the students serve as resources for one another. In a program with Spanish-speaking students, the students learning Spanish use their ELL peers as language tutors, and ELLs use their partners to tutor them in English. The growing need in the world, especially in the United States, for linguistic diversity and cultural competence should be the catalyst for Americans developing a more pluralistic attitude toward the value of diverse languages and cultures.

> ✓ **Self-Check 4.4** Complete this self-check quiz to check your understanding of attitudes toward the cultural and linguistic diversity of the United States and which educational approaches have been most effective for learning English.

Afterword

"America, it would seem, is miraculously both singular and plural, organized and scattered, united and diffused."

— HENRY KARIEL (1924–)

The history of immigration demonstrates that there have been and still are diverse but clearly defined attitudes toward immigration on the part of American citizens, political leaders, and representatives of business and industry. Although workers sometimes resent the economic competition, our society has always benefited from the willing labor of immigrant workers. We have also benefited from the cultural diversity of immigrants from so many different nations. Although some Americans have railed against current immigrants not assimilating and have repeatedly insisted that immigrants should rid themselves of their old culture, history teaches us that there is no royal road for immigrants trying to adjust or adapt to a new culture; in reality, there are diverse pathways. Each immigrant may take a different route, but if they remain in the United States, each will likely end at the same destination—becoming an American.

Summary

- Because British colonists were trying to recreate the Old World in the New World, they were not receptive to immigrants from cultures that were not of Anglo Saxon origin.

- The anti-immigrant ideology of Nativism rejected Catholics and all immigrants perceived as radical, and nativists engaged in political activities to control them.

- The eugenics movement in the past and the English Only movement today are examples of organizations that have fueled anti-immigrant sentiment that

has resulted in a variety of hostile actions toward immigrants; despite the documented contributions that immigrants make to the American economy, Americans continue to believe negative myths about current immigrants.

- Although the United States is still a monolingual society, many recent immigrants are promoting bilingualism, and studies have shown that bilingual education is not only the best way to learn English but also the most effective way to preserve native language and culture.

Terms and Definitions

Americanization The demand that immigrants to the United States reject their ethnic or cultural heritage and conform to American ways as defined by the dominant group

Anti-Semitism Having anti-Jewish prejudices or stereotypes, or engaging in discrimination against Jewish people

Assimilation A process whereby immigrants adopt cultural traits of the host country in order to be identified with that country and integrated into the immediate society

Asylum A safe place; a shelter from danger (pertaining to refugees)

English Only A movement in various states demanding that legislatures make English the official language of the state, with the eventual goal of having the federal government make English the official language of the United States

Eugenics The study of agencies under social control that may improve or repair the racial qualities of future generations, either physically or mentally (Lynn, 2001)

Linguistic diversity The range of variation exhibited by human language (Skutnabb-Kangas, 2000)

Nativism An anti-immigrant ideology advocating the protection of "native" inhabitants of a country from new or potential immigrants who are viewed as threatening or dangerous (Feagin & Feagin, 1996)

Oppression When any entity (society, organization, group, or individual) intentionally or unintentionally distributes resources inequitably, refuses to share power, imposes ethnocentric culture, and/or maintains unresponsive and inflexible institutions toward another entity for its supposed benefit and rationalizes its actions by blaming or ignoring the victim (Andrzejewski, 1996)

Refugee An individual "unable or unwilling to return to his or her country because of a well-founded fear of persecution . . . based on race, religion, nationality, or membership in a particular social group or political party" (Pipher, 2002)

Xenophobia Fear of or prejudice against people from other nations

Discussion Exercises

Exercise #1 Believing in Myths

Directions: Chapter Four described myths about immigrants, including the following:

1. They are ignorant, arrive penniless, have very little formal education, and immediately go on welfare.
2. They cling to their culture, language, and traditions, and refuse to assimilate into the American "melting pot."
3. A large percentage of them are illegal.

4. They are taking jobs away from Americans.

In discussing these myths, start by identifying which ones you once thought were true and why you thought them. Then discuss what made you realize they were not true. Conclude by identifying which myth does the most damage in promoting negative attitudes toward immigrants, and explain why.

Exercise #2 The Immigration Letter to the Editor

Directions: This letter appeared in newspapers across the United States, in each one signed as if written locally. Discuss your understanding of its message, and then move to the Questions for Discussion. As you read, consider which of the four ethnic perspectives presented in this chapter is illustrated.

I am tired of this nation worrying about whether we are offending some individual or their culture . . . I am not against immigration, nor do I hold a grudge against anyone who is seeking a better life by coming to America. Our population is almost entirely made up of descendants of immigrants. However, there are a few things that those who have recently come to our country, and apparently some born here, need to understand.

This idea of America being a multicultural community has served only to dilute our sovereignty and our national identity. As Americans, we have our own culture, our own society, our own language and our own lifestyle. This culture has been developed over centuries of struggles, trials, and victories by millions of men and women who have sought freedom.

We speak ENGLISH, not Spanish, Portuguese, Arabic, Chinese, Japanese, Russian or any other language. If you wish to become part of our society, learn the language! "In God We Trust" is our national motto. This is not some Christian, right wing, and political slogan. We adopted this motto because Christian men and women, based on Christian principles, founded this nation, and this is clearly documented. It is certainly appropriate to display it on the walls of our schools. If God offends you, then I suggest you consider another part of the world as your new home, because God is part of our culture.

We are happy with our culture and have no desire to change, and we really don't care how you did things where you came from. This is OUR COUNTRY, our land, and our lifestyle. Our First Amendment gives every citizen the right to express opinions and we will allow you every opportunity to do so. But once you are done complaining, whining, and griping about our pledge, our national motto, or our way of life, I highly encourage you to take advantage of one other great American freedom, THE RIGHT TO LEAVE.

God Bless America

Questions for Discussion

1. What do you think the writer means in saying that the view of America as a multicultural community "has served only to dilute our sovereignty and our national identity"?
2. Are large numbers of immigrants not learning English?
3. Should immigrants who are learning English be criticized for trying to maintain fluency in their native languages?
4. Are immigrants complaining about the use of "God" in the Pledge of Allegiance?
5. If "God is part of our culture," do you have to believe in God to be an American?
6. Who is intended to be included in the "we" of the last paragraph?
7. How could the letter be written to reflect any of the other ethnic perspectives?

Chapter 5

Race and Oppression: The Experiences of People of Color in America

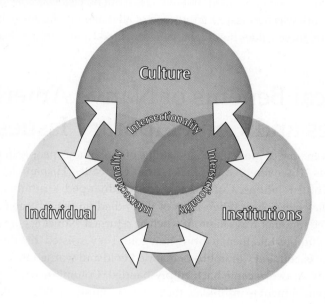

 ## Learning Outcome

After reading this chapter you will know and be able to:

5.1 Describe potential benefits inherent in indigenous cultures, and explain the ongoing significance of Indian treaties and contemporary issues affecting Native Americans.

5.2 Discuss resistance to slavery by both Black and White people in the United States, and describe the struggle of Black people after the Civil War to attain their civil rights as American citizens.

5.3 Describe and give examples of the historic hostility of White Americans toward Asian immigrants, and explain how the model minority myth recognizes Asian American achievements while still stereotyping the group.

5.4 Identify and discuss the diverse Latino groups that have immigrated to the United States, and give examples of the different obstacles each group has encountered.

"Everyone likes to give as well as to receive. No one wishes only to receive all the time. We have taken much from your culture. I wish you had taken something from our culture for there were some good and beautiful things in it."

—CHIEF DAN GEORGE (1899–1991)

The categorizing of human beings into racial groups has resulted in a history of racial oppression in America, beginning with the colonial period and continuing as rebellion against England created a new nation. Although all immigrants to the United States encountered obstacles and opposition, being perceived as White initially or eventually proved an enormous advantage. Whether they came voluntarily as immigrants or were brought involuntarily as slaves, people of color had to contend with blatant forms of oppression. Some of these experiences were similar for all groups, but other forms of oppression were unique to each particular group.

The quotation from Chief Dan George describes a problem for **indigenous people**, those who were established in the New World, and all immigrants of color in their encounter with European colonists. Differences perceived as "race" were actually differences of culture, so by rejecting other races, the majority was actually rejecting the cultural gifts each group could have shared. Diversity in the United States began with the American Indians, with most of the nations having egalitarian social structure when Europeans first arrived. Men and women performed different tasks, but no task was considered inferior to another. All work was necessary for the good of all (Lajimodiere, 2013). European settlers did not share these values but might have benefited from learning them.

Historical Benefits of Native American Cultures and Contemporary Issues

The Arawaks were one of more than 500 nations of indigenous people in the Americas when Columbus "discovered" a Caribbean island he called Hispaniola. After a brief period of peaceful relations, Columbus's crew kidnapped a number of Arawaks to auction as slaves in Spain. When most of them died on the voyage back to Spain, Columbus looked for other ways to profit when he returned. Noticing gold jewelry worn by Arawaks, Columbus told them to bring him gold. They insisted that there was only a little gold on the island, but Columbus demanded gold and warned them not to return without it. If any Arawaks came back empty-handed, Columbus had his men cut off their hands as punishment to intimidate the rest into complying (Zinn, 2003). Although historians cannot give a precise number for the population of indigenous people living in North America in 1492, their best estimate is that the number probably exceeded ten million people. By the 1920 Census, there were less than 100,000 American Indians left (Cox, 2015). According to Josephy (2005), Europeans exterminated half of the 500 nations and nearly eradicated the cultures of many Indian nations that managed to survive.

What did Europeans learn from native Americans?

English settlers in America tended to build on existing Indian settlements and walked on Indian paths, many of which eventually became the roads of the new nation. Benjamin Franklin studied the governance structure of the Iroquois League and borrowed heavily from it to create his "Albany Plan," the basis for the Articles of Confederation that was the first form of government implemented in the United States (Weatherford, 1988). Even though he borrowed ideas from the Iroquois League, Franklin's prejudice against Indians appears in a letter to James Parker:

> It would be a very strange Thing, if six Nations of ignorant Savages should be capable of forming a Scheme for such an Union and be able to execute it in such a Manner, as that it has subsisted for Ages, and appears indissoluble; and yet that a like Union should be impracticable for ten or a Dozen English Colonies, to whom it is more necessary. (Le May, 1987, p. 444)

Unlike Franklin, most colonists did not care to learn from Indians. Their ethnocentric goal was to establish the culture and traditions of their own European heritage in

> **What's in a Name**
>
> Although the term *Native American* has become widely used, there is still not a consensus for a single term among native peoples. The only consensus is their preference to be identified by their tribal affiliation, such as Hopi, Apache, Sioux, Mohican, or Inuit. Author Sherman Alexei rejects the term *Native American*, preferring *American Indian*. Some prefer to be called *indigenous people*; others are content with the traditional label of *Indian*. In this chapter, all four terms are used to reflect this diversity of preferences. In conversations with individual American Indians, the best option is to ask the individual what his or her preference is, and then use that term.

America. **Ethnocentrism** is the belief that your own race, nation, or culture is superior to all others, as illustrated by colonial choices for settlement names. Dutch settlers called their town New Amsterdam until the English captured it and renamed it New York. Many settlements were named without even adding the term *new*, which can be seen by comparing city names on current maps of New England states with city names on maps of England. English colonists called a bird a robin because it reminded them of an English robin. We still call this bird a robin today, but it's not an English robin, nor is it related to the English robin (Williams, 1954).

What did European settlers fail to learn from native Americans?

If Europeans had been willing to listen, they could have learned much from Native Americans. The following five areas provide a few examples.

Foods and medicines. European settlers did not want to eat food initially unfamiliar to them, such as potatoes, peanuts, corn, squash, tomatoes, peppers, and pumpkins. Later, these foods came to be exported around the world and had a major influence within countless nations. As Weatherford (1988) wrote, "It is difficult to imagine what Ireland would be today without the potato" (p. 64). Similarly, it is difficult to imagine what Italian food was like before the American tomato became part of its cuisine.

Europeans did not try to acquire the indigenous people's knowledge of medicinal properties of plants. (See Figure 5.1.) As an example, scurvy is a disease resulting from vitamin C deficiency, causing bleeding gums and fatigue; it often afflicted people voyaging on ships because fruit didn't last long at sea. Native Americans knew how to cure scurvy long before Europeans found a cure by noticing that German sailors on boats stocked with sauerkraut did not tend to get this illness (Weatherford, 1988). Suzuki and Knudtson (1992) estimate that 75 percent of prescription drugs derived from plants have been discovered based on clues stemming from the healing practices of the indigenous peoples of the world. According to Harvard botanist Richard Schultes, every time a shaman dies, "it is as if a library had burned down" (Gell-Mann, 1994, p. 339).

> "God teaches the birds to make nests, yet the nests of all birds are not alike."
>
> —DUWAMISH PROVERB

Hygiene. According to Spring (2001), European descriptions of Indians as "filthy savages" had nothing to do with hygiene but with their "seemingly unrepressed sexuality" (p. 10). American Indians practiced frequent bathing while Europeans did not. Europeans believed that exposing the body to the air could cause colds and other health problems. Christian church leaders also disapproved of public bathing, fearing that nude people mingling in a public bath might inspire lust. Instead, throughout Europe, many, including the aristocracy, would dry-rub themselves with sand, ashes, or pumice stone. For the rich or royal, perfume disguised body odor. According to Smith (2001), England's Queen Elizabeth I took a bath once a month, and Spain's Queen Isabella proudly claimed that she had only taken two baths in her life: when she was born and when she was married. No wonder perfume was so expensive and so highly valued!

Figure 5.1 Kickapoo Sagwa Bottle

The use of Indian images on medicine bottles in the 1800s suggests that Americans were aware that Indians understood the medicinal value of plants. Instead of acquiring that knowledge, entrepreneurs created concoctions (usually including alcohol), put an image of an Indian on the bottle, and sold the bogus medicine to naive customers.

SOURCE: Kent Koppelman

Governance and gender equality. Indian women who owned property maintained control of it regardless of their marital status (White, 2001). Women elders in clans often had the power to select tribal leaders, and they had a voice in important decisions. Some women even participated in battles. Among the Cherokee, such women were called "war women" and were given a place on the nation's governing council; Lakota women warriors constituted four military groups (Lajimodiere, 2013). In 1642, Virginians met with a Cherokee delegation to negotiate for a peaceful resolution of their recent conflicts. As their leader approached the colonial delegation, he asked them why he saw no women. Hearing that the colonists had brought no women, the leader said he could not negotiate since the colonists did not have half of their people. Despite this historic reality about Indian women, Europeans created and disseminated stereotypes about them that persist today—both the negative stereotype portraying them as drudges who were restricted to domestic work and the "positive" stereotype of the Indian Princess. The latter image pertained to Indian women saving or giving aid to White men (Lajimodiere, 2013).

Childcare. Europeans might also have benefited from learning childcare practices from American Indians. Children of European immigrants, like children in Europe, were expected to work on domestic chores at an early age. If they misbehaved, they were punished severely with beatings and whippings to teach them obedience to parental authority, just as parents had to be obedient to their superiors. Children were rarely shown overt affection and were allowed little freedom. By contrast, European observers of American Indian societies were surprised by the amount of freedom given to Indian boys and girls. Young children were not expected to assist their parents with farming, hunting, or household tasks. There were few restrictions on their activities as they became intimately familiar with their surroundings. Instead of punishing with straps or rods, Indian children were scolded and made to feel a sense of shame about misbehaving. The parents' goal was to promote a sense of personal pride and an independent, courageous spirit. They believed that threats and physical punishment would cause children to become passive and fearful (Mintz, 2004). European children who were captured and raised by Indians were called "White Indians." Even if offered a chance to return to their families, many of these children refused to leave. When "White Indian" children were returned to colonial society, most preferred to return to their Indian families. Benjamin Franklin addressed this phenomenon in 1753 (Mintz, 2004):

> When white persons of either sex have been taken prisoners young by the Indians, and lived awhile among them, tho' ransomed by their Friends, and treated with all imaginable tenderness to prevail with them to stay among the English, yet in a Short time they become disgusted with our manner of life . . . and take the first good Opportunity of escaping again into the woods, from whence there is no reclaiming them. (p. 8)

Ecology. Native Americans have expressed the belief that human beings share a spiritual kinship with the natural world and are obligated to live in harmony with it. Suzuki and Knudtson (1992) cite a declaration by the Iroquois Confederacy deploring the destruction of forests by entrepreneurs, the depletion of wildlife by sports hunters and pesticides, the pollution of the air by factories, the pollution of water and poisoning of fish by industry and agribusiness, and the depositing of toxic wastes in chemical dumps across the country. The Iroquois declaration calls on people to preserve life around us, to "carry out our function as caretakers of the land" (pp. 240–241).

What was the main source of conflict between Europeans and Indians?

> "Take only what you need and leave the land as you found it."
> —ARAPAHO PROVERB

The primary contention between European colonists and Indians was about land ownership. In school, children are often taught that Columbus planted Spain's flag in the New World to claim the land for Spain, implying that Spanish and Indian representatives would resolve the competing claims either by negotiating a treaty or by warfare. Engaging in war based on claims to land was common in European history. Nations gained or lost inhabited land through conquest because only uninhabited land could be claimed, a principle identified as *vacuum domicilium* (Berkhofer, 2004). Even in 1492, international law recognized the rights of indigenous people to own the land where they lived. Explorers were given charters to allow them to claim land under the legal principle of *terra nullius*, an ambiguous term suggesting lands without people but interpreted as including land inhabited by a people not possessing religions and customs equal to those of Europeans.

When Columbus planted the Spanish flag, he was establishing the legal right for Spain to possess uninhabited land or to purchase the land if indigenous people had a legitimate claim to it. But most legal claims for land inhabited by Native Americans were not made under the principle of *vacuum domicilium* because natives made it clear that the land where they lived belonged to them collectively, and they belonged to the land. To resolve the ambiguity of making a *terra nullius* claim, European nations wanting to take possession of Indian land created a new concept called *occupatio bellica*, referring to peaceful seizure of land underutilized by the indigenous people. Although indigenous people might not agree with what was viewed as "underutilized," the principle allowed Europeans to take possession of land by peaceful means, such as by erecting crosses marked with the royal seal throughout the land or by bribing a few indigenous individuals to sign an agreement conceding the land.

Nomads were the exception. Defined as "pastoral people" wandering on the land and never staying in one place, **nomads** were not granted a legal claim to land. In making land claims, colonists described indigenous people as "nomadic" because they would move their villages every few years because of soil depletion and decreasing crop productivity. After many years at another site, they might move again, eventually returning to a site abandoned decades before where the soil would now be replenished (Berkhofer, 2004). Such a pattern does not fit the definition of nomadic. Although Plains

> "They made many promises, so many I can't remember, but they only kept one. They promised to take our land, and they took it."
> —RED CLOUD (1822–1909)

Indians, such as the Sioux or Cheyenne, were nomadic and followed historic migratory patterns, most indigenous people lived in villages. If villagers resisted encroachment on their land, the result was often armed conflict ending with a treaty mandating the loss of land and Indian resettlement.

Why are Indian treaties still important today?

A **treaty** is a legal document negotiated between two (or more) sovereign nations involving terms of peace, trade, and other matters. Indian treaties document the cession of Indian lands to the U.S. government that were then made available for settlement. Land was also confiscated for resources. As described in Gedicks (1993), historian David Wrone has calculated that 19.5 million acres of land taken from just one indigenous group, the Chippewa, resulted in the United States gaining significant wealth. Besides taking possession of the land, the resources from the land included "100 billion board feet of timber; 150 billion tons of iron ore; 13.5 billion pounds of copper" (p. 51). Other resources taken from Indian land included water, ports, fish, fowl, and game, all contributing to a profitable tourism industry that has yielded considerable wealth to members of the dominant society who gained access as a result of treaties.

A treaty signed by an Indian nation and the United States was an agreement between sovereign nations. Treaties were written with provisions to be maintained in perpetuity, yet the U.S. government has violated virtually every treaty made with indigenous peoples, often during the lifetimes of those who signed the treaty (Josephy, 2005; Wilson, 1998). Yet treaties continue to be important documents because they affirm the status of Indian Sovereignty. Deloria (2001) described **Indian Sovereignty** as a principle affirming the legal right of Indian nations to define themselves on their own terms and to behave as unique cultural and legal entities.

An ongoing controversy related to Indian Sovereignty was the announcement of the proposed Keystone pipeline that would carry oil from Canada to the Gulf Coast, crossing treaty land and sacred sites belonging to indigenous people. In April 2016, the Standing Rock Sioux established the Sacred Stone Camp in North Dakota, where they were joined by more than 300 nations of indigenous people to protest the pipeline. By December there were 2000 permanent camp residents and a population that rose as high as 10,000 on the weekends (Wolfe-Rocca, 2017). Other allies included farm families who were concerned about the risks to their precious water resource, the Nebraska aquifer. Supporters of the pipeline emphasized the value of increased oil supplies and the jobs the project would create, but critics pointed out that there was no oil shortage today, and only 35 permanent jobs would be created since most jobs would last for only the two years of construction (Baker & Davenport, 2017). Protest organizers told everyone who came to the Sacred Stone Camp that they could engage in only nonviolent activities such as demonstrations, ceremonies, and prayer meetings, but protestors were subjected pipeline security forces using tear gas, security dog attacks, and security forces firing on them with rubber bullets or spraying them with water hoses in subzero temperatures (Editors of *Rethinking Schools*, 2016–2017). On December 4, 2016, the Army Corps of Engineers denied permission to Energy Transfer Partners to build the proposed pipeline. In 2017, newly elected President Donald Trump signed a series of executive orders allowing the Keystone pipeline to be built as well as a pipeline through North and South Dakota, another point of contention for American Indians and environmentalists (Baker & Davenport, 2017). Once again, it appears that the U.S. government will ignore the principle of Indian Sovereignty by violating a treaty.

Why were native American treaties consistently violated?

The United States negotiated over 400 treaties with various Indian nations. When Indian treaties were signed, the land designated for indigenous people was often regarded as expendable; yet if the land became desirable, Indians were forced to surrender it.

The Cherokee possessed legal deeds to Georgia land where they had built homes and businesses. When ordered to go to Oklahoma territory, they took their case to the U.S. Supreme Court, which ruled in their favor; however, President Andrew Jackson refused to enforce the ruling. In 1838, he ordered federal troops to march the Cherokee to Oklahoma, a journey now called the Trail of Tears because of numerous deaths that occurred on the way (Wallace, 1993).

Because of treaties, several Indian nations were forced to occupy Oklahoma territory until White demands for cheap land led the United States to renegotiate the treaties, restricting Indians in Oklahoma to the least desirable land and allowing settlers to claim the rest. Americans had little interest in Indian land in Oklahoma—until oil was discovered. The treaty was renegotiated. Similarly, an 1868 Treaty of Fort Laramie declared that the Sioux would permanently retain lands sacred to them in the Black Hills—until gold was discovered. The treaty was renegotiated (Josephy, 2005; Wilson, 1998). This pattern has continued.

Many treaties signed over a century ago relegated Indians to small reservations but affirmed their right to hunt and fish on tribal lands beyond reservation boundaries. For native people, being able to hunt and fish on former tribal land was a critical concession that may have seemed an innocuous benefit to the other side when the treaty was signed. As hunting and fishing became profitable tourism activities, complaints that the treaties should be abrogated or renegotiated have increased. People promoting outdoor recreational activities have protested Indian hunting and fishing privileges, even though the treaties guarantee them. Indigenous people have responded by insisting on maintaining the treaties and respecting their rights as sovereign nations.

One consequence of this history of treaty violations is that American Indians have historically been the most impoverished racial group in the United States, a fact reflected in health data. Health issues have plagued American Indians for a long time, but Pember (2015) highlights a new perspective from a 2014 report concluding that when earlier generations have struggled with a traumatic experience, their responses seem to have an effect on their genetic structure, making them more susceptible to future stress or trauma. Further, genetic research has found evidence supporting the concept of intergenerational trauma. One expert described this phenomenon as a process beginning with the experience of a significant trauma such as losing one's homeland or one's culture. Over time, victims' negative responses, in terms of physical and psychological health, are passed on to subsequent generations, who manifest similar symptoms, contributing to such adverse health conditions as diabetes, depression, and post-traumatic stress disorder. Poor health is also reflected in longevity data, which reports that American Indians are more likely to die before reaching the age of 45 than members of any other racial or ethnic group in the United States (Cox, 2015).

What are other contemporary issues affecting Indigenous people?

Most students in American K–12 schools are not given much information about the cultures of American Indians, even when Native American students are in the school. The latter are likely to be affected by stereotype threat, which scholars say is a major factor contributing to the achievement gap between American Indian students and others (Warner, 2015). Schools need to provide accurate information about Native Americans, especially on the diversity of American Indian cultures, to debunk Indian stereotypes. The responsibility to provide accurate information about American Indians is mandated by social studies standards, but according to a Penn State Study of all 50 states, 87 percent of the references to American Indians in state academic standards pertain to Indians living in the nineteenth century (Editors of *Rethinking Schools*, 2016–2017). Warner (2015) cites studies finding that curricula in K–12 schools provide inadequate coverage of American Indians or no coverage at all. One study reported that in

Figure 5.2 Protesting Stereotypes

A group of American Indians gather at a statue to protest its stereotypical portrayal of Indians and other Indian stereotypes such as sports mascots.

SOURCE: Kent Koppelman

nine states where standards require content on American Indians, nearly all did not require content after the 1830s when many tribes were forced to relocate, leaving a final image of American Indians as powerless people being victimized. Such an image does not enhance the self-esteem of an American Indian student. Further, the disappearance of Native Americans from textbooks distorts history and makes Indian students feel invisible (Wolfe-Rocca, 2017).

Warner (2015) cites a review of American Indian representations in seven popular U.S. history textbooks that found two themes: the "dead and buried" approach and the "tourist" approach. The first portrays American Indians as existing primarily in the past with only brief references to contemporary events. Both approaches fail to address the diverse cultures of American Indian nations and current issues confronting them. Instead, any mention of contemporary Indians tended to focus on Indians living on reservations, even though they represent only 35 percent of indigenous people today. Even worse, these accounts often replace older stereotypes with new stereotypes based on Indians operating casinos. Only four states require content on contemporary American Indians from elementary school through high school, but outcomes vary widely based primarily on state funding. The best outcome has been achieved in Montana, which passed a Constitutional mandate in 1999 entitled the Indian Education for All Act (IEFA), but it had to pursue a successful lawsuit to get appropriate funding in 2004 to implement the law (Constantin, 2015). Tribal leaders contributed to identifying "Essential Understandings" about American Indian history and culture, and scholars say a major factor in its success is that the knowledge was integrated into the curriculum rather than being offered as separate courses (Carjuzaa, Baldwin, & Munson, 2015). Another major factor in the success of IEFA was the presence of support specialists working with preservice teachers. The result is that Indian students finally get to see people from their group portrayed accurately in their classrooms, and non-Indian students have an opportunity to understand a perspective different from their own. Other states are looking at Montana, and in 2015, Washington passed its version of IEFA (Constantin, 2015). Unfortunately, we continue to be surrounded by Indian stereotypes, such as the images used for sports teams, even in K–12 schools.

Many Native Americans and tribal councils have spoken out against these Indian logos and mascots, saying they are racist and offensive and asking schools and colleges displaying such images to discontinue this practice. (See Figure 5.2.) Some white people say that Indian mascots honor and respect a proud, fighting spirit, but it shows a lack of respect to ignore Indians who proudly fight to eliminate mascots because they are offensive. Indian women are also trying to dispel their stereotypes by taking leadership roles in tribal governments, and both genders are increasingly pursuing careers in such areas as higher education, medicine, law, politics and the arts (Lajimodiere, 2013). Instead of reinforcing stereotypes, multicultural education advocates encourage teachers to talk about Indians living in urban areas and discuss Indian achievements in the twentieth century, such as the Navajo code talkers.

Although American Indians have consistently joined the military in numbers far disproportionate to their percentage of the population over the years, and many have been awarded medals for their heroism, the Navajo code talkers made an especially critical contribution. Navajos were not the first Indian code talkers. During World War I, Choctaws were code talkers for Company D, 141st infantry. After the Pearl Harbor tragedy, several American Indian languages were under consideration for use in radio communications as the nation prepared for war. The challenge was to find skillful interpreters who could easily translate their native language into English. The Navajo language was selected, and Navajos developed a code in which bomber planes were called *chicken hawks*, an observation plane became a *staring owl*, and a fighter plane was referred to as a *little hummingbird*. The code was developed in secrecy and by 1943 was being used successfully when an article in the June issue of *Arizona Highways* noted that the U.S. military was using a Navajo language code, with Navajo soldiers as interpreters. Despite this revelation, the code was never broken, making it the only military code language that was never deciphered. In 1968, Navajo code talkers were recognized in an official ceremony in Chicago (Bixler, 1992). On June 4, 2014, 93-year-old veteran Chester Nez died—the last remaining member of the 29 Navajo code talkers.

One fact about contemporary Indians that seems to be widely known is that they operate casinos, but because most non-Indians tend to have a superficial knowledge of the history of Indian gaming, this activity has become controversial. The first Indian gaming operation was a bingo parlor that opened in Florida in 1979. Because of Indian sovereignty accorded in federal treaties, reservations primarily negotiated directly with the federal government, but in 1988, Congress passed the Indian Gaming Regulatory Act, which mandated that state governments were responsible for negotiating contracts for tribes wanting to create gaming venues. This has resulted in some states approving the establishment of Indian gaming operations and taking a share of the profits, while other states have refused to approve Indian gaming proposals. Despite such obstacles, Indian gaming venues have become well established in several states.

One consequence of these casinos is that many non-Indians believe that gaming revenues have solved economic problems confronting American Indians, but two-thirds of the tribes in the United States have no casinos, and of the one-third who do, only a small percent enjoy significant revenues (Cox, 2015). Yet a new stereotype is emerging of a "casino Indian," based on the assumption that all Indians share in the gaming revenues wealth and that problems of poverty and unemployment on reservations have been eliminated. Some tribes receiving significant profits from casinos have had positive outcomes when revenues are used to provide services in support of infrastructure needs, such as tribal administration, education, and healthcare, rather than simply engaging in profit sharing by distributing checks to tribal members (Hansen & Skopek, 2011).

Video Example 5.1

In this video, two teachers discuss the history of names, such as "redskin" in the context of the debate on sports team names. What misconceptions are there about the term *redskin* and its history? What role do these misconceptions play in the context of the prevalence of American Indian stereotypes today?

"All wars are civil wars because all men are brothers. . . . Each one owes infinitely more to the human race than to the particular country in which he was born."

—FRANCOIS FENELON (1651–1715)

Among tribal nations earning significant profits from gaming activities, three broad goals have emerged in addition to improving the financial status of individual tribal members. The first goal is to maintain Indian Sovereignty, the second is to lobby the regulatory body in their state to implement policies favorable to the perpetuation or increase of profits from gaming operations, and the final goal is to use their profits to reacquire ancestral lands. Those who have been successful are often regarded with what has been called "casino envy," stemming from erroneous assumptions about the success of Indian gaming across the United States (Hansen & Skopek, 2011). Such assumptions overlook the states still refusing to approve Indian gaming proposals and ignore the enormous disparity that exists for gaming operations with minimal economic gain compared to highly publicized gaming operations that have made impressive profits.

One final issue: Beginning in the late 1970s, a study reported that when state services took Indian children into state custody, 85 percent of them were placed in non-Indian homes or institutions. Congress passed the Indian Child Welfare Act to protect the interests of Indian children and to promote stability in Indian tribes and families. The law created standards that had to be met before children could be taken from their parents and mandated that if children were taken, they should be placed in settings that reflected Indian cultural values. Despite the law, some states persisted in separating Indian children from their parents and placing them in non-Indian settings (Brewer, 2015).

Since then, thousands of Indian families have been torn apart and the children placed in non-Indian foster homes, severing them from their cultural heritage. South Dakota appears to be the worst offender. Even though Indian children are only 13 percent of all children in the state, they represent 53 percent of children in foster care. Indian children are 11 times more likely than White children to be taken from their families. When these cases went to court, South Dakota judges defended the Department of Social Services (DSS) by claiming the likely emotional or physical harm children would sustain if returned to their parents, but they offered no proof of this claim (Brewer, 2015). This ruling is not surprising since the courts have not been sympathetic to Indian families. After an Indian father was arrested for driving under the influence, DSS immediately removed the father's two children from their home, even though the mother had not been involved in her husband's arrest. She went to court to get her children back, and her hearing lasted less than two minutes, with the judge ruling that the children should be placed in foster care. The mother engaged in two months of persistent activity before her children were returned to her (Brewer, 2015). This child removal controversy remains unresolved.

Video Example 5.2

This video features Bryant Chapo, a skateboarder from the Navajo Nation Tribe. How does this presentation of American Indian contemporary culture challenge stereotypes about indigenous peoples? What are some of the ways that skateboarding culture responds to American Indian histories and contemporary issues facing tribal nations?

https://www.youtube.com/watch?v=CEoMigMxbXw&index=5&list=PL6F43EC9B22CF3317

> **Self-Check 5.1** Complete this self-check quiz to check your understanding of the potential benefits inherent in indigenous cultures and the ongoing significance of Indian treaties and contemporary issues affecting Native Americans.

The African American Struggle for Freedom and Civil Rights

The first Africans in the New World came not as slaves but as soldiers and explorers. Although we do not have individual names, records indicate that Africans came with Cortez and Pizarro in the early 1500s, that 30 Africans sailed with Balboa, and that 200 accompanied Alvarado to Quito. The names of a few Black adventurers have survived. In the early sixteenth century, Estevanico (from Morocco) explored the American Southwest, preparing the way for later Spanish conquest. In the late eighteenth century, Jean Baptist Point du Sable (from Haiti) came with French explorers and founded a permanent trading post in a settlement called Chicago (Painter, 2005).

The first Africans in the American colonies arrived in 1619. A Dutch ship traded 20 Africans to Jamestown settlers for food and water (Reiss, 1997). The 17 men and 3 women were not slaves but indentured servants, able to gain their freedom after specified years of servitude. During the seventeenth century, 75 percent of American colonists came as servants, many of them indentured servants (Takaki, 1993), but Zinn (2003) argues that English colonists regarded African indentured servants as inferior to White servants and treated them accordingly.

How were the Black indentured servants treated differently?

A few Africans were able to earn their freedom, and some had to resort to courts to free them from unwilling owners, but most were never free. A few free Black people bought property, even including slaves, but by the mid-1800s, the colonies were establishing different rules for White and Black servants. Based on assumptions of Black inferiority, Africans were often forced to accept permanent servitude status. A 1662 Virginia statute decreed that children born to a woman who was a permanent indentured servant must take her status (Reiss, 1997). Not surprisingly, 70 percent of Africans in Virginia at this time were permanent indentured servants (Takaki, 1993).

As southern agriculture gravitated toward large plantations for the export of crops, the use of slaves became increasingly attractive. Indian workers knew the region and easily escaped, and White indentured servants escaped and passed as free White people. Black people could be easily identified, captured, and returned to their owners. Because England was already invested in the slave trade, exporting Africans to America was simply an expansion of an existing business. From the late 1500s to the early 1800s, more than 10 million Africans were brought to America, but many of them died on the trip from Africa during what is called the **Middle Passage**.

Why did so many Africans die during the middle passage?

Conditions on slave ships were horrendous. According to Reiss (1997), a full-grown man was allotted a space 6 feet long and 18 inches wide in the hold. Women and children were given even less. There was no room to sit up. Slaves were chained together and packed into the hold in a "spoon" position to maintain maximum space. Reiss quoted Lord Palmerston, "They had less room than a corpse in a coffin" (p. 34).

En route, slaves were fed twice a day and given buckets to relieve themselves; the buckets were seldom emptied and frequently overflowed. Many were unable to get to the buckets and soiled themselves where they lay. Not surprisingly, disease was a major cause of death, including typhoid, smallpox, yellow fever, and malaria (Painter, 2005).

Because bodies of the dead were tossed overboard, sharks routinely accompanied slave ships. As slaves were brought up on deck during the day, some took the opportunity to escape by leaping into the shark-infested waters. Scholars estimate that from five to six million Africans died during Middle Passage, and some who survived were left with permanent disabilities (Reiss, 1997). As bad as conditions were on slave ships, slavery was even more brutal. A day of work could be as long as 18 hours during harvest, with brief rest periods to eat. Overseers punished those who didn't appear to be working hard enough, usually by whipping. Women worked with men and often endured sexual assault from masters and overseers. It is not surprising that so many slaves rebelled against slavery.

How did Africans resist the oppression of slavery?

African captives engaged in a range of activities in their resistance to slavery. Some cut off their toes or mutilated themselves in other ways so they would be less useful workers for their masters. In addition, some slaves murdered their masters; many slave

> "Until lions have their historians, tales of the hunt will always glorify the hunter."
>
> —AFRICAN PROVERB

owners lived in fear of being poisoned by their slave servants (Franklin & Moss, 2000). Some slaves learned to read and write either by tricking their masters into teaching them or by converting to Christianity and persuading their master to give them the literacy skills needed to read the Bible (Cornelius, 2000). They perceived competent literacy skills to be a useful tool to assist themselves and other slaves, as well as an important asset if they managed to escape from slavery.

When slaves converted to Christianity, their owners tried to use aspects of the faith to manipulate them into being more docile and obedient. For example, although White owners exhorted slaves to obey the commandment against stealing, slaves continued to steal. They justified their thefts by regarding their owners as hypocrites: White people were responsible for stealing Africans from their homeland and their families. The captive Africans also rejected "moral" precepts emphasized by White ministers. Raboteau (2000) described a service for slave converts in which a White clergyman used a passage from the Apostle Paul in a sermon condemning slaves who ran away. During the sermon, the clergyman reported that "one half of my audience deliberately rose up and walked off" (p. 31).

Why did Black people fight on the American side during the revolutionary war?

When the war began, George Washington and his aides agreed that the Continental Army would not recruit Black people. Alexander Hamilton warned that if they did not, the British would (Chernow, 2004). In November 1775, Washington issued his policy against recruiting Black people, and British supporters quickly recruited slaves by promising emancipation for military service. Washington issued a new policy in December, permitting free Black men to serve in the Continental Army. Meanwhile, colonial militias were already recruiting slaves as well as free Black men. According to Franklin and Moss (2000), 5000 of the 300,000 colonial troops were Africans, primarily free Black men from northern colonies. The bravery of Black soldiers refuted the pervasive stereotypes, but their achievements were betrayed when the U.S. Constitution was drafted.

How did the U.S. constitution address the issue of slavery?

Although slaves represented 20 percent of all Americans at this time, the word *slave* does not appear in the Constitution of the United States (Painter, 2005); instead, it refers to "unfree persons." Article II, section 9, states that "importation of such persons as any of the States now-existing shall think proper to admit, shall not be prohibited by Congress prior to the year 1808." In other words, in deference to southern plantation owners and businesses, the new nation had agreed to ignore the slave trade for 20 years; however, taxes were to be collected on imported slaves. Even northern states that had abolished slavery profited from the continued importation of slaves.

Another issue in drafting the Constitution concerned the question of whether slaves should count in determining political representation. With 300,000 slaves representing 40 percent of its population, Virginia wanted slaves counted, as did North and South Carolina, with over 100,000 slaves in each state (Painter, 2005). The constitutional compromise was to count each slave as three fifths of a person, giving significant political power to southern states: Ten of the first 15 American presidents were slaveholders. Nevertheless, anti-slavery organizations became increasingly influential.

Who opposed slavery, and what did they do?

In 1775, Quakers organized the first anti-slavery society in Philadelphia; 10 years later another was formed in New York. Anti-slavery societies soon formed throughout New England (Chernow, 2004). In 1777, Vermont abolished slavery in its state constitution, and in 1783, New Hampshire and Massachusetts did the same. In two decades, all northern states had abolished slavery or legislated a timeline for its extinction. Some organizations lobbied to end the slave trade, and others wanted to deport slaves, but all agreed on the principle of abolishing slavery. When the 20-year constitutional hiatus ended in 1808, anti-slavery groups successfully lobbied Congress to pass a law that prohibited importation of slaves to the United States. The law was primarily a moral victory because the American coast was too long and the U.S. Navy too small to stop the smuggling of slaves.

Africans, enslaved or free, adamantly opposed slavery. Thousands of slaves ran away, and many successfully escaped. Former slaves Harriet Jacobs and Frederick Douglass gave speeches and wrote books denouncing slavery. In addition, between 1750 and 1860, there were an estimated 250 slave rebellions, each involving 10 or more slaves (Zinn, 2003), as well as numerous smaller rebellions. In February 1831, a solar eclipse inspired perhaps the best-known rebellion. Nat Turner interpreted the eclipse as an omen, and six months later he led a slave rebellion that began with the killing of Turner's owner and family, and went on to result in the deaths of 60 other slave owners before the slaves were overpowered by federal troops (Franklin & Moss, 2005).

As early as the 1770s, free Black people petitioned colonial legislatures to emancipate slaves. Using the words of revolutionary leaders, they challenged White people to live up to their ideals of democracy and equality by making them a reality for all (Painter, 2005). The original draft of the Declaration of Independence denounced slavery as an "execrable" practice, but the Continental Congress deleted that particular passage at the insistence of southern slaveholders. Many slaves began using the Underground Railroad to escape from slavery.

What was the underground railroad?

Named in the 1800s because of the popularity of steam railroads, the **Underground Railroad** existed as early as the late 1700s as a network of people helping slaves escape. Franklin and Moss (2000) quote a 1786 letter from George Washington complaining that one of his slaves escaped and went to Philadelphia, where "a society of Quakers, formed for such purposes, have attempted to liberate (him)" (p. 205). By 1804, this informal network had become more organized and had established "stations" 10 to 20 miles apart for runaways to rest and eat after traveling all night. The organization eventually included over 3000 people of all races (Painter, 2005). They had to be careful because helping slaves escape was a criminal activity, violating federal fugitive slave laws that compelled the return of any runaway slave.

Some slaves had a "conductor" to help them escape; one of the best known was Harriet Tubman, who made 19 trips and freed over 300 slaves. Plantation owners offered $40,000 to anyone who caught her, but they never did (Painter, 2005). Although it is impossible to determine how many slaves escaped using the Underground Railroad, one southern governor estimated that from 1810 to 1850 the South had lost 100,000 slaves worth $30 million (Franklin & Moss, 2000). Still, all enslaved Africans in America would not gain their freedom until the end of the Civil War.

Did slaves and free Black people fight for the union during the Civil war?

Slaves supported the North during the Civil War by disrupting southern productivity. Many refused to work even though they were severely punished; others engaged in subversive tactics such as supplying information to approaching Union troops. When Union soldiers came near a plantation, slaves would abandon it. Early Union victories in western states liberated slaves, but the federal government had not allocated resources to assist them. In northern cities, relief societies formed to raise money for food, clothing, and shelter and provided some education and job training for newly freed Black people.

When the war began, free Black men offered to enlist, but once again they were rejected. Few people believed the conflict would last long, but when it did, the need for more soldiers intensified. In September 1862, the **Emancipation Proclamation** freed Black people in rebellious states, but slave owners in Delaware and Kentucky kept slaves until the 13th Amendment was ratified. Issued in January 1863, the final version of the Emancipation Proclamation allowed free Black men to enlist in the army. Over 200,000 Black men enlisted. By August, 14 Black regiments were trained and ready for service, with 20 more regiments in preparation (Franklin & Moss, 2000).

Black soldiers protested the Congressional Enlistment Act that established lower compensation for them. Two Black regiments from Massachusetts refused their wages rather than receive less pay than White soldiers. When the Massachusetts legislature offered them money to make up for the difference, the Black soldiers refused that offer. They were fighting for the Union, and they insisted that the Union pay them fairly. In 1865, the War Department finally approved equal pay for Black and White soldiers (Painter, 2005), even though it came too late for the 38,000 Black soldiers who had died. For those who survived the war, the next task was to create a new society in the South that would include a significant number of free Black people.

Did Black people play a role in shaping the new south?

Black men (but not women) could vote and run for office, and 16 were elected to the U.S. House of Representatives. There was one Black governor (Louisiana) and six Black lieutenant governors, and over 600 Black people were elected to state legislatures and participated in drafting new state constitutions (Goldstone, 2011). In response, angry southern White people formed secret societies such as the Knights of the Ku Klux Klan to bribe or intimidate Black people and ostracize those White people who seemed to support the developing new social order. Many racist groups began to use violence to reestablish White supremacy in the South, usually engaging in activities at night.

Black people who registered to vote were harassed; some were forced to leave their communities, and some were lynched. In 1871, Black men elected to the South Carolina legislature were given 15 days to resign. State laws prohibited such harassment, but even Union troops stationed throughout the South were ineffective at stopping it. The U.S. Congress passed laws giving the president broad powers to punish anyone interfering with a citizen trying to vote. Hundreds were imprisoned, but violence persisted.

"The basic race hatred in the United States is a matter of the educated and distinguished leaders of white civilization."

—W. E. B. DU BOIS (1868–1963)

Throughout the 1870s, the Democratic Party, led by White southerners, elected majorities to state legislatures. Congress no longer required federal troops at all southern polling places during elections. By 1877, when President Harrison withdrew federal troops, efforts to re-establish White power accelerated. During the last two decades of the nineteenth century, the U.S. Supreme Court enacted rulings sanctioning southern legislation that prevented Black people from voting, removed them from jury rolls, maintained their segregated schools, and required racial segregation in public transportation and public facilities (Goldstone, 2011). With these Supreme Court decisions, the transformation to the "Jim Crow" South with complete racial segregation was concluded.

How did Black citizens in the south respond to this transformation?

Southern Black people did not accept the threats and harassment passively, yet without support from the federal government or northern organizations, they did not have the resources to combat White supremacists. They regarded education as the best way to acquire resources and power on their own, but with minimal state funding for schools, educational opportunities were limited. As late as the 1890s, southern states supported segregated private schools, spending an average of less than $2 annually per student in public schools compared to the $20 per student provided in northern states (Lewis, 1993).

In 1881, Booker T. Washington came to Tuskegee Institute and created an educational approach that appealed to White people and many Black people. Washington wanted Black people to carve out a niche in the southern economy, and he knew that White people could accept Black people doing agricultural, domestic, and factory work. Washington cultivated good relations with local leaders by having his students provide food and services to the community, and he promoted his school as a model for Black education in the South. Eventually Washington attracted interest and funding from northern White people, many of whom were industrialists who wanted a better trained workforce in the South.

At the Atlanta Cotton Exposition of 1895, Washington declared that he believed Black people would be willing to accept social inequality in exchange for economic opportunity. White politicians, business leaders, and the press claimed that Washington spoke for Black Americans, but some Black people, notably W. E. B. Du Bois, believed Black Americans deserved more.

What did Du Bois want for Black Americans?

Based on his own experience as the first Black graduate from Harvard, Du Bois felt that Black people could demonstrate academic ability if given an opportunity. Du Bois rejected the idea that social inequality for Black people was acceptable under any conditions. He supported vocational training for Black students, but not for those who demonstrated academic ability. Du Bois's approach was overt and confrontational. Although Washington worked within the status quo, secretly donating money in support of legal efforts opposing racial segregation, Du Bois challenged the status quo, publicly denouncing all racial discrimination, as in the following statement (Lewis, 1993):

> Such discrimination is morally wrong, politically dangerous, and industrially wasteful and socially silly. It is the duty of whites to stop it, and to do so primarily for their own sakes. (p. 208)

In 1910, Du Bois helped found the **National Association for the Advancement of Colored People (NAACP)**, and for 25 years he served as editor of its main publication, *The Crisis*. For 18 years he hosted a conference on race problems at Atlanta University, and he helped found the American Negro Academy for Black intellectuals. Throughout his life, Du Bois attacked racism and promoted racial equality in his research, reports, essays, and even fiction (Lewis, 2000).

What were Black Americans doing to cope with race problems?

In the late 1800s, southern Black people began to migrate to northern cities, driven by economic need and persistent violence in the South, especially lynching. (See Figure 5.3.) For more than thirty years, Ida Wells-Barnett took a public stand against lynching, ignoring many death threats. In 1914, *The Crisis* published the names of 2732 Black people lynched between 1885 and 1914, and the NAACP challenged Congress to pass anti-lynching laws (Lewis, 1993). According to Feagin and Feagin (2008), at least half of all lynchings were not recorded, so the total number is estimated to be over 6000. The House of Representatives passed anti-lynching bills in 1922, 1937, and 1940, but southern senators blocked them. It was not until June 2005 that the Senate finally took a stand, voting to issue a public apology for its failure to pass an anti-lynching law.

Southern migration to the north was not dramatic until the twentieth century. According to Feagin and Feagin (2008), 90 percent of all Black Americans still lived in the South in 1900. Migration increased significantly between 1914 and 1918, when

Figure 5.3 "THE REASON"

Cartoonist Albert Smith illustrated "The Reason" for Black people to migrate north in the 1920s.

SOURCE: Albert Smith

World War I created labor shortages because few Europeans immigrated. By the end of the war, a million Black people had moved to northern cities. Over 360,000 out of more than two million registered Black people served in World War I, and many returning southern Black soldiers settled in northern cities (Franklin & Moss, 2000). In 1900, Chicago had 30,000 Black people by 1920, it had over 109,000. By 1930, two million southern Black people had migrated to northern cities (Takaki, 1993). Even with this larger urban population, discrimination persisted. W. E. B. DuBois and other African American leaders joined with White allies such as Charles Edward Russell and Mary White Ovington to found the National Association for the Advancement of Colored People (NAACP), an organization committed to confronting the nation's White supremacist attitudes and actions.

As Americans welcomed war heroes from World War I, buried the dead, and cared for maimed and suffering veterans, they were ready for a new era. As F. Scott Fitzgerald said, "The uncertainties of 1919 were over—there seemed little doubt about what was going to happen—America was going on the greatest, gaudiest spree in history" (2005, p. 188). Prohibition drove drinking into the shadows of speakeasies. Jack Dempsey drew the first million-dollar gate in boxing. Babe Ruth became the highest paid baseball player in history. And in New York City, Black people began a cultural and literary development called the *Harlem Renaissance.*

What was the Harlem renaissance?

White people came to Harlem in the 1920s to enjoy the clubs, dancing, and jazz, creating an open community where people from all races would dance to Duke Ellington at the Cotton Club or listen to Louis Armstrong at the Savoy. As Americans enjoyed a variety of new music, new dances, new artists, and new writers, Harlem contributed the novels of Jean Toomer, the poetry of Langston Hughes, and the creative works of many others who expressed the uniqueness of the Black experience in America. Although it was a racially segregated community, Harlem was home to diverse Black peoples, including newly arrived southern Black people, Africans, and West Indians. Spivey (2003) notes that this mix of people produced a new kind of Black individual, quoting Alain Locke's description of how this "New Negro" emerged: "Each group has come with its own separate motives and its own special ends . . . but their greatest experience has been the finding of one another" (p. 165).

Was there a decrease in discrimination against Black people after World War I?

Many African Americans were upset that the U.S. military did not recognize the achievements of Black soldiers during World War I. For more than six months, the Black first battalion of the 369th infantry endured continuous fire while fighting in France. The French awarded the Croix de Guerre to the battalion, but the U.S. Army did not invite the first battalion (or any Black units) to Paris for the victory parade in August 1918 (Lewis, 1993). Many Black mothers received Gold Stars symbolizing the loss of a son, but when the French government invited American Gold Star mothers to France to honor them, the Army only paid for the White mothers. Black mothers who attended had to pay their own way (Painter, 2005).

> "Had it not been for our art and our culture, when all else was ripped from us, we would never have been able to survive as a people."
>
> —HARRY BELAFONTE (1927–)

The 1920s saw the rebirth of the Ku Klux Klan, reaching a peak of five million members in 1925. In 1921, a White mob in Tulsa, Oklahoma, set fire to all of the buildings in the Black community and burned them to the ground. In 1923, White people also destroyed the Black community of Rosewood, Florida. The NAACP experienced dramatic growth at this time, expanding from 50 chapters to more than 500 between the two world wars (Woodward, 1966). Attitudes were slowly changing about race, thanks to the work of scholars such as Franz Boas, who questioned the soundness of "scientific" studies of race. He noted that intelligence scores, supposedly not malleable, changed when an individual's environment changed significantly. Boas emphasized culture instead of race and asserted that culture was dynamic rather than unchanging (Painter, 2010).

As the Great Depression began, Black farmers suffered even more than White farmers, with many being ejected from their land. As for black workers in northern cities, over 26 unions did not accept Black members in 1930, and Black unemployment was three to four times higher than that of White unemployment (Feagin & Feagin, 2008). In October 1933, 18 percent of Black people were receiving government assistance ("relief") compared to 10 percent for White people, and relief programs often provided Black families less than the amount given to White families (Takaki, 1993). The best hope for Black people seemed to be the nominee of the Democratic Party, Franklin Delano Roosevelt and his "New Deal."

Did the new deal programs help black Americans?

Millions of Black people benefited from New Deal programs, yet millions of others did not. The Social Security Act provided financial security for older Americans, and the Fair Labor Standards Act established a minimum wage, but both excluded agricultural and domestic work—jobs largely held by Black people (Lui, 2004). Black union leader A. Philip Randolph threatened to organize a march on Washington until President Roosevelt issued Executive Order 8802 banning racial discrimination in defense industries and creating a Federal Employment Practice Commission, but he was criticized for appointing a White Mississippian to head the commission (Lewis, 2000).

Despite the president's mixed record, Black people appreciated the social activism of Eleanor Roosevelt and her close relationship with Black activist Mary McLeod Bethune. In 1936, while heading the Division of Negro Affairs, Bethune helped create the Federal Council on Negro Affairs, an advisory group to the president consisting of 30 Black professionals. Media soon referred to them as FDR's **Black Cabinet**. FDR appointed Black people to serve in the Federal Housing Authority, Department of the Interior, and other federal agencies; during this time Black Americans increasingly changed their allegiance to the Democratic Party, but their participation in the nation's economic recovery was not meaningful until World War II began.

What gains did Black Americans make during World War II?

With so many men enlisting in the military, more than a million were Black, jobs were available for Black men and women, especially in defense industries. Black people in the military were selected for programs that had not been permitted before, such as the engineer corps, pilot training, and officer training. For the first time in its history, the Marine Corps recruited African Americans. When the Navy restricted Black men to mess hall duties, they protested, and within a year they were given general assignments and included in officer training programs (Franklin & Moss, 2000). In 1948, President Truman issued Executive Order 9981, officially desegregating the U.S. Armed Forces.

What happened to African Americans after the war?

Many Americans regarded the defeat of Germany as a victory over Nazi beliefs of racial superiority. By the war's end, half of the major unions had accepted Black members (Feagin & Feagin, 2008), and Black veterans symbolized to all Black people that they earned the right to have the same rights and opportunities as other Americans. In business and industry, however, the percentage of Black men and women laid off during the postwar period was considerably higher than that for White people, suggesting a return to "business as usual" attitudes. Racial discrimination in the implementation of the GI Bill was especially frustrating for African Americans.

For World War II veterans who wanted to attend college, the GI Bill covered all of their tuition, fees, and even subsistence payments. As early as 1947, 49 percent of all students attending college were veterans, and over twice that number used the GI Bill to attend vocational or business schools, or participate in apprenticeships and other on-the-job training (Schuck, 2014). Because of overt racism, most colleges and universities were racially segregated and refused to admit veterans of color; historically Black colleges were small institutions with too few openings to accommodate the demand from returning veterans of color. The GI Bill resulted in more money being spent on education than was used in the Marshall Plan to rebuild Europe (Hamilton, Cottom, Darity, Aja, & Ash, 2015). By 1956, when the GI Bill ended, almost half of the 16 million veterans who returned home after the war had enrolled in college or in a job-training program (Friedman & Mandelbaum, 2011), but the GI Bill ended up being "an affirmative action program for white males" (Schuck, 2014, p. 340).

Despite such overt racial discrimination, the NAACP and its allies were successful in court case rulings against racial desegregation in transportation and education, and in 1954, *Brown v. Board of Education* overturned decades of legal discrimination based on race. It was a victory more in principle than in practice as segregation in America persisted; nevertheless, in the context of such moral victories, the civil rights movement was born, opposing discrimination but also challenging Americans to recognize their prejudices and stereotypes.

With more Black people demanding their rights as American citizens, the response from southerners became more violent. In August 1955, a 14-year-old Black youth from Chicago came to Mississippi to visit relatives. After Emmett Till showed a group of Black friends a picture of a White girl he knew in Chicago, one of the boys dared him to go into the nearby store and talk to the White woman working there. After buying candy in the store, Emmett turned before leaving and said, "Bye, Baby." The woman's husband was out of town but soon returned. It was shortly after midnight when he and two friends came to the home of Mose Wright, where Till was staying, and dragged the boy out of bed. They brutally murdered him and threw his body in the Tallahatchie River. When his corpse was found three days later, it was so badly mutilated that Mose Wright could only identify the boy by a ring on Emmett's finger (Williams, 1987).

Emmett's mother demanded an open casket at his funeral so that mourners could see what had been done to her son. Photographs of the boy's mangled face appeared in newspapers across the nation, shocking most Americans. The three men responsible were arrested and brought to trial. Despite the courageous testimony of Mose Wright, who identified the accused men as the ones who took Emmett Till from his house, the all-White jury acquitted all three men of kidnapping and murder. People of all races expressed outrage at the injustice (Williams, 1987).

What did the civil rights movement achieve for African Americans?

In Montgomery, Alabama, Rosa Parks and Martin Luther King Jr. inspired African Americans to conduct a boycott of city bus services to end racial segregation. The boycott lasted over a year; then in 1957, the U.S. Supreme Court upheld a federal court ruling to desegregate public bus transportation systems. In February 1960, four Black college freshmen in Greensboro, North Carolina, entered a Woolworth store and deliberately sat at a lunch counter that served only White people. When refused service, the Black students opened their textbooks and read. They eventually left, but they returned, and other students came with them. The idea spread across the nation as 70,000 students, mostly Black but some White, staged more than 800 sit-ins in over 100 southern cities. As more than 4000 students were arrested, White people stayed away from lunch counters, and many would not shop in stores where sit-ins were occurring. The economic losses forced many businesses to begin offering services to Black people (Lomax, 1963).

Although Martin Luther King Jr. encouraged nonviolent tactics, younger, radical Black leaders encouraged Black Americans to return violence for violence. The passionate oratory of Malcolm X may have predisposed some White people to begin listening to the peaceful rhetoric of King and his followers. Even after Malcolm X ended his association with the extremist Nation of Islam to pursue a more authentic Islamic faith, he insisted that Black people should demand the same rights as White Americans—not just civil rights but their human rights (Malcolm X, 2000).

Another militant voice came from the Black Panther Party founded in 1966 by Huey Newton and Bobby Seale. The Black Panthers attracted Black youth, especially in urban areas. Despite the Panthers' sponsoring community service activities such as a free breakfast program for Black children, White authorities saw them as a paramilitary organization. FBI Counterintelligence kept its leaders under surveillance, and Panther offices were subjected to police raids. Newton's 1967 arrest and imprisonment on murder charges weakened the Panthers, as did the violent assaults on party members that left 28 dead (Sanchez & Hagopian, 2017). By the mid-1970s, most Panther leaders either had been expelled from or had voluntarily left the organization.

Throughout the 1960s, the South was the primary scene for marches, protests, and demonstrations. In 1963 alone, the Department of Justice recorded over 1400 events in three months (Zinn, 2003). As usual, the White response was immediate and violent, but this time some of the violence was recorded by the national press and witnessed by a national audience. The images of law enforcement officers using dogs, fire hoses, and clubs to assault unarmed Black people left many White viewers appalled, and yet even more violence took place. Mississippi civil rights leader Medgar Evers was shot and killed on his front porch. A bomb placed in the basement of a Birmingham church killed four Black children, and in 1968, Martin Luther King Jr. was assassinated in Memphis.

Being White did not protect protestors from southern wrath. When Freedom Riders rode integrated buses to test southern compliance with desegregation laws, mobs

> "Non-cooperation with evil is as much a duty as is cooperation with good."
> —MOHANDIS K. GANDHI (1869–1948)

Video Example 5.3

In this video, a teacher discusses how students define diversity. Pay attention to how the students respond. How might the students' desires for "more things for Black kids to get excited about" reflect the effects of historical oppression in schools?

attacked the buses, assaulting White and Black people as local law enforcement and the FBI observed the violence but did nothing (Zinn, 2003). In Mississippi, authorities found the bodies of three young civil rights workers who had been murdered. During a Selma-to-Montgomery march in Alabama, a White minister was beaten to death, and a White housewife transporting marchers to Selma was shot and killed (Painter, 2005).

Amid this turmoil, Congress passed the Civil Rights Act of 1964, forbidding discrimination in public accommodations, federally assisted programs, public facilities, and education, followed by the Voting Rights Act (VRA) of 1965. By outlawing voter suppression tactics such as literacy tests and by sending federal observers to southern states to assist in the law's enforcement, the VRA was extraordinarily successful in expanding the opportunity for African Americans and other racial minorities to register and vote in local, state, and national elections. In 1952, 20 percent of eligible southern Black people were registered to vote; because of this legislation, 40 percent of eligible southern Black voters were registered in 1964, and by 1968, 60 percent of Black people were registered, the same percentage as for White people (Zinn, 2003).

In less than a decade, rates of voter registration and voting were almost the same for Black and White voters in the targeted states, and since the passage of the VRA there has been a significant increase in Black people and other minorities being elected to public office. The number of Black elected officials increased from 500 in 1965 to 10,500 in 2011 (Schuck, 2014). Because of its success, many VRA supporters were critical of the 2013 *Shelby County* decision where the U.S. Supreme Court declared Section 4 of the VRA unconstitutional; it required designated states to secure federal preclearance before making any changes to voting laws or practices. The Court said this section of the law was an anachronism that no longer made sense, but critics point out that the designated states (as others) are still engaged in voter suppression tactics (Schuck, 2014).

> ✓ **Self-Check 5.2** Complete this self-check quiz to check your understanding of Black and White resistance to slavery in the United States and the struggle of Black people after the Civil War to attain their civil rights as American citizens.

Historic Hostility Against Asian Immigrants and Contemporary Stereotypes

The first Asian immigrants to the United States were from four villages in the Canton province of China. Arriving in 1850, they set the Chinese pattern of predominantly male migration to America with a ratio of 10 men for every 1 woman (Lowe, 2000). Chinese immigrants were lured to California by the thought of finding gold and returning to China. San Francisco welcomed the new arrivals by inviting them to participate in California's statehood ceremonies, but by 1870, 63,000 Chinese immigrants had arrived, with more than 75 percent in California, representing 25 percent of the state's workforce (Fong, 2000). Nativists accused these "aliens" of bringing "moral chaos" to California because they were from a non-European culture, which meant they brought "foreign" cultural beliefs and practices that did not correspond with our national identity as Americans (Lee, Kumashiro, & Sleeter, 2015).

What actions did nativists initially take against the Chinese in America?

Nativists lobbied the California legislature for a tax on non-U.S. citizens who were mining for gold (Takaki, 1993). Although the tax penalized any immigrant, the passage of the "foreign miners" act was a major setback for the Chinese. Most had borrowed money and were expected to repay their debts on arriving in America. In addition to paying for their passage, they were expected to send money home to support their wives and families, and two thirds of them managed to earn enough money to take care of their financial obligations and return to China (Glenn & Yap, 2000). Because of the 1790 law restricting U.S. citizenship to "Whites only," there was little incentive to remain in the United States.

Why didn't Chinese men bring their wives and families?

In places like Singapore and Hawaii, Chinese men who chose to remain either married local women or sent for their wives, but neither option was possible in America. California law forbade interracial marriage, and entrepreneurs imported Chinese women to work as prostitutes. In 1870, the California legislature passed the Page Law to stop the immigration of Chinese prostitutes, but this resulted in the exclusion of almost all Chinese women. By 1890, the ratio of Chinese men to women was 26 to 1 (Fong, 2000).

Who employed Chinese immigrants?

Unable to mine for gold, many Chinese men found work as laborers on the western portion of the transcontinental railroad. Railroad owners paid the Chinese less than other workers and forced them to work during the winter of 1866, despite snowdrifts as high as 60 feet. They had to tunnel under the snow, digging shafts to allow for air so they could work. After that winter, Chinese workers went on strike for higher wages, only to be denounced by local newspapers and literally starved into submission when railroad owners cut off food supplies (Takaki, 1993). When the railroad was completed, most Chinese laborers returned to China, but some chose to stay, particularly in the area of San Francisco.

Wherever they settled, Chinese men continued to be paid low wages. In addition to agricultural jobs, they worked in factories or were employed as houseboys, gardeners, and cooks, and a few started small businesses. Starting a laundry was especially tempting because it required a small investment for equipment and minimal English skills. Being self-employed enabled them to avoid both exploitation by employers and competition with hostile White laborers.

What kind of hostile actions did the Chinese encounter?

The resentment of White laborers was not the only source of hostility; the White population in general tended to perceive the Chinese as refusing to give up their "foreign" identity and become "Americanized." Some White men would occasionally target Chinese men who maintained traditions such as the "queue," a long single braid of hair worn down their back. (See Figure 5.4.) Chinese laborers complained of White men grabbing or even cutting off their queue. It wasn't long before such hostility escalated to violent confrontation.

The U.S. economy experienced a depression in the 1870s, yet the numbers of Chinese increased, and many were becoming visibly prosperous. Looking for a scapegoat, White politicians and labor leaders blamed economic problems on the Chinese, and newspapers published and disseminated their views. In 1871, mob violence resulted in the deaths of 21 Chinese men in Los Angeles; in 1885, 28 Chinese railroad workers were killed in Rock Springs, Wyoming (Fong, 2000; Wu, 1972). Although Chinese immigrants constituted less than 1 percent of the U.S. population in 1882, Congress passed the **Chinese Exclusion Act** to prohibit Chinese immigration for the next 10 years; it was renewed for another 10 years in 1892, and renewed indefinitely in 1902. The door to the "Gold Mountain" closed.

Figure 5.4 Anti-Chinese Attitudes

Newspapers often expressed their hostility to Chinese immigrants in cartoons.

SOURCE: The Bancroft Library, University of California, Berkeley

PACIFIC CHIVALRY.
Encouragement to Chinese Immigration.

© 1999 HARPWEEK®

During another economic recession in the 1890s, unemployed White workers rioted, beating and shooting Chinese workers. Such violence often discouraged the Chinese from continuing to work as laborers, except for employers who were also Chinese. The Chinese created their own communities in urban areas—Chinatowns—where they felt safe establishing businesses and homes, and less vulnerable to White discrimination and violence. Chinese entrepreneurs often pooled their resources to start a business, and they would employ other Chinese. By 1890, the 6400 Chinese workers employed in California laundries constituted 69 percent of all laundry employees in the state (Takaki, 1993).

Although they were willing to live in separate communities, most Chinese who remained in America were unwilling to be perceived as foreigners in the land. By 1924, Andrew Kan had lived and worked in the United States for over 40 years, and he took his case to court to insist on his right to be an American citizen; the courts disagreed. In fact, anti-Asian sentiment would intensify during World War II as the United States fought a Japanese enemy portrayed as treacherous and brutal.

How did Americans view the Japanese before World War II?

By 1880, only 148 Japanese lived in the United States (Fong, 2000); however, 150,000 Japanese immigrated to the mainland between 1880 and 1908. By the 1920s, the Japanese population in America was twice as large as that of the Chinese (Zia, 2000). Unlike the Chinese, Japanese immigrants tended to include women. By 1920, women constituted 46 percent of the Japanese in Hawaii and 35 percent in California (Takaki, 1993). Based on their awareness of the hostility toward the male Chinese immigrants, Japanese government officials screened immigration applications to ensure that those approved included married couples.

In 1905, California newspapers initiated a campaign against the **Yellow Peril** based on the belief that the Japanese, like the Chinese, could not or would not adopt the American culture (Feagin & Feagin, 2008). In reality, many Japanese immigrants had assimilated and desired to become American citizens. In 1922, Takao Ozawa challenged the 1790 law restricting U.S. citizenship to White people. Ozawa had been educated in American schools, belonged to a Christian church, and spoke only English at home. Ozawa's argument to the U.S. Supreme Court was that he had done everything that any immigrant could be asked to do to assimilate into the culture, and the only thing that prevented his citizenship was his race. The Supreme Court said that was all that mattered and rejected his appeal.

Before the Supreme Court made its decision, California legislators in both houses passed a resolution calling for the prohibition of further Japanese immigration. Responding to such nativist sentiment, President Theodore Roosevelt met with Japanese officials in 1908 and reached the **Gentleman's Agreement** that Japan would prohibit further immigration except for the close relatives of those already in the United States. Japanese immigrants could use this loophole until 1920 to bring family members—including "picture brides"—to join them in America.

> "If we believe absurdities we shall commit atrocities."
>
> —VOLTAIRE (1694–1778)

What was a picture bride?

Japanese culture regarded marriage as an affair negotiated between families. In the **picture bride** system, matchmaking resulted from an exchange of photographs. Combining those who came with their husbands and those who came as picture brides, 60,000 Japanese women immigrated to America (including Hawaii) and gave birth to almost 30,000 children. These children, **Nisei**, were Americans by right of birth. Most Japanese immigrants still lived in Hawaii, constituting 40 percent of the population; they were less than 2 percent of California residents (Zia, 2000).

Where were Japanese immigrants employed?

The Japanese often worked in canneries and took a variety of jobs, but many worked as agricultural laborers, as they had done in Japan. Some began to contract for land, negotiating a share of the profits with the owner or guaranteeing a set price after the crop was sold. The owner provided seed and equipment, so with minimal investment and intense labor, Japanese farmers were able to be quite successful. Some saved enough money to secure a loan and lease or purchase land, giving them the opportunity for higher profits. By 1910, Japanese farmers in California owned or leased about 200,000 acres of land, producing almost all of the state's celery and snap beans, three quarters of the strawberries, and almost half of the onions and green peas (Takaki, 1993).

In 1913, California legislators passed the Alien Land Law to prohibit any immigrant ineligible for citizenship from owning land or leasing land for more than three years. Because their children, the Nisei, were American citizens, the Japanese leased or purchased land in their children's names; those who had no children paid other families for the right to use their children's names as their "landlords" (Zia, 2000). This prompted the California legislature to pass a new Alien Land Law in 1920, prohibiting the use of children's names to lease or purchase land.

Japanese immigrants were disappointed that their success, efforts to assimilate, and children's citizenship status did not reduce hostility against them. Even when they possessed a college diploma, Nisei children were not likely to find work. Many returned to the family business, and those who were doctors or dentists tended to work in the Japanese communities (Takaki, 1993). Then World War II began, and Japan became America's enemy.

How did the war affect American attitudes toward Japanese families living in the United States?

Given the history of anti-Japanese sentiment, it is not surprising that rumors of spying and sabotage began circulating immediately. Japanese farmers were accused of planting flowers in a particular pattern to guide airplanes carrying bombs to their target (Feagin & Feagin, 2008). Fearing a broad anti-Asian backlash, many Asian-owned businesses posted signs saying that the owners were Asian but not Japanese. Some shops sold buttons that said, "I am Korean" or "I am Chinese" so Americans would not confuse them with Japanese (Koppelman, 2001).

What actions were taken against the Japanese during World War II?

Barely two months into the war, President Roosevelt issued Executive Order No. 9066 that was the basis for taking Japanese Americans from their communities and relocating them in federal "camps." Japanese families were given a week or less to sell property and possessions, packing what remained into their suitcases. More than 100,000 people, two thirds of them American citizens, lost almost everything as they were evacuated to 10 federal camps. The path to these relocation camps was paved with widespread prejudices that were affirmed by political leaders at all levels of state and national government. (See Figure 5.5.)

Figure 5.5 Defining "The Enemy"

The Japanese American relocation camps of World War II illustrate the perception of these American citizens as "foreign." Rumors that there were spies from Japan circulating among them were enough to justify confiscating their property and keeping them behind barbed wire for the duration of the war.

SOURCE: Seattle Museum of History and Industry.

Once at the camps, Japanese families were informed that the U.S. government required them to take a loyalty oath renouncing their allegiance to Japan. The Nisei were already American citizens, so this was not an issue for them, but for their parents, renouncing Japanese citizenship with no chance of becoming American citizens meant that they would become people without a country. When 4600 of them refused to sign the oath, they were sent to federal prisons (Zia, 2000). Despite such treatment, 23,000 Japanese men joined the army to prove their loyalty. The army segregated its troops by race, and a Japanese American regiment, the 442nd, became the most highly decorated unit of the war. Yet until the war's end, Japanese families continued to be kept in camps with barbed wire and armed soldiers. It is a tribute to the tenacity of Japanese Americans that so many were able to rebuild their lives and their finances after the war.

What other Asian immigrants faced anti-Asian attitudes?

Between 1907 and 1910, large numbers of Filipinos immigrated primarily to Hawaii as agricultural laborers. When the 1924 immigration law prohibited Asian people from entering the United States, Filipinos immigrated not as Asians, but as "nationals" because the Philippines had become American territory after the Spanish-American War. Of the 45,000 who had entered the United States by 1930, most were young men who worked as agricultural workers or domestic servants. Filipinos tended to be active in labor unions, causing resentment among both White landowners and other laborers (Fong, 2000).

In 1934, Congress passed legislation restricting Filipino immigration to 50 people annually. Filipinos were prohibited from entering many professions and were declared ineligible for federal aid during the Great Depression. Yet during World War II, the army recruited 30,000 Filipinos to fight the Japanese in the Philippines. Although Filipino soldiers were promised full citizenship, the promise was not kept until 1990, long after many had died (Feagin & Feagin, 2008).

Koreans first began immigrating to the United States in the early 1900s to work in agriculture or as domestic servants. Like other Asian immigrants, they encountered oppression. They were refused entrance into some restaurants, not allowed access to some public places, and restricted to racially segregated neighborhoods. Because Japan had conquered Korea in the late 1930s, Koreans hoped that the allies would defeat their historic enemy during World War II; instead, the U.S. government classified Koreans as "Japanese" during the war because Japan governed Korea (Feagin & Feagin, 2008).

After the war, the total ban on Asian immigration was slightly modified, but the number of Korean immigrants was minimal until the Korean War. Because the U.S. Army maintained a presence in South Korea, many American soldiers returned with Korean wives who were exempt from Asian immigration quotas. As with other Asian groups, the number of Koreans in America has increased dramatically since the Immigration Reform Act of 1965. There have also been significant increases in the numbers of other Southeast Asian immigrants, such as Vietnamese, Cambodians, Laotians, and Hmong. Even though they have encountered prejudice, most refugees emigrated to escape violence in their native countries. Because they are able to live safely with their families in the United States, they tend to be more optimistic about overcoming difficulties here (Pipher, 2002).

In the early 1900s, Sikh farmers were the first Asian Indian immigrants to America. Landowners employed them instead of East Asian people who had been targets of nativist outrage. In 1923, a Punjabi immigrant named Bhagat Singh Thind applied for U.S. citizenship using "scientific" race theories to prove he was White. Having cited race theories to deny citizenship to previous non-White applicants, the U.S. Supreme Court nevertheless chose to ignore "science" in this case, asserting that Thind was not White because the justices did not believe him to be White (Zia, 2000).

> "Almost all people have this potential for evil, which would be unleashed only under certain . . . social circumstances."
>
> —IRIS CHANG (1968–2004)

Most Asian Indian immigration has occurred since 1965, with 80 percent of Indo-Americans being the first generation of immigrants. Yet Asian Indian immigration has involved significant numbers of people, producing an Indo-American population that is the fourth largest among all Asian groups (after Chinese, Japanese, and Filipinos). Asian Indians are notable for linguistic and religious diversity, and they are culturally diverse, being more likely to identify with a province such as Bengal or Punjab than the country of India. Migrating Asian Indians often have academic qualifications in fields such as engineering, medicine, mathematics, and computer management. In one study of Asian immigrants employed as physicians, over half were Asian Indians (Kar, Campbell, Jiminez, & Gupta, 2000). Their success has contributed to the "model minority" myth that has been used to counter claims of discrimination by other minority groups.

What is the model minority myth?

Beginning in the 1960s, White Americans praised Asian Americans as a **model minority** because they had overcome all obstacles and achieved success. People of color were told that if they were willing to work as hard as Asian Americans, they could be just as successful, and if they failed, it was their own fault. The model minority myth has created resentment among people of color, particularly African Americans, toward Asian Americans. Takaki (1993) suggests that this was the intent of those promoting the model minority myth: "Our society needs an Asian American 'model minority' in an era anxious about a growing black underclass" (p. 416). The model minority myth has often been criticized as a distraction that avoids the reality of ongoing discrimination against Asian Americans.

How does the model minority myth distort reality?

As a group, Asian Americans exist on both extremes of social status, but the model minority myth focuses on the upper extreme. Data that seem to document their financial success need to be put in context. Asian Americans tend to live in urban areas of states where the cost of living is high, inflating salary data. According to the 2010 census, California had far more Asian Americans than any other state, with New York a distant second (East-West Center, 2012). Asian American incomes are also inflated because they are reported as household incomes. Although most American households consist of dual wage earners, Asian American households often have additional earners as well.

At the other extreme are Asian Americans working for low wages. In California and New York, most garment workers are Asian American or Hispanic women working over 40 hours a week for less than minimum wage (Freeman, 2013). Their wages are low because they are competing against Third World workers who are hired by companies outsourcing jobs or establishing factories in other countries, making multiple incomes a necessity for many Asian American households. Although it is appropriate to celebrate the success of those who overcome oppression, the model minority myth actually harms Asian Americans, as Fong and Shinagawa (2000) have explained:

> [It] diverts attention away from serious social and economic problems that affect many segments of the Asian American population, detracts from both the subtle and overt racial discrimination encountered by Asian Americans, places undue pressure on young Asian Americans to succeed educationally and professionally, and fuels competition and resentment between Asian Americans and other groups. (p. 191)

Application Exercise 5.1
This video features a student who identifies with "the Asian community." Think about the assumptions and stereotypes of people with Asian heritage that the speaker in the video discusses and how these relate to the "model minority myth." Consider the ways in which she both challenges and reproduces these assumptions and stereotypes in her responses. Review the video and complete the activity.

 Self-Check 5.3 Complete this self-check quiz to check your understanding of the historic hostility of White Americans toward Asian immigrants, and explain how the model minority myth recognizes Asian American achievements while still stereotyping the group.

Diverse Latino Immigrants and the Obstacles They Encountered

There is no clear consensus on an appropriate term that includes all the diverse Spanish-speaking ethnic groups in the United States, but the immigration of Mexicans, Puerto Ricans, Cubans, Central Americans, and South Americans has created a need for an inclusive generic term. In 1980, the U.S. Census Bureau suggested *Latino* as the generic term; however, some critics said that sounded like "Ladino," an ancient form of Castilian Spanish spoken by Spanish Jews. The Bureau chose *Hispanic*, a label rejected by many Spanish-speaking people as a contrived, bureaucratic term (Shorris, 2001). Although *Hispanic* seems to be the preferred term in the southeastern United States and Texas, it is rejected in many other places, including most of California and much of the Midwest. Given this lack of consensus, both *Hispanic* and *Latino* are used in this final section.

Which Spanish-speaking group was the first to come to the United States?

The Spanish established the first permanent U.S. settlements in 1565 at St. Augustine, Florida, and in 1598 at Santa Fe, New Mexico, yet rarely do American history books mention this. Historically, school textbooks have focused on the English settlements in 1607 at Jamestown and in 1620 at Plymouth (Loewen, 2008). When the United States annexed Texas, Mexicans living there (Tejanos) found themselves in America; as the Tejanos like to say, "We didn't cross the border; the border crossed us" (Shorris, 2001, p. 37). After the Mexican-American War, Mexico signed the Treaty of Guadalupe Hidalgo, giving up a million square miles of land, half of its territory. Mexicans living in newly declared American territory were given six months to decide either to stay and become U.S. citizens or to move to the redefined Mexico. Of the more than 82,000 Mexicans who had to choose, about 80,000 chose to stay (Duignan & Gann, 1998).

Article X of the treaty promised to honor the land claims of Mexicans who became citizens, but when the American Congress ratified the treaty, they rejected Article X. To reassure Mexico that the land titles and civil rights of Mexicans would be respected, American representatives presented a "Statement of Protocol" to the Mexican government with assurances that the U.S. government would not annul Mexican land grants and that these claims would be considered legitimate in American courts (Vento, 1998). That promise proved to be false.

Only a few **Anglos**, as Mexicans called White settlers, came to the new territory at first, but after gold was discovered in California, they flooded the land. Anglos settled on Mexican American land, refusing to move, and authorities took no action against the "squatters." When Anglos made legal claims to the land, Mexican Americans were forced to retain White lawyers to represent them because court proceedings were conducted in English. Although courts confirmed land grants for more than two million acres owned by Mexican Americans, they rejected Mexican American claims for almost 34 million acres (Vento, 1998). Even when the courts affirmed their claims, landowners often had to sell portions of their land to pay legal fees. Aggressive Anglo efforts soon created a society in former Mexican territory consisting of Anglo landowners and entrepreneurs and a pool of primarily Mexican laborers. As Shorris (2001) observed: "In less than a quarter of a century California changed from Spanish to Anglo" (p. 31), and with that change came an enormous transfer of wealth and culture.

> "Poor Mexico, so far from God, so near to the United States."
> —PORFIRIO DÍAZ (1830–1915)

What was the experience like for Mexicans immigrating to the United States?

In the 1880s, Mexicans began crossing the border into the United States, recruited by American employers after the Chinese Exclusion Act was passed in 1882. Mexican immigrants tended to take jobs in agriculture, mining, and construction; they constituted 70 percent of workers laying track for the Southern Pacific and Santa Fe railroads. Although American businesses actively recruited them, many Anglos perceived Mexicans as inferior. Mexicans were refused admission to public places such as beaches and restaurants. All members of Mexican families participated in agricultural work; child labor laws were not enforced. Experienced workers might make up to $1.50 per day compared to $4 to $5 a day earned by miners (Duignan & Gann, 1998).

Mexicans did not passively accept such exploitation. In 1903, Mexican and Japanese farm workers formed the Japanese-Mexican Labor Association (JMLA) and engaged in a strike to increase hourly wages. They were successful, but they couldn't survive without support from national labor organizations. They petitioned the American Federation of Labor (AFL) to accept JMLA members, but AFL president Samuel Gompers insisted that the JMLA would be granted a membership charter only if it excluded Asian members. The Mexicans refused to betray their Japanese co-workers, so the charter was not granted (Takaki, 1993). Although the JMLA did not survive, Mexican farm workers continued to strike and protest against low wages.

Because of the Gentleman's Agreement of 1908 and the restrictive 1924 immigration law, Mexico was regarded as an excellent source of cheap labor. By 1910, 222,000 Mexicans lived in the United States, some as far north as Montana. Many migrated to escape the violence of the Mexican Revolution from 1910 to about 1920. When the revolution was over, only 10 percent of Mexico's citizens were landowners, and the northern migration continued (Vento, 1998). By 1930, 90,000 Mexicans lived in Los Angeles, representing about 10 percent of the city's population. Smaller numbers settled in Denver, Pittsburgh, and St. Louis, and over 20,000 Mexicans lived in Chicago (Duignan & Gann, 1998). Only a small number of these immigrants applied for citizenship, perhaps because the proximity of Mexico made it easier to consider returning.

To promote Latino immigrants applying for citizenship, the **League of United Latin American Citizens (LULAC)** was formed in the 1920s. In addition to being American citizens, members promoted assimilation by encouraging the use of English and affirming the virtues of citizenship. Although criticized for its middle-class bias, for many years LULAC was the only Latino organization to have a national presence. LULAC worked to improve education for Latino students, protest discrimination, and promote civil rights for Hispanic Americans (Vento, 1998). LULAC also encouraged Latinos to become citizens so they would be less vulnerable to nativist activities. LULAC's efforts were only marginally successful, but World War II would cause a more significant change in American attitudes toward Mexican immigrants.

Why did attitudes toward Mexicans change during World War II?

When the United States entered the war, the government began negotiations for Mexicans to replace the workers who had joined the military and the Japanese workers who had been taken to relocation camps. The U.S. government proposed a **Bracero Program** (*braceros* referring to contract laborers), which offered transportation and jobs; the Mexican government felt that this program would also provide Mexicans with an opportunity to learn about American agricultural practices. In 1942, the Bracero Program was implemented.

The U.S. government had guaranteed that Mexican workers would be paid the "prevailing wage" for their labor, but supervision of the program was inadequately funded, and many growers abused it by failing to pay the promised wages. In Texas, growers with a history of employing illegal immigrants continued to use them because they were less costly to hire. Although the Bracero Program was criticized on both sides of the border, it lasted well beyond World War II. When it ended in 1964, the program had issued almost five million contracts to Mexican workers (Vargas, 2000). In addition to the contribution of Mexican workers, more than 500,000 Spanish-speaking soldiers, primarily Mexican Americans, joined the American armed forces, the highest percentage of soldiers from any ethnic community (Takaki, 1993). Despite their willingness to fight for the country, many Latino soldiers encountered prejudice from fellow soldiers and in communities where they were stationed. One of the most publicized examples of anti-Latino prejudice was the **Zoot Suit Riots**.

What were the zoot suit riots?

On June 3, 1943, 11 sailors on shore leave in Los Angeles claimed to have been attacked by a gang of Mexican youth. Local media often stereotyped young Mexicans wearing flamboyant "zoot suits" as criminals and gangsters. (See Figure 5.6.) On June 4, soldiers and sailors rented 20 taxicabs and cruised the barrio, attacking those who looked Latino, especially anyone wearing a zoot suit. At the Carmen Theater, sailors charged in and grabbed youth wearing zoot suits, ripping off their clothes and beating them severely. The police arrested several Mexican American youth, and the local media portrayed the sailors as heroes (Banks, 2009; Vento, 1998).

The following night sailors and soldiers marched into the barrio, invading bars and businesses, destroying property, and attacking patrons. Local police refused to charge them with destruction of private property or assault. On June 7, civilians and servicemen formed a mob of thousands, attacking anyone who looked Latino, including several Filipinos and Black people. Some were left naked and bleeding on the streets. Los Angeles police arrested 600 Mexican American youth. Eleanor Roosevelt declared in her newspaper column that the riots were the result of "long standing discrimination against Mexicans" (Vento, 1998, p. 187). Los Angeles police and city government denied the accusation, but as they followed the events in the newspapers, Latinos, especially Latino soldiers, were angry that they were still not accepted in their adopted land.

> "I believe cruelty is the inability to assign the same feelings and values to another person that you harbor in yourself."
> —CARLOS FUENTES (1928–2012)

Was it better for Latinos after the war?

Latino communities felt a great deal of pride in their returning veterans. Latino soldiers earned numerous bronze and silver stars given for bravery in battle, and 17 Latino

---

Figure 5.6 Zoot Suit

A soldier appears to be admiring a zoot suit, but servicemen would justify attacking Mexican American youth during the Zoot Suit Riots by claiming it was unpatriotic to wear zoot suits requiring so much cloth when cloth was being rationed because of the war.

Photograph by John Ferrel (1942). Library of Congress Prints and Photographs Division [John Ferrell/LC-USF34-011543-D]

soldiers received the nation's highest military award—the Congressional Medal of Honor (Duignan & Gann, 1998). Because Latino soldiers had not been segregated and had served with White soldiers, some also rose to positions of command. As Shorris (2001) stated, "Men who had commanded Anglo troops in battle did not cringe before them in civilian life" (p. 97).

Although they had encountered difficulty getting home loans before the war, Latino soldiers now had their loan applications approved. The GI Bill allowed many to pursue a college education. These soldiers represented only a small portion of Latinos, but their experiences demonstrated that Latinos could receive equitable treatment. Yet the majority of Latinos still encountered prejudice and discrimination, even those who had served in the military. At Three Rivers, Texas, a funeral home director refused to bury Felix Longoria, a Mexican American who had been decorated for heroism in World War II. After Mexican Americans protested, Longoria was finally buried with military honors at Arlington National Cemetery (Shorris, 2001).

How did Mexican Americans respond to discrimination after the war?

Challenging racially segregated schools, Mexican Americans brought *Mendez v. Westminster School District* to California courts in 1946; the judge ruled it was unconstitutional to segregate Mexican American children. This case and others helped the NAACP to bring *Brown v. Board of Education* to the Supreme Court in 1954. Recognizing the need for a legal organization similar to the NAACP, an attorney in San Antonio named Pete Tijerina persuaded the Ford Foundation to provide $2.2 million to establish the **Mexican American Legal Defense and Educational Fund (MALDEF)**. MALDEF continues to confront discrimination against Mexican Americans.

To establish a fair wage for agricultural workers in California, Cesar Chavez assisted farm workers in creating a union. Chavez led a strike lasting from 1965 until 1970, resulting in a contract with one of the major growers. After another seven years of activism, the remaining growers agreed to pay farm workers standardized wages and benefits. Also in the 1960s, some Mexican American youth began to refer to themselves as "Chicanos," a term that had historically been used as a slur directed at Mexican migrant labor (Kazin, 2011). In Crystal City, Texas, Mexican Americans, who were a large majority of the residents, formed a third party called La Raza Unida and won control of the city council and the school board. They instituted bilingual education programs and hired numerous Mexican American administrators and teachers.

In 1957, El Paso citizens elected Raymond Telles as the first Mexican American mayor in the United States. In 2005, Antonio Villaraigosa was the first Mexican American mayor of Los Angeles. Political candidates in the Southwest, urban areas, and California court Mexican American voters, and in 2011, there were 5850 Latinos in public office. According to the U.S. Census Bureau (2016), Mexican Americans are almost two thirds of all Latinos in the United States, followed by Puerto Ricans (9.5 percent), Salvadorans, and Cubans (almost 4 percent for each). Unlike other Latino immigrants, however, Puerto Ricans came to America already claiming U.S. citizenship.

How did Puerto Ricans become citizens of the United States?

When Spanish ships arrived in 1493, they called the island San Juan Batista and the harbor Puerto Rico; over time the names reversed and the "rich port" of San Juan became the capital of the island of Puerto Rico (Fitzpatrick, 1971). The 70,000 Tainos inhabiting the island were almost exterminated, so Africans were imported to work as slaves. Because Spain mainly sent soldiers, marriages and relationships took place between Spaniards, Tainos, and Africans, producing the range of skin colors from light to dark that can be found among Puerto Ricans today. In 1897, the Spanish government agreed to give Puerto Rico more autonomy, but the Spanish-American War made Puerto Rico a U.S. possession.

After almost 20 years of autocratic rule by the United States, Congress responded to Puerto Rican demands for more autonomy by passing the Jones Act in 1917. Puerto Ricans elected representatives to their two legislative bodies as well as a resident commissioner, but the U.S. president still appointed the governor and maintained veto power (Fitzpatrick, 1971). The Jones Act also provided the opportunity for Puerto Ricans to become U.S. citizens, giving them six months to make a decision. Although it made them eligible for military service, only 287 out of more than a million people rejected U.S. citizenship (Perez y Gonzalez, 2000).

What effect did becoming part of the United States have on Puerto Rico?

When the United States assumed control, Puerto Rican farmers owned 93 percent of the farmland. By 1930, 60 percent of sugar beet production and almost all tobacco production came from farms with absentee owners, primarily American corporations. Although the United States built more roads and schools, the basis of the economy was transformed from small farms producing food to meet the local need to large farms hiring low-wage workers and exporting their products (Feagin & Feagin, 2008). Soon the island was not producing enough food for its own people, and malnutrition became common. Because of improved health care, Puerto Rico's population doubled by 1940, but jobs did not. Agriculture jobs paid as little as six cents an hour. By 1910, about 1500 Puerto Ricans had come to America because of economic hardship, with a third of them living in Spanish Harlem in New York City (Duignan & Gann, 1998).

In the 1930s, Luis Marín formed the Popular Democratic Party (or "Populares") to address Puerto Rico's economic problems. The party sponsored legislation to limit the amount of land that absentee owners could control; land returned to the government was redistributed to small farmers, but two thirds of American corporations refused to cooperate with the law (Perez y Gonzalez, 2000). Puerto Ricans expressed their frustration by demanding more autonomy from the United States.

In 1949, the United States allowed Puerto Ricans to elect their own governor, and they elected Luis Marín. Three years later, Congress approved the proposed Puerto Rican Constitution, giving the island the status of a commonwealth. Although it now had more autonomy, Puerto Rico also had significant economic problems. After sixty years of American rule, more than 50 percent of the total national income went to 20 percent of the people, and there was persistent unemployment and underemployment (Duignan & Gann, 1998).

Governor Marín proposed an ambitious economic plan called **Operation Bootstrap** that offered incentives such as a large supply of cheap labor and tax exemptions for businesses moving to Puerto Rico. Many corporations took advantage of this offer. Throughout the 1950s and 1960s, Operation Bootstrap expanded the island's industrial base and created 140,000 manufacturing jobs. Personal income rose from an annual average of $118 in 1940 to $1200 by 1970 (Perez y Gonzalez, 2000). Tourism increased, and Puerto Rico was called the "Showcase of the Americas," but economic problems persisted. With so much land being used for industry, the number of agricultural jobs decreased, resulting in unemployment rates as high as 10 percent. So much land was given over for industrial use that Puerto Rico had to import food. Corporate tax exemptions required Puerto Ricans to pay higher taxes to fund the necessary improvements in sewers, roads, electricity, and water (Feagin & Feagin, 2008).

For many Puerto Ricans, the primary economic benefit was the opportunity to earn enough money to migrate to the United States. By the 1980s, more than 900,000 were living in New York City alone, comprising about 12 percent of the city's population, and the three million Puerto Ricans living in the United States represented 11 percent of all Latinos. Approximately 60 percent of Puerto Ricans lived in either New York or New Jersey, but with unemployment rates as high as 23 percent, nearly 60 percent of these Puerto Rican families lived in poverty (Banks, 2009; Duignan & Gann, 1998).

How do the experiences of Puerto Ricans in the United States compare to those of other Latino groups?

Puerto Ricans have encountered many obstacles in the United States. The percentages of Puerto Ricans who are unemployed or on welfare have been higher than for other Latino groups. In part, the high unemployment rate is the result of a decline in unskilled and semiskilled jobs in the urban areas where they have settled. Puerto Rican children living in poverty have attended racially segregated urban schools without resources to provide the quality of education necessary for their students to compete for better paying jobs. One consequence of these economic and social problems is that Puerto Ricans have historically had higher rates of drug use, drug addiction, and crime than other Latino groups (Perez y Gonzalez, 2000).

"Come from where it may, racism divides."

—JOSÉ MARTÍ (1853–1895)

Yet Puerto Ricans have succeeded in a variety of fields, including literature, sports, politics, the arts, music, medicine, and more. For over 40 years the Puerto Rican organization called Aspira has supported high school clubs to encourage Puerto Rican youth to graduate and go to college. Regardless of their success or failure, Puerto Ricans resent other Americans perceiving them as foreigners rather than regarding them as the fellow citizens that they are. If they migrate from Puerto Rico to a state, or from one state to another, Puerto Ricans should be viewed the same as a Minnesotan who moves to New York.

Today, there are over a million more Puerto Ricans living in the United States than in Puerto Rico, and the majority of them were born here. Puerto Ricans tend to be bilingual and bicultural, identifying themselves as Puerto Ricans but proud of their status as American citizens. Like other Latinos, they often speak Spanish at home, but young people are more likely to speak English to their peers. Although Puerto Rican Americans have attained higher levels of education and income compared to all U.S. Latinos, the percentage of them who are unemployed (12.8 percent) or living in poverty (27 percent) is also higher compared to all other U.S. Latinos (Perez & Patten, 2015). Despite the mixed outcomes, Puerto Ricans encourage their youth to strive for success, regardless of the difficulty of the goal.

Why has the experience of Cubans been so different from that of Puerto Ricans?

The islands of Cuba and Puerto Rico have similar histories. Columbus and his men conquered the Taino Indians, inhabiting both islands and enslaving the residents. Yet by 1762, Cuba's capital city was twice the size of New York or Philadelphia; Havana was a port of such significance that the British captured the city and refused to give it back until Spain agreed to give up Florida in exchange. In addition to being a major trading center in the Caribbean, Cuba prospered because of its sugar production carried out by imported African slaves. By 1830, the combination of free and enslaved Black people was larger than the population of White people. By 1870, Cubans were trying to win independence from Spain; a few Cubans immigrated to the United States during the lengthy struggle that ended in 1898 when American troops prevailed in the Spanish-American War.

After four years of military rule, the United States agreed to make Cuba a sovereign nation, but the Platt amendment gave the United States the right to intervene in Cuba's affairs at any time to protect property and liberty in Cuba. For the next two decades, no Cuban who did not gain U.S. approval could be elected president nor stay in that office (Feagin & Feagin, 2008).

Even under American dominance, Cuba prospered; few Cubans immigrated to the United States until Fidel Castro's successful revolt against dictator Fulgencio Batista. After Castro announced that Cuba would be a communist nation, Cubans began leaving, most immigrating to Florida. The wealthiest Cubans left first. Those who followed in the 1960s were a heterogeneous group but with a disproportionately high number of businessmen, professionals, and entrepreneurs. Many had been in the merchant navy; others were former government officials or were revolutionaries who were disillusioned with Castro (Duignan & Gann, 1998).

What happened to the Cubans who came to the United States?

A federally funded Cuban Refugee Program (CRP) was established to assist Cubans coming to Florida. CRP refugee centers provided resources rarely given to other immigrants (Portes & Bach, 1985). Cuban businessmen who had salvaged some of their wealth relied on traditional business methods called *socios* or *socioismo*, in which loans were approved not by an objective analysis but because the applicant was a friend. Cuban immigrants tended to be educated, and many had business experience. For the next two decades, Cubans used their resources to engage in business enterprises as well as to provide services such as grocery stores, legal assistance, and funeral homes for fellow Cubans. As Shorris (2001) stated, "The Cuban exiles, primarily middle- and upper middle-class, soon became middle- and upper middle-class again" (p. 67). Attracted by Cuban success in the United States and disenchanted with Castro's communism, more Cubans came.

The next wave of Cuban immigrants tended to be working-class people from urban areas (almost half from Havana alone). Many found work in businesses owned or managed by Cubans, where they tended to earn higher wages. By the mid-1980s, Cuban Americans were the majority in Dade County and in Miami. Although 40 percent of Cuban immigrants settled in Florida, they also settled in New York, New Jersey, and California (Duignan & Gann, 1998). A 1953 Cuban census identified 72 percent of Cubans as White, but the 1970 U.S. census identified 95 percent of Cubans living in the United States as White (Portes & Bach, 1985).

Compared to other major Latino groups in the United States, Cuban Americans have recorded the highest median household incomes. One reason for their success is that, similar to Asian American families, they tend to have multiple wage earners in a household. According to a study of Cuban immigration from 1960 to 1980, about two thirds of Cuban American wives worked outside the home, and 27 percent of these households had additional family members earning income. The presence of Cubans in Florida has attracted an increasing number of tourists and entrepreneurs from both Central and South America, providing additional business opportunities.

Although Cuban immigrants have traditionally viewed themselves as a people in exile, that view is not shared by Cuban American youth. According to Shorris (2001), "Older Cubans say they will return to Cuba as soon as Castro dies or is deposed. The younger generation is interested only in going back to visit" (p. 75). Their attitudes are similar to Mexican American and Puerto Rican youth, as well as other Latinos living in the United States. Some pundits have suggested that this change in attitude among the youth was a factor in President Obama issuing the executive order to restore U.S. relations with Cuba. Although tourism was banned, travel restrictions were reduced significantly, and those young people who wanted to return to Cuba for a visit could now do so.

Predictably, when President Trump promised to cancel President Obama's agreement with Cuba, most young Cuban Americans and many of those in the business community were opposed, consistent with a 2016 poll that found a majority of Cuban Americans against the U.S. embargo and in favor of better relations. Perhaps this change

Video Example 5.4

This video discusses the fears and challenges that immigrant students face when they have undocumented family members. What are some of the ways discussed in which certain assignments or school environments create challenges for undocumented students and families? What might be some other ways in which schools can create challenges for undocumented students and families that are not discussed in the video?

"What the people want is very simple. They want an America as good as its promise."

—BARBARA JORDAN (1936–1996)

in Cuban American attitudes was the reason the President Trump did not go as far as he initially indicated. Even so, critics say that the new policy will adversely affect Cuban entrepreneurs and that limiting travelers to tour groups will reduce the number of people who are able to travel to Cuba. Following Trump's announcement of his new Cuba policy, a Florida poll reported that 47 percent supported Obama's attempt to normalize relations with Cuba, and only 34 percent supported Trump's more restrictive policy (Persio, 2017), which may be modified at a future date.

What other Latino groups live in the United States?

Other Hispanic immigrant groups have come to the United States in the twentieth century. Since the 1960s, there has been a small but steady stream of immigrants from the Dominican Republic, surging in the early 1980s because of the global recession that drove down sugar prices, creating a huge foreign debt and an unemployment rate of 30 percent. By the time the crisis was over, 10 percent of Dominicans had immigrated, primarily to the United States, with 90 percent settling in New York City (Duignan & Gann, 1998).

Immigrants from Central America have usually come to the United States to escape political turmoil and violence in places like Guatemala, Honduras, Nicaragua, and El Salvador. In 2015, there were 3.4 million Central Americans living in the United States, nearly half of them in three states: California, Texas, and Florida. Compared to other immigrants, Central Americans tend to have less education; about 67 percent had limited proficiency in English compared to 49 percent for all other immigrants. On the other hand, Central American immigrants were more likely to be employed, but even though 73 percent of their adults were in the labor force, 22 percent of Central American immigrants live in poverty (Lesser & Batalova, 2017). Central Americans have tended to settle in urban areas, and so many Salvadorans have settled in Los Angeles that it is now the second largest Salvadoran city in the world after San Salvador, the nation's capital.

> ✓ **Self-Check 5.4** Complete this self-check quiz to check your understanding of the diverse Latino groups that have immigrated to the United States and the different obstacles each group has encountered.

Afterword

Human evolution is a story of survival, but once physical survival is assured, human beings create culture. The struggle to maintain one's culture while living in a new homeland with its own culture is no easy task, especially because physical and cultural differences have been used to create the concept of race. Race has then been used to divide human groups, creating subordinate races that are forced to struggle against a dominant race.

For the indigenous people in America, this struggle began when European colonists stepped on American shores. The roots of oppression expanded across the nation in the cultural and physical conflict that followed. The oppression eventually encompassed African slaves, Chinese and Japanese laborers, Mexican migrant workers, and other immigrants of color. This oppression was even directed against groups considered White today, like Irish, Italian, and Slavic immigrants, but all European groups would eventually be offered the freedom and opportunity they sought in the United States while these continued to be denied to people of color.

Oppression based on race and extended to include ethnic groups has been sustained by the descendants of the original European settlers, affecting people of color living in the United States and those who are coming with the same vision of freedom and opportunity that brought the first colonists. We are now a nation of nations with people from all over the world pursuing the happiness promised by a free society. If the United States is to be a pluralistic society embracing diverse groups, it must make sure that all people living in America are respected as part of our diverse national family.

Summary

- European colonists rejected many cultural benefits offered by indigenous people who persisted in maintaining their cultural differences and their tribal sovereignty, but all tribes are still encountering issues that affect the lives and well-being of their people.

- Slavery was disputed during the colonial period as both Black and White people took actions to end it prior to the Civil War, and afterward Black people continued to struggle against oppression, culminating in the civil rights confrontations following World War II.

- White American attitudes toward Asian immigration reveal a historic pattern of rejection until more recently when the development of the model minority myth illustrated respect for Asian American achievements while misrepresenting the reality of their diversity.

- The immigration experiences of Mexicans, Cubans, Puerto Ricans, and other Latinos have involved some similarities but more differences, especially the historic obstacles that have confronted each group.

Terms and Definitions

Anglos A term identifying White people who settled in Mexican territory, eventually becoming a generic term for White people

Black Cabinet The Federal Council on Negro Affairs, consisting of 30 Black professionals, served as an advisory group to President Franklin Roosevelt

Bracero Program Initiated during World War II, this program continued to import Mexicans to work as manual laborers in the United States for 22 years

Brown v. Board of Education The 1954 Supreme Court decision overturning *Plessy v. Ferguson* by declaring racial segregation unconstitutional

Chinese Exclusion Act An 1882 law prohibiting Chinese immigration to the United States, renewed in 1892, and making exclusion permanent in 1902

Emancipation Proclamation Issued by President Lincoln to free slaves only in Confederate states and permitting free Black men to enlist in the Union Army

Ethnocentrism Believing your race, nation, or culture is superior to all others; also individual actions or institutional practices based on that belief

Gentleman's Agreement The Japanese government assured the U.S. government it would issue no more passports (as of 1908) to Japanese workers except those already in the United States or their close relatives

Indian Sovereignty Legal rights of Indian nations, confirmed by treaties with the U.S. government, to define themselves and to act as unique cultural and legal entities

Indigenous people A racial or ethnic group that is well established in an area before the arrival of a new group; a group that may be but does not need be native to the area in which it is established

League of United Latin American Citizens (LULAC) A national organization for members of Spanish-speaking ethnic groups who are American citizens that is dedicated to promoting the value of citizenship, protesting discrimination, and advocating for civil rights for Latinos

Mexican American Legal Defense Fund (MALDEF) An organization opposing discrimination and advocating for Mexican Americans' civil rights

Middle Passage The ocean crossing of slave ships resulting in the deaths of an estimated five to six million Africans being transported as slaves

Model minority The belief that Asian Americans have been successful because they have been willing to work hard and that all other minorities could be just as successful if they emulated Asian American behavior

National Association for the Advancement of Colored People (NAACP) An organization opposing racism and advocating for Black civil rights

Nisei The term for children of Japanese immigrants who were born in the United States and therefore possessed U.S. citizenship

Nomads A group of individuals with no single fixed abode who move from place to place in search of food and water

Operation Bootstrap An economic plan for Puerto Rico during the 1950s and 1960s to boost its industrial base and create more manufacturing jobs

Picture bride A modification of the Japanese system for arranged marriages involving the exchange of photographs between families negotiating marriage for Japanese men who had immigrated to the United States

Treaty A legal agreement between two or more nations involving terms of peace, trade, and other matters as agreed to by the negotiating parties

Underground Railroad An organization that established "stations" where runaway slaves could get food and rest as they escaped north to freedom

Yellow Peril The term for the belief that Chinese and Japanese immigrants could never be assimilated into American culture and therefore threatened the unity of American society

Zoot Suit Riots Several days of mob violence in 1942 in Los Angeles that demonstrated anti-Latino prejudice as U.S. servicemen (later joined by civilians) attacked Mexican American youth, especially targeting those wearing zoot suits

Discussion Exercises

Exercise 1: Understanding Recollections of Larry Kobori Activity

Directions: Read to learn the feelings that Larry recounts having had about the incident that he describes. Then respond to the Insight Builder Questions below.

Larry Kobori's School Story

When I was young I noticed I was a little different from my friends. My father told me I was Japanese and that I should never be ashamed of being Japanese. When I started school everything was perfect until the fourth grade. Some kids called me a "Chink." I told them I'm Japanese, not Chinese. If I was going to be called a dirty name, at least use the proper dirty name. My friends always told me to forget those kids, that those kids were stupid. I was glad to hear my friends say that.

In the seventh grade we started to read about World War II. I knew Japan had attacked Pearl Harbor. I never answered any questions. I would just slouch in my chair. I was feeling ashamed and embarrassed at the atrocities of Japan during World War II. But I didn't understand why the textbooks and my teacher glorified America's bombing of Hiroshima and Nagasaki. Thousands of civilians, including women and children, were killed by the atom bombs to make Japan surrender. She added that the bombings had saved many American lives.

I asked my teacher, "Wouldn't that be considered an atrocity since so many civilians died? That's the way you describe Japanese atrocities." I'll never forget the way she stared at me and said, "There's a difference." Even today that episode is still clear as a bell for me.

My three years in high school were the best years. I was really accepted. I couldn't compete on the high school level so I did what I could to help. I was the varsity scorekeeper in football, basketball, and baseball. I learned the plays and found myself getting to know the other guys. I was encouraged to write sport stories in the local newspaper, and the players liked what I wrote.

Outside of class sometimes it was a different story. Traveling with the basketball team, some Black and Mexican players called me a "Jap." Remembering my promise, I restrained myself and did not retaliate.

I'll never understand why those people called me a "Jap."

Insight Builder Questions

1. What are your impressions of Larry Kobori?
2. Do you think Larry Kobori's responses to the racial incidents were appropriate ways to deal with the discrimination he experienced?
3. What alternatives did Larry have, and which would you recommend as the best strategy?
4. In your opinion, how should teachers present the Japanese role in World War II? The use of atomic bombs on Hiroshima and Nagasaki?

Exercise 2: College Racial Incidents Activity

Directions: Imagine you are a college counselor or residence hall assistant when the student of color in each incident comes to you to report what happened. What sort of advice would you give to this student? Explain why your advice represents the best course of action for the student to follow.

1. A Puerto Rican American, Jorge, interviewed for a graduate assistantship position. The director discussed the role and responsibility of the assistantship position and indicated that the primary responsibility would be to supervise outreach activities for Hispanic students who were not using available student services. The director believed that Jorge would be a good role model and could convince students to use services since there were biological factors resulting in some people being able to learn more and to be more intelligent than others. Noting Jorge's negative response, the director said he just wanted to be open and honest about his opinions.

2. When in the Marine Corps, Leonard, a Lakota Sioux, had been stationed in the United States and Germany. After serving three years, he returned to his reservation and enrolled in a nearby college. Visiting a sweat lodge, Leonard's friends and older members of the tribe shared stories of their ancestors. When Leonard had been a child, he remembered listening to his father telling stories about his great-grandfather; he had always enjoyed learning about his family history. Now Leonard realized, however, that the stories had no meaning for him. He found himself in conflict with his family and friends. He considered dropping out of college to get a job, but he knew there weren't many jobs for people with only a high school diploma. Leonard became more depressed and began to think that the only resolution was to drop out of college and reenlist in the Marines.

3. Jessica, a 22-year-old Mexican American from Illinois, left home to attend college in California. A few weeks into the semester she noticed that the majority of Hispanic students were able to speak both English and Spanish fluently. Although her parents spoke Spanish at home, they did not insist that their children become bilingual, so Jessica could understand Spanish if someone spoke to her, but she was not a fluent Spanish speaker. Jessica talked to the Chicano studies professor after class, who assured her that not all Mexican Americans share the same sociocultural experience, but that all people needed to understand and respect the values of others. He also suggested that if this situation continued to bother Jessica, she should consider seeing a counselor. In her English class, consisting primarily of White students, Jessica felt comfortable and relaxed; however, in a Chicano studies course, she felt out of place because she did not share the experiences of the other Hispanic students.

Chapter 6
Religion and Oppression: The Struggle for Religious Freedom

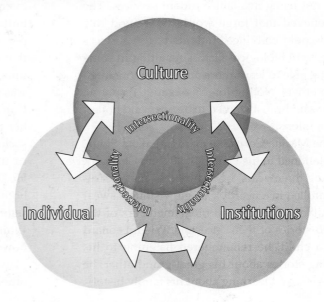

 ## Learning Outcomes

After reading this chapter you will know and be able to:

6.1 Describe religious diversity during America's colonial period, and explain how it led to support for the principle of religious freedom.

6.2 Discuss the reasons behind the virtual exclusion of religion from the U.S. Constitution and the inclusion of religious freedom in the First Amendment.

6.3 Describe and give examples of religious intolerance in the United States as reflected in anti-Catholic and anti-Semitic attitudes from the colonial period to the twentieth century.

6.4 Explain how increased religious diversity resulted from immigration reform and how this diversity presents new challenges to the principle of religious freedom.

"All religions are but stepping-stones back to God."

—PAWNEE PROVERB

In a play based on the popular book *The Diary of Anne Frank,* the authors have Anne make a comment similar to this Pawnee proverb because she wishes Peter had a religion—but she emphasizes that it doesn't matter to her what the religion is (Goodrich & Hackett, 1956). Her story has frequently been used to introduce students to the horrors of the Holocaust, perhaps because despite the Nazis' persecution of the Jewish people, Anne continues to believe in the goodness of human beings. Her comments affirm the decency of humanity, regardless of the differences between people. Such a comment or a belief should not be controversial, yet some Christians have demanded that children not read the play because the remark about religion suggests that all religions are equally valid. Usually those who complain believe that one religion, their religion, is the only true faith.

Religious Diversity in Colonial America and How it Led to Religious Freedom

Americans have confronted religious controversy since early colonial times when immigrant groups arrived with an array of diverse beliefs and minority faiths contended with the power of a dominant faith to survive. Honoring the principle of **religious freedom/religious liberty**—the right to worship according to individual beliefs—has been an ongoing struggle in America, and the history of our efforts to achieve it is the focus of this chapter.

Although religious freedom does not deny an individual's right to disagree with the beliefs and practice of another religion, it does require acceptance of divergent beliefs, as long as they don't infringe on the rights of others. The constitutional separation of church and state principle was established to resolve issues related to diverse faiths in America, but efforts to achieve religious liberty have been a source of dramatic conflict throughout American history.

How did the first colonists deal with religious diversity?

Puritans came to the New World to practice their religion freely but had no intention of allowing others the same freedom. When Anne Hutchinson expressed sentiments contrary to Puritan beliefs, she was excommunicated and exiled. Roger Williams was also exiled for advocating respect for all religious faiths and for separation of church from state, a principle not found in European cultural heritages. To reestablish Old World practices, dominant religious groups such as the Anglicans in Massachusetts expected their faith to be designated the **established church** of their colony and to be supported by an allotment of local tax dollars. Miller (1976) described this perspective: "The established religion with its educated ministers and stately rituals was an important element in creating or re-creating the world they left behind" (p. 26).

English colonists discovered that it was difficult to create an established church in the New World. Parishioners wishing to take care of their families could not afford to give their churches much financial support, so the need for support from colonial governments was greater than had been required in England, which placed a significant fiscal burden on colonial revenues. Furthermore, immigrants represented diverse faiths—Presbyterians, Quakers, Baptists—and were resentful when colonial tax revenues were expended to support a church to which they did not belong.

Religious resentment was mutual. Northern colony Puritans particularly disliked Quakers because of their ecstatic worship and their practice of allowing women to be church leaders. In Massachusetts, blasphemy laws were enacted to force Quakers out, threatening them with death if they returned. When they did return, authorities promptly arrested them; four Quakers were executed between 1659 and 1661. The executions stopped when embarrassed authorities in Britain insisted that Quakers be sent to London for proper trials (Miller, 1976).

Most American colonies enacted blasphemy laws for those not belonging to the colony's majority faith. *Blasphemy* was defined as denying the truth and authority of the Bible. If anyone denied the divinity of Christ, he could lose his property or even be executed. Although violating blasphemy laws usually did not result in death, punishments could be quite severe, especially for freethinkers and atheists. According to a 1699 Maryland law, blasphemers, typically people who made comments degrading Christ, the Apostles, or the Trinity, were branded with a "B" for a first offense, had a hole burned through their tongue with a red-hot iron for a second offense, and had their property confiscated for a third offense. In a humanitarian gesture, some colonies allowed blasphemers to avoid punishment by publicly asking to be forgiven (Myers, 1960).

As colonies designated "established churches," blasphemy laws required ministers from other churches to register as "dissenters" and agree to practice only after receiving colonial approval. Some dissenting ministers refused to register and preached whenever they wished, but there were consequences. Baptist ministers were aggressively pursued, arrested, and jailed for unauthorized preaching, but the number of Baptist converts increased dramatically (Miller, 1976). By 1775, over 150 years since the first colonists arrived, only 10 percent of Americans were church members (Lippy, 1994). Conversion efforts were usually focused on colonists who attended but were not members of a church or on those not attending a church—a majority in the colonies. Their goal was material success: to own land and to provide for their families. They wanted a better life on earth, not in heaven.

How did the colonies promote the concept of religious freedom?

Because of the influence of Roger Williams, William Penn, and Lord Baltimore, the colonies of Rhode Island, Pennsylvania, and Maryland declared religious freedom for all faiths. Puritans regarded their faith as a "light to the world," so they forced people to accept it. Williams argued that people could not develop true faith through coercion and expressed the need for a "wall of separation between the garden of the church and the wilderness of the world" (Nord, 1995, p. 135). Without this wall, Williams felt that both church and state would be corrupted (Lindberg, 2015). In Rhode Island, the arrival of Quakers tested the Baptist majority's commitment to religious freedom. Williams personally disliked Quakers and attacked them in his writings, but tolerance prevailed, attracting even a small group of Jewish people to Newport. Quakers eventually became the dominant group in Rhode Island (Miller, 1976).

William Penn believed that God spoke directly to individuals through the conscience and that this was the basis for a commitment to religious freedom. Penn undertook deliberate efforts to bring to Pennsylvania people from diverse faiths: Anabaptists, Presbyterians, Puritans, Roman Catholics, and others who had no religious conviction. Pennsylvania was the first colony to experiment with the idea of denominational churches instead of an established church; no church received state assistance, nor did the state interfere in church affairs. Pennsylvania's "holy experiment" was not without problems. Because Penn was a Quaker, Quakers had more government influence than other denominations, and for a time they functioned as an informal established church. Yet Pennsylvania and Rhode Island provided the clearest alternative to the Old World tradition of state support for an established church.

Founded by Lord Baltimore, Maryland was originally intended as a refuge for English Catholics. The principle of religious freedom was self-serving because Catholics constituted a minority even among the first contingent settling Maryland, and Catholicism remained a minority faith throughout the colonial period. Baltimore's commitment to religious tolerance attracted immigrants from diverse faiths, but Maryland's experiment failed when the Church of England became its established church in 1702. Because three other faiths had more members—Presbyterians, Anabaptists, and Quakers—the Church of England was established on condition that religious tolerance would be maintained for current groups, but when Jews and Unitarians migrated there, they were not allowed to settle in Maryland (Hudson, 1973).

How was the principle of religious freedom established in all the colonies?

As the mid-eighteenth century approached, a significant event (later termed the "Great Awakening") promoted the principle of religious freedom, beginning with ideas in the widely read writings of Jonathan Edwards and other New England ministers. Concerned about the "extraordinary dullness" of people's faith, Edwards challenged individuals to demonstrate personal commitment to their faith in their everyday lives, and he spoke of the necessity of faith being deeply felt as well as rational.

In 1740, English preacher George Whitefield presented a similar challenge to colonial people. (See Figure 6.1.) Protestant ministers invited him to preach, but Whitefield avoided churches, preferring to speak in open fields. His sermons stimulated emotion as much as intellect, and audiences responded enthusiastically. Whitefield said that being a Christian was not about belonging to a particular church but being committed to a faith. Nord (1995) describes a sermon in Philadelphia in which Whitefield looked up to the sky and shouted:

> Father Abraham, whom have you in heaven? Any Episcopalians? No! Any Presbyterians? No! Any Independents or Methodists? No, no, no! Who have you there? . . . We don't know those names here. All who are here are Christians . . . Then God help us to forget party names and become Christians in deed and truth. (p. 103)

The impact of the Great Awakening on religious freedom was that it denied the significance of differences between Protestant sects. Prior to the Great Awakening, Protestants

---

Figure 6.1 George Whitefield

Whitefield's impact on colonial America is commemorated in this statue on the University of Pennsylvania campus.

SOURCE: Kent Koppelman

belonged to one sect or another, each defining itself as the "true faith." This **sectarian** view of Christianity gave way to a consensus about what it meant to be Christian: accepting others, doing good deeds, and ignoring theological controversy. The Great Awakening replaced a sectarian approach to Christianity with a **denominational** view based on the perception of a singular Protestant church that is called—denominated—by many different names, such as Anglican, Lutheran, or Baptist. Although the denominational view united Protestants, Catholics were not included.

 Self-Check 6.1 Complete this self-check quiz to check your understanding of religious diversity during America's colonial period and how it led to support for the principle of religious freedom.

The Exclusion of Religion from the Constitution and the Need for the First Amendment

In the mid-eighteenth century, Europeans were making significant discoveries based on scientific inquiry. Isaac Newton discovered the principles of gravitation and light, developed differential calculus, and even had time to invent the reflecting telescope. There was an increased respect for science and a diminished belief in the supernatural. Some argued that religious truths, like scientific truths, would be discovered by human reason, not through divine revelation. Such thinking led to the birth of **Deism**, a religious philosophy based on rationality that was devoid of mysticism. Deists acknowledged that God created the universe but argued that humans had to use their intellects to understand the rational principles by which the universe functions. In response to the increased emphasis on rationality and the scientific method as the preferred means of ascertaining truth, many intellectuals rejected all religious faiths. Although some American colonists declared themselves **atheists**, denying the existence of God, the religious philosophy of Deism was more appealing than atheism to Christian intellectuals in the colonies.

> "I do not believe in the creed professed by the Jewish church, by the Roman church, by the Greek church, by the Turkish church, by the Protestant church nor by any church that I know of. My own mind is my own church."
>
> —THOMAS PAINE (1737–1809)

What was the relationship between Deism and Christianity?

Deism dismissed much of what constituted traditional Christian beliefs. Deists believed God created the world and a system of natural laws that governed it. Although they believed that God would reward or punish the soul after death, they did not believe that God was an active force in the everyday world. Thomas Jefferson and Benjamin Franklin were among many who were attracted to Deism as a religious philosophy. Although Deists denied the divinity of Christ, they tended to admire his moral teachings; therefore, many Deists attended churches of various denominations, whereas others never went to church. Although Deist views were not popular among the general public, the principles of Deism influenced several people who would write the documents that transformed the 13 colonies into the United States of America. Curiously, these "enlightened" founders included little about religion in the Constitution.

Why was there so little reference to religion in the original Constitution?

Although the majority of men responsible for writing the U.S. Constitution were Protestant and of European descent, they chose to defy their European traditions and create the first secular government. For centuries, the governments of most European nations claimed to derive their authority from God; therefore, the state had both the right and the responsibility to intrude into religious issues and attempt to resolve religious controversies, usually in favor of a majority faith. The Articles of Confederation referred to "the Great Governor of the World" (Jacoby, 2005, p. 30), but the authors of the U.S. Constitution cited "We the People" as the source of the government's power and authority, deliberately excluding any reference to God. When challenged to explain this omission, Alexander Hamilton's tongue-in-cheek response was "We forgot" (Chernow, 2004, p. 235).

They did not forget. When the delegates met in Philadelphia in 1787, they were well aware of the debate that had recently occurred in Virginia. In the early 1780s, Patrick Henry unsuccessfully lobbied to have Christianity declared Virginia's established religion. In 1784, he introduced a resolution calling for a tax on Virginians to promote Christianity but allowing them to designate their denomination or even a particular church as the recipient of their tax dollars. Those belonging to no church could contribute their taxes to a general education fund. This resolution gained wide support, even receiving George Washington's endorsement. On November 11, the Virginia legislature voted 47 to 32 in favor of the resolution, but the legislative session was dismissed shortly after this vote.

> "The government of the United States of America is not in any sense founded on the Christian Religion."
> —TREATY OF TRIPOLI (1797)

James Madison led the opposition to this resolution. He wrote a pamphlet describing the dangers inherent in such legislation: "Who does not see that the same authority which can establish Christianity, in exclusion of all other Religions, may establish with the same ease any particular sect of Christians, in exclusion of all other Sects?" (Waldman, 2006, p. 36). Madison's pamphlet generated widespread support. By the time the Virginia legislators reconvened, they were inundated with petitions and documents espousing staunch opposition to establishing Christianity as Virginia's state religion, some even coming from Christians—especially evangelical Christians.

When Patrick Henry brought his bill to the Virginia legislature to establish Christianity as the state religion, it was soundly defeated. Later, the legislators discussed Thomas Jefferson's "Statute for Religious Freedom," which they modified slightly before passing, making this legislation not only state law but also a model for other states and for the first amendment that guaranteed religious freedom in the United States.

Why wasn't religious freedom guaranteed in the Constitution?

By the time of the Revolutionary War in 1776, four colonies had guaranteed the right of people to worship as they chose: Rhode Island, Pennsylvania, Delaware, and New Jersey. The Church of England remained the established church in other colonies; however, during the war one colony after another ceased providing church support. By the war's end, only Massachusetts, New Hampshire, Connecticut, and Virginia continued to have established churches. In 1786, the new nation was still struggling to function under its first constitution, the Articles of Confederation, when the delegates met in Philadelphia to write the new Constitution. Especially after what had just transpired in Virginia, they did not question nor did they debate the issue of religious freedom.

The delegates did debate other issues, however, such as which civil rights should be granted to those who were not Protestant. New Jersey's constitution stated that every officeholder had to be Protestant, a provision not revised until 1844. Some states required all those seeking public office to recite an oath that they had no allegiance to any foreign power—"ecclesiastic as well as civil" (Myers, 1960, p. 46). Of course, a devout Catholic could not take such an oath, which was the reason it was required. Some states merely demanded that an officeholder be a Christian; Maryland, which eventually permitted Jewish people to settle, stood alone as the only state that allowed Jews to vote and hold public office. Obviously, Jefferson's wall between church and state had yet to be built.

As they wrote the Constitution, the authors affirmed the principle of religious freedom by stating, "No religious Test shall ever be required as a Qualification to any Office or public Trust under the United States" (Article VI). When completed, this was the only reference to religion. To secure consensus for the Constitution, the question of having an established church was left to each state. Because religious freedom was a well-established principle in most states, the authors may have thought there was no need to include such a statement until it became obvious that several amendments would be necessary before enough states would ratify the Constitution. Eck (2001) describes how Jefferson used the "Statute for Religious Freedom" he had written for Virginia's legislature in 1786 when he drafted the First Amendment's explicit guarantee of religious freedom.

Nord (1995) argued that much of the impetus for religious freedom stemmed from the Enlightenment belief that "natural reason, operating in a free culture, was the way to the truth" (p. 108). Most church leaders, especially evangelical Christians, supported the First Amendment for similar reasons. Evangelicals were concerned about separating church and state because they had already been persecuted and harassed. Jefferson's letter espousing a "wall of separation between church and state" was written to Connecticut evangelicals who applauded his comments.

Did the First Amendment establish religious freedom in the new nation?

Although the freedom to worship according to personal religious beliefs was guaranteed in the Bill of Rights, it was guaranteed in principle more than in practice. Of the two states still supporting an established church, Connecticut ended its tax subsidies to the Congregational Church in 1817, and Massachusetts did the same in 1833 (Myers, 1960). Yet having a minority faith could still affect political rights. As the Constitution was being ratified by the 13 states, only three of them—Pennsylvania, Maryland, and Delaware—permitted Catholics to vote. Within five years of the Constitution's ratification, three more states—South Carolina, Georgia, and New York—granted the vote to its Catholic citizens, and eventually the remaining states did the same (Myers, 1960).

All states denied Jewish people the right to hold political office by requiring officeholders to take an oath that they believed in Jesus Christ, but in 1818, a Scottish Presbyterian named Thomas Kennedy introduced a bill to the Maryland legislature to end what he called this prejudice against Jews. Even though Kennedy was defeated in two subsequent elections, he continued to lobby for his bill, and after eight years it was approved, making Maryland the first state to grant full political rights to Jewish people (Niebuhr, 2008). Although their numbers were limited, Jewish people continued to encounter intolerance and a refusal to allow them to have political influence. Their political vulnerability was illustrated during the Civil War when General Ulysses S. Grant expelled Jewish people from areas he had reclaimed by military conquest for the United States; however, President Lincoln rescinded Grant's order (Miller, 1976). North Carolina granted civil rights to Jewish people in 1868; New Hampshire granted Jewish people the right to vote in 1876.

Was any group actively persecuted for their religious beliefs?

Religious freedom was violently denied to the followers of Mormonism, the Church of Jesus Christ of Latter-Day Saints, which was founded on the revelations of Joseph Smith in the early 1800s. After his *Book of Mormon* was published in 1830, Smith found followers captivated by his new vision and his responses to major religious controversies. He aroused animosity among traditional Christian denominations because of his promotion of polygamy and other unconventional ideas. Smith's first church in Ohio was not welcomed, and when the members moved to Missouri, they were attacked and forced to leave, eventually settling in Nauvoo, Illinois. They lived there for only a few years before Smith was arrested and incarcerated at nearby Carthage, where a masked mob broke into his cell and shot and killed him. Miller (1976) declared, "The rise of Mormonism tested the American dedication to religious liberty, and the nation ultimately failed the test" (p. 111).

When Brigham Young was chosen to replace Smith, he was convinced that the Mormons would not be granted religious freedom anywhere in the United States. In 1847, Young and his followers began an ambitious journey of a thousand miles, finally stopping to settle on land that belonged to Mexico. (See Figure 6.2.) One year later, as the Mexican-American War ended, the Great Salt Lake Valley where the Mormons had settled became part of the United States. Because there was no one close enough to persecute the Mormons, they successfully populated the territory of Utah and applied for statehood. Their application was denied six times until 1897, when they changed their state constitution to renounce polygamy (Kosmin & Lachman, 1993).

Religious freedom was also not extended to those who rejected religious beliefs. Atheists in Virginia could be arrested for publicly professing that God did not exist. In 1833, Abner Kneeland was arrested and incarcerated in Massachusetts for questioning the divinity of Jesus, his miracles, and his resurrection. Kneeland was convicted under the state's blasphemy law and sentenced to 60 days in jail; however, his conviction resulted in vigorous protests. Kneeland was the last individual convicted of blasphemy in Massachusetts, although the law was not repealed for many years (Miller, 1976).

Video Example 6.1

In this video, two teachers discuss the genocide of tribal nations in the United States. How does the main speaker relate this genocide to religious ideology and theology? And how does he discuss this within the context of religious freedom?

 Self-Check 6.2 Complete this self-check quiz to check your understanding of the reasons behind the virtual exclusion of religion from the U.S. Constitution and the inclusion of religious freedom in the First Amendment.

The Rise and Fall of Anti-Catholicism and Anti-Semitism: 1800 to 1970

In contrast to the slow but steady growth of members in Protestant churches, membership in the Catholic Church increased dramatically. By 1850, the number of Catholics in the United States had expanded from several hundred thousand to nearly 2 million.

Figure 6.2 Mormon Trail Map

This map documents the route that the Mormons took, leaving the United States and settling in Mexican territory.

Between 1820 and 1865, of the approximately 2 million Irish immigrants to the United States, over a million were Catholic (Kosmin & Lachman, 1993). Because of its assistance to Irish immigrants, the New York City political and labor organization known as Tammany Hall became a powerful force influencing the city and state of New York, which intensified anti-Catholic sentiments.

What was the impact of large numbers of Catholic immigrants?

Immigrants have often provoked hostility in some Americans, but the arrival of so many Catholics fueled Protestant fears. Because the Catholic Church had persecuted, tortured, and even killed those who defied its authority in the past, Protestants believed that Catholics would not hesitate to employ any tactic that would convert Protestants to the Catholic faith. Several popular novels, including *The Awful Disclosures of Maria Monk*, described Protestant women being kidnapped and confined in underground cells in convents and subjected to unspeakable tortures.

Following a fistfight between laborers at a Charlestown, Massachusetts, convent and brickyard workmen, the workmen spread rumors that the convent had imprisoned a woman just as the novels suggested. Although published results of an investigation said there was no truth to the rumor, a mob gathered and set fire to the convent. No police or militia appeared. Ten fire engines responded to the call, but the fire brigades insisted they could not act without orders from a magistrate, so they watched as the convent was destroyed (Myers, 1960).

"We have just enough religion to make us hate, but not enough to make us love one another."
—JONATHAN SWIFT (1667–1745)

Why was hostility directed toward Catholics?

The 1830s and 1840s was the era of Native American and Know-Nothing parties promoting **anti-Catholicism** and anti-immigrant sentiments. The Know-Nothings dedicated themselves to reducing the growth of Catholic power. Anti-Catholic prejudices were reflected in public school textbooks in which priests were depicted as living in luxury, oblivious to the poor, and the Catholic Church was denounced for its history of religious persecution (Miller, 1976). The Catholic Church felt compelled to create an alternative school system, increasing Protestant animosity.

Protestants were not opposed to separate schools for Catholics, but in 1840, Bishop Hughes of New York created controversy when he petitioned the New York Public Schools Society for funds to support Catholic schools. Hughes argued that separate schools for Catholic children had become necessary because of anti-Catholic materials in public schools. Protestants objected to using tax dollars to teach "Catholic dogma" and accused the bishop of trying to undermine public schools. Hughes provided excerpts from textbooks that ridiculed Catholicism (Myers, 1960). Although the New York Public Schools Society denied Hughes's petition for funds, they agreed to remove anti-Catholic content from textbooks and to exclude from school libraries books that clearly promoted anti-Catholic prejudice (Myers, 1960). Although this seemed to solve the problem in New York, growing anti-Catholic sentiment would lead to the shocking events of the Philadelphia Bible Riots.

What were the Philadelphia Bible Riots?

In 1844, the Philadelphia School Board approved the substitution of the Douay (Catholic) Bible for Catholic students when Bible reading was required. An anti-Catholic group called for a meeting in Kensington, an Irish Catholic district in Philadelphia, to protest the use of the Catholic Bible in public schools. The meeting provoked area residents, who attacked participants and forced the meeting to end. The leaders of the anti-Catholic group insisted on a second meeting in Kensington, which resulted in violence that left one individual dead and 50 wounded.

The following day, a large crowd gathered to approve a resolution in support of teaching the Protestant version of the Bible in public schools. The meeting soon became uncontrollable, and when the mob heard shots fired from a nearby building, they set fire to that building and went on a rampage. Troops were called in, but before they could restore order, several homes had burned, eight men were dead, and 16 were wounded. The night was quiet, so the next morning most of the soldiers withdrew.

By mid-afternoon, a Protestant mob gathered once again, setting fire to a Catholic Church and a nearby row of houses whose tenants were Irish. Troops were recalled, but before they arrived, the mob attacked another church. This time the police surrounded the church, but the mob drove them off with bricks and stones and set fire to that church and a Catholic school; then the fire spread to frame houses nearby. The troop commander declared martial law. Property losses from the riots included 45 homes, two churches, and a school. Violence flared again a month later, and by the time the Philadelphia Bible Riots were finally over, 58 people had been killed and 140 wounded. The anti-Catholic group blamed the Irish for the riots (Myers, 1960; Ravitch, 1999).

People settling in frontier areas were initially more receptive to Catholics because of the need to attract more people and establish communities. In the early 1800s, there was a wave of migration to Kentucky, and Louisville was one of the early settlements. Methodists built the first church in 1809; Catholic settlers constructed their church just two years later, and the majority of donations were from members of the Methodist Church. As the number of Catholics increased, they needed a bigger church, and the celebration of the laying of the cornerstone took place in the Presbyterian Church with Protestants representing the majority of those attending the ceremony. Then came the surge of nativism in the 1850s. For the 1855 elections, Louisville newspapers endorsed a slate of anti-immigrant candidates, predicting dire consequences if they were not elected. On the day of the election, mobs assaulted Catholic voters and attacked Catholic property (Niebuhr, 2008). Anti-Catholicism had come to the frontier. Although anti-Catholic sentiment continued to be strong, other issues commanded the nation's attention.

What caused anti-Catholic sentiments in the United States to subside?

Nord (1995) concluded, "The politics of race and the Civil War put the politics of anti-Catholicism to rest" (pp. 73–74). Although the Great Awakening unified Protestant churches, they were split over the slavery issue. During the Civil War, Catholic soldiers fought and died as bravely as the Protestant soldiers beside them, and anti-Catholic sentiments declined. After the war, anti-Catholic prejudice still existed and flared up on occasion, yet it never reached the level that fostered the rise of the Native American and Know-Nothing parties. Another factor in the decline of anti-Catholic prejudice after the Civil War was that the Catholic Church was no longer the only serious opponent for Protestant churches. Religious diversity in the United States was about to increase dramatically.

How did religious diversity increase following the Civil War?

After the Civil War, immigration to the United States surpassed prewar levels. By 1900, there were 75 million Americans, 25 million of whom were foreign-born adults and their children. The number of Roman Catholics in the United States increased from 2 million in 1850 to 4 million in 1870, and to 12 million by 1900. Although Protestants continued to be the dominant group, a third of Americans who claimed church membership in 1920 were members of the Catholic Church (Hudson, 1973).

Catholic immigrants came from Germany, Ireland, Poland, Italy, and Czechoslovakia, and their ethnic diversity created tension within the church. Not only did they speak different languages, but also they had different traditions and customs related to their worship. The church's inability to resolve ethnic differences led to the creation of the Polish National Catholic Church in the 1890s and the Lithuanian National Catholic Church in 1914. Protestant churches faced similar challenges. The majority of Protestant immigrants were Lutherans whose diversity resulted in Finnish, Icelandic, Swedish, Danish, German, and Norwegian Lutheran churches. According to Hudson (1973), there were at least 24 different kinds of Lutheran churches by 1900.

Diversity also resulted from missionaries proselytizing Native Americans and former slaves. Minimal efforts to reach either group had been made prior to the Civil War because both groups had been perceived as heathen. The Great Awakening had generated some enthusiasm for seeking Indian converts, but Native Americans who accepted Christianity usually blended new beliefs with their old ones. Following the Civil War, the federal government banned many tribal religions and provided missionaries with funding to build schools for Native American children. Protestants often established off-reservation boarding schools, whereas Catholics tended to establish boarding schools and day schools on reservations (Hendry, 2003).

After the Civil War, Protestant missionaries actively recruited the 3.5 million newly freed slaves. Former slaves who were Christians no longer wanted to attend the churches their owners had forced them to attend, especially when the church members still expected former slaves to sit in the back seats. Separate churches for freedmen were established, the majority being Baptist with Methodists a distant second. By 1916, 43 percent of Black people were members of a church, a higher percentage than for the White population (Hudson, 1973).

As racial and ethnic groups added to the diversity, so did the creation of new faiths. Mary Baker Eddy responded to the growing importance of scientific research by founding Church of Christ, Scientist. Eddy believed that an Eternal Mind was the source of life and that disease was a consequence of mental error (Lippy, 1994). In 1884, William Miller was abandoned by "Millerites" when his predicted second coming of Christ did not happen. Many of his followers turned to Ellen Harmon White, whose revelations included hygienic practices and dietary restrictions to ensure the return of Jesus. White's followers became Seventh-Day Adventists. Adding to the complexity of diverse faiths in the late nineteenth century was the fact that not all immigrants were Christian.

What non-Christian religions were included among immigrants?

Immigrants to the United States included members of non-Christian religious groups. On the West Coast, Buddhists among Chinese and Japanese immigrants established a Young Men's Buddhist Association in 1898. On the East Coast, 1.5 million Jewish people came to America between 1880 and 1905 to escape anti-Semitism in Russia, Poland, Rumania, and Austro-Hungary. Hudson (1973) cites an adviser to the czar predicting the consequences of new Russian policies: "One-third of the Jews will emigrate, one-third will be baptized, and one-third will starve" (p. 332).

Diversity increased within the Jewish community as well. In 1880, most of the 250,000 Jewish people in the United States were descendants of German-speaking Jews from central Europe affiliated with reform Judaism; Jewish people emigrating later from Eastern Europe were more likely to be orthodox. According to Hudson (1973), more than 3 million Jewish people had immigrated by 1920, with orthodox Jews outnumbering reform Jews. The group larger than the total number of all religious Jewish people combined, were those not affiliated with any synagogue; many of them were Zionists.

America also experienced an increase in people professing no religion. Darwin's theory of evolution and other scientific advances caused many people to question the validity of religious faith. English scientist Thomas Huxley declared himself an **agnostic**, believing that one could neither prove nor disprove the existence of God. Lawyer and orator Robert Ingersoll published *Why I Am an Agnostic* in 1896 and traveled across America questioning many aspects of Christianity. Some scholars reconciled Darwin's ideas with religion by believing in God, not in specific denominational doctrines. The Christian majority reacted by punishing those who strayed from conventional beliefs as well as nonbelievers. In 1878, Alexander Winchell publicly rejected the Genesis version of creation, and Vanderbilt University trustees asked him to resign. When Winchell refused, they abolished his position (Hudson, 1973).

Did increasing numbers of non-Christians cause anti-Catholic prejudice to diminish?

Although racial prejudice became more dominant than religious prejudice after the Civil War, a large Catholic immigration fueled anti-Catholic attitudes. Protestant leaders called for tolerance, yet others said tolerance meant a lack of religious commitment and an indifference to the true faith, and they urged Protestants not to give equal status to any other religion.

Forced to disband by federal troops during Reconstruction, the Ku Klux Klan was revived in 1915. In their efforts to promote and maintain Caucasian supremacy in the United States, the Klan employed tactics of intimidation including threats and violence. Although their primary targets were Black people and foreigners, as a Christian group, its members were also hostile to Catholics and Jews. Membership in the Klan increased every year for 10 years, peaking at 2 million in 1925. (See Figure 6.3.) It fell to 100,000 by 1928 (Myers, 1960). The last time the Klan's anti-Catholicism would be seen on the national stage was in the 1928 presidential election of 1928.

> "A believer is a bird in a cage; a freethinker is an eagle parting the clouds with tireless wing."
> —ROBERT INGERSOLL (1833–1899)

Figure 6.3 The Klan on the March

The Ku Klux Klan had its highest membership when the group sponsored this 1925 march in front of the nation's capitol.

SOURCE: Library of Congress, Prints and Photographs Division [LC-DIG-npcc-16225].

How did the 1928 election demonstrate anti-Catholic prejudice?

The Democratic Party nominated Alfred E. Smith, the first Catholic to run for President. Some political and religious leaders hailed the nomination as evidence of growing religious tolerance; others saw it as a threat to the social order. The Klan and other anti-Catholic organizations insisted that the Vatican was directing Smith's campaign with a Jesuit committee assigned to persuade Protestants to ignore Smith's religion as an issue. Methodists were urged to vote for the man who prayed the same way they did. Myers (1960) quoted an excerpt from an anti-Catholic magazine claiming that Smith would get not only the Catholic vote but also "the Jew and Negro vote . . . gamblers, the red-light and dope-ring vote . . . the Jew-Jesuit movie gang (vote) who want sex films and Sunday shows to coin millions through the corruption of youth" (p. 268).

Although anti-Catholic prejudice contributed to Smith's defeat, it is not clear how large a role it played. Democrats were the minority party, the economy was doing well, and Republican candidate Herbert Hoover was widely respected. Despite the anti-Catholic assault, Smith received 40 percent of the vote, more than the Protestant Democratic candidates had received in the two previous elections (34 percent in 1920; 28 percent in 1924). Smith had a higher percentage of votes than a majority of Democrats running for Congress in that election (Hudson, 1973).

After Franklin Roosevelt was elected president in 1932, Catholic participation in national politics became common, and the question of whether a Catholic could be elected president was answered in 1960 when Americans chose John F. Kennedy. It is possible that Kennedy's election was not so much a measure of increased religious tolerance as it was an indication of what has been called the "Americanization of religion." Since World War II, attitudes of American Catholics gradually diverged from a strict recognition of Roman Catholic Church doctrine and became more closely allied with attitudes of the Protestant majority. By the 1990s, polls documented Catholic attitudes as being similar to Protestant attitudes on such issues as abortion, birth control, ordination of women, and marriage of priests (Kosmin & Lachman, 1993). Despite the decline of anti-Catholic attitudes, anti-Semitic attitudes continued to flourish, with prejudices stemming not only from their religion but also from the perception of Jewish people as a separate race.

Why were Jewish people regarded as a separate race?

In 1451, the King of Castile (Spain) endorsed a blood purity statute declaring that Jewish converts could not hold office in the Catholic Church. This statute transformed the perception of Jewish people to a racial rather than a religious group. In the 1870s, American public school textbooks referred to Jews as "a race," using traditional stereotypes of Jewish people as greedy, selfish, and manipulating. Jewish people were described as unethical entrepreneurs who tried to monopolize certain professions and as the devious power behind the throne in many European countries (Miller, 1976). In 1879, the term **anti-Semitism** was employed for the first time by a German journalist to express his opposition to the Jewish "race." In his essay, Wilhelm Marr made the paradoxical argument that although Jewish people were inferior to Aryans, they were a threat to Aryan world dominance (Carroll, 2001). Reacting against such stereotypes, one Jewish writer complained, "In the popular mind, the Jew is never judged as an individual, but as a specimen of a whole race whose members are identically of the same kind" (Eck, 2001, p. 303). All of this anti-Semitism culminated in the Holocaust where the Nazis even arrested Jewish people who had converted to Christianity because "once born a Jew, always a Jew" (Wegner, 2002, p. 152).

From 1890 to 1914, Jewish people accounted for 10 percent of all immigrants. With increased numbers of Jews in America, anti-Semitism was at least as strong as earlier anti-Catholicism. Ironically, despite their experience of oppression, Catholics joined Protestants in vilifying Jewish people. In the popular press, Eck (2001) found Jewish people

"Anti-Semitism is a noxious weed that should be cut out. It has no place in America."

—WILLIAM HOWARD TAFT (1857–1930)

presented as undesirable aliens who could not assimilate because they were "incapable of grasping American ideals" (p. 50), although many Jewish people refuted the view by achieving extraordinary success, especially in higher education. As the number of Jewish people at Harvard escalated from 6 percent in 1908 to 22 percent in 1922, the president of Harvard proposed establishing a quota for the number of Jewish people Harvard would accept. Faculty rejected his plan, but Harvard still limited the number of Jewish people for many decades. Other colleges established quotas for Jewish enrollment at anywhere from 3 percent to 16 percent (Dinnerstein, 1994).

In what ways was anti-Semitism promoted?

Anti-Semitism had several popular advocates. In the 1920s, one was Henry Ford. In his role as publisher of a weekly newspaper, *The Dearborn Independent*, Ford printed the text of "The Protocols of the Elders of Zion," which documented the activities of a Jewish conspiracy plotting a revolution to undermine Christian civilization and establish Jewish supremacy throughout the world. Ford's popularity made it likely that his readers would take his warning seriously. In a poll taken in 1923, *Collier's* magazine reported that 260,000 people—over a third of those polled—endorsed Ford to run for president (Ribuffo, 1997).

Shortly after Ford published "Protocols," the document was exposed as a forgery concocted in the late 1890s by Russian loyalists supporting the czar. In response to this revelation and to a legal action for slander brought by a Jewish businessman, Ford wrote a letter of apology, promising not to publish anti-Semitic articles again, but the damage had been done. Ford ceased publishing his newspaper, yet he continued to maintain and express anti-Semitic attitudes. In 1938, Ford traveled to Germany to receive a medal from Adolf Hitler in honor of his anti-Semitic actions, and two years later in England during an interview with the *Manchester Guardian*, Ford insisted that "international Jewish bankers" caused World War II (Ribuffo, 1997).

In the 1930s, President Franklin Roosevelt invited many Jewish people into his cabinet, and over vigorous objections, he appointed Felix Frankfurter, a Jew, to the Supreme Court. However, anti-Semitism found a spokesman in a priest named Charles Edward Coughlin. In his popular radio show, Father Coughlin attacked President Roosevelt, communists, and Jewish people. Although reprimanded for his attacks on the president, Coughlin was not criticized by church superiors for his anti-Semitism because he disguised it in anti-communist rhetoric (Myers, 1960).

In 1938, Coughlin revealed his anti-Semitic attitudes by reprinting "The Protocols of the Elders of Zion" despite the evidence of its forgery. Nineteen thousand people attended a gathering in Madison Square Garden where Coughlin gave a speech, surrounded by banners declaring "Smash Jewish Communism!" and "Stop Jewish Domination of Christian America!" Coughlin's use of rumor and distortions of fact to castigate Jewish people was challenged by Jewish groups, denounced by many Protestants, and contradicted by his embarrassed superiors in the church. He was forced to abandon his radio program in 1940, but for the next three years, young men belonging to his "Christian Frontier" organization roamed the streets in several large cities, affixing obscene materials to Jewish businesses or synagogues and even assaulting Jewish people they chanced to encounter (Myers, 1960). Anti-Semitism intensified during World War II. According to one poll, over half of Jewish soldiers in the armed forces had changed their names to generic American surnames to avoid anti-Semitic remarks from other soldiers. By the end of the war, 58 percent of Americans agreed with the statement, "Jews have too much power in the United States" (Dinnerstein, 1994, p. 146).

What influence did the Holocaust have on American attitudes?

Learning about the horrors of the Holocaust changed American attitudes toward Jewish people after World War II. Many returning veterans deplored anti-Semitism and other prejudices they had witnessed. In 1945, Bess Meyerson became the first Jewish woman to be crowned Miss America, despite her refusal to change her Jewish-sounding name (Painter, 2010). Hollywood produced films addressing anti-Semitism in America, and one of them, *Gentleman's Agreement*, won the Oscar for best picture in 1947. Editorials in many newspapers and magazine articles reinforced the idea that anti-Semitism was no longer acceptable. Although it was in the 1950s that "under God" was added to the Pledge of Allegiance and "In God We Trust" to U.S. currency to emphasize U.S. opposition to "godless communism," being Catholic, Protestant, or Jewish was less important than someone believing in the Judeo-Christian God (Fraser, 1999).

> "[The Jew] always talks about the equality of all men, without regard of race or color. Those who are stupid begin to believe that."
>
> —ADOLF HITLER (1889–1945)

In his analysis of religion in America, *Protestant-Catholic-Jew*, sociologist Will Herberg (1955) wrote that Catholics and Jewish people reflected American attitudes as much as Protestants did. An "Americanization" of religion meant that each faith "regards itself as merely an alternative and variant form of being religious in the American way" (p. 278). Herberg said the majority of Americans were still anti-Semitic, but they knew it was inappropriate to act on their feelings. Despite his advocacy for Jewish people, Herberg did not include Black Protestants among American Christians, and in a 1965 article, he accused the civil rights movement of demagoguery that undermined the essential order of society (Painter, 2010). A series of polls in the 1950s reported Americans expressing increasingly positive attitudes toward Jewish people. By 1965, *Time* magazine reported that "anti-Semitism is at an all time low," and that overt expressions of anti-Semitism were "out of fashion" (Dinnerstein, 1994, p. 171). In 2015, the Anti-Defamation League reported a dramatic increase in anti-Semitic incidents in the United States (Markoe, 2015). The 2017 ADL report found a 60% increase in anti-Semitic incidents, the biggest increase since the 1970s when the ADL began collecting such information. In a time of increased polarization and more blatant expressions of racism and xenophobia, some experts view this as part of an overall trend of incivility and intolerance, while others fear that American Jews and Jewish institutions will be increasingly targeted for attacks. This perspective was unfortunately reinforced by the 2018 shooting at a Pittsburgh synagogue. Forms of religious bigotry are still pervasive on the Internet, especially web sites with anti-Jewish and/or anti-Muslim content. This will necessitate continued monitoring by groups like the ADL.

 Self-Check 6.3 Complete this self-check quiz to check your understanding of religious intolerance in the United States as reflected in anti-Catholic and anti-Semitic attitudes from the colonial period to the twentieth century.

Immigration and Increasing Religious Diversity Creating New Issues for Religious Freedom

The 1924 U.S. immigration law had prohibited Asian immigration, and strict quotas ensured that the majority of American immigrants would be White and Christian. When President Lyndon Johnson signed the Immigration and Nationality Act of 1965, not only did the racial makeup of incoming immigrants change dramatically but so did their religious affiliation. From 1960 to 1990, of 15 million immigrants, more than 5 million were Asian, and according to the Pew Research Center (2012), there are now 18.2 million Asian Americans, almost 6 percent of the total population. They increased the religious diversity within and outside of Christianity; among them were 4 million Buddhists and enough Korean Christians to form 2000 congregations. Jainists have established 60 temples and centers, Sikhs have almost 250 gurdwaras, and more than a million Hindus have established 700 temples (Gaustad & Schmidt, 2002; Niebuhr, 2008). From 1992 to 2012, immigrants to the United States included 1.7 million Muslims, almost a million Hindus, and almost a million Buddhists (Pew Research Center, 2013). There are increasing numbers of children from diverse faiths: As the twenty-first century began, about 20 percent of students attending public school in the United States identified as "religious minorities" (Clark et al., 2002).

Although proportions of those representing different religions in the United States have changed, what has not changed is the importance of religion. According to a 2014 study, more than 90 percent of Americans believed in God and as many as 69 percent claimed to attend church regularly or at least occasionally, although some critics challenge this finding (Paulson, 2014). To appreciate this variety of faiths, Americans must confront stereotypes. We often make assumptions about an individual's religion based on ethnicity, but there is diversity within any religion. An old stereotype is that Irish Americans are Catholic, but the majority of them are not. For more than two decades, scholars have reported that most Asian Americans are not Buddhist or Hindu but Christian, as are most Arab Americans, and most American Muslims are not Arabs (Kosmin & Lachman, 1993; Pew Research Center, 2012). In fact, Islam is a global faith with over 60 nationalities, which affects the way they practice their faith as described in a study of diverse cultural groups among American Muslims (El-Atwani, 2015).

How have Americans responded to the increasing religious diversity?

Unfortunately, recent immigrants continue to encounter prejudice as Americans have persisted in their past religious animosities and have reverted to learned stereotypes. Muslim Americans have received the brunt of these negative reactions, in part because they are one of the fastest growing religious groups in America. Although some studies claim the number of Muslims already exceeds the number of Jewish people, a 2015 Pew Research study disputes that claim but predicts that the number of American Muslims will surpass American Jews by 2050 (Lipka, 2015). Despite these numbers, many Americans have little contact with Muslims and have negative stereotypes of them, including the perception that many of them are terrorists. Barrett (2007) reported that 75 percent of Muslims have personally experienced or know someone who has encountered anti-Muslim behavior.

According to data collected since 9/11 concerning acts of terrorism, Muslim terrorists have been responsible for 45 deaths in the United States, but White supremacists and other anti-government radicals have caused 48 deaths (Associated Press, 2015). In 2017 alone, 34 people were victims of domestic terrorism and white supremacists murdered 18 of them. (Dupuy, 2018). Since 9/11, Americans have murdered over 150,000 of their fellow citizens, which means that 0.02 percent of American homicides are the result of Muslim terrorists (Rendall & McCloskey, 2013). Instead of fearing a terrorist attack, this data would suggest that Americans would be safer if they lobbied Congress to pass stricter gun safety laws. And yet the stereotype that American Muslims are terrorists persists, and many Muslims argue that American media plays a role in perpetuating the terrorist stereotype. According to a University of Illinois study, from 2008 to 2012 Muslims represented only 6 percent of the people that the FBI suspected of engaging in terrorism, but during that same four-year time period, Muslims accounted for 81 percent of FBI terrorism suspects identified in television news coverage (Naureckas, 2015).

Media accounts of Muslim violence overseas such as the attack on Benghazi and other American embassies in Muslim countries often describe the attackers as mainstream Muslim believers. The fact that "the cumulative total of protesters so far in about 30 countries" is well under 100,000 out of a world population of 1.6 billion Muslims calls into question the claim that those involved are average Muslims. In addition, anti-American violence in Muslim nations pales in comparison to the violence inflicted on Arabs and Muslims by the United States during the 10-year time period from 2002 to 2012. Further, Cole has analyzed deaths caused by wars in the twentieth century and reported that less than 2 percent of these deaths can be attributed to nations having a majority of Muslims (Rendall & McCloskey, 2013). In addition to the hundreds of thousands killed in the wars in Iraq and Afghanistan, the United States has killed

Video Example 6.2
In this video, Farah Pandith, the first U.S. Special Representative to Muslim communities for the United States Department of State, discusses why Americans value religious diversity and pluralism. Thinking back to Chapter 1 and the discussion of the common disconnect between American values and behavior, what incidents discussed in this chapter or that you know of from contemporary society exhibit this disconnect?

https://www.youtube.com/watch?v=Iemw8vqt-54

thousands of civilians as a consequence of air strikes and missiles fired at countries such as Pakistan, Libya, Yemen, and Somalia and from increased use of drones. Some of the protests in Muslim nations have been against the violence that the United States has used against their people.

American Muslims want to be perceived simply as mainstream believers who embrace many traditional American values rather than being associated with radicals or extremists, and there is evidence to support their assertion. In a recent survey that included a question asking if there was an acceptable justification for an individual or a small group of people to target and kill civilians—89 percent of Muslim Americans said that such killings could never be justified; this percentage was the highest of any of the American religious groups surveyed. In addition, a majority of American Christians (both Catholic and Protestant) and American Jews said it was acceptable for the military to kill civilians during wartime, but a majority of Muslim Americans disapproved of such killings (Rendall & McCloskey, 2013). According to a study by the Gallup Center for Muslim Studies, over 90 percent of Arabs and Muslims support the constitutional concept of free speech and the right to engage in protests as long as they are nonviolent (Rendall, 2012). Following the 1995 bombing of the Murrah Federal Building in Oklahoma City, many television broadcasts suggested that it was a terrorist attack and that authorities were pursuing "Middle Eastern-looking" men. In the aftermath of these news reports, Islamic centers across the nation became targets of drive-by shootings and bomb threats. Muslim parents kept their children home for fear they would be taunted or even assaulted in school.

What the media did not report was the presence of Muslim firefighters rescuing victims of the bombing, Muslim physicians working to save victims' lives, and individual Muslims and Muslim organizations donating money to help the families of the victims. Yet Muslims were denied an opportunity to participate in the nationally televised memorial service featuring speeches by President Clinton and representatives of Catholic, Jewish, and Protestant faiths.

Abdo (2006) has argued that: "television news programs (portray) Muslims as the new enemy of the West" (p. 5). Other American Muslims have accused the news media of including misinformation in their coverage that promotes anti-Muslim prejudices. For example, some American politicians have described Islamic "Sharia Law" as a threat to our legal traditions in the United States, but Berlet (2012) called this "a bigoted falsehood" (p. 14). Yet at least seven states have passed laws banning the imposition of Islamic Sharia law on the American judicial system. Legal scholars say such laws reflect unfounded fears and are completely unnecessary, but this has not been clearly addressed in media coverage (Potok, 2015). Historically, news media has been charged to hold people in leadership positions accountable for any claims they make by fact checking and finding credible sources concerning the issue. Imagine a newspaper headline saying: "Some Experts Say Nazi Genocide a Hoax; Others Disagree." Instead, we have seen journalists confront Holocaust deniers and challenge them for making false statements They should do the same with lies coming from any source. Berlet (2012) addressed this issue of media responsibility: "When . . . should we call a blatantly false statement false? Isn't the ethical answer 'always?'" (p. 14).

Because there is widespread acceptance of stereotypes for American Muslims, it is not surprising that anti-Muslim activity increased after the destruction of New York City's World Trade Center on 9/11, 2001. Over 8000 Muslim Americans and Arab Americans were interrogated, and within weeks approximately 1200 were incarcerated. This action was called a "preventive detention"; the prisoners were held without charges, denied the opportunity to post a bond, and not allowed any contact with their families (Abdo, 2006). Two months later, 600 were still in custody, yet the FBI eventually admitted there was no evidence linking any of the incarcerated people to terrorism. Of the 82,000 Muslim immigrants who were fingerprinted and interrogated under the Patriot Act, there was only enough evidence found to declare 11 of them as "suspected" terrorists (Lee, 2004). Such actions caused McCloud (2006) to claim that no other religion has been treated in such fashion in the history of America.

According to Nimer (2004), in the 30 days following 9/11, Muslims filed 1700 complaints of harassment and hate crimes. In Tennessee, citizens of Murfreesboro protested the construction of a mosque in their community, and an arsonist damaged construction equipment at the site. In New York, a teenager fired a shotgun at a mosque, and several teenagers assaulted a Muslim worshipper. Graffiti has been painted on many mosques (see Figure 6.4), and in Texas, vandals started a fire that destroyed the mosque's playground equipment. Mosques were vandalized in Tallahassee, Cleveland, and Seattle. In Florida, a pipe bomb exploded in a Jacksonville mosque, injuring 60 people. Even Buddhist and Hindu temples were vandalized in Boston, Houston, and Detroit. An Egyptian businessman who had resided in the United States for 20 years was shot and killed in his California store. He was a Christian (Intelligence Report, 2010).

American anti-Muslim attitudes and behavior have continued. A 2015 study found 27 percent of Americans believing that the actions of the terrorist group ISIS reflected the true nature of the Islamic faith; even more discouraging was that this group included 45 percent of participants who identified as "senior Protestant pastors." Further, a 2015 poll reported that over half of Americans believed Muslims were more likely than other world faiths to encourage the use of violence to achieve their goals (Potok, 2015). Yet in response to a question about terrorist violence in a Pew Research survey, 75 percent of Muslims from diverse nations such as Nigeria, Indonesia and Pakistan said suicide bombings and other acts targeting civilians cannot be morally justified (Fasciano, 2015). Perhaps because Americans continue to associate American Muslims with violence, many of them are engaging in verbal and physical abuse against Muslims. In Long Island, New York, bystanders heard a White man shouting Osama just before driving his pickup truck into a Sikh man whom he mistakenly thought was a Muslim. In Dallas, two men shot an Iraqi immigrant who was simply out walking with his family; the FBI investigated the incident as a possible hate crime. In Florida, a teacher was reported

Figure 6.4 Mosque Graffiti

An American Muslim walks in front of a mosque that has been defaced by graffiti linking its worshippers with the terrorist Osama Bin Laden.

SOURCE: Photograph by Gregory Rec, courtesy of the *Portland Press Herald*.

to have called a student a "rag-head Taliban." In Iowa, an Ames mosque received an anonymous letter containing anti-Muslim slurs and threats (Potok, 2015). In one poll of Muslims, 22 percent said they had encountered racial slurs (Chalabi, 2015).

These negative attitudes and behaviors have even invaded American schools. In California, a survey of Muslim-American youth found that nearly half of them had been bullied in school because of their faith; the actions ranged from women having their hijabs pulled off their heads to accusing students or their families of being terrorists. In Brooklyn, a 15-year-old Muslim student wrote a report for her class on global issues concerning the violence of Boko Haran in Nigeria. In response, a student asked why all Muslims were terrorists, and she was intimidated into silence when it became clear that the other students shared the questioner's belief. A study found that two-thirds of Sikh students who wore turbans to school also encountered bullying behavior, and in Atlanta a Sikh youth was attacked so viciously he had a broken nose and a swollen jaw and had to undergo two surgeries (Fasciano, 2015).

By contrast, most Americans reject bigotry against Muslims. Since 9/11, neighbors, churches, and community groups have offered support to American Muslims. In Seattle, an ecumenical group created a program called "Watchful Eyes" to prevent or minimize anti-Muslim violence. In Denver, volunteers stood with linked arms in a circle around a mosque to create a "ring of protection." In other cities, Christians and Jewish people cleaned graffiti sprayed on to mosques and some purchased new items to replace ones that vandals had damaged (Niebuhr, 2008). Despite these activities, Muslims continue to be victims of prejudice and violence.

A Gallup Poll (2010) found that 43 percent of Americans admitted to feeling at least "a little" prejudiced against Muslims compared to only 15 percent who admitted prejudice against Jewish people. This negative attitude is illustrated in a 2017 study reporting that from 2014–2016, incidents stemming from a religious bias (e.g., verbal abuse) increased by 70 percent, and hate crimes (e.g., physical violence) increased by almost 600 percent. In response to such negative attitudes and behaviors, American Muslims have tried to emphasize that Islam is a religion of peace. Over 150 Muslim scholars signed an "Open Letter" to ISIS leader Al-Baghdadi that included passages from the Quran to refute and denounce religious beliefs that terrorist groups have asserted to justify their use of violence (Fasciano, 2015). Specifically, American Arab and Muslim organizations have denounced the violent activities of ISIS, especially the beheading of hostages (Hanania, 2014), but American media has rarely reported these proclamations. In addition, American Muslims have interacted with people from other faiths to clarify their beliefs and practices. In one survey, 63 percent of all mosques in the United States indicated that they had hosted an open house during the previous year where non-Muslim community members were invited to come for a tour, a meal, or a presentation on Islam. Further, 79 percent of these mosques had been involved in an interfaith program with people from one or more different faiths (Bagby, 2012). In support of our religious freedom in America, some organizations have engaged in activities to support religious diversity. Administrators of the Mall of America in Minneapolis, the nation's largest enclosed shopping facility, created an interfaith group called the Mall Area Religious Council to promote dialogue between people of different faiths. Harvard has established the Pluralism Project to engage students in the study of religious diversity.

In politics there have been some efforts to be inclusive of diverse faiths. Since 1991, Muslim and Hindu chaplains have joined Protestant, Catholic, and Jewish chaplains to provide invocations at opening sessions of Congress. In the 115th Congress, religious diversity is illustrated by 30 Jewish members (22 in the House, 8 in the Senate), 3 Buddhist members (2 in the House, 1 in the Senate), and 2 Muslims and 3 Hindus in the House (Manning, 2017). But politics has also stirred up religious controversy. In 1990, the U.S. Supreme Court heard the case of two American Indian counselors denied unemployment compensation after being fired by their employer for taking an illegal hallucinogenic drug, peyote. Both counselors were members of the Native American

"The First Amendment has erected a wall between church and state. That wall must be kept high and impregnable."

—JUSTICE HUGO BLACK (1886–1971)

Church, which uses peyote in its ceremonies, but the lower court ruling was that being an illegal drug took precedence over religious practice. In response, Congress passed a Religious Freedom Restoration Act (RFRA), which stated that federal laws, rules, or regulations could not substantially burden an individual's free exercise of religion unless there was proof of a "compelling interest." The law was intended to strengthen federal protection of minority faiths (Lindberg, 2015). In recent years, RFRA laws have been passed by various state legislatures, but the intent has been altered dramatically. Following U.S. Supreme Court rulings affirming civil rights for gay people and lesbians, especially the right to marry, these new RFRA laws allow Christians to deny civil rights to sexual minorities. A Columbia law professor stated: "They are being written . . . and used by people who are actually already members of a majority religion, and who actually want other people to have to follow their religion" (Lindberg, 2015, 39).

During the 2016 presidential campaign, Muslims accused Donald Trump of promoting anti-Muslim stereotypes numerous times. On January 27, 2017, President Trump kept a campaign promise by issuing a Muslim travel ban, and in response American Muslims and their supporters flocked to airports around the nation to demonstrate against it. On March 8, a federal court in Seattle issued an injunction against enforcing the policy. Trump reissued the executive order after removing U.S. ally Iraq from the list of seven countries covered by the ban, exempting people with visas or green cards and eliminating the special treatment accorded to Christian refugees. On March 15, a federal judge in Hawaii issued a nationwide order blocking the travel ban, followed by a federal judge in Maryland. Both judges alluded to Trump's anti-Muslim rhetoric during the presidential campaign as providing a legitimate basis for challenging this executive order on the grounds of religious discrimination (Burns, 2017).

A panel of 13 judges representing the Fourth Circuit Court of Appeals did not rule on the travel ban but met to review a lower court's injunction to keep the executive order from being enforced. Trump's revised executive order mandated a ban against travelers from six majority Muslim nations, including a temporary ban on acceptance of refugees. On May 25, by a vote of 10 to 3, the judges upheld a lower court's ruling preventing the ban from being implemented. The chief judge was quite explicit in his ruling that the travel ban "drips with religious intolerance, animus and discrimination". The ruling noted that White House claims for national security was not a "silver bullet" always taking precedence over other consideration (Domonoske, 2017). In June of 2018, the U. S. Supreme Court ruled that the Trump Administration's third version of a travel ban was constitutional. Chief Justice Roberts acknowledged President Trump's incendiary public comments, but argued that the Constitution gives the President broad powers to restrict entry into the United States for national security issues. In a scathing dissent, Justice Sonia Sotomayor argued that the travel ban "masquerades behind a façade of national security concerns" and read numerous examples of the President's anti-Muslim comments, saying they clearly reflected "hostility and animus toward the Muslim faith." Opponents of the travel ban have vowed to continue exploring legal options for challenging this policy.

How have K–12 schools taught students about the concept of religious freedom?

The history of American education reveals a gradual secularization of public schools. Public schools in the United States originally did not teach about religious freedom; they reinforced Protestant beliefs, causing Catholics and Jewish people to establish schools for their children in addition to or instead of public schools. History credits Horace Mann with shaping public schools in the United States, yet he was denounced as the "archenemy of the Christian church" for advocating that the Bible should be read—but not interpreted—in school because biblical interpretation should be a parental prerogative (McMillan, 1984, p. 85). When Bible reading was eliminated, *McGuffey's Reader* became the most popular public school textbook. It referred to God and used Protestant perspectives to deliver its moral lessons. Later revisions of *McGuffey* eliminated overt religious language but maintained a sermonizing tone. By 1870, most Protestants agreed that a sectarian religious perspective should not be presented in public schools but felt that a nonsectarian Christian perspective was essential (Nord, 1995).

Starting in the 1940s, U.S. federal courts wrote several decisions related to the constitutional guarantee of religious freedom being enforced or contradicted in schools (see Table 6.1). The next 60 years of court rulings would challenge schools to eliminate their Christian bias and become more **secular**, reflecting the civic culture and not promoting any religious perspective. U.S. courts have ruled that schools are forbidden to force students to say the Pledge of Allegiance; compel students to pray; begin the day with devotional reading from the Bible; have a minister, priest, or rabbi give a prayer at graduation; post the Ten Commandments in classrooms or hallways; or teach religion disguised as science—"creationism"—as a scientific alternative to evolutionary theory (Allen, 1996; Fraser, 1999; McMillan, 1984). Yet despite the consistent court rulings against teaching creationism as science, a research study has found that in nine states and the District of Columbia, over 300 private schools that accept public vouchers are teaching creationism in their science classes. The issue of vouchers has come before the courts, and although Louisiana's voucher system was declared unconstitutional, the Supreme Court upheld Ohio's voucher program (Goodavage, 2013).

In 2002, the Ninth Circuit court created a controversy in *Newdow v. United States Congress* by ruling that the inclusion of the phrase "under God" meant the Pledge of Allegiance served a religious, not a secular, purpose. The court concluded that schools could not have students recite the pledge even if they are allowed to choose to not

Table 6.1 Court Rulings on Religion in Public Schools

A selection of significant cases:	
1943	*West Virginia v. Barnette* (brought by a Jehovah's Witness family): No child can be forced to recite the Pledge of Allegiance.
1947	*Everson v. Board of Education:* Students attending parochial schools to be transported to their schools on buses provided for public school students.
1962	*Engel v. Vitale:* Students attending public schools could not be forced to recite state-written prayers.
1963	*Abington Township v. Schempp:* Public schools could not insist that students recite the Lord's prayer or any prayer nor require "devotional Bible reading."
1968	*Epperson v. Arkansas:* An Arkansas law forbidding the teaching of Darwin's theory of evolution in school was ruled unconstitutional.
1971	*Lemon v. Kurtzman:* Established that the separation of church and state principle was not violated if the statute, policy, or practice under consideration: (1) had a secular legislative purpose; (2) did not foster excessive government entanglement with religion; or (3) neither advanced nor inhibited religion as its primary purpose.
1980	*Stone v. Graham:* A Kentucky law requiring a copy of the Ten Commandments posted in every public school classroom was declared unconstitutional.
1985	*Wallace v. Jaffree:* Since the intent of an Alabama law requiring a moment of silence was "to return prayer to the public schools," it was unconstitutional.
1987	*Edwards v. Aguillard:* Schools could not teach creationism as an alternative to evolutionary theory because creationism was based on religious beliefs and did not satisfy the criteria to constitute a scientific theory.
1990	*Westside Community Schools v. Mergens:* If a public school allows community groups to use its facilities, religious groups must have equal access.
1992	*Lee v. Weisman:* Schools could not include prayers offered by religious leaders (of any faith) at graduation ceremonies; if a school policy or practice has a coercive effect, it is unconstitutional.
2000	*Santa Fe School Independent School District v. Doe:* Student-led prayers at football games violated separation of church and state.

SOURCE: *The Religious History of America: The Heart of the American Story from Colonial Times to Today* by E. Gaustad and L. Schmidt, 2002.

participate because the school setting is a coercive context that puts pressure on students to conform to the majority (Pauken, 2003).

How can public schools teach about religion in a way that respects all religions?

As federal and district courts ruled on what schools could not allow, they also provided guidelines for constitutional activities. Schools were encouraged to teach objectively about all religions and even about the Bible. As Justice Clark wrote,

> It might well be said that one's education is not complete without a study of comparative religion or the history of religion and its relationship to the advancement of civilization. It certainly may be said that the Bible is worthy of study for its literary and historic qualities. (McMillan, 1984, p. 163)

Although schools cannot force students to pray, they cannot prevent a student from praying, as long as the prayer does not create a disruption. If students representing a religious group want to use school facilities, they have the same right of access as any community group.

Another action that schools can take is to permit the formation of a Secular Student Alliance (SSA). These groups are intended as a safe place for students who are atheists or agnostics or who have more questions than answers when it comes to religion. In the past, nonreligious students were not open about their beliefs for fear of being harassed or bullied, and this has happened to students who openly admitted a lack of faith. A Pew Research survey reported that Americans felt more antagonistic to atheists than to immigrants, Jewish people, Muslims, or lesbians and gay men (Lim, 2011). Youthful nonbelievers have encountered hostility not only from students at school but also sometimes from family members. In addition, some schools have refused to allow students to establish SSA groups, in violation of the 1984 law that requires schools receiving federal funds to allow the formation of such a group if the school sponsors other student groups. Ironically, this law was the result of intense lobbying by conservative Christians to ensure that schools would have to allow their children to form student groups. Many schools are already providing support for student nonbelievers. By 2012, the Secular School Alliance reported that they had established about 365 affiliates, more than double the number in 2009. At SSA meetings, students discuss issues related to religion, but they also discuss politics and current events, and many have fundraising events for charities. More importantly, such student groups provide an affirmation of religious freedom by reminding students that faith is a choice and not an obligation, and all choices should be respected.

In 1999, the U.S. Department of Education sent comprehensive guidelines on issues related to religion in public schools to every public school in the nation. A committee of diverse religious and educational leaders had developed the guidelines that include legal assurances for recommended practices (al-Hibri, 2001). Teaching about religions has now been incorporated into national and state standards for teachers (American Academy of Religion, 2010; Douglass, 2002); following the guidelines will ensure that schools address those standards by providing accurate information about fundamental beliefs of the world's major religions.

Finally, Aronson and Amatullah (2016) offer a compelling argument for teaching about religion in public schools. The say the three primary reasons are: (1) widespread lack of knowledge about world religions among Americans, (2) prejudice stemming from this lack of knowledge creates difficulty in promoting respect for diverse faiths, and (3) teaching about world religions diminishes ignorance and promotes acceptance of religious diversity. Those educators who don't feel they know enough to teach about world religions should be reminded that if they don't provide students with accurate information, there are numerous websites on the Internet for students to access that

Video Example 6.3
In this video, two teenage girls perform for a Brave New Voices, Youth Speaks event. Think about the role that religious stereotypes play in society and their performance. What kinds of responses to religious diversity do you hear them speak about, and how do they relate to those discussed in this chapter?

https://www.youtube.com/watch?v=tv00xjClbx0&t=

Application Exercise 6.1

In this video, a teacher is interviewed about one of the school's students, Harjar, who is a practicing Muslim. Pay attention to the story of Harjar's arrival at the school and how this teacher responds to her family. Review the video and complete the activity.

promote negative attitudes and stereotypes regarding diverse faiths. Without intervention to disrupt inaccurate portrayals, students from diverse faiths will continue to be marginalized and will be more likely to encounter discrimination. Many religious organizations also have websites and offer accurate information and resources to interested teachers. One change that should promote more instruction on religions is for teacher preparation programs to include instruction on diverse world religions and provide opportunities for pre-service teachers to incorporate religious content into their lessons. These programs should also challenge students to discuss Christian privilege with the goal of promoting a deeper understanding of the role of religion in America and a greater acceptance of diverse faiths (Aronson & Amatullah, 2016).

 Self-Check 6.4 Complete this self-check quiz to check your understanding of how increased religious diversity resulted from immigration reform and how this diversity presents new challenges to the principle of religious freedom.

Afterword

Although historically the Protestant majority in the United States vigorously, at times violently, resisted accepting other faiths, Protestants of all denominations accepted each other on equal terms and eventually accepted Catholics and Jewish people. Will the faiths of new immigrants—Islam, Hinduism, Buddhism, and other non-Christian religions—become acceptable to the dominant Judeo-Christian groups in America? Further, will Americans accept the fastest growing group among all the diverse faiths? Whether they call themselves agnostics, atheists, or they simply have no interest in religion, the number of Americans not affiliated with any specific religious faith continues to increase, reaching its highest level so far of 56 million people, or almost 25 percent of the U.S. population. According to a 2015 Pew Research Report, there are now more unaffiliated Americans than there are Catholics and mainline Protestants combined. Demographers predict that in another decade or so, the largest "religion" in the United States as determined by the box people check on the Census Bureau surveys may be "None" (Schrobsdorff, 2016). As the religious landscape continues to change, schools will have an important role to play.

In the past, public schools promoted Protestantism and reinforced anti-Catholic and anti-Semitic attitudes. As schools became more secular, they contributed to the acceptance now commonly seen among Protestants, Catholics, and Jewish people. Because current immigration has increased non-Christian religious diversity in the United States, public schools need to affirm court decisions and use the guidelines on religious diversity offered by the Department of Education. Students need to learn more about other religions, and as they learn they may also come to appreciate why religious freedom was guaranteed in the Bill of Rights and why it has been so difficult to achieve that ideal.

"We establish no religion in (America), we command no worship, we mandate no belief, nor will we ever. Church and state are, and must remain, separate. All are free to believe or not to believe, all are free to practice a faith or not, and those who believe are free, and should be free, to speak of and act on their belief."

—RONALD REAGAN (1911–2004)

Summary

- Religious diversity in the United States has existed since colonial times, and it was a major factor in political leaders promoting the concept of religious freedom.

- The Constitution had minimal reference to religion, but leaders of diverse faiths insisted that it should guarantee religious freedom, and this became part of the First Amendment.

- From colonial times, anti-Catholic and anti-Semitic attitudes existed among Protestant Americans, and they would persist into the twentieth century.

- As twentieth-century Americans became more accepting of diverse faiths, immigration reform resulted in a dramatic increase in religious diversity that offered new challenges for citizens to promote and adhere to the principle of religious freedom.

Terms and Definitions

Agnosticism A belief that human beings cannot prove or disprove the existence of God

Anti-Catholicism Expressing stereotypes about or prejudices against Catholics or discriminating against Catholics

Anti-Semitism Having anti-Jewish prejudices or stereotypes, or engaging in discrimination against Jewish people

Atheism A belief that God does not exist

Deism A belief that God created the world and the system of natural laws that governed the world but was not a presence (and did not play a role) in everyday life

Denominations A perspective on diverse Protestant faiths that views all of them as a singular Protestant church with different names (denominations)

Established church When one church is declared the official faith of a political unit (a colony or state), and tax revenues are used to fund this church

Religious freedom/religious liberty The right to worship in any church of one's choice consistent with that church's beliefs and practices

Sectarian A perspective on diverse Christian churches or sects in which an individual regards her own sect as the "true faith"

Secular The civic culture of a society not reflective of religious perspective

Discussion Exercises

Exercise 1: Separation of Church and State Activity

Directions: Read the situation below, and decide which requests for changing school policy from the following list will be implemented (Agree) and which requests for change will be rejected (Disagree). On completion of your group's consideration of the 12 proposed rule changes, compare your recommendations with those of other groups.

The Situation: It is December 5. As a citizen and parent, you have been publicly assigned to a select committee to examine a list of new school district policies that has been proposed by a group of Jewish parents. In the district, 25 percent of the students are Jewish, 15 percent have no religious affiliation, and 60 percent declare some sort of Christian affiliation.

Proposed District Policies: Breaks and Absences

_____ 1. Vacation breaks during the school year will be established without regard to religious holidays.

_____ 2. Jewish children will be excused when they are absent on Jewish holidays.

_____ 3. Jewish teachers will not be charged with personal leave when they are absent during Yom Kippur and Rosh Hashana.

Religious Holidays

_____ 4. No celebration of Christmas as part of the school curriculum.

_____ 5. No celebration of Hanukkah as part of the school curriculum.

_____ 6. No creche will be displayed in school.

_____ 7. No Christmas trees will be displayed in school.

_____ 8. No gift exchanges or Christmas parties in class.

Curricular and Extracurricular Activity

_____ 9. Impact of religious values on historic or current events and issues will be examined and discussed in the classroom.

_____ 10. Holocaust will be studied as part of the World War II unit and as part of the history of Western civilization.

_____ 11. No extracurricular activity will be scheduled on Friday evening.

_____ 12. No songs that refer to Jesus Christ will be sung in the winter music program.

Exercise 2: Religious Freedom in the United States: What Is Your Judgment?

Directions: The following list contains incidents that have actually occurred. Determine which items you believe violate the rights of people to behave in accordance with their chosen faith.

Religious Freedom in the United States

1. Should a Sikh be allowed to wear his turban on a hard-hat job even though it appears to be a violation of safety regulations?
2. Can a soldier who is a member of Wicca practice his religion on an army base?
3. Should Hindus be forced to build their temple with a "Spanish" architectural style that will match the other buildings in a Southern California community instead of building it based on their traditional temple architecture?
4. Because a Jainist student attends the high school, must the cafeteria staff clearly mark the contents of the meals prepared so that the student can be assured of eating only vegetables?
5. Can a Muslim woman teaching in a public school wear her traditional head covering in her classroom?
6. Should members of the Native American Church be allowed to ingest peyote because this drug has historically been part of their religious rituals?
7. Should a Florida city council allow members of the Santeria faith to engage in animal sacrifice because it is traditionally part of their religious practice?
8. Should a Sikh student come to school with the symbolic knife (kirpan) he is required to wear following his initiation?
9. Should Muslim employees be given time to perform obligatory prayers during the workday?
10. Do Seventh-Day Adventist or Jewish employees have the right to be excused from work on Saturday because it is their Sabbath?

Chapter 7
Rejecting Oppressive Relationships: The Logic of Cultural Pluralism for a Diverse Society

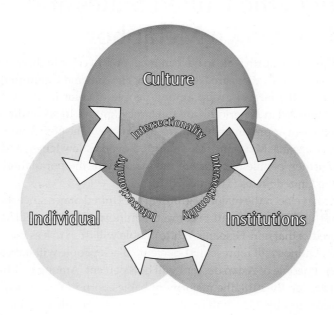

Learning Outcomes

After reading this chapter you will know and be able to:

7.1 Provide examples of the increasing diversity in the United States, and describe Terry's up/down metaphor.

7.2 Describe four historic perspectives on diversity in America and the rationale for advocates who promote pluralism for our diverse society.

7.3 Discuss the available strategies to achieve social change, and explain why it is not possible to claim sympathy for social change but not be actively involved in it.

> "In the United States, we have the richest mix of ethnic groups, of racial groups, of global experience that the world has ever known and it is this richness of this mix that yields our incredible creativity and innovation. We have not even begun to experience the real potential of our fantastic human resource mix—our competitive edge in the global economy."
>
> —JAMES NAISBITT (1929–)

James Naisbitt, author and consultant, provides corporate clients with analyses of data and trends to facilitate corporate decision making related to many pertinent social issues. In his comment, Naisbitt is describing the possibilities for America because of our diversity. Schuck (2014) argues that the United States can provide evidence in support of the claim that we are the most diverse society in the world regardless of how diversity is defined or what specific aspect of diversity is being measured. Because some demographic changes are not obvious in certain areas of the United States, some people think that talk of diversity is about the future. Demographers agree that America is going to be increasingly diverse in the coming decades, but changes are already happening in urban areas and in bellwether states such as California and Texas.

Diversity in the United States and Terry's Up/Down Metaphor

In 2005, Texas became the fourth state to have more people of color in the state's population than White people (the others are New Mexico, Hawaii, and California). Hispanic Americans constitute the largest group among people of color in all of these states except Hawaii, where Asian Americans are the largest group. In six additional states, people of color represent approximately 40 percent or more of the population—Arizona, Florida, Georgia, Louisiana, Maryland, Mississippi, Nevada, New Jersey, and New York (Maciag, 2015). Further, people of color are the majority of the population in the 106 largest cities in the United States (Thomas, 2012).

White people have been the majority group in the United States since the founding of the nation, but in 2043, they will become the minority. Between 2050 and 2060, demographers predict that non-Hispanic White people will drop to less than 47 percent of the population, Latinos will represent 31 percent, Black people will increase slightly to 14.7 percent, and people of Asian descent will be 8 percent. Among children, change will occur much earlier. By 2018, the majority of babies born in the United States will be children of color, and by 2020, half of all youth will be people of color (Teixeira & Halpin, 2013; Yen, 2012). For the social security system to provide its promised benefits, people of color will need jobs that pay living wages. Americans should care about diversity because in our complex, technological society we are highly dependent on each other.

According to the Pew Research Center (2015), 13 percent of people living in the United States were born in another country. Almost 42 percent of them are naturalized citizens, and nearly 12 percent have permanent legal status. Historically, immigrants have tended to settle in urban areas of a few states, primarily New York, California, and Florida, but beginning in the 1980s, more immigrants were sent to live in smaller cities. Pipher (2002) was one of the first to observe this phenomenon in Lincoln, Nebraska, noting: "Our obituary column . . . is filled with Hrdvys, Andersens, Walenshenkskys, and Muellers. But the births column . . . has many Ali, Nguyen, and Martinez babies" (p. 6).

In 2015, 10 percent of married people in the United States were in an interracial marriage, but of those people who were married during 2015, 17 percent of these marriages were interracial. Interracial marriages are more common for Asian Americans (29 percent) and Hispanic Americans (27 percent). Only 18 percent of African Americans were involved in an interracial marriage, and Black men were twice as likely as Black women to be in an interracial marriage. In response to a question about whether interracial marriages are good or bad for our society, 39 percent said they are good for our society, and 52 percent says they make no difference, which implies that as many as 91 percent of Americans are not opposed to interracial marriages (Livingston & Brown, 2017). Demographers predict that by 2050, more than 50 percent of Latinos, Asian Americans, and American Indians, and 10 percent of White and Black people, will be married to someone from another race (Painter, 2010). One consequence of increasing interracial marriage is that 12 percent of our youth today identify themselves as multiracial (Bouie, 2012), and it is likely that those numbers will increase significantly. The future will require the collaboration of diverse groups, so we need to understand strategies Americans may employ to promote changes that address the needs and aspirations of these diverse groups. First, it is important to examine how Americans have responded to our consistently diverse population.

How have members of the majority responded to diverse groups?

Despite what media coverage might suggest, a majority of Americans appear to accept diversity. In fact, White people tend to overestimate present levels of diversity in the United States by saying they believe almost half of Americans are people of color (Teixeira & Halpin, 2013). This represents a change in historical attitudes toward diversity. In any society, there is often a group hierarchy where preferred groups in an advantaged position disregard groups devalued by that society. As described in the historical information provided in previous chapters, the majority group in the United States frequently has not respected minority group rights. Terry (1993) described the relationship of dominant and subordinate groups with an "up/down" metaphor. To determine who is up or down in a society, observe which groups have the most wealth, status, and power, and which have the least. In the United States, an individual is an "up" by belonging to these groups: White, men, middle or upper class, Christian, without disabilities, and heterosexual. A "down" belongs to one or more of these groups: people of color, women, lower class, non-Christian, people with disabilities, and gay, lesbian, bisexual, or transgender. Most individuals represent a mixture of memberships in these up or down groups.

Terry insists that ups don't know much about downs, and they think they don't need to know about them because downs are not regarded as socially important. This sort of ignorance causes prejudice, which Eck (2001) described as "being down on something you're not up on" (p. 300). Ups do not compete with downs; they move in different circles. The only time ups become concerned about downs is when downs start getting "uppity" by challenging the power structure or the status quo and engaging in marches, demonstrations, or other forms of protest. The response of ups is likely to be "What do these people want?" And ups genuinely do not know. They are "dumb ups" when it comes to understanding issues affecting downs. By contrast, downs know a great deal about ups because they must; it is essential for their survival and success. To achieve whatever goals they have set for themselves, downs have to know, as Terry says, what the ups are up to (pp. 194–196).

It is tempting to assume that if someone is a down in one category, that individual will be more sensitive to downs in another category in which she functions as an up, but it doesn't work that way. When people are behaving as part of an up group, they tend to be "dumb ups." It's as if there are separate file folders; their experiences in one category stay in that file and don't influence other files. People living in poverty can be racist; people of color can be homophobic; gay men and lesbians can be prejudiced against immigrants; immigrants can be sexist; women can be prejudiced against people with disabilities; and people with disabilities can be prejudiced against welfare recipients.

> "It is well to remember that the entire universe, with one trifling exception, is composed of others."
>
> —JOHN ANDREW HOLMES (1789–1876)

Terry's "up/down" metaphor provides a useful way of thinking about the complexity involved in a society that includes such diverse minority groups.

When the topic of diversity is addressed in the media, especially racial and ethnic diversity, pundits rarely employ Naisbitt's positive language. Columnist George Will has criticized higher education's efforts to advocate for diversity, chastising institutions for engaging in "political correctness." Margai and Frazier (2010) have concluded that opponents of multiculturalism see it as an attack on the shared American culture and even on English as the national language that has unified the country even with its enormous diversity. They embrace the concept of American individualism and deplore efforts to emphasize the group instead of the individual. Some opponents even view civil rights advocacy for groups as a smokescreen for limiting the rights and the opportunities of individual White people. Such beliefs so not generate optimism about the future of the United States with its diverse population.

It is imperative that Americans understand how we benefit from diversity and that we learn more about previous and current contributions of diverse groups in our society because the real threat to our nation is not diversity but ignorance. Americans need to be aware of opportunities offered by a diverse society and not focus only on group conflicts. This issue goes beyond the United States; it is global. Naisbitt and Aburdene (1990) were among the first to describe global societies becoming culturally homogenized in the 1980s. They predicted a "backlash against uniformity" in the twenty-first century as people struggled to "assert the uniqueness" of their culture in the global village: "As our outer worlds grow more similar, we will increasingly treasure the traditions that spring from within" (p. 120). In all nations, people are being challenged to develop new, more positive attitudes about diversity.

 Self-Check 7.1 Complete this self-check quiz to check your understanding of the increasing diversity in the United States and Terry's up/down metaphor.

Attitudes about Diversity and Promoting Pluralism

Historians have long maintained that to understand the present, we must understand the past. The best way to understand historic attitudes toward societal diversity is to examine how Americans have responded to immigration, the primary source of our diversity. Although some Americans have been (and still are) guilty of anti-immigrant sentiments, many have expressed positive beliefs about immigrants. By reviewing past and present attitudes concerning immigration, Gordon (1964) described consistent ideological perspectives with regard to ethnic diversity: Anglo conformity, melting pot, and pluralism. Brooks (1996) and others have described a fourth perspective: separatism. These four perspectives represent historic and contemporary American views on ethnic diversity, and Anglo conformity is a good place to begin because it has been and continues to be the dominant perspective on racial and ethnic diversity in the United States.

What does it mean to have an Anglo conformity perspective?

Cole and Cole (1954) first identified **Anglo conformity** as the efforts of English colonists to maintain particular American values, norms, and standards. Anglo conformity is an extension of English culture and European civilization. It rejects diversity in favor of homogeneity, requiring that everyone conform to values, norms, and standards determined by the Anglo founders of the country and modified by a continuing White majority.

Anglo conformity requires that immigrants stop speaking native languages and use only English as soon as possible. It also requires immigrants to abandon their ethnic heritages, including customs, ceremonies, and traditions, and to adopt American ways to be similar to everyone else. Barrett and Roediger (2002) explained that people of color have found Anglo conformity to be a problem because: "For new immigrant workers the processes of 'becoming white' and 'becoming American' were connected at every turn" (p. 30). Because immigrants of color could never become White, they could never achieve the goal of Anglo conformity: to look and act just like the members of the White majority. Essayist Randolph Bourne was an early critic of Anglo conformity, arguing that America could never benefit from its diverse population until we eliminated our historic belief in White superiority; unless this was done, America would be "guilty of what every dominant race is guilty of in every European country, the imposition of its own culture upon the minority peoples" (Kazin, 2011, p. 144). Bourne also insisted that a belief in White supremacy contradicted the nation's ideals concerning individual freedom.

When referring to individuals assimilating into society, social scientists often use the term *Americanization*, yet it still refers to Anglo conformity. Americanization was a process of assimilation applied even to children of indigenous people. In the late 1800s, public schools were viewed as responsible for the Americanization of immigrant children, so schools created by the Bureau of Indian Affairs (BIA) were expected to "Americanize" Indian children. American Indians had long been viewed as an obstacle to U.S. expansion and occupation of new territories; so in order to Americanize Indian children, the BIA established boarding schools to "educate" them. As illustrated in the photographs of Navajo student Tom Torlino (Figure 7.1), these schools insisted on the Anglo conformity ideal.

Video Example 7.1

In this video, a speaker discusses how children learn systems of knowledge and interaction through a socialization process. How does this socialization process of learning relate to the idea of "Anglo conformity"/"Americanization" and assimilation for immigrant groups? What role do schools play in this process of learning culture?

Figure 7.1 Tom Torlino from Beinecke Library

Anglo conformity is vividly illustrated in these two pictures of a Navajo student, Tom Torlino, before and after being enrolled in a BIA boarding school.

SOURCE: Photo by J.N. Choate, Beinecke Rare Book and Manuscript Library, Yale University.

How did the BIA boarding schools promote Anglo conformity with Indian children?

At first, Indian schools were established on reservations, but being close to parents meant Indian children would return home and, as BIA officials feared, "go back to the blanket"—back to Indian values and behaviors. Parental influence interfered with one of the major purposes of BIA schools, which was, as Adams (1995) explained, to teach values: "to respect private property . . . to realize that the accumulation of personal wealth is a moral obligation" (p. 22). To be more confident of success in its Americanization efforts, the BIA built boarding schools away from reservations, and Indian students were not allowed to return home even on weekends. Although years passed before anyone recognized the absurdity of trying to Americanize Native Americans, the boarding school experiment was an unmitigated failure. Emphasis on conformity, uniformity, and individual achievement were too contrary to intrinsic Indian values. The Americanization experiment was much more successful with immigrant children.

Which immigrant groups benefited from Anglo conformity?

Northern European ethnic immigrants to the United States could more easily achieve Anglo conformity. To insist that people Americanize—dress, talk, think, behave, and conform fully to the White majority—is easier for those with White skin. However, when people of color rejected their heritage and native language and imitated White behavior, they still could not overcome the disadvantage of skin color—they could not be as successful as their White peers. As Americans of color were denied rewards given to White ethnic groups, those with lighter skin sometimes opted to claim White skin—"passing for White." Although some were successful, they paid a psychological price. Their success illustrated the power of Anglo conformity and contradicted the concept of America as a melting pot.

What does it mean to describe America as a melting pot?

The **melting pot** perspective is that immigrants to America need not relinquish their entire racial or ethnic heritage. Instead, the idea was that ethnic differences would blend into the dominant culture to create a new identity, an American identity, made up of cultures and customs carried to America by all immigrants (see Figure 7.2). This perspective was first articulated by eighteenth-century French immigrant Hector St. John de Crèvecoeur, who said of the United States: "Here individuals of all nations are melted into a new race of men" (Schlesinger, 1991, p. 12). A few intellectuals alluded to the melting pot concept, but Americans scarcely responded.

In 1908, there was a tidal wave of immigration at the time Israel Zangwill's play, *The Melting Pot*, opened in the nation's capital, and this engaging metaphor quickly became firmly established in the American imagination. The melting pot has been especially attractive in intellectual, artistic, and political circles with its compelling image of Americans as a blend of many cultures. In the following excerpt, the character David, a Russian Jew, describes the metaphor but also defines the limits of the melting pot:

> America is God's Crucible, the great Melting Pot where all the races of Europe are melting and re-forming! Here you stand, good folk, think I, when I see them at Ellis Island, here you stand in your fifty groups, with your fifty languages and histories, and your fifty blood hatreds and rivalries. But you won't be long like that, brothers, for these are the fires of God you've come to—these are the fires of God. A fig for your feuds and vendettas! Germans and Frenchmen, Irishmen and

Englishmen, Jews and Russians—into the Crucible with you all! God is making the American! (1915, p. 33)

Despite the rhapsodic oratory, notice the absence of references to people of color. Black, Latino, and Asian people, as well as Native Americans, are excluded. Only northern Europeans are invited to this highly selective melting pot; even members of certain darker-skinned White ethnic groups such as Greeks or Italians need not apply! The melting pot favored "the white Anglo-Saxon Protestant (WASP) group and . . . [neglected] certain 'culturally different' groups" (Laosa, 1974, p. 136). Anglo conformity continued to be reflected in government policy and educational programs, but the idea that America was a melting pot was an image that many White Americans embraced.

From the beginning, people of color questioned the melting pot concept, viewing it as a myth that had nothing to do with the reality of America's diversity. It wasn't just that people of color were excluded from the melting pot; they weren't sure they wanted to be included. Melting implied giving up their ethnic identification, with its history and traditions, to be acceptable to White people. The melting pot was supposed to be the combination of all subcultures into a new and superior culture, but as Sue (2015) pointed out, the concept of the melting pot was simply used "to mask White supremacy and White privilege" (p. 89).

The melting pot perspective became popular among White people because it deemphasized differences and emphasized the need to accept immigrants as Americans as long as they learned to speak English and became citizens. The most common expression of the melting pot perspective today is the argument that people should be **color blind**; that is, we should ignore an individual's skin color. Americans will often say, "When I look at you I don't see color, I just see an American (or a student or a neighbor)."

People of color often are offended by the color-blind approach, arguing that it disguises a negative attitude about race. Sue (2015) refers to studies of organizations promoting a color-blind attitude that were more likely to implement policies and practices that discriminated against employees of color and were used to justify the resulting inequality. Further, when individual White people say they don't notice skin color, people of color question why we should be oblivious to skin color but not to other colors in the world such as in flowers, animals, sunsets, or rainbows. White Americans advocate being color blind only when it relates to skin color. Seldon (1996) observed that being color blind indicated a discomfort with those whose skin is not white; it involved pretending that an individual was White in order for a White individual to be comfortable associating or working with him.

Foner (2000) offered historical evidence that America has never been color blind, even before the passage of the 1790 naturalization law that limited citizenship to White immigrants; yet many Americans still lobby for a color-blind society. Advocacy of a color-blind approach in education is especially problematic. Nieto (2011) describes the U.S. Supreme Court's 1974 decision in *Lau v. Nichols*, in which the San Francisco schools were sued for not providing an equal education for Chinese students. The schools' lawyer argued that Chinese students had the same curriculum, teachers, and instruction as other students. The Supreme Court ruled that taking the same approach with diverse students, as if all of them had the same needs, did not fulfill the goal of providing an equal education since students whose first language was Chinese would not benefit from curriculum and instruction in English, as would students who were native speakers. And if being color blind results in problems at the institutional level, it is even more disastrous at the individual level. After describing teachers who took a color-blind approach in teaching diverse children, Sleeter (1993) asked: "What does it mean to construct an interpretation of race that denies it?" (p. 161). The answer to this

Figure 7.2 "The Melting Pot"

A political cartoon illustrating the idealistic image of the melting pot. Even though Japanese and Black people are included in the pot, anti-Irish prejudice is revealed in the caricature of an Irishman with a knife in one hand, the Irish flag in the other, and the caption that reads, "The Mortar of Assimilation—and the One Element That Won't Mix."

SOURCE: Courtesy of Michigan State University Museum.

"Two deer, two owls will behave differently from each other. I have studied many plants. The leaves of one plant, on the same stem, none is exactly alike . . . . If the Great Spirit likes the plants, the animals, even little mice and bugs to do this, how much more will he abhor people being alike, doing the same thing."

—JOHN LAME DEER (1903–1976)

critical question illustrates why many racial and ethnic minorities view a color-blind attitude toward skin color as being just as negative as many of the ideas advocated by those who promote a separatist perspective.

How is the separatist perspective negative?

Separatism is the most pessimistic of the four perspectives, yet it may also be the easiest to recognize. Separatists believe that different racial and ethnic groups ought to be apart; they should have their own places and "be with their own kind." The goal of separatism is for diverse groups to tolerate each other. Separatism is based on the premise that ineradicable differences exist between groups of people and that differences inevitably cause hostility. The logical outcome is to believe that different groups must have their own places separate from others and should interact only when necessary. The best an individual can hope for is peaceful coexistence.

At various times, both majority and minority group members have advocated for a separatist perspective. Before the Civil War, White separatists advocated for African Americans being relocated to Africa, and some Americans assisted a number of former slaves in creating a new African nation called Liberia. Even President Lincoln considered the idea, but he abandoned the project after hearing a vehement rejection of the proposal at a White House meeting with a group of prominent African Americans, including Frederick Douglass (Martin, 1984). In the 1920s, Marcus Garvey promoted the goal of supporting Black entrepreneurs in creating a self-reliant Black society (Cronon, 1955). For a more contemporary example, Appleton (1983) described Switzerland as a "segregated pluralism where the country is divided into four distinct cultures" with four languages (p. 26). Although German speakers in the northern and eastern cantons constitute 70 percent of the population, 21 percent live in western cantons and speak French, 8 percent live in south-central cantons and speak Italian, and 1 percent living in the Alps speak Romansh.

There are separatist groups in the United States today, but they attract few followers and most, such as the Aryan Nation or Black Muslims, are perceived as hate groups. Not all separatists advocate hatred, but they tend to subscribe to the pessimistic separatist premise about human differences. Some call for a separate state for African Americans; others reject the concept of integrated schools in favor of returning to the *Plessy v. Ferguson* principle of a separate but equal education for children of color. Although these three perspectives continue to be in the mix of voices reacting to diversity, pluralism has become the first alternative perspective to challenge the dominance of Anglo conformity.

What attitudes about diversity does pluralism promote?

Pluralism (also known as **cultural pluralism**) refers to the equal coexistence of diverse cultures in a mutually supportive relationship within the boundaries of one nation (Pai & Adler, 1997). The United States has been diverse since colonial times, but immigration significantly increased the extent of the country's diversity. In the early 1900s, journalist John Reed wrote about taking a walk in a public park in New York City: "within a mile was every foreign country" (Kazin, 2011, p. 143). When Horace Kallen coined the term *cultural pluralism* in 1906, his focus was ethnic diversity, arguing that immigrants' cultural differences were essential to American democratic life. Alain Locke advocated a pluralism that encompassed racial groups as well.

In the 1920s, pluralists insisted that people in a diverse society such as the United States should have the right to preserve their cultural heritage and not be forced to abandon it to conform to a dominant culture (Menand, 2001). In an article published in the *Atlantic Monthly*, Randolph Bourne challenged Americans to view the United

States as an "embryo" of a better world to come: "The failure of the melting-pot, far from closing the great American democratic experiment, means that it has only just begun . . . building up the first international union" (Kazin, 2011, p 144). Bourne predicted that if Americans could eradicate White supremacist attitudes and adopt a pluralistic perspective, the United States could become "the first truly democratic society on earth" (p. 144).

Today, most advocates would agree with Pai and Adler (1997) that pluralism is based on "equality of opportunity for all people, respect for human dignity and the conviction that no single pattern of living is good for everyone" (p. 102). Further, advocates argue that diversity is not a difficulty to be overcome but a positive attribute of a society. American pluralists do not refer to being tolerant of others because tolerance is an inadequate response in a nation as diverse as the United States. As Eck (2001) writes, "Tolerance can create a climate of restraint but not one of understanding . . . . It is far too fragile a foundation for a society . . . [as] complex as ours" (p. 72). In a society guided by pluralistic beliefs, people appreciate differences because everyone is enriched by diversity. Pluralists insist that individuals have the right to maintain and be proud of their racial, cultural, ethnic, or religious heritage. Pluralistic attitudes have been steadily increasing in the United States. A 2013 survey reported that 70 percent of Americans agreed with the idea that our diverse society means we have more to learn from each other and are "enriched" by our exposure to many different cultural groups (Teixeira & Halpin, 2013).

Separatists say that human differences will always cause conflict and will never disappear. Melting pot advocates ignore differences to avoid problems arising from them. Anglo conformity advocates demand the elimination of differences based on the assumption that a homogeneous society will be a more harmonious one. By contrast, pluralism encourages individuals to identify themselves in terms of their heritage in addition to identifying themselves as American. Individuals who embrace pluralism might claim an identity as an Italian American or Polish American, as an African American or Arab American, as a Mexican American or Cuban American, as a Chinese American or Hmong American. The identification means their identity is shaped by their racial or ethnic heritages as well as by the American culture. With regard to preserving cultural heritage, some have asked how Italian must an Italian American be? From a pluralist perspective, it is up to each individual to decide how much of the customs, traditions, and language of an ethnic heritage to maintain.

Because pluralism promotes bilingual education and maintenance of one's native language, those in the English Only movement misunderstand the pluralist position as a rejection of the need for English as a common language. A society with diverse language groups needs a common language, and English has been and continues to be the common language for the United States. The more important question is: Can people become fluent in English without losing the language spoken in their home? Students around the world are taught to be fluent in more than one language. Since there are children and youth in America who are fluent in a language learned at home, it makes more sense for schools to teach them English but also help them maintain their first language. Pluralists argue that people should not be forced to give up the language associated with their cultural heritage because these languages are part of the diversity that enriches our society. The concept of pluralism is consistent with American values concerning individuality and freedom; as our diversity increases, it becomes increasingly necessary for Americans to reject Anglo conformity in favor of pluralism.

Video Example 7.2

In this video, a speaker discusses students and intercultural competence. Think about the speaker's notion of cultural competence and the concept of cultural pluralism discussed here in Chapter 7. What are some ways in which intercultural competence aligns with cultural pluralism?

What are some arguments from people who are opposed to pluralism?

Opponents of pluralism insist that it contradicts the American emphasis on the individual by placing more importance on group membership. They argue that emphasizing groups in a society will encourage identification with a group rather than with the nation, and that animosity will arise between individuals who identify with a group and those who simply perceive themselves as "American." In response, pluralist advocates have said that this criticism is a misinterpretation of pluralism (Appleton, 1983; Greeley, 1975; Pai & Adler, 1997). One of the goals of pluralism is to encourage people to shape their own identity. Cultural pluralism does not require mindless conformity to a group's cultural heritage; it fosters a dynamic process that allows individuals to decide the extent to which they choose to embrace their cultural heritage exclusively or to integrate certain aspects of other cultures or the dominant culture into that heritage. Pluralists support individuals who have chosen to maintain their heritage as well as those who choose to adopt other cultural ways while retaining important aspects of their cultural heritage.

Opponents maintain that there is still a problem with pluralism because it places so much emphasis on being proud of your cultural group. They argue that any level of individual identification with a cultural group inflates the importance of that group and exacerbates the potential for conflict between groups. They believe that the best way to avoid such conflicts is for all people living in the United States to identify themselves as Americans. Without this common bond, pluralism's critics believe that group conflicts are inevitable and will lead to fragmentation and conflict in our society. Yet when Chua (2007) examined the historical record of the achievements of the most successful nations, she found that a common thread connecting them was the promotion of pluralistic attitudes toward their diverse inhabitants. From the Roman Empire to the Mongol Dynasty to the British Empire, the central government encouraged people under its rule, including conquered people, to maintain their culture and religion. The most gifted people from all groups were solicited and employed so the empire could benefit from their talents, and the government provided opportunities for diverse individuals to achieve, regardless of their background or their differences.

At the end of her book, Chua acknowledges that the United States is now a superpower, and she insists that: "Tolerance played a critical role in every dimension of the United States' rise to superpower status" (p. 254). But tolerance is no longer enough; Chua says the United States will not benefit from its diverse population until it begins to promote pluralistic attitudes. For those critics who remain skeptical, pluralist advocates insist that pluralism is consistent with both democratic principles and American values for individuality and freedom. As diversity in the United States increases, it becomes even more necessary for Americans to end our historic practice of demanding Anglo conformity in favor of promoting cultural pluralism.

Why should American society become pluralistic?

Although pluralist advocates have challenged the appropriateness of Anglo conformity in our diverse society, it is still the dominant perspective. These advocates have generated arguments in support of promoting pluralism in America around five major themes:

1. *The failure of Anglo conformity* has been described by many social critics. Although a majority of Americans have historically endorsed Anglo conformity, this effort has been ineffective because conformity contradicts the historic experience of the United States. Eck (2001) observed, "America is a nation formed not by a race or a single people, but by the ideals articulated in the succession of founding documents, beginning with the Declaration of Independence" (p. 74). American immigrants have succeeded because they have accepted the civic culture of the United States as described by those founding documents; to require conformity based on race, religion, or other human differences in a society with such diversity is by nature unrealistic and illogical (Dickens, 2011; Fuchs, 1990).

Video Example 7.3

In this video, a teacher discusses the challenges of educating individuals within cultural groups. In what ways does he suggest immigrant students need to assimilate? How can schools help immigrant children in this process? What are some of the challenges to teaching individual students who come from immigrant cultures? Finally, how does this discussion relate to cultural pluralism and what pluralism opponents argue?

Sociologists who note that Anglo conformity has failed in America argue that it is inherently unjust to those who cannot conform adequately because they are not White or Protestant (or at least Christian). People unable to conform have endured oppression, and many are still oppressed. Racial and ethnic minorities are disproportionately represented in the data on human suffering such as infant mortality rates, unemployment statistics, welfare rolls, inadequately funded schools, and unsafe neighborhoods. The availability of goods and services and accessibility to education and opportunity have been inequitable because access and distribution have been affected by factors such as race, gender, social class, disability, and sexual orientation. Feelings of respect and self-respect have also been inequitable—which goes beyond equity to raise an ethical question about a lack of human compassion.

2. *The impact on self-consciousness and self-determination* refers to the effect of being perceived as "different" on an individual's efforts to develop the kind of positive self-consciousness that is essential to be confident in the ability to determine goals and achieve them. If people consciously feel proud of who they are, it is easier to set goals and believe they can be reached. Appleton (1983) argued that a primary purpose of democracy is to "provide an opportunity for individuals to choose who and what they will become" (p. 57). It is difficult for people to develop a sense of personal pride and believe they can achieve their goals when they feel their abilities are constantly being doubted.

   In one study, researchers reviewed the Graduate Record Examination (GRE) taken by undergraduates across the country as part of their applying for admission to graduate school. Twenty questions from the GRE were selected to create a "test" that was given to Black and White undergraduate students. In testing sessions where they were asked to identify their race on a pretest questionnaire, African American students only answered half as many questions correctly as compared to testing sessions where they were not asked to identify their race. After the test, African American students were asked if anything had happened that would interfere with doing well on the test. They typically said, "No." Even when asked specifically if identifying their race on the pretest questionnaire bothered them, they said it did not. Yet several African American students admitted that they questioned their ability to achieve academic success at the graduate level (Gladwell, 2005). It is essential that people function in a context in which their abilities are clearly respected if they are to develop a positive consciousness of self and a belief that they can determine their own goals and achieve them.

3. *The necessity for human interdependence* concerns the extent to which people depend on others. Individuals interact in any society; as a society becomes more complex, people inevitably become more dependent on each other. A complex society relies on technology, cooperation, and division of labor. Some people grow food, some build homes and furniture, some sell and service cars, and so on. People rely on others to provide the goods and services needed in their daily lives. It is also essential that those in the workforce be paid well enough to support the social security system for retired workers. In any society, but especially in a democratic society, people rely on each other. According to Pai and Adler (1997), "a democratic society is necessarily pluralistic . . . because it is founded on a belief in the intrinsic worth of individuals and their unique capacities to become intelligent human beings" (p. 109). Becoming a pluralistic society is necessary to promote positive relations among individuals in all areas and from all groups within that society.

   The lack of a pluralistic perspective concerning racial and ethnic interdependence in the United States contributed to problems in the past. When drug use began to increase in urban ghettos and barrios in the 1950s and 1960s, the larger society ignored it. No one seemed to care what "those people" did to themselves because we did not understand that interdependence means that social problems cannot be confined. By the 1970s, drug use by urban and suburban White people increased significantly, and today, the entire society is confronted with an enormous health and economic problem because of the availability and use of illicit drugs. Drug use became a significant problem in the United States because the majority did not appreciate the interdependence of diverse groups in American society.

> "Pluralism is the greatest philosophical ideal of our time."
>
> —JOHN DEWEY (1859–1952)

White people are not alone in misunderstanding social interdependence. When AIDS first appeared, most people, including people of color, ignored the disease because it seemed to affect only the gay community. Some people said—and some still say—that AIDS was a punishment from God on gay men. It was only when the virus spread to heterosexuals in highly publicized cases that the U.S. government began providing funds for research to find a cure. In the meantime, thousands of human beings died.

Human interdependence exists everywhere, but in a diverse, democratic society such as the United States, citizens must advocate for and practice pluralistic attitudes to ensure that society functions as effectively as possible to be a good place for all (Locke, 1989). The Boy Scout study described in Chapter 2 illustrates this point. When boys competed with each other, hostility developed between groups, but hostility was eliminated when they cooperated to achieve a mutual goal. As Aronson (2012) concluded, "The key factor seems to be mutual interdependence—a situation wherein individuals need one another and are needed by one another in order to accomplish their goal" (p. 345). This is not a new insight. More than three centuries ago, poet John Donne wrote, "Any man's death diminishes me . . . therefore never send to know for whom the bell tolls; it tolls for thee" (Simpson, 1967, p. 101).

4. *The recognition of diversity as an ideal* implies that people must recognize that diversity constitutes the best possible situation. We need only consider what has occurred as a result of the diversity of the United States: Some of the best art, music, and literature ever created in America was a consequence of borrowing from different cultural traditions. Our modern English language has evolved by adopting words from languages of cultures as diverse as Germany, France, Italy, and Mexico, as well as from African and Native American dialects (Claiborne, 1983). A major argument for English as a world language is its flexibility and accessibility in accommodating an infusion of words from other cultures.

Diversity is regarded as an asset when people engage in solving problems. If we all examined problems the same way, we would generate similar solutions. Williams (2003) described a problem-solving conference in which a chemical company invited 50 employees who were women and people of color along with the company's top 125 predominantly White male managers. When divided into problem-solving teams, half of the groups consisted of White men only and half were diverse in both gender and race. Afterward, the company CEO said, "It was so obvious that the diverse teams had the broader solutions . . . . We realized that diversity is a strength as it relates to problem-solving" (pp. 442–443).

Diversity is also valued in the natural world: The more diversity there is in nature, the more likely it is that human life will adapt as new conditions arise. We have become concerned about endangered species and the destruction of rain forests: If diversity in nature is diminished, whatever potential usefulness exists in a species of plant or animal will be lost permanently.

> "Commandment Number One of any truly civilized society is this: Let people be different."
>
> —DAVID GRAYSON (1870–1946)

5. *The current existence of diversity* is perhaps the most compelling argument for promoting pluralism. If some quality is characteristic of a society, it makes sense that we value it rather than deny it or try to pretend that it doesn't exist. If most of the players on a basketball team are tall, a coach will take advantage of their height to create offensive and defensive strategies. If the tall players graduate and next

year's team is short and fast, the coach will take advantage of quickness and speed by creating new offensive and defensive strategies. As the most multicultural society in the world today, we must realize the advantages of diversity and embrace pluralism to capitalize on our advantages.

Other arguments for pluralism challenge us to think about how our society is changing and what sort of society it could become. To maintain Anglo conformity reinforces the current fear and hostility that certain groups have for each other and perpetuates conflicts between them. However, changing societal attitudes to a pluralistic perspective offers hope. Human beings have always encountered problems and conflicts, but in a diverse society, conflicts and problems are more likely to be resolved if people have pluralistic attitudes. There is some evidence that Americans are becoming more favorable to pluralism, especially people of color and young people who tend to express attitudes reflecting a greater acceptance of diversity.

In a questionnaire on openness to diversity based on 160 as the highest possible overall score, the mean scores for people of color were: 93 for African Americans, 90 for Latinos, 97 for Asian Americans, and 84 for non-Hispanic Whites. These scores were higher for younger Americans from all racial or ethnic groups—the age group from 18–29 had a mean score of 92. Analyzing responses coming from members of all racial and ethnic groups, there were three statements about outcomes from America's growing diversity that attracted the strongest support:

1. Americans will learn more from one another and be enriched by exposure to many different cultures.
2. A bigger, more diverse workforce will lead to more economic growth.
3. Diverse workplaces and schools will help make American businesses more innovative and competitive.

Participants in this study also expressed a major concern that society was not providing enough jobs for people entering the workforce and that this problem might eventually create a burden on government services. Although a majority of conservatives expressed their belief that Americans are on their own to solve problems that may arise, a majority of participants who were people of color and liberal White people agreed that these challenges could be met if all Americans worked together (Teixeira & Halpin, 2013). Such responses represent a step toward Americans becoming a society that genuinely values individual differences and collaborates effectively with each other.

Application Exercise 7.1

In this video, a speaker discusses ways in which students' cultures can be brought into the classroom and how it can benefit students. Think about the five themes for promoting pluralism in America and the three statements about outcomes from America's growing diversity that attracted the strongest support from the diversity questionnaire discussed in Chapter 7. Review the video and complete the activity.

 Self-Check 7.2 Complete this self-check quiz to check your understanding of the four historic perspectives on diversity in America and the rationale for advocates who promote pluralism for our diverse society.

Strategies to Achieve Social Change and the Need to be Actively Involved

The evidence that Americans have already learned to value diversity on a basic level becomes most apparent when people are asked, "Would you want to live in a society where everyone was the same?" Most Americans reply that they would not want to live in such a society. It is an American belief that each individual is unique, and most of us are proud of those factors that establish our individuality. The United States has always consisted of people from different races, cultures, and religions. If we value our own uniqueness, it is logical and consistent to value what is unique in others. Pluralists value human differences. Sooner or later, all Americans should embrace pluralism because no other perspective regards differences as an asset for a society. Still, to be a pluralist requires more than claiming to value diversity; pluralism must be practiced. As Eck (2001) noted, "diversity alone is not pluralism. Pluralism is not a given but must be created. Pluralism requires participation and attunement to the life and energies of one another" (p. 70). Individuals and organizations committed to pluralism are actively working to bring about social change in the United States and to transform social attitudes from our traditional acceptance of Anglo conformity to acceptance and promotion of pluralism.

Must you be actively involved in change to be a pluralist?

Terry (1975) developed a matrix (see Figure 7.3) based on the idea that people can either be prejudiced against one or more groups (racist, sexist, homophobic) or demonstrate pluralistic attitudes toward diversity. According to Terry, people also can be active or passive in their prejudices or their acceptance of diversity. The matrix identifies four different positions: (1) People may actively assert and promote their prejudices; those with such strong prejudices are typically perceived as extremists (such as a bigot or a male chauvinist). (2) People may be prejudiced without expressing those ideas or behaving in ways that obviously reflect prejudice; they do not disagree with bigots or chauvinists but also do not tend to articulate their ideas on behalf of causes. People in this group passively accept the status quo that has been shaped by past prejudice and thereby perpetuate injustice in our society. They are conformists. They like things as they are, and they would like to see them stay that way.

In another position, (3) people may reject prejudiced ideas and sympathize with victims of social injustice but not express their views. Although opposed to prejudice and discrimination, they don't want to risk causing trouble or upsetting anyone, so they say nothing—and do nothing. Similar to those who are passive in their prejudice, people in this group conform to the status quo. By their conformity they help perpetuate problems that are known to be part of the status quo. There is little difference between prejudiced people and those opposed to prejudicial ideas and actions if they are both passive in their behavior. It is not possible to claim to have pluralistic attitudes and be passive, because passivity perpetuates social injustice.

Tatum (1997) describes the existence of prejudice and its benefits for the dominant group as similar to a moving walkway at an airport. People who actively engage in prejudice not only step on the walkway but keep walking as well. People who are passive, whether their attitudes are prejudiced or opposed to prejudice, merely step on

Figure 7.3 Matrix for Oppressive and Anti-Oppressive Behaviors

Terry's Matrix illustrates why it is not possible to claim to be anti-oppressive while being passive on social issues.

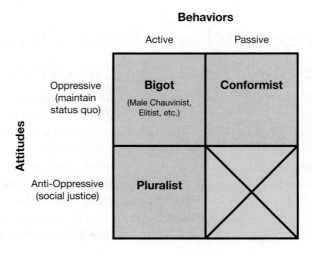

the walkway and let it carry them along. To be actively opposed to prejudice and the benefits it brings to the dominant group, people must step off the walkway as soon as they recognize its function. Using Tatum's metaphor, to escape the moving walkway means to be actively involved in promoting social justice.

To promote social justice, (4) people must reject prejudiced ideas, articulate pluralistic attitudes, and act on a new consciousness of human differences. To be a pluralist requires not only positive attitudes but also a commitment to engage in activities to change social injustices in our society. Contrary to those who promote being color blind, pluralists argue that it is not consciousness of color that is the problem, but rather that people's consciousness of color and reactions to other differences have tended to be negative. White people may feel uneasy around someone who is not White. Middle- or upper-class people may have contempt for welfare recipients. People without disabilities feel pity for people with disabilities. Men may be condescending to women. What is needed is not to ignore differences but to consciously develop a positive attitude toward human differences. Put simply, unless we are part of the solution, we are part of the problem.

What kinds of activities can create social change?

If you have power to address a problem, you need only decide how to use that power to solve the problem. If individuals or groups do not have power to make a desired change, they may employ tactics to persuade those with power to implement the solutions they advocate. The tactics—deliberate and conscious strategies—employed to achieve social change in the United States are as old as the birth of our country, as illustrated in the Declaration of Independence and in the writing of John Adams, Thomas Jefferson, Thomas Paine, and others responsible for revolution against England and for eventual American independence. Terry (1975) identified six tactics historically employed to promote social change.

The most basic tactic is to engage in (1) a dialogue with those in power to convince them to implement a proposed change. If dialogue fails, people might organize (2) a confrontation of some kind: a march, a sit-down strike, or a rally. Confrontation dramatizes the need for change by public demonstration to show that people are concerned about an issue. The goal of confrontation is either to revive a dialogue that had been terminated or to pressure those in control to develop a greater sense of urgency about finding a solution.

If both dialogue and confrontation fail, those advocating change might (3) apply economic pressure to those individuals or organizations unwilling to change. Pressure usually takes the form of a **boycott** of products or services related to the issue in dispute. For example, the Montgomery bus boycott lasted more than a year and ended when the courts ruled in favor of desegregation of public transportation. The bus boycott launched the career of Martin Luther King Jr. and brought national attention to the civil rights movement (Williams, 1987). Other examples include the 1995 boycott of Shell Oil by Greenpeace that had a dramatic effect in Germany, where sales plummeted by nearly 40 percent. In 2009, animal activists called for a boycott of McDonald's based on reports of unethical and inhumane practices being employed in the slaughter of chickens sold to the fast food chain. Experts say the most effective boycotts occur when media is used effectively to gain the sympathy of a wide audience (Diermeier, 2012).

Economic pressure can also be applied through discrimination litigation calling for major economic penalties. In the 1990s, 1300 African American employees at Coca-Cola brought a class-action lawsuit charging the corporation with discrimination in performance reviews, pay, and promotions. They won the case and were awarded $192 million. To improve the corporate image in the aftermath of the lawsuit, Coca-Cola committed additional resources to diversity issues, including "increasing its use of minority suppliers, instituting a formal [diversity] mentoring program, and instituting days to celebrate diversity with its workforce" (Jones & George, 2003, p. 130).

People demanding change often initiate or support (4) research designed to examine data relevant to the issue being confronted. Research about a specific issue might define the nature of the problem and perhaps identify its causes. Researchers may or may not recommend specific solutions to address problems, but the purpose of research is to provide information in support of a persuasive argument about changes being proposed to those in control.

Another tactic is to establish (5) an inside-outside alliance in which a member of a decision-making body (such as a board of directors, city council, or school board) collaborates with a group demanding change. This tactic may involve persuading someone who is already in the decision-making group about the benefits of the changes being advocated, or it may mean working to elect a candidate or influence the appointment of someone who is sympathetic to the need for change. Once elected or appointed, this individual can articulate arguments for change advocated by outside groups. Jones and George (2003) provide the example of an insurance and annuity company committed to diversity that owned almost a million shares of Nucor Corporation; they exerted pressure on Nucor to add more women and people of color to its board of directors.

When all else fails, people resort to (6) violence to demonstrate their frustration and to dramatize the need for change. This tactic might involve destruction of property or an assault on people, or both. The use of violence is typically an unplanned and spontaneous reaction, as when 10 businesses were destroyed by fire and vandalism during the 2014 riots in Ferguson, Missouri, in response to the shooting death of an unarmed Black teenager, Michael Brown, by a police officer (Stewart, 2014). When violence is planned, most often it is meant primarily to be a symbolic gesture, such as the Boston Tea Party of 1773.

In the past, violence erupted when frustration over an issue reached a point where the people most affected could no longer control their rage, usually responding destructively to a specific incident. During the Civil War, if wealthy young men were drafted, they avoided military service by paying poor and often unemployed men to take their place. The poor knew that these young men were being exploited and that most of them would probably be killed in the war, and their anger resulted in the 1863 Draft Riot in New York City. More recently, riots occurred during the 1999 World Trade Organization protests in which some protesters smashed windows and vandalized businesses in response to police using pepper spray, tear gas, and stun guns against them. In 2015, people of color in Baltimore wanted a peaceful protest in response to the death of a young Black man, Freddie Gray, who died of a spinal injury while in police custody, but some protesters engaged in violence, resulting in 15 buildings and 144 cars being set on fire (Stolberg, 2015). Violence rarely resolves problems, primarily because incidents igniting riots are typically only symptoms of larger problems. Even if symptoms are addressed following a riot, the causes of those symptoms will eventually create new problems.

In the last half of the twentieth century, people of color participated in riots, especially in urban areas. This has caused many Americans to associate violent tactics for change with people of color, but many groups have resorted to violence in the past. The history of riots in the United States reveals that White people have most often been the group causing riots (see Table 7.1). Jones (1997) addressed this history: "With few exceptions . . . previous racial riots had consisted of interracial fighting or the destruction of black communities by white mobs" (p. 46).

In identifying tactics, Terry noted that the first five represented nonviolent approaches and also illustrated the critical role education must play if individuals and groups are to engage in nonviolent change. The skills and means necessary to engage in nonviolent tactics are related to what we teach in our schools. To be persuasive in dialogue requires the kinds of communication and problem-solving skills students are taught. To engage successfully in confrontation, it is essential to understand how to

Table 7.1 Riots in America: A Selected List of Riots in the United States Since the Nation Began

Year	Name/Location	Cause
1788	Doctors' Riot/New York City	Medical students digging up bodies
1834	Election Riots/Several cities	Allowing recent immigrants to vote
1835	Abolition Riots/Several cities	Opposing abolitionist efforts
1844	Bible Riots/Philadelphia	Use of Catholic Bible in public schools
1863	Draft Riots/New York City	Corruption and injustice in draft laws
1877	Railroad Riots/Baltimore, Pittsburgh, Chicago, others	Workers striking for fair pay riot in response to militia being called in
1885	Anti-Chinese Riots/Rock Springs, Wyoming	Opposing the railroad's use of Chinese labor
1908	Race Riot/Springfield (IL)	(False) allegation by a White woman of being raped by a Black man
1917	Race Riot/East St. Louis	Black workers hired to replace White workers on strike
1921	Race Riot/Tulsa (OK)	(False) allegation by a White woman of an attempted rape by a Black man
1942	Zoot Suit Riot/Los Angeles	Allegation that sailors were assaulted by *pachucas* in zoot suits leads to sailors attacking Mexican Americans
1965	Watts Riot/Los Angeles	"Routine" traffic stop sparks protest against unjust treatment by police and legal system
1967–1968	Race Riots/Detroit, Newark, and other cities	Protesting police brutality against Black suspects, other local racial injustices, and the assassination of Martin Luther King Jr.
1992	Race Riot/Los Angeles	Protesting White jury acquitting White police officers caught on videotape beating a Black man (Rodney King)

work effectively in groups; from elementary school through college, students are provided opportunities to participate in collaborative activities. Students are also taught how to deliver an effective speech in school, and successful confrontation requires one or more individuals with an ability to articulate the group's concerns to the public.

Although economic pressure may not seem to relate to schools but simply to the economic resources an individual controls, studies show that people earn higher salaries based on the level of education they have completed (Bonilla-Silva, 2001; U.S. Department of Labor, 2009). Organizing a successful boycott requires sufficient numbers of people in a community with economic resources to create pressure on those resisting change, and that largely depends on how much education the people have completed. The level of education an individual has completed is also a major factor in employing the tactic of an inside-outside alliance. The perception of an individual's credibility as a legitimate candidate for election or appointment to a decision-making body is typically influenced by educational achievements.

Finally, education also plays a pivotal role in research. Although studies can be conducted by anyone with a basic knowledge of principles of effective research, those results that are widely disseminated and that influence public and corporate policies tend to come from studies conducted by people with college experience. Violence is the only tactic that does not require education; as Jefferson wrote in the Declaration of Independence, it is the approach people will choose when they believe no other options exist. It is essential that schools provide people with the skills and means for engaging in nonviolent tactics to address issues of social injustice.

> "We are all Americans who, because of our cultural heritage, contribute something unique to the fabric of American life. We are like the notes in a chord of music—if all the notes were the same, there would be no harmony, no real beauty, because harmony is based on differences, not similarities."
>
> —ROSA GUERRERO (1934–)

 Self-Check 7.3 Complete this self-check quiz to check your understanding of the available strategies to achieve social change and why it is not possible to claim sympathy for social change but not be actively involved it.

Afterword

The United States today is a society struggling with its internal diversity at the same time that it is attempting to understand and adjust to the external diversity of the global village. Americans have much to learn from other nations' experiences with diversity. Historically, societies dominated by Western Europeans have been intolerant of differences, persecuting those who did not think or act in accordance with what religious or political authorities deemed acceptable, causing conflicts between religions, ethnic groups, and countries. Even when tolerance was practiced, Zeldin (1994) argued that it was for the wrong reasons: "Not out of respect for other people's views, not out of deep knowledge of what they believe, but in despair of finding certainty. It meant closing one's eyes to what other people believed" (p. 272).

Being more diverse than all of Europe, the United States is engaged in a debate between maintaining Anglo conformity or promoting pluralism in response to diversity. Zeldin (1994) explained why advocating tolerance is inadequate: "The tolerated are increasingly demanding to be appreciated, not ignored, and becoming more sensitive to [the] contempt lurking behind the condescension. They do not want to be told that differences do not matter" (p. 272). Pluralism goes beyond tolerance, requiring understanding and acceptance of differences. Many American institutions are responding positively to diversity and taking public positions on the issue. Eck (2001) praised the following statement from the Girl Scouts:

> Pluralism means being inclusive and respectful of people or groups with different backgrounds, experiences, and cultures . . . although you can have diversity without pluralism, you cannot have pluralism without valuing diversity. (pp. 76–77)

If Americans are to demonstrate pluralistic attitudes, educators must teach all students about diversity and how individuals from diverse groups have contributed to our society. If the changes needed to improve and sustain this society are to come as a consequence of nonviolent tactics for change—from discussion and debate in the context of mutual respect—teachers must help students develop the abilities to use nonviolent tactics effectively. How schools can fulfill this role and what pluralistic policies and practices illustrate the changes happening in the United States will be the focus of the final section of this text, but first it is necessary to understand the problems experienced by diverse groups in our society.

Summary

- Statistics illustrate the current diversity in the United States, and Terry's up/down metaphor is one way to understand what it means to be a member of an advantaged or disadvantaged group and how group members view each other.

- The four historic perspectives on diversity in America include Anglo conformity, the melting pot, separatism, and pluralism. Advocates for pluralism have created a compelling rationale for promoting that perspective in our diverse society.

- Six strategies to achieve social change include dialogue, confrontation, economic pressure, research, inside-outside alliances, and violence, and individuals typically take one of four perspectives on the need to take action for social change.

Terms and Definitions

Anglo conformity Views the values, norms, and standards of the United States as an extension of English culture because the English were the dominant group during the colonial era and when the new nation was emerging

Boycott To abstain from using, buying, or associating with a group, organization, or nation to protest an injustice and to force the other to address this injustice

Color blind A response to race based on the belief that an individual should not notice or consider the skin color of another

Melting pot The conceptual belief that when immigrants from diverse racial/ethnic backgrounds come to the United States, they blend into the culture and, mixed together with those who have come before, develop into a new, distinctly American identity

Pluralism (cultural pluralism) The equal coexistence of diverse cultures in a mutually supportive relationship within the boundaries of one nation

Separatism The conceptual belief in the notion of establishing entirely separate societies for each distinct racial or ethnic group or other groups that exist within a society

Discussion Exercises

Exercise #1 Differing Views: America's Ethnic Composition Activity

Directions: Identify each of the following statements by its perspective on ethnic diversity: Anglo Conformity (AC), Melting Pot (MP), Separatism (S), or Pluralism (P).

_____ 1. My parents decided not to teach us Laotian. They hoped that this would enable us to move more quickly through the process of becoming an American.

_____ 2. More and more I think in family terms, less ambitiously, on a less than national scale. The differences involved in my being from an Italian family, and Catholic, and even growing up in a lower middle-class home seem more and more important to me.

_____ 3. Marcus Garvey once said that the reliance of his race on the progress and achievements of others for a consideration in sympathy, justice, and rights is like a dependence on a broken stick: Resting on it will eventually consign you to the ground. The Negro needs a nation and a country of his own, where he can best show evidence of his own ability in the art of human progress.

_____ 4. Now listen to me, Nikki, you are beginning to understand our American ways, so the sooner you drop your Puerto Rican notions, the more successful you will be.

_____ 5. Our blood is as the flood of the Amazon, made up of a thousand noble currents all pouring into one. We are not a nation, so much as a world.

_____ 6. To justify placing Japanese-Americans in "relocation camps," a U.S. military leader made the following comments during a congressional hearing after World War II: The Japanese race is an enemy race, and while many second- and third-generation Japanese born on United States soil possess U.S. citizenship and have become "Americanized," the racial strains are unchanged.

_____ 7. Outwardly I lived the life of the White man, yet all the while I kept in direct contact with tribal life. While I learned all that I could of the White man's culture, I never forgot that of my people. I kept the language, tribal manners, and usages, sang the songs, and danced the dances.

_____ 8. A few years ago, these Greek immigrants had nothing, and now most of them have made it. They're all well off. Of course, the richest ones have left the Greek neighborhoods and live in the suburbs.

_____ 9. Teachers must teach our children what they need to know, but the teachers must also have a profound knowledge of our culture when they work with our children. This is of paramount importance to the preservation of the Cherokee nation.

_____ 10. The Amish keep to themselves. They are tied together by religion, kinship, and custom, and they want to keep it that way.

_____ 11. That's right, I was ashamed of my name. Not only that, I was ashamed of being Jewish. There you have it. Exit Abraham Isaac Arshawsky, Enter Art Shaw! You see, of course, how simple this little transformation was. Presto, change-o! A new name, a new personality. As simple as that!

_____ 12. Indian children are taught to "be like a White man, and think like a White man." They completely lose their self-identity as Navajos.

_____ 13. What I should like to do is come to a better and more profound knowledge of who I am, whence my community came, and where my son and daughter, and their children's children, might wish to head in the future: I want to have a history.

_____ 14. I only ask of the government to be treated as all other men are treated. If I cannot go to my own home, let me have a home in some country where my people will not die so fast.

_____ 15. It makes no difference to me whether my students are Black, White, brown, green, red, yellow, or purple. They are students, and I treat them all the same. After all, we are all human beings. Why can't we forget about color entirely and just treat each other like human beings?

Adapted from _Education in a Multicultural Society_ by Fred Rodriguez, University Press of America (1983).

Exercise #2 Are You an Advocate for Gender Equality?

Directions: In our everyday language we make implicit comments that signal oppressive relationships. Read each of the following statements; then respond _Yes_ or _No_ and write a brief comment of explanation. Check for assumptions that are contained in the item before writing your response.

1. Should a husband help his wife most of the time with homemaking and child care?
   Yes _____ No _____ Comment:

2. Should a husband usually ask his wife's opinion before making decisions about major purchases or investments?
   Yes _____ No _____ Comment:

3. Should a husband approve of his wife's working outside of the home, although it interferes with her homemaking and child-care duties?
   Yes _____ No _____ Comment:

4. Should a husband be willing to let his wife take the initiative sexually?
   Yes _____ No _____ Comment:

5. Should a husband be pleased when his wife expresses informal opinions about political or intellectual matters, even if her views differ from his?
   Yes _____ No _____ Comment:

6. Should a husband agree to babysit the children when his wife is unable to do so?
   Yes _____ No _____ Comment:

7. Do you rate yourself relatively liberated?
   Yes _____ No _____ Comment:

Chapter 8
Racism: Confronting a Legacy of White Domination in America

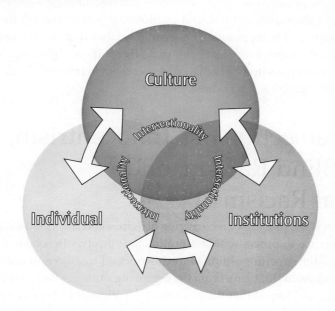

Learning Outcomes

After reading this chapter you will know and be able to:

8.1 Define and provide examples of ethnocentrism in our culture, and explain how color-blind racism represents cultural racism.

8.2 Provide examples of frontstage and backstage racism, and discuss how the ideology of individualism reinforces individual racism.

8.3 Describe and give examples of institutional racism in employment, housing, education, and politics, and discuss the consequences of racism for people of color.

> "To deny a man his hopes because of his color or race . . . is not only to do injustice, it is to deny America and to dishonor the dead who gave their lives for American freedom."
>
> —LYNDON JOHNSON (1908–1973)

If we added the numbers of all people of color living in the United States, the total would be over 100 million. Comparing that number to population figures for nations around the world, this "nation" would be the twelfth most populous, occupying a rank between Mexico and the Philippines (Davis, 2009). The diversity of such a significant group of people could be an enormous asset for the United States, but racism causes many Americans to have a negative reaction to racial diversity. Although popular culture presents racism as something all races can engage in, scholars have described **racism** as a system of unequal power and privilege by which one racial group dominates others. David Wellman (1977) defined racism as a *system* of advantage based on race. Because the dominant group in the United States has historically been White, racism is a product of White racial prejudice and discrimination, reinforced intentionally or unintentionally by institutional power and authority, and used to the advantage of Whites and the disadvantage of people of color (Hilliard, 1992). Even though individual Whites may be "against" racism, they still benefit from a system that privileges Whites as a group. People of color may hold prejudices and discriminate against Whites, but they do not have the social, cultural, and institutional power backing their prejudice and discrimination that is necessary to be accurately labeled *racism*; the impact of their prejudice on Whites is temporary and contextual. By contrast, White people hold social and institutional positions in society that empower them to infuse their racial prejudice into laws, policies, practices, and norms.

The Intersection of Ethnocentrism, Color-Blind Racism, and Cultural Racism

Cultural racism is the practice of recognizing activities and contributions of one racial group in preference to others within a multiracial society, often taking the form of **ethnocentrism**—the superimposition of the history and traditions of one racial group over others (Andrzejewski, 1996). From the beginning, America had a mix of races, but a dominant culture emerged that did not reflect this diversity. Our society has historically continued to disseminate the message that it's better to be a White person than it is to be a person of color (DiAngelo, 2006).

White people are presented as the dominant group in our culture in a variety of ways: in textbooks and other curricular materials; in media and advertising; in comprising the majority of our teachers, role models, heroes, and heroines; in norms and standards of beauty that emphasize conventional White features; in popular television shows featuring friendships among individuals who are all White, even in racially diverse settings such as New York City; and in art, especially religious iconography that depicts God, Adam and Eve, and other special individuals as White. Holidays in the United States include Columbus Day, honoring a man responsible for initiating slavery and genocide of indigenous people that would last for over three centuries (but relegated to a sidebar in history textbooks). Cultural racism is reflected in the return to pre-integration levels of segregation in schools and neighborhoods.

For many years scholars believed that children were not aware of racism and that such an awareness did not develop until early adolescence, but since the 1990s, research has reported children as young as 3 years old being aware of race and susceptible to race bias (Quintana, 2008). Children do not process information the same way adults do, but if a young child is exposed to racial biases against another group, they may internalize it and exhibit this bias in their words or actions. In one study, researchers showed 263 White children between ages 3 and 14 drawings of people in different skin tones, asking the children to say if the individual in each drawing was happy or angry. When children were shown faces that were a light tan color that could have been perceived

"At the start of the twentieth century, over 98 percent of blacks in the United States were native-born, a much higher percentage than for whites. Blacks are as American as you can get."

—MARGUERITE WRIGHT (CONTEMPORARY)

as a White or Black individual, most of the children said the individual was Black and angry, regardless of the facial expression in the drawing. When children believed they were looking at White faces, they said the individual was happy, even when the face was drawn with an obvious frown. When shown Asian faces, White children again described the people as angry. A separate group of Black children were included in the study, and they tended to show no bias but identified drawings as happy or angry depending on the facial expression (Burnett III, 2012).

Cultural racism is reinforced by a racist socialization influenced by media representations. Of 50 top-grossing films worldwide, 46 were directed by White American men. Consider the implications of a racially homogenous group empowered to tell our culture's stories. The problem is not that privileged White men are bad people—it is that their worldview is necessarily limited, especially regarding race; yet it is virtually the only worldview many of us see (Sensoy & DiAngelo, 2012). Videogames are enormously popular with children and youth, and White men dominate the industry. In one game, the story line begins with Africans who are living in poverty being exploited by a pharmaceutical company; yet the character of the game player, a muscular White man, must kill hordes of these Africans who are portrayed as sick and savage human beings. To be fair, most videogames do not employ characters representing familiar racial or ethnic groups in the United States, but they have characters associated with darker or lighter skin color. In one game players must choose between an avatar with dark skin who is athletic or an avatar with light skin who is smart, reinforcing historic racial stereotypes (Sargent, 2012).

The implicit messages of racism from the media and other sources are an example of what has been termed "new racism" (Bonilla-Silva, 2009). New racism refers to how racism has adapted over time so that modern norms, policies, and practices produce discriminatory outcomes without appearing to be explicitly racist. For example, what is termed **color-blind racism** is an example of racism's ability to adapt to cultural changes (Bonilla-Silva, 2009). This ideology asserts that by *ignoring* race we will end racism. This idea was inspired by a misinterpretation of one line from Martin Luther King Jr.'s 1963 "I Have a Dream" speech—a speech that was a turning point in the adaptation of racism. In the period before King gave this speech, many White people felt quite comfortable, even proud, to express their internalized sense of racial superiority and even to admit some of their racial prejudices. But one statement of King's speech—that one day he might be judged by the content of his character and not the color of his skin—struck a moral chord with the public. Seizing on this part of King's speech, the dominant culture began promoting the idea of "color-blindness" as a remedy for racism. However, King presented this speech at the "March on Washington for Jobs and Freedom"; its focus was economic justice, and King was advocating for the elimination of poverty. King did not mean that Whites should deny that race mattered but instead advocated that they should actively work to create a society in which it *actually* didn't matter. But once the civil rights movement became more mainstream, and civil rights legislation was passed, there was a significant change in dominant culture; it was no longer as acceptable for White people to admit to racial prejudice (Picca & Feagin, 2007).

People who say they are color blind argue that all people are the same and that to be aware of group differences is divisive, but critics say that it is not the differences but the perception of differences that is divisive. Historically physical differences have been associated with negative attributes that reinforce prejudice and stereotyping, and we need to talk about those perceptions. As Sue (2015) has asserted, to be color blind is to be color mute. If you don't acknowledge skin color differences, you can't discuss issues related to skin color. By denying racial differences, the color-blind individual denies the existence of prejudices and stereotypes based on perceptions and assumptions stemming from group differences as well as institutional racism that accounts for differences in opportunity and outcomes for people of color compared to White people. The concept of color-blindness may have started out as a well-intentioned strategy, but

Video Example 8.1

In this video, Lilly Wong Fillmore discusses how teachers' bias and racism plays a role in how they interpret children's behavior. What implicit and explicit insight does she give about interpreting student behavior? And how might teachers' interpretations of student behavior be related to aversive racism?

in practice it has served to deny the reality of racism and thus perpetuate it. Scholars have termed this *aversive racism*.

What is aversive racism?

Sue (2015) has noted that as overt acts of racism such as hate crimes have diminished, White attitudes and behaviors "have morphed into a more subtle, covert and insidious form of racial bias known as **aversive racism**" (p. 99). Joel Kovel coined this term in the 1980s to describe the racism that well-intentioned, educated, and progressive people are more likely to enact (Hodson, Dovido, & Gaertner, 2004). It often exists below the surface because it conflicts with consciously held beliefs about equality and justice among racial groups. Aversive racists act in ways that allow them to maintain a positive self-image (i.e., "I am not prejudiced") demonstrated in a variety of ways and to rationalize racial segregation as necessary in order to access "good schools." They explain a lack of cross-racial friendships as a result of few people of color living in their neighborhood or claim relationships with diverse colleagues if their workplace is diverse. They use racially coded terms such as "urban," "underprivileged," "diverse," "sketchy," and "good neighborhoods," and they attribute inequality between Whites and people of color to causes other than racism. Regardless of a White individual's racial beliefs, most are subjected to individual racism expressed by friends or family who will at least occasionally make direct comments and jokes about people of color. Despite the claims of many young White adults that racism is in the past and that they were taught to see everyone as equal, research on individual racism shows otherwise.

> **Self-Check 8.1** Complete this self-check quiz to check your understanding of ethnocentrism in our culture and how color-blind racism represents cultural racism.

Frontstage and Backstage Racism, and How Individualism Reinforces Individual Racism

Individual racism includes both racial prejudice and racist behavior. Racial prejudice refers to negative attitudes an individual holds toward racial groups; these attitudes are learned in many ways—from stereotypes in the media to myths and misconceptions passed on from one generation to the next. Racist behavior occurs when someone acts upon racial prejudices by saying or doing something degrading or harmful toward an individual or group. In a study by Picca and Feagin (2007), 626 White college students at 28 different colleges across the United States kept journals recording every instance related to racial issues, images, and understandings that they observed for six to eight weeks. They recorded over 7500 accounts of blatantly racist comments and actions by the White people in their lives (friends, family members, acquaintances, strangers). This study provided empirical evidence that racism continues to be explicitly expressed by Whites, even those who are young and profess to be progressive. Another example comes from an ABC television program that staged two situations where a young man appeared to be stealing a bicycle by trying to break its lock. The young men were of comparable age and dressed in similar clothes, but the young man who was White was ignored by those passing by and was only confronted once in a one-hour period. The young man who was Black was quickly confronted by several people who accused him of being a thief, and others passing by called the police on their cell phones (Jackson, 2013). Both the study and the staged situations address the difference between what has been termed *front-* and *backstage* racism.

What are front- and backstage racism?

In Picca and Feagin's study, *front-* and *backstage racism* referred to a pattern in people's racist comments and actions. The majority of incidents occurred in what the researchers described as "backstage"—in all-White company. Whites often played predictable roles. There was a protagonist who initiated the racist act, a cheerleader who encouraged it through laughter or agreement, spectators who stood in silence, and (rarely) a dissenter who objected. Virtually all objectors were subjected to a form of peer pressure in which they were told it was "only a joke" and that they should "lighten up." The student journals documented that in "frontstage" settings (i.e., people of color were present), the White participants behaved differently and displayed racially conscious behaviors including acting overly nice, avoiding contact (e.g., crossing a street or not going to a particular bar or club), using stereotypical Black expressions in order to fit in with Black people, and avoiding racial terms or labels by using code words to talk negatively about people of color. In "backstage" settings (i.e., people of color were not present), White students often used humor to reinforce racial stereotypes about people of color, particularly Black people, and occasionally made blatantly racist comments. Picca and Feagin (2007) argue that the purpose of these backstage performances is to create White group solidarity and reinforce the ideology of White (and male) supremacy. This behavior reinforces individual racism in all people, albeit in less formal but perhaps more powerful ways than in the past.

Jackson (2013) described a particularly blatant example of backstage racism. Nicole Cogdell, a Black woman who had been a successful store manager for the retail outlet Wet Seal, was fired after a corporate vice president visited her store. The vice president allegedly told Cogdell's supervisor that he preferred a store manager to have blonde hair and blue eyes. A spokesperson for Wet Seal denied that they engaged in racial discrimination and insisted that they had many African American employees, but in May 2013, the corporation settled a $7.5 million class-action lawsuit after the Equal Opportunity Employment Commission said the evidence of the corporation's racial discrimination was "unusually blatant" (p. 7). When such examples surface, many White people outspokenly deplore such behavior, but too often that becomes an excuse to not believe that it is necessary to look inside themselves for influences of racism.

In what ways are all people affected by individual racism?

The presence of racism in society means that all individuals will internalize it, including people of color, but these messages have a different impact on people of color than on Whites. For people of color, these messages promote what is termed **internalized racial oppression**—the largely unconscious beliefs of racial inferiority and related behaviors that are accepted by people of color who have been raised in a White supremacist society. Conversely, the socialization of White people resulting in their acceptance of largely unconscious beliefs of racial superiority is termed **internalized racial dominance**. An internalized sense of racial dominance is evident in some White individuals by their blatant dislike for people of color, but for most White people, the feeling of racial superiority is more subtle; it is a sense of entitlement to White privileges, reinforced by the ideology of *individualism*.

How does the ideology of individualism reinforce individual racism?

The ideology of individualism emphasizes that we are each unique individuals and that categories such as race have no relevance to our life outcomes. Many examples of **White privilege**, as described by McIntosh (2001), are in large part the result of the privilege

Table 8.1 White Privilege

Because of White privilege, the following activities illustrate assumptions White people can make that people of color cannot make:
1. If I should need to move, I can be pretty sure of renting or purchasing housing in an area that I can afford and in which I would want to live.
2. I can be pretty sure that my neighbors in such a location will be neutral or pleasant to me.
3. I can go shopping alone most of the time, pretty well assured that I will not be followed or harassed.
4. When I am told about our national heritage or about "civilization," I am shown that people of my color made it what it is.
5. I can be sure that my children will be given curricular materials that testify to the existence of their race.
6. Whether I use checks, credit cards, or cash, I can count on my skin color not to work against the appearance of financial reliability.
7. I can swear, or dress in secondhand clothes, or not answer letters, without having people attribute these choices to the bad morals, poverty, or illiteracy of my race.
8. If a traffic cop pulls me over or if the IRS audits my tax return, I can be sure I haven't been singled out because of my race.
9. I can easily buy posters, postcards, picture books, greeting cards, dolls, toys, and children's magazines featuring people of my race.
10. I can choose blemish cover or bandages in "flesh" color and have them more or less match my skin.

SOURCE: Adapted from "White Privilege: Unpacking the Invisible Knapsack" by Peggy McIntosh in *Race, Class, and Gender in the United States: An Integrated Study*, P. Rothenberg, Ed.

of being perceived as an individual rather than as a member of a racial group (see Table 8.1). But there have always been racial groups in the United States, and Whites have historically been the dominant group. As Sue (2015) says, "White privilege cannot exist outside the confines of white supremacy" (p.32). Affirming the ideology of individualism is an attempt to reject the reality of White supremacy and racism by projecting a sense of fairness to everyone but insisting that there is a "level playing field" where the best will experience success denies the existence of discrimination. In a study asking about the extent to which discrimination affects Black people today, only 10 percent of White people said "a lot" compared to 57 percent of Black respondents (Sue, 2015).

Individualism positions the group at the top of the social hierarchy (i.e., Whites) as a collection of outstanding (and unraced) individuals who value hard work, education, and determination. Simultaneously, groups of color that have been consistently denied institutional access and have not had similar achievements are assumed to lack these values (Meizhu, Robles, & Leondar-Wright, 2006). If we believe that we are all individuals and that social categories such as race, class, and gender don't matter but are just "labels" that stereotype us, then logically it follows that we all end up in our appropriate place. Those at the top succeeded on their individual merits, and those at the bottom failed because of individual shortcomings. Individualism upholds the myth of meritocracy—that success is the result of ability and hard work—and a belief in the superiority of those at the top (Bonilla-Silva, 2009; Wise, 2005).

This belief in a "level playing field" where merit is rewarded crumbles before even a cursory examination of the American reality. Rothstein (2017) reports that families of color overwhelmingly tend to live in racially segregated neighborhoods and send their children to schools that are often deteriorating. A disproportionate number of people of color live in poverty, and even when people of color earn a college degree, they do not gain the same financial reward for that achievement as a White individual. Rehmeyer (2007) described a study demonstrating how economic forces arising from racial segregation created economic inequities even when there was no history of discrimination between two groups, concluding: "even when social groups are economically equal, continued segregation may result in inequality over time" (p. 2). Racial issues can be simple or complex. At times White Americans seem to be confused and express contradictory sentiments. In one survey, 61 percent of White Americans agreed that being White was an advantage, but in the same survey, 65 percent of them denied that discrimination against people of color benefited White people. People of color are not confused. In that same survey, 66 percent of the Black respondents said White people have benefited from racial discrimination (DiJulio, Norton, Jackson, & Brodie, 2015).

Because so many Whites choose to live racially segregated lives—another manifestation of racism—their sense of entitlement is seldom challenged, and when it is, lack of experience often leaves Whites unsure of how to respond in constructive ways. One common way that racism is manifested toward people of Asian heritage is through the idea that they are not regarded as American but as *perpetual foreigners* (Howard, 2006). Individuals of Asian heritage frequently encounter such sentiments when they are asked, "Where are you from?" If their answer is "Chicago," the next question often will be, "Okay, but where are you *really* from?" If the individual responds by saying he has always lived in Chicago, the next question may be "Okay, but where did you come from?" This attempt to ascertain the individual's ethnicity implies that Asian Americans are seen as foreigners. Most White Americans have not learned the skills that promote constructive engagement across racial divides. Instead, they tend to express rationalizations that prevent them from seeing and understanding racism.

What are some examples of rationalizations justifying individual racism?

It has been over 60 years since the U.S. Supreme Court's *Brown v. Board of Education* decision ruled segregated schools inherently unequal, mandating racial desegregation "with all deliberate speed," but Schuck (2014) reports that there has been little change as 75 percent of Black children attend schools that have a majority of non-White students. One reason is that few White students attend urban schools because their families participated in the migration to segregated suburbs termed **White flight** (Thompson, 1999). Despite the persistence of segregated schools, many White Americans express the denial rationalization that schools are no longer segregated by race. Yet when Massey (2003) analyzed multiracial societies around the world, he found that the only nation as segregated as the United States was South Africa under apartheid.

In the 1960s, affirmative action programs were instituted to address the well-documented problem of discrimination against hiring people of color. Many White people believe the myth that affirmative action required an employer to give hiring preference to a person of color over a qualified White applicant in order to achieve a racial quota, even if the person of color was not qualified. Using affirmative action to deny racial discrimination is a denial rationalization. In reality, affirmative action was a way to ensure that qualified minority applicants were given the same opportunities for employment as White people; the program never mandated racial quotas in hiring decisions, and employers were never required to hire unqualified people of color. In fact, there is still evidence of employer preference for White applicants today.

Imitating the design of some academic studies, the staff of an ABC news program investigated racial discrimination in employment and housing by providing equal credentials to Black and White individuals. They filmed these individuals going to job interviews and talking with potential landlords; the cameras recorded the dramatic contrast between the friendly, reassuring responses to White people and the curt and dismissive responses to Black people as they were told that the job had been filled or the apartment was no longer available (Jackson, 2013). The preference for White applicants, whether conscious or unconscious, may be seen in the workplace concept of "fit," the tendency to prefer people whose cultural style matches the workplace culture. Since White people are the dominant group in workplace leadership positions, they may be more likely to view White applicants as a better "fit" with the workplace culture (Bohonos, 2013). After all, despite the perception that affirmative action primarily benefits people of color, White women have been the greatest beneficiaries of affirmative action programs. Favoring White women over people of color in employment has contributed to the creation of what some have called a "persistent White ceiling." Reed (2011) has noted that when corporations demonstrate a concern for diversity in hiring executives, they tend to favor White women and those people of color who come from elite backgrounds outside the United States.

Victim-blaming rationalizations are a common White response to allegations of prejudice or discrimination. An Associated Press (2012) poll found that 40 percent of White people viewed both Black people and Hispanics as violent. In a UCLA study, White college students were asked to assess the age and "innocence" of Latino, Black, and White boys. The students saw Black boys as more intimidating and overestimated their age by 4.5 years. Since teachers in K–12 schools are predominantly White, some are likely to view Black children's misbehavior through a harsher lens, seeing the behavior as threatening, requiring sterner discipline, and justifying their actions by blaming the victim (Editors of *Rethinking Schools*, 2015). Studies have reported that White people often view Black children as young as 13 as adults. Overestimating the age of Black men may have serious consequences for these children. A 2014 report found that police officers across America were responsible for the deaths of Black youth (ages 15–19) at a rate of 31 out of one million compared to 1.5 out of one million for White men in the same age range. Often the police have blamed the victim, and juries have accepted these rationalizations and acquitted most of these officers. In Cleveland, a 12-year-old Black child named Tamir Rice was playing with a toy gun in a public park and a police officer shot and killed him within seconds of arriving on the scene. Tamir's 14-year-old sister ran over to help him but an officer tackled her and handcuffed her as she lay on the ground. The officer who did the shooting called the dispatcher he described the victim as a 20-year-old Black man (Editors of *Rethinking Schools*, 2015).

Another especially offensive use of victim-blaming rationalizations occurs when White people hear Black people complaining about racism and perceive them as not being patriotic Americans. If you accept the conventional measure of patriotism as the willingness to risk your life by enlisting in one of the military services to fight for our nation, most people of color clearly emerge as being patriotic, especially Black people. Buckley (2001) described the history of African Americans who volunteered, fought, and died in every war in which the United States was involved: the Revolutionary War, the Civil War, the Spanish-American War, and all conflicts, large and small, in the twentieth century. (See Figure 8.1.) Further, Black people enlisted in today's military services far outnumber their proportion of the population.

When White Americans acknowledge problems of discrimination against Americans of color, they often express no sense of responsibility. History provides numerous examples of the White majority in the United States discussing "the Negro problem" as if it had nothing to do with Whites. Novelist Richard Wright contradicted that assertion: "There isn't any Negro problem; there is only a white problem" (Lipsitz, 2008). Wright meant that the racial attitudes and behaviors of White people were the problem—that racism in America meant White racism. Saying that racism is only a problem for people of color allows White people to rationalize their unwillingness to do anything to address this issue. If White people genuinely want to confront racism, they must be willing to challenge their worldviews. This requires not only an honest exploration of the ideology of individualism that perpetuates racism but also an overhaul of the institutional policies and practices that continue to create unequal opportunity for people.

Figure 8.1 African Americans in the American Military

Members of the segregated 10th Calvary, called Buffalo soldiers, were part of the "Rough Riders" led by Teddy Roosevelt who took San Juan Hill during the Spanish-American War; African American soldiers are rarely acknowledged in films or in history books.

SOURCE: Library of Congress Prints and Photographs Division

 Self-Check 8.2 Complete this self-check quiz to check your understanding of frontstage and backstage racism, and how the ideology of individualism reinforces individual racism.

Institutional Racism and the Consequences for People of Color

Jones (1997) defined **institutional racism** as "established laws, customs, and practices that systematically reflect and produce racial inequities in American society" (p. 438). We rely on institutions in America. Although individual racism is damaging, institutional racism is far more devastating because of the broader impact institutions have on people.

Institutional racism can be intentional when it is a result of a prejudiced individual making a conscious decision about an individual or group based on their race. Williams (2013) described a study in which pairs of Black and White men and pairs of Hispanic and White men applied for the same jobs. Identical qualifications were created on their résumés. The men were trained to present themselves in similar ways to minimize differences during interviews; still, White men received three times as many job offers as did Black or Hispanic men. We also know that institutional racism can be unintentional. For more than two decades, multiple studies on racial gaps in high stakes tests has reported that social stigma results in lower test scores for stigmatized groups. The lower test scores promote negative attitudes among White faculty and students, reinforcing the stereotype that Black students are cognitively inferior to Whites. This is not a new problem. In a 1935 essay, W. E. B. Du Bois described how White administrators, faculty, and students without conscious intent shape the learning environment in a way that stigmatizes students of color and diminishes their motivations and aspirations (Hamilton, 2015).

Because most Americans appear to agree that it is wrong to discriminate based on race, ethnicity, gender, or other factors, it is important to understand how institutional discrimination occurs. Whether intentional or unintentional, institutional racism has negative consequences for people of color. Unemployment statistics document how race makes a difference when decisions are made about hiring people.

How is institutional racism reflected in statistics on employment?

Disproportionate numbers of people of color work in low-paying, low-status jobs, and people of color tend to have significantly higher unemployment rates compared to Whites. The data for youth of color is troubling. The U.S. Bureau of Labor Statistics (2014) reported a 33.4 percent unemployment rate for Black teenagers and 23.8 percent for Hispanic teenagers compared to 18.9 percent for White teenagers. Black teenage unemployment is as high as 60 percent in some urban areas. The employment discrepancy continues after graduation from high school. Higher percentages of African Americans are unemployed in the year after they graduate from high school than White graduates, regardless of whether the graduates were from rural or urban schools. The unemployment rate for Black graduates was higher than that for Whites regardless of socioeconomic status, type of high school attended, or type of academic program in which they were enrolled. Studies of comparable job applicants reporting that three times as many White applicants were called back compared to Black applicants caused Aronson (2008) to conclude: "Skin color, it seems, still outweighs character where hiring is concerned" (p. 307).

Despite affirmative action programs, studies by the U.S. Bureau of Labor Statistics (2014) document that the disparity in adult unemployment has continued with a 4.8 percent rate for Whites, 6.5 percent for Latinos, 11.1 percent for African Americans, and 11.3 percent for Native Americans. On some reservations, Native Americans unemployment is higher than 80 percent, and this group is three times more likely than Whites to live in poverty (Jenkins, 2009). Urban areas showed even larger disparities in jobless rates for White and Black workers. In a study by the Center for Economic Development at the University of Wisconsin-Milwaukee, Levine (2010) compared Black and White jobless rates in Milwaukee with those in selected cities such as Chicago, Buffalo, Cleveland, and Detroit. Levine looked at jobless rates rather than unemployment rates because the latter does not include adult people in the workforce who have given up on finding a job, often because no jobs appear to be available. This is especially a problem in urban areas. Levine's data (see Table 8.2) reveals that urban Black workers are almost twice as likely not to have a job as urban White workers. Milwaukee had the most significant problem, with 53.3 percent of its Black workers jobless, almost two and a half times the rate for White workers. Such data clearly suggest that race, whether intentional or unintentional, was a factor in hiring employees.

Table 8.2 Black/White Unemployment in Selected Metropolitan Areas

	Black	White	Black/White Ratio
1. Milwaukee	23.7	4.8	4.94
2. Cleveland	15.5	5.1	3.04
3. Chicago	14.1	5.6	2.52
4. Detroit	15.1	6.6	2.29
5. Buffalo	9.2	5.7	1.61

SOURCE: Bureau of Labor Statistics (2015).

How does institutional racism influence hiring decisions?

To understand why disparities in Black and White unemployment exist, examine how hiring decisions are made. Studies repeatedly show that one of the most important methods used to recruit and hire employees is **word-of-mouth hiring**. If job seekers have relatives or friends already working for the company to recommend them, they have a better chance of being hired. Research suggests that 60 percent to 90 percent of blue-collar workers were hired because of recommendations from family or friends—and the same pattern has been observed in hiring decisions for white-collar jobs. For example, a Rutgers study involved interviews with hundreds of people and confirmed that White people tend to help other White people to find jobs. In these interviews, White people said they received help from either family or friends to get 70 percent of the jobs that they held during their work career (Jackson, 2013).

Employers feel they benefit from the word-of-mouth approach. If a trusted employee recommends someone, the employers believe that the risk in determining the quality of the individual being hired is greatly reduced. Another benefit is that hiring costs are minimal; jobs are filled without having to pay to advertise them. Because of word-of-mouth hiring, Lipsitz (2008) found that 86 percent of available jobs never appeared in the classified ads of local newspapers.

Word-of-mouth hiring disadvantages people of color because of the history of segregation and discrimination in the United States. In the past, White male employees were blatantly favored over applicants who were women or people of color. At one time, the preference was so obvious that state and federal governments passed anti-discrimination laws to address the problem; still, White men constituted a disproportionate share of the workforce. Schaefer (2008) reviewed social distance studies indicating that people consistently indicate a preference for people most like themselves; therefore, White people may recommend other White people simply to make sure they will be with people with whom they are comfortable.

Furthermore, because of ongoing housing segregation, White Americans have not tended to become friends with people of color. When White workers recommend a friend or relative for a job, they may insist that they are not trying to prevent a person of color from being hired but instead are helping someone they know. Intentional or not, word-of-mouth job recruitment offers a distinct advantage to White job applicants and contributes to discrimination documented by statistics on unemployment disparities between Black and White workers.

Discrimination also occurs in decisions regarding company location. Because neighborhoods in the United States still reveal a pattern of racial segregation, a company's decision to locate in a White suburb means that the employees hired will be primarily or exclusively White. Studies show that when a new company selects a location or an established company expands to a new location, employees who live within a 30- to 40-mile radius of the worksite tend to be hired.

Wilson (1996) reported a trend toward the suburbanization of industry in the 1990s, especially among retail trade companies. The trend has continued. White suburbs are advantaged because they tend to be more affluent than urban areas and usually offer more incentives to influence a company's decision to relocate. Wilson reported that when a number of low-income Black people were placed in suburban apartments, they were significantly more likely to find work than the low-income Black people placed in apartments in the city; the reason was the higher availability of jobs in the suburbs. According to data from the federal government, America's suburbs are dominating employment growth in metropolitan areas, responsible for almost 70 percent of that growth with another 11 percent happening in exurbs (Cox, 2016). A company's reasons for selecting a location may have more to do with economic incentives than with race, but the consequences of that decision have a racial impact.

> "The sad truth is that most evil is done by people who never make up their minds to be either good or evil."
>
> —HANNAH ARENDT (1898–1989)

How has institutional racism influenced the development of segregated neighborhoods?

Studies report that neighborhoods in the United States continue to reveal a pattern of racial segregation (Bonilla-Silva, 2001; Farley, 2010). Although there has been some improvement since the 1980s, Massey (2003) described the level of Black and White segregation in urban areas using an index where a score of "0" means Black and White people are evenly distributed in a neighborhood, and a score of "100" identifies a neighborhood where Black and White people are completely segregated. Any score over 50 is regarded as "high," and a score over 70 is viewed as an example of "extreme" segregation. Massey identified the most highly segregated metropolitan areas:

> Detroit, with an index of 85, followed by Milwaukee (82), New York (81), Newark, N.J. (80), and Chicago (80). Other areas with "extreme" segregation scores include Buffalo, Cincinnati, Cleveland, Kansas City, Philadelphia, and St. Louis. (p. 22)

Studies have documented that White families will stay in a neighborhood as long as Black families do not exceed 7 percent or 8 percent of its residents; once that percentage is exceeded, White families leave (Bonilla-Silva, 2001). It is not surprising that a report from the National Fair Housing Alliance (2017) found that housing segregation persists in America, and that the average White American is living in a neighborhood that is almost 80 percent White. Further, when middle class Black families live in White majority neighborhoods, they are more likely to be living near low-income areas. One study reported that 32 percent of middle/upper income Black people live in communities that border severely disadvantaged neighborhoods, compared to only 7 percent of middle/upper income Whites (Rothstein, 2014).

Neighborhood segregation is assured when realtors engage in a practice known as **steering**. The term refers to keeping files of homes for sale in White neighborhoods separate from those for sale in areas consisting predominantly or exclusively of families of color. In a multi-year study by the National Fair Housing Alliance (2017), Black and Latino testers contacted realtors to ask that they be shown prospective homes. About 20 percent of the realtors refused to meet with them, and those who did steered the testers to segregated neighborhoods 87 percent of the time. If clients make a specific request, realtors may show them homes in racially mixed neighborhoods, if there are any. If accused of racism, realtors may claim that White homeowners who don't want people of color moving into their neighborhoods will not list their home with a realtor whom they believe will show their home to people of color. Realtors could insist that they are not being racist but are simply respecting the wishes of their clients.

Zoning ordinances might also contribute to racial segregation of neighborhoods. City councils often approve ordinances excluding multifamily dwellings in certain residential areas. The cost of homes in such areas is usually well beyond the means of many families of color, but the rental price of units in a multifamily dwelling might be affordable. So the passage of a zoning ordinance expressly prohibiting multifamily housing virtually eliminates the possibility of families of color moving into the neighborhood.

Segregation aside, it is often more difficult for people of color to finance the purchase of homes. Between 1998 and 2008, banks and other lending institutions began to approve more home loans to people of color as part of the subprime mortgage fiasco. When the financial collapse happened, many critics blamed lenders for making too many bad loans to people, especially people of color, whose finances were inadequate to pay off their home loans. Yet data collected over this 10-year period from the Community Advantage Program that facilitated loans to families with low incomes or single-headed households showed that even though these clients presented a greater risk, they were no more likely to default on conventional home mortgage loans than the rest of the population (Oliver & Shapiro, 2008). The problem was that subprime mortgage loans involved hidden costs, wildly adjustable rates, and severe prepayment penalties. Yet African American families who qualified for conventional mortgages often were steered to the more profitable subprime home loans; twice as many

"An illustration of the craving people have to attach favorable symbols to themselves is seen in the community where white people banded together to force out a Negro family that had moved in. They called themselves 'Neighborly Endeavor' and chose as their motto the Golden Rule."

—GORDON ALLPORT (1897–1967)

Video Example 8.2
Begin this video at 1:15 and play it until 6:46. In this video, Yale School of Management's Michael Krauss discusses misconceptions about the reality of the wealth and income gap between Black and White Americans and the myth of the American Dream. What role does institutional racism play in creating a wealth and income gap between Black and White Americans? How does institutional racism as referred to in Chapter 8 in relationship to the development of neighborhoods, hiring, and employment relate to what Kraus discusses? Even further, what role does institutional racism play in perpetuating the myth of the American Dream?

http://www.youtube.com/watch?v=QMgKl3n_c1w

African American and Latino homeowners lost their homes because they defaulted on the subprime loans. One estimate of the loss of wealth to African American homeowners was somewhere between $72 billion and $93 billion (Oliver & Shapiro, 2008). In 2011, the Bank of America paid $335 million to settle a lawsuit accusing the bank of engaging in discriminatory practices against Latinos and African Americans stemming from subprime lending; it was the largest settlement ever with regard to residential loans (Stiglitz, 2012). Yet this settlement did not redress the harm done. The National Fair Housing Alliance (2017) reported that the loss of net worth for Black homeowners was 53 percent and for Latinos was 66 percent compared to White homeowners who lost only 16 percent of their net worth.

How does institutional racism occur in K–12 schools?

Maintaining segregated schools is the obvious example of institutional racism in K–12 schools. In 1954 the U.S. Supreme Court ruled that racially segregated schools were unconstitutional and that schools should be desegregated "with all deliberate speed," but there was little change until Congress passed the 1964 Civil Rights Act. According to Gary Orfield of the UCLA Civil Rights Project, U.S. schools were engaged in court-ordered desegregation for slightly more than two decades; during that time the numbers of students of color graduating from high school increased significantly, and the race gap in test scores decreased substantially (Epperly, 2014). As schools began resegregating in the 1990s, the gap in racial test scores widened, and multiple studies found that American schools were more segregated than they were before the passage of the 1964 Civil Rights Act (Carjuzaa, Baldwin, & Munson, 2015). One study conducted by the UCLA Civil Rights Project reported that Latinos are even more segregated than African Americans in suburban schools, and that both Black and Latino students tend to be in schools with a large majority of poor children compared to White and Asian American students who are more likely to attend schools with a majority of middle-class students (Epperly, 2014).

In response to the increasing presence of students of color, some schools, especially in urban areas, have implemented curricula more inclusive of the achievements of people of color, but critics complain that portrayals of Black historical leaders are "whitewashed" by eliminating controversial information (Quinlan, 2016). At the heart of the problem is that textbooks have historically demonstrated a Eurocentric bias in history, literature, art, and music (Kirp, 1991; Loewen, 1995; Quinlan, 2016). As Tobin and Ybarra (2008) state: "Bias plagues textbooks by choosing one group's narrative over another—when that narrative is historically wrong and the facts are not the facts" (p. 7). The prevalence of textbook bias requires that teachers develop supplementary materials to provide students with information about multicultural perspectives. This is a difficult task because the major function of teaching is delivering curriculum, and teachers have limited time and resources to develop new material.

Another significant issue in K–12 schools today involves racial disparities in the suspension of students. This is a critical issue because suspensions are a major factor in predicting which students will drop out of school. Losen (2011) reported that in 1973, suspensions for White, Hispanic, and Native American students were equal, with 3 percent of each group having been suspended at least once, while twice as many Black students (6 percent) had been suspended. By 2013, Black student suspension rates had almost tripled (16 percent), followed by Native Americans (10 percent) and Hispanic students (6.5 percent), while White student suspensions remained low at 4 percent (U.S. Department of Education, 2014). It was even worse for all groups in middle school, where 10 percent of White students were suspended, but approximately 16 percent of Hispanic and Native American students and over 28 percent of Black students were suspended. Among middle school girls, four times as many Black women had been suspended as White women (Losen, 2011). One study reported that White students were more likely to be suspended for offenses that could be objectively documented such as smoking, using profanity, and vandalism, but Black students were more likely to be suspended for behaviors requiring a subjective judgment such as being disrespectful,

> " . . . if we were to select the most intelligent, imaginative, energetic, and stable third of all mankind, all races would be represented."
>
> —FRANZ BOAS (1858–1942)

being too loud, and loitering. Losen (2011) referred to the conclusion from a study of 21 schools that found "no evidence that African-American over-representation in school suspension is due to higher rates of misbehavior," but that "Black students were more likely to be sent to the office for disciplinary reasons" (pp. 6–7).

Another example of racism in schools is **tracking**—grouping students into categories by ability and assigning them to specific, ability-related classes. Most public elementary, middle, and high schools in America engage in some form of tracking. Students of color tend to be overrepresented in classes for slow learners, underrepresented in accelerated classes, and placed in vocational or remedial classes in disproportionate numbers (Oakes, 2005; Oakes et al., 2000). According to Callahan (2005), tracking is also harmful to English Language Learners (ELLs) because teachers tend to regard these students as having cognitive deficits instead of realizing their difficulties may be related to their learning in another language. Researchers have concluded that tracking results in both race and class segregation because low-income students are typically placed in different tracks than middle- or upper-class students. In a meta-analysis of over 300 studies, Hattie (2009) concluded that tracking resulted in minimal benefits, even for high-achieving students, and significantly negative consequences for low-track students.

Another ongoing controversy is the closing of public schools. In 2013, the Chicago Board of Education closed 49 elementary schools, the largest mass closing of schools in American history. The Board argued that the closings would save millions of dollars and improve the education of students from the closed schools. The decision primarily impacted African American families; their children accounted for 88 percent of students whose schools were closed. In Philadelphia, Black students represented 81 percent of the students who saw their schools shut down. African American parents in Chicago have complained that their children's quality of education has not improved and the closures had a negative economic impact due to weakened property values and the harm done to small businesses that destabilized the affected communities. Although the Chicago Board tried to sell the closed schools, many remain vacant, are often vandalized, and are sites for criminal activity. School boards defend these decisions as a budget reduction strategy, saying the closed schools were expensive to operate because too few students attended them, but critics note that many children in these schools were students enrolled in early childhood programs or students with special needs that required additional space (Cohen, 2016).

Research on students relocated from a closed school does not support claims of higher academic achievement. In Chicago, Newark, and Philadelphia, the typical portrait of these students was that their academic performance initially decreased at their new school but eventually returned to the level they achieved before but with no additional improvement. Further, these students often encountered bullying and violence as teachers struggled with increased numbers of student in their classes. Some students were relocated more than once because their new school was underperforming and eventually was closed. As for the justification of saving money, the reality is that it is expensive to close schools due to increased transportation costs, decreased value of school properties, and the cost to demolish buildings. In Washington DC the school closings cost the school district $40 million. Parents in Chicago, Newark, and New Orleans filed federal complaints alleging racial discrimination against students of color and their communities. They are supported by studies reporting that the higher the percentage of students from low-income families in a school, the lower is the level of funding to maintain the facilities. Despite multiple studies on the negative impact of unsafe and inadequate schools on student academic achievement, research on schools report that the students most at-risk get about half the funding available to students from wealthier families (Cohen, 2016). School closings were supposed to result in students performing at a higher academic level, giving them a better chance to go on to college, but this is not what has happened, and even if it had worked, these students would have still encountered problems in higher education as well.

What is the nature of institutional racism in higher education?

According to a report by Georgetown University, increasing numbers of Hispanics and African Americans are enrolling in postsecondary institutions. New freshman enrollments grew 107 percent for Hispanics and 73 percent for African Americans, compared to a 15 percent increase for Whites (Carnevale & Strohl, 2013). The report also found that White, Hispanic, and African American students with higher test scores attended college at about the same rate, but it also showed evidence that higher education is contributing to the perpetuation of White privilege. Based on a survey of newly enrolled students at 4400 postsecondary institutions from 1995–2010, 82 percent of White students were enrolled in the 468 most selective colleges and universities in the nation, while 72 percent of Hispanics and 68 percent of African Americans were enrolled in two-year, open-access colleges. Over 30 percent of Hispanics and African Americans who maintained a high school grade point average above a 3.5 attended community colleges. The result is that White people constituted 75 percent of students at the most selective four-year colleges, while only 14 percent were Black and Hispanic, which gives White students four major advantages: (1) greater access to financial resources, (2) higher completion rates, (3) higher rates of graduate school enrollment and attainment of advanced college degrees, and (4) higher future earnings (Carnevale & Strohl, 2013).

Student debt is an issue affecting all college students, but it affects students of color even more. A 2015 study of student loans in higher education reported that not only have Black students typically had to borrow more money than White students to complete their education and graduate, they more often have to resort to the most costly loans with higher interest rates, the least generous repayment terms, and higher default rates. In addition, many for-profit institutions that encourage students to get loans by making exaggerated claims for the success rates of their graduates have disproportionately and aggressively recruited students of color (Hamilton, Cottom, Darity Jr., Aja, & Ash, 2015). Such forms of institutional racism are difficult to address. It is especially difficult for people of color because successful confrontation requires political power at local, state, and federal levels. Institutional racism curtails opportunities to be elected to local governing bodies—school boards, city councils, or county commissions—and makes it even more difficult to win party primaries or elections at the state and national levels.

Video Example 8.3

In this video, a speaker discusses cultural differences between home and school cultures. How do the examples she uses align with examples of institutional racism discussed in this chapter? What are some other ways that cultural differences between home and school cultures might relate to institutional racism and its effects on students?

How does institutional racism affect politics?

In the early 1960s there were virtually no Black people in public office, but the 1965 Voting Rights Act enfranchised over 20 million people. After the 2000 elections there were 9000 African Americans in public office. In the 2012 presidential election, 66 percent of African Americans voted, higher than any other racial group, but there was a 10 percent gap between men and women. A Harvard University scholar argued that this gap is explained almost entirely by the number of African American men who were denied the right to vote (Bouie, 2013). Although the Justice Department had previously rejected strict voter identification laws, after the 2013 U.S. Supreme Court decision overturning Section 4 of the Voting Rights Act, six southern states immediately implemented restrictive voting laws. In 2016, a federal appeals court struck down North Carolina's law, ruling that the law was clearly intended to discriminate based on race. There are likely to be other court cases to come.

Although the situation has improved today, people of color still tend to be underrepresented in the House of Representatives and Senate at both state and federal levels. People of color constitute more than 36 percent of the U.S. population, but in the 115th Congress there were only 11 (22 percent) in the Senate, with five Latinos (setting a new record), three African Americans and three Asian/Pacific Island Americans (also a new record), and 97 people of color (22 percent) in the House—49 African Americans, 45 Latinos, 18 Asian/Pacific Island Americans, and two Native Americans (Manning, 2017). Politicians often use their seat in the House of Representatives as a springboard to running for the Senate; prior to the 2012 elections, nearly half of the Senators had previously served in the House. Yet only four of the 46 Black members of the House have run for the Senate, and none of them were successful, in part because of the problems uniquely affecting candidates of color.

> "In a democracy, the majority of citizens is capable of exercising the most cruel oppression upon the minority."
>
> —EDMUND BURKE (1729–1797)

Bouie (2012) explained that many Black House members are elected from districts with a significant percentage of African American voters and only need minimum support from White voters to get elected. These housing patterns are a consequence of historic discrimination, but the result is that a Black candidate for a statewide office such as Senator or Governor will need the support of White voters to be elected. In addition, the districts these Black officials represent tend to be less affluent because of historic discrimination in Black employment and other financial opportunities. Since fundraising for most candidates for statewide office tends to be based on the district they represent, Black representatives are typically at a disadvantage in fundraising. As the first African American woman to be elected to the Senate, Carol Moseley Braun had firsthand knowledge of this dilemma: "If a person does not have access to very deep pockets, they really don't have much of a chance" (Bouie, 2012, p. 7).

In New Mexico, some Hispanic candidates have been successful by emphasizing their Spanish (i.e., White) ancestry. Shorris (2001) noted that such candidates were elected to local and state offices "long before other Latinos could get past gerrymandering, ward politics, and at-large elections" (p. 167). The use of **at-large candidates** involves members of city councils or school boards being elected by the entire city instead of by their respective districts or wards. If the majority of voters in a city are White, electing at-large candidates will assure all-White representation on councils or boards, despite having areas within the city consisting primarily or exclusively of people of color.

An Associated Press (2010) story described how the at-large issue was resolved in the wake of a discrimination lawsuit from Latinos living in Port Chester, New York. Port Chester is a community of 30,000 residents, half of whom are Latinos, but only one quarter of the Latino residents are voters. Every two years, Port Chester voters would elect two of the town's six trustees from a slate of at-large candidates, and even with the influx of Latino residents, all six trustees continued to be White. After reviewing the evidence, Judge Stephen Robinson ruled that Port Chester was in violation of the federal Voting Rights Act. The judge ordered the community to revise its electoral process so that Latino voters were not unfairly denied their political voice by "diluting" their votes. The village still wanted to elect trustees who were concerned for the entire community and not just one district within the community. Instead of creating districts, Port Chester approved an electoral process called "cumulative voting," in which each voter can vote for an at-large candidate more than one time. The plan called for all six trustees to be selected in a single election, and in casting their six votes, all voters were given the option of voting up to six times for the same candidate. In the first election implementing this new approach, Luis Marino, a Peruvian immigrant, received the fourth highest number of votes, becoming Port Arthur's first Latino trustee.

In the 2008 presidential campaign, the Democratic Party exemplified the changing face of America by fielding three highly regarded candidates who were not White men. The Latino candidate, Governor Bill Richardson (New Mexico), dropped out of the race, but Hillary Rodham Clinton and Barack Obama competed for the nomination. Perhaps the most significant achievement of Obama's campaign organization was its ability to overcome fundraising problems that have tended to disadvantage candidates of color at all levels in the past. His campaign's phenomenal fundraising during the primaries was surpassed after he received the party's nomination for President. Much of the fundraising was done on the Internet as 3.1 million contributors gave an average of $86. Despite this fundraising success and Senator Obama's impressive oratory, pundits still wondered if White voters would vote for an African American candidate, but on election night, Barack Obama emerged as the first African American and the first openly biracial individual to become President of the United States. Many Americans viewed President Obama's election as a major blow against racism in the United States, and they hoped that his victory would promote even more aggressive challenges to institutional racism (see Figure 8.2).

Since the election, examples of both individual and institutional racism have demonstrated that neither can be expected to decline in the immediate future. Evidence comes from predatory lending practices that have disproportionately targeted families of color, employment data that have continued to document higher unemployment rates for workers of color, racial profiling implicitly endorsed in anti-immigrant statutes approved by state legislatures in Arizona and Alabama, and the continued growth and expansion of hate groups (Potok, 2013). The Associated Press (2012) poll documented that negative attitudes among Americans have increased since the 2008 election, perhaps related to the declining economic conditions for much of the middle class. Wages have been stagnant, some middle-class neighborhoods are deteriorating, and schools are consistently underfunded. The major accomplishment of the Obama Administration was the passage of the Affordable Care Act (ACA) in 2010 with the immediate result that 16 million more Americans were covered by health insurance, and the number of uninsured Americans was cut in half (Diamond, 2015). Following the passage of the ACA, there were economic benefits such as an increase in consumer spending and a decrease in unemployment that some experts attributed in part to the ACA (Furman, 2014). Yet problems have persisted. Health care bills are still one of the biggest expenses for Americans. In 2015, the average family of four with a median income of $53,000 spent over $10,000 for care that insurance didn't cover (Edwards, 2016). As of this writing, the ACA remains a controversial program that Republicans are trying to replace since they took control of the House and Senate in the 2016 elections. Americans who finally received health insurance under the ACA are actively protesting efforts to eliminate their coverage. The difficulties are complex, and this debate is likely to continue for some time to come.

Figure 8.2 A Historical Appointment

President Barack Obama's nomination of Judge Sonia Sotomayor meant that she would become the first Latina to serve on the Supreme Court. Although widely regarded as one of the best qualified nominees in recent years, Republican opponents demonstrated the persistence of historic prejudices as they questioned her abilities and even accused her of being "a racist" for arguing that her ethnicity provided a valuable perspective for her judicial decisions.

SOURCE: Whitehouse.gov, Stacey Ilyse Photography

How can institutional racism be reduced in the United States?

In our K–12 schools, one promising program is called "restorative justice," which is based on viewing a school as a community. Restorative practices are a preventive rather than a reactionary approach. When misbehavior occurs, it is regarded as harming not just the individuals involved but also the community. In response, restorative justice implements practices that address the harm done to both. Such practices have been described as a tool kit for teachers to foster positive relationships in the school community among students and between students, teachers and staff. In response to a student conflict, restorative justice provides students with the opportunity to engage in discussions of the problem to identify who was harmed, how the individual or individuals were affected, and what actions are most likely to resolve the problem (Kline, 2016). Restorative justice includes strategies such as "victim offender mediation" (VOM), where juvenile offenders meet with their victims to repair the damage done and restore the bonds of community. One Midwestern school reported that students participating in VOM listened thoughtfully to their victim and began to view their behavior differently, with many expressing remorse and even empathy for their victim. Urban schools in Philadelphia and San Diego are implementing restorative justice, and the early results appear positive. The approach has even gone global, being adopted by schools in New Zealand and Scotland (Kline, 2016).

But institutional racism involves confronting complex problems that are not easily solved. In the 1970s, scholars began to emphasize that intent was not necessarily relevant to the issue of whether institutional policies and practices created advantages for White people and disadvantages for people of color. In the 1980s, however, the U.S. Supreme Court ruled that to prove a claim of discrimination, plaintiffs had to demonstrate that the intended purpose of institutional policies or practices was to discriminate against a particular group. Producing statistics documenting racial inequities was not enough; plaintiffs had to prove that those who developed policies or engaged in practices alleged as discriminatory were guilty of an evil intent. As Bonilla-Silva (1999) noted,

> The standards that the Supreme Court enacted . . . on discrimination (plaintiffs carrying the burden of proof in discrimination cases and the denial of statistical evidence as valid proof of discrimination) help to preserve intact contemporary forms for reproducing racial inequality in America. (p. 85)

The Supreme Court's ruling illustrates the difficulties involved in making much progress on institutional racism unless the people of the United States and the legal system acknowledge that evil intent is not always the cause of discrimination. When courts are willing to examine the issue of who is advantaged or disadvantaged by institutional policies or practices—regardless of the original goals that these policies or practices were intended to address—then we may see progress in the United States against subtle but widespread institutional practices of racism. In the meantime, people of color must rely on affirmative action programs and legal recourse to respond to blatant discrimination within American institutions. Affirmative action has been effective to a degree, but it also has produced vigorous criticisms.

How do advocates and critics assess the effectiveness of affirmative action programs?

Affirmative action advocates cite studies beginning in the 1960s showing that the number of workers of color decreased in traditional occupations and increased in other occupations. For example, the percentage of African Americans employed as domestic servants or other service occupations decreased, while their numbers have increased in the ranks of bank tellers, police officers, firefighters, and electricians. Larger numbers of professionals of color have moved into high-status positions (Hacker, 1992). Critics argue that these gains have primarily benefited people of color, especially Black people, who were already middle class. They propose changing affirmative action policies to focus on socioeconomic status rather than race, but Miah (2010) described the racism still encountered by middle-class Black people despite their economic success.

Critics of affirmative action charge that these programs engender **reverse discrimination** by giving applicants of color preferential treatment over Whites, especially White men. Historically, studies have not supported this allegation. Kivel (2002) summarized a report reviewing opinions rendered by U.S. District Courts and Courts of Appeal for over four years. There were 3000 discrimination cases, of which 100 alleged reverse discrimination. The courts found merit in only 6 of the 100 claims and ordered restitution. Stainback (2013) engaged in a review of employment since the passage of the 1964 Civil Rights Act and found no evidence of reverse discrimination against White applicants. Affirmative action advocates argue that White men have historically benefited from preferential treatment, beginning with the U.S. Constitution and sustained in most policies and practices implemented since then. In addition to historical examples, we currently have ample evidence that racial discrimination persists, requiring that the United States maintain a commitment to the goals of affirmative action programs.

Critics of affirmative action insist that the most pernicious discrimination occurring today is reverse discrimination against White men, and some refer to studies showing that African Americans were almost 40 percent of new hires for police officers in U.S. cities from 1970 to 2000 (Reaves & Hickman, 2002). Since African Americans constitute only 12 percent of the population in the United States, this appears to justify the accusation that urban police departments had hired an excessive number of Black applicants. However, Vick (2015) reported that of the approximately 680,000 police officers in the United States, 80 percent of them were White with African Americans and Latinos accounting for most of the remaining 20 percent. These figures are similar to their percentage of the overall population, but for many years the African American share of urban populations has been much higher than their share of the general population, and Latinos are catching up with them. Analyzing the population of almost any specific urban area will show that people of color are not represented on these police forces at a similar percentage to their share of the urban population. Ashkenas and Park (2014) reviewed the percentage of officers of color in urban areas and reported that in almost all of them, including cities such as Boston, St. Louis, Cleveland, Atlanta, Miami, Chicago, Kansas City, Phoenix, and Los Angeles, officers of color still did not equal the percentage of the city's residents of color.

Concern about the need for more officers of color in urban areas has increased following the death of Michael Brown, an unarmed young Black man who was shot and killed by a White police officer in Ferguson, Missouri. At the time, about 67 percent of Ferguson's residents were Black, but 49 of its 53 police officers were White (Ashkenas & Park, 2014). Protests against predominantly White police forces where White officers have killed unarmed Black men have occurred in South Carolina over the killing of Walter Scott; in Cleveland, where Freddy Gray died while in police custody; and in Minneapolis, where Philandro Castile was shot at point-blank range after telling the police officer that he was licensed to carry a gun (perhaps hoping that by honestly providing this information the officer would not shoot him). In 2015, police officers killed more African Americans than were lynched in the year of the Jim Crow era that recorded the highest number of lynchings (Editors of *Rethinking Schools*, 2016). What is making a difference now is that many of the victims are being filmed with cell phones and in some cases by body-cams that are being used by one-third of all local police departments (Vick, 2015). The anger that has fueled the protests against these killings has resulted in the formation of a group called "Black Lives Matter" (BLM), who call for changes in police training and address other forms of oppression in urban communities. BLM grew out of a Facebook post by Alicia Garza following George Zimmerman's acquittal of the murder of Treyvon Martin. In the wake of the shooting deaths of other unarmed Black men by police officers, BLM became a significant voice protesting these injustices, but the movement claims no centralized leadership and no hierarchy in its organizational structure. The Occupy Movement was another protest group that used this model, and the failure of that movement to sustain its momentum has caused many who support BLM goals to worry that this movement may share the same fate. The existence of 30 BLM chapters in the United States and one in Toronto provides the best sense of hope that the movement is now firmly established and will continue to grow.

To determine if affirmative action hiring decisions by urban police departments have been fair, the most useful measure is to compare the percentage of officers of color with the percentage of people of color in an urban community. For example, in 2013 less than half of New York City's population was White, and a little over half was equally split between Hispanic and Black, but 52 percent of its police officers were White, 30 percent were Hispanic, and only 16 percent were Black (Goodman, 2013). The fact that Hispanic officers were proportional to the city's Hispanic population is an anomaly according to a 2014 analysis that found Hispanics to be the most underrepresented group among police officers, even in smaller urban areas such as Waco, Texas, which is over 30 percent Hispanic but has fewer than 12 percent Hispanic police officers, and Anaheim, California, with over half of the population Hispanic but only 23 percent of its police officers. The 2014 study identified 49 urban areas where Hispanics were the majority population, but the majority of police officers were White (Sullivan & Gillum, 2014). Although people of color have comprised a significant percentage of the officers hired over three decades, the data over that time period have not illustrated reverse discrimination but rather an ongoing problem of disproportionate representation and a justifiable effort to correct a history of discrimination.

What are some consequences of racial discrimination?

A major consequence of racial discrimination can be seen in the asset inequalities based on race. One study reported that the median net worth of White households was well over $100,000 but only a little over $7000 for Black households. If the head of household had not earned a high school diploma, the net worth of Black families was only one-third the net worth of White families, and if the head of household had a college degree, the net worth of White families increased to $180,500 compared to $23,400 for Black families. Finally, if the head of household had a graduate or professional degree, the net worth of White families was over $293,000 but only $84,000 for Black families. Yet Black families at all economic levels have significantly higher rates of charitable donations than White people (Hamilton, Cottom, Darity, Aja, & Ash, 2015). The disparities in net worth stem from a history of racist obstacles such as inequality of educational opportunities, discrimination in being hired and in wages and promotions, and difficulties related to stable home ownership. A Fannie Mae consultant calculated the economic difference if racial equality existed in the United States; African Americans would have $120 billion more in their retirement accounts and $80 billion more in their bank accounts, and the wealth they controlled would be $1 trillion higher than it is (Packer, 2005).

A consequence of racism stemming from asset inequality is diminished health and longevity. In the past and still today, Black people were much more likely to die before age 65 than White people, but in 1950, Black and White people who made it to their sixty-fifth birthday had the same longevity, which was to live to be 77-years-old. By 2010, less than 70 percent of Black men lived to be 65 years old compared to 80 percent of White men. Further, Black and White people turning 65 no longer had the same years left; White men were living two years longer than their Black peers, and White women were living one year longer than Black women. As for their health, a Center for Disease Control and Prevention study reported that the average Black man will reach his sixty-first year before developing chronic conditions that limit activities, but the average White man will reach his sixty-seventh year without such limitations (Ghilarducci, 2015).

"Washing one's hands of the conflict between the powerful and the powerless means to side with the powerful, not to be neutral."

—PAOLO FREIRE (1921–1997)

Another consequence of institutional racism is the incarceration of disproportionate numbers of African Americans, especially men. The United States has less than 5 percent of the world's population but incarcerates over 20 percent of global prison population. Although only one-third of American adults are people of color, they represent two-thirds of adults in our prisons or jails (Steinzor, 2016). Six times as many Black men are in prison compared to White men, and twice as many Black women are incarcerated as White women. Latinos represent about 17 percent of U.S. residents but constitute 22 percent of incarcerated adults (Center for American Progress, 2016). The FBI's Universal Crime Reports Index reflects societal biases by providing data on street crime but not white-collar crime, which is largely committed by White people. In an analysis of criminal activity for one year, Arielly (2008) reported that the total cost of all robberies was $52 million compared to the cost of white-collar crimes such as employee theft and fraud ($600 billion) or income-tax fraud ($350 billion). A University of Texas study found that 80 percent of federal criminal prosecutions were for immigration issues, weapons charges, or drug-related activities. This focus on individual crimes has been accompanied by a decrease in prosecutions for corporate "regulatory offenses," which have declined since 1980, when they represented 7 percent of all federal criminal defendants, to a mere 2 percent in 2015 (Steinzor, 2016). Further, the American Civil Liberties Union engaged in a 10-year study and found that African Americans were more likely than White people to be incarcerated for drug use even though drug usage in both groups occurs as a similar level, and the Bureau of Justice reports that 65 percent of Americans in prison for a drug-related offense were people of color (Center for American Progress, 2016). Ultimately, all American taxpayers have to bear the burden for the cost of incarcerating all these people—an annual rate of $80 billion (Steinzor, 2016).

The number of African Americans in prison exceeds the number of Black people who were slaves in 1850, and on leaving prison they have encountered what Alexander (2010) has called a new "Jim Crow." The old Jim Crow system took away the voting rights of an individual who had committed a felony or even petty theft. These laws were written to appear to be racially neutral, but they resulted in far more Black people being disenfranchised than White people (Bouie, 2013). In the new Jim Crow system, when a Black man is released from prison, a felony conviction once again means the loss of voting rights. Every state except Virginia and Maine deprives felons of the right to vote for some period of time, and in four states they are disenfranchised permanently (Bouie, 2013). A felony conviction is also used to justify excluding a felon from juries and to allow for discrimination in employment and housing. Aronson (2008) cited research that developed résumés and trained equal numbers of Black and White male college graduates to apply for jobs, with half of each group saying they had served a year and a half in prison for a drug conviction. Of the applicants acknowledging a criminal record, White applicants were called back twice as often as Black applicants, and White applicants with criminal records were slightly preferred over Black applicants with no criminal record. As for housing issues, felons are not allowed to live in public housing for five years after their parole, keeping them away from their families. Such actions seem draconian since the majority of these "felons" are not violent criminals but were primarily arrested for using drugs, with only one out of five arrests for selling drugs (Alexander, 2010). As incarceration issues illustrate, the problem caused by institutional racism cannot be resolved by piecemeal action but will require aggressive proposals targeting particular areas of concern such as unemployment, housing, and education.

What remedies have been proposed to address institutional racism?

To speak of remedies for problems as complex and widespread as those stemming from institutional racism is to speak of partial solutions and of good faith efforts. Ongoing research must be conducted on institutional racism because racist outcomes of policies and practices often are not easily identified and vary from one region and one institution to the next. Remedies proposed to address problems stemming from racism have come from scholars such as Bonilla-Silva (2009), Feagin and Feagin (1986), Massey (2001), Sensoy and DiAngelo (2012) and Editors of *Rethinking Schools* (2015). Among their proposed solutions for institutional racism are the following:

1. A national agency should be created that has regional offices to coordinate anti-discrimination activities across the nation. Such an agency would improve enforcement of anti-discrimination legislation and provide better documentation and dissemination of information. Most experts agree there are adequate laws against discrimination, but enforcement of those laws is not adequate because the responsibility for enforcement is currently assigned to the Justice Department, which has so many other areas of responsibility.

2. There must be a national and statewide commitment to stop the deterioration of inner cities in America. By providing resources, we could better address conditions that create misery and despair. Examples of resources include tax incentives to attract businesses to inner cities, federally funded jobs similar to the 1930s Works Progress Administration, training programs to give people skills related to available jobs, and day care subsidies to provide quality and affordable childcare so that more people could work.

3. Schools and individual teachers need to implement anti-racist curricula with social justice topics in addition to the traditional grounding in literacy skills. Students need a safe place to deal with the emotional intensity often aroused by discussing topics like police brutality, especially the numerous instances where police officers have killed Black youth. To provide such a safe place, teachers need to build a sense of community in their classrooms, sharing stories to create a sense of trust that allows for discussions of racism. This can only be achieved by engaging in reading and writing to address social or personal issues, sharing that writing accompanied by respectful discussions, and choosing meaningful group projects. The goal is to have a community of learners who are capable of empathy and consistently demonstrate mutual respect.

4. Teachers must be taught how to work effectively with diverse student populations. They need to learn about diversity, not just students of color, but students with disabilities, low-income students, and students marginalized by the society or by other students. Teachers must learn how to support positive intergroup relationships between students in their classrooms. They also must be able to identify bias in instructional materials and to teach students how to recognize bias. Until textbooks reflect multicultural content, schools must have resources to purchase multicultural instructional materials to supplement textbooks.

Application Exercise 8.1

In this video, a speaker discusses teachers and cultural understanding, and how he asks teachers to reflect on their own degree of cultural understanding in his district's training. Review the video and complete the activity.

 Self-Check 8.3 Complete this self-check quiz to check your understanding of institutional racism in employment, housing, education, and politics, and the consequences of racism for people of color.

Afterword

In *The Souls of Black Folk* published originally in 1903, W. E. B. Du Bois (1994) wrote that the problem of America was the problem of the "color line," that skin color divided America as if it were a line drawn in the sand, never to be crossed. The color line continues to prevent Americans from being united by a common vision, strengthened by an appreciation of diversity. Du Bois challenged Americans to solve the problem of the color line in the twentieth century. That challenge still has not been met even in the second decade of the twenty-first century.

What must Americans do to confront the problem of the color line? For people of color, the challenge continues to be the same as it was for Du Bois, to overcome barriers created by racism. The challenge for White Americans is first to acknowledge the existence of racism, then to understand blatant and subtle ways it operates in society, and, finally, to join with Americans of goodwill to reduce racism in America's schools, neighborhoods, and institutions. If those of us who will commit to this goal are successful, we will bring this society closer to the ideals for which it stands: freedom, equality, and the opportunity for all people to pursue their vision of happiness. When we come closer to that goal, it will not just be a victory for Americans of color, it will also be a victory for America.

> "[America is] a vast and quarrelsome family, a family rent by racial, social, political and class division, but a family nonetheless."
>
> —LEONARD PITTS (1957–)

Summary

- From movies to videogames to textbooks, our culture reveals an ethnocentrism based on the experience of White people that is reinforced by pretending to be "color blind."

- The ideology of individualism fosters individual racism by denying the significance of race as a category while covertly engaging in backstage racism.

- The consequences of institutional racism for people of color includes higher jobless rates, segregated neighborhoods and schools, being "tracked" in K–12 schools, less access to quality higher education, obstacles to political power, and higher incarceration rates.

Terms and Definitions

At-large candidates Refers to candidates for local offices being elected by an entire community rather than by districts or wards within that community

Aversive racism Forms of racism that allow well-meaning people to maintain a positive ("not racist") self-image while still perpetuating racism

Color-blind racism Pretending not to notice race or asserting that race has no meaning

Cultural racism The societal recognition and promotion of activities and contributions of one racial group in preference to others within a multiracial society; the superimposition of history and traditions of one racial group over other racial groups

Ethnocentrism The belief that your race, nation, or culture is superior to all others; also individual actions or institutional practices based on that belief

Individual racism Prejudiced attitudes and behavior against others based on skin color demonstrated whenever someone responds by saying or doing something degrading or harmful about people of another race

Institutional racism Established laws, customs, and practices in a society that allow systematic discrimination between people or groups based on skin color

Internalized racial dominance The socialization of White people that results in their acceptance of these largely unconscious beliefs of racial superiority

Internalized racial oppression The largely unconscious racist beliefs and related behaviors that are accepted by people of color raised in a White supremacist society

Racism The creation of categories of human beings according to color, with one group establishing an artificial superiority to others; an attitude, action, or institutional structure that subordinates or limits an individual on the basis of race

Reverse discrimination The allegation that people of color are receiving preferential treatment with regard to decisions about hiring, promotion, participation, and admission to schools

Steering The practice by realtors of showing homes to prospective buyers in neighborhoods where residents are predominantly or exclusively of the same race

Tracking The process in which students are divided into categories so that they can be assigned in groups to various kinds of classes

White flight The migration of White families from an urban to a suburban location because of court rulings to desegregate urban schools

White privilege A set of options, opportunities, and opinions that are gained and maintained at the expense of people of color

Word-of-mouth hiring Employment of a job applicant based on the recommendation of current employees

Discussion Exercises

Exercise #1 My Feelings About Race—A Personal Questionnaire

Directions: The nine statements below could be a reaction that you might hear concerning another individual's feelings about race. Create a response you think would be appropriate.

1. People should not be forced to integrate if they don't want to.
2. I don't believe I'm racist, but when it comes right down to it, I wouldn't marry an individual of another race.
3. On the whole, the educated, the upper classes, the more sophisticated, or the more deeply religious people are much less racist.
4. I should not be held responsible for what my ancestors did a hundred years ago.
5. When I am around an angry person of another race, it makes me feel defensive because it's as if they want me to feel guilty or something.
6. Other ethnic groups had to struggle, so why should certain groups get bilingual education and other special accommodations today?
7. How can I support my own ethnic group without being against another?
8. Don't tell me that certain racial groups aren't more violent than others. If you look at the statistics, you have to admit that there is a higher crime rate with some groups.
9. In many situations some racial and ethnic groups are paranoid and oversensitive; they read more into a situation than is really there.

Exercise #2 My Experiences with Culture, Race, and Ethnicity

Directions: Reflect on at what age(s) over your life span you have had personal, direct contact with someone of a different culture, race, and ethnicity. Begin with the earliest recollection, and move forward to the present.

1. Identify your first personal experiences with people different from you. What was the setting: home, school, family? What was the basis for the contact: dinner guest, classmate, or playmate? What was your age at the time? Who was the individual, and how was he or she different?
2. Identify your earliest exposures to people who were different from you through movies or television shows, or reading novels or nonfiction. What was the story about? What was your age at the time? Who was the individual, and how was he or she different? What impressions did you gain from each of these visual media experiences?

Chapter 9
Classism: Misperceptions and Myths About Income, Wealth, and Poverty

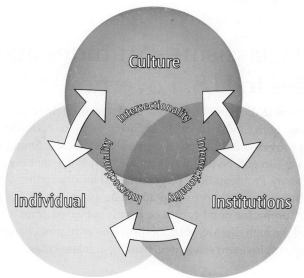

After reading this chapter you will know and be able to:

9.1 Describe historic attitudes and responses to poverty in the United States.

9.2 Explain the negative contemporary attitudes, myths, and misconceptions about poverty, especially those pertaining to welfare recipients.

9.3 Provide examples of institutional classism, and describe the impact of such practices for American families living in poverty.

9.4 Define ageism, and explain how age can be the cause of negative consequences for both older adults and youth.

> "The greatest of evils and the worst of crimes is poverty."
> —GEORGE BERNARD SHAW (1856–1950)

Classism refers to attitudes and discriminatory actions toward others based on their low socioeconomic status. It is nearly impossible to grow up in the United States without being affected by pervasive cultural messages that engender antagonism and sometimes contempt for poor people. In our American capitalist economic system, which emphasizes competition for opportunity and reward, there are winners and there are losers. Americans are encouraged to admire winners. Stories of winners are told daily in newspapers and magazines, and we applaud their success. Americans do not tend to identify with losers, who are usually perceived as low-income individuals or families. Historically, many negative messages have asserted that low-income people are deficient and inferior; these negative cultural messages represent **cultural classism**, and they constitute one factor influencing the process by which Americans have learned to devalue low-income people.

Cultural Classism—Attitudes and Responses to U.S. Poverty

When colonists came to the New World, they had a well-established tradition that caring for the poor was both a local responsibility and a religious obligation. The European Catholic Church provided food to the hungry, shelter for the homeless, and care for the sick; the legacy can still be found in Catholic and Protestant hospitals and social service agencies today. Problems of poverty remained local, affecting a small percentage of people, and church resources provided adequate assistance. But in fourteenth- and fifteenth-century Europe, the number of poor people increased dramatically. Rural families lost their land through disease, wars, and various economic changes, which forced them to search for employment elsewhere, usually in major cities.

What was the response to poverty during the colonial period?

In England, communities provided food, health care, and other assistance as needed; this was called *outdoor relief*. In the colonies, outdoor relief included providing common grazing land and building shelters for homeless families. To reduce burdens of poverty, potential settlers often were required to prove they could care for themselves. If they failed to take care of their own needs as promised, they could be *warned out*— notified that they must leave the community. Komisar (1977) reported that in 1790, one Massachusetts community warned out almost a third of its population. In England, they passed vagrancy laws that punished beggars with forced labor or public whippings.

Later English poorhouses were established to provide food and shelter as an alternative to outdoor relief. People living in poorhouses were required to work to pay for their care, reducing the need for local revenue. Americans liked this idea, and Boston established the first colonial poorhouse in 1664 (Katz, 1986). Poorhouses were not compassionate places; they were "the best means of frightening the able bodied into going to work and discouraging people from applying for aid" (Komisar, 1977, p. 21). The physical conditions in many poorhouses were atrocious: too many people crowded together, many with contagious diseases, and often too little food or medical care. Poorhouses also admitted alcoholics and people with mental illness. Anyone applying for outdoor relief could be referred to a poorhouse based on the assumption that the threat of referral to such a place would reduce relief applications. Yet poorhouses were established across the nation. (See Figure 9.1.)

Figure 9.1 An Iowa Poorhouse

If you were in a poorhouse, you might be able to let friends and family know where you were by sending a postcard like this one from the County Poor House in Burlington, Iowa, early 1900s.

SOURCE: Courtesy of the Poorhouse Lady.

County Poor House, Burlington, Iowa.

What happened to the "religious obligation" to help the poor?

Christians in America contributed to the harsh attitudes toward the poor. Many colonial Protestants believed that poverty was a consequence of sin and slothfulness, while the rich were rewarded for their thrift and virtue. Americans often expressed their belief that anyone who wanted to work could find a job, as Matthew Carey noted in 1828:

> Many citizens entertain an idea that in the present state of society . . . every person able and willing to work may procure employment . . . [and that] the chief part of the distresses of the poor arises from idleness, dissipation, and worthlessness. (Katz, 1986, p. 7)

Carey believed that poverty was not so much a consequence of personal failure as it was from low wages, poor working conditions resulting in accidents or illness, and economic downturns. Those who actually worked with poor people understood that many were industrious and virtuous but still lived in poverty because of circumstances beyond their control. Despite the efforts of Carey and others, negative attitudes prevailed, not only toward paupers but also toward the working poor who lived perilously on the brink of poverty.

Why were people who had jobs so close to poverty?

Komisar (1977) described an 1833 economic analysis of a construction worker's salary that showed it was hardly enough to support a wife and two children. The influx of immigrants exacerbated the problem by increasing competition for jobs, allowing employers to keep wages low or reduce them. Schwarz (2000) quotes social reformer Joseph Tuckerman explaining that wages in 1830 were so low "because the number of laborers [was] essentially greater than the demand for them" (p. 17). Because unemployment remained high, poorhouses never lacked occupants in spite of their deplorable conditions.

Poorhouses included primarily children, older adults, and people with disabilities or illness. Komisar (1977) referred to an 1848 report of a Philadelphia poorhouse where only 12 percent of the residents were capable of working. In some places, poorhouses were built on farmland, hoping that residents could pay for their care by operating the farm, yet "poor farms" often hired people to do the work because there were not enough healthy, able-bodied people in residence. Men who could work stayed out of poorhouses and tried to find a job, but it wasn't easy.

Why was it so difficult to find work?

The rapid development of machines throughout the second half of the nineteenth century increased unemployment, even in rural areas, where hand threshing was eliminated by threshing machines. In urban areas, unskilled factory workers replaced skilled artisans. Men's wages were low, but women's were even lower, and even children had to work. If everyone in the family worked and stayed healthy, it was possible to save money to be self-sufficient in old age. Workers didn't usually retire, but when they could no longer work, they typically lived with their adult children. When a family could no longer afford to take care of older adult parents, they had to live in poorhouses.

Why did people think poorhouses were the solution to poverty?

In the early 1800s, institutions were promoted as a solution to social problems: prisons for criminals, mental hospitals for the insane, orphanages for children, reform schools for juvenile delinquents, and poorhouses for the poor. In addition to rehabilitating inmates, these institutions were supposed to require minimal tax dollars from state and local governments. By 1850, many people had been placed in institutions, but expenses proved more costly than anticipated. To make matters worse, "Mental hospitals did not cure; prisons and reform schools did not rehabilitate" (Katz, 1986, p. 25). In fact, from the beginning, institutions tended to provide primarily custodial care.

In the late 1800s, the few men still in poorhouses were expelled. They moved to cities to find work and often sought lodging with poor families needing the extra money. This arrangement gave the men sexual access to women in the home, and the word *lodger* became a derisive term. The housing need could not be ignored, so lodging houses, nicknamed *flophouses*, provided inexpensive rooms for single men. Later, after children were also removed from poorhouses, they evolved into nursing homes exclusively for older adults (Katz, 1986).

Why were children removed from poorhouses?

Social activists believed that poverty was caused in part by *hereditary pauperism*, as if being poor was a genetic defect. Although adult paupers were viewed as beyond help, children could be saved. Many states passed legislation mandating placement of children in orphanages if their caretaker had been admitted to a poorhouse. By 1875, most children in orphanages were not orphans but had living parents who were poor. Adoption patterns began to change. Low-income families used to adopt children old enough to assist with chores, but middle- and upper-class families were increasingly adopting children based on the assumption that these infants would remember nothing of their impoverished origins and could be "saved" by being raised in good homes. Such negative attitudes toward the poor resulted in a minimal response to the needs of poor people.

What was the response to the needs of poor people?

In the 1880s and 1890s, American society tended to regard poverty as proof of moral misconduct, so organizations denied aid to drunkards and would only help their families if the wife and children left the drunkard. By the late 1890s, studies began to suggest that misconduct, especially alcohol abuse, was not a major cause of poverty. One study reported that alcohol abuse and other forms of misconduct affected only 10 percent to 30 percent of families living in poverty, but that circumstances beyond anyone's control accounted for 65 percent or more situations of poverty. Schwarz (2000) described social reformers such as Josephine Lowell defending poor people "who are not drunken and shiftless, but who lead lives of . . . heroic self-sacrifice and devotion" (p. 101). Social reformers began to challenge Americans, especially Christians, to demonstrate an altruistic attitude to the poor, and they often identified capitalists as the true cause of suffering among the poor.

In the early 1900s, social reformers no longer supported the practice of taking children from poor parents. Buttressed by new child development theories, they denounced orphanages as harmful to children. They lobbied for funds to keep poor families together, believing that the presence of children was an incentive for parents to work, and many states began to provide financial assistance to single-parent mothers regardless of whether they had been abandoned by their husbands or had never married. This was essential because it was hard for single women to earn enough to cover their own expenses, and even more difficult if they had children. Women workers were paid much less than men, so women workers were the first to form unions and initiate strikes demanding wage increases and better working conditions.

> "It is the function of religion to teach society to value human life more than property."
> —WALTER RAUSCHENBUSCH (1861–1918)

What did workers do to protest employer exploitation?

Throughout the 1800s, many women workers—and men—joined unions as their best option to stop exploitation by employers. Most early labor strikes were unsuccessful because impoverished women workers desperately needed money and could not afford to be out of work for long. In the early 1870s, 20,000 unemployed workers in Chicago marched to City Hall, demanding food, clothing, and shelter; textile workers went on strike in Massachusetts; and coal miners struck in Pennsylvania. In 1877, railroad owners drastically cut worker wages, causing strikes in several states, and they hired immigrants to break the strikes, fueling anti-immigrant sentiments among workers. Local citizens often supported strikers, but railroad owners had the law on their side. As strikers barricaded buildings and blocked tracks, police and state militias were called in to drive striking workers away, resulting in many injuries. In a strike in Pittsburgh, owners feared that local militias would not fire at strikers and demanded federal troops be summoned. In the first confrontation with strikers, federal troops killed 10 people; local residents responded angrily, surrounding the troops as they retreated to a roundhouse. The citizens surrounded the roundhouse and set fire to the building, but the troops managed to escape and left the city (Zinn, 2003).

How did unions ultimately help workers to gain higher salaries?

Despite union efforts, wages remained low. A 1904 economist reviewed available jobs and reported that a third of the jobs paid less than $300 a year (Komisar, 1977). If more than one individual in a family worked, they might manage to save money, but their savings would often be used against them: "When employers discovered that their workers earned enough to put something by, they concluded that they had been overpaying them" (Schwarz, 2000, p. 43).

Laborers toiled in dangerous workplaces. In 1908, the federal government reported more than 35,000 workers killed and 536,000 injured on the job every year. The U.S. rates for worker injuries and deaths were much higher than in most European countries. Unions lobbied state legislators, and between 1909 and 1920,

43 of 45 states passed workers' compensation laws over the objections of the employers, who complained of the financial burden of compensating workers for injuries sustained at work (Katz, 1986). Being paid a daily wage was the norm throughout the nineteenth century, but during the twentieth century, unions helped to persuade employers to pay a monthly wage, which gave workers a predictable rate of compensation (Piketty, 2014). Americans continued to debate what was fair for employees and employers until the 1930s, when the federal government was confronted with the issue of widespread unemployment.

How did the federal government address unemployment in the 1930s?

During the spring of 1931, there were five million unemployed U.S. workers. By 1933, when Franklin Roosevelt began his first presidential term, between 12 and 15 million workers were unemployed, a third of the U.S. labor force. Federal programs were installed to keep Roosevelt's campaign pledge to offer a "New Deal" for American workers. When Roosevelt signed a Federal Emergency Relief Act (FERA) to provide assistance for people in poverty, he ended a tradition of local and state governments having exclusive responsibility for the poor. FERA distributed $250 million to the states based on a formula of $1 of federal money for every $3 the state spent for relief or economic assistance to individuals; another $250 million was given to states with the most severe poverty. In some states, 40 percent of the people were on relief. As if to punish people for taking federal funds, 14 states passed laws preventing people on relief from voting.

> "The test of our progress is not whether we add more to the abundance of those who have much; it is whether we provide enough for those who have too little."
>
> —FRANKLIN DELANO ROOSEVELT
>
> (1882–1945)

In addition to providing money for relief, the federal government became an employer. The Civilian Conservation Corps recruited 250,000 young men (but no women) to work on projects to prevent floods, fires, and soil erosion, and to develop recreational areas. The Works Progress Administration (WPA) employed about two million men, a fourth of the workforce, to build roads or to construct bridges, public buildings, and parks. Some Americans did not support these actions; Komisar (1977) quoted a conservative bank president who said, "I profoundly believe that society does not owe every man a living" (p. 56).

Although federal employment programs provided jobs, the numbers of unemployed continued to be significant, and employers took advantage of the oversupply of labor to keep wages low or reduce them, resulting in more worker protests and strikes. The Wagner Act, passed in 1935, created a National Labor Relations Board and granted unions legal status as collective bargaining agents. The Board encouraged peaceful resolutions of labor disputes through negotiation, not strikes. During World War II, the National War Labor Board supported unionization after getting a "no strike" agreement with the unions for the duration of the war. After World War II, union membership kept increasing until reaching a high of 34 percent of those employed in the private sector. By 2015, private sector workers who were members of a union had declined to 6.6 percent (Bensman, 2015).

What was the outcome of the New Deal?

During World War II there were so many jobs available that the federal government saw no reason to continue the New Deal work programs. Although European democracies had maintained social insurance programs since 1833, conservative critics accused Roosevelt of aspiring to be a dictator and attacked his poverty programs as a threat to "the integrity of our [capitalist] institutions" (Komisar, 1977, p. 62). Yet programs created by the Economic Security Act of 1935 such as unemployment insurance, Social Security, and welfare have been maintained to support people in need. A 1939 Gallup poll reported that 70 percent of Americans believed the federal government should address

Figure 9.2 The Legacy of Programs for Youth

The Civilian Conservation Corps (CCC) gave young men jobs in the 1930s when jobs were scarce (top photo). The federal government continues to engage young adults to work on conservation projects (bottom photo), but unlike the CCC, the Student Conservation Association's diverse membership also includes women.

SOURCE: Library of Congress Prints and Photographs Division [Carl Mydans/LC-USF33-T01-000067-M3] (left photo) and Student Conservation Association (right photo).

the needs of unemployed people, and the same 70 percent approved the amount of relief available to the poor. These programs still function because they have been successful and enjoy widespread public support.

The legacy of Roosevelt's New Deal was not only social programs but also the principle of federal government involvement in poverty issues. The Civilian Conservation Corps was the forerunner of such programs as Peace Corps and AmeriCorps (see Figure 9.2). Few Americans would question the need for the federal government to support welfare programs or Social Security. Because of the New Deal, Americans developed new perceptions of poverty, but some cling to old attitudes and accuse poor people of having deficiencies that cause their poverty.

 Self-Check 9.1 Complete this self-check quiz to check your understanding of historic attitudes and responses to poverty in the United States.

Individual Classism and Misconceptions about Poverty and Welfare

Individual classism refers to attitudes and discriminatory actions stemming from prejudice against poor people (see Figure 9.3). Most Americans don't seem to understand that capitalism requires a certain percentage of workers to be unemployed in order to keep wages low and control inflation. A 2012 Pew Research Center poll found that 77 percent of Americans believe success is determined by individual effort, compared to two thirds of Europeans who believe success is more likely determined by forces beyond an individual's control. These contrasting beliefs are reflected in research reporting that 60 percent of Europeans support programs assisting low-income families, but only one third of Americans say they "completely agree" that our government should provide a "safety net" for the most economically vulnerable citizens (Schuck, 2014). Historically, Americans have tended to view their nation as a land of opportunity; therefore, if someone was poor, it was because they lacked the motivation to get out of poverty, but in recent years there are signs that American attitudes may be changing. In a 1998 Gallup poll, 68 percent of Americans said they believed our economic system was fair, but in 2013 only 44 percent believed this. Further, a 2015 Pew Research poll asked

Americans if given a choice, would they opt for financial security or a chance to move up the economic ladder, and 92 percent chose to be financially secure (Cooper, 2015).

Gillespie (2014) reports that tax credits, food stamps, and Social Security allowed 40 million Americans to live above the poverty line, but more than 48 million Americans live in poverty, including almost 15 million children (Children's Defense Fund, 2017). The Census Bureau identifies an additional 51 million Americans classified as "near poor," meaning they earn an annual income of between $11,000 and $17,000. The nearly 100 million Americans living below or near the poverty level represents one-third of our population, and a significant portion of them are children (Hightower, 2013). To assess poverty issues in Third World nations, the World Bank defines "extreme poverty" as an individual living on $2 a day or less, and Feeney (2015) reported that 1.5 million American households, which include 6.5 million children, were living in extreme poverty. Despite having the largest economy of the world's 35 industrial nations, the United States ranks thirty-fourth in terms of child poverty with only Romania ranked below us (Children's Defense Fund, 2017).

A major factor affecting poverty in the United States is health care; medical expenses not covered by insurance have forced 11 million Americans into poverty (Gillespie, 2014). Another factor is the increasing number of low-wage jobs. About 42 percent of workers are paid an hourly wage of less than $15; even if the minimum wage was raised to $14 an hour, that would still only produce an annual salary of less than $30,000. One third of all American households earn less than $30,000 a year. Some of these workers receive tips, but do tips add up to a decent salary? Since 1991, the federal minimum wage for workers who receive tips has been stagnant at $2.13 an hour. In 2016, the median hourly pay for a restaurant worker was $9.25 an hour, producing an annual salary of less than $20,000. This is why tipped workers are twice as likely to be living in poverty as the average worker (Hanauer, 2016; Howell, 2016). Their salary is consumed by basic expenses such as transportation to and from work, rent, and groceries.

Whether they have tipped workers or offer primarily minimum wage jobs, some large corporations in the United States pay such low wages that many of their workers have to rely on government programs. Federal assistance comes in the form of

Figure 9.3 Legal Advocates for Low-Income Families

The Southern Poverty Law Center (SPLC) is dedicated to combating economic injustices, providing its services free of charge. SPLC offices are located in Montgomery, AL, along with the Civil Rights Memorial, designed by Maya Lin, and the Civil Rights Memorial Center, which serve tens of thousands each year.

SOURCE: Photo courtesy of Valarie Downes // SPLC.

$58 billion for the Child Tax Credit (CTC), $80 billion for food stamps, and $38 billion for housing vouchers and rental assistance, all of which primarily benefit poor people who have jobs. Additionally, 47 percent of all babies born in 2015 received some support from the Women, Infants, and Children program that provides services to babies and young children up to the age of five who lack adequate nutrition. Having to rely on federal programs because of their subsistence salary means that these families have no additional income to spend. Every dollar added to a worker's hourly salary would provide $2080 to that worker's annual income (Hanauer, 2016). If low-wage workers had this additional money, they could afford to purchase more products, and that would stimulate the economy, which is why some economists argue that low wages are bad for business. For example, over half of fast food employees receive assistance from at least one federal program. As one American entrepreneur bluntly stated, "This is a ridiculously inefficient way to run an economy (Hanauer, 2016, p. 37).

How are children from low-income families disadvantaged in schools?

Some Americans argue that low-income children should use free education provided in public schools to escape from poverty, but the appalling conditions of the schools these children attend have been well documented for many years. Even before the children from low-income families start coming to school, there is already an achievement gap. The Children's Defense Fund (2017) reported on a study looking at 4-year-old children and found that high-income children had heard 30 million more words than low-income children. Further, preschoolers from low-income families are less likely to recognize letters, count up to 20, or be able to write their first name. The study said that gaps in cognitive skills can be observed before a child's first birthday, and the gaps typically increase over time. By the time they start kindergarten, children from low-income families are more than a year behind the children whose parents were college graduates in terms of reading- and math-related abilities (Porter, 2015). Another factor in this achievement gap relates to experiences outside school. One study reported that in the first six years of their lives, when compared to poor children, wealthier children experienced 1300 more hours each year engaging in enrichment activities such as travel, music lessons, or attending a summer camp. These children would go on to achieve much higher math and reading scores in school than their low-income counterparts (Collins, 2013).

Since the 1970s, class-based disparities in math and reading test scores have increased at a pace consistent with increasing disparities in income and wealth. For children born in 2001, the income gap between high- and low-income families is 30–40 percent higher than it was for children born five years earlier (Collins, 2013). A study of data from 2001 to 2011 reported that the achievement gap between students from high- and low-income homes was twice as large as the gap between Black and White students (Tavernise, 2012). Yet too many Americans simply blame low-income children for their poor performance in school; Pipher (2002) commented on attitudes of Americans who are not poor: "We were born on third base and we think we hit triples" (p. 21).

American schools are designed for middle- and upper-class children, and that's a major reason why they are failing to educate low-income students, a failure that has been exacerbated by the focus on standardized testing, first with President Bush's No Child Left Behind initiative and later with President Obama's Race to the Top program. Experts point out that it is absurd to think that simply by testing and having high expectations you can improve the educational achievements of a student coming from a low-income home, where the family has minimal literacy (and may not even have books at home), and the children may not always get adequate nutrition and often have health problems. Achieving equitable funding for poor students is typically defined as requiring 40 percent more spending on these students to effectively address their

> "For every talent that poverty has stimulated it has blighted a hundred."
>
> —JOHN GARDNER (1912–2002)

additional learning challenges. Alaska is the only state to meet that standard (Children's Defense Fund, 2014).

Other nations in the industrialized world have tried to address class-based income disparities by investing in programs to improve the lives of low-income families; these programs provide good health care, job training, and educational opportunities, and this has resulted in improved social mobility for the children of these families (Collins, 2013). For children from low-income families to achieve success in their adult lives, they must have access to the following:

- good nutrition
- health care
- high-quality preschool education
- good K–12 public schools
- early diagnosis of learning disabilities and other special needs

The educational advantages for children of the middle and upper classes can be ascertained by analyzing student SAT scores in relation to family income. According to multiple studies, higher family income in all races—socioeconomic standing—translates into higher scores on SAT tests (deMause, 2014). Two major reasons for such a test score discrepancy based on family income is that wealthier families can readily afford to pay for courses to prepare for taking the SAT. These courses can cost up to $10,000 if they involve one-on-one tutoring. The data show that students who have taken test-prep courses tend to score much higher than students who have not taken such courses. Also, students score higher on the SAT if they have taken the PSAT, and this is more commonly offered at high schools serving higher income students. As a result, students from families with incomes over $200,000 have an average combined SAT score of 1714, and as income levels drop each category has a lower combined SAT score until you get to families earning less than $20,000, where students have the lowest score of 1326 (deMause, 2014). Even when the children from low-income families overcome the obstacles to achieve academic success, research finds that they are still less likely to graduate from a college or university than students from higher income families who were not as academically successful (Stiglitz, 2012).

The most disadvantaged children are those who are homeless. Prior to 1980, homelessness was primarily a problem for people with alcohol or drug addictions or mental illness. In his first year in office, President Reagan slashed the budget for housing subsidies for low-income families by 50 percent, and homelessness increased so much that by the end of Reagan's second term, the number of homeless people had doubled. Since many of the homeless were now families with children, Congress passed the McKinney Act in 1987, and over the next decade the bill was amended to increase funding and expand its services (Drier, 2004). In its 2000 version, the renamed McKinney-Vento Act provided funds for various programs to assist homeless people, including the Education of Homeless Children and Youth Program in the Department of Education. This law mandated that homeless children should be given a "free and appropriate education" and required public schools to remove barriers to enrollment, attendance, and achievement of these students (National Coalition for the Homeless, 2006). The Department of Education provided funds to assist homeless children in such areas as transportation, school supplies, and academic assistance.

"A decent provision for the poor is the best measure of civilization."

—SAMUEL JOHNSON (1709–1784)

According to the National Center on Family Homelessness (2014), there are now over 2.5 million homeless children in the United States, with 1.2 million of them attending public schools. America has more homeless women and children than any other industrialized nation. As with other poverty measures, a disproportionate number of families of color are affected; for example, Black families are three times more likely to be homeless than White families (Austin, 2013). Homeless children are more likely to live in food-insecure homes, which means they lack sufficient food to maintain good health. In addition to poor physical health, they often struggle with depression over being evicted from their home, anxiety about their family, and fears resulting from family instability and violence. Because homeless families move frequently, the children are often at one school for a brief period before transferring to another school. It is often difficult for teachers to determine whether a child has special needs such as a learning disability. The revised McKinney-Vento law required public schools to identify all homeless children at their school and monitor them carefully for warning signs of a disability. When there was evidence of a possible disability, the school was to initiate the diagnostic process, and if the child transferred to another school during the process, the school was directed to forward the paperwork to the new school so that the process could be completed (U.S. Department of Education, 2008).

Despite the good intentions of the McKinney-Vento Act, homeless children remain extremely vulnerable, and their numbers are increasing. Following the 2008 recession, even suburban families became homeless when they could not make mortgage payments. According to a 2011 analysis of Census data by the Brookings Institution, American suburbs have become the site of the fastest growing population of people living in poverty. From 2000 to 2010, poverty in the suburbs increased by 53 percent, making them the site of the largest segment of our population living in poverty. Around 33 percent (15.4 million people) of people living in poverty reside in the suburbs compared to 28 percent (12.7 million) who live in urban areas, and the remaining 39 percent (18 million) are divided between those who live in small cities or rural areas (Wilson, 2012). For example, Colorado ranked eighth among all states in foreclosures, and the number of homeless students in just one county increased from 59 in 2001 to 2812 in 2012 (Potts, 2013). Most suburban parents had jobs but struggled with their finances, creating stress for the entire family. Research on Adverse Childhood Experiences (ACE) has reported that occasional stress can be healthy, but when stress experiences for children (such as being homeless) are sustained, the results can include "damage (to) parts of the developing mind crucial for memory, learning, cognition, planning, impulse control, and judgment" (Tillman 2013, p. 65). Researchers have described the effect of ACE on learning by noting that children sitting in a classroom thinking about the stress in their lives might feel an enormous desire to run out of that classroom. One researcher described this as "a little like gunning a car at 110 miles per hour with the brakes on" (Tillman, 2013, p. 66). Needless to say, students whose minds are in such a state are going to have difficulty learning even if they stay in the classroom.

How can schools make a difference in the lives of low-income children?

A scholarly review of numerous studies concluded that conditions associated with poverty are likely to have an adverse effect on a child's developing brain (Jairrels, 2008), but these effects are not permanent. Researchers in France tracked a group of children who had come from abusive homes, foster care, or institutional settings after the children were adopted by financially secure parents. When the children were adopted, they were regarded as borderline for a diagnosis of mental retardation with an average IQ score of 77. Just nine years after their adoption, the IQ scores for all of these children had improved significantly, with the highest increases appearing in those children who were adopted into the most affluent families (Kirp, 2007). It is not feasible to place all poor children in affluent homes, but they could be enrolled in school, especially preschool. In 2012, only nine states had implemented preschool programs for four-year-old children, and because of inadequate funding, these states did not enroll most of the eligible children. The exception was Oklahoma, with 75 percent of its four-year-old population enrolled in preschool, the highest in the nation, where preschool teachers were paid salaries comparable to K–12 teachers. Research on such high-quality early childhood programs has reported that they have an especially significant impact on low-income children (Lerner, 2012).

Video Example 9.1

In this video, Ms. Adimoolah discusses socioeconomic status and its role in her classroom. Think about how children from lower socioeconomic groups are disadvantaged in schools and then how schools can help them. Ms. Adimoolah talks about the students being aware of "have and have-nots" and that ultimately, everyone can learn from one another in her classroom. What might be some ways her students are made aware of socioeconomic status in schools? When she talks about taking a risk, what might she be referring to? Are these risks the same for all students?

A study of Oklahoma's pre-K programs found that the gains achieved during a single academic year were among the largest ever reported for a pre-K program. The students were nine months ahead of students not in pre-K programs with regard to skills such as recognizing letters and telling stories. They were seven months ahead of their peers in pre-writing skills and five months ahead in pre-math skills. The gains were comparable to children enrolled in a Head Start program. Although the children from low-income families made the largest gains, students from all socioeconomic levels benefited from their enrollment in the pre-K program (Lerner, 2012). A North Carolina study reported that low-income students participating in a state-funded preschool program had higher scores in math and reading than their low-income peers who were not enrolled in the program (Webley, 2011). Other studies of pre-K programs have found that these students are less likely to be held back in a grade, less likely to require special education assistance, and more likely to graduate from high school (Lerner, 2012).

In addition, high-quality early-childhood education programs have lasting benefits for low-income children. The researcher studying the Oklahoma pre-K program calculated the potential impact of the program on the future annual income of these students and estimated that it could increase their annual income by an average of $30,548 for children from low-income homes, and $24,610 for middle-class children (Lerner, 2012). A Michigan study initiated in 1972 tracked two groups of low-income children with similar IQ scores—one group had attended preschool, but the other had not. At the age of 40, those participants in the study who had attended preschool had higher levels of education, earned higher incomes, were more likely to be homeowners, and were less likely to have spent time in jail (Webley, 2011). Despite these impressive findings, across the United States, less than 30 percent of 4-year-old children and only 4 percent of 3-year-old children are enrolled in preschool programs (Lerner, 2012).

Educational gains are not limited to programs for young children. Kahlenberg (2016) argues that K–12 schools segregated by social class have an adverse effect on the academic achievement of students from low-income homes, and that reorganizing schools to eliminate such segregation benefits all students. He cites four decades of research reporting that the lives of low-income students are qualitatively better if they attend schools with predominantly middle-class students, including data from the National Assessment of Educational Progress (NAEP), which found that low-income 4th grade students in schools with a majority of middle-class students had math scores that were almost two years ahead of their low-income peers in high-poverty schools. Attending a largely middle-class school means students are more likely to have peers motivated for academic achievement as well as to have high-quality teachers with high expectations for students (Kahlenberg, 2016). If we are serious about meeting the needs of low-income students, the federal government must assist state and local governments in addressing this problem.

How has the federal government addressed the disadvantages for low-income students?

In 2003, President Bush signed the No Child Left Behind (NCLB) Act requiring rigorous testing and identification of students not achieving designated test scores. If scores were below the Adequate Yearly Progress (AYP) benchmarks for two consecutive years, the school was labeled as "failing" (later softened to "in need of improvement"). In 2006, more than a fourth of all public schools failed to reach their AYP (Karp, 2006). Many educators criticized NCLB for relying on standardized tests to determine student learning. Even creators of standardized tests admit that these tests measure only a portion of what a child learns, and that multiple measures are necessary for authentic assessments. NCLB made no distinction between students attending underfunded schools in high poverty areas and students attending well-maintained schools with state-of-the-art facilities. They all had to pass the same tests. According to a Harvard study, NCLB failed to improve student scores on reading and math achievement, and made no progress on reducing achievement gaps between students based on race or income differences (Lee, 2006).

In 2007, Congress was supposed to pass a reauthorization of NCLB, but because of the criticisms, there was no agreement on how the program should be modified. The Obama Administration provided almost $4.4 billion from stimulus funds for its "Race to the Top" initiative to promote innovation and reform. Critics pointed out that this initiative still emphasized testing and also proposed including test scores in teacher evaluations, a controversial suggestion since a student's test score is a product of many factors, not just the performance of the teacher (White, 2011). Criteria in scoring rubrics for awarding "Race to the Top" funding included the development and adaptation of a common set of educational standards (*Rethinking Schools*, 2013). In 2015, President Obama signed a bipartisan bill, the Every Student Succeeds Act (ESSA). Although it replaced NCLB, it still emphasized teachers having high expectations for students and improving academic achievement for students in low-performance schools. Prior to the passage of the ESSA, the Council of Chief State School Officers and the National Governors Association Center for Best Practices promoted the development of the Common Core State Standards (Common Core State Standards Initiative, 2014). In 2010, this "state-led effort to establish consensus on expectations for student knowledge and skills that should be developed in Grades K–12" led to the creation of academic standards for mathematics and English language arts/literacy known as the Common Core (Porter et al., 2011, p. 103). Outlining learning goals for what every student should know and be able to do at the end of each grade, the Common Core were designed to provide equity and consistency across schools, districts, and states. Having consistency across schools no matter their location was touted as a means of increasing college-readiness for students from low-income families (D'Alessio, 2014).

By the 2014–2015 school year, 43 states, the District of Columbia, and four territories had adopted the Common Core for implementation, but criticisms continued from educators, families, the media, and schools about who wrote the standards, what adoption and assessment would cost, the process of implementation and teacher preparations, and their overall quality. By 2017, several states opted out, leaving only 35 states committed to implementation. President Trump and Education Secretary Betsy DeVos expressed opposition to the Common Core Curriculum, but the federal government is prohibited from making curricular decisions for K–12 schools. Nevertheless, in April 2017, President Trump signed an executive order creating a task force to review policies and regulations for the past eight years to determine which ones need to be eliminated to reassert local control of K–12 schools (Klein, 2017). In addition, the president's proposed budget includes about $10 billion in cuts to education at all levels, specifically reducing funds for programs providing advanced course work, after-school programs (serving mostly low-income children), and efforts to reduce class sizes (Brown, Strauss, & Douglas-Gabriel, 2017). Advocates for children from low-income homes are redoubling their efforts to lobby for federal assistance to improve low-income students' academic achievements but also to address problems these children encounter outside of school.

Why should problems outside of school affect a child's performance in school?

Urban sociologist Pedro Noguera argues that the only crisis in American education exists in schools with a concentration of low-income children (*Extra!*, 2011). In 2014, over 48 million Americans were living in poverty, and 16 percent were children (Gillespie, 2014); yet about 75 percent of these households had one or more employed adults, with 80 percent having full-time jobs (Children's Defense Fund, 2014). According to a 2017 report from the Children's Defense Fund, 45 percent of low-income children lived in homes where they received inadequate nutrition, termed "food insecurity," which is associated with not only lower scores in reading and math but also more physical and mental health issues and more emotional and behavioral problems. Children from food-insecure homes rely on free or reduced price meals during the school year, but 89 percent of them did not receive meals from the Summer Food Service Program. Inadequate nutrition is not just a health problem; it is also an educational problem that affects children before they are born. If pregnant women aren't getting adequate nutrition, neither are the babies they are carrying; this often results in premature births and low-birth-weight babies. Low-birth-weight babies often have problems with cognitive development; they tend to have lower IQ scores and are more likely to be diagnosed with a learning disability or attention disorder. Low-income children enrolled in kindergarten tend to have lower test scores when their height and weight are below normal (Shepard, Setren, & Cooper, 2011). In one study that compared them with children from food-secure homes, children in kindergarten from food-insecure homes had 13 percent lower scores in both reading and math by third grade. A longitudinal study found that children receiving food assistance before the age of five were in better health as adults than children not receiving such assistance, and female students receiving food assistance in the study were more likely to graduate, earn more money, and not rely on safety net programs as adults (Children's Defense Fund, 2014).

Berliner (2005) noted that there are: "thousands of studies showing correlation between poverty and (low) academic achievement" (p. 11). He suggested a number of reasons to explain the correlation, including inadequate nutrition, impeding cognitive development, and less stable home lives, but also children living in poverty are more likely to sustain environmental deficiencies that often lead to health problems. The Children's Defense Fund (2017) reported that children living in poverty are five times more likely to have health concerns than children living above the poverty level, and yet poor children are less likely to have access to health care. Further, the health problems that poor children have tend to be more severe. In recent years asthma has become the leading cause of chronic absenteeism in K–12 schools. Even when asthmatic children attend school, breathing problems may have kept them up at night so that they are sleepy and unable to focus on academic tasks. Middle-class children with asthma are typically treated for it so that their asthma is controlled, while low-income children are far less likely to receive such treatment. In addition, having asthma makes children less likely to exercise so they become less physically fit and more irritable, contributing to behavioral problems in school (Rothstein, 2009; Children's Defense Fund, 2017).

> "It is easy to protect the interests of the rich and powerful. But it is a great labor to protect the interests of the poor and downtrodden."
>
> —THADDEUS STEVENS (1792–1868)

Largely because of medical debts, one third of Americans slip in and out of poverty each year. According to a report from the Urban Institute, 51 percent of Americans will experience poverty at some time in their lives before they reach the age of 65 (Garces & Rendall, 2012). About 1.3 million public school students drop out of high school each year (Gavett, 2012); yet Georgetown University's Center on Education and the Workforce reported that in 2018, more than 60 percent of job openings in the United States required some post-secondary education (Carey, 2012). By 2014, all states were spending twice as much housing prisoners as they did on K–12 education, with 21 states spending over three times as much (Children's Defense Fund, 2014). Shepard, Setren, and Cooper (2011) examined the costs of poverty related to inadequate education, illness, and charitable programs (many simply providing food), and reported that poverty costs each American household $1410 annually. The authors concluded: "The nation pays far more by letting hunger exist than it would if our leaders took steps to eliminate it" (p. 17).

How will addressing health issues for low-income children improve their academic achievement?

For a long time, advocates such as Schwartz-Nobel (2002) have explained that the bodies of undernourished children use food energy first to maintain critical organs and next for growth, with the remaining energy being used for cognitive development. Even short-term nutritional deprivation diminishes the ability to learn. "Children who come to school hungry are known to have shorter attention spans. They are unable to perform as well as their peers" (p. 139). Although poor nutrition interferes with academic achievement, good nutrition enhances it. Studies of federal nutrition programs such as SNAP report that eligible children receiving food assistance before the age of five were in better health as adults than those who had not received such assistance; in addition, children who had received food assistance were more likely to have completed more years of school, to be earning higher salaries, and to have no need for social services programs. According the Children's Defense Fund (2017), increasing the SNAP program by 30 percent would move almost two million more children above the poverty line. Further, studies of school breakfast programs have found that students participating in these programs demonstrate enhanced academic performance because of improvements in memory and other cognitive skills. In one study, students participating in the breakfast program had reduced tardiness and absenteeism as well as significant increases in standardized test scores. A number of these studies are cross-cultural. For example, Chinese researchers found that kindergarten children who ate breakfast "often" or "always" had higher IQs than those who ate breakfast "sometimes" or "rarely" even when the researchers controlled for such factors as parental education and family economic status (Carroll, 2014).

The ongoing existence of poverty comes at a cost. The Children's Defense Fund (2014) reported that the United States spends over $500 billion annually on child poverty. It's estimated that each of the more than one million high school students who drop out each year will cost taxpayers $13,890 every year (Rowe, 2014). At the beginning of the twenty-first century, Schwartz-Nobel (2002) cited a projection that the U.S. labor force would lose "as much as $130 billion in future productive capacity . . . for every year that 14.5 million American children continue to live in poverty" (p. 224). Closing the achievement gap in schools is perhaps one of the most effective ways to improve the American economy. Friedman and Mandelbaum (2011) cite a study that assessed the economic impact if schools had eliminated these achievement gaps in 1998 and all students achieved at the same level from 1998 to 2008. They concluded that by 2008, the gross domestic product (GDP) of the United States would have been $310 billion to $525 billion higher. The additional income represented by increased GDP levels means more money would have been generated for all Americans. Yet efforts to persuade Americans to support programs that address poverty are persistently sabotaged by myths and misunderstandings concerning poverty, especially about welfare recipients.

What are some myths about welfare recipients?

> "Men in search of a myth will usually find one."
> —PUEBLO INDIAN PROVERB

There is confusion in the United States about who qualifies for welfare assistance. Americans have historically believed that it was possible for able-bodied men to receive welfare, but with the exception of programs for widows, orphans, and people with disabilities, over 90 percent of social support has come through Transitional Assistance for Needy Families (TANF) since 1996. TANF is supposed to assist single-parent families, rarely including men but typically consisting of women with dependent children; children represent the majority of recipients.

Numerous scholars have identified a variety of myths about welfare; many have been around for a number of years. The following list includes examples of myths that have fostered negative or even hostile attitudes and actions toward recipients; further information is included to provide a more accurate picture about people receiving social assistance.

Myths about social assistance have shaped American attitudes and promoted negative reactions to welfare recipients. Although negative actions illustrate individual classism, the inadequacies of American social assistance programs illustrate institutional classism.

MYTH #1:

Welfare rolls are increasing. Although the number of people in poverty has increased, the number of people on welfare has decreased. In 1994 prior to the passage of TANF, 5.1 million families, a total of almost 14 million people, were provided with cash assistance, but after the passage of TANF the numbers plummeted to a low of 1.6 million families assisting 4.1 million recipients (Falk, 2016). From the time TANF was being debated, critics argued that this welfare "reform" was more concerned with reducing tax dollars spent on welfare than providing assistance to low-income people.

MYTH #2:

Welfare families are large. In 2014, about 50 percent of all TANF families had one child and 28 percent had two children, which is consistent with the average size of American families. Further, 38 percent of TANF families do not include an eligible adult for a variety of reasons but were "child only" recipients (Child Trends, 2013; Falk, 2016).

MYTH #3:

People on welfare abuse the welfare system. According to Couch (2014), families receiving public assistance spend about 40 percent of their budget on housing, over 20 percent on food, 17 percent on transportation, and 9 percent on health care and insurance, leaving only about 14 percent of their budget to purchase school supplies, clothes, and other necessities. As for abusing the system, less than 2 percent of recipients have been documented as being engaged in welfare fraud; yet Internal Revenue Service estimates of tax evasion have found that every year approximately $30 billion of income taxes owed by middle- or upper-class Americans will not be collected (Laws.com, 2013).

MYTH #4:

The government only helps people on welfare. In 2012, funding for all welfare programs was less than 0.5 percent of the federal budget (Eichelberger, 2014), but the federal government has a history of giving large sums of money to corporations. Kivel (2002) reported that federal subsidies for wealthy corporations cost each taxpayer about $1400 annually compared to $400 per taxpayer spent on TANF and food stamps. Federal subsidies to corporations are estimated to cost at least $100 billion taxpayer dollars each year, and it isn't just the federal government. A *New York Times* study reported that state and local governments spend over $80 billion annually in subsidies for corporations (Quigley, 2014).

MYTH #5:

Welfare recipients are too lazy to get a job. Over 75 percent of TANF recipients are children, with 44 percent being five years old or younger (Falk, 2016). Studies have consistently found that the majority of adults without disabilities in the TANF program are employed. Eichelberger (2014) cites a study of families receiving food stamps, reporting that 60 percent included at least one adult who had a job. These adults work despite the fact that the jobs they are most likely to have only pay minimum wage, which hardly covers the cost of child care and work-related expenses such as clothing and transportation. Further, minimum wage jobs frequently lack health insurance, and if insurance is provided, it is likely restricted to employees only, not their families.

Self-Check 9.2 Complete this self-check quiz to check your understanding of the negative contemporary attitudes, myths, and misconceptions about poverty, especially those pertaining to welfare recipients.

Institutional Classism and the Impact for Families in Poverty

Individual prejudice based on socioeconomic status and negative behaviors rooted in prejudice are problematic in a society with as wide a disparity in wealth and income as the United States. Yet **institutional classism**—institutional policies and practices that exploit low-income people and benefit middle- or upper-class individuals—has contributed even more to that disparity. The increased economic disparity in the United States has made it more difficult for individuals from one class to move up to a higher class. If a society provided opportunity for social mobility to individuals from all income levels, only 20 percent of the families in the bottom 20 percent of the economy would see their children remaining in the bottom 20 percent. Denmark comes close with 25 percent of children from low-income families unable to move upward. In the United States, 42 percent of low-income children don't escape the lowest percentile, and of the 58 percent who move up, most only move up a little (Stiglitz, 2012). Noah (2014) concluded that social mobility in the United States began to decline in the 1970s and now lags behind Canada and many European nations such as France and Germany. Americans are apparently becoming aware of this change. In a *Washington Post*/ABC News (2014) poll, 71 percent of Americans said our economic system was not fair and that it favors the wealthy. Scholars agree that the single most important factor in predicting an individual's future wealth is the wealth of that individual's family; some say a family's wealth has a predictive value of at least 40 percent, and others claim it is as high as 60 percent (Noah, 2014).

And yet the optimism reflected in the American Dream dies hard. Despite the fact that social mobility in the United States appears to be stagnating or decreasing, a recent Pew Foundation Poll reported that almost 70 percent of Americans said they had either achieved the American Dream already or they believed they were on their way toward achieving it (Stiglitz, 2012). According to the Pew Research Center, two-thirds of Americans were middle class in 1971, but by 2015 less than 50 percent were middle class (Geewax, 2015) The best hope for social mobility has been education, and today this bodes well for families in the top 25 percent in the United States whose children increased their proportion of those earning college degrees by 40–80 percent, while children of families in the bottom 50 percent stagnated at only 10–20 percent of those earning college degrees (Piketty, 2014). For Harvard students, their parents' average income equals the average income of the top 2 percent. As Piketty (2014) notes, "Such a finding does not seem entirely compatible with the idea of selection based solely on merit" (p. 485). As social mobility declines and the middle class becomes smaller, the disparity between the rich and poor is becoming larger.

Why is the disparity between the richest and poorest Americans increasing?

Federal policies have played a major role in diverting resources to the richest Americans. Some people regard income redistribution as a socialist scheme, but it is a function of government. Each year the U.S. Internal Revenue Service (IRS) collects income taxes—scaled according to income—to fund programs and projects approved by our elected representatives. During the 1980s, $160 billion collected from middle- and low-income

Video Example 9.2
In this video, the speaker discusses how culture affects students' and families' attitudes toward school. Think about the role institutional classism might play in the lives of the students she is referring to. Compare and contrast how social mobility and success are discussed in the chapter and in the video. How might these definitions of social mobility affect student's school experiences and relationship with a school?

taxpayers replaced tax dollars lost due to capital gains tax cuts benefiting wealthy Americans (Phillips, 1990). Social economists call this a *redistribution of income*, and in the United States, the redistribution has continued to go upward. According to Longman (2012), each year about $500 billion of American taxes are used to subsidize home-ownership and savings through property tax deductions, mortgage interest deductions, and preferential rates for capital gains. About 80 percent of recipients are Americans in the top 20 percent of the economy, and 45 percent of the benefits go to households whose average annual income is greater than a million dollars (Longman, 2012). In 2016, the top 1 percent controlled over 30 percent of American wealth, while the bottom 50 percent controlled only 2.5 percent (Teachout, 2017).

Corporations have also contributed to the growing economic inequality. The IRS is supposed to collect 35 percent of corporate income in taxes, but the IRS reports that many businesses employ tax-dodging practices. According to Citizens for Tax Justice, at least 55 companies in the Fortune 500 avoided paying $147.5 billion in corporate income taxes by shifting domestic profits to offshore accounts where, on average, they paid only a 6.7 percent tax rate. This watchdog group also reported that 362 of the Fortune 500 companies have almost 8000 accounts in tax havens (Johnston, 2014). Another popular tactic is called "tax inversion," where a corporation moves its headquarters overseas to avoid paying taxes; the result is corporations keeping an estimated $2 trillion of untaxed revenue (Feyman, 2014). Employing such tax-dodging practices, corporations have increased their wealth by depriving our society of its legitimate tax revenue; some of these corporations (and the taxes they have not paid) include Wells Fargo ($6 billion), AT&T ($4.8 billion), Verizon Communications ($4.1 billion), General Electric ($2.8 billion), and more than $1 billion each for IBM, Exxon-Mobil, and Goldman Sachs Group (Stucki, 2013).

At the start of the twentieth century, the United States had a more equitable distribution of income and wealth than the nations of Europe, but by the end of the century, the United States had become more inequitable than European nations. The dramatic change began in the 1980s, with the bulk of this change occurring for people in the top 1 percent in the American economy. In 1980 their share of the national income was 9 percent (compared to 11 percent for the next 4 percent of Americans), but by 2010 their share increased to 20 percent. In terms of the economic growth during this 30-year time period, 60 percent of it went to the top 1 percent (Piketty, 2014). From 1970 to 2014, the share of the nation's income that went to middle-class Americans decreased by almost 20 percent, dropping from 62 percent to 43 percent, but a 20 percent increase was reflected in upper-class income, which increased from 29 percent to 49 percent. Economists say that the erosion of the middle class has been steady, but a major factor was the 2008 recession and the lackluster economic recovery. Many Americans over 50 who lost their jobs have not been able to find another job with a comparable salary. As a result, the debt that millions of middle-class Americans had accrued to maintain their living standards must be paid off, and this has increased the economic stress for these families. Even those with a college diploma have seen their incomes decline (Meyerson, 2016). Many young wage earners have found it necessary to live at home while trying to gain access to better paying jobs that will allow them to live on their own (Arvedlund, 2017). As income declines, so does wealth. Middle-class Americans now control only 26 percent of the nation's wealth, and their share consists primarily of the homes they own (Piketty, 2014).

This widening gap in economic inequality contributed to financial instability, a key factor in the 2008 recession, as the purchasing power of lower- and middle-class consumers stagnated and their debt increased due to banks and other lenders offering generous credit rates. Before the recession began, the wealthiest Americans in the top 0.1 percent of the economy had incomes 220 times larger than the average income of the bottom 90 percent. As another way of comparing these two groups, the top 0.1 percent made in one and a half days what the bottom 90 percent earned for a year's

Video Example 9.3

In this video, a teacher discusses students' experiences of culture shock. Pay attention to how the teacher subtly approaches their economic situations and challenges in the conversation. How might institutional classism play a role in their experiences and contribute to the challenges they cite?

worth of work. This disparity continued even during the recession. Of the additional income created in 2010 compared to the previous year, the top 1 percent of Americans were recipients of 93 percent of those additional dollars (Stiglitz, 2012). One of the signs of America's growing economic disparity is the dramatic increase in billionaires. In 1980 there were only two billionaires in the United States, but more than 50 emerged by the end of the decade (Phillips, 1990). According to the Billionaires Mailing List (2017), there are 540 billionaires in the United States, more than in any other nation; China is second with 190 billionaires. Assessing the growing economic inequality in the United States, economist Thomas Piketty (2014) observed: "It is hard to imagine an economy and society that can continue functioning indefinitely with such extreme divergence between social groups" (p. 297). Some economists argue for increasing the minimum wage, which would raise salaries in general, addressing the problem of income inequality.

How have salaries in the United States been affected by recent economic changes?

> "Wealth is a power usurped by the few to compel the many to labor for their benefit."
> —PERCY BYSSHE SHELLEY (1792–1822)

In 1938, Congress passed the Fair Labor Standards Act that established a minimum wage of 25 cents an hour, and it stipulated that Congressional action would be necessary for any future increases. In 1950, when Congress increased the minimum wage from 40 cents to 75 cents, some economists predicted higher unemployment and other dire results, but the unemployment rate decreased by more than half. Further, from 1991 to 2015, the State of New York increased its minimum wage eight times, and each time its Department of Labor reported an increase in employment rates (Howell, 2016). Until the 1980s, federal minimum wage laws varied between 40 percent and 50 percent of the median wage, but since the 1980s, that percentage has dropped to 30–40 percent of the median wage (Holzer, 2012). The 2008 recession made a bad situation worse. The economy lost 8.2 million jobs, and 75 percent of the new jobs had salaries ranging from $7.50 to $13.50 an hour (Connell, 2011). In part this change was influenced by the Walmart business model introduced in 1962, which emphasized low-wage jobs. It continues to be widely imitated, primarily because of the profits made by the Walton family; four of its members are on *Forbes* magazine's list of the 20 richest Americans. As for the people who have to work at those low-paying jobs, their average wage in 2014 was almost exactly what the average wage was in 1979 when about 36 percent of employed workers were low-wage earners, but in 2014 these workers constituted 61 percent of all employed workers. Finally, it should be noted that the shift to more low-wage jobs is not related to worker performance since measures of the productivity rate for U.S. workers have found that they have more than doubled (Howell, 2016).

A 2008 study of over 4000 workers in such low-wage jobs found that over 25 percent were paid less than minimum wage, and 75 percent worked overtime without receiving overtime pay despite labor law mandates. Further, 70 percent of these employees worked "off the clock" (working additional hours for no pay). Of the workers who complained or initiated efforts to form a union to gain better protection, 43 percent experienced retaliation ranging from being fired to having their hours cut, despite laws that forbid such retaliation (Bernhardt, Milkman, & Theodore, 2009).

Historically, White men have enjoyed an economic advantage resulting in their salaries being the highest in all worker categories, yet even wages for White men declined, and having full-time work no longer provides adequate financial support. According to Cooper and Hall (2013), having a minimum wage job in 1980 was enough to keep a single parent above the poverty line, but that was not true in 2014. In the late 1960s, the minimum wage was 53 percent of the average worker's wages, but today it is only 37 percent of the average wage; if the minimum wage had been maintained at the 53 percent level it would be $10.50 today, enough to keep a couple with two children above the poverty line. Although more than 30 million low-wage workers would benefit from a higher minimum wage, women would be among the major beneficiaries, followed by people of color, especially Latinos (Cooper & Hall, 2013).

While wages for workers have declined, management has prospered. U.S. chief executive officer (CEO) salaries have climbed astronomically since 1983 when the average CEO earned 46 times the average worker's salary. By 2013, American CEOs were making an average of 331 times the average worker's salary (Wong, 2014). German, Japanese, and British CEOs earned average annual salaries of about $500,000, but the average CEO salary in the United States is $2 million; if you add their stock options, their average total compensation is $11.4 million (American Federation of Labor, 2011). The extravagant rise in salaries of CEOs is often a consequence of this elite group being able to dictate their pay packages or have their demands approved by a compensation committee of their peers who earn similar salaries and benefits. These dramatic increases could perhaps be justified if they were related to higher production under the CEO's leadership, but typically they are not. Piketty (2014) notes that executive pay tends to rise more rapidly when sales and profits increase for reasons that are external to the corporation (e.g., a booming economy), a phenomenon that has been called "pay for luck" (p. 335).

How large is the disparity of wealth in the United States?

Income is generated by toil or investment; *wealth* refers to assets you control. Because wealth is an obvious means of designating upper class, that group controls much of our wealth. But what level of concentrated wealth results in excessive influence? Wealth controlled by the top 1 percent of U.S. families declined slightly in each of the four decades after 1940 until 1980. The slight decrease in assets, related in part to higher tax rates, helped fund valuable social programs such as the GI Bill, FHA loans, and college loans that provided economic assistance to middle- and low-income families, creating a larger and more robust middle class.

By 1959, the top 4 percent of Americans had accumulated as much wealth as the lowest 35 percent; but in the 1980s, wealthy Americans began amassing even more wealth. According to U.S. Census data, between 1979 and 2008, wealth for 90 percent of Americans was stagnant or increased only slightly, and wealth for the lowest 20 percent decreased, but the incomes of the top 5 percent of American families increased by 73 percent (Johnson, 2011). This difference was reflected in a 2012 Federal Reserve survey reporting that the top 10 percent owned 72 percent of the wealth in the United States, while the bottom 50 percent only had 2 percent of the wealth. For the bottom 50 percent, wealth typically refers to wages available in a checking or savings account, a few possessions, and a home owned or being purchased (Piketty, 2014). There has been little protest from most Americans about the tax cuts for the wealthy that have caused this upward redistribution and loss of wealth for people regarded as being in the middle class. Perhaps these people view the tax cuts as being to their benefit either now or in the future. Graham (2013) reported that average Americans believe that at some time in the future their incomes will be above the mean. Such a belief may explain why there is such a high tolerance for income inequality in the United States and for its impact on Americans at different income levels.

How do income levels determine social class in the United States?

Scholars have long struggled to determine who comprises the middle class. According to a study by the Pew Charitable Trusts, Americans tend to view the middle class as people with incomes between $33,000 and $64,000 a year, yet most Americans earning more than $64,000 are likely to call themselves middle class. A *Gallup/USA Today* poll reported

Application Exercise 9.1

In this video, several teachers discuss the culture of schools, communicating with families, and family involvement. Pay attention to the teachers talk about some of the instances in which they communicate with families and the kinds of events and meetings that they expect to have with families. Think about the role that socio-economic status plays in this context of family involvement and communication with schools. Review the video and complete the activity.

that only 10 percent of Americans describe themselves as "lower class" and that to be middle-class status meant having a secure job and owning your home (Springer, 2013). Some American politicians lobbying for economic relief for the middle class have argued for extending tax cuts to those with annual earnings of up to $200,000 or higher. Even government experts like Longley (2014) say that middle class is a state of mind more than being clearly defined by income or wealth. Wolfe (1998) conducted a survey asking Americans how large an annual income would have to be for someone to be considered too rich to be middle class. The answers were diverse but caused Wolfe to define **middle class** not as a specific income range but as a combination of attitudes, beliefs, and practices that characterize someone who is "not too poor to be considered dependent on others and not too rich to be so luxuriously ostentatious that one loses touch with common sense" (pp. 2–3). This is as close to a definition of middle class as any expert has offered.

It is not difficult to define *low income*. The federal government established criteria for determining poverty based on earnings and number of people in a family (see Table 9.1). In 2014, federal definitions of **poverty levels** designated an income of $12,119 for an individual (under 65) living alone; $16,057 for a single individual with one child; and $18,769 for a single individual with two children (U.S. Census Bureau, 2014). Keeping these poverty levels in mind, a full-time worker being paid the minimum wage will earn $15,080 a year. Recognizing the inadequacy of the federal minimum wage, many U.S. cities are proposing to raise the local minimum wage, and some are considering the implementation of a "living wage" to meet the needs of low-income families.

According to Levinson (2012), the history of determining poverty thresholds illustrates why they are now outdated. In the 1960s, a Social Security administrator named Mollie Orshansky proposed a standard to measure poverty. At this time, the typical family spent one third of its household budget on food. Orshansky developed an emergency food budget providing a family with adequate nutrition for a short time, and a low-cost budget providing a family with adequate nutrition for a year. She lobbied for using the latter, but the Johnson administration chose the less adequate emergency food budget. Since then, this standard has only changed to reflect increases due to inflation. When first established, the poverty line was approximately 50 percent of the median income, consistent with other industrialized democracies, but by 2010, the poverty line in the United States had declined to 36 percent of the median income. For most families today, purchasing food only accounts for one eighth of their expenses, whereas costs for health care, childcare, and housing have increased significantly. To determine if families are living in poverty, federal authorities use their income prior to taxes being taken out, which inflates family resources available for their basic needs. The Economic Policy Institute has proposed a budget that accurately reflects the needs of American families, and it requires an average income that is twice as much as current poverty levels just to cover basic expenses. Their higher budget does not include money for savings accounts or other resources for escaping poverty (Levinson, 2012).

Table 9.1 Official Poverty Levels in the United States

Members in Family	Annual Income
Single	$12,119
Single 1 child	$16,057
Single 2 children	$18,769
Single 3 children	$23,707
Two adults 1 kid	$18,751
Two adults 2 kids	$23,624
Two adults 3 kids	$27,801
Annual Income for Minimum Wage Earner ($7.25/hr) = $15,080	

SOURCE: United States Census Bureau 2014. Available at www.census.gov

Who suffers most from poverty?

Many experts agree that women and children are most affected by poverty. Although the percentage of children in low-income homes with married parents has increased to 32 percent, 70 percent of children living with a single parent were in low-income homes. Gender is a significant factor because a female tends to be the head of household in most single-parent families. The fact that the parent had a job did not guarantee that families would be lifted above the poverty line: 75 percent of children living in poverty were living with at least one parent who worked at least part time. Even having some college education did not provide an escape from poverty—47 percent of low-income children and 39 percent of children living in poverty had at least one parent who had completed some post-secondary education (Skinner, 2013). Further, older adult women are more likely than older adult men to live in poverty, in part from their greater reliance on Social Security. They were more likely to work in low-wage jobs, resulting in less lifelong earnings and lower Social Security payments. These women were also less likely to have jobs offering pensions (Pyke, 2013). In the United States, *extreme poverty* is defined as a family's annual income being less than half of the poverty level. A family of four would be living on less than $30 a day. From 2011–2012, the numbers of older adult single women living in *extreme poverty* increased by 31 percent (Eichelberger, 2014).

Historically, one of the most vulnerable groups affected by poverty has been our children. The U.S. federal government response to help children in poverty began with the Economic Security Act of 1935 that included Aid to Dependent Children (ADC), a program intended for mothers widowed or abandoned by a husband. In 1950, ADC was expanded to include any single parent with children and was renamed Aid to Families with Dependent Children (AFDC). In 1964, food stamps were made available to low-income families. In the late 1970s, studies assessed the impact of the 1960s war-on-poverty programs initiated in the 1960s by President Lyndon Johnson. One study reported that hunger had been virtually eliminated (Edelman, 2001). Yet in 2010, the Children's Defense Fund (2011) estimated that 16.4 million children were living in poverty, with seven million in *extreme poverty*; for these children, not receiving proper nutrition is a regular feature of their lives. What had changed?

In 1996, Transitional Assistance for Needy Families (TANF) replaced AFDC. A welfare system needs to increase assistance to the poor during periods of economic downturn when the numbers of poor people inevitably increase. The AFDC program was able to expand automatically with increases of eligible recipients, but the Temporary Assistance to Needy Families (TANF) program was not designed to assist increased numbers; it required a vote of Congress to get increased funding and failed to meet the needs of eligible recipients during the recession that began in 2008. Although unemployment doubled in a number of states, TANF recipients increased only marginally and in some areas declined (Abramsky, 2012). A major factor for this decline is that TANF is funded by fixed block grants to states that can be used for other budgetary issues. Less than 25 percent of TANF funds are used for cash support of eligible recipients, and only 8 percent are used to assist recipients in finding a job. This significant reduction in cash support occurred as the numbers of families living in extreme poverty, the recipients most in need of cash support, was increasing dramatically (Harris & Shaefer, 2017). TANF has clearly been an inadequate program to assist families, especially children, living in poverty.

In 2000, among American cities with populations of 200,000 or higher, only one reported a child poverty rate as high as 40 percent, but in 2010, eight urban areas surpassed this rate, topped by Detroit with a 50 percent child poverty rate and Cleveland close behind at 49 percent. Related to this, urban children living in poverty are disproportionately in families of color. A child from a Black, Latino, or Native American home is almost three times as likely as a White child to live in poverty, and yet because White people are still the largest overall population, about 33 percent of all children living in

> "Of all the preposterous assumptions of humanity over humanity, nothing exceeds most of the criticisms made on the habits of the poor by the well-housed, well-warmed, well-fed."
>
> —HERMAN MELVILLE (1819–1891)

poverty are White compared to 25 percent for African Americans and 36 percent for Latinos. In addition, immigrant children constitute 25 percent of all American children, and they are more likely than native children to live in poverty or in near-poverty conditions (Skinner, 2013).

In the United States, one out of five children lives in poverty; over 40 percent of them live in *extreme poverty*. America has the second worst child poverty rate in the world among industrialized nations, with the United States ranking thirty-first in infant mortality rates and twenty-fifth in low birth weight rates. Low birth weight means a baby is born weighing 5-1/2 pounds or less. These babies tend to come from low-income families, and their problems are largely a due to a lack of health care (Children's Defense Fund, 2014). The Affordable Care Act (ACA) allowed states to expand Medicaid, which significantly increased the numbers of people having health insurance. The response was initially bipartisan. Of the 31 states implementing an expanded Medicaid program, over half had Republican governors. With this expansion, Medicaid covered 20 percent of all Americans, surpassing Medicare to become the largest health care provider in the United States. Medicaid covered 40 percent of America's children and paid for half of all births. It insures one-third of Americans with a disability and two-thirds of all older adults in nursing homes (Rosenbaum, 2017). Among its recipients, 42 percent were White, 31 percent were Latino, 19 percent were Black, and 8 percent were mixed race individuals (Gurley, 2017). In 2017, the new Republican-controlled Congress tried to replace the ACA, but its proposals involved at least 20 million Americans losing their health care. Another issue is that many states like Tennessee that did not expand Medicaid have been struggling with economic consequences of this decision, such as forcing rural hospitals to close. Tennessee already had the second largest rate of hospital closings, and an additional 40 or more rural hospitals were on the brink of closing (Gurley, 2017). These hospital closings not only affect access to health care but also have economic repercussions for people living in those rural areas.

Another group of people significantly affected by poverty is older adults. Many Americans believe that the United States effectively addressed the problem of poverty for older adult Americans with the establishment of the Social Security system in 1935, and there is some truth to this belief. Social Security was a major reason why only about 10 percent of people living in poverty in the United States are older adults, although a 2011 study found their numbers increasing up to 14 percent (Smith, 2013). Older adult Americans encounter a number of serious problems related not just to poverty but also to a form of prejudice scholars have termed "ageism."

 Self-Check 9.3 Complete this self-check quiz to check your understanding of institutional classism and the impact of such practices for American families living in poverty.

How Ageism Negatively Affects Both the Elderly and Youth

Although research on age prejudice is relatively recent, it is not a new problem. According to Macnicol (2006), anthropologists have reported that in all societies, age is one of the major factors fo-r determining an individual's status. In the United States, status is primarily determined by age, race, class, and gender, and yet historically age has been the least acknowledged. As scholars began investigating bias and prejudice against older adults, they linked many negative attitudes to the fear of mortality. Nelson (2009) wrote: "Older people are a very poignant and salient reminder to younger people that they are mortal, that life is finite" (p. 436).

How do scholars define ageism?

Butler (2008) originally coined the term *ageism* in 1968, defining it as "a form of systematic stereotyping and discrimination against people because they are old" (p. 41). At first social scientists were reluctant to accept this concept, but by 2000, the term *ageism* was widely viewed as a phenomenon that justified research to clarify its impact on older adults (Levy & Banaji, 2002). An emerging view among some social scientists has been to argue for a broader definition of ageism, one that includes both the young and older adults.

The trend toward a broader definition began in the 1980s with the formation of the Americans for Generational Equity (AGE). AGE focused on concerns related to the increasing use of resources to provide health care for older adult Americans, asserting that such an unbalanced distribution of resources was provided at the expense of the young, representing prejudice against the young. Bytheway (2005) supported the idea of a broader definition of ageism that included all age groups: "We are all, throughout our lives, oppressed by ageism, by dominant expectations about age, expectations that dictate how we behave and relate to each other" (p. 338). Two prominent researchers in the field have offered a broader definition of **ageism** as "an alteration in feeling, belief, or behavior in response to an individual's or group's perceived chronological age" (Levy & Banaji, 2002, p. 50); nevertheless, most of the research on ageism pertains to older adults more than to any other age group. Studies of ageism have not only described current issues but also explored how perceptions based on age have changed over time and influenced the creation of stereotypes and prejudices.

How has ageism manifested itself in American society?

During the colonial era, an elder was a highly respected member of the community, but as the United States became industrialized, urban areas expanded and attitudes toward older adults changed. Increased emphasis on a nuclear family resulted in parents living apart from their adult children, and older adults spent less time with their grandchildren. With the growth of technology, younger workers were more likely to have the most highly valued skills and knowledge, transforming the ideal of the wise elder into a perception of older adults as people who cannot learn, are out of touch, are cantankerous, and are set in their ways, unable to change (Schmidt, 2011).

In addition, there was a dramatic change in psychological views of the individual. According to Gullette (2011), American psychologists historically viewed mental ability in terms of an individual *mind* associated with personality, individuality, and moral or religious sentiments. In the twentieth century, the concept of mind gave way to an emphasis on the brain as the seat of mental activity, and scientists studied how the brain functioned. In recent years, this emphasis has been reduced to memory, with considerable research devoted to the study of memory loss. A decline in the ability to remember information, including nonsense syllables, has become the defining measure of mental decline. Ageism scholars have noted the increased use of the term *senility* in the medical profession and in society. Gullette (2011) observed that in the past, senility "was available as a medical label, but it was much harder to apply to a particular old person when many valuable qualities were simultaneously observable" (p. 177).

As with other forms of prejudice and discrimination, ageism tends to replace individual identities with myths and stereotypes of the group. Older adults are often viewed as frail, lonely, depressed, and socially isolated, and it is widely believed that aging is accompanied by a significant loss of cognitive ability leading to dementia. While it is true that aging often results in a slight loss in cognitive ability, only 5 percent of people over 65 years old develop dementia (Anderson, 2017). As for frailty, older workers take fewer sick days than younger workers. Yet prejudices can be powerful.

"There is a wicked inclination in most people to suppose an old man decayed in his intellects. If a young or middle-aged man, when leaving a company, does not recollect where he laid his hat, it is nothing; but if the same inattention is discovered in an old man, people will shrug up their shoulders, and say, 'His memory is going.'"

—SAMUEL JOHNSON (1709–1784)

Television programs portraying older adult characters as being forgetful, irritable, or easily confused reinforce ageist stereotypes, and older adults who are the most avid televisions watchers tend to have a more negative view of their own peer group (Scheve & Venzon, 2017). Even so, numerous studies report older people as achieving higher levels of happiness, and lower levels occur during the mid-life of adults (Anderson, 2017). Finally, older people do not tend to be isolated but remain connected to family and friends and are typically active at local senior centers or in their churches. This relates to a positive stereotype about older people—that they tend to be religious, but Anderson (2017) argues that this is a generational phenomenon. Older people are more likely to have grown up attending church, and it has continued to be a place where they socialize or engage in volunteer work. More than half a million adults over the age of 55 volunteer with Senior Corps alone (Scheve & Venzon, 2017). Many of the prejudices against older adults are implicit rather than explicit. As Levy and Banaji (2002) noted: "One of the most insidious aspects of ageism is that it can operate without conscious awareness, control or intent to do harm" (p. 50). They argue that many Americans do not take ageism seriously because it is not characterized by explicit emotions such as the vitriolic bigotry directed against certain communities.

Individuals who might be accused of ageism will not respond with the same sense of shame or defensiveness as would someone accused of racism or harboring anti-gay attitudes. Ageism is so subtle and pervasive that it even affects the attitudes of older adults. Whereas most groups reveal a bias favoring in-group members, Barber and Mather (2014) report that implicit negative attitudes about aging were stronger than any other implicit attitudes, even about race. In one study, half of the participants read articles describing older adults maintaining their memory abilities over their lifespan, and the other half read articles about how memory declines as people age. Both groups then took a memory test. In the first group there was no difference in the scores of younger or older participants, but in the second group, younger participants had significantly higher scores than older participants on the memory test.

Ageist stereotypes and assumptions are part of our culture. Aging expert Steve Scrutton says, "Ageism surrounds us . . . but it is so engrained within the structure of social life that it is unlikely to be (noticed or) challenged" (Macnicol, 2006, p. 10). Children learn such stereotypes. Several studies have documented children's preference for young adults and their bias against older adults (Barber & Mather, 2014). When children describe older people, they tend to focus on physical aspects of aging such as baldness, wrinkles, and poor vision or hearing, and they use negative descriptive terms such as being sad, lonely, or boring. In one study, children who were four, six, or eight years old were paired with an adult who was either 35 or 75 years old. The adults were all dressed according to current fashion, in good health, and instructed to act very friendly toward the children. Yet when paired with the 75-year-old adult, all three age groups of children tended to sit farther away, make less eye contact, and engage in fewer interactions, including fewer requests for assistance. Although children do learn some positive stereotypes about older adults, several studies document that negative attitudes are predominant, and they intensify as children enter their adolescent years. A recent study conducted online included 60,000 respondents and reported strong implicit associations between the words *bad* and *older*; these negative responses were consistent among all participants, even those who were older adults (Barber & Mather, 2014).

This result parallels studies of other minority groups in which some individuals view themselves in ways influenced by negative stereotypes. Barber and Mather (2014) report that older adults do not do as well on tests when they are told that the purpose is to examine memory performance; this suggests that the older adult participants have internalized negative stereotypes about aging associated with cognitive decline and memory loss. Internalizing ageist stereotypes may even affect longevity. Gullette (2011) described the results of a longitudinal study of 660 people over the age of 50 in a small Ohio town in which individuals who had positive views about aging lived 7.5 years longer than those who had negative views about growing older. This represented a bigger increase in longevity than factors associated with exercise and the cessation of smoking. Numerous studies concerning the impact of ageist stereotypes on older adults have reported evidence of an age-based stereotype threat (ABST). Effects were observed whether the research overtly introduced these stereotypes or whether they were expressed more subtly—for example, the instructions being given in a patronizing tone or with frequent offers of help. In a meta-analysis of articles based on 37 experimental studies, researchers concluded that exposure to ABST had an adverse effect on the performance of older adult research participants (Lamont, Swift, & Abrams, 2015).

> "Life's Tragedy is that we get old too soon and wise too late."
>
> —BENJAMIN FRANKLIN (1706–1790)

In part because of the findings from ongoing research in medicine and gerontology, life expectancy in the United States has risen dramatically. Americans are not only living longer but are also healthier and living more vigorously into their 70s and 80s, with an increasing number holding full- or part-time jobs. Of all adults over 80, only 30 percent require assistance with basic activities of daily life, and they tend to be housed in nursing homes (U.S. Department of Health and Human Services, 2011). Americans who are 90 or older are the fastest-growing age group in the United States (Scheve & Venzon, 2017). Yet because older adult Americans live in a culture that emphasizes youth and beauty, aging is still regarded as a time of inevitable physical and mental decline and social marginality.

For individuals from a minority group already marginalized, ageism increases the problems. For example, many heterosexuals believe that most gay men and lesbians are affluent, but a higher percentage of older adult gay men and lesbians (also bisexuals and transgender people) live in poverty than their heterosexual peers. Arana (2013) reports that half of LGBT individuals have only $10,000 in savings when they retire and are far less likely than younger LGBT people to have a domestic partner or spouse. Because prejudice against them was much more widespread and overt when they were younger, older adult LGBT individuals are more likely to lack family support. The 2013 U.S. Supreme Court ruling on the Defense of Marriage Act provided equal rights for LGBT couples, but it came too late for older adult LGBT partners to recover years' worth of tax and insurance benefits. Finally, older adult LGBT people in nursing homes have encountered anti-gay prejudice from staff. LGBT people in nursing homes report hearing anti-gay slurs, or they have been excluded from social occasions. A 2011 study found that less than one third of older adult care institutions provided workshops to increase staff sensitivity to LGBT clients (Arana, 2013). Older adult LGBT people who have been out of the closet for most of their lives may return to the closet after moving into care institutions if they encounter staff with homophobic attitudes or behaviors. But the marginalization of older adults is not the only manifestation of ageism in our society; there are also negative attitudes toward youth.

Is there evidence to support claims of prejudiced attitudes toward youth?

In the media, terms like "Generation X," "Generation Y," or the "Millennial Generation" reinforce the use of generalizations about these cohort groups that are often stereotypical assumptions about the attitudes and behaviors of all members of each group. Specific negative stereotypes relate to perceptions of youth as drug users, irresponsible, sexually promiscuous, lacking ambition, and not valuing education.

Macnicol (2006) discussed how these stereotypes are reinforced by the correlation between youth and higher crime rates, unemployment, homicides and other traumatic deaths, drug abuse, car accidents, and higher health costs. Much of this correlation is a consequence of economic and cultural factors, and of course, data about a few members of a group should never be used to characterize an entire group. Negative attitudes about youth have resulted in institutionalized discrimination against young people through what critics view as an arbitrary establishment of a minimum age for activities such as driving a car, serving on a jury, consuming alcohol, voting, running for public office, and attending adult films. In schools, some educators use the concept of "age-appropriate" curricula to avoid dealing with serious and controversial issues. Such discrimination against youth has been observed in other cultures. After he was elected President of South Africa, Nelson Mandela wanted to reward the country's youth for their participation in the struggle against Apartheid, but when he proposed lowering the voting age to 14, he encountered such vigorous resistance within his own political party that he withdrew the proposal (Mandela, 2010). Ultimately, the harshest impact of ageism on youth, as is true for older adults, will always be found in the economic consequences stemming from their age. As most Americans continue to struggle in the aftermath of one of the deepest recessions in the history of the global economy, it is important to understand the consequences of poverty in conjunction with ageism.

What are some economic consequences of ageism for both older adults and youth?

By the 1980s, almost 60 percent of employed Americans had a pension that was managed by their employers. When they retired, their pension provided a check every month for as long as they lived. Some pension plans even included health benefits and pension benefits that went to their spouses when they died. By 2009, only 7 percent of private employees had an employer-managed pension plan, and among corporations established since 1980, almost none provided the kind of pension plan that used to be commonly funded (Kuttner, 2012). Retirement packages today are usually 401(k) plans that rely on the significant contributions from the individual worker, and as retirement approaches, the median balance of these plans is slightly over $110,000, which will only pay for a few years of retirement. Further, a majority of workers in the lower two-thirds of income distribution do not have any savings for their retirement. Social Security has been an important source of retirement funds, but the average benefit today is only $1200 a month. If individuals delay retirement until they are 70, their benefits are 76 percent higher than if they retire at 62, but many low-income workers do not have good job prospects to rely on, and they tend to die sooner. For them, it makes more sense to collect benefits at age 62, but over time they will receive fewer benefits than those who wait to retire until they are 70, typically higher income workers (Ghilarducci, 2015).

It may not seem surprising to be told that poor Americans die at a younger age than wealthy Americans and have fewer years to enjoy retirement, but what may be surprising is to learn that there used to be a more equitable term of retirement in the United States and that it was a direct result of egalitarian government policies dating from the 1930s to the 1960s. By the 1980s, thanks to programs such as Social Security, Medicare, and private pension plans, low-income Americans were spending approximately the same amount of time in the workforce as high-income earners, and they were enjoying retirement for about the same number of years. Now Social Security and Medicare are being attacked relentlessly, and the traditional pension plans that once covered almost half of the American workforce have almost disappeared (Ghilarducci, 2015).

The current Social Security policy represents institutional ageism because it is based on an assumption that all retirees will have the same or a similar longevity rate. That would mean that people retiring at 62 or at 70 would receive similar benefits over their lifetimes but paid at a lower or higher rate depending on when they retired. This is not true because of the disparate longevity rates based on social class, race, and educational attainment. If politicians arguing for increasing the retirement age are successful, the inequities would increase. Proposals to raise the retirement age from 67 (scheduled for implementation in 2022) to 70 would drastically reduce benefits for the recipients in the early years, and many will not live long enough to collect the higher benefits (Ghirladucci, 2015). Some advocates for older adults insist that we need to increase Social Security benefits and create a universal pension plan to offset the unequal earnings of workers over their lifetimes. If this were done, the United States could once again achieve the economic equality that had been established in the twentieth century.

There is a gender dimension to poverty. Twice as many women as men live in poverty. Social Security checks constitute 70 percent of the total income for nearly two-thirds of older adult Americans, and women represent 75 percent of this group (Kuttner, 2012). Almost one-fourth of older adult, unmarried women live in poverty, and for almost half of them, Social Security checks constitute 90 percent or more of their income (Hinden, 2017). The median income of Social Security benefits for retired men is $27,612, but for women it is only $16,040 because women earn less than men and are not able to save as much money (Hicken, 2014). A major factor in this difference is that women face not only additional stress from their traditional role in our culture as caregivers but also sustain economic consequences. Over the course of their career, women tend to work 12 years less than men, largely due to leaving a job in order to care for children or aging parents. Women of color are also affected, as over 20 percent of Black and Latino women live in poverty (Hicken, 2014). Finally, because women live longer than men (2.1 years if both genders reach 65), women are more likely to have to spend more on medical costs (Hinden, 2017). Yet the gender gap between men and women remains, with men receiving a typical monthly benefit in the $1400 to $1800 range, while the typical monthly benefit for women falls in the $700 to $900 range (Caplinger, 2014).

Despite such minimal support, Social Security is regarded as a successful anti-poverty program. From 1959 to 2006, the rate of older adults living in poverty declined from 35 percent to 10 percent, causing Whitman and Purcell (2007) to conclude: "The reduction in poverty among older Americans is one of the most significant public policy successes of the past half century" (p. 194). Each year, Social Security checks keep 21 to 22 million people above the poverty level, including over a million children who receive Social Security benefits if one or both parents die or if they live with a family whose income comes in part or wholly from Social Security. Without Social Security checks, over 44 percent of Americans past the age of 65 would be living in poverty as opposed to the current rate of less than 9 percent. Finally, Social Security Disability Insurance represents 75 percent or more of the income for 60 percent of people with a disability who are not institutionalized (Lawson, 2015).

The economic consequences of poverty for older adult Americans are likely to become even more significant in the next two decades. Demographers at the U.S. Census Bureau predict that from 2000 to 2030, the number of people over 65 will double (Nelson, 2009). In the workplace, policies and practices based on the ageist assumption that increased age brings a decline in mental capabilities may have a powerful negative impact, and the consequences are already being experienced. Those at the top of the economic hierarchy will never share the fate of the masses, yet they are likely to have a significant influence on what that fate may be. Wealthy and powerful people do not end up in nursing homes or rely on Social Security checks to survive, but for the majority of Americans, fears about aging are largely related to the concern about what will happen after they have exhausted their financial resources.

The economic consequences of ageism for youth are especially significant for those living in poverty, but many issues have had an adverse impact on the young. For most of the twentieth century Americans assumed that having more college-educated people in the population would contribute to our prosperity and approved the use of tax dollars to support post-secondary public institutions. By subsidizing these institutions, tuition was kept low enough to make college affordable for those who had the requisite academic abilities. Enrollments in higher education increased, and premier universities in America were recognized internationally. The contributions of higher education were regarded as a major factor in the United States becoming the richest nation in the world. The transformation of American attitudes began with the belief that higher education was a private benefit rather than a public good. Fewer tax dollars supporting university budgets resulted in higher tuition costs. Compared to 1980, attending a public institution today costs students three times as much. In 2000, only three states provided less state revenue to public higher education than students paid in tuition, but by 2012, the three states had increased to 24 states. In the process, college students have accrued a debt of over $1.2 trillion, approximately $300 million more than the debt all Americans have accumulated on their credit cards (Kirp, 2015). The financial burden is most difficult for the poor. About 50 percent of students earning a bachelor's degree come from financially secure homes, compared to the 10 percent of degrees earned by low-income youth who are increasingly forced to drop out for financial reasons. About 60 percent of students in two-year community colleges drop out, as do 40 percent of students enrolled in a four-year institution. These numbers have little to do with academic ability. A Stanford study reported that roughly 35,000 low-income students in high school have test scores and grades in the top tenth percentile. The Stanford researcher observed: "The amount of untapped talent out there is staggering" (Kirp, 2015, p. 120).

Historically, young people interested in attending college could contribute to the cost by saving money from their summer jobs, but summer jobs are getting harder to find. In the 1970s, 60 percent of American teenagers looked for a summer job, but in 2016 only 35 percent were looking (Vick, 2017). In 2017, 41 percent of companies responded to a survey saying they planned to hire summer workers, but 84 percent admitted that they already knew the individual they were going to hire (e.g., family member or friend). American youth have more competition today: Foreign students come in the summer looking for a travel experience as well as a job, and retired Americans are often financially forced to look for part-time or seasonal work. The competition for jobs has forced many young people to accept unpaid internships, thinking that this experience will look good on an application to college or for a job. Further, according the Bureau of Labor Statistics reports that 40 percent of youth between 16 and 19 enrolled in summer classes, knowing that they could not save much for college from the low-wage job they might get and hoping that an advanced academic experience was a better investment of their time (Vick, 2017).

A final point: College is not able to offer the same fiscal incentives as in the past. For the generation born during World War II, 90 percent earned more than their parents did, but for the generation born in the 1980s, only 50 percent are achieving that fiscal milestone. This decline is happening in all 50 states, and the research suggests that a major factor is the increasing economic inequality in the United States (Wong, 2016). Declining incomes has forced many young adults (ages 18–34) to live at home. In 2005, the majority of young adults lived alone or with a spouse or an unmarried partner, a dominant pattern in 35 states, but in 2015, this pattern was the norm in only six states. Analysis of the young adults living at home has found that the majority are male, about half of them are White, and 20 percent have at least one child. Further, 90 percent of the young adults who were living in the parental home a year ago are still there (Arvedlund, 2017). These examples of ageism affecting older adults and the young should be important to all of us since both groups are simply part of the human experience, and we should always remember that no matter what form exploitation takes, it is most damaging to the poor, who are the most vulnerable portion of our population.

How do institutions exploit low-income families?

Financial institutions exploit poor families simply by enforcing policies meant to protect them from losses. **Redlining** refers to banks and other lenders identifying a deteriorating area in a city and refusing to lend money for mortgages or business loans in that area. For low-income workers, such areas are most likely to offer the best opportunity to purchase affordable homes, yet when they apply for mortgage loans, their applications may be denied. In such cases, denial is not based on bad credit ratings or lack of skills to maintain and improve property; it results from the age and/or current condition of properties in the redlined area and the average income levels of its residents.

"Nobody talks more of free enterprise and competition and of the best man winning than the man who inherited his father's store or farm."
—C. WRIGHT MILLS (1916–1962)

Although the 1968 Fair Housing Act outlawed redlining, communities of color argue that it persists by taking on new forms such as "retail redlining." For example, when Minority entrepreneurs interested in opening a business in a largely minority neighborhood cannot get the bank loans needed if the area is redlined (Badger, 2015). Banks insist that it is just good business practice not to invest in declining areas, but refusing to lend money for purchase or improvement of property makes deterioration inevitable, making the bank's "prediction" a self-fulfilling prophecy. The federal government has attempted to stop redlining practices, encouraging some corporations to offer low-interest loans to promote minority-owned businesses in redlined areas, but they have not been able to overcome the difficulties that banks have created. Although the reason for redlining is supposedly based on objective economic factors, this practice has had a significant impact on low-income people of color. As Shorris (2001) observed, "Redlining by the bank has taken the economic heart out of Latinos, as it did (for) blacks" (p. 323).

Another way financial agencies discriminate against low-income families is by insisting on a minimum balance of $150 or $200 for checking accounts, making it impossible for workers living from paycheck to paycheck to maintain checking accounts. Cramer (2012) says banks have little interest in accounts from low-income people because they are likely to be small-scale savers if they save at all; so, a large portion of low-income families are "unbanked," or they are considered "underbanked" if they have to use the services of payday lenders and check-cashing stores that charge high rates (Steinzor, 2017). According to a report from the Federal Deposit Insurance Corporation (2015), American households consisting of 15.6 million adults and 7.6 million children were unbanked, and households consisting of an additional 51.1 million adults with 16.3 million children were underbanked.

Finally, banks, thrifts, and credit unions found in higher income areas are not as available in low-income areas. For example, Manhattan boasts one bank per 3000 residents, but there is only one bank available per 20,000 people living in the South Bronx (Steinzor, 2017). When banks abandoned the central cities, check-cashing stores and payday lending outlets proliferated. Ratcliffe (2009) reported that there were 4000 more check-cashing stores and payday lending businesses in the United States than the total combined retail stores for McDonald's, Burger King, Target, Sears, JCPenney, and Walmart. Ratcliffe also reported that a 400 percent annual interest rate is standard for payday lenders, and they make an annual profit of $4 billion. Some of this profit stems from the practice of payday lenders combining several high-interest loans and selling them to a bank for the interest owed. The bank owning the high-interest loans can then collect interest at a rate well above what it would normally be permitted to charge. But banks and private lenders are not the only businesses involved in the exploitation of low-income families and individuals.

How do businesses discriminate against low-income people?

One basic way businesses discriminate is to charge higher prices for products in stores serving low-income people than in stores in the suburbs with similar merchandise. Such tactics have been going on for a long time, and Feagin and Feagin (1986) described several practices that merchants engaged in (and continue to employ) to exploit the poor:

Blank price tags Blank price tags on merchandise force the customer to ask for the price of an item, allowing merchants to quote higher prices to customers who seem particularly naive.

Bait and switch Although the practice is illegal, stores may advertise a product at a low price to attract customers, who are then told that the product is of poor quality. Customers are encouraged to buy a similar product of better quality at a higher price.

Rent-to-own Customers rent a product that they can own by making weekly payments over a specified time, but only 25 percent eventually own the product. Rent-to-own stores across the nation earn annual revenues of $8.5 billion by charging up to four times the retail price of the item. For example, a computer that retails for $851 could be rented for weekly payments of $49 for 91 weeks; the renter would own the computer after having made payments for 21 months totaling $4449 (Ratcliffe, 2009). If the renter missed a payment, the store could legally demand that the computer be returned with no refund. Some lawmakers believe these excessive charges should be capped at 24 percent, but store owners say they are exempt from laws limiting interest rates because they are renting a product, not charging interest (Hirschfeld, 2015).

Pawnshops Every year more than 30 million people have to resort to the expensive option of taking a possession to a pawnshop as collateral for a loan. The average loan is $150, but one company's report noted that 30 percent of these people never return for the item they pawned (Quigley, 2016). In Atlanta, a mother living in public housing was given a $75 loan at a pawnshop and paid $15 a month interest. With a credit card she would have paid a little over $1 a month interest (Hudson, 2011). Even when customers pay the interest and reclaim the property, the loan repayment does not go on their credit record, so the transaction does not improve their credit rating.

Poor people are exploited in other ways in America, but the preceding examples illustrate that exploitation occurs. One must overcome numerous economic obstacles to escape poverty, and no simple solutions exist. As was demonstrated in the 1930s, federal and state governments must address issues of poverty if any progress is to be made concerning the exploitation of and discrimination against poor people.

> "Governments exist to protect the rights of minorities; the loved and the rich need no protection."
> —WENDELL PHILLIPS (1811–1884)

What can federal and state governments do to assist families living in poverty?

Scholars and activists such as Harris and Shaeffer (2017), Piketty (2014), Lerner (2012), Schmidt (2012), Goldstein (2012), and Haycock (2001) and organizations such as the Children's Defense Fund (2017) have made recommendations regarding the role government must play in assisting people in poverty or in supporting those struggling to stay out of poverty:

1. Provide services to address critical needs such as subsidizing childcare services for low-income women who are enrolled in education or training programs.
2. Currently the Child Tax Credit (CTC) program does not provide the poorest families with the full lump sum that is supposed to be distributed for each dependent child. Fully fund the CTC, and transform it into a Universal Child Allowance where the cash assistance is distributed monthly with payments based on a realistic income floor; this would provide financial stability for low-income families to escape extreme poverty.
3. Raise the federal minimum wage. Raising the minimum wage to $10.10 would move over 400,000 children above the poverty line. Several studies have concluded that the current minimum wage is so low it could be increased without causing any decrease in employment. In 2017, 29 states had a minimum wage higher than the federal level.
4. Restructure public school funding so that taxes to support schools are collected by the state and disbursed to schools according to a variable per pupil funding formula that takes into account factors such as (a) the number of low-income students in a given school, (b) the amount of budget devoted to special learners, and (c) the mobility rate of students. In 1990, the New Jersey Supreme Court ruled that such plans are economically feasible and morally justified (*Abbott v. Burke*).

Only by making such a commitment can we reap the benefits of children becoming adults who develop and use their abilities to the fullest.

5. Provide tax relief for low-income families. Tax relief for wealthy Americans already exists as capital gains tax cuts. If tax relief is good for the wealthy, then it should be good for the poor. Some tax relief exists in the Earned Income Tax Credit (EITC) and childcare allowances, although some politicians want to eliminate both. Another form of tax relief for low-income workers is to exempt home purchases to allow time to make improvements and save money so the owner can pay the resulting higher taxes assessed because of improvements.

6. Offer tax incentives for corporations to locate in inner cities and tax incentives for corporations creating day care centers at the worksite if they allow low-income families in the area to place children in the centers. Some scholars have argued that the reduction of businesses in inner cities has been a major factor in the increase of drug use and crime, and the general deterioration of those communities.

7. Strengthen educational opportunity by increasing support for Head Start programs and funding quality preschool programs for all eligible children but especially economically disadvantaged children. Oklahoma's program should be the model to achieve maximum benefits for enrolled children, including subsidizing teacher salaries to attract experienced, quality teachers, especially for schools in low-income areas.

8. Increase subsidies for affordable housing. Currently only 25 percent of eligible recipients received such assistance. The federal government could add 300,000 more housing vouchers each year for the next 10 years. Badger (2014) advocates for incentives to local housing agencies to assist families in using their vouchers to rent housing in neighborhoods that are not low-poverty areas. In addition, the Low-Income Home Energy Assistance Program could be expanded so low-income families can meet rising energy costs.

9. Provide reasonable regulation of the private sector to maintain jobs. The federal government should review policies pertaining to multinational corporations relocating outside the United States. Although inevitable in a global economy, there should be disincentives for locating abroad, and offering incentives might keep those jobs in the United States. American corporations currently have more incentives to locate overseas.

 Self-Check 9.4 Complete this self-check quiz to check your understanding of ageism and how age can be the cause of negative consequences for both older adults and youth.

Afterword

Oppression is an inevitable consequence when power and resources are concentrated in one group. During the 1930s, U.S. Supreme Court Justice Louis Brandeis expressed his concern for the future of democracy in America by proposing that the United States could continue to be a democracy, or it could continue to allow great wealth to be accumulated by a few people, but it was not possible to accomplish both. Equity and justice depend on transferring resources and power to oppressed groups. People sustain the misery of poverty not because they deserve it but most likely as a consequence of birth. The consequences of poverty affect youth as they are becoming adults and continue throughout their lives. As soon as they are perceived as "senior citizens," people may find themselves struggling against stereotypes and prejudices based simply on their age, affecting even those in the middle class.

If needs of adults living in poverty are neglected, we will perpetuate a despair that often produces drug abuse, crime, and violence. In America today, one of every five babies is born into poverty. If the needs of children living in poverty are neglected, we will be guilty of abandoning American ideals and betraying the decency and compassion Americans have long associated with those ideals. If Americans reject our social conscience, we make achievement of social justice impossible. When we look at faces of children deprived of their basic needs, we are confronted not only with a moral dilemma in the present but also with a question about what kind of society America will be in the years to come.

> "Until the great mass of the people shall be filled with the sense of responsibility for each other's welfare, social justice can never be attained."
>
> —HELEN KELLER (1880–1968)

Summary

- Cultural classism is illustrated by historic American attitudes and responses to poverty.

- Americans continue to have negative attitudes, myths, and misconceptions about people living in poverty, especially welfare recipients.

- Institutional classism has contributed to an increasing disparity in income and wealth, and institutional policies and business practices often exploit low-income people.

- Ageism not only involves prejudices and stereotypes of both older adults and youth but also has economic consequences for both groups.

Terms and Definitions

Ageism An alteration in feeling, belief, or behavior in response to an individual's or group's perceived age (Levy & Banaji, 2002)

Bait and switch An illegal strategy in which a merchant advertises a cheap product, and when the customer comes in to purchase it, he is persuaded to buy a more expensive product

Classism An attitude, action, or institutional structure that subordinates or limits an individual on the basis of her low socioeconomic status

Cultural classism The societal promotion of negative beliefs and practices that tend to portray poor, less educated, or socially unacceptable persons as deficient, inferior, and responsible for their own situation; the assumption of superiority by people or groups based on wealth, employment, education, or social standing

Individual classism Prejudiced attitudes and behavior against others based on the perception of level of income, education, or status as inferior

Institutional classism Established laws, customs, and practices in a society that allow systematic discrimination against low-income individuals or groups to the benefit of middle- or upper-class individuals or groups

Middle class A socioeconomic status determined partly by income and primarily by a cluster of attitudes, beliefs, and practices of someone not too poor to be considered dependent on others but not living in an ostentatious manner associated with being wealthy

Pawnshops Businesses that receive individual possessions as collateral for loans

Poverty levels Income levels established by the federal government based on earnings and the number of individuals in a family

Redlining The practice of banks and other lenders of designating certain areas, especially inner-city neighborhoods (ghettoes or barrios), as "deteriorating," which means they are viewed as bad risks for mortgage loans

Rent-to-own Businesses that offer merchandise on a rental basis to customers who cannot afford the purchase price of that merchandise, stipulating that at the end of the rental period the merchandise will become the property of the renter at an exorbitant cost

Discussion Exercises

Exercise 1 Broadening the Wealth in America: Can We Avoid Economic Domination by the Wealthy?

The Proposal: Ideas for a more equitable distribution of economic resources in the United States have been implemented, including pension plans, profit sharing, the GI Bill, FHA loans, and Social Security. Proponents argue that the money for the proposal below could be raised by increasing income tax on the wealthiest 40 percent of Americans (those making $80,000 or more) by 2 percent.

Directions: Review the plan. Does it seem to be a reasonable way to obtain funding to fulfill its objective? What special considerations might need to be made in its implementation?

Proposal

Every American would have a "wealth account" of $80,000 established for him at birth. Individuals could have access to this account upon turning 21 but only upon graduation from high school. For the rest of their life, people could use this account to achieve desired goals, but anything taken from the account must be paid back. As an example of how the account could be used: 18-year-olds attending college would be permitted to access the account early to pay for college expenses (including the high school graduate trying to escape a violent and drug-ridden neighborhood); workers who are laid off from their job could live off the interest until they found a new job, or they could pay for further training for a related or different occupation; a young couple who just had their first child and wanted to buy a house could use the money for a down payment; a truck driver could use the money to begin her own trucking company. Any of the interest or principal used from this "wealth account" would eventually be repaid so that when an individual died, the money plus interest from the wealth account would be reclaimed by the government and used to finance an account for another individual. If an account did not have the full amount it should have, the government would get to make the first claims on whatever assets the dead individual left behind in order to get the full amount repaid.

(Adapted from Ackerman, B.A., & Alstott, A. (n.d.). "$80,000 and a Dream. The American Prospect Online," *The American Prospect*, http://www.prospect.org/print/V11/16/ackerman-b.html.)

Exercise 2 The Manager's Dilemma

Directions: The following dilemma is based on a true story. Read the description below, and respond to the following questions: What would you do if you were the manager? What reasons would be primarily responsible for your decision?

You are the manager of a popular urban restaurant whose customers are mostly young professionals and office workers. The restaurant franchise has established strict rules for employee schedules with regard to how many hours an employee can work and what days and times employees must be available for work. These rules exist to reduce employees being paid to work overtime hours and to minimize the number of full-time employees eligible for benefits. Further, during their shift employees cannot leave work and then return, and they are not allowed to bring their children to the restaurant while they are working. All of your racially mixed wait staff are mothers (many are single parents) so the franchise rules create problems for taking care of their family obligations. To address their concerns, the women develop a plan and meet with you to discuss it.

They propose that employees commit to working for a minimum length of time during their shift—for example, four hours. Once those minimum hours are completed, they can leave if they need to take a child to the doctor, pick a child up from school, or meet some other obligation. The women have agreed to collaborate with one another to ensure that there will always be enough people working, especially during the busiest hours of the day. They ask that their children be allowed to come to the restaurant and eat lunch when their mother is getting off shortly after the lunch hour. Their proposal is based on the experience of a friend of one of your wait staff who works at another restaurant where they use this kind of flexible scheduling. The woman gives you the telephone number of that restaurant's manager.

When you call the manager, she says that the flexible scheduling has been in place for several years, and it has worked well. In fact, she believes the schedule is the main reason why employee morale is high and turnover is low. She often sits with the children when they come to eat lunch and even helps them with their homework. The manager admits that the franchise would probably not approve of the flexible scheduling if they knew about it, so she keeps two time sheets—one that she sends to the corporate office and another that she keeps with the actual hours her employees have worked. The hours of work indicated for each employee on the official time sheet accurately reflect the hours actually worked according to the unofficial time sheet. The manager admits that she would probably be fired if her bosses discovered what she was doing, but she says the franchise is primarily interested in profit, and her restaurant has been even more profitable since she implemented the flexible schedule—largely because of low turnover. Asked why she has done this when it places her own job at risk, she said, "I just want to treat my employees as human beings; if I had to abide by the company rules, I would end up becoming a person I wouldn't like very much." Your employees ask you to think about their proposal and give them your decision in the next few days.

Adapted from Lisa Dodson (2009). *The Moral Underground: How Ordinary Americans Subvert an Unfair Economy*. New York, NY: The New Press.

Chapter 10
Sexism: Where the Personal Becomes Political

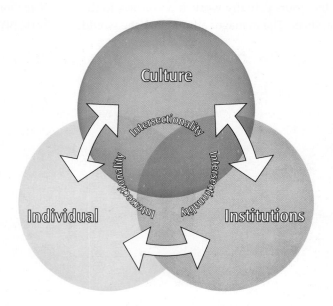

∨ Learning Outcomes

After reading this chapter you will know and be able to:

10.1 Discuss early forms of sexism in the United States and the role of language and media portrayals of female beauty on women's perceptions of their body image and attractiveness.

10.2 Define the terms *male chauvinist* and *feminist*, and describe the nature of violence against women in the United States.

10.3 Explain how institutional sexism affects women's opportunities in school and especially in the workforce, and discuss the economic consequences of sexism.

> "Male supremacy has kept woman down. It has not knocked her out."
>
> —CLAIRE BOOTHE LUCE (1903–1987)

Segregation is the normal pattern for the relationship between dominant and oppressed groups. Americans have been segregated according to such differences as race and social class. Sexism, however, is a unique form of oppression because people who belong to the dominant and subordinate groups live together. Andrzejewski (1996) defines sexism as "an attitude, action, or institutional structure that subordinates or limits a person on the basis of sex" (p. 56). Although sexism is customarily regarded as the oppression and exploitation of women, the concept of sexism includes both men and women, and it is a type of oppression stemming from cultural norms for femininity and masculinity that limit men and women. Most other forms of oppression are influenced by the isolation and alienation of dominant and subordinate groups; yet because daily personal relationships exist between most women and men, we believe we have intrinsic, intimate knowledge about sexism. For this reason, men are more likely to take gender issues lightly, discussing them without the discomfort that often affects discussions of racism. Men are also more likely to make insensitive comments about women that they would never make about people of color.

To illustrate men's insensitivity, consider the *natural* argument. White Americans used to say people of color were naturally—meaning genetically—inferior to Whites, a belief now mostly relegated to the ranks of White supremacists. Yet many American men, even males of color, have employed the natural argument in discussing the differences between males and females to defend beliefs about males' superiority. These males claim that "the male animal" is always larger than the females, illustrating nature's intent to make males the protector of females. Gould (1983) corrected this assumption by explaining that larger males are only true for mammals, and not all of them, whereas in the entire animal world—think of insects and fish—the more typical pattern is that females are larger than males.

Americans are usually more comfortable talking about gender issues than racial issues; men and women joke about the "war between the sexes." When Virginia congressman Howard Smith amended the Civil Rights Act of 1964 by adding gender, he was not expressing concern about gender discrimination in this country; to the contrary, as a Southerner, he wanted the bill defeated. Smith gambled that the "absurd" addition of women as a group whose civil rights needed protecting would appear so ridiculous that it would prevent or at least delay the bill's passage, but the tactic backfired. The majority of members of the House of Representatives and the Senate were committed to voting for civil rights, and the bill was passed (Branch, 1998).

A particularly unique perspective of how gender can impact behavior comes from Alter (2016) and her interviews with almost two dozen transgender people. One participant said that after transitioning from Sheila to James, he noticed he no longer had men correcting him in his job as a radio broadcaster. James said, "I'm the same person, (but) the men are less critical" (Alter, 2016, p. 24). After transitioning to a man, several interview participants noted they felt safer walking alone at night and noticed that women walking toward them appeared to be nervous, a reminder of how women have concerns about safety every where they go. Several of the men also noticed major differences at work. As a woman at work, they often faced subordinates challenging their authority, but as men they noticed male colleagues minimizing their mistakes and celebrating their successes, and they also overheard male bosses belittling female subordinates. One interview subject had worked at a family clinic for six years as a woman, but after transitioning to a man he was suddenly promoted to a leadership role (Alter, 2016).

On the other hand, transgender men reported struggling more in their professions after transitioning to be women. A biology professor published many articles with only rare requests for changes. After becoming a woman, she found it harder to publish under her female name. Her papers were criticized more harshly, and she faced more problems getting approval for grant writing proposals (Alter, 2016). All of these examples illustrate individuals displaying sexist attitudes, and these attitudes have been shaped by the American culture.

A History of Cultural Sexism and Contemporary Issues Concerning Body Image

Cultural sexism in the United States originated in the gender roles brought by the English and other European colonists. Men were expected to be in a superior role as head of the household, whereas women were assigned the subordinate role as the individual responsible for domestic chores and childcare. English law stipulated that any property a woman owned became her husband's property after marriage, and any money a wife earned had to be given to her husband. As Sir William Blackstone expressed it, "The husband and wife are one, and the husband is that one" (Collins, 2003, p. 12). These gender roles shaped our culture's ideals for masculine and feminine behavior in ways that have been modified but not radically changed.

What gender biases did women confront in the earliest years of the United States?

Although men were expected to provide for the family's needs, their wives could earn extra money working at home. In the early 1800s, women produced four times the amount of textiles that were manufactured in textile factories. To support the family, some women took in laundry or sewing, taught neighbor children, or made things to sell or barter. Although an unmarried woman could own property and engage in business activities on her own, a married woman could not. She could not sign a contract or request a loan without her husband's approval. Women began to protest against the common law stipulation that their property and earnings must be given to their husbands. During the American Revolutionary War, women had to assume additional responsibilities. For example, women joined together to protest against certain merchants who were suspected of inflating prices. Angered by one exceptionally greedy merchant, a group of women attacked the man, took his keys, and helped themselves to the coffee stored at his warehouse (Riley, 1986).

How and when did forms of discrimination change?

Activists such as Elizabeth Cady Stanton and Susan B. Anthony lobbied successfully for women's property rights in many states, but they were not as successful in their demand for women's right to vote. By the 1830s, individual states began to pass legislation to grant women the right to own property and keep their earnings. Meanwhile, more textile factories were built, employing more young women, and factory owners exploited them. Women workers formed unions to strike for better pay and working conditions. With the number of schools increasing and so few men willing to take the low salary of a teacher, public schools reluctantly began to hire women, reducing the salary even further. One Ohio superintendent boasted that he was able to hire twice as many women teachers as other school districts that hired only men (Collins, 2003).

In addition to demanding gender equality, women became active in the anti-slavery movement. The Grimke sisters shocked those who felt it wasn't women's place to speak in public, especially not passionately about political issues. Women who defied society's norms provoked harsh criticism, as illustrated by this explanation of their "unladylike" behavior: "Some of them are old maids, whose personal charms were never very attractive and who have been sadly slighted by the masculine gender" (Evans, 1989, p. 102). These unladylike women continued to lobby for gender equality and against slavery as the Civil War approached.

What effect did the Civil War have on women's demands for gender equality?

During the Civil War, the wives of soldiers once again had to provide for themselves and their children. Women were hired to be office workers, government workers, factory workers, nurses, and teachers, yet they encountered a gauntlet of critics. Their morals were questioned, and they were said to be a distraction to male workers. After the war, women continued to work and to lobby for causes such as women's suffrage and temperance.

After the Civil War, many people migrated west—more men than women. In 1869, Wyoming became the first state to give women voting rights as well as to pass laws guaranteeing married women's right to own property and requiring equal pay for female teachers. With so few women in Wyoming, this legislation gave the *Cheyenne Leader* the hope of seeing "quite an immigration of ladies to Wyoming" (Collins, 2003, p. 235). The need for women may explain why the first 12 states giving women the right to vote were all in the West.

New employment opportunities for women arose as the establishment of department stores required personnel who could assist predominantly female customers. By 1900, more than a third of all clerical workers were women; 20 years later, women would be the majority. Women already constituted the majority of teachers, and their numbers steadily increased among librarians, social workers, and nurses (Evans, 1989). But as women tried to redefine their "place" in the early twentieth century, they encountered strong resistance.

What progress and what resistance to women's rights occurred in the early twentieth century?

By 1920, 50 percent of college students were women. Women held a third of all federal government jobs and pursued a greater variety of careers, especially if they were not married. In the 1890s, only 3 percent of married women worked outside the home, increasing to 10 percent by the 1920s (Collins, 2003). Many women were politically active, especially for women's suffrage, and a few began to call themselves *feminists*. Using recently created psychological language, critics called them *lesbians*, accusing them of hating men. Yet women's efforts on behalf of suffrage succeeded after almost a century of struggle. Women cast their first votes for president in 1920, but one year later, the first Miss America Beauty Pageant was held in Atlantic City, New Jersey, reminding women of their place and purpose. When World War II began and men left the workforce to join the military, many women were hired to replace them.

Did women workers during World War II prove their competence?

During the war, women became the majority (57 percent) of the workforce for the first time (Faludi, 2006). When jobs had been scarce during the Great Depression, studies concluded that menstruation reduced women's ability to be effective at work. One researcher even described the effects as debilitating; later, that same researcher conducted a study of working women during World War II and reported that menstruation caused no adverse effects on their ability to perform their jobs (Tavris, 1999).

During wartime, women workers were praised for the quality of their work (see Figure 10.1), including advertising campaigns with "Rosie the Riveter," but no one expected them to stay in those jobs permanently—no one except the women. Seventy-five percent of women surveyed wanted to keep their jobs after the war, but industry had other ideas. Businesses that had praised women's work during the war suddenly found them to have "bad attitudes" or to be incompetent. Two months after the war

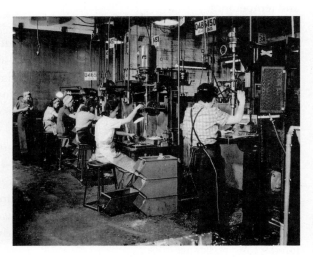

Figure 10.1 Relying on Women Workers During Wartime

Advertisements like the one on the left glorified efforts of working women during World War II. Although pictures such as the one below often depicted White women, a significant number of wartime workers were women of color.

SOURCE: (left) The U.S. National Archives and Records Administration; (right) Courtesy FDR Library, Hyde Park, New York.

ended, the aircraft industry fired over 800,000 women (Faludi, 2006). Blatant media bias helped to force women out of the jobs they had performed competently.

What role did the media play in women being forced out of their jobs?

In 1945, a *Fortune* magazine poll reported that most Americans believed if a husband earned enough money to provide for his family, his wife should not work—even if she wanted to (Evans, 1989). The media was telling women to stop taking men's jobs and to go home where they belonged. By 1946, more than 3 million women were eliminated from well-paying industrial jobs. More than 80 percent did not quit working but took jobs with lower salaries. Three years after the war, America was the only nation in the Western Hemisphere that refused to sign a statement from the United Nations supporting equal rights for women (Faludi, 2006).

"I'm just a person trapped inside a woman's body."

—ROBIN MORGAN (1941–)

How did women respond to the pressure to stay home and not have a career?

By the 1950s, more women were enrolling in college even though a Cornell University study warned that 65 percent of college women were more likely to not get married (Faludi, 2006). But women, especially middle-class married women "entered the labor force faster than any other group in the population through the 1950s and 1960s" (Evans, 1989, p. 254). By 1980, women represented 43 percent of the workforce, and they attended college in record numbers.

A 1986 Harvard–Yale study predicted that if women postponed marriage to get a college diploma, they would find few marriage partners available. According to the study, women had a 20 percent chance of marrying if they were 30 years old, a 5 percent chance at 35, and a 1.3 percent chance at 40. But the prediction was based on an erroneous assumption: Earlier studies of marriage patterns had found that women tended to marry men two to three years older, and that assumption was used to produce the results of the Harvard–Yale study. By the 1980s, this pattern had changed as more women were marrying men closer to their age and even younger. Two other studies reported findings contradicting the conclusions of the Harvard–Yale study, but the popular press did not report on them (Faludi, 2006), once again revealing a sexist bias in our culture, pressuring women to marry and gain the benefits of marriage. Some research suggests attitudes about marriage are changing. Women born in the 1980s and 1990s are getting married much later than their parents or grandparents. In the 1940s, about 25 percent of women were still unmarried at age 23, but for women born in the 1990s, that number has gone up to 81 percent (Downey, 2016).

What do studies say about who benefits from marriage?

Storrs (2011) reviewed several research studies and found that marriage appears to have different benefits for men and women. One study reported that married men tend to be physically healthier than unmarried men, and that a major factor in this difference was that after getting married, men tended to reduce risky behaviors such as binge drinking and smoking. Further, heart disease is the major cause of adult deaths, and unmarried men are three times as likely to die from heart disease as married men. A 2015 study analyzed medical records of 10,000 middle-aged people looking for links between marital status and health. The researchers found that marriage had clear benefits for men for physical health concerns such as blood pressure, diabetes, and heart disease. Unmarried men were at a 14-percent higher risk of heart disease compared to unmarried women. Marital status did not appear to impact women's risk of serious illness (Knapton, 2015). In addition to being healthier, married men and women tend to live longer than single people. In one study of people over 40, death rates for unmarried men were twice as high as for married men; the difference was far less between unmarried and married women. Finally, 49 percent of married men said they received "extreme" emotional satisfaction from sexual activity compared to only 33 percent of unmarried men. On the other hand, depression is twice as likely to affect women as men, but married women report lower levels of depression than unmarried women. These studies appear to contradict the traditional American belief that women are the primary beneficiaries of marriage.

What sexist messages still exist in American culture and how are they being addressed?

For decades there have been (and continue to be) professions that are dominated by men, and traditional terms such as *policeman, fireman,* and *mailman* imply that these jobs are exclusively for men. Feminists have long recognized such gender prejudice in language, and they have been committed to changing the language by replacing sexist terms with nonsexist alternatives (Arliss, 1991; Nilsen, 1977a, 1977b). Their efforts are reflected in language changes that have become common usage, such as *police officer, firefighter,* and *letter carrier*. In addition to including women, this language is more descriptive of the job responsibilities. Since these examples show that language has changed, have attitudes and behaviors changed as well?

There is some evidence of changing attitudes among youth. Shapiro (2012) conducted a study of almost 1200 middle school students from urban, suburban, and rural schools, and found that girls were more likely than boys to work outside of school and home, and more likely to hold a leadership position. More girls than boys planned to go to college and anticipated going on to a graduate or professional school. Further, 78 percent of the girls believed they would have to fully support themselves as adults, and 87 percent assumed they would have full-time jobs. As for what jobs they would prefer, more girls (27 percent) than boys (12 percent) said they would enroll in medical school, and more girls (24 percent) than boys (14 percent) anticipated a career in a professional field. There is also evidence from higher education. According to National Center for Educational Statistics (NCES; 2013) data, the number of women graduating with a master's degree or PhD in engineering has jumped from 1 percent in 1970 to 27 percent in 2012. In addition, the number of women graduating with a bachelor's or master's degree in physical sciences and technology has gone from 14 percent to 52 percent, and women graduating with a bachelor's or master's degree in natural resources and agriculture increased from 9 percent to more than 50 percent.

Even with these increases, traditional occupations still exert a strong attraction, especially for men. Data on students graduating with a bachelor's or master's degree reveal that women earn almost 79 percent of education degrees and 84 percent of degrees in the health professions. The gap between the numbers of women and men with degrees in mathematics and business is narrowing significantly, but men still dominate in the fields of engineering and computer science (NCES, 2013). Shapiro (2012) defined a gender-dominated occupation as one in which 65 percent or more of workers are men or women. Over 90 percent of middle school boys in this study said they would only consider jobs dominated by men, but 74 percent of the middle school girls chose a male-dominated job as their preferred career choice. The lingering influence of sexism is illustrated by 35 percent of middle school boys saying they believed men had more career options than women, and 73 percent agreeing that men are better at doing some jobs than women. Although it is true that women who graduate from high school today are more likely to pursue a nontraditional career than in the past, the numbers are still small (NCES, 2013), and it is likely that sexist language contributes to that outcome.

To address sexism in our language, feminists have lobbied professional organizations, businesses, and institutions to promote the use of **inclusive language** (terms that include both men and women). In response, several organizations have changed the guidelines in their writing manuals to promote nonsexist language for their professional publications. The style manual of the American Psychological Association includes writing conventions employing language free of sexist implications. Despite such progress, feminist scholars continue to criticize sexist language reflected in common words and phrases. Do we have a man-made product if it comes from a factory employing only women? Can an organization "man the desk" with women? Does brotherly love include sisters? Alternatives for sexist terms exist: a product is handmade, and women can staff the desk. Opponents question the need for such changes, but after men won the right to work in the formerly all-female occupation of stewardess, airlines uniformly and rapidly revised the name to *flight attendant*. If it was so easy to change the language to be inclusive of men, why can't women be similarly accommodated?

In American English, there is a pattern of condescending language toward women illustrated by the use of diminutive endings of words as in "poetess." Although the Academy Awards still has a "Best Actress" category, most women who receive the award refer to themselves as actors. American feminists have also explained that the term *coed* is a condescending reference from an era when men believed that women lacked the intelligence required for college studies—comparable to the condescending phrase *colored people* for African Americans. Colleges permitting women to attend were "coeducational"; therefore, the term *coed* reflects the historic perception of women as intellectually inferior to men. Oberlin College became the first coeducational campus in 1833. Although the college deserves credit for offering the opportunity, the school also had a policy that female students were to be dismissed from classes on Mondays so they could take care of the male students' laundry (Parker, 2015). This example illustrates the reality that change rarely occurs without some sacrifice.

Another sexist pattern is the denigration of aging women, reinforcing the importance of female appearance: Women are valued only if they are beautiful. Attractive young women are referred to as "kittenish," but with age they become "catty." The sexy young "chick" becomes the "old biddy" who "henpecks" her husband. A man is considered a "good catch," but a woman is a "ball and chain." Valuing women for their beauty has led to research on body image, finding that our culture's ideals for beauty can have a negative impact on girls and women.

> "The limits of my language are the limits of my world."
> —LUDWIG WITTGENSTEIN (1889–1951)

How does the culture's image of ideal beauty adversely affect women?

In American culture, the ideal body image for women is slender yet toned, and for men it is slim yet muscular. According to scholars, this cultural ideal for beauty is transmitted in diverse ways and internalized by men and women, resulting in a sense of satisfaction or dissatisfaction with their own body image. According to Levine and Chapman (2011), almost 70 percent of female adolescents identify magazine images as an influence on their beliefs about an ideal body shape. Further, the amount of time spent viewing media that is focused on appearance (e.g., fashion magazines or music videos) correlates with adolescents reporting dissatisfaction with their body. This negative feeling persists into adulthood. In the United States, almost 80 percent of women express dissatisfaction with their body (Javier, Abrams, Maxwell, & Belgrave, 2013).

Body dissatisfaction is one component of an individual's body image and is defined as a negative evaluation about one's body in general or a specific part of one's body (Javier et al., 2013). Tiggemann (2011) has argued that most women in Western societies have such a negative experience concerning body image that he referred to their feelings of discomfort about their shape as "normative discontent" (p. 12). According to McKinley (2011), *normative discontent* is not an individual phenomenon but a systemic one. Female beauty is presented according to cultural standards that objectify the female body shape and women's consciousness of their own body, making them dependent on the approval of others. In the last few years, more research has been examining how social media impacts body image and whether it is also responsible for setting up unattainable "ideal" body shapes. Even though interactions are with peers, studies find people are comparing themselves to their attractive friends and then end up feeling bad about themselves. Some studies suggest that people active in photo sharing on social media are especially prone to feelings of negative body image and eating disorders (Holland, 2016).

The role of culture becomes clear when comparing attitudes toward body image in the United States with attitudes from other nations. The Japanese appear to be more accepting of larger bodies, and in many Pacific Island cultures and African cultures, large women not only are valued for child bearing but also are regarded as more healthy and attractive. Yet there seems to be a growing body of evidence that attitudes toward body image in some cultures may be changing toward a more positive perception of people who are slender, especially among those who have considerable contact with American culture through media (Grogan, 2008). As a consequence, future research may discover an increase in body dissatisfaction among those populations.

Feminists argue that media images of ideal female bodies have contributed significantly to a widespread sense of inadequacy among American women. In a study of older and younger women who were given an array of images of female body shapes from extremely thin to obese, most women identified a larger shape for their "current image" than the shape that they felt represented the one the majority of American men would find attractive. These studies reported that almost every woman expressed a desire to be at least a little slimmer (see Figure 10.2). In a study using a similar range of male body shapes, young men tended to select their current body shape as the same one that they believed women would be attracted to (Grogan, 2008).

Figure 10.2 Women's Body Shapes

Researchers show female participants in their studies a diagram with a range of body shapes similar to what is presented here to ascertain their view of their own body shape and what they consider to be the ideal body shape.

SOURCE: Pearson Education.

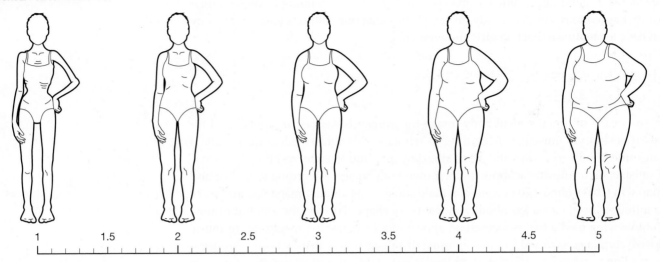

Media now places more emphasis on ideal male body images, and more men are becoming critical of their bodies. Fifteen years ago researchers thought the rate of male eating disorders was about one in ten; newer research suggests it's closer to one in four. Today, 18 percent of boys now say they're "highly concerned" about their weight and build, and 25 percent of average weight men perceive themselves to be underweight. Perhaps this is a reaction to movie stars and action figures increasingly featuring chiseled men with six-pack abs, but only 1–2 percent of men have that kind of physique (Santa Cruz, 2014). Of the boys who acknowledged being highly concerned about their weight, about one-third were concerned with being both muscular and thin. That suggests that boys are facing pressure to both gain weight and lose it. One study found that one-third of middle school and high school aged boys were using protein powders and shakes to bulk up, while 16 percent admitted to using steroids or other muscle enhancing substances. Long-term use of unregulated substances increases risk of depression, rage attacks, suicidal tendencies, and heart conditions. The researchers found that boys who are willing to take extreme measures to achieve their ideal body image are at increased risk of obesity, drug use, and binge drinking (Santa Cruz, 2014).

Research on African American women has found that they are more likely to be satisfied with their body shape, not only in comparison to White women but also to other ethnic minority women. In one study of over 4000 women from diverse ethnic groups, African American women preferred larger body silhouettes and were less likely to express body dissatisfaction than the other women in the study. In addition, African American women were less likely to overestimate their weight or to engage in dieting or other strategies intended to control their weight. One reason why African American women express greater body satisfaction was their emphasis on "style" as a major factor in determining attractiveness; "style" was defined by the way an individual dressed and presented herself in a positive manner when interacting with others (Javier et al., 2013). Although these findings have been consistent, recent studies report a diminishing difference between body dissatisfaction expressed by White and Black women as well as other women of color. Scholars speculate that this change may signify an increasing internalization of the dominant culture's ideal body image, especially among young African American women.

As for Asian American and Latina women, some studies report that they express feelings of body dissatisfaction similar to those of White women, while other studies report them having a greater acceptance of their body image. Such contradictory findings could be a result of the ethnic diversity within both groups, but studies have also reported that in a comparison of ethnic minority women, Asian American women were more likely than other women of color to affirm the thin female body as an ideal image. Another clue could be in the findings of a meta-analysis reporting that the highest levels of body dissatisfaction for Asian American women came from the 18–25-year-old age group. The diverse responses of Latinas may be explained by research finding that across subgroups of Latinas, "closer identification with native culture was associated with better body image" (Javier et al., 2013, p. 152).

 Self-Check 10.1 Complete this self-check quiz to check your understanding of early forms of sexism in the United States and the role of language and media portrayals of female beauty on women's perceptions of their body image and attractiveness.

Application Exercise 10.1

In this video, a teacher discusses her action research in which she investigates gender bias in basal readers mandated by a school district. Review the video and complete the activity.

Individual Sexism, Feminism, and Violence Against Women

As a result of learning sexist cultural attitudes, people of both genders may engage in **individual sexism** involving prejudiced attitudes and actions against women or men because of rigid beliefs about gender and gender roles. Both men and women can be "male chauvinists," but they can also choose to be "feminists" in support of gender equality.

What does it mean to be a "male chauvinist" or a "feminist"?

The term *chauvinist* is reported to have originated with a Frenchman named Chauvin, a zealous soldier intensely loyal to Napoleon Bonaparte. To be a *chauvinist* has evolved to designate someone who believes in the superiority of someone or something (Partridge, 2009). Kimmel (2006) referred to people being chauvinistic about their culture. French scholars have been accused of being chauvinistic about their language, as demonstrated by their attempts to prevent foreign words, especially American phrases—"le hamburger" or "le week-end"—from polluting their native tongue. To call someone a male chauvinist is to accuse that individual, who could be either a man or a woman, of believing men are superior to women. A **male chauvinist** is an individual who believes that men ought to be the leaders and decision makers and women should be subordinate. It is interesting that there are American men who publicly declare themselves male chauvinists, yet they would bristle at being called racists or bigots.

Confusion also exists with the word *feminist* and with those labeled as *feminists*. Too many people perceive a feminist as an angry woman; our media has reinforced that view by focusing on feminists who represent radical perspectives. In reality, a **feminist** is a woman—or a man—who advocates for the personal, social, and economic equality of women. The goal of feminist activists is to increase the opportunities available for both men and women as part of the larger goal of eliminating traditional, stereotypical gender roles. To eliminate gender stereotypes, feminists have advocated androgyny, a concept that promotes interchangeability of female and male roles or responsibilities in all areas beyond fundamental biological ones.

> "People call me feminist whenever I express sentiments that differentiate me from a doormat or a prostitute."
> —DAME REBECCA WEST (1892–1983)

Video Example 10.1

In this video, teachers discuss how to empower students related to gender issues and identity. What are some of their concerns about gender? What are some of the ways they respond to these concerns? How do their responses relate to feminism as it is discussed in Chapter 10?

What does it mean to be androgynous?

Androgyny has been confused with the unisex concept illustrated by unisex clothing, hair styling, and toilets, but the unisex concept denies differences between men and women and advocates treating members of both genders as if they were exactly the same. **Androgyny** is the belief that men and women share a variety of human traits that should be encouraged in both, as opposed to fostering certain traits in each gender based on traditional cultural stereotypes about masculinity and femininity.

Androgynous people respond to situations as needed, without being limited by their gender. If a situation calls for aggressive behavior, an androgynous individual responds aggressively; if the situation requires a nurturing response, the androgynous individual is nurturing. The individual's gender does not matter because aggression and nurturance are traits every human being possesses. Does each androgynous individual respond the same way in a given situation? No, because each individual is different, but if everyone in a society were androgynous, the differences between people would derive from their individual abilities and preferences, not from artificial differences created by teaching children to conform to rigid stereotypes about aggressive men or passive women that can lead to abuse.

What kind of abuse do women encounter in the United States?

According to a Bureau of Justice study, over 2.5 million adult women in the United States were stalked, and 70 percent of them knew their stalker (20 percent were stalked by a former intimate partner, 15 percent by a friend or neighbor). In this study, 25 percent of the victims report stalkers using technology such as monitoring them with global positioning systems (GPS) or sending them unwanted messages via email or instant messaging (Catalano, 2012; Stalking Resource Center, 2014). Almost 240,000 women in the United States are sexually assaulted annually, meaning that a sexual assault occurs every two minutes (525,600 minutes in a non-leap year divided by 250,000 victims; the math is simple). One of six American women has been a victim of sexual assault, 80 percent were under the age of 30, and almost 75 percent of the victims knew the perpetrator. About 44 percent of sexual assault victims are under the age of 18 (15 percent were less than 12 years old), and 93 percent of them knew their attacker (RAINN, 2014). Experts say the actual number of incidents is probably even higher. According to Gonnerman (2005), 73 percent of domestic violence incidents are not reported; more than 60 percent of women who did not report such an incident said they did not think the police would believe them.

Colleges and universities should be role models in their policies regarding allegations of rape, especially since one in five women are sexually assaulted while attending college. According to a 2014 Congressional survey of over 400 colleges and universities, more than 40 percent conducted no investigations of sexual assault from 2009 to 2014. Almost 73 percent do not have a clearly defined process that works with local law enforcement. Some campuses do not even have a designated coordinator for sexual assault complaints, even though that is required by federal statute. In cases where student athletes were involved, 20 percent of the largest public institutions and 15 percent of the largest private institutions sent these complaints to the athletic department. In July 2014, the Office of Civil Rights in the Department of Education added 12 college campuses to the 55 already being investigated for a Title IX violation for reporting sexual assaults. This institutional failure to react appropriately to rape allegations is part of a broader problem.

Rape is a significant aspect of the violence against women in America; almost 84,000 women are victims of rape annually, which means a woman is raped every six minutes. Young women are especially vulnerable. One survey reported that over 67 percent of rape victims were raped when they were 11 to 24 years old, and approximately half of all date rapes occur among teenagers (Centers for Disease Control, 2012). There is often confusion when discussing rape because it has a history of being misrepresented. In 1927, the Federal Bureau of Investigation defined rape as "the carnal knowledge of a female, forcibly and against her will," but that excluded oral rape, anal rape, male rape,

"There is no difference between being raped and being run over by a truck, except afterwards men ask if you liked it."

—MARGE PIERCY (1936–)

penetration by an object, and more. In 2012, the FBI finally issued a revised definition of **rape**: "The penetration, no matter how slight, of the vagina or anus with any body part or object, or oral penetration by a sex organ of another person, without the consent of the victim" (FBI, 2012). The new definition addresses some of the past misunderstandings about rape, and it should enhance the gathering of data with regard to this crime.

How has rape been misunderstood in the United States?

In January 2017, a police commander in Brooklyn came under fire for downplaying a recent surge of sexual assaults in the area, saying they were less "troubling" because many were actually date rapes and not "true stranger rapes." The commander said the acquaintance rapes were sometimes committed when women met men on dating sites like Tinder, so they were not the "abominable" action of a stranger attacking a victim on the city streets (Feuer, 2017). The mayor's office condemned the comments, and the police commissioner issued a public editorial to respond to the controversy, calling the commander's comments "insensitive" (O'Neill, 2017). Recognizing misperceptions about rape is necessary to understand the reality of that experience. Some generally conceded myths and realities about rape are listed next.

MYTH: Rape is an act of sexual arousal caused by an attractive, sexy woman who stimulated such sexual tension and passion that the man could not control himself.

REALITY: Rape is an act of power and humiliation, and any woman of any age is a potential victim regardless of her physical appearance.

MYTH: Rapes usually occur in dark alleys or poorly lit parking lots where the woman is isolated and therefore vulnerable.

REALITY: More than 60 percent of rapes occur in the victim's home or in a place where the woman would normally feel safe—the home of a friend, relative, or neighbor.

MYTH: Rapes are usually committed by violent strangers concealed somewhere usually at night waiting for an unwitting and unknown victim.

REALITY: Almost 66 percent of rapes are committed by someone the victim knows, such as a lover, friend, relative, or acquaintance; other potential rapists may be trusted authority figures such as a teacher, minister, counselor, or therapist.

These rape myths have an impact on men and their perception of rape. In one study of 73 male college students, 31 percent said they would force a woman to have sex "if nobody would ever know and there wouldn't be any consequences." But when researchers asked the same question changing the language from "forcing sex" to "rape," the number dipped to 13 percent (Edwards, Bradshaw, & Hinsz, 2014). The confusion about rape can affect both sexes and may influence a woman's decision not to report a rape.

Why do women choose not to report a rape or attempted rape?

Rape is an underreported crime. According to the Justice Department, for every 100 rapes, only 40 percent are reported to the police, only 10 percent lead to an arrest, and only 8 percent are prosecuted (RAINN, 2014). Because of changes in police departments' processing of rape cases and new guidelines for rape trials, this crime is now more likely to be reported. Still, fear affects a woman's decision to report a rape. According to

MacKinnon (1987, p. 82), victims have given one or more of the following four reasons for not reporting a rape:

Threats: Rapists often threaten to return and to inflict even more violence if victims go to the police. Some rapists even threaten to kill their victims, and just by reading newspapers, women know this has happened to others.

Reactions: Some victims fear the reactions of their significant others. Women have been verbally abused, beaten, and even abandoned by partners who would not believe that the woman did nothing to incite the rape.

Disbelief: Some women fear that if they report the rape, the police might not believe them. Even if the police are convinced, some women fear they may not be able to persuade a jury. There is no guarantee of justice from the legal system.

Publicity: Some women fear the loss of privacy and the feeling of being exposed and vulnerable, as well as being subjected to embarrassing allegations about their personal lives in court. They are also reluctant to recall and relive (in front of an audience) a painful, humiliating incident they would rather forget.

The concerns of rape victims are the reason why law enforcement and experts agree that rape happens more often than we think. A study by the Department of Justice (2013) examined sexual crimes over a five-year time period and found that many victims did not report a sexual crime because of their fear of retaliation (20 percent), belief police wouldn't help them (13 percent), or belief it was a personal matter (13 percent). Rape and domestic violence are painful consequences of sexism played, principally by men, as a power game in our culture.

 Self-Check 10.2 Complete this self-check quiz to check your understanding of the terms **male chauvinist** and **feminist** and the nature of violence against women in the United States.

The Impact of Institutional Sexism on Opportunities for Women

Institutional sexism is the consequence of established laws, customs, and practices that systematically discriminate against people or groups based on gender. One institution that hits many people close to home is the family structure. In the 1950s, two-thirds of American children under the age of 15 lived in homes with both parents where the mother stayed home with the kids. For families with children under the age of six, only 19 percent of the mothers worked outside the home. Sixty years later, researchers now find that 64 percent of mothers today with children under age six are back in the workforce, and 26 percent of American children live in a single-parent home (Coontz, 2016). This is a significant change, but American employers are not adapting. Only 13 percent of full-time employees in the United States have the opportunity to take a family leave, and 44 percent do not even have the option of requesting *unpaid* family leave. According to a Health and Human Services study, the average length of time women employees took for maternity leave was only 10 weeks, and a Department of Labor study reported that almost 25 percent of women taking maternity leave were back to work less than two weeks after giving birth. In contrast to comparable nations in the developed world, only the United States did not mandate that workers receive paid sick leave and vacation time.

This is a problem not only for families with children but for over 40 million Americans who provide unpaid eldercare for family members even though 60 percent of them have a job. There is some evidence that implementing policies to assist workers in meeting family obligations is not simply a good ethical choice but a pragmatic one. A survey conducted after the implementation of paid leave in California found that the new policy not only benefited workers but their employers as well. The savings for businesses come in the form of increased staff loyalty, morale, retention, and productivity (Coontz, 2016).

A persistent form of institutional sexism has been the ongoing gender discrimination in hiring. Business school professors from Columbia University conducted a study asking both male and female managers to hire people for a job that required simple mathematical tasks. The applicants were an equal mix of men and women with equal skill sets, but the managers more often hired the men. Even when the applicants were tested, and both applicants performed equally, the men were 1.5 times more likely to be hired. At times managers would even hire people who they knew had performed worse on the test, and in those cases the hires were two-thirds more likely to be men (Reuben, 2014). Although women represent about 47 percent of the workforce and hold 51.5 percent of high-paying management and professional positions, they are still a minority in the most highly paid positions, with only 27 percent being chief executive officers and 29 percent working as general operations managers. The numbers of women remain low in highly paid occupations such as law, engineering, and computer specialties, whereas they dominate professions that are less well paid such as teaching, nursing, social works, and other service occupations. Women represent only 38 percent of physicians but almost 70 percent of physician's assistants (U.S. Bureau of Labor Statistics, 2017).

Historically, there is ample evidence of inequities in the salaries of men and women, but attempts have been made to address this gender gap. There is disagreement about the extent to which gender salary inequities are being resolved, but most people concur that men earn more than women, even when they work in the same jobs (see Table 10.1). Researchers used to estimate women would close the wage gap well before the end of this century. However, the rate of narrowing that gap has slowed since 2001, and if this new rate continues, women will not close the wage gap until more than halfway through the twenty-second century (Miller 2017).

Why are men earning more than women in the workforce?

Four arguments address the issue of salary inequity between men and women. The first argument is that significant progress has been made in closing the income gap. According to the U.S. Bureau of Labor Statistics (2013b), American women were earning about 62 cents for every dollar a man made in 1982; by 2012, women earned an average of almost 81 cents for every dollar a man earned. The answer to the salary inequity question would seem to be that men are still earning more but that women are gradually catching up.

Careful analysis of salary data tells a different story: The primary reason for the decreasing gap is that the salaries of male workers have not been increasing; they have even been decreasing in some areas. The claim that women's salaries are becoming closer to men's salaries is based on the reality of salary stagnation for men (Zumbrun, 2014). In addition, 76 percent of the workers in low-wage jobs earning less than $22,000 a year are women (Entmacher, Robbins, & Frohlich, 2014). It seems debatable to say that "progress" is being made concerning men's and women's salaries if closing the gender gap is based on women making small wage gains while men are receiving no wage increases.

A second argument regarding gender salary inequity is based on data showing that young women aged 16–24 entering the workforce are making 89 percent of what their male peers earn, and women aged 25–34 are making 90 percent of what men in their age group earn (U.S. Bureau of Labor Statistics, 2013b). Such statistics have been

> "The Glass Ceiling hinders not only individuals but society as a whole. It effectively cuts our pool of potential corporate leaders by half. It deprives our economy of new leaders, new sources of creativity."
>
> —LYNN M. MARTIN (1939–)

Table 10.1 Median 2012 Earnings

Rank Earnings Gap	State	Men	Women	Women's Earnings per Dollar of Men's Earnings
1	District of Columbia	$66,754	$60,116	90 percent
2	Maryland	$57,447	$49,000	85 percent
3	Nevada	$42,137	$35,941	85 percent
4	Vermont	$44,776	$38,017	85 percent
5	New York	$51,274	$43,000	84 percent
6	California	$50,139	$41,956	84 percent
7	Florida	$40,889	$34,202	84 percent
8	Hawaii	$45,748	$38,040	83 percent
9	Maine	$42,280	$35,057	83 percent
10	Arizona	$43,618	$35,974	82 percent
11	North Carolina	$41,859	$34,421	82 percent
12	Georgia	$43,707	$35,479	81 percent
13	Delaware	$50,689	$41,120	81 percent
14	Rhode Island	$50,975	$41,074	81 percent
15	New Mexico	$41,211	$33,074	80 percent
16	Colorado	$50,509	$40,402	80 percent
17	Minnesota	$50,885	$40,595	80 percent
18	Texas	$44,802	$35,453	79 percent
19	Massachusetts	$60,243	$47,651	79 percent
20	Oregon	$47,402	$37,381	79 percent
21	Virginia	$52,125	$41,104	79 percent
22	New Jersey	$60,878	$47,878	79 percent
23	Illinois	$51,262	$40,309	79 percent
24	Connecticut	$61,097	$47,900	78 percent
25	Washington	$52,529	$41,062	78 percent
26	South Dakota	$40,721	$31,792	78 percent
27	Wisconsin	$46,898	$36,535	78 percent
28	South Carolina	$41,740	$32,402	78 percent
29	Iowa	$45,305	$35,106	77 percent
30	Nebraska	$42,878	$33,218	77 percent
31	Tennessee	$41,828	$32,398	77 percent
32	New Hampshire	$54,136	$41,774	77 percent
33	Ohio	$46,789	$35,984	77 percent
34	Arkansas	$40,153	$30,843	77 percent
35	Missouri	$42,974	$32,868	76 percent
36	Montana	$41,656	$31,775	76 percent
37	Kansas	$44,765	$34,131	76 percent
38	Oklahoma	$41,415	$31,543	76 percent
39	Kentucky	$42,321	$32,157	76 percent
40	Pennsylvania	$49,330	$37,414	76 percent
41	Mississippi	$40,081	$30,287	76 percent
42	Idaho	$41,664	$31,296	75 percent
43	Alaska	$57,068	$42,345	74 percent
44	North Dakota	$45,888	$33,877	74 percent
45	Michigan	$49,897	$36,772	74 percent
46	Indiana	$45,620	$33,419	73 percent
47	Alabama	$44,567	$31,674	71 percent
48	Utah	$48,540	$34,062	70 percent
49	West Virginia	$44,159	$30,885	70 percent
50	Louisiana	$47,249	$31,586	67 percent
51	Wyoming	$51,932	$33,152	64 percent

SOURCE: Adapted from AAUW (2014), Data from Bureau of Labor Statistics and U.S. Bureau of the Census.

used to argue that the gender inequity problem is being solved and to predict that the salary gap will eventually disappear as more highly paid young women pursue their careers. Although entry-level salaries are becoming more equal, feminists argue that women who stay in the workforce lose ground to their male peers because they are not promoted as readily as men. The term **glass ceiling** was coined to refer to an upper limit, usually middle management, beyond which women are not often promoted. In male-dominated fields where women make less than men at the start of their career, the gap continues to widen until retirement, with women's savings significantly affected because of the lower salary. In fields where women are the majority, such preschool teachers, secondary school teachers, librarians, and social workers, women begin (at ages 22–25) making 10 percent more than men, but by their thirtieth birthdays there is no difference between the women's and men's salaries. Just five years later the men are making a higher salary. When analyzing salary by age groups, women typically start out their careers making 15 percent less than men. By the time men reach the end of their work years (ages 51–64), they are making almost 40 percent more money than women. That widening gap over time was true for all professions. For example, a male delivery truck driver earns approximately $12,000 more than a woman, and male physicians earn $125,000 more than their female peers (Showalter, 2016).

In addition, our dominant cultural expectation for women to perform housekeeping duties and raise children results in less opportunity for them to develop abilities, experience, contacts, and a reputation in their field. Businesses could do more to encourage women to maintain their careers while being a parent. According to Hall and Spurlock (2013), Australia passed a parental leave law in 2010, making the United States the only industrialized nation not to provide paid parental leave to women or guarantee them a job when their leave is finished. The reduction of the gap between men's and women's salaries for entry-level jobs is important, but the economic penalty women pay for bearing and raising children still contributes significantly to the disparity between men's and women's salaries.

A third argument about gender salary disparity is based on the fact that more American women earn college diplomas than ever before. Because more education is assumed to mean more access to careers with higher salaries, gender disparity is predicted to decrease further and eventually to disappear. Yet according to the U.S. Bureau of the Census (2012), the median annual income for a woman who had completed two years of college was $33,432 compared to $35,468 for a man with only a high school diploma. The median annual income for a woman with a bachelor's degree was $43,589 compared to $69,479 for men. Women with doctorates made $83,708 compared to $114,347 for men, and women with a professional degree made $89,897 compared to $150,310 for men.

A fourth argument for gender salary inequity is that women tend to choose careers that pay lower salaries than the highly paid professions men select. Although women hold two thirds of minimum-wage jobs as well as 75 percent of jobs with low salaries partially paid by tips ($2.13 hourly wage), comparing the salaries of women and men within the same profession reveals that men are paid more—even in professions where women constitute the majority of workers (National Women's Law Center, 2014; U.S. Bureau of Labor Statistics, 2013b).

What are economic consequences of institutional sexism for women?

Gender disparity in earnings has an enormous impact on women over the course of a lifetime, no matter what education level. Lifetime losses of income for women compared to men are an estimated total of $700,000 for a high school graduate, $1.2 million for a college graduate, and $2 million for a professional school graduate (Miller, 2017). This means women in low-income jobs are more likely to live below the poverty line than men. Women of all income levels will continue to feel the wage gap into retirement because their lower income (compared to men) means less income from Social Security, pensions, and other retirement sources. Further, 10 percent of women over 65 years old live in poverty compared to 7 percent of men. Closing the wage gap for some women would mean raising them up out of poverty (Miller, 2017).

For middle- and upper-class women, these economic disparities make it difficult for them to pursue political power by campaigning for national or state offices. Such campaigns are expensive and require personal funds as well as aggressive fundraising. One hundred and five women (19.6 percent) are in the 115th U.S. Congress—84 of 435 seats in the House of Representatives and 21 Senate seats (Manning, 2017). In the 2016 election, Hillary Clinton became the first female presidential candidate nominated by a major party and the first woman to win the popular vote in a presidential election, but the United States lags behind many other nations with regard to women leaders. As of 2017, the United States ranked 100th in the world (tied with Kenya) regarding numbers of women legislators, surpassed by such nations as Rwanda, Bolivia, Cuba, and even Iraq and Saudi Arabia (Inter-Parliamentary Union, 2017). Women have been appointed to only 45 Cabinet positions in the history of our country. In 2017 women were only 35 percent of legislative directors in the House of Representatives but they dominated the lesser administrative positions such as "office manager" (95 percent) and "scheduler" (83 percent) (Burgat, 2017).

At the state level, only six women served as governors in 2017 (two were elected as lieutenant governor, but presidential appointments left a vacancy filled by the women). Women made up 24.8 percent of the legislators with approximately 1830 women serving in 50 states. The states with the highest percentage of women legislators included Nevada (39.7 percent), Vermont (39.4 percent), and Colorado (39 percent). Among the 100 largest cities, 20 had female mayors, including Fort Worth, Baltimore, and Las Vegas (Center for American Women and Politics, 2017). Why don't more women run for political office? Researchers polled men and women from various jobs that would typically lead to a political career (e.g., law or business) and found that only 57 percent of the women with the skill sets beneficial to hold a public office thought of themselves as qualified, while 73 percent of men with similar skill sets felt they were qualified to run (Boschma, 2017).

> "Whatever women do they must do twice as well as men to be thought half as good."
>
> —CHARLOTTE WHITTON (1896–1975)

Part-time employment also illustrates the economic exploitation of women. Approximately 23 million U.S. workers are in low-wage jobs, making less than $15 an hour (Close, 2016). An Oxfam America study found that the vast majority, 19 million, of those workers are women. One-third of these women workers were mothers, and 15 percent were single mothers. The study also reported that in 2024, one in six of all jobs will be low-wage positions with predominantly women workers (Close, 2016). Women who chose to leave their jobs to give full-time care to their children will often take part-time, low-salary jobs with no benefits. About 28 percent of women have part-time jobs compared to 14 percent of men (Edwards, 2015). This loss of income will hurt women as they age, especially if they never married. According to 2013 Census Bureau data, there were three times as many single women aged 65 or older living in poverty as married women. Some critics cite the declining marriage rates for all age groups and argue that if these single women married, they would be better off financially, but according to Terry O'Neill of the National Organization for Women: "People aren't poor because they're not getting married. People aren't getting married because they are poor" (Edwards, 2015, p. 52). Her argument is supported by data showing that young men aged 25–34 who might want to get married are earning 20 percent less than the same age group earned in 1980.

Nearly 50 percent of American families get critical financial support from a working wife, but these women often give their families a higher priority than work. According to a MetLife study, choosing to reduce hours, avoid overtime, decline a promotion because it would involve longer hours, or other similar choices adds up to an average loss of more than $324,000 over a woman's work career in terms of wages, pensions, and Social Security benefits (Edwards, 2015). Further, the Bureau of Labor Statistics found that over 22 million women are giving up at least three hours a day to provide unpaid care for an older adult. The Social Security Administration reports that between childcare and care for an older adult, women are absent from the workforce for an average of 12 years. An individual's Social Security check is calculated on wages earned over 35 years, so earning little or nothing for more than 10 years significantly reduces this benefit. Taking into account all individual retirement assets, including pensions, savings accounts, and other earnings, retired men received an average of more than $27,600 a year, but retired women received a little over $15,300. Half of all single older adult women rely on Social Security as their only source of income compared to less than a fourth of married couples (Edwards, 2015).

Another economic consequence of institutional sexism is payment of child support. When the family unit is broken, mothers are most often awarded custody of children and, as part of legal divorce settlements, fathers are almost always required to provide child support for children under the age of majority. According to Grall (2016), mothers represented almost 83 percent of all custodial parents, and over half of them were awarded child support. However, less than half received their full payments, and another 26 percent never received any payments. The average amount for those with legal child support agreements was $5770, or about $480 a month. For mothers living below the poverty line, receiving full child support payments is critical because it constitutes two thirds of their annual income. Despite lower salaries, lack of child support, and other economic consequences, most women will become part of the workforce, regardless of discrimination in salaries and promotions, and despite another frustration encountered on the job: sexual harassment.

How is sexual harassment a significant problem for women in the workforce?

The behavior called *sexual harassment* is not new, but it wasn't until 1979 that Catherine MacKinnon created the term in her writings on workplace behaviors and gender discrimination (Wetzel & Brown, 2000). In 2016, 12,860 sexual harassment complaints were filed with the Equal Employment Opportunity Commission (EEOC); the total of monetary compensation awarded was $40.7 million (Equal Employment Opportunity Commission, 2016). Sexual harassment in the workplace is not just a problem for women; men filed over 16 percent of those complaints. Typically, **sexual harassment** is defined as unwelcome deliberate and repeated behavior of a sexual nature that is neither requested nor returned. Men tend to be responsible for sexual harassment, even when men are the victims. Sexual harassment is an issue of power, not sex. The role of power became clear in 2017 as Hollywood actresses who had some wealth and power went public with accusations of sexual harassment, and there have been consequences for the men they accused. Their stories prompted the #MeToo movement where any woman who had experienced sexual harassment or assault could tell her story. These stories have accused a variety of men from entertainers to politicians to simply men in the workplace, and as of this writing the stories are being reported sympathetically and widely in the news media. Many feminists and social commentators have speculated that these developments may significantly impact cultural and institutional sexism, accompanied by significant changes in the attitudes and behaviors of men at all levels of power and status.

What are the most common behaviors that women regard as sexual harassment?

Two common reasons for women complaining about sexual harassment could be regarded as illustrating a "cultural" conflict between men and women. One complaint: Men make a nuisance of themselves by persistently asking women for dates.

Video Example 10.2
In this video, three teachers discuss the ways in which young people become aware of cultural sexism. What does the main speaker in the black shirt say about how people become aware of being part of an "oppressed group"? How is this related to sexism as it is discussed in Chapter 10?

In response, the explanation is that during childhood and adolescence, American men are taught some version of the cliché "if at first you don't succeed, try, try again." Men view persistence as a positive attribute and are encouraged to be persistent in anything they do. Accused of harassment, some men have yet to understand that persistently approaching women for dates may initially be regarded as obnoxious but eventually becomes threatening. American women tend to regard such harassment as a verbal form of stalking, and it is interesting that many teenage victims describe harassers as disgusting, even ugly, regardless of the physical attractiveness of the harasser (Strauss & Espeland, 1992).

A second complaint has to do with men making unwelcome, sexually suggestive remarks to women, often in the form of sexual jokes that men tell to each other. Now constituting almost half of the workforce, most women find this kind of humor patently offensive. As our workforce continues to change, it is inevitable that some previously established norms and behaviors have to change. Men must recognize the need for reform and respond appropriately. Men must also understand that respecting rather than resisting reasons for reform demonstrates their respect for women. Meanwhile, courts have ruled that it is sexual harassment when employees are subjected to verbal or physical conduct of a sexual nature, and the EEOC has established guidelines for monitoring such inappropriate behavior (Kitchin, 2010).

What are the workplace guidelines for sexual harassment?

If sexual harassment is not severe—persistent requests for a date or telling sexual jokes—victims must tell the harasser that they regard this behavior as offensive. If the harasser continues the behavior despite the victim's repeated objections, the victim can contact a supervisor to ask that she intervene or file a sexual harassment complaint. If the behavior is not considered severe, it must be repeated several times before a sexual harassment complaint is filed.

How many times must the victim be subjected to the behavior before filing a complaint? The courts use a "reasonable person" standard, meaning how long a reasonable person should have to tolerate such behavior before it is considered intolerable. Conversely, if the behavior is considered severe, such as demanding sexual favors from an employee in return for a raise or promotion, it only has to occur once for the victim, or an advocate aware of the behavior, to file a sexual harassment complaint (Webb, 2000).

Are American employers following sexual harassment guidelines?

Most American employers have demonstrated a willingness to take aggressive action against sexual harassment, perhaps because courts have ruled that they have a "vicarious liability" for what happens at their worksite, but even more persuasive is the impact such harassment has on a company's profits. This is one of the reasons that some companies are working to end blatant sexual harassment, and yet forms of what has been called "selective incivility" remain prevalent in the workplace (Kabat-Farr & Cortina, 2012). Disrespectful and degrading comments and behavior affect women in similar ways as sexual harassment: increased job stress, job dissatisfaction, reduced worker creativity, and declining desire to be part of the team. Other workers who observe but are not victims of this incivility are still affected, reporting lower job satisfaction and expressing their intent to look for another job. Consequences for the company include more worker conflicts, loss of productivity, and a higher turnover rate, all of which reduces company profits. Selective incivility or even outright sexism typically exists where there is organizational tolerance, although at times it is because managers are not aware of the problem (Kabat-Farr & Cortina, 2012). Most women do not report incidents to their company or other reporting agencies because of various fears: that their complaint will be ignored, that the harassment will increase, that they will be fired and their career damaged as a result (Knapp, 2016). Ultimately it is in the employer's own best interests to take aggressive action against sexual harassment in the workplace, and such actions are also needed in our schools.

How much of a problem is sexual harassment in the schools?

In 2011, the AAUW conducted a national survey (the third time since 1993) examining sexual harassment in America's schools. Nearly 2000 students in grades 7 through 12 responded, with 56 percent of the girls and 40 percent of the boys indicating that they had experienced sexual harassment at least once during the past school year. Although these figures represent a significant decline from the previous two studies, a new factor that could increase sexual harassment in the future is the use of technology. Almost one third of all students in the 2011 survey were sexually harassed by email, Facebook, and text messaging, and 87 percent of students said that whether the harassment was in person or via technology, the experience had negative consequences, including skipping school and not being able to focus on homework. Common forms of sexual harassment included sexual comments, jokes, and gestures, but 13 percent of girls reported being touched inappropriately. For 18 percent of boys and girls, harassment involved being called gay or lesbian. Perpetrators of sexual harassment were usually peers (96 percent), with 66 percent involving one or more male students, 19 percent one or more female students, and 11 percent involving a mixed group of boys and girls. About 44 percent of students who admitted to engaging in harassment said it was "not a big deal," and 39 percent claimed they were just trying to be "funny" (AAUW, 2011).

Schools have both an ethical and a legal obligation to respond aggressively to such behavior. In 1999, the U.S. Supreme Court decision on *Davis v. Monroe County Board of Education* ruled that schools were legally liable if they did not take appropriate action to eliminate sexual harassment. The AAUW study and other studies have documented the impact of harassment, which reinforces the ethical obligation to address this problem. According to Meyer (2014), consequences have included declining academic performance, increased absenteeism, abuse of alcohol and drugs, and even some instances of suicidal behavior. To reduce sexual harassment, educators must confront sexist attitudes that encourage such behavior.

Some schools have responded to this issue by declaring any kind of harassment as a form of bullying behavior, but this is not likely to be effective because, as the AAUW noted in its 2011 report, calling harassment bullying tends to obscure the fact that gender is the main factor in selecting a victim. Meyer (2014) argued that bullies tend to target a specific individual victim with the intent to cause harm, but the harm caused by harassers is sometimes unintended, and even if it is directed at a specific individual, sexual harassment (and the school's response to it) has a more widespread impact that could potentially affect the entire school.

Technology has also given sexual harassers more tools to work with—cell phones, email, instant messaging, camera phones, personal websites, and social-networking sites. Schools have felt pressure to further protect students, especially because of media attention and public response. Most schools are revising bullying policies to clarify rules about cyberbullying, and some states are passing laws that require school districts to address cyberbullying; however, many higher education institutions are lagging behind and are not prepared to handle cases of cyberbullying (Goshe, 2016). It's a question of health and safety, and sometimes life or death for kids. In 2012, 15-year-old Audrie Pott passed out at a party, and three 16-year-old boys sexually assaulted her, drew lewd messages on her body, and then took pictures. The girl was humiliated and ultimately committed suicide (Wakeman, 2016). In other instances, girls are having their

Video Example 10.3

This video features a discussion on interactions between boys and girls in schools related to bullying. What are some of the issues related to gender and bullying/harassment that the teachers discuss? How are these issues related to the statistics discussed from the AAUW survey examining sexual harassment in America's schools?

nude images shared to humiliate them, often for ending a relationship. This so-called "revenge porn" has become such a concern that 39 states have passed laws protecting people from having their private images shared without their consent. Often victims are incredibly young, like one 14-year-old girl who described the humiliation she felt when a boy she sent naked photos to decided to share them with her classmates and online. At the time she was too scared to tell any adults, but now she's leading a movement for women and girls to know they're not alone, should not be ashamed, and can speak out against this violation of an individual's body and trust (Natham, 2017). A national study reported that 90 percent of revenge porn victims are women, nearly all (93 percent) reported significant emotional distress, and about half (51 percent) thought about suicide (Nathman, 2017).

What are some other gender issues in schools?

Nonsexist educators have long advocated teaching strategies to confront sexist attitudes because gender problems are not limited to sexual harassment. Based on several years spent collecting observational data in K–12 classrooms, Sadker and Sadker (1994) were among the first to report sexist behavior patterns that disadvantaged female students. Boys were more likely to call out answers without raising their hands, and they interrupted when others gave answers. Because boys were more aggressive, teachers tended to call on them, praise them, and discipline them more often than girls. Teachers were more likely to challenge boys to finish their homework, whereas they would help girls finish theirs. Despite the efforts of some teachers to address such issues, these behaviors persist.

Are there gender equity issues for boys?

Some scholars question whether schools have gone too far in promoting gender equity because boys are having more problems today. Gurian (2010) was an early critic, noting that girls were consistently earning higher grades than boys—60 percent of all A grades—while boys were recipients of 70 percent of all D and F grades and were 80 percent of all dropouts. According to the U.S. Department of Education (2012), boys are more likely than girls to be held back one year (61 percent of boys compared to 39 percent of girls), and male students are suspended at a higher rate than girls. One study looked at how schools respond to boys and girls who had similar behavior problems such as not paying attention to the teacher, not being able to control their emotions, having difficulty making friends, or having conflicts with their teachers. The study followed the children through adolescence and into adulthood, reporting that boys with higher levels of behavior problems as young children struggled more in high school, often having to repeat grades, and ended up completing less schooling by their mid-twenties. The researchers said they set out to see why girls were succeeding more in school and ended up with the question of what schools needed to do to help boys become more successful (Camera, 2016).

As for academic issues, there are equal numbers of boys and girls in high school biology classes, but more boys are enrolled in physics; however more girls are enrolled in chemistry. Despite women's increasing academic achievement, boys are still more likely to enroll in Advanced Placement (AP) courses and to sign up for AP tests, and they pass these tests at a higher rate than females. After graduation, a majority of high school girls are still interested in traditional careers such as in education and health, but over half express an interest in marketing, and over 40 percent are interested in information technology (U.S. Department of Education, 2012). The central issue in this debate over gender equity in schools should be whether all students, both boys and girls, are being given the opportunity in curricular and extracurricular programs to learn and develop their talents and abilities. Gender equity in education is not about winners and losers in a competition between boys and girls but about making the educational experience as fair and as equitable as possible for both boys and girls.

What evidence indicates that gender equity issues are being addressed in schools and society?

One issue that has evoked concern for men is access to higher education. More women are entering college, earning 57 percent or more of all bachelor's degrees, 60 percent of all master's degrees, and 51 percent of all doctorates (NCES, 2013). After combining graduates with a bachelor's degree, master's degree, or doctorate, the data show that women constitute 58 percent of biology/biomedical science majors, 79 percent of majors in health professions and related clinical sciences, 47 percent of business majors, and 63 percent of communication/communication technology majors (NCES, 2013). Women continue to account for 49 percent of all students in law schools and in medical schools (American Bar Association, 2017; Association of American Medical Colleges, 2016).

In addition to academics, women are increasingly involved in athletics. In 1972, less than one half of 1 percent of girls participated in high school sports, but by 2016, 42 percent (3.3 million) were involved, compared to 58 percent of boys. However, by the age of 14, girls drop out of sports at twice the rate of boys. Some educators argue that despite laws requiring equal access, girls still have 1.3 million fewer opportunities to participate in high school sports than boys (Women's Sports Foundation, 2016). Another concern is the underrepresentation of girls of color in high school sports, with three fourths of White girls involved compared to less than two thirds of Black people and Latinas and less than half of Asian American girls. This gap is wider in urban schools and for youth from low-income families (Dusenbery & Lee, 2012).

In college sports, only 30,000 women competed in 1972, but by 2016 there were over 211,000 female participants. Minority participation continues to be low, with a slight increase in Black (1 percent) and Hispanic (3 percent) women athletes in 2016. There is also a disparity with funding. In 2015, Division I athletics departments in the National Collegiate Athletic Association (NCAA) allocated 2.5 times more money on men's programs than on women's, spending $45,000 more on each male athlete than on a female athlete. There have also been complaints about the lack of women in leadership roles. Men represent more than 60 percent of all coaches for NCAA women's teams (Wilson, 2017). The NCAA also rewards men for their success. Basketball teams that make it to the tournament could earn approximately $260,000 for each game played in the tournament, plus $260,000 a year for the next five years. That means a total value for a victory in the men's tournament is about $1.56 million. However, women are not paid anything for playing in or even winning the tournament (Zimbalist, 2016).

Such inequities underscore a major flaw of Title IX—lack of enforcement. When a Title IX complaint is submitted, investigators from the Office of Civil Rights often respond by conducting a "desk audit" rather than visiting the school to determine the degree of compliance. Although violations of Title IX should put schools in jeopardy of losing federal funding, this penalty has never been recommended. Even when Title IX complaints are upheld, monetary damages have never been awarded (Kilman, 2012). Yet there is evidence that women benefit significantly from participating in sports. Studies show health benefits such as decreased risk of obesity, increased confidence, and less risk of depression (Women's Sports Foundation, 2016). Other studies report that women who play sports are more likely to graduate college, get a job, and work in male-dominated fields. One survey of senior business women found that nearly all (94 percent) played sports, and half played at the university level; 75 percent of these women leaders said they'd be more likely to hire someone who had a background in sports (Brooke-Marciniak, 2016).

Despite the ongoing issues stemming from the persistence of sexism in our society, the pattern of women's increasing involvement in sports, the workforce, politics, and other activities was reinforced by the White House Council on Women and Girls, which reported that women are marrying later in life and having fewer children; in addition,

"What is enough? Enough is when somebody says, "Get me the best people you can find," and nobody notices when half of them turn out to be women."

—LOUISE RENNE (1937–)

Video Example 10.4
This video features a news story about how a high school is changing their policies with regard to sports and cheering to comply with Title IX. Note the difference in response from the faculty member and the student interviewed. Compare the different speakers' responses to the policy changes. How do their responses relate to the issues surrounding Title IX discussed in Chapter 10? How do they relate to the history of cultural sexism discussed in Chapter 10?

https://www.youtube.com/watch?v=ZJs-6tw3egU

more are choosing not to have children. More American women appear to be making choices about what sort of life they want to have. Along with their significant gains in educational attainment, it is clear that women are going to be an important factor in shaping the changes to come in this century.

 Self-Check 10.3 Complete this self-check quiz to check your understanding of how institutional sexism affects women's opportunities in school and especially in the workforce, and the economic consequences of sexism.

Afterword

This description of cultural, individual, and institutional sexism is the tip of an iceberg. Gender discrimination occurs in our laws and in our court system, in the arts and in athletics, and in the images encountered in media and in school textbooks. Sexism permeates our institutions. Some men believe that sexism works to their advantage and resist efforts to promote gender equality, but sexism hurts men and women, boys and girls. Anything that prevents people from using their talents and abilities results in a loss for us all. When anyone is denied a chance to contribute to our society, the result is a nation that is less than it could have been. If Americans create a society that offers opportunities to all and receives the gifts each individual has to offer, the male–female power game could cease to exist—and that would be a victory for everyone.

Summary

- Sexism in the United States has existed since colonial times, and the cultural history of sexist language as well as media portrayals of female beauty have influenced the way women have viewed themselves, especially in terms of body image and attractiveness.

- Americans have been confused about terms like *male chauvinist* and *feminist*, and they have also not understood the reality of violence against women.

- Institutional sexism affects women's opportunities in education and especially in the workforce, resulting in significant economic consequences for women.

Terms and Definitions

Androgyny The interchangeability of men's and women's roles and responsibilities in all areas beyond fundamental biological ones

Cultural sexism The societal promotion of negative beliefs and practices that reinforce rigid gender roles in which men are traditionally accorded a superior role in society while women are assigned to subordinate roles; the artificial superimposition of authority of one gender over another

Feminist A woman or man committed to the struggle for the social, economic, and personal rights of women and men; an advocate for equality between women and men

Glass ceiling An informal upper limit that keeps women and minorities from being promoted to positions of greatest responsibility in work organizations

Inclusive language Words or phrases that are not gender specific but inclusive of both genders

Individual sexism Prejudiced attitudes and behavior demeaning to women, or to men, because of beliefs about gender and gender roles, demonstrated whenever someone responds by saying or doing something degrading or harmful about individuals of the other gender

Institutional sexism Established laws, customs, and practices in a society that allow systematic discrimination against people or groups based on gender

Male chauvinist A man or woman who believes that men ought to be the leaders and decision makers and women should be subordinate to them

Rape "The penetration, no matter how slight, of the vagina or anus with any body part or object, or oral penetration by a sex organ of another person, without the consent of the victim" (FBI, 2012)

Sexism An attitude, action, or institutional structure that subordinates or limits an individual on the basis of sex (Andrzejewski, 1996)

Sexual harassment Deliberate and repeated behavior that has a sexual basis and is not welcomed, requested, or returned

Discussion Exercises

Exercise 1: Find the Problem: Analyzing Sexist Language

Directions: Determine why the language in each statement has been termed "sexist." Write an appropriate nonsexist message to replace the sexist one. [*Example*: The average American drinks his coffee black. *Nonsexist revision*: The average American drinks black coffee.

1. Dear Sir:
2. Any student who is not satisfied with his performance on the pretest may take the posttest.
3. Mr. McAllister runs the garage in partnership with his wife, a striking blonde who mans the pumps.
4. Housewives are feeling the pinch of higher food prices.
5. A writer can become so involved in his work that he neglects his family.
6. We are asking all the mothers to send cookies for our field trip tomorrow.
7. Black people finally received the vote in 1870.
8. While lunch was delayed, the women gossiped about last night's meeting.
9. The ancient Egyptians allowed women considerable control over property.
10. One of the political debates in the racial struggle taking place in South Africa is over the concept of "one man, one vote."

Exercise 2 Sexual Harassment: Case Studies from Higher Education

Directions: Sexual harassment may take several forms: innuendo or overt action toward either gender by those of the same or opposite sex, unwanted sexual advances, sexual assault, or sexual coercion (rape). In each situation below, respond to the following three questions:

- Is this a case of sexual harassment? If yes, when did the harassment begin to occur?

- What are the harassing behaviors in this situation?

- What can the individual(s) involved in each situation do to address the harassment?

1. Kevin is taking an introductory English course. His first writing assignment dealt with his uncertainties about being a new student in college and on his own for the first time. When the essays are returned, his has no grade and only the comment, "Please see me." Kevin goes to the teacher's office during the posted office hours. His teacher suggests that they go out for a drink to discuss the essay.

2. Connie is taking a math course that includes a unit on statistics. Connie has been having some difficulty understanding probability theory. She knows that this course is important to her career, and a good grade in math can increase her chances of getting into graduate school. She contacts her teaching assistant and explains her concerns about the material and her wish to get a good grade to qualify for graduate school. They set up a series of tutoring sessions, and by the third session have not only become friends but have also begun to date outside of the sessions.

3. In her introductory psychology class, Sonia, a Latina, notices that her professor smiles and comments on her appearance as a greeting each morning, but he does not greet any other student in that way. Before his lecture on contemporary sexual roles and behavior, he says to the class, "Sonia can probably help us understand this topic because she has to put up with macho types."

4. In an undergraduate literature class, Professor Helmsley, the director of Graduate Studies, expresses his opinion that courses in literature offered under the Women's Studies Program are useless preparation for graduate study. He has recommended that all such courses be dropped from the list of acceptable courses for the undergraduate major in literature.

Adapted from *Sexual Harassment and the University: Seven Cases.*

Chapter 11
Heterosexism: Challenging the Heterosexual Assumption

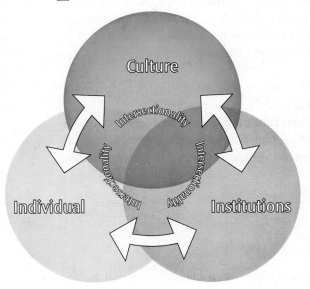

After reading this chapter, you will know and be able to:

11.1 Discuss the history of gay people in ancient societies up to the present, and describe the evolution of American attitudes from accepting the heterosexual assumption to being more consistent with scientific research.

11.2 Describe the groups included under the broad "transgender" label as well as the ongoing myths about being gay.

11.3 Provide examples of institutional discrimination against LGBT individuals, and discuss why the privileges that heterosexists believe should be considered for LGBT individuals are in fact rights for all people.

"The only abnormality is the incapacity to love."

—ANAIS NIN (1903–1977)

The word *homosexual* and the concept of homosexuality originated in the 1860s in the German medical writing of Dr. Karl Ulrichs, but it was not until 1892 that the term and concept entered into public discourse when scholars such as Havelock Ellis and Magnus Hirschfeld published essays and books describing theories and research concerning human sexuality. In one highly regarded book, Richard von Krafft-Ebing chose not to use "sexual inversion," the common term in America, but Ulrichs's word, translated into English as *homosexuality*. Krafft-Ebing described a **homosexual** as someone sexually attracted to members of the same sex. The introduction of this new concept was met with a backlash of prejudice and bigotry in many cultures.

Cultural Heterosexism: Historical and Scientific Perspectives on Human Sexuality

Cultural heterosexism refers to a dominant culture defining heterosexuality as the norm and anything else as deviant. The heterosexual assumption is an example of cultural heterosexism. Although science has attempted to explain the complexity and variations in human sexual response, some people insist that the only acceptable way to love and make love is to be a heterosexual couple. History tells us, however, that being gay is not a new aberration but has been reflected in human behavior in all cultures, in every era. Because same-sex liaisons have been documented throughout human history, the new term challenged the Western world's traditional heterosexual assumption.

What is the heterosexual assumption?

Non-Western cultures have a history of acknowledging and accepting sexual variation in human beings (Williams, 2001). Western cultural attitudes about sexuality have been based on a **heterosexual assumption**: that all people were born **heterosexual** and that being attracted to opposite-sex partners was the natural condition of human beings. People who engaged in any sexual activity not conforming to heterosexual norms were assumed to be making deviant and unnatural choices, especially when sexual activity took place with a same-sex partner. The Bible was often used to justify beliefs about deviant sexual behavior, and even twentieth-century psychologists reinforced the assumption by regarding being gay as a mental illness. Gay people were widely perceived as aberrations in need of correction (a cure) to bring them back to their true heterosexual nature (Duberman, Vicinus, & Chauncey, 1989).

> "In my relationship with others, I have found that it does not help, in the long run, to act as if I am something I am not."
> —CARL ROGERS (1902–1987)

When was the heterosexual assumption challenged?

Krafft-Ebing provided the term that challenged the heterosexual assumption. Although he still believed that being gay was immoral and unacceptable, he defined it as one of many forms of sexual desire. Krafft-Ebing argued that like fetishism or masochism, being gay was a condition, a mental defect that could be cured. His assertion was addressed by the evolving field of psychology as its practitioners searched for a way to remedy deviant behavior. The suggested "cures" included castration, sterilization, electric shock, and occasional lobotomies; however, none proved to be successful (Katz, 1985).

Although conventional wisdom among psychologists continued to regard being gay as deviant and unnatural—a mental defect—the failure of recommended remedies in the clinical setting caused several respected people in the field, including A. A. Brill, Magnus Hirschfeld, and even Sigmund Freud, to conclude that homosexuality could not be cured and was probably a permanent condition. As psychologists became convinced that deviant sexual desires could not be redirected, they adopted approaches such as "adjustment therapy" to control "homosexual behavior." These practices were the norm when the Kinsey Report was published in 1948.

How did the Kinsey Report challenge the heterosexual assumption?

With funding from the Rockefeller Foundation, a zoologist named Alfred Kinsey with a research staff engaged in a study of human sexual behavior from 1938 to 1956. The Kinsey Report (Kinsey, Pomeroy, & Martin, 1948 issued in 1948 was controversial and included the proposition that **sexual orientation** was not a singular phenomenon but instead was a continuum of multiple possibilities ranging from exclusive heterosexuality to exclusive homosexuality, with diverse bisexual orientations in between (see Figure 11.1). Based on self-reports of dreams, fantasies, and behaviors, Kinsey and his staff concluded that only a small percentage of their subjects were exclusively heterosexual or exclusively homosexual. (Later a figure of 10 percent became widely used.) Most appeared to have some potential for **bisexual** behavior—being sexually attracted to members of either gender—although sexual attraction might be biased more toward one gender than another.

The 1948 Kinsey Report on male sexuality (and the 1953 report on female sexuality) challenged the general assumption that all human beings possess a heterosexual orientation. Americans were confronted with the radical concept of sexual orientation: Human sexuality includes categories of different sexual attractions and behaviors, including a desire for same-sex partners.

What was the impact of the Kinsey Report?

The term *homosexuality* provided a label for what Oscar Wilde's lover had called "the love that dare not speak its name," but most Americans were uncomfortable with the subject and refused to discuss it. Most psychologists still regarded being gay as a form of mental illness, but gay people themselves began to reconsider their situation. There were, and always had been, same-sex–oriented people who were comfortable with their sexuality while being discreet in their behavior. These men and women became

Figure 11.1 The Kinsey Diversity of Sexual Orientation

SOURCE: J. K. Graphics.

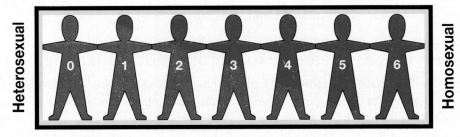

The Kinsey Continuum of Sexual Orientation

0 = Exclusively heterosexual
1 = Predominantly heterosexual, only incidentally homosexual
2 = Predominantly heterosexual, but more than incidentally homosexual
3 = Equally heterosexual and homosexual
4 = Predominantly homosexual, but more than incidentally heterosexual
5 = Predominantly homosexual, only incidentally heterosexual
6 = Exclusively homosexual

convinced that attitudes in America needed to change, but they weren't sure how that could happen.

Gay male friends of psychologist Evelyn Hooker argued that psychologists persisted in regarding being gay as a mental illness because gay clients who sought treatment were not comfortable with their own sexuality. These individuals were often filled with guilt and anxiety because of society's condemnation or their religious upbringing. One gay man urged Dr. Hooker to engage in research involving well-adjusted gay men, and he volunteered a number of such men for the research (Marcus, 1992).

Hooker took her client's suggestion and conducted a study with 30 gay men and 30 heterosexual men. She gave her subjects three different personality tests and submitted the results to a panel of internationally respected psychologists. None of the panelists could discern heterosexual from gay subjects, and they gave two thirds of the subjects from each group a score of average or higher, clearly refuting the belief that being gay was associated with inherent mental problems. Hooker presented the findings of the panel evaluations in her research at the national conference of the American Psychological Association (APA) in 1956. It would take another 17 years for APA members to admit they had been wrong and take appropriate action.

In 1973, the APA voted to remove homosexuality from its list of mental illnesses. The American Medical Association (AMA) would later join the APA in declaring that being gay was not a mental illness and that gay men and lesbians could be just as healthy, competent, and capable of functioning effectively in society as heterosexuals. The APA and AMA decisions challenged people who believed they had been justified in discriminating against individuals who were not heterosexual. This resulted in the concept of **heterosexism**—the oppression or exploitation of human beings not biologically heterosexual.

What has the current research reported?

Ever since the 1973 APA statement, research on human sexuality has increased, and researchers largely agree that sexual orientation has a significant biological basis. Based on anthropological evidence and child development studies, Pillard (1997) proposed that sexual orientation was an innate characteristic, a deeply embedded personality trait that can be observed in young children:

> There seems to be a fundamental bias toward either a heterosexual or a homosexual developmental path, prefigured early in life, neither taught nor learned, and profoundly resistant to modification. (p. 233)

In 2008, the world's largest study of twins confirmed that sexual orientation is influenced by genetics as well as by a mix of environmental factors. The researchers emphasized that this was true for heterosexuals as well; their sexual behavior was also shaped largely by genetics and random environmental factors (Schlatter & Steinback, 2010). According to a comprehensive review of research on sexual orientation, the authors concluded that various biological factors appear to contribute to the determination of sexual orientation, as do environmental factors. Further, the researchers found little evidence that the LGBT population increases significantly when there is more social tolerance for LGBT people (Bailey, 2016).

Reinforcing the idea of sexual variation among humans, animal studies report same-sex sexual activities. By 2000, there were so many observational studies of various animals engaged in same-sex sexual activities that virtually no credible scientists disputed this claim. Further, for some animals such activity is not simply a rare occurrence that could be attributed to confusion but a regular event (Hogenboom, 2015). Same-sex sexual activity has been observed among lions, dolphins, and killer whales, and it seems particularly common among animals living in herds. Even among animals

"I can't understand any discussion of gays and lesbians as if they were something immoral or unsatisfactory. They're just doing what nature wants them to do."

—R. BUCKMINSTER FULLER (1895–1983)

that mate for life such as ducks or geese, scientists have identified 4–5 percent of the pairs as same-sex couples. Scientists have long been interested in the dwarf chimpanzee because it is a close relative to humans. Based on their observations, it seems that the entire species is bisexual (Ellerton, 2011).

Research regarding human sexual variation parallels the role that variation plays in nature. Gould (1983) describes striping patterns for zebras as an illustration. One pattern has numerous narrow, parallel stripes configured relatively straight up and down the body. Another pattern has fewer, thicker stripes on the body and three broad slightly curved stripes on the haunch. A third pattern has even fewer and thicker stripes on the front of the body, and even broader stripes starting from the middle of the belly and curving back to the haunch (see Figure 11.2).

The three striping variations result from the striping mechanism being initiated at different times during fetal development. Because variation occurs in something as simple as the striping pattern for zebras, it is difficult to maintain that all human beings possess the same heterosexual orientation, given the complexity of factors involved with the sexual development of the human fetus. It is far more logical to expect the kind of sexual variation described in the Kinsey Report, in the research conducted since 1948, and as recorded in human history.

What historical evidence has described the existence of same-sex attraction?

Love and sexual desire between men was widely practiced by ancient Greeks who wrote openly about the love of one man for another. Although Sappho's poetry described women's love for other women, men were primarily the authors of Greek literature that was preserved. Approving of same-sex attraction wasn't an Athenian idiosyncrasy; it

Figure 11.2 Striping Patterns in Zebras

A simple genetic striping mechanism occurring at different times during fetal development produces these three striping patterns.

SOURCE: Alan Jeffery/Shutterstock (top left); Kent Koppelman (bottom left); Mogens Trolle/Shutterstock (right).

was widely accepted in Sparta and other city-states. One of the most famous military units in Greek history was the Band of Thebes—150 pairs of lovers—300 men pledged to stand by their lover in battle until death took one or both. They played a heroic part in Sparta's siege of Thebes as fewer than 6000 Thebans defeated more than 10,000 Spartan soldiers, a setback from which Sparta never recovered, which paved the way for the conquest of Greece by Philip of Macedonia. Philip's son, Alexander the Great, would become famous for conquering the known world during his lifetime and, according to contemporary accounts, was known to engage in sexual activity with male partners (Rowse, 1977).

One of the ironies of the history of gay people occurred in nineteenth-century England. At a time when English society was quite homophobic, wealthy families sent their sons to boys' boarding schools, where they learned to read Latin and Greek texts, some with gay themes. Many memoirs recall upper-class boarding schools where English boys engaged in behavior they called **Greek love**, a euphemism for "homosexual activity" (Crompton, 1998).

Anthropologists have observed that culture often determines societal attitudes toward being gay. Some Native American cultures believe that a gay man is a special human being, possessing traits of both men and women, and thus endowed with great power. Williams (2010) provides historical and anthropological documentation as evidence of the acceptance of being gay and other sexual anomalies in various Native American cultures.

Some Polynesian and Caribbean cultures also view same-sex desires as acceptable. The Mediterranean region, including southern Italy and countries such as Greece, Morocco, and Turkey, has historically been a haven for gay people from Europe because same-sex relationships were tolerated. Aristocratic gay people traveled there primarily to act on their sexual attraction to same-sex partners (Williams, 2001). According to Zeldin (1994), being gay has been accepted at one time or another by about two thirds of human societies.

Early on, the Catholic Church played a major role in the denunciation of homosexuality in Europe. The church regarded homosexuality as a sin, yet in 1102, the Archbishop of Canterbury called for lenient punishments for people engaging in same-sex activity because "this sin has been so public that hardly anyone has blushed for it" (Zeldin, 1994, p. 123). In the thirteenth century, church persecution of homosexuals was part of the Inquisition investigations as the Vatican sought to eliminate various heresies. The Inquisition lasted about 400 years, but being gay would be persecuted in Europe for the next 600 years (Boswell, 1994).

Medieval churchmen executed both gay men and lesbians, although women were equally likely to be executed as witches, which was also justified by the Bible. Even royalty were not immune from persecution. Kings and queens were permitted a variety of sins as long as they used discretion, but English monarch Edward II was not discreet. His coronation festivities were almost disrupted by public reaction to the king's obvious preference for his friend Piers Gaveston rather than his queen. Offended by the king's outrageous behavior, English nobles sent Gaveston back to France. Edward could not bear to be separated from his lover and pleaded that Gaveston be allowed to come back. Shortly after Gaveston returned to England, he was murdered, which led to a civil war that ended with Edward's death at the hands of Queen Isabella and her lover, Mortimer (Rowse, 1977). Still, for royalty, aristocrats, or even an artist under their protection, it was usually possible to escape persecution for being attracted to same-sex partners or even acting on that feeling. Yet England continued to reflect homophobic attitudes that forced even those with a title and wealth or even fame, like the poet Lord Byron, to seek sexual pleasure outside the boundaries of Britain for fear of punishment. For example, Oscar Wilde's popularity as a playwright was not enough to protect him from being tried and sent to prison (1895–1897) for being gay.

By the middle of the twentieth century, attitudes about gay people in Europe and England were changing, yet despite Alan Turing's significant contribution to deciphering the German Enigma code during World War II, he was convicted for engaging in "homosexual behavior" and punished by having to submit to chemical castration, and he eventually committed suicide. By the 1990s British and European attitudes became more accepting in contrast to American attitudes, illustrated by the Clinton administration's appointment of James Hormel, an openly gay man, as U.S. ambassador to Luxembourg. Although government officials in Luxembourg raised no objection to Hormel, his appointment was stalled in the Senate for two years because of objections from conservative senators, forcing the president to avoid Senate approval by appointing Hormel during a Congressional recess.

How have attitudes of the American people changed concerning gay people?

World War II had an impact on American gay men returning from the war, as it had with racial minorities. The 1948 Kinsey Report refuted the heterosexual assumption, and many gay and lesbian veterans thought their military experience earned them the right to be accepted regardless of their sexual orientation. Since California courts had upheld the right of openly gay men and lesbians to patronize certain bars and businesses, it seemed the safest place to live. San Francisco had been a major port of departure for men and women sent to the Pacific; therefore, many returning gay men and lesbians chose to remain there. As their numbers grew, so did their political activism; by the 1970s, mayoral candidates such as George Moscone openly courted gay voters.

San Francisco was one of many cities across the United States to witness gay and lesbian political activism. When Harvey Milk, an openly gay candidate for a city supervisor position in San Francisco, was elected in 1977, national media reported the story. One year later, a city supervisor, Dan White, who objected to serving with a gay man, murdered both Milk and Mayor Moscone. As an indication that anti-gay prejudice had not disappeared, the jury convicted Dan White of the minimal penalty possible in such a case, manslaughter. The White verdict sparked a riot lasting more than two hours in gay areas of San Francisco with police shouting homophobic slurs and brutally beating any gay man or lesbian they encountered (D'Emilio, 1989).

The San Francisco riot on the West Coast, like the Stonewall riot a decade earlier in New York City, were two of many events in the late twentieth century that forced Americans to acknowledge the presence of gay people (see Table 11.1). The word **gay** became accepted as the self-chosen label of the community, but usage was eventually limited to men. By the 1970s, columnist Abigail van Buren ("Dear Abby") responded to questions about gay people by emphasizing the need to accept it, based on her understanding of scientific research. In 1975, David Kopay, a retired National Football League running back, published an autobiography in which he said that he was gay and alleged that many professional athletes were gay. In the 1970s and 1980s, the revelation of the sexual identity of popular culture celebrities such as Rock Hudson and Liberace, along with increasing numbers of prominent people openly accepting gay men and lesbians, were important factors in changing anti-gay attitudes. As the 1980s began, gay men and lesbians were encountering more tolerant attitudes, especially in urban areas.

Most Americans tended to ignore the AIDS epidemic that arose in the early 1980s, although some radio and television ministers blamed homosexual behavior and called it a "gay disease." As Sontag (1989) explained, "The unsafe behavior that produces AIDS (was) judged to be more than just weakness. It is indulgence, delinquency—addiction to chemicals that are illegal and to sex regarded as deviant" (p. 25). As the epidemic continued, Americans were forced to confront their historic cultural bias against gay men as people increasingly recognized that HIV was a virus, not a punishment from God.

Table 11.1 A Timetable of Important Events in the Recognition of Gay Rights in the United States

1924	Formation of the first recognized activist group for gay men and lesbians (Chicago).
1962	Illinois is the first state to repeal its sodomy laws.
1969	Police raid of the Stonewall Inn (a gay bar in New York City) results in riots that spark the beginning of the gay rights movement.
1970	First "gay pride" march (New York City) commemorates the Stonewall Riot.
1978	Harvey Milk, San Francisco's first openly gay city supervisor, is assassinated.
1981	The Centers for Disease Control reports on the first case of what later becomes known as AIDS (initially called the "gay plague").
1982	Wisconsin is the first state to prohibit discrimination based on sexual orientation.
1984	Hollywood's legendary leading man Rock Hudson admits to being gay.
1987	Formation of ACT UP, which advocates for more funding for AIDS research.
1993	U.S. military adopts "don't ask, don't tell" policy as a compromise to address the problem of harassment of gay and lesbian soldiers.
1993	Hundreds of thousands participate in a march for equal rights for gay men and lesbians (Washington, D.C.).
1996	U.S. Supreme Court declares equal rights for gay men and lesbians.
1997	The popular television show *Ellen* is the first program to have a main character who admits to being gay (as does the actress Ellen DeGeneres).
1998	The murder of Matthew Shepard gains national attention and is the catalyst in many states to include gay people in hate-crime legislation.
2003	U.S. Supreme Court rules that sodomy laws are unconstitutional, reversing its 1986 decision in *Hardwick v. Bowers*.
2011	U.S. military lifts ban on openly gay soldiers serving in the military.
2013	U.S. Supreme Court rules that the Defense of Marriage Act denying federal benefits to gay couples legally married in their states was unconstitutional.
2015	The U.S. Supreme Court rules that gay marriages must be recognized in all 50 states in *Obergefell v. Hodges*.

The fact that a young boy, Ryan White, could contract this fatal disease from a blood transfusion illustrated the point dramatically. For seven of his eight years as president, Ronald Reagan never publicly acknowledged the spread of AIDS (Shilts, 1987). It took another presidential election before Congress passed the Ryan White Comprehensive AIDS Resources Emergency Act in 1990. But anti-gay attitudes in the United States have persisted, in part because of religious and cultural beliefs.

What are some heterosexist cultural and religious beliefs?

Many Americans still cling to the cultural belief that being gay is unnatural, an accusation that calls for reasonable people to consider what it would mean for something to be natural. Some sexual activity, such as incest, is forbidden in every known culture; on the other hand, being gay has been or still is accepted in most world cultures (Chiariello, 2013). Scientists have argued that anything observed in nature should be considered natural. According to Ellerton (2011) researchers have documented examples of same-sex sexual activity in every species except those that never have sex, such as sea urchins. This would suggest that sexual activity between same-sex partners normally occurs in nature.

Although the Catholic Church accepts that being gay is a natural predisposition (one is born with it), church officials continue to denounce "homosexual activity" as a sin—the only instance of the church forbidding something it admits to be natural. Yet attitudes of Catholics appear to be changing. The Human Rights Campaign (2015) cited a Pew Research poll that found 75 percent of young Catholics (aged 18–29) support

> "God loves homosexuals as much as he loves everybody else."
>
> —RYAN WHITE (1971–1990)

marriage for same-sex couples, and the majority of all Catholic age groups except for those 65 or older support inclusion of LGBT people in the Catholic Church.

Protestant churches are divided on the issue of accepting gay people. Some Protestant theologians continue to condemn being gay. Others argue that certain biblical passages have been mistranslated to justify regarding same-sex sexual activity as a sin; these passages actually denounce male and female prostitution, not being gay. Some feel biblical criticism of men engaging in same-sex acts was based on the biblical authors assuming that everyone was heterosexual and that anyone engaging in a same-sex act betrayed human nature (Doupe, 2001). Another argument that has arisen is that since biblical injunctions against eating pork or making clothes out of two types of material are now regarded as historic and no longer relevant, any biblical passage interpreted as an injunction against same-sex acts could also be regarded as an example of historic prejudice. Protestant debates about these issues will continue, but some degree of acceptance appears to be developing. Duke University's recent study of over 2700 Christian and Jewish congregations in the United States reported that 38 percent of them (with almost half of those who attend religious services) accepted gay men and lesbians as church members. On the other hand, less than 20 percent of these congregations accepted gay men and lesbians in volunteer leadership roles. (Chaves, 2014).

> **Self-Check 11.1** Complete this self-check quiz to check your understanding of the heterosexual assumption concerning human sexuality and the evolving scientific understanding of sexual orientation.

Individual Heterosexism: Ongoing Myths About Being Gay and the Growing Awareness of Transgender Individuals

Despite increasing acceptance of being gay in the United States, a persistent minority of Americans still regards being gay as sexual deviance, illustrating **individual heterosexism**—negative attitudes and behaviors based on the belief that sexual orientations other than heterosexual are unnatural. Although the term has become somewhat controversial, **homophobia** refers to a more extreme feeling, defined as fear or hatred of gay people. These negative attitudes are not limited to gay men and lesbians but to a variety of people who are perceived as sexually deviant. For that reason, gay men and lesbians today are more likely to refer to themselves as part of the Lesbian, Gay, Bisexual, and Transgender (**LGBT**) community, and sometimes more letters are added to the acronym, like "Q" for "Queer" or "Questioning."

What groups are included in the LGBT community?

All of the groups and the terms for them relate to the issue of sexual orientation, and even though some terms are new, the issues are not. As Sullivan (2003) observed: "Although the terms *transsexual* and *transgender* have been coined only relatively recently, a variety of forms of gender ambiguity can be found throughout history" (p. 99). Introduced in 1949, *transsexual* was one of the first terms for a category eventually classified as "Gender Identity Disorder." A transsexual was someone who could not psychologically identify with his or her biological gender—a man identifying as a women or a woman identifying as a man. By the 1970s, medical professionals regarded transsexuals

Application Exercise 11.1

In this video, a young man talks about the stereotypes he encountered during his coming out process. Think about the cultural and individual heterosexism discussed in Chapter 11. Review the video and complete the activity.

as different from gay people; they established gender identity clinics and developed sex reassignment procedures.

Part of the confusion over sexual orientation is the tendency to think of sex and gender as two different concepts, with sex being determined biologically based on fetal anatomy, whereas gender is cultural and determined by a set of learned behaviors. It may be easier to understand transgender people by thinking of gender as a spectrum of behaviors rather than a dualistic phenomenon. People who identify as transgender feel that the sex they were assigned at birth because of their genitalia or other physical attributes does not match their innate sense of gender identity. According to one LGBT advocacy group, *gender identity* refers to an individual's "deeply-felt inner sense of being male, female, or something other or in-between," whereas gender expression refers to "a person's "characteristics and behaviors such as appearance, dress, mannerisms and speech patterns that can be described as masculine or feminine" (Terry, 2015, p. 28). Gender identity and gender expression are unrelated to sexual orientation. Whether their gender identity is male or female, transgender people may identify as heterosexual, bisexual, gay, lesbian, or other. The Internet has helped transgender people find answers to their questions. They also go online to chat with people who have similar feelings. Sexual identity is viewed as more fluid today; it is still consistent with the Kinsey Continuum, but locations along that continuum are not rigid. For example, one Cornell researcher is studying people who consider themselves straight but with "a bit of gayness," estimating this group as 15 percent of women and 5 percent of men (Steinmetz, 2017).

There are also individuals who identify as transvestites (cross dressers) or drag queens/kings, and the outdated term *hermaphrodites* has been replaced by the term *intersexuals*, referring to people whose genitals, chromosomes, or hormonal systems (or some combination of these) do not fit the standard parameters for men or women (Schwartzapfel, 2013). The term *transgender* now encompasses a broad range of identities viewed as "gender nonconforming"; it became more widely accepted in the 1990s when public health officials adopted it (Steinmetz, 2014). Based on the work of several scholars, Rankin (2005) defined **transgender** as "individuals whose gender identity conflicts with biological sex assignment or societal expectations for gender expression as male or female" (p. 29).

Although transgender is a broad term, a medical study reported that it represents only 0.5 percent of the U.S. population, or about 1.5 million people, but a middle school study found that 1 percent of the students were transgender (Schwartzapfel, 2013). Their small numbers are part of the difficulty transgender people encounter in their efforts to be recognized and accepted. In a recent survey, the Public Religion Institute reported that 65 percent of Americans have a close friend or family member who is a gay man or lesbian, but only 9 percent said they knew someone who is transgender (Steinmetz, 2014). The lack of knowledge about and acceptance of transgender youth produces the sort of psychological stress that gay and lesbian youth have had to overcome. A major clinic dealing with transgender adolescents and young adults reported that 20 percent of them had engaged in some form of self-mutilation, and almost 10 percent had attempted suicide (Schwartzapfel, 2013).

Transgender people struggle with many issues, including the perception that they have a mental illness. After removing the term *homosexuality* from its *Diagnostic and Statistical Manual of Mental Disorders* in 1973, the APA added the term *transsexual* to the manual in 1980; transsexual was eventually replaced by *gender identity disorder* and then by *gender dysphoria* in 2013, and this term remains in the manual (Steinmetz, 2014). In the popular culture, transgender people have to confront confusion in mainstream media. For example, media stories often refer to transgender men being "born a girl," but many transgender men reject such a statement and argue that they were not "born a girl," but they were a born a boy in a girl's body (Schwartzapfel, 2013). With such complexity and the subsequent increase of nonconforming gender behavior, new labels are being

Video Example 11.1

In this video, one counselor is seeking help from a mentor counselor on working with a client who identifies as transgender. How does the client inform the counselor that they identify as transgender? What are some of the suggestions that the mentor counselor gives to the other counselor about working with her client that might relate to some of the challenges that transgender youth in schools might be facing?

generated. In a large 2016 survey asking subjects to provide a label that best fit how they viewed their gender, over 500 different terms were submitted (Steinmetz, 2017).

Another issue related to sexual orientation concerns people who openly identify themselves as bisexual (attracted to sexual partners of either gender). For many years bisexuals received the least attention of all groups in the LGBT community, perhaps because their sexual orientation may be viewed as disconcertingly fluid and ambiguous. As gay and lesbian activism increased in the 1980s and 1990s, activists resisted adding "bisexual" to the names of their organizations or to the titles of their conferences. But a 2014 survey of 9000 Americans aged 18–44 reported more men and women identifying as bisexual than in past surveys (Storrs, 2016). This could represent a more positive attitude about bisexuality consistent with the increasing acceptance of sexual orientation. Past studies reported that bisexual people were often stereotyped as sexually promiscuous and that they spread sexually transmitted diseases. Although one study found that bisexuals have high rates of depression, anxiety, and self-harm, including suicide attempts, another study reported that bisexuals who were comfortable with their sexuality had strong feelings of independence, greater self-awareness, and positive relations with others (Pauwels, 2012). Regardless of how LGBT individuals self-identify, all members of their community are still likely to encounter prejudice, discrimination, and even violence based on their sexual orientation.

What examples of violence against LGBT people have been reported?

Sociological studies confirm that individual heterosexism is a major factor promoting one of the most common hate crimes in the United States—**gay bashing**. The term refers to the physical assault of an individual perceived to be gay, but that perception could include anyone in the LGBT community. Although hate crimes appear to be declining for other groups, they remain steady for LGBT individuals. In 2014, 20 percent of single-bias hate crimes targeted LGBT individuals, twice the number of hate crimes against African Americans (Park & Mykhyalyshyn, 2016). Transgender women were as much as three times more likely to encounter physical violence, including police violence, than victims who were not transgender. Further, race makes a difference—nearly one-third of Americans who identify as LGBT are people of color, and LGBT people of color were almost twice as likely to report being victims of hate crimes as White LGBT people (Center for American Progress, 2016; Mitchum, 2013).

One of the most infamous gay bashing incidents occurred on October 7, 1998. Matthew Shepard, a 22-year-old University of Wyoming student, was savagely beaten, tied to a fence in a remote area, and left to die. (See Figure 11.3.) He suffered for 18 hours before he was found. At the hospital, doctors reported that his skull was fractured and there had been brain stem damage. He never regained consciousness and died just six days later. During the trial of the two young men who murdered Shepard, the prosecution argued that the crime resulted in large part because of the victim's sexual orientation. The killers could not be charged with a hate crime because sexual orientation was not included in the federal hate crimes law that had been passed in 1968 following the assassination of Dr. Martin Luther King Jr. That law defined a hate crime as one motivated by the victim's race, religion, or national origin. In response to Matthew Shepard's murder, gay activists and allies began an intense lobbying effort to expand the hate crimes act to include crimes committed because of the victim's sexual orientation, but they encountered resistance from some members of Congress.

Figure 11.3 Matthew Shepard

Matthew Shepard's legacy is not limited to his brutal and tragic murder, but to the expansion of the federal hate crimes law to include those motivated by the victim's sexual orientation and gender identity.

SOURCE: *Photo courtesy of the Matthew Shepard Foundation.*

Although the House of Representatives and the Senate each passed a version of the law over a 12-year period, both bodies could not agree on one version until 2008. The various versions of the bill had been supported by over 300 activist groups, over half of the state attorneys general, and almost all major national law enforcement agencies. As politicians in Washington delayed in taking action, 30 states amended their hate crime laws to include sexual orientation or disability, and 12 states added gender identity (Anti-Defamation League, 2009). Further, polls indicated growing public support. In a 2007 Gallup poll, 68 percent of Americans favored expanding the definition of hate crimes to include sexual orientation and gender identity. A 2007 Hart Research poll reported that even groups often viewed as not sympathetic toward gay causes expressed support for this change to hate crime laws—56 percent of Republican men and 63 percent of evangelical Christians (Human Rights Campaign, 2009). Finally, the House and Senate reached an agreement, and on October 28, 2009, President Barack Obama signed the bill that added sexual orientation, gender identity, and people with a disability to the groups identified under the Hate Crimes Prevention Act.

Although this act will assist law enforcement after a crime has been committed, it has not yet produced a reduction of anti-gay violence. Young men are the primary perpetrators of anti-gay violence, and studies of their motivations have revealed that young men often believe cultural myths about being gay and use them to justify their verbal abuse and physical attacks (Franklin, 2013). This finding suggests that a more effective way to reduce gay bashing is for teachers in K–12 and postsecondary schools to provide accurate information about sexual orientation to refute myths that too many Americans still believe.

What are some myths about being gay?

Myths regarding being gay contribute to individual prejudice and homophobia in the United States (Schlatter & Steinback, 2010). Following are examples of myths still perpetuated in American society about gay men and lesbians, along with refutations based on reality.

MYTH: Anyone who has ever engaged in sexual activity with an individual of the same sex is a gay person.

REALITY: To identify as a gay person means that an individual demonstrates a persistent erotic attraction for people of the same sex. Gay men and lesbians are not attracted to every same-sex individual they see, but when they feel physically and emotionally attracted to someone, that individual is consistently someone of the same sex.

Some people engage in sexual activity with an individual of the same sex one time and never again. Some people only engage in same-sex sexual acts during unusual and temporary circumstances, such as being in situations where there is no easy access to members of the opposite sex (e.g., in prison or in the military). Men or women who engage in sexual acts with a partner of the same sex in an unusual situation generally do not persist in this behavior when circumstances return to the more typical situation and thus should not be identified as gay or lesbian.

MYTH: Gay men tend to engage in criminal activity and are especially likely to prey on children and molest them.

REALITY: Studies of criminal activity report that gay men are no more likely to engage in criminal activity than heterosexual men, and a study of convicted child molesters revealed that 79 percent were White and 77 percent were married or formerly married heterosexuals (Child Molestation Research & Prevention Institute, 2014).

Child molesters are **pedophiles**—adults who desire sexual contact with children. There are heterosexual pedophiles who desire children of the opposite sex and gay pedophiles who desire children of the same sex. As the data show, children are at greater risk from heterosexuals than from gay men and lesbians. Pedophilia has nothing to do with being gay.

MYTH: Gay men and lesbians attempt to seduce vulnerable adolescents and recruit them into their "lifestyle".

REALITY: Individuals who engage in sexual activity with an individual of the same sex during adolescence tend to do so with other adolescents, not adults.

The accusation of corrupting the youth is an ancient one, as we know from the life of Socrates, who was accused of this crime, found guilty, and ordered to drink a poisonous cup of hemlock for his punishment. Because the primary group responsible for gay bashing in the United States is adolescent men, gay men would be risking the possibility of a violent response if they approached adolescents for sexual purposes.

MYTH: Gay men and lesbians do not have loving relationships but are only interested in sex and engage in sexually promiscuous behavior.

REALITY: Until recently, most Americans agreed that same-sex couples did not have the right to marry; they tolerated sexual activities of gay men and lesbians who were discreet but did not sanction their relationships. Today, a slim majority of Americans accept gay marriage.

This myth is especially egregious because American society has created conditions that promote the behavior being condemned. Gay men and lesbians were historically limited to gay bars and bathhouses to engage in sexual activity, and they were not allowed to declare their affection publicly or to have their relationships acknowledged. Americans have long rejected gay men and lesbians seeking public sanction for their relationships by demanding the right to marry or to be recognized in domestic partnerships. Although heterosexuals may engage in public displays of affection, gay men or lesbians have been verbally or physically assaulted for the same behavior.

By contrast, heterosexuals are encouraged to marry and to be monogamous, yet the percentage engaging in premarital sex with many partners has increased, over 20 percent of Americans are currently divorced, and over their lifetimes it is projected that 40–50 percent of married couples in the United States will get divorced (Stanton, 2015). Given such projections, it is hypocritical for heterosexuals to accuse gay men and lesbians of promiscuity and to insist that marriage is sacred and should be reserved exclusively for heterosexual couples. According to psychologists, gay men and lesbians have the same need as heterosexuals for long-term stable relationships. The 2013 U.S. Supreme Court decision declaring the Defense of Marriage Act unconstitutional mandated that gay spouses should receive the same benefits that heterosexual spouses enjoy, and the 2015 *Obergefell v. Hodges* decision affirms the right of gay people to marry and requires all 50 states to recognize gay marriage. Perhaps gay couples may not have more lasting relationships than heterosexual couples, but now they have the opportunity to try.

"If . . . marriage can keep you in touch with your past, your emotional self, and your humanity, the notion that this should be any less true for gay or lesbian couples than it is for heterosexuals is absurd."

—DERRICK BELL (1930–2011)

MYTH: People become gay because they had a bad experience while involved in heterosexual activity; therefore, gay men or lesbians could change their sexual behavior if they had a positive heterosexual experience.

REALITY: Many gay men and lesbians have been involved in heterosexual relationships, including marriage, because of the hostility directed against gay people.

Many gay men and lesbians have engaged in heterosexual activities in an effort to convince themselves that they were "normal" according to societal standards, but sexual orientation is not a choice. Some people still refer to sexual orientation as if lesbians and gay men *prefer* same-sex partners. But human sexuality is not a matter of preference. Evidence from "sexual reorientation" therapies like reparative therapy documents that they have not been successful, and the APA has repudiated them. Yet there are almost 70 therapists in 20 states who still advertise their use of reparative (or "conversion") therapy (Schwartzapfel, 2014).

MYTH: Close personal relationships between adolescents or adults of the same sex could stimulate sexual or romantic feelings and behaviors, so intimate friendships should be avoided, especially between men.

REALITY: It is perfectly normal for a man or a woman to feel and express love and affection for an individual of the same sex as can be readily observed in other cultures.

Displays of affection between men and between women are common in many cultures. In American culture, women are allowed some degree of public intimacy with each other, such as holding hands, dancing together, or even kissing (as long as they don't kiss on the lips). Men are not allowed to engage in similar public behaviors with other men without being perceived as being gay; this creates a burden for American men, who have the same human need for affection and intimacy as women.

MYTH: People become gay because of negative childhood experiences such as being sexually abused or having parents who were not good heterosexual role models.

REALITY: Based on reviews of research, the American Psychiatric Association has stated that there is no evidence that parental deficiency is a cause of being gay. Further, the studies related to sexual abuse report that it is no more prevalent among children who identify as LGBT when they are adolescents or adults than among children who identify as heterosexual during adolescence and when they become adults (Schlatter & Steinback, 2010).

In addition to having no foundation in reality, this myth attempts to demonize parents of gay men and lesbians. It is rooted in the past perception of being gay as a perversion of normal sexual behavior; therefore, it must have been caused by an abuser or by some negative sexual experiences. This myth is also a denial of research conclusions that numerous studies have reported since the Kinsey Report was first published in 1948—that sexual orientation is a diverse human attribute, and that influences shaping sexual orientation are complex, including environmental as well as genetic factors.

Figure 11.4 Advocating for LGBT People

Parents, Families, and Friends of Lesbians and Gays (PFLAG) is an advocacy organization that started when the mother of a gay man participated in a 1972 gay pride march in New York City after her son had been assaulted because of his sexual orientation. Today, PFLAG has a national office in Washington, D.C., with 500 affiliates that promote respect for human differences and the acceptance of all people regardless of sexual orientation or gender identity.

SOURCE: Photo courtesy of PFLAG.

 Video Example 11.2

In this video, Boston Public Schools Counseling & Intervention Center Director Jodie Elgee discusses bullying and LGBTQ youth. What clarification about bullying and LGBTQ youth does she make that relates to public perception? How might her discussion about "normalizing" relate to combating myths about the LGBTQ community in schools?

https://www.youtube.com/watch?v=GMYZgrWu0Yw

Because of myths such as these, it should be easy to understand why most people would be reluctant to identify with such a reviled and persecuted group. Civil rights activists claim that LGBT people encounter more blatant discrimination than any other minority group. In response, LGBT activists have intensified their efforts to promote **LGBT rights**, which means LGBT individuals having the freedom to openly identify their sexual orientation and not be discriminated against with regard to civil rights available to other citizens. (See Figure 11.4.)

☑ **Self-Check 11.2** Complete this self-check quiz to check your understanding of the history of people attracted to same-sex partners in ancient societies up to the present and the evolution of American attitudes toward the LGBT community.

The Impact of Institutional Heterosexism and Recognizing Gay Rights as Human Rights

Although Kinsey suggested that the sexual orientation of approximately 10 percent of Americans is exclusively gay, a National Health Interview Survey reported that 1.8 percent of men identify as gay 1.5 percent of women identify as lesbian, 0.7 percent are bisexual, and 1.1 percent are "something else" (Volokh, 2014). Interestingly, a Gallup poll found Americans estimating a much higher number, believing that as many as one in four Americans identified as gay or lesbian (Morales, 2011). But it is difficult to determine an accurate census of all LGBT people because of the number who deny their sexual identity or conceal it to protect themselves from prejudice and discrimination. **Institutional heterosexism**—established laws, customs, and practices that systematically discriminate against people who are not heterosexual—has been so prevalent and so blatant that LGBT activists have intensified their efforts to promote LGBT rights.

Is the demand for LGBT rights really a demand for special privileges?

The goal of LGBT rights is to make it possible for LGBT people to be honest about their sexual orientation without being deprived of civil rights. These rights do not entail special privileges, but rather the rights of citizens in our democracy. On the most basic level, it is about tolerance: One can support civil rights for LGBT individuals without necessarily condoning their sexual behavior. This means that if LGBT people identify their sexual orientation publicly, they should not be discriminated against when applying for jobs, renting or purchasing a home, running for political office, enlisting in the military, attending their place of worship, or any other situations that heterosexuals take for granted. In much of the United States, LGBT people are often not extended the same civil rights that heterosexuals enjoy unless they are **in the closet**, meaning they deny or disguise their sexual orientation.

As an example of discrimination based only on an assumption that someone was an LGBT individual, one study used pairs of fictional résumés to apply for 100 jobs advertised by federal contractors. One résumé listed the applicant having a leadership role in an LGBT organization, and the other had a leadership role with another cause such as women's rights. The LGBT résumé was made more attractive on such features as grade point average or related work experience. Of the 100 résumés that were sent to eight federal contractors, the LGBT applicants were 23 percent less likely to be called back for an interview (Equal Rights Center, 2014). In 2014, President Obama issued an executive order forbidding federal contractors to engage in employment discrimination based on sexual orientation and gender identity, providing LGBT employees with legal avenues to pursue if a federal contractor discriminates against them.

There is other evidence of discrimination as well. After reviewing multiple studies, Gaille (2017) reported that almost 60 percent of LGBT employees have heard derogatory comments or demeaning jokes about LGBT people at their workplace, and 10 percent reported such comments coming from their supervisor. Over 20 percent of lesbian and gay employees and almost half of transgender employees have experienced discrimination with regard to decisions about hiring, promotion, and salary. About 40 percent of LGBT employees have had their workplace vandalized or have been verbally or physically abused by co-workers, and 97 percent of transgender employees reported experiencing harassment or mistreatment at their workplace. Such experiences could explain why almost one fourth of lesbian and gay employees and almost half of bisexuals have not openly acknowledged their sexual orientation at work. In the 1990s, only one state included gender identity in its nondiscrimination policies, but by 2014, 17 states had revised or passed new nondiscrimination policies that now exist in 21 states, with 19 of them including gender identity as well sexual orientation (see Table 11.2).

Despite these state laws, some small businesses are exempt. For example, several states only require compliance from businesses with at least 15 employees. In addition, there are 29 states where it is still legal for a business to refuse to hire or to be able to fire someone simply for being an LGBT individual. About 200 cities have passed ordinances against LGBT discrimination, and the governors of 11 states that don't include LGBT people in their antidiscrimination laws have issued executive orders forbidding LGBT discrimination (Eidelson, 2014). Yet LGBT discrimination is still taking place; there are numerous examples of gay men and lesbians who were dismissed from jobs not because they were incompetent but because employers discovered their sexual orientation. A Baltimore civil rights advocate told the story of a lesbian manager of a diner who hired a gay dishwasher. When the owner of the diner became aware of the dishwasher's sexual orientation, he told the manager to fire the man because he did not want gay employees on his payroll. The woman enjoyed a good relationship with the owner and had proven her competence as a manager over the past 10 years. She took a chance. She told the owner he already had a gay employee and he was looking at her.

> "Tolerance is the positive and cordial effort to understand another's beliefs, practices, and habits without necessarily sharing or accepting them."
>
> —JOSHUA LIEBMAN (1907–1948)

Table 11.2 States with Nondiscrimination Policies That Include Sexual Orientation

Wisconsin—1982
Massachusetts*—1989
Connecticut*—1991
Hawaii*—1991
New Jersey*—1992
Vermont*—1992
Minnesota*—1993
New Hampshire—1997
Nevada*—1999
Rhode Island*—2001
Maryland*—2001 (added transgender in 2014)
New York*—2002 (added transgender in 2014)
New Mexico*—2003
California*—2003
Illinois*—2005
Maine*—2005
Washington*—2006
Colorado*—2007
Iowa*—2007
Oregon*—2007
Delaware*—2009 (added transgender in 2013)
Utah*—2015

*The asterisks identify those states that include gender identity as well as sexual orientation in their nondiscrimination policies.
SOURCE: Human Rights Campaign (2017).

He fired her. The civil rights advocate said this story was not unusual and that the only way gay men and lesbians could be certain of keeping their jobs was to stay in the closet. And many do, but even then they may still encounter discrimination.

How can LGBT people be discriminated against if they don't reveal their sexual identity?

Some people argue that attitudes have changed so much that it is no longer necessary for LGBT people to be in the closet. For example, a 2014 study found that 81 percent of heterosexual workers believed their LGBT co-workers should not have to conceal their sexual orientation. Yet that same study reported that over half of these heterosexual workers admitted they would be uncomfortable if an LGBT co-worker began to talk about dating experiences at work. The study also found that 25 percent of LGBT people report hearing anti-gay comments at work, so it should not be surprising that the study found over half of the LGBT people they surveyed were in the closet at their workplace (Human Rights Campaign, 2014). If gay men and lesbians are in the closet—not perceived by their employers, supervisors, and co-workers as being gay—it seems logical to assume that they should not experience discrimination, but that assumption is only accurate for blatant discrimination. Subtle forms of discrimination may influence promotion decisions. Lawrimore (2014) discussed a study reporting that being in the closet was a distraction, creating anxiety and social isolation at work. LGBT people in the closet avoided casual conversations and did not socialize after work or on weekends. This social isolation in an effort to protect their identity was a factor for LGBT people being passed over for promotions.

Another form of discrimination based on sexual orientation involves employee benefits. LGBT employees who are in the closet don't receive compensation for their partners that are offered in benefits such as insurance (life, health, and dental), retirement (pension, health care), and leaves (bereavement, family). Heterosexual employees who receive such benefits for their spouses are being paid far more than co-workers who may be in a committed relationship such as a marriage or civil union. The Bureau of Labor Statistics reports that about 30 percent of the compensation employees receive is in benefits (Burns, 2012). Now that the Supreme Court has ruled gay marriage as a constitutional right, it must be accepted in all 50 states, but half of those states had not recognized gay marriages prior to the Court's decision, and there remains strong opposition.

Why are Americans so divided on the issue of gay marriage?

LGBT individuals who desire a state-recognized marriage give reasons similar to those of heterosexuals: to make a public statement about being committed to each other, including the pledge to maintain a monogamous relationship. Rather than being a special privilege, marriage is a decision to participate in a legally and socially sanctioned activity. Church leaders may insist that marriage is a sacred rite reserved exclusively for people in heterosexual relationships, but many gay men and lesbians want to participate in a secular marriage ceremony performed in accordance with state law, not necessarily a religious ceremony. (See Figure 11.5.) To assert that marriage is a legal contract exclusively for heterosexual couples is to engage in discrimination based on sexual orientation. In 2014, the U.S. Supreme Court refused to hear the appeals of five states that had banned gay marriage, thus legalizing gay marriage in 30 states that had tried to prohibit it. Then, in 2015, the U.S. Supreme Court ruled that no state can refuse to recognize gay marriages that have been conducted and sanctioned in other states. The United States joins the ranks of nations around the world accepting same-sex marriage, including the Netherlands (2000), Belgium (2003), Canada and Spain (2005), South Africa (2006), Norway (2008), Sweden (2009), Portugal and Argentina (2010), Denmark, (2012), and 14 additional nations that now include the United States (Pew Research Center, 2017).

According to a UCLA study, much of the opposition to same-sex marriage comes from historic stereotypes about gay men and lesbians—for example, that they are sexually promiscuous—and from a belief in traditional gender roles, including the belief that marriage should be between a man and a woman. Many women, in particular, regard their marital vows as sacred and believe that it demeans what they pledged to their

Video Example 11.3
In this video, PBS NewsHour features a transgender high school student and her school's changing policies. What are some examples of institutional heterosexism discussed in the video? What perspectives advocating for and arguing against LGBT-inclusive policies are discussed in the video and in Chapter 11?

https://www.youtube.com/watch?v=wGtu62lQNfM

"If what we think is right and wrong divides still further the human family, there must be something wrong with what we think is right."
—WILLIAM SLOANE COFFIN (1924–2006)

Figure 11.5 Images from Two Gay Marriages

SOURCE: *Burton Altman (left); Nicholas Perkins (right).*

husbands to have same-sex couples making a similar pledge. Especially for people who call themselves conservative or traditional, opposing same-sex marriage is their attempt to protect the sanctity of their marriage; they literally view the acceptance of same-sex marriage as a threat to their way of life (Wolpert, 2016). Supporting this argument is the belief that same-sex couples do not have the same commitment as heterosexual couples, and that as conflicts emerge, same-sex couples will not try to get through the hard times but will separate or divorce. Further, their actions will contribute to a deterioration within heterosexual marriages where one partner or the other will be tempted to take the easy way out by thinking, "If they can do it, why can't I?" (Carmon, 2015)

In 2015, when the U.S. Supreme Court ruled in favor of same-sex marriage, numerous amicus briefs were filed in opposition to the eventual decision. Anyone who has an interest in a case can file an amicus brief, which is a "friend of the court" document. Arguments in amicus briefs from opponents to same-sex marriage included concerns that more same-sex marriages would result in fewer children being born, which would have an adverse impact on our economy. Another concern: If the court sanctioned same-sex marriage, some K–12 teachers, especially those with children in their classrooms who were being raised by same-sex parents, might present the concept of same-sex marriage as simply an alternative to traditional marriage, which would contradict what some parents were teaching their children, creating confusion and conflict. Another argument was that children being raised by same-sex couples were more likely to be exposed to verbal or physical abuse and sustain psychological damage. Many opponents of same-sex marriage insist that having same-sex parents is potentially harmful to children (Carmon, 2015). These arguments were largely based on assumptions, stereotypes, or prejudice, and they were ineffective in persuading the Supreme Court justices, but the argument about the quality of parenting provided by same-sex couples has been studied, and the results of this research are available.

Are LGBT couples good parents?

Some people claim that it is harmful for a child to be raised by an LGBT couple, but what harms a child is to be abandoned, untouched, unloved, ridiculed, and physically or sexually abused. It is not harmful for a child to be cared for by his or her biological mother or father or to be adopted by caring couples, regardless of their sexual orientation. According to one study, the percentage of Americans rejecting the right of LGBT people to have and care for children has fallen from 50 percent in 2007 to 35 percent in 2011. Over 20 percent of Americans believe gay men and lesbians do a good job raising children, and 40 percent say there is no difference for children raised by a same-sex couple or a heterosexual couple (Pew Research Center, 2013a).

Based on an analysis of multiple sources of data, over 125,000 same-sex couples are raising about 220,000 children in the United States, and 37 percent of LGBT adults have cared for a child at some point in their lives. The children may be a biological child of one parent, a step child, or an adopted child; in addition, the LGBT couple could be foster parents. It is estimated that six million Americans were raised or are being raised by an LGBT parent. Further, almost 40 percent of same-sex couples with children under 18 years old are people of color (Gates, 2013). Regardless of the reason for having children, studies suggest that same-sex couples are conscientious parents.

According to a 2013 report from the American Academy of Pediatrics, three decades of research has found that children raised by same-sex couples are thriving. Several studies report no differences between children raised by same-sex couples and those raised by heterosexual couples. One study of lesbian parents reported that their children had high levels of both social skills and academic competence, and that the children also exhibited fewer social problems such as aggression and breaking rules. In general, the studies found that factors far more significant for children than the sexual orientation of their parents included parental ability to provide social and economic support for the family and the children's relationship with their parents (Perrin & Siegel, 2013). Even before this most recent report, the Child Welfare League and the APA had responded to research on parenting by releasing statements supporting the right of same-sex couples to be parents (Schlatter & Steinback, 2010).

Why have gay men and lesbians always been excluded from military service?

Historic evidence indicates that gay men and lesbians have served in the military in the United States and in other nations. In addition to the Greek Band of Thebes, historic leaders such as Alexander the Great and Richard the Lion-Hearted had male lovers. As Western attitudes became more negative toward gay people, same-sex behavior in the military became more carefully concealed. Activities occasionally were exposed, as in Germany's Eulenberg Affair (1907 to 1909), when accusations of being gay were directed toward officers in the German army, the diplomatic corps, and Kaiser Wilhelm's cabinet (Steakley, 1989). Allegations were well documented, leading to resignations by cabinet members and military officers.

In America, a Navy investigation at Newport Naval Training Station following World War I similarly revealed widespread homosexual activity (Chauncey, 1989). During World War II, the army conducted an investigation of alleged lesbian activity in the Women's Army Corps (WAC) in which a WAC officer testified about a letter she received from the Surgeon General's Office that said "homosexual relationships should be tolerated" as long as they were discreet and did not lead to disruptions in the unit (Bérubé, 1989, p. 384).

Gay service members in the American armed forces is not new, but a new direction was taken in 1981 when the Pentagon instituted a policy banning all gay men and lesbians from the armed forces because the leaders believed that being gay was incompatible with military service. Patriotic gay and lesbian soldiers serving their country could be discharged, not for incompetence or misbehavior, but because they were gay. In 1993, the Clinton Administration modified the policy, forbidding the military to inquire into the sexual orientation of recruits or of those already serving in the armed forces.

The "Don't Ask, Don't Tell" (DADT) policy was intended to discourage attempts to identify and remove gay people from the military. Gay men and lesbians could be silent or they could lie about their sexual identity, but they could still be discharged if their identity was discovered or if they admitted to it. In a study of discharges over a 10-year period after DADT was first implemented (1993–2003), the military discharged over 10,000 service members, including many with critical military skills or other highly important skills such as being fluent in Arabic, Korean, or Farsi. The case for repealing DADT gained strength over the years because of the need for quality recruits. The Pentagon found that 75 percent of young Americans were ineligible for military service because of issues such as weight problems, inadequate education, or having a criminal record (SLDF, 2010). It was becoming increasingly difficult to justify rejecting otherwise qualified soldiers or recruits simply on the basis of their sexual orientation. The repeal of DADT came in the wake of a 2010 CNN poll reporting that 72 percent of Americans supported repealing DADT and a 2009 Gallup poll reporting that support came from 60 percent of people who were "churchgoers" and 58 percent of people identifying as "conservative" (SLDF, 2010).

According to Bumiller (2011), U.S. military leaders asked President Obama to delay the repeal so that they would have time to prepare for the end of DADT by revising regulations and implementing new training programs. Also in anticipation of the end of DADT, the Pentagon began accepting applications from openly gay men and lesbians. Critics of repealing DADT insisted that gay men and lesbians serving openly in the military would adversely affect unit cohesion and military preparedness; however, military

> "You don't have to be straight to be in the military; you just have to shoot straight."
> —BARRY GOLDWATER (1909–1998)

leaders anticipated a smooth transition based on a survey finding that an overwhelming majority of troops already served with someone they knew to be gay or lesbian and were accepting of them. A 2012 report on the consequences of the DADT repeal one year after it was implemented found that there were no negative effects and that the repeal had improved the ability of the military to pursue and complete its missions. There was no significant increase in resignations, no increased problems with anti-gay violence, and no reports of a widespread decline in troop morale. In fact, individual service members were just as likely to re-enlist as they were prior to the DADT repeal, and there has been no impact on either recruitment or retention of service members (Burns & Rothman, 2012).

Many gay men and lesbian service members have expressed positive feelings about being able to serve openly, and some have reported that they are better able to resolve disputes stemming from their sexual orientation. Their primary concern was that their spouses were still not able to enjoy all of the benefits given to their heterosexual peers because the military was limited by the restrictive definition of "spouse" in the Defense of Marriage Act. Same-sex military couples could not be recognized with regard to housing allowances, relocation assistance and other family programs, legal services, and health insurance (Burns & Rothman, 2012). The U.S. Supreme Court's 2013 ruling that the Defense of Marriage Act was unconstitutional allowed the military to implement changes giving gay and lesbian spouses the same benefits as heterosexual spouses (Philpott, 2013). The next challenge for the U.S. military was the issue of transgender soldiers. In 2015, the Pentagon established a working group to determine the best way to lift the ban on transgender soldiers. In July 2016, the military announced a new policy allowing transgender soldiers to serve openly, but in July 2017, newly elected President Donald Trump announced that the military should not accept transgender soldiers. This created enormous controversy, and military leaders said they would proceed slowly in considering the president's directive. In December 2017, the military announced that it would not implement the president's directive but would continue to allow transgender soldiers to serve openly in the military. The response of military leaders to this issue reflects the growing acceptance of LGBT people in a variety of professions, including those like education, where past LGBT educators tended not to be open about their sexual orientation. Today they are encouraged to consider teaching for a career choice.

Why should LGBT people be encouraged to become teachers?

Anti-gay attitudes and behaviors in K–12 schools have declined slightly, but they persist and need to be addressed, especially because studies report that the average age for gay and lesbian youth to identify themselves publicly, called **coming out**, has been declining dramatically. One study found that LGBT youth reported feeling same-sex attractions as young as 8 years old; although the average age for coming out is about 16 years old, many are coming out in middle school (Goodman, 2013). According to a National School Climate Survey of LGBT youth, almost all of them had heard anti-LGBT comments at school, 67.4 percent had heard them frequently, and 85.7 percent heard specific remarks denigrating transgender people. In the past school year, over 85 percent of LGBT students encountered verbal harassment in school, 27 percent of them were physically harassed (e.g., pushed or shoved), and 27 percent were physically assaulted (kicked, punched, or hit with a weapon). In addition, over 56 percent of students heard homophobic remarks from teachers or school staff (GLSEN, 2015). Over 63 percent of LGBT students chose to report an anti-gay incident in school but said that nothing was done in response, and in some cases students were told to ignore it; it is not surprising that over 57 percent of LGBT students who were harassed or assaulted in school did not report the incident. The lack of intervention has negative consequences for LGBT students because the more frequently they were harassed, the more likely it was that their grade point average would decline, and they were twice as likely to say they did not plan to pursue any post-secondary education compared to students experiencing less harassment (GLSEN, 2015). The most effective way to address this problem is for K–12 teachers and school administrators to be more aggressive about ensuring the safety of LGBT students and more committed to hiring LGBT teachers.

Being confronted with such hostility while receiving little support from teachers and staff has consequences. According to the National School Climate Survey, almost 58 percent of LGBT students reported feeling unsafe at school because of their sexual orientation, and these students were three times as likely to have missed school during the month before the survey (GLSEN, 2015). Another 2015 survey of students in all 50 states reported that LGBT students were twice as likely to have been electronically bullied via e-mail, chat rooms, texting, or instant messaging, and LGBT boys were three times as likely to have been cyber-bullied as heterosexual boys. Twice as many LGBT students were physically assaulted on a date as heterosexual students, but the numbers are closer if LGBT students are compared only to heterosexual girls. Faced with such animosity, LGBT students were three times as likely to have considered committing suicide in the previous year compared to heterosexual students, and 30 percent of them had attempted suicide at least once during the previous year (Kann, Olson, & McManus, 2016).

There was some good news from the GLSEN National Survey; LGBT students in schools with an inclusive curriculum (i.e., one that provided accurate historic and current information about LGBT people) are less likely to miss school, are more likely to view their peers as accepting of them, and report a stronger sense of being part of their school community than LGBT students in schools not using an inclusive curriculum. In addition, over 50 percent of schools have a Gay-Straight Alliance (GSA) support group—usually consisting of LGBT students and supportive non-LGBT students. LGBT students who attended schools with a GSA group were more likely to feel safer in school. They were less likely to have heard homophobic comments, they experienced less victimization based on sexual orientation or gender expression, and they were more likely to report that school personnel intervened upon hearing homophobic remarks. Although LGBT students attending a school that enforced an anti-bullying policy addressing sexual orientation and gender identity reported feeling much safer in school, only 10 percent of students said their schools had such policies (GLSEN, 2015). In addition to the value of an inclusive curriculum and GSA support groups, it is important that schools hire not only LGBT teachers but also heterosexual teachers who are comfortable with and supportive of LGBT youth. Such teachers can be role models for students and also can create a more positive learning environment, an outcome that would benefit all students.

> "Good citizens around the world continue to (assert) the simple truth that LGBT rights are human rights."
>
> —BARACK OBAMA (1961–)

 Self-Check 11.3 Complete this self-check quiz to check your understanding of institutional discrimination against LGBT individuals and why the privileges heterosexists believe should be considered for LGBT persons are rights for all people.

Afterword

One of the most important changes needed in the United States is for institutions to establish policies and practices that promote an acceptance of people across the spectrum of sexual orientation so that all LGBT people feel safe at school, at work, and in their neighborhoods. Some LGBT individuals are trying to change the language of hate by using the term **queer** to describe people with diverse gender identities, including those who are gay or lesbian, bisexual, transsexual, and transgender. They argue that the term helps to simplify a discussion of the issues affecting this diverse group. As one gay man said in an interview with the *New York Times*, "When you're trying to describe the community you have to list gays, lesbians, bisexuals, drag queens, transsexuals (post-op and pre), it gets unwieldy. Queer says it all" (Duggan, 2004, p. 59). Although not everyone in the LGBT community agrees about using the term *queer*, on many college campuses scholars have established Queer Studies programs to examine and disseminate information about the history of LGBT people and the contemporary issues they face.

Changing cultural attitudes will take time, but as it becomes more acceptable for individuals to be open about sexual identity, it is more likely that heterosexuals will find that they know an LGBT individual. A national survey by the Pew Research Center (2013b) reported that when people know an LGBT individual, they tend to be less homophobic and to have a more positive attitude about issues related to sexual orientation. Change is possible if conditions are created to allow it. Accepting LGBT people is an ethical challenge confronting all nations, but in the United States, American institutions and individuals have a special responsibility to meet that challenge because of America's longstanding commitment to individual freedom in our society and individual rights.

Summary

- The heterosexual assumption is the conviction that all people are heterosexuals at birth and that being gay is somehow deviant; this belief was prevalent until the 1948 Kinsey Report introduced the concept of sexual orientation.

- Prejudice against people who were sexually different has existed throughout the history of Western cultures, but starting in the nineteenth century, scientists began to explore human sexuality and gain a better understanding of the concept of sexual orientation. The LGBT community encounters attitudes of homophobia, including, in extreme cases, violence such as gay bashing. Although American attitudes are changing toward gay men and lesbians, homophobia persists, as well as prejudice against transgender individuals.

- Institutional discrimination against LGBT people is often blatant if they are open about their sexual identity, but it takes more subtle forms for those who are in the closet.

Terms and Definitions

Bisexual A normative category of sexual identity referring to lifelong sexual desires or erotic relations with members of both genders

Coming out When gay and lesbian youth publicly announce their sexual orientation

Cultural heterosexism The societal promotion of negative beliefs and practices that reinforce dominant culture traits that define heterosexuality as the norm and anything else as deviant and unacceptable; the assumption of superiority of heterosexuals over those who are not heterosexual

Gay A term in reference to homosexuality in general, but specifically to sometimes specifically to gay men.

Gay bashing Physical assault on an individual who is perceived as being gay, which is motivated by the individual's sexual orientation

Greek love The nineteenth-century code phrase invented by boys at British boarding schools to describe their sexual activities with other boys

Heterosexism The systematic oppression and exploitation of bisexuals, lesbians, gay men, and transgender individuals, especially policies and practices reinforcing heterosexuality as the only option for relationships and families

Heterosexual A normative category of sexual identity referring to exclusive lifelong sexual desire and erotic relations with the opposite gender

Heterosexual assumption The assumption that every human being is born a heterosexual

Homophobia The culturally influenced fear and hatred of homosexual individuals, acts, and events

Homosexual A normative moral category of sexual identity referring to exclusive lifelong sexual desire and erotic relations with the same gender

Individual heterosexism Prejudiced attitudes and behavior against others based on the assumption that sexual orientations other than heterosexual are unnatural; this is demonstrated whenever someone responds by saying or doing something degrading or harmful about individuals who are not heterosexual

Institutional heterosexism Established laws, customs, and practices in a society that allow systematic discrimination against people or groups who are not heterosexual

In the closet The concealment of sexual orientation from colleagues, heterosexual friends, or family

LGBT An acronym identifying a group defined by sexual orientation and consisting of lesbians, gay men, bisexuals, and transgender people

LGBT rights The demand that LGBT individuals be able to openly identify their sexual orientation and not be

discriminated against with regard to civil rights available to other citizens

Pedophiles Adults who desire sexual contact with children

Queer Generic term used to refer to people who are gay, lesbian, bisexual, transgender, and transsexual (LGBT)

Sexual orientation The sexual identity of an individual based on lifelong sexual fantasies, desires, and practices

Transgender An individual whose gender identity or gender expression does not conform to concepts conventionally associated with his or her biological gender

Discussion Exercises

Exercise 1 Testing Your Knowledge

Directions: Misconception and myth typically contradict what is actually known about sexual orientation. Decide if each statement below is true or false.

1. Child development studies suggest that an individual's sexual orientation is established at an early age.
2. Gay men and lesbians are attracted to members of the same sex because they psychologically desire to be members of the opposite sex.
3. Most gay men and lesbians report being seduced during middle or high school years, usually by an older adult of the same sex.
4. If they undergo what is called "reparative therapy," gay men and lesbians can re-establish their original heterosexual orientation.
5. Researchers have documented same-sex sexual activity among most species of animals.

6. Beginning in the early 1970s, the APA responded to research findings and removed homosexuality from its list of mental illnesses.
7. The majority of states in the United States maintain "sodomy laws" making it a crime for two people of the same sex to engage in sexual activity.
8. According to studies of men imprisoned for child molestation, heterosexual men are more likely to molest young girls than gay men are to molest young boys.
9. Despite claims about gay bashing, gay men are no more likely to be victims of criminal violence than heterosexual men.
10. Some church denominations have welcomed gay men and lesbians into their congregations and have made public statements denouncing anti-gay discrimination.

Adapted from James T. Sears, *Coming Out of the Classroom Closet*, 1992, Harrington Park Press.

Exercise 2 Integration in the Military

Directions: The statements below represent some original responses to the proposed U.S. military policy of racial integration. Review this chapter's discussion about gay men and lesbians being excluded from military service. As you read the statements below, think about how they reflect some of the current arguments concerning the integration of openly gay men, lesbians, and transgender individuals

into the military. What do you make of the connection between the historical and current responses?

1. The opinion of soldiers: Army studies show that 80 percent of White soldiers oppose racial integration in the armed forces.
2. The opinion of generals: Respected generals such as Dwight David Eisenhower and current military

leaders have been and remain staunchly opposed to racial integration in the armed forces.

3. Objections based on unit cohesion: According to the Secretary of the Army, racial integration would undermine unit cohesion—"Effective comradeship in battle calls for a warm and close personal relationship within a unit"; an Army Report opposing racial integration argued, "The soldier on the battlefield deserves to have, and must have, utmost confidence in his fellow soldiers."

4. Objections based on opposition to using the military for social reforms: As one general has said, "the Army is not out to make any social reforms." It will change its policy on racial integration "when the Nation as a whole changes . . . experiments within the Army in the solution of social problems are fraught with danger to efficiency, discipline and morale."

5. Objections based on privacy: A Georgia senator says racial integration in the armed forces would compromise the privacy rights of the White soldiers—"There is no more intimate relationship known to men than that of enlisted men serving together at the squad level. They eat and sleep together. They use the same facilities . . . They are compelled to stay together in the closest association."

6. Objections based on health concerns: The senator from Georgia went on to say he had statistics "which will show that the incidence of (all venereal diseases) is appallingly higher among Black people than among White people."

7. Objections based on religious beliefs: A congressman from Alabama has argued that racial integration in the armed forces would lower not just the morale but the "morals" of soldiers.

8. Objections based on the will of the majority: The Department of Defense has taken the position that racial integration in the armed forces would erode public confidence in the military—"The Army can under no circumstances adopt a policy which is contrary to the dictates of a majority of people (because) to do so would alienate the people from the Army and lower their morale."

Chapter 12
Ableism: Disability Does Not Mean Inability

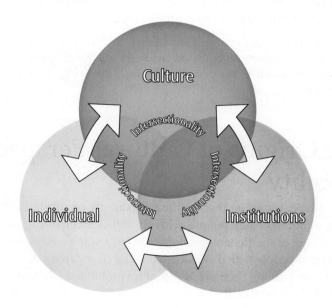

 ## Learning Outcomes

After reading this chapter you will know and be able to:

12.1 Identify and describe historic cultural perspectives of people with disabilities.

12.2 Explain language, labels, and assumptions related to disabilities in terms of their negative impact on the perceptions of people with disabilities.

12.3 Describe the history of the institutionalization of people with disabilities and some of the barriers encountered by people with a disability who are living in a community.

> "All governments treat disabled people badly. They all see us as a burden. All governments, whether capitalist or socialist, have separated us from the rest of society. . . . Until we are businessmen, politicians, community leaders, people at all levels of society, we will be marginalized and segregated."
>
> —JOSHUA MALINGA (CONTEMPORARY)

In 1993, members of the United Nations declared people with disabilities an oppressed minority group. Writers of the UN Human Rights and Disabled Persons Report documented that around the world, people with disabilities were being treated as outcasts and that the situation was getting worse as their numbers increased. The 1995 representatives at the World Summit on Social Development in Copenhagen described people with disabilities as "one of the world's largest minority groups facing poverty and unemployment as well as social and cultural isolation" (Erevelles, 2001, p. 93). Despite the statements of these global organizations, the concept of *ableism* has yet to be accepted by many people, including Americans.

Linton (1998) has provided a definition of **ableism** as the negative determination of an individual's abilities based on his or her disabilities. Ableism promotes the belief that people with disabilities are inferior to able-bodied individuals in order to justify discrimination against them. Linton's definition asserts that people with disabilities are oppressed just as other minority groups are. Filler (2017) agrees:

> Historically and across societies people with disabilities have been stigmatized and excluded from social opportunities (based on) assertions that people with disabilities are biologically defective, less than capable, costly, suffering, or fundamentally inappropriate for social inclusion. (p. 1)

Historic Origins of Cultural Perspectives on Disability

Some disability advocates argue that a primary example of cultural ableism is the ongoing debate about whether people with disabilities constitute an oppressed minority. The passage of the Rehabilitation Act in 1973 was perhaps the first public acknowledgment that people with disabilities could be considered a minority group in need of civil rights protections. Section 504 of that act prohibited discrimination against people with a disability who had appropriate qualifications for jobs in federally funded programs. In 1990, Congress addressed the issue of discrimination against people with a disability by passing the Americans with Disabilities Act (ADA) to provide a legal recourse. Hahn (1994) argued that policies and practices in a democratic society reflected people's attitudes, and that American social attitudes were a major source of problems for people with disabilities. Yet some people still questioned the appropriateness of viewing persons with disabilities as a minority group.

The Fall 2001 issue of the *Journal of Disability Policy Studies* addressed the question of whether people with disabilities could be regarded as an oppressed minority. The contributors agreed that people with disabilities were oppressed, but guest editor Andrew Batavia (2001) strongly disagreed. While acknowledging there were problems in the past, Batavia argued that people with disabilities in the United States lived in conditions "dramatically better" than those in other countries. Regarding the high rate of unemployment for people with disabilities in the United States, Batavia said employers had the right to hire the most qualified individual for a job regardless of disability, implying that applicants with disabilities were often not the most qualified.

Because of the efforts of disability rights advocates and with the passage of the ADA in 1990, Batavia argued that people with disabilities no longer experienced the discrimination that occurred in the past and therefore did not qualify as an "oppressed minority." Apparently Batavia had not reviewed statistics from 10 years after the ADA was passed: A survey of people with disabilities found that the percentage of unemployed adults had increased, as had the percentage of people living in poverty (Wilson & Lewicki-Wilson, 2001). And the problem has continued: With a poverty rate of 29 percent, people with disabilities aged 18–64 are almost twice as likely to live in poverty as people without disabilities (DeNavas-Walt & Proctor, 2014). This denial that discrimination has a significant effect on people with disabilities is unusual only because Batavia was a person with a disability.

Another argument denies that people with disabilities are oppressed because having a disability makes one part of the majority. According to the rationale of this argument, having a disability places an individual on a continuum ranging from mild physical disabilities such as poor eyesight, easily corrected by wearing glasses, to a more severe physical disability requiring the use of a wheelchair. The argument is that whether minimal or severe, almost all of us have a disability in one way or another and must learn to live with the condition. But Gill (1994) argued that to be a person with a disability means the disability has a significant impact on daily life: For example, the disability influences an individual's sense of identity, or others' perceptions of the disability have a significant influence on their reactions to the individual, including the likelihood of negative attitudes of rejection or even discrimination, similar to those experienced by other minority groups. Schroeder (2015) argued that people with disabilities are a minority group "in every legitimate sense of the word" because their lives are restricted by socially constructed barriers that they must overcome to participate fully in our society. Instead of being given their full civil rights, people with a disability are given limited civil rights or conditional civil rights. "People with disabilities are members of a minority group, but it is an orphan minority, a subordinate minority" (p. n/a).

Negative portrayals of people with disabilities in America and derogatory attitudes are not a recent phenomenon. Whether perceived as wicked, violent, or merely foolish, people with physical, emotional, or mental disabilities have been identified consistently as **deviant** because they were not viewed as normal. In the early 1900s, the U.S. Public Health Service categorized people with mental retardation as "defectives" along with criminals and delinquents, later labeling them "mental defectives" to distinguish them from prostitutes, pimps, pickpockets, and paupers. These human beings were frequently placed together in institutions because their perceived deviance from the norm required their removal from communities. The historical record reveals a pattern of **cultural ableism**, images and beliefs perpetuated in society that promote the perception of people with disabilities as deviant or incompetent. Members of the disability community continue to challenge these negative images and beliefs. (See Figure 12.1.)

> "The disability rights approach views disability as a natural phenomenon which occurs in every generation, and always will. It recognizes people with disabilities as a distinct minority group, subject at times to discrimination and segregation . . . but also capable of taking our rightful place in society."
>
> —LAURA HERSHEY (1962–2010)

Figure 12.1 Confronting Stereotypes

To confront negative attitudes toward people with a disability, many states have sponsored pageants since 1972 to select Ms. Wheelchair America; pictured here is Tamika Citchen, Ms. Wheelchair Michigan.

SOURCE: *Ms. Wheelchair Michigan promotional photo.*

What are the historical perceptions of people with disabilities?

Having knowledge about how societies have regarded people with various kinds of disabilities can help us understand not only negative individual attitudes but also why different societies institutionalized people with disabilities. Wolfensberger (1970) was one of the first to identify and describe some of the major historical perceptions of people with disabilities in the following categories.

A subhuman organism. Although other groups (such as African Americans, Native Americans, and Jewish people) were historically regarded as subhuman, the perception is still associated with people with disabilities, especially those labeled "mentally retarded" who have at times been referred to as "vegetables," alluding to medical terminology for performance of vital functions (heart rate, blood pressure) as vegetative functions. Logical thinking and other higher brain activity were assumed impossible for persons with retardation. Even in the last half of the twentieth century, caregivers for institutionalized people with mental disabilities used cattle prods for control. Once we degrade a group to subhuman status, there are few limitations to what can be done. A more recent example of the subhuman perception was articulated in a 2012 article in which two bioethicists argue that organs should be harvested from people with profound disabilities and given to those on organ waiting lists, suggesting that these vulnerable human beings are not worthy of life but are simply a human resource whose organs should be used to help others (Sinnott-Armstrong & Miller, 2012).

Menace to society. This perception regards people with disabilities as evil. It is fostered in children's literature with villains such as Captain Hook and Long John Silver and in fairy tales that portray an array of wicked goblins, giants, and other weird, frightening characters who are ultimately subjugated or eliminated (Fiedler, 1993). Adult literature continues the pattern, portraying people with disabilities as criminal, homicidal, or maladjusted monsters who are often sexual deviants as well. Charles Dickens created a dwarf called Quilp to be the evil villain in pursuit of the innocent Nell in *The Old Curiosity Shop*. Popular literature is often made into popular films, and there are several versions of *The Hunchback of Notre Dame* and *The Phantom of the Opera* to remind us that a person with a disability is a "monster" whose fearful features suggest a distortion of his personality that mirrors a "deformity" of the soul (Winzer, 1997).

Object of dread. The origin of this perception is the medieval myth of the changeling in which people believed that upon the birth of a normal child, evil spirits came in the night and stole the child, replacing it with a defective child such as one who had mental retardation or cerebral palsy. In Grimm's fairy tale "The Elves," a changeling with "fixed staring eyes" is substituted for the original baby. The belief that evil spirits were the source of changelings may have influenced Martin Luther's perception of children with deformity or disability as spawn of Satan, denouncing them as a "mass of flesh" without a soul (Winzer, 1997). Today it is not unusual for mothers to sustain depression and seek therapy after the birth of a child with disabilities. Some conservative Christians believe that a disability is a visible sign of sinfulness. In 2014, a Christian conservative who campaigned for a Congressional seat in Virginia insisted that a child born with a deformity or disability was a punishment from God for a woman having an abortion (Stone, 2014).

Object of pity. This perception may not seem negative because it appears to include compassion for individuals with disabilities, but it is a compassion seldom accompanied by respect. Fundraising campaigns by well-meaning organizations work to arouse pity by using posters of children with disabilities or by featuring the children in telethons to stimulate viewers to make contributions. In the 1990s, surveys conducted in the United

States concluded that more people formed their attitudes about people with disabilities from telethons than from any other source (Charlton, 1998). Because telethons tend to reinforce images of people with disabilities as helpless or dependent, the disability community in America has voiced objections to them; however, Horn (2012) reports that emphasizing pity is still common in fundraising campaigns despite the protests of people with disabilities and disability organizations.

Diseased organism. This perception views an individual's physical or mental disability as a temporary condition that can be cured by chemical or psychological treatments. Ancient Egyptians often regarded disability as a condition for which medical "cures" were prescribed. Egyptian doctors hoped to restore eyesight to blind people by applying a special solution to their eyes. Greek physicians rejected superstition but attempted to identify physiological causes of a disability (Winzer, 1997). In the United States, fund drives soliciting money for research to find medical cures portray people with that disability as having an incurable disease until a cure can be found. Because of such perceptions, people with disabilities have been placed in institutions, punishing them for the crime of having a disability.

Holy innocent/eternal child. This perception is normally identified with one group: people labeled "mentally retarded" (the current term is "person with intellectual disabilities"). Viewed as incapable of sin, the Holy Innocent image can be found in most nations, religions, and cultures. The perception suggests that people with this disability need to be protected and sheltered, isolated from the outside world to perpetuate their innocent, childlike qualities. But encouraging these individuals to maintain childish behaviors rather than learn adult behaviors is a barrier to empowering them to live independently. This perception can become a self-fulfilling prophecy, illustrated in past reports of people diagnosed with "mental retardation" who had been constantly treated as children even during adolescence and who persisted in childlike behaviors as adults, requiring constant care (Wehmeyer, 2000). Today, advocates emphasize the importance of teaching age-appropriate behavior to people with intellectual disabilities.

Object of ridicule. In literature, folk stories, and jokes, people with disabilities are subject to humiliation for the sake of humor. People with intellectual disabilities have been portrayed as village idiots and ridiculed in moron jokes. According to Fiedler (1993), pagan practices of displaying freaks for public entertainment were revived in the Middle Ages by the Catholic Church, which displayed disabled or deformed "monsters" on feast days. In the nineteenth century, carnival side shows with magicians and sword swallowers also featured freaks: giants, dwarves, human skeletons, and other people with physical malformations or disabilities. Legendary showman P. T. Barnum popularized the freak show in the United States by exhibiting Siamese twins, midgets, pinheads, and armless or legless "wonders," now immortalized in wax at the Circus World Museum in Baraboo, Wisconsin. People with deformities are still often perceived as odd, ridiculous, or bizarre—anything but human. (See Figure 12.2.)

Each of these historical perceptions has stigmatized various disabilities and dehumanized people who had them. Today, many disability advocates in the United States are combating such negative images by insisting that people with disabilities are one more cultural group in a culturally diverse society, that these individuals are part of the disability culture and have a unique history shaped by common perceptions of disability, causing their life experiences to be different from those of Americans without disabilities (Brown, 2011). These arguments are supported by an emerging discipline called Disability Studies, a field that did not exist just two decades ago. Students explore disability issues and are taught to think critically about them (Simon, 2013). Further, scholars in this field have identified characteristics that describe what advocates mean when they talk about a disability culture.

Figure 12.2 "The Elephant Man"

In the 1800s, people reacted to Joseph Merrick with dread, pity, and ridicule and as if he were sub-human. But Merrick worked at normal jobs until his tumors made that impossible, and only then did he put himself on display as the "Elephant Man" to earn a living. His story was told with compassion in the 1980 film *The Elephant Man*, nominated for several Academy Awards.

SOURCE: *Royal London Hospital Archives.*

How do scholars describe a disability culture?

Because of past rejection, many people with similar disabilities have come together to support each other in their efforts to achieve the goal of living a normal life that includes a job, a home, a family, and so on. As a result of this collaboration, they have had similar experiences and developed cohesiveness based on common needs and shared aspirations. A traditional concept of culture suggests that a group's historical experience together will create a "pattern of knowledge, skills, behaviors, attitudes and beliefs, as well as material artifacts" (Pai & Adler, 1997, p. 23). Langtree (2017) argues that artists create culture by describing and explaining aspects of a group's experiences, and he notes that over the past several decades, people with a disability who are authors, artists, and performers (comedic and dramatic) have described the experience of having a disability. This is the basis for what has become a disability culture, teaching people with a disability to value their experiences and perspectives; as a consequence, they have emerged from the shadows and are more likely to be acknowledged by people without disabilities. Their increased visibility has produced more self-awareness in the disability community and more awareness in our society.

Reagan (2005) was one of the first to describe components of culture as a way to understand disability culture. He identified four components that must be shared by all members of a culture: (1) historical knowledge and awareness, (2) a common language, (3) awareness of a cultural identity supported by cultural artifacts and identified by distinctive norms and patterns of behavior, and (4) a network of voluntary, in-group social organizations. There is evidence for each of these components in support of a disability culture, but perhaps the clearest example is the deaf culture since it represents both cultural and linguistic diversity.

With regard to the first component, scholars in disability studies have written about the shared historical experience that has shaped the deaf community and individual identities. As Padden and Humphries (1998) noted: "[The] knowledge of Deaf people is not simply a camaraderie with others who have a similar physical condition, but is, like many other cultures . . . historically created and actively transmitted across generations" (p. 2). The issue of transmitting the culture leads to perhaps the most compelling argument for a deaf culture in the United States: the existence of American Sign Language (ASL). In the early 1970s, linguistic research concluded that ASL was a language characterized by its unique grammar and syntax, and that "manual language developed naturally in deaf children similarly to the way oral language developed in hearing children" (Hehir, 2005, p. 21). Deaf children usually become fluent in ASL early in their lives, and information being transmitted by this language is at the center of what is called deaf culture. Many deaf parents advocate that teachers recognize deaf culture and challenge the idea of deafness as a deficit. Deaf advocates argue that hearing students could benefit from learning about historical events affecting the deaf community and issues confronting deaf people today. These arguments are similar to other minority groups who advocate for bilingual/bicultural education for their children.

As for the two remaining components, deaf people often express their sense of a shared cultural identity. Reagan (2005) said a distinctive artifact of deaf culture was the Telecommunications Device for the Deaf (TDD) combined with a Teletypewriter (TTY)—a computer with a keyboard input and printer or display output; other cultural artifacts include closed-caption programming on television and personal devices such as doorbells connected to lights in their homes. These cultural artifacts exist to assist deaf people in functioning effectively in everyday life. In addition to communication devices, ASL includes a rich literary trove of stories, anecdotes, poetry, plays, and humor, and deaf theater has unique conventions for use of choreography and mime (Seligson, 2011). Reagan (2005) has identified cultural patterns among deaf people such as a high rate of endogamous (in-group) marriage and behavioral differences such as establishing eye contact or the acceptability of physical contact. These cultural norms for deaf people have sometimes created misunderstandings similar to what has been experienced by ethnic groups during cross-cultural interactions. As for the fourth component, the deaf community has established numerous social organizations related to sports, theater and the arts, and social clubs, as well as state and national organizations.

Many deaf people and disability advocates are working to remove the stigma historically associated with disabilities. In the United States, they are challenging people to reject the assumption that regards any disability as a deficit and to understand disability as one more example of human diversity. According to the U.S. Bureau of the Census, 19 percent of Americans have some form of disability, which makes it surprising that so many Americans maintain negative attitudes about people with physical or mental disabilities (Brault, 2012). Finding the reasons requires identifying factors that contribute to perpetuating these negative attitudes.

> "Before I was paralyzed, there were 10,000 things I could do. Now there are 9,000. I could dwell on the 1,000 I lost or focus on the 9,000 I have left."
>
> —WALTER MITCHELL (CONTEMPORARY)

 Self-Check 12.1 Complete this self-check quiz to check your understanding of historic cultural perspectives of people with disabilities.

Individual Ableism as an Outcome of Negative Language, Labels, and Assumptions

Negative attitudes are reflected in the language we employ to identify people with disabilities. The word *disabled* implies inability; the prefix *dis* is generally regarded as signifying *not* or *no*. Derived from Latin, the prefix actually means *apart* or *asunder*, which is consistent with the historic practice of keeping people with disabilities apart from society.

People with disabilities are described as being "afflicted with" or a "victim of" a disability. Affliction is associated with disease, as is being a victim, so this language relates to the cultural image of the person with a disability as a diseased organism. Using words or phrases like *crippled, handicapped, impaired*, or *confined to a wheelchair* foster the belief that people with disabilities are incompetent or damaged, not capable of being independent. The term *confined to a wheelchair* is especially absurd. People in wheelchairs are not confined but liberated by them. Wheelchairs provide mobility to people who might be "confined" to their apartment or home if they did not have one. Physical barriers can be identified easily, but it is much more difficult in America today to identify and overcome barriers created by **individual ableism**—prejudiced attitudes and actions toward people with a disability based on our assumptions about them.

What assumptions are made about people with disabilities?

Based on research, Fine and Asch (2000) identified and discussed five erroneous assumptions that are still made today about persons with disabilities:

1. **Disability is a biological problem of a particular individual.** This assumption is related to the medical model of disability. Block (2014) discusses the stereotype of seeing a person with a disability as needing to be cured and lamenting "tragic" cases where there is no cure. This assumption overlooks the influence of prejudices, stereotypes, and discrimination. People with disabilities react to their environmental circumstances. Putnam (2005) commented that the absence of disability accommodations by architects, urban planners, and public officials suggests to people with disabilities that they are not being recognized or included as part of a community. That is a problem not created by their disability but instead by their being omitted from the thoughts and decisions of others.

2. **Any problems for a person with a disability must stem from the disability.** People with disabilities may have health problems like anyone else, but they are not "unhealthy," nor is a disability a cause of disease. If a man with a disability is upset because he feels he has been discriminated against, it is discrimination and not the disability that is the cause of his anger. Being in a wheelchair is not necessarily frustrating, but a woman in a wheelchair may be frustrated when confronted with no curb cuts, no ramps for her to enter a building, or inaccessible restrooms within the building.

3. **A person with a disability is a "victim."** This assumption may suggest a humane and even compassionate attitude, but it is steeped in pity and lacks respect for the person with a disability. Such perceptions relegate people with a disability into something not fully human, which is alienating (Block, 2014). Studies of people with disabilities often report that the participants do not view themselves as victims but are more concerned about how to function effectively in their environment.

4. **Having a disability is central to self-concept and social comparisons for a person with a disability.** Having a disability is usually a factor in shaping an individual's sense of identity, but self-concept refers to how an individual feels about himself or herself. People with a disability will develop their self-concept in ways similar to others who rely on factors such as academic achievement, awards, aesthetic interests, good relationships with others, demonstrating competence at work, and so on. People with a disability who are employed are likely to compare their job performance with that of *all* of their co-workers, not just others with disabilities. A paraplegic woman "may be as likely to compare herself with other women her age, others of her occupation, others of her family, class, race or a host of other people and groups who function as (her) reference group" (Fine & Ash, 2000, p. 334).

5. **Having a disability means a person will need assistance.** This assumption comes from the historical notion of "handicapped people" as helpless and dependent. In the 1930s, people with a disability were classified as "unemployable," preventing them from being considered for jobs in federal and local work relief programs (Longmore, 2003). People with disabilities are not blamed for having a disability, but they are seen as an unending burden, needing the kindness of others to assist them (Block, 2014). Yet people with disabilities are only as dependent as the environment makes them. The blind man on the elevator may ask someone to push the button for the right floor unless the elevator panel has floor numbers in Braille. A hard of hearing woman may have to ask her friend to summarize the speech of a speaker who said, "I have a loud voice; I don't need a microphone." A wheelchair user will have to ask family members or strangers for help getting past a flight of steps if there is no ramp allowing wheelchair access. Because of these assumptions, advocates have had to aggressively demand that people with disabilities be given opportunities to achieve their goals.

For example, a young woman who was born without arms chose to attend a large Midwestern university and enrolled in the nursing program. Although she had an excellent academic record, the nursing faculty was opposed to accepting her based on concerns that she would not be able to perform the physical tasks required of nurses. A campus disability advocate became involved, and a compromise was reached. The young woman would be admitted to the nursing program but not be allowed to take licensure exams. Her primary interest was in the subject matter, so she agreed. After graduation, she engaged in research, wrote and published articles for nursing journals, and eventually became editor of a journal. Nursing faculty had not focused on what the young woman could do, so they had not anticipated this outcome. Instead, the nursing faculty created barriers based on their assumptions, but is it possible to change such negative assumptions? Dollar (2014) described one specific and one general strategy: (1) Lobby higher education institutions preparing students for positions in the medical profession to provide opportunities for interaction with people who have a disability in contexts that are outside of the clinical setting. The goal is for these students-in-training to hear real stories of what it is like to live with a disability and become more focused on people with disabilities as individuals; (2) challenge simplistic and distorted media representations of disability by providing more complex and positive examples of people living with a disability.

What labels represent legitimate ways of identifying people?

In recent years, the label *mentally retarded* has been replaced by the term *"person with intellectual disabilities"*. Most Americans appear to believe that regardless of the label, this condition is a well-defined, scientifically determined, unambiguous way to categorize human beings: It is not. In the early 1900s, people with Down syndrome were considered to have profound retardation; today, it is estimated that 20 percent to 50 percent of people with Down syndrome have a mild disability. In 1952, the American Psychological Association (APA) considered people with IQs of less than 50 as having severe retardation and recommended institutionalization (Adelman, 1996). The current APA categories for intellectual disability include Mild (IQ of 50–70, can learn practical life skills, has social skills, and functions well in everyday life); Moderate (IQ of 35–49, competent at self-care activities, can learn basic health and safety skills, but may have developmental delays); Severe (IQ of 20–34 can learn self-care activities and daily routines but has significant delays in development and requires direct supervision in social situations); Profound (IQ of less than 20, has major developmental delays, needs assistance in self-care activities, requires close supervision, and is not capable of independent living). Further, 85 percent of all people diagnosed as having intellectual disability have a mild disability, and another 10 percent are categorized as moderate (Gluck, 2016).

Another disability that professionals had to reevaluate was cerebral palsy. In 1960, experts assumed that 75 percent of people with cerebral palsy also had an intellectual disability. After some alternative methods of communication and assessment were developed, including adaptations for typewriters and later special computers, assumptions about an intellectual disability diminished significantly (Kliewer & Biklin, 1996). According to the National Institutes of Health (2013), experts now estimate that about 30–50 percent of individuals diagnosed with cerebral palsy may also have an intellectual disability, but in those instances, the vast majority are diagnosed as mild or moderate. These examples demonstrate why disability advocates are concerned about the labels given to people, especially children, and the consequences of such labeling.

What are some current controversies about labeling children?

For many years studies have reported an overrepresentation of children of color among those labeled as needing special education services, and the pattern continues today (Cardichon, 2014). For example, African American children are still the most overrepresented racial group in diagnoses of *intellectual disability* or *emotional disturbance*. In one study, African Americans represented only 14 percent of the K–12 students but constituted 32 percent of students labeled as having an intellectual disability; White students were more likely to be placed in categories that are less stigmatized, such as having attention deficit hyperactivity disorder (ADHD), where they constituted 68.4 percent of students with this label (Colker, 2013). This is an important difference because these labels can affect teacher responses. If a Black child who is energetic and has difficulty sitting still is labeled emotionally disturbed, a teacher's response to that child may be more forceful and perhaps more punitive than his response to a White child labeled as having ADHD.

American Indian children are also overrepresented in being labeled with a disability and placed in special education, and their overrepresentation shows up in data on disciplinary actions. In general, students identified with a disability are twice as likely to be suspended from school and even more likely when they are students of color. According to the U.S. Department of Education (2014), 29 percent of all boys with a disability who were suspended from 2011 to 2012 were American Indians, followed by another 27 percent who were African Americans, compared to only 12 percent who were White. Similarly, 20 percent of all girls with a disability who were suspended were American Indians, and 19 percent were African Americans, compared to only 6 percent of girls who were White. Finally, although students with disabilities made up only 12 percent of the K–12 population, they comprised 75 percent of students subjected to physical restraints, and over half of these students were children of color. This disparity betrays the schools' fundamental purpose of providing a safe and appropriate setting for all students. A school environment should encourage all students to develop their abilities and receive support when needed. When schools reinforce negative attitudes toward students with disabilities, they reinforce the negative perception of people with disabilities as "not able."

How can negative attitudes be changed?

The first step is to use labels that promote positive images. The use of *people with disabilities* began to be widely accepted in the 1970s as a substitute for *the disabled* and *the handicapped*. The term places people first to emphasize the humanity of the group and retains the word "disability" to acknowledge an existing mental or physical problem. Linton (1998) defined **people with disabilities** as referring to "people with behavioral or anatomical characteristics marked as deviant . . . that makes them targets of discrimination" (p. 12).

There is still debate about some alternative terms, but there is agreement on the offensiveness of negative terms such as *impaired, crippled,* and *handicapped*. These words contribute to the perception of people with disabilities as not being able to manage for themselves or contribute to society. According to the World Health Organization, a disability is not a handicap. **Disability** refers to "a restriction of functional ability and activity caused by an impairment (e.g., hearing loss, reduced mobility)," but **handicap** is a reference to "an environmental or attitudinal barrier that limits the opportunity for an individual to participate fully in a role that is normal (depending on age, sex, and social and cultural factors) for that individual" (Bernell, 2003, p. 41).

Imagine a woman in a wheelchair approaching a building. Her legs do not function well enough for her to walk; the wheelchair provides mobility. As she nears the steps of the building, she discovers it has no access ramp. Now she is handicapped. She has found a way to be mobile, but because of the insensitivity or prejudice of the architect and building owners, the lack of a ramp is a barrier that denies her and any wheelchair user access to that building.

> "It is not the fact that [a person] cannot walk that is disabling but that society is organized for walking and not wheelchair-using individuals. [A person's] disability is not paraplegia but steps, pavement kerbs, buses and prejudiced shopkeepers."
>
> —VICTOR FINKELSTEIN (CONTEMPORARY)

 Self-Check 12.2 Complete this self-check quiz to check your understanding of how language, labels, and assumptions related to disabilities have a negative impact on the perceptions of people with disabilities.

Historic Foundations of Contemporary Institutional Ableism

Institutional ableism is a consequence of established laws, customs, and practices that systematically discriminate against people with disabilities. A unique consequence for this minority group has been their placement in institutions, comparable only to nineteenth-century poorhouses for paupers. Poorhouses and poor farms have come and gone; yet institutions for people who have mental or physical disabilities remain.

Why were people with disabilities placed in institutions?

The first institutions charged with caring for people with disabilities were hospices built within monasteries. An early reported example comes in the fourth century: a hospice for the blind at a monastery in Caesarea, now Turkey. According to the legend of St. Nicholas, as bishop of Mya in southwestern Turkey, he provided care for "idiots and imbeciles." For his efforts he was named the patron saint of the "mentally retarded", although that part of his history was lost in his transformation into the American Santa

Video Example 12.1
In this video, special education teachers discuss their perceptions of students and how they view their jobs. Notice how these teachers discuss their students and how they conceive of their jobs. How do the teachers describe their students and their job as special education teachers? What assumptions, negative attitudes, prejudices, and labels about special educations students do they mention?

Claus (Winzer, 1997). As monasteries were built in Europe, many included hospices to care for the poor, the homeless, or people with disabilities. Yet the Catholic Church contributed to negative attitudes toward people with disabilities. St. Augustine refused to allow deaf people to become church members because of his literal interpretation of St. Paul (Romans 10:17): "Faith comes by hearing." These negative attitudes intensified during the Middle Ages when Europe was devastated by plague and pestilence, especially the Black Death; fear fostered hostility toward people exhibiting strange appearances or odd behavior (Barzun, 2000).

In the sixteenth century, the Reformation did not reform the Catholic Church but created an alternative to it, and before long monasteries were abandoned and inhabitants evacuated. Communities were confronted with the problem of people with disabilities and beggars wandering the streets. Not surprisingly, attitudes toward the newly released people became increasingly negative. Laws were passed that vagrants were to be whipped (Ribton-Turner, 1972). By the fifteenth century, the Catholic Church declared a virtual war on witches, which resulted in the arrests, torture, and deaths of people who were considered unusual or deviant. Evidence suggests that people who had mental illness and people with intellectual disabilities were among those serving as scapegoats.

The association with witchcraft often stemmed from these odd people making strange comments. Some citizens believed their mutterings were a dialogue with the devil; others regarded the conversations as divinely inspired. Whether talking to God or the devil, deviants were not tolerated on the streets. Some communities placed vagrants with intellectual disabilities in the old city wall guard towers, which came to be called a "Fool's Tower" or "Idiot's Cage" (Winzer, 1997). In other communities, homeless people were charged with vagrancy, tortured, and expelled, or if they could work, they were forced into slavery (Ribton-Turner, 1972). Reformation leaders John Calvin and Martin Luther did not question the prejudices behind this behavior. Calvin believed Satan possessed people with intellectual disabilities; Luther believed Satan was responsible for fathering children with intellectual disabilities (Winzer, 1997).

When the scourge of leprosy ended as the seventeenth century began, buildings used to quarantine lepers (leprosaria) became vacant. Communities found a solution to their dilemma of what to do with deviants: Europe initiated *the great confinement* to these "lunatic hospitals" (Foucault, 1989). Although initially used to house people with mental illness, the hospitals accepted "mental defectives," including people with physical and mental disabilities, and eventually amassed a wide assortment of "defectives." Before long, only about 10 percent of inmates were considered insane in the average lunatic hospital. Inmates included prostitutes, beggars, alcoholics, social dissidents, and people with syphilis (Winzer, 1997). Whereas hospices had protected people with disabilities from the wickedness of the world, lunatic hospitals protected the world from the wickedness of human beings perceived as morally, mentally, and physically deviant.

These hospitals did not provide treatment to rehabilitate inmates. Their purpose was to remove defective people from society, and the quality of "care" was not good. In England, the Hospital of St. Mary of Bethlehem was referred to as "Bethlehem," which reduced to "Bedlam," coining a word to describe chaotic conditions there. By the nineteenth century, reformers visiting lunatic hospitals were appalled by the horrible conditions: some inmates wandering around naked and shivering, others chained to beds, some sitting in their own excrement, many bitten by rats. Reformers advocated for "moral treatment" of people in the institutions: eliminating chains, giving clients work, and treating clients with respect to develop self-esteem (Foucault, 1989).

Moral treatment involved not defining clients as deviant so much as regarding their defects as conditions requiring accommodations for them to function more effectively. Foucault (1989) told the story of a man with mental illness who refused to eat because he thought he was dead and that dead people did not eat. One night, institutional staff came to the client's bed looking pale, ashen, and dressed in clothing to simulate the look of a corpse. They brought in a table and some food, then sat down and began eating. The client asked why they were eating when they appeared to be dead, and they replied that dead people had to eat like anyone else. They finished their meal and left. The next day the client resumed eating.

Instead of being defined as insurmountable deviance, *disability* gradually came to be regarded as a human condition; institutional staff began to provide accommodations to help individuals to take better care of themselves and to function more effectively with others. Although moral treatment reforms were not universally applied, they constituted a practical alternative to the punitive treatment that had characterized previous institutional practices.

How were institutions for people with disabilities established in the United States?

When the United States entered the global community as a new nation, people with disabilities simply lived in communities and were cared for primarily by their families, and some religious facilities provided assistance. Individual situations varied widely— from having employment to being the town fool or even a pariah whom the family hid from the community. In the nineteenth century, attitudes toward people with disabilities were challenged. Americans no longer viewed people's disabilities as an act of God but instead in a biological context, and rehabilitation was emphasized as the appropriate response.

Following the Civil War, a transformation of public attitudes seemed to be demonstrated by the construction of numerous institutions and residential schools that were often dedicated to a particular kind of disability. Institutionalizing people with disabilities was especially popular in urban areas, indicating a shift in responsibility for care from families and communities to the state. Based on a biological view of human disability, the institutions were usually administered by people with medical training who claimed to use rehabilitative strategies. In reality, the function of institutions was usually custodial care, reflecting society's real attitudes toward people with a disability.

> "Progress, far from consisting in change, depends on retentiveness . . . . Those who cannot remember the past are condemned to repeat it."
> —GEORGE SANTAYANA (1863–1952)

What evidence exists that negative attitudes prevailed in institutions and in society?

The negative attitude toward institutionalized people is documented. A 1913 Wisconsin law institutionalized people with disabilities who were a "menace to society." A similar law passed in Texas stated that people with disabilities mingling in the community was "a most baneful evil" because people with disabilities were "defect(s) . . . [that] wound our citizenry a thousand times more than any plague . . . [they are] a blight on mankind" (Garrett History Brief, 2001, p. 72). With support from the **eugenics** movement after World War I, every state in the United States passed laws to institutionalize people with mental or physical disabilities. Some states authorized removing children with disabilities from their homes, even against the wishes of parents.

Even after most people with disabilities were confined to institutions, continuing prejudice was demonstrated in the 1930s when over 30 states enacted laws permitting involuntary sterilization of people in state-funded institutions. Among the targets were those identified as feeble minded, idiots, morons, and mental defectives. States justified their actions by claiming the need to eradicate the possibility of procreation for people who were such burdens on society (Garrett History Brief, 2001). German Nazis implemented a program of involuntary sterilization that continued until the end of World War II. Forced sterilization of people with disabilities was initially included on the list of Nazi war crimes but was deleted when the United States and others noted that such laws existed in their own nation.

People with disabilities who were institutionalized in the United States were largely ignored until 1972, when appalling conditions at New York's Willowbrook State School were exposed: "one hundred percent of all residents contracted hepatitis within six months of entering the institution . . . . Many lay on dayroom floors (naked) in their own feces" (Linton, 1998, p. 40). The description parallels conditions denounced by "moral treatment" reformers a century earlier, yet 10 years after the Willowbrook scandal, problems persisted in American institutions. Linton (1998) cited a *New York Times* article about a community facility for people with physical and mental disabilities in California that described staff serving spoiled food, not repairing malfunctioning toilets, and physically and sexually abusing clients.

Are institutions for people with disabilities providing good care today?

Although reduced in number, institutions for people with physical and mental disabilities still exist despite the fact that national and state political leaders know they are harmful to the people in them. In Oregon, workers in institutions locked people with a disability in closets, beat them, and punished misbehavior by throwing scalding water at them. In 2012, the National Council on Disability issued a report denouncing such treatment and identifying and censuring the use of other inhumane practices at institutions to restrain people with a disability including employing leather cuffs, helmets, and straitjackets or excessive dosages of sedatives or psychotropic medications. The report described harm to residents, including injuries, unnecessary illnesses, and physical degeneration—and in some instances, the institutional "care" contributed to a resident's death. In Iowa, 13 workers at one institution were fired or resigned in response to allegations that they had humiliated residents or in some cases physically abused them. Eventually criminal charges were filed against six former staff members (Leys, 2017). Perhaps the most egregious example of mistreatment occurred in the state of New York. Nurses caring for a man who was not mobile, could not speak, and required a ventilator discovered that he had maggots growing near a hole in his throat next to his breathing tube. The man was only one of 4169 cases of abuse or neglect reported in 2016 against private and public institutions that were supposed to be regulated by the state (Klepper, 2017).

The National Council on Disability (2012) reported that most states have attempted to eliminate institutions by passing "deinstitutionalization" laws. In 1977, about 54,000 children and youth had been institutionalized because they had been diagnosed with a disability, either developmental or intellectual. By 2008, the total of those who were in institutions had declined by 97 percent to slightly less than 1800 people (Pollack & Bagenstos, 2015). By 2013, states had closed 219 institutions, and Medicaid was providing about three million people with disabilities with community-based services (Ne'eman, 2017). These services were threatened by the Republicans' proposed health care plan to replace the Affordable Care Act (ACA), and hundreds of people with a disability protested at the nation's capitol. For these protestors, living in communities rather than in a nursing home or institution was not an issue of receiving different kinds of care but a civil rights issue. Institutions are regimented with residents denied basic choices such as when and what to eat, when to sleep at night, even the people they associate with. In addition, studies have shown that life skills deteriorate in institutions, whereas people with a disability have improved functional skills when they are in community-placements (Ne'eman, 2017). Advocates for deinstitutionalization emphasized cases such as a 41-year-old man with Down syndrome, released after 20 years in an institution, who began eating solid foods again and walking after spending years in a wheelchair. His caregivers reported that he was shopping in local stores, having meals in restaurants, and socializing with friends (Pollack & Bagenstos, 2015). Unfortunately, when institutions close, residents may not receive a community placement but are relocated to another form of institutional care—nursing homes. Care in nursing homes is reportedly no better, and sometimes worse, than institutional care.

What is the best alternative to placing people with disabilities in institutions?

Instead of being placed in institutions, most people with disabilities prefer to live in family homes or group homes in their communities, but there has been resistance to this approach. A 1996 federal court ruling found that some city zoning ordinances had limited or prevented the establishment of group homes in neighborhoods by including "density laws" restricting the number of "unrelated persons" in a house or the number of group homes in a certain area (Garrett History Brief, 2001, p. 72). Further, it was easier for state governments to place people in nursing homes and institutions. In 1999, the U.S. Supreme Court reviewed research findings and the law and ruled that the ADA required Medicaid to offer community-based options to any person with a disability who preferred to live in a home. As of 2015, there were over 640,000 people on waiting lists for community placement; most of them were people with a disability (Ne'eman, 2017). A final note: It is against federal law to refuse to rent or sell housing in a community to an individual because of a disability, and landlords are required to make reasonable accommodations such as building a ramp for entry into the home or installing grab bars in a bathroom (Castro, 2014). Resistance to placing people with a disability in the community is ironic because community placement is much more cost effective for taxpayers than providing care in nursing homes or institutions.

What is the cost of care for people with disabilities?

Fitfield (2016) reported that the yearly cost of being cared for at a state institution ranged from $129,000 in Arizona to over $600,000 in New York. The Scan Foundation (2013) says nursing home costs average $73,000 to $81,000 a year. Critics say the low cost reflects the minimal services nursing homes provide to residents. By contrast, a national study reported that the average state cost of providing community-based services was around $43,000 (Fitfield, 2016). Whether people with a disability are living in the community, in nursing homes, or in institutions, taxpayers fund over 60 percent of their expenses (Rudowitz, 2016). Several studies report that moving people from institutions into community settings resulted in savings from 5 percent to 27 percent, and the savings today would be higher because the cost of institutional care has continued to increase significantly (National Council on Disability, 2012).

Community settings are more cost effective because institutions have a high fixed cost related to maintaining the facility, and the costs for staff far exceed what is required in the community. Institutions are providing 24-hour care for clients who may need only a few hours of care a day. Further, studies have found that living in a community results in people with a disability reporting positive outcomes such as acquiring new skills, developing existing skills, gaining a feeling of competence in daily living activities, experiencing better health, and having a larger social network and more friends (National Council on Disability, 2012). Reviewing the evidence related to moving people from institutions to community settings, Pollack and Bagenstos (2015) concluded: "Despite inadequate resources and other limitations, the deinstitutionalization of people with intellectual and developmental disabilities has been a quiet triumph" (p. 19).

Advocates for **normalization** oppose confining people with disabilities in institutions. The concept of normalization refers to implementation of policies and practices to help create life conditions and opportunities for people with disabilities that are at least as good as those of average citizens. Strategies are employed to assist people with a disability to live and work in communities, and the concept challenges people without a disability to eliminate barriers that prevent people with a disability from being involved in community life. Based on normalization, disability advocates help people with disabilities move out of institutions and into communities, and they have lobbied for legislation to protect the civil rights of people with disabilities living in communities. (See Figure 12.3.) Despite the clear advantages of community-based services, cuts to the Medicaid budget could still potentially threaten these services.

Another issue concerning advocates for community placement is the availability of caregivers. In 2014, workers providing direct care to people with disabilities in residential or community settings were paid an average salary of less than $12 an hour. These direct-care workers tried to organize unions to address this issue, but the decision by the U.S. Supreme Court in *Harris v. Quinn* did not support their efforts to collectively bargain for better wages and improved working conditions. The low salaries contribute to a high turnover rate for employees and low morale (Pollack & Bagenstos, 2015). According to a 2014 study, six out of 10 home-care workers leave their job every year. One reason for this turnover rate was that median annual salary for these workers is less than $21,000, which keeps a family of three barely above the poverty line. This annual salary is far less than the median annual salary of $35,000 for all occupations in the United States. Because of their inadequate compensation, almost half of home-care workers received some form of public assistance such as food stamps or Medicaid. Further, there is a gender and race component to this underpaid group of workers: Approximately 90 percent are women, and almost half are people of color (Rogers, 2015). Disability activists have been lobbying state and federal governments to address this problem.

How does the United States support people with disabilities who want to live independently?

In 1973, the Supplemental Security Income (SSI) program was created to assist people with disabilities. The means-tested program offers a range of $400 to $700 per month, but recipients must remain without other means of support to receive SSI funds. If recipients make extra money, they are likely to lose the benefit. Individuals with a disability

Figure 12.3 A Disability Protest

Today people with a disability are just as likely to protest discrimination and demand their rights as any other minority group.

SOURCE: *Tom Olin*

receiving SSI support cannot have more than $2000 in assets, a figure unchanged since the program was initiated. If this asset limit had been modified to account for inflation, the amount of assets today would be over $8500 (Vallas & Fremstad, 2014). In 2014, Congress finally addressed this problem by passing the Achieving a Better Life Experience (ABLE) Act. The new law increases the assets an individual can amass to $100,000 in a special account (similar to college savings accounts), and the money can be used for education, transportation, housing, health care, or other necessary expenses (Diament, 2014b).

In recent years there have been news stories about the abuse of programs supporting people with a disability. The allegation is that increasing numbers of people living in poverty are applying for disability payments instead of welfare to avoid welfare's work requirements. Since welfare payments are given overwhelmingly to young single mothers, this should mean that the numbers of young single mothers receiving disability payments have increased significantly. Yet a recent study of disability benefits found no significant increase in benefits being paid to young single women (deMause, 2013). The reality is that it is quite difficult for Americans to qualify for and receive financial support for having a disability. A review of disability benefits in over 30 nations found that the United States is one of the most restrictive and least generous nations in providing disability benefits (Vallas, 2013). Less than 40 percent of American applicants are approved to be recipients, and many of the 60 percent being denied have significant disabilities or illnesses. Even after an applicant is approved, his or her status is reviewed every three years to determine if he or she is still eligible or if the assistance should be reduced or stopped (deMause, 2013). As an indication of how serious an individual's condition must be to receive disability benefits, of those Americans who are approved, 20 percent of the men and 17 percent of the women die within five years of being recipients of financial support (Vallas, 2013).

What are some examples of discrimination against people with disabilities living in communities?

People with disabilities fortunate enough not to be institutionalized encounter various forms of discrimination in the community. First, the poverty rate for people with a disability is almost two and a half times higher than that of people without a disability. According to Vallas and Fremstad (2014), half of working-age adults living below the poverty line have a disability, and two thirds of adults coping with long-term poverty have a disability. Many people with a disability living in a community struggle with food insecurity and have difficulty paying rent or utilities or getting health care. They are twice as likely not to have even modest savings to deal with unexpected expenses. In one study, 70 percent of people with a disability said they were not likely to be able to procure as little as $2000 for an emergency compared to 37 percent of individuals without a disability. There are four areas where discrimination has a significant impact on people with a disability: jobs, mobility/accessibility, health care, and education.

Jobs. Just as women worked in traditionally male jobs during World War II because of the shortage of male workers, people with disabilities also experienced increased employment during the war. And similar to women workers, unemployment rates for people with disabilities increased after the war as jobs were given to returning soldiers. The work performance of people with disabilities during the war proved that they wanted jobs and could competently perform their tasks, but this lesson was lost on employers: People with disabilities continue to be discriminated against in hiring decisions. Critics argue that employers don't want to make expensive accommodations for a worker with a disability, but the reality is that two thirds of accommodations cost less than $500, and many can be done at no cost (U.S. Department of Labor, 2014). Repa (2017) provides several examples, such as when a worker complained that the glare from the computer screen caused fatigue, the employer purchased an antiglare screen

Video Example 12.2
This video features a vocational training program for students with cognitive delays and multiple handicaps. What kinds of strategies does this program employ to help serve these students' needs? And how might these experiences help students live more independently in the future?

for $39. When the desk assigned to a wheelchair user was too low for the individual's knees to go under it, wooden blocks were put under the desk legs to raise it up to an appropriate level at no cost.

A survey by the Kessler Foundation (2015) reported that 68.4 percent of working-age adults with a disability want to work rather than rely on SSI benefits, but in 2016, only 35 percent were employed compared to 76 percent for people without disabilities, a gap that has steadily increased for the past eight years. In addition, the median income for workers with a disability was a little more than $21,500 compared to almost $32,000 for people without a disability (Kraus, 2017). About one-third of Americans with disabilities who have a job are employed in sheltered workshops (Kardish, 2015), which are allowed to pay less than the minimum wage. At one Tennessee workshop, the 70–80 employees only earned $25 to $100 a week (Nelson, 2017). To reduce the number of people with disabilities employed in sheltered workshops, Congress passed a law in 2014 increasing federal funding for programs that assist people with a disability with getting a job in a regular workplace and requiring people with a disability who are younger than 25 to sign up for these vocational rehabilitation services (and other resources) before they could apply for a job paying less than the minimum wage (Diament, 2014a).

Although the 1990 ADA was supposed to reduce discrimination against people with a disability, problems persist. In 2014, the Equal Employment Opportunity Commission (EEOC, 2014) reported that in the previous year, people with a disability had filed 25,957 discrimination complaints, and 10.2 percent were resolved with monetary compensation of over $109 million. Charges of discrimination because of a disability are second only to complaints of race discrimination. The most common complaint concerned being fired for having a disability (58.4 percent), and the next most frequent complaint concerned the employer's refusal to make reasonable accommodations (28.2 percent). About 42 percent of unemployed people with a disability say that employers are not willing to provide the accommodations needed to perform the job successfully (Orkis, 2010). More corporations and businesses should look at the example of Walgreens, which established a goal of filling 20 percent of the jobs at its distribution centers with workers who have a disability. Over 40 percent of the workers at its distribution center in South Carolina are people with a disability (DeRose, 2012). A workplace study reported that the performance of these workers with a disability was at the same level as their peers without disabilities, the distribution centers had better retention of employees and less turnover, and the workplace culture was improved. According to the study, 99 percent of workers with a disability met or exceeded productivity requirements (Smith, 2014).

> "I am not broken! I am not broken! I am a representative of the diversity of the human race."
>
> —NORMAN KUNC (1957–)

In a case illustrating discrimination complaints, an employee who had worked for over 24 years and had been promoted to store manager was diagnosed with a disability that would not affect her performance at work. Her supervisors began to treat her differently, and in a few months she was fired. She filed a discrimination complaint charging retaliation for complaining of discrimination and harassment. The jury agreed, awarding her $3,500,000 (Greenwald, 2012). In another case, a man with bipolar disorder who had been open about his disability before he was hired worked successfully for six months and received an achievement award before asking for time off to deal with problems related to his disability. His request was rejected, and soon after he was fired. In response to his discrimination complaint, the employer gave other reasons for firing him, but the District Court judge said the reasons were obviously a pretext and the bipolar disorder was the real reason. The employer was fined $6500 in back pay and $50,000 for emotional pain and suffering (Ellin, 2012). Given this kind of discrimination, it is obvious why half of the working-age adults living in poverty are people with a disability (Vallas & Fremstad, 2014).

Mobility/accessibility. According to a national survey, people with a disability are less likely than people without a disability to engage in community activities such as socializing with others or attending church services, and far less likely to go out to a restaurant (Taylor, Krane, & Orkis, 2010). In another study, people with a disability said lack of accessible public transportation was a major problem, and one interviewee described long waits at transfer stops requiring two hours to travel only nine miles to get to work (Vallas & Fremstad, 2014). The ability of people in wheelchairs to function effectively in the community is dramatically affected by the existence of wheelchair lifts on public buses, elevators, curb cuts, and ramps; yet even buildings with ramps are not necessarily accessible. Many ramps are too narrow or too steep, or they lack handrails. Theaters, sports facilities, and other public settings may provide space for wheelchairs segregated from the other seats so wheelchair users can't be with colleagues or friends. Wheelchair users do not insist on special consideration, but they do want the same opportunities as other people (see Figure 12.4).

Accessibility problems can also impede a citizen with a disability's right to vote. Although the Voting Accessibility for Elderly and Handicapped Act of 1984 mandated accessible voting facilities, there are still polling places that interfere with a citizen with a disability's right to vote. In a national survey, 10 percent of people with a disability said they had problems getting to the polling place or getting inside the building. A federal study found that 73 percent of polling places had one or more potential impediments that might limit access by an individual with a disability (Schur, 2013). The Census Bureau reports that about 57 million Americans have a disability, representing about 19 percent of Americans (Brault, 2012), but a recent study said they were less likely to vote than citizens without a disability, and that if they voted at the same rate as Americans without disabilities, they would be casting three million more votes (Schur, 2013). About 25 percent of people with a disability have expressed a preference for voting with absentee ballots to avoid voting difficulties. But 21 states require the voter to give an excuse for requesting an absentee ballot; many people with a disability are reluctant to identify their disability on a public form because of the stigma associated with disabilities. In places where no excuse is required or where there are policies for people to receive an absentee ballot for each election with no excuse required, officials have reported significantly higher voter turnout for individuals with or without a disability (Schur, 2013).

Although the passage of the ADA required public buildings to be accessible, most are still not, and the ADA did not require accessibility for nonpublic buildings. A concept promoting accessibility to all buildings is termed "visitability"; advocates encourage the construction of homes, businesses, and non-public buildings to accommodate people with disabilities. The primary accommodations required are level entryways, wide doorways, and an accessible bathroom. This concept not only benefits people with disabilities but their family, friends, and neighbors. This idea was proposed three decades ago when Ron Mace introduced the **universal design** concept in 1985, advocating

---

Figure 12.4 An Inclusive Comic Strip

In the 1980s, Berke Breathed's "Bloom County" was one of the first comic strips to feature a character using a wheelchair.

SOURCE: *Bloom County used with the permission of Berkeley Breathed and the Cartoonist Group. All rights reserved.*

creation of products capable of being used by all people and constructing environments that are accessible to everyone. A ramp instead of steps leading to the entrance of a building provides access for people with disabilities but also makes access easier for parents with baby strollers or workers carrying heavy items. Some communities have promoted visitability, and in 2014, the Austin (TX) City Council approved changes in its building code to require that all designs be "disabled accessible" (Krupa, 2014).

Health care. According to Krahn, Walker, and Correa-De-Araujo (2015), adults with disabilities are more likely than adults without a disability to report their health as "fair" or "poor." Yet a national health organization reported that people with disabilities were more likely than people without a disability to encounter difficulties or delays in getting standard care. For example, they were more likely to say that in the past three years they had not visited their dentist, not engaged in fitness activities, and had high blood pressure rates. Not surprisingly, they were also more likely to report symptoms of psychological distress. Factors contributing to the health care disparities between people with a disability and Americans without a disability included physical barriers (e.g., inaccessible diagnostic equipment such as examination tables), health programs that excluded people with a disability, transportation problems, and stigmatizing attitudes from clinical staff (Peacock, Iezzoni, & Harkin, 2015). Many Americans reject these claims of health care disparities by saying either (1) having a disability makes it more likely that an individual is in poor health, or (2) the individual was already in poor health and the "disability" was a consequence of that. Yet the reality is that with the use of preventative services (e.g., blood pressure checks or mammograms), many of the health problems experienced by people with a disability are preventable, just as they are for people without a disability (Krahn, Walker, & Correa-De-Araujo, 2015). Yet Barnett and Vornovitsky (2016) found that adults with a disability were less likely than their peers without a disability to receive preventative care.

In response to these disparities, Congress included provisions in the ACA to prevent insurers from rejecting applicants because of a disability, to establish caps on the amount of money people with a disability would personally have to pay for health care, and to separate health care from employment since a high percentage of people with a disability are unemployed. Another ACA provision provided federal funding for training health care professionals in specific competencies related to disability culture (Peacock, Iezzoni, & Harkin, 2015). The ACA expanded eligibility for low-income Americans, but this benefit is only available in those states that have agreed to implement the Medicaid expansion and accepted federal funding. Despite talk of "repeal and replace," the ACA is still in effect, but Congress needs to make further changes if it is to be an effective means of addressing America's health care needs.

Access to Medicaid is essential for people with disabilities who need services and equipment not provided by private insurance. Medicaid is the primary provider of health care for more than nine million people under age 65 who have disabilities (Institute on Disability, 2014). Social Security's regulations concerning employment for people with a disability penalizes workers who earn too much money. Such penalties can include losing health care benefits. Even without the threat of a penalty, if workers with a disability are covered by the employer's health care plan, they can lose their federally funded medical benefits. If a person with a disability loses his or her job, it often takes up to two years to be approved for federally funded health care. Fearful of losing their health care benefits, many people with a disability who would prefer to have a job do not seek employment (Ellis, 2016).

Education. Since the United States began, children with disabilities were kept at home or sent to segregated institutions. From 1930 to 1960, the number of children and youth with a disability increased significantly. By the 1950s, public schools were creating special education programs for these students, and from 1948 to 1956, schools providing such programs increased by 83 percent (Osgood, 2005). Even so, the assumption persisted that a segregated setting was the best way to teach these students. In the 1960s, researchers coined the term "learning disability," identifying various conditions that interfered with a child's ability to learn. Following several court decisions and passing of state legislation, the federal government passed the Education for All Handicapped Children Act (EAHC) in 1974, requiring public schools to educate students with a disability in the "least restrictive environment." More than a million children with a disability were being excluded from public schools; many were in institutions. The EAHC did not use the term **mainstreaming**, but the idea that students with disabilities should be educated in the least restrictive and most acceptable environment was now the goal. By 2013, 90 percent fewer children with developmental disabilities were in institutions or otherwise excluded from public schools (Colker, 2013).

The problem was that the concept of mainstreaming had different meanings for different people, including parents, teachers, and administrators. Some viewed it as promoting the placement of students with disabilities into regular classes with support services to help them become academically successful; others argued that the "least restrictive environment" for academic achievement was occasionally a regular classroom but often a special education classroom where special accommodations could be made (Osgood, 2005). Research studies tended to support the position of disability advocates, who insisted that students with physical and mental disabilities learned more when they were integrated into regular classes than when they were taught in separate classes (Hines, 2001; Kochhar, West, & Taymans, 2000). Yet the pace of change was slow. A Massachusetts report quoted a student with a disability newly graduated from high school who said he and his peers felt unprepared because "a segregated environment just will not do as preparation for an integrated life" (Osgood, 2005, p. 162).

The U.S. Supreme Court's (1988) *Honig v. Doe* decision affirmed the rights of students with an emotional disability. In two separate incidents, students with emotional disabilities had been suspended from the San Francisco Unified School District (SFUSD) for disruptive and violent behavior, and eventually they were expelled. The parents sued on the basis of a provision in the 1974 EAHC Act that stated schools could not change a student's placement without the parents' consent. State School Superintendent Bill Honig justified his actions by arguing that both students represented a danger to others, but the court sided with the parents since the nature of each student's emotional disturbance made them prone to exactly the kind of violent and disruptive behavior that resulted in their expulsion.

In 1990, the EAHC was renamed the Individuals with Disabilities Education Act (IDEA), and legislators included a provision that a student could be suspended for up to 45 days for coming to school or a school function with a weapon or with drugs, or if he or she physically assaulted someone. Despite these exceptions, IDEA continued to reinforce the rights of all students, even those who are emotionally disturbed, to have a "free and appropriate public education" (Whitted, Cleary, & Takiff, 2011), but the *Honig v. Doe* decision was a major factor encouraging parents and advocates for students with disabilities to become more assertive in promoting their vision of an "appropriate" education for these students.

In the 1990s, disability advocates began arguing for the merger of regular education and special education both in schools and in teacher preparation programs. They had abandoned mainstreaming to lobby for **inclusion**—a total integration of students with disabilities in regular education classrooms. Advocates insisted that inclusion would benefit all students, and they were assisted by a series of court decisions ruling in favor of families with children with a disability that ordered schools to adapt regular classrooms to meet the needs of students with a disability (Osgood, 2005). Despite these rulings, the debate has continued. Opponents argue that most students with a disability are uncomfortable in regular classrooms because of the negative attitudes and reactions (i.e., teasing) from students without a disability, and that the students with special needs demand too much time from teachers at the expense of the other

Video Example 12.3

In this video, speakers discuss a brief history of special education and inclusion in education. What have been the key movements in that history that the speakers mention? One of the speakers discusses the benefits of inclusion for special education students. What are some of the benefits of inclusion discussed in Chapter 12? And what are some of the challenges of inclusion discussed in Chapter 12?

students (API Healthline, 2012). Mihail (2014) reports that research has consistently described benefits of inclusion for all students when it is implemented competently. To do so requires teachers to utilize aides, peers, and classroom strategies to ensure that all students receive appropriate educational experiences.

Despite these arguments, the reality is that major problems remain for students with a disability. An ongoing and troubling issue is that although students with a disability represent less than 12 percent of all K–12 students, they account for almost 25 percent of school suspensions (General Accounting Office, 2018). This is particularly a problem for students diagnosed with mental health issues. Another persistent problem is the low graduation rate. In 2014, the national graduation rate was 82.3 percent, but that figure dropped to less than 70 percent in most states for students with disabilities, and in seven states it was less than 50 percent. A recent report stated that almost 90 percent of students with disabilities were capable of graduating from high school if given appropriate academic support (Diament, 2016). In addition to academic concerns, a 2010 report from the Office of Government Accountability found that students with a disability participated far less in athletics than their peers without disabilities.

Analyzing School Curricula Regarding Portrayals of People with a Disability

1. Absence of people with a disability

Inclusion is an issue for all minority groups in fiction and nonfiction texts. The omission of any group suggests that they are not part of the diverse human family. This is especially important for people whose disabilities aren't obvious (visible).

2. Use of stereotypes to represent people with a disability

In the text or in illustrations, people with a disability may be portrayed with stereotypical attributes such as being helpless, childlike, or with little emotional range (e.g., always happy). People with disabilities should be portrayed as people with diverse personalities, and when they are included, they should be one of the main characters in some books rather than always being minor characters.

3. Content that promotes ableism

Curricula may intentionally or unintentionally reinforce negative cultural attitudes and actions toward people with a disability. Are the problems faced by a character with a disability (CWD) presented as personal challenges to be overcome, or do the problems stem from societal prejudice and discrimination against people with a disability? Is the CWD presented as a resourceful problem solver (for self or others), or are the problems of a CWD resolved through the intervention of a character without a disability? Does a person with a disability have to be an extraordinary individual (i.e., "supercrip") to be accepted or admired?

4. Use of words with negative messages about disability

Derogatory views of people with disabilities are promoted by the use of loaded words such as *lame, suffer from, confined to a wheelchair (or wheelchair-bound), victim,* and, of course, *crippled,* and also by culturally derisive phrases such as *blind as a bat, deaf as a post, lame joke, blind drunk,* and *idiot proof.* If such words are included, teachers should use them as a "teachable moment" and have students analyze the negative perceptions such language promotes.

5. People with disabilities presented in passive roles

Every person with a disability should not be presented as heroic since that would simply be a positive stereotype and not a realistic portrayal; nevertheless, people with a disability should be portrayed as often as possible as people who play a significant role in the development of a story. They should be rescuers as well as rescued, leaders as well as supporters, problem solvers as well as people with problems. People with disabilities encounter many problems in daily life related to transportation, housing, education, employment, and self-determination, so it is important for students to be provided with realistic accounts of such problems. It is also important that people with disabilities are shown responding actively to their problems whether they are able to resolve them or not, including their efforts to reach out to allies to work with them in solving problems as opposed to simply being "rescued" by others.

NOTE: In reviewing curricular materials, make sure the text includes "People First" language (e.g., using "people with epilepsy" instead of "an epileptic"; and always check the copyright dates of books and curricular materials because portrayals of people with disabilities have improved significantly in more recent publications.

Adapted from: Myers, C., & Bersani, H. Jr. (2008–2009). Ten Quick Ways to Analyze Children's Books for Ableism. *Rethinking Schools, 23*(2), 52–54.

In response, the Department of Education disseminated a letter in 2013 informing K–12 school administrators that they should make reasonable accommodations to ensure that students with a disability have an equal opportunity to participate in sports. If a deaf student has the ability to be a competitive runner, the school should provide a visual symbol (e.g., a flag) to signal the start of the race. If there aren't enough wheelchair users among students to field a basketball team, a school could team with another school to offer this opportunity. The American Association of Adapted Sports Program has already helped numerous schools cooperate to form teams for wheelchair basketball and handball (Gregory, 2013). As of 2014, 12 states offered sports to accommodate students with a disability. Golf for girls with disabilities was initially offered at two schools and has expanded to 18 schools. One sports advocate said the goal was to get 30 schools involved in accommodating students with disabilities, but 106 schools are participating (Haddix, 2014).

Finally, multiple studies report that children are curious and interested in human differences and that they do not demonstrate a fear of differences unless they are taught to do so (Coleman, 2006). According to Stephens (2007), children initially respond to faces and similarities (i.e., two eyes, one nose), but by ages three or four they begin to notice differences. They are so curious and honest that their observations can create awkward situations, but the solution is not to teach them to ignore human differences. Classrooms with diverse students can benefit all students by confronting stereotypes and stigmatizing labels, and the presence of students with disabilities can benefit other students by providing opportunities to develop attitudes and skills that will enable them to work with people who may be different from themselves (Tirrell-Corbin, 2017). For these reasons, disability advocates believe that inclusion is the best strategy to improve attitudes toward people with disabilities.

How difficult is it to change people's attitudes?

As Fiedler (2008) wrote, "Perhaps the greatest obstacle to school change efforts is the attitudes of the individuals who must implement the change" (p. 258). The effectiveness of school change efforts has varied according to the attitudes of teachers and administrators; this is true for community change efforts as well. Posner (1979) described an incident from Israel illustrating the difficulty of changing attitudes. Two villages did not have enough orange pickers at harvest time, so they arranged for young men at an institution for people with intellectual disabilities to help with the harvest. Before the young men arrived, researchers came to the villages and conducted an attitude survey. The researchers reported that 66 percent of villagers said there should be no contact between people with intellectual disabilities and children; 68 percent thought people with intellectual disabilities should be permitted to work only in sheltered workshops; 95 percent said institutions were the best place for people with an intellectual disability; and 58 percent believed that people with an intellectual disability should be forbidden to marry.

When the workers with intellectual disabilities came, they picked oranges with great care and an enthusiasm not often displayed by other workers. All workers were told that if fallen oranges had not been bruised, they could be used; only men with intellectual disabilities inspected oranges that had fallen or been dropped. They also climbed to the tops of ladders to pick oranges from high branches; no other workers were willing to climb so high. As the days passed, townspeople invited the workers to join them for lunch, and the men with intellectual disabilities played with the children from the village. When the harvest was over, the young men returned to their institution.

The researchers returned to conduct a second attitude survey to see if changes had occurred in the attitudes of village residents. They found that the same 66 percent still believed there should be no contact between people with an intellectual disability and children; the same 68 percent still thought people with intellectual disabilities

Video Example 12.4

This video features a tour of an inclusive school. Pay attention to the rhetoric that Principal Jackson uses when talking about her students. What assumptions about disabilities does she refer to? And what adaptations for students in and around the school does she discuss?

Application Exercise 12.1

This video features an inclusive classroom. Pay attention to the role that the peer students play in the inclusive strategies in this classroom. Also, notice the goals of the inclusive classroom and how they relate to changing attitudes about ableism and disability. Review the video and complete the activity.

"But in the ideal world, my differences, though noted, would not be devalued. Nor would I. Society would accept my experience as 'disability culture,' which would in turn be accepted as part of 'human diversity.' . . . In such a world, no one would mind being called Disabled."

—CAROL GILL (CONTEMPORARY)

should not work alongside others; the same 95 percent said people with an intellectual disability should be in institutions; and the same 58 percent believed people with an intellectual disability should not marry. But please, all the villagers asked, will you make sure they send those nice young men back again next year?

> ✓ **Self-Check 12.3** Complete this self-check quiz to check your understanding of the history of the institutionalization of people with disabilities and some of the barriers encountered by people with a disability who are living in a community.

Afterword

Attitudes are resistant to change: Change occurs when people examine their attitudes for myths, misperceptions, or stereotypes. It is especially important for aspiring teachers to reflect on their attitudes because all of them will teach children or youth with disabilities. Assessing personal attitudes is appropriate for others as well: It is important for employers who have the choice of hiring a person with a disability and for employees who may work with that individual. Cornell University reports that 12.6 percent of people living in the United States have a disability (Yang & Tan, 2016), and those who do not have a disability should acknowledge the possibility that anyone can acquire a disability as a consequence of an accident or an unexpected health problem. With that in mind, we should all be committed to having a just society that provides opportunities for people with disabilities to live full, engaging, and productive lives. We should advocate for a society that provides opportunities for education and employment for those with disabilities rather than creating obstacles for them. Working together as allies, we could be a force for change that has a positive impact on our communities and the people with disabilities who live in them.

Summary

- There has been a history of negative perceptions of people with a disability in Western culture that continues to influence Americans today.

- The use of certain terms and labels and the belief in negative assumptions about people with disabilities has contributed to negative perceptions of them.

- The previous institutionalization of people with disabilities was a consequence of historic prejudices, and although people with disabilities are more likely to live in a community today, they still encounter barriers that negatively affect their lives.

Terms and Definitions

Ableism The determination of an individual's abilities based on his or her disabilities; any policy or practice promoting the belief that people with a disability are inferior to able-bodied individuals to justify discrimination against people with disabilities

Cultural ableism The societal promotion of negative beliefs and images concerning people with disabilities that tend to portray the less able as deviant or incompetent; an assumption of superiority by people or groups based upon physical, mental, and emotional attributes

Deviant/Deviancy Someone whose appearance or behavior differs from the norm, from acceptable standards, in society

Disability A restriction of functional ability and activity caused by an impairment (such as hearing loss or reduced mobility) (Bernell, 2003)

Eugenics The study of agencies under social control that may improve or repair the racial qualities of future generations, either physically or mentally

Handicap An environmental or attitudinal barrier that limits the opportunity for an individual to participate fully in a role that is normal (depending on age, sex, and social and cultural factors) for that individual (Bernell, 2003)

Inclusion Integration of all students with a disability into regular education classrooms

Individual ableism Prejudiced attitudes and behavior against others based on the assumption that one's level of ability is deviant from the norm, demonstrated whenever someone responds by saying or doing something degrading or harmful about persons whose ability is looked on as unacceptable

Institutional ableism Established laws, customs, and practices in a society that allow systematic discrimination against people with disabilities

Mainstreaming The responsibility of schools to educate all students, regardless of disability, in the least restrictive and most normally acceptable environment

Normalization Policies and practices that help create life conditions and opportunities for people with disabilities that are at least as good as those of average citizens

People with disabilities People with behavioral or anatomical characteristics marked as deviant, which identify them as targets for discrimination (Linton, 1998)

Universal design Designing and creating products and constructing environments that are accessible to everyone

Discussion Exercises

Exercise #1 Group Home Discussion Activity

Directions: Imagine that you are a supervisor for people with various disabilities living in a group home. Identify activities listed below that a person with an intellectual disability (ID), cerebral palsied (CP), epilepsy (E), or a physical disability (PD) should be permitted to do. Write the abbreviation for the particular disability next to each activity. If you feel that all people with the disabilities listed here should or should not be allowed to do the particular activity, write "all."

Category/Activity

I. Interpersonal Relationships
1. Date
2. Engage in safe sex
3. Marry
4. Have and raise children

II. Lifestyle Concerns
1. Choose their own clothing
2. Dress the way they want
3. Participate actively in the church of their choice
4. Plan their own leisure time
5. Engage in recreational activities of their choice

III. Economic Issues
1. Choose the job they want
2. Support themselves
3. Be financially independent
4. Enter into contracts
5. Live where they choose

IV. Rights and Responsibilities
1. Vote in political elections
2. Drive a car
3. Drink beer or liquor
4. Have medical insurance
5. Be educated to their fullest potential
6. Be held responsible for their actions

Exercise #2 Disability Awareness Activity

What is a disability? How much do we know about disabilities? How prevalent are our disabilities?

Part One: List all the disabilities that you can think of; you will be reminded of additional disabilities as you listen to the suggestions of others. Attempt to identify a minimum of 20 different disabilities (but feel free to add more).

Part Two: Sort your disabilities list into three principal groups: physical, emotional, or physiological. (For example, multiple sclerosis is a physical degeneration of the muscular system; schizophrenia is commonly identified as a brain chemistry imbalance.) If you are uncertain of the category of a disability, discuss it with others. Recall from the chapter that disabilities may be permanent or temporary, evident and observable, or invisible.

Personal Insight Builder: Make three generalizations regarding how humans are different according to disability. Can you identify instances of unjustifiable discrimination against persons with disabilities? What attitudinal adjustments might be made within the general U.S. population regarding our attitudes toward persons with disabilities?

Chapter 13
Pluralism in Schools: The Promise of Multicultural Education

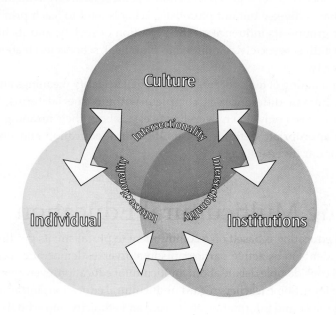

 ## Learning Outcomes

After reading this chapter you will know and be able to:

13.1 Distinguish between the terms *diversity*, *pluralism*, and *multicultural*, and provide an accurate description of the educational reform called *multicultural education*.

13.2 Explain the assumptions, beliefs, and pedagogical practices of the traditional approach in American education called *essentialism*.

13.3 Explain the assumptions, beliefs, and pedagogical practices that are promoted by advocates for multicultural education.

13.4 Describe the pedagogical approach called *culturally responsive teaching*, and explain how it addresses the goals of multicultural education.

> "Learning to read was, for slaves, not an immediate passport to freedom but rather a way of gaining access to one of the powerful instruments of their oppressors: the book."
>
> — ALBERTO MANGUEL (1948–)

Learning and schooling are critical for every individual in any society. The future of our diverse society will depend on how schools educate coming generations, and pluralism must be a significant factor in that education. During an interview for a college administrative position, an African American candidate asked about his views on diversity responded, "First, let me say that I'm a pluralist. After all, we had a diverse society when we had slaves." This is an important distinction. Many people refer to *diversity* and *pluralism* as if the two terms were synonymous, but **diversity** simply describes the existence of many different groups of people within a society, whereas **pluralism** describes a society in which diversity is accepted and supported. In a pluralistic society, diverse groups function together effectively, with mutual respect. In a society that is diverse but not pluralistic, schools tend to teach principally about the dominant group—its influence on the evolution of society, and its literature, art, and music. In a diverse society committed to pluralism, schools teach about all groups within the society.

Misunderstanding of terms occurs when we fail to clarify meanings and intentions. No study of human differences is complete without special terms, and precise communication exists only when everyone is clear about their meaning. So we must start with an appropriate definition of multicultural education and understand its importance for our diverse society.

Defining Multicultural Education

Multicultural education is based on a commitment to pluralism; its guiding purpose is to prepare students to be active participants in a diverse, democratic society. There is confusion and considerable debate about multicultural education, even among educators who advocate for it. Some teachers regard multicultural education simply as the process of integrating issues and information about race and ethnicity into school curricula, but that describes what Banks (2006) defines as **multiethnic education**. Other educators regard multicultural education as a curriculum for teaching about cultures around the world, but that is usually called **global (or international) education** (Aintablian, 2014; Gayle-Evans & Michael, 2006). Some advocates say multicultural education includes recognition of women, gay men and lesbians, people with disabilities, and other minority groups; opponents to this idea argue that such groups do not constitute distinct cultures and therefore should not be included. This confusion raises many questions that must be answered before we can understand what multicultural education is and recognize schools that are engaged in an authentic form of this educational approach.

In addition to conflicting opinions about the definition of the term *multicultural education* and who should be included, there are numerous perceptions about who benefits from it. Americans seem to agree that students of color benefit from multicultural education, especially in urban multiracial and multiethnic classrooms; yet many educators and parents in suburban or rural school districts consisting predominantly or exclusively of White students appear to believe that multicultural education provides no benefits. Gayle-Evans and Michael (2006) review several studies reporting that many teachers were uncomfortable incorporating multicultural issues into their content because they felt that the topics were "too sensitive"; educators also said they did not feel that their teacher education programs adequately prepared them to implement multicultural education practices. Kumashiro (2010) has argued that much of the reluctance to implement multicultural education stems from the social justice issues that are addressed. For White students in particular, multicultural education challenges what students think they know—assumptions that seem "natural" or just "common sense." Hines (2007) has argued that students in multicultural education classes must rethink their assumptions by asking questions such as "What are the alternatives?" and "Who benefits from this (policy/practice/outcome)?" Kumashiro (2010) also asserts that concepts learned in multicultural education often require that students unlearn some of their assumptions first, a process that may make them uncomfortable—so uncomfortable that they begin to resist the theories and research presented to them. Teachers may avoid the issue by simply including contributions of a few people of color in the curriculum, but this does not adequately provide an education that can be called *multicultural*.

What does it mean for education to be called *multicultural*?

As early as 1974, Hilliard wrote that **multicultural** refers to a society "made up of a number of cultural groups based upon race, ethnicity, religion, language, nationality, income, etc." (Hillard, 1974, p. 41). Because income level is not usually regarded as representing a different culture—rich or poor, we're all Americans—Hilliard's comment is assumed to mean that the term *multicultural* includes other subordinate groups that he did not specifically identify, such as women, gay men and lesbians, and people with disabilities.

As for the term *education*, we must distinguish between *education* and *training*. Some dictionaries suggest that education and training are synonyms, but people take classes to train them in a particular skill. An individual can be trained to drive or cook, or be trained to train a dog. Education is a broader concept. Partridge (1983) explained that *educate* derives from the Latin word *ducere*, which means "to lead"; *educere* means "to lead out or bring forth" (p. 169); *education* means "to bring forth the potential of an individual." In addition to developing cognitive skill and affective sensitivity, education entails developing an understanding of previous achievements in subjects such as history, literature, and science as a basis for making individual and societal choices in the future. Carse (1986) distinguished education from training:

> Education discovers an increasing richness in the past because it sees what is unfinished there. Training regards the past as finished and the future to be finished. Education leads toward a continuing self-discovery; training leads toward a final self-definition. (p. 23)

Multicultural education integrates information about past issues with achievements of diverse groups to describe how they have influenced our society. Children and youth from all groups are thereby provided with a sense of belonging to our society by understanding how their group has helped to shape what our society is and by appreciating the potential they have for influencing what it will become.

What is an appropriate definition for multicultural education?

Multicultural education is a journey that leads students to self-discovery and to a sense of personal efficacy. Nieto (2012) provides a comprehensive definition and description of multicultural education that includes the components to be addressed in this chapter:

> **Multicultural education** is a process of comprehensive school reform and basic education for all students. It challenges and rejects racism and other forms of discrimination in schools and society and accepts and affirms the pluralism (ethnic, racial, linguistic, religious, economic, and gender, among others) that students, their communities, and teachers reflect. Multicultural education permeates the schools' curriculum and instructional strategies, as well as the interactions among

Figure 13.1 A New Perspective

©1998 Thaves/Reprinted with permission.

Frank and Ernest

© 1998 Thaves / Reprinted with permission. Newspaper dist. by NEA, Inc.

teachers, students, and families, and the very way that schools conceptualize the nature of teaching and learning. Because it uses critical pedagogy as its underlying philosophy . . . multicultural education promotes democratic principles of social justice. (p. 42)

Nieto's definition and description of multicultural education emphasizes that it is not a "business-as-usual" approach to schooling. It requires changes in teaching methods and perspectives on learning because of critical philosophical differences between traditional education and multicultural education (see Figure 13.1).

 Self-Check 13.1 Complete this self-check quiz to check your understanding of the terms *diversity*, *pluralism*, and *multicultural*, and provide an accurate description of the educational reform called *multicultural education*.

Traditional Assumptions in American Education

The development of American schools has been based on a conservative philosophy that was eventually labeled *essentialism*, and essentialist assumptions are still in place. The term stems from the belief that an essential body of knowledge and essential human values that have stood the test of time can be identified and transmitted to students. Essentialists describe the purpose of schools as the transmission of the most significant accumulated knowledge and values from previous generations to the coming generation.

What body of knowledge have essentialists identified?

Essentialist scholars maintain that knowledge from four disciplines is essential: social studies, science, mathematics, and English language and literature; therefore, these four subjects are emphasized in elementary, middle, and high school. Graduation requirements for high school students usually include a minimum of two years of course work, often three or even four, in social studies, science, mathematics, and English. To essentialists, subjects such as art, music, and physical education are accepted principally to make school more enjoyable, but they are regarded as additional rather than essential. When administrators consider budget reductions, programs in art, music, and physical education are scrutinized and are most likely to be reduced or eliminated. Similar assumptions continue into college, where general education programs often require students to choose among a selection of courses in social studies, science, math, and English literature and composition.

What essential human values do schools teach?

As indicated in Chapter 1, Myrdal (1944) identified core American values that are embraced by most citizens and taught in most schools. In addition, Americans presume that there are certain values that represent the American middle class: promptness, honesty, hard work, competitiveness, and efficiency. Teachers implement traditional approaches to teaching values (see Chapter 1) to convince children and youth that the core values are worthwhile and should be adopted. Students may say they believe in these values because it's expected of them, even though their behavior often does not suggest that they have a genuine commitment to them.

How do essentialists define or describe learning?

Essentialists define learning as the acquisition of essential knowledge and values. Metaphors used by essentialists to describe learning portray knowledge as water and students as empty vessels to be filled or as sponges ready to absorb. To assess learning, essentialists favor objective tests with questions about factual information to ascertain whether students absorbed the information. If they did not, teachers may review the information and test students again. In extreme cases, students may repeat a grade to have a second chance to learn material in the hope that the teacher, perhaps a different teacher, will be more successful in helping them acquire the information. Maturity and readiness are considered secondary in this process.

What is the role of the essentialist teacher in helping students learn?

An essentialist teacher is supposed to be a skillful transmitter of information and an advocate for American values. Teachers are expected to be role models of our society's values—both inside and outside the classroom. As transmitters of information, teachers are expected to use technology to make information interesting and thereby promote acquisition of knowledge. Although teachers may select from a variety of pedagogical techniques, the goal is to motivate students to remember information provided in textbooks, lectures, and media. The problem is that few students can demonstrate that they are learning what teachers are teaching.

> "Teachers open the door, but you must enter by yourself."
> —CHINESE PROVERB

Why are students not learning in essentialist schools?

The first problem has to do with what has been considered essential. During the past several decades, research in various fields, especially the sciences, has generated what scholars have called a *knowledge explosion*. Given so much new knowledge, how is one to determine which facts are most important? Feminists and scholars of color have developed alternative interpretations of historical events that challenge conventional views; they believe their perspectives should be included in school curricula. Whereas women and writers of color were minimally represented in previous literature anthologies, advocates are increasingly demanding that their voices be acknowledged. Curriculum reformers suggest that most students regard traditional essentialist curriculum as inaccurate, irrelevant, and not at all motivational.

Another problem is that we know students learn at different rates. If teachers transmit information at a certain prescribed rate, some students learn all of it, some learn most of it, and some retain very little of it; yet teachers often must proceed as if all students learned equally. The solution essentialists have developed to address incomplete learning is to group students according to ability, which is known as *tracking*.

Studies of tracking have found that excellent students learn just as well in heterogeneous groups as in homogeneous groups where they are grouped by ability, but that the achievement of moderate and slow learners improves significantly when they are in mixed groups rather than when they are grouped according to academic ability (Hattie, 2009; Oakes, 2005; Oakes et al., 2000). Despite these consistent research conclusions, essentialist schools tend to continue to group students according to ability (Toppo, 2013).

Perhaps the most significant obstacle to learning in essentialist schools is the problem of retention and transfer. **Retention** refers to student recall of knowledge; **transfer** is the ability of students to apply that knowledge both inside and outside the classroom. Students have long complained about cramming before taking exams that require them to memorize material. Studies have consistently found that students tend to forget 50–80 percent of the new information they supposedly learned (Hoffman, 2014). Many reform-oriented educators have promoted the concept of constructivism, the belief that students do not passively acquire knowledge but actively construct their knowledge, and that students forget what they have learned when the teaching occurs in isolation from any meaningful context. Constructivists challenge teachers not to lecture use other methods to dispense knowledge but to provide a context that allows students to make their own mental constructions based on information and ideas they encounter (Dornoo, 2015). Educational research documents that K–12 teachers tend to teach in a style that is consistent with traditional educational strategies. Yet the constructivists point to studies where reform-oriented instructional strategies were implemented with the result that students earned higher test scores, even on high-stakes tests (Doorno, 2015).

Charter schools represent another response to the problem of how to improve student learning. In 2013, the Center for Research on Educational Outcomes (CREDO) at Stanford University conducted a study of charter schools analyzing data from 1.7 million students attending over 5000 charter schools that were supposed to engage in innovative educational practices that would foster more effective ways of teaching diverse students. Yet the CREDO (2013) study found no significant difference in the reading scores for 56 percent of charter school students compared to public school students, and the reading performance of 19 percent of students in charter schools was significantly worse than public school students. Further, a 2017 Associated Press study reported that charter schools represent some of the most racially segregated schools in our nation. The enrollments of more than 1000 charter schools were 99 percent students of color; only 4 percent of public schools have similar minority enrollments compared to 17 percent of charter schools. Research has consistently found that students of color attending racially segregated schools demonstrate significantly lower levels of academic achievement. As one civil rights advocate stated: "There is no amount of money you can put into a segregated school that is going to make it equal" (Moreno, Fenn, & Melia, 2017, A2). Public schools are also obligated to meet the needs of special education students, requiring increased resources, but charter schools, which do not tend to enroll special needs students, are taking these resources away. One study found that public schools were underfunded by about $2 billion. As one University of Illinois education professor stated: "The poorest kids and the kids with the most costly special needs still go to public schools" (Gurley, 2016, p. 55). As an alternative to the failed charter school approach, many educators advocate multicultural education, which requires a transformation of the assumptions essentialist schools have made about schools, teaching, and learning.

✓ **Self-Check 13.2** Complete this self-check quiz to check your understanding of the assumptions, beliefs, and pedagogical practices of the traditional approach in American education called *essentialism*.

Assumptions of Multicultural Education

To resolve problems related to student learning, as parents or educators, we must change our assumptions about curriculum content, learning, teaching, and the purpose of schools. As described by Banks (2014), Nieto (2012), Gollnick and Chinn (2013), and others, multicultural education challenges those assumptions.

What assumptions do multicultural educators make about curriculum?

Nieto's widely accepted definition of multicultural education includes an affirmation of diversity that must permeate the curriculum to provide honest representations of diversity in American society. According to reviews of their content, textbooks continue to be dominated by the art, music, history, literature, perspectives, and images of White Americans (Stanton, 2015; Sleeter, 2011). Portrayals of Black people are still largely associated with slavery, Latinos and Asian Americans are usually in the background with no attention given to their role in history or contemporary society, and American Indians are primarily historical figures encountered as White people move westward to "settle" America. If racism is described, it tends to be in the context of a historical account (e.g., slavery) with no connection to or mention of contemporary racism; in addition, usually a few individuals are portrayed as perpetrators of racism rather than racism being presented as a system of oppression. As Stanton (2015) concluded, "Textbook authors frequently privilege Eurocentric narratives and perspectives" (pp. 183–184).

According to Sleeter (2011), studies of students of color in high school report that not only are they aware of the Euro-American bias in their classes, but they are also able to describe it in detail. This bias is identified as a contributing factor for those who admit to a growing lack of interest in school. A study of Black middle school students in a talented and gifted program found that all of these students wanted to learn more about Black people in their school curricula and believed that such curricular content would make their classes more interesting. Almost half of the students said they were tired of the constant focus on White people in their curricula. Students of color attending college have the same concern. A survey of over 500 university students reported that most of them, especially students of color, identified the inclusion of perspectives from people of color in course curricula as the most significant factor in their judgment of a university's commitment to diversity.

To present a realistic understanding of our multicultural society and the influence of diverse groups on our society, advocates support a multicultural curriculum for all students, not just for students of color. Based on her review of studies assessing academic and social outcomes for students introduced to racial and ethnic issues, Sleeter (2011) reported that White students as well as students of color benefited from their exposure to this curricula. A multicultural curriculum examines the influences of diverse groups on historical events, literary developments, musical styles, artistic expression, athletic achievements, and other facets of American society—but the goal is not simply to memorize facts. Appleton (1983) described multicultural curriculum as "a conceptual approach that provides a framework for understanding the experience and perspectives of all the groups" (p. 211). The need for a conceptual approach is another assumption about curriculum by multicultural educators.

> "It is probably never really wise, or even necessary, or anything better than harmful, to educate a human being toward a good end by telling him lies."
> —JAMES AGEE (1910–1955)

Why is it necessary to take a conceptual approach to curriculum?

Because of the knowledge explosion, it is impractical to emphasize memorization. It is not possible for us to remember all available information in every subject; we also know that much information soon will be obsolete or supplanted by new knowledge.

In a multicultural curriculum, understanding broad concepts is preferable to memorizing facts. An early advocate for multicultural education, Gay (1977) described multicultural curriculum designs based on a thematic approach and a conceptual framework. In the thematic approach, students employ information from different disciplines to explore universal themes such as the search for identity, communication and conflict resolution, human interdependence, economics and exploitation, or the struggle for a just society (see also Gay, 2010).

Curriculum based on a conceptual framework requires an interdisciplinary approach. Beginning with a concept such as power, alienation, or socialization, students collect data from various sources addressing the concept, leading them to the identification and exploration of related concepts. Dover (2013) described a *social justice* conceptual framework that incorporated aspects from multicultural education in ways that challenged students to confront injustice based on their understanding of oppression theory (multiple forms of oppression), and social identity. Although this approach was initially implemented in higher education, the idea of "teaching for social justice" is being implemented by teachers in K–12 schools in conjunction with addressing academic standards being promoted by state and federal governments.

Because multicultural curriculum is based on concepts rather than on specific content, students are involved in a dynamic search for knowledge that is never finished, whereas the monocultural curriculum traditionally presented in schools is a finished product. As Nieto (2008) wrote,

> When reality is presented in schools as static, finished, and flat, the underlying tensions, controversies, passions and problems faced by people throughout history and today disappear. (p. 55)

Identifying concepts for students to analyze and discuss to clarify their understanding is the foundation of multicultural curriculum; to be effective, it is critical that the curriculum not be sabotaged by the hidden curriculum in school.

What is the hidden curriculum?

Pai and Adler (1997) define **hidden curriculum** as the indirect means by which schools teach students "the norms and values of their society" (p. 148). They describe the hidden curriculum as subtle messages learned from pictures displayed on bulletin boards or from school policies such as tracking. Intentional or unintentional messages can promote values but often vary, such as high income children being taught leadership and problem solving skills and low-income children being taught to respect authority and being rewarded for compliance. The messages may not seem so hidden when you look at curricular content. Teaching that Columbus discovered America tells children that Native Americans were irrelevant and can be ignored; perhaps it is no coincidence that the White majority ignores Native Americans who protest Indian mascots for school sports teams. Brigham Young took his followers to Mexican territory because of the oppression and violence Mormons had encountered in the United States. Teaching that Mormons settled in Utah instead of Mexican territory implies that religious groups have always been able to practice their beliefs freely in the United States and ignores the difficulty America has experienced living up to the principle of religious freedom. Teaching that Old World art refers only to ancient Greek and Roman cultures denies the artistic heritage of many—especially non-Western—countries. Educators implementing multicultural curricula must be especially sensitive to subtle messages provided by the hidden curriculum.

Why have schools implemented multicultural curriculum?

Many schools across the United States, especially in urban areas, have developed their own multicultural materials to supplement inadequate textbooks. Banks (2008)

"The wise person can see a question from all sides without bias. The foolish person is biased and can see a question only from one side."

—CONFUCIUS (551–479 BCE)

categorized the efforts into four approaches: the contributions approach, the additive approach, the transformation approach, and the social action approach. The first two approaches address multicultural education minimally by including heroes, holidays, and other cultural information (*contributions*), and then adding some multicultural concepts and perspectives to the curriculum (*additive*), but leaving its basic structure unchanged. The last two approaches come much closer to satisfying Nieto's definition of multicultural education.

A *transformation* approach to multicultural curriculum design emphasizes concepts and themes. Students are presented with multiple perspectives on issues, and the goal is not to identify a "right perspective" but to understand how each perspective contributes to a richer understanding of issues. Critical thinking skills are emphasized as students develop their own insights and conclusions and logically justify them.

A *social action* approach to multicultural curriculum design encourages students to take action based on their ideas and conclusions. Students individually or collectively pursue projects at school and in their community to address problems they identify and study. The goal of a social action approach is to empower students and to demonstrate that learning is not a game of *Trivial Pursuit*. Knowledge can lead to social action and create positive change. By encouraging critical thinking and active learning, multicultural educators combine theory and practice about conditions necessary to promote effective learning.

How do multicultural educators describe learning?

Advocates for multicultural education rely on cognitive development theory to describe how people learn. In essence, learning is a process of meaning making. Learners organize ideas, information, and experiences they encounter in order to make sense of them. They may categorize, find relationships, and simplify complex issues to achieve understanding. According to Sleeter and Grant (2003), "Learning is a process of constructing knowledge through the interaction of mind and experience" (p. 196). Piaget (1974) observed that children learn by interacting physically and intellectually with their environment. If students are provided information through lecture, they may attempt to extract relevant meaning from it, but if they perceive no relevance in the information, they are not likely to make the effort.

Learning results from the active interaction of individuals with information. Learning also requires meaningfulness. Information regarded as meaningless will not be learned. Active learning promotes the development of competence and confidence, the basis for Dewey's insistence that children "learn by doing." Feeling competent and gaining self-confidence leads to a sense of power. As Hilliard (1974) wrote, "Learning is related to a sense of power over some of the forces which impinge upon our lives" (p. 47). If students feel powerless, they have little motivation to learn; when students are active, they develop skills and demonstrate abilities that reinforce self-confidence and give a sense of personal competence, and they acquire an enthusiasm for learning.

With regard to skill development, learning must not be limited to basic academic skills—reading, writing, computing—but must include a multitude of skills related to critical thinking, creativity, decision-making, problem solving, information accessing, interpersonal and cross-cultural communication, conflict resolution, visual literacy, and self-analysis. Gay (1977) said education that "does not include the development of skills that will increase and enhance students' capabilities to live and function in a culturally pluralistic setting is incomplete" (p. 98). Although students may develop skills, an obstacle they face to facilitating skill development is that there are multiple ways of learning; therefore, a single teaching strategy may be inadequate. Teachers committed to multicultural education believe that all children can learn—as long as learning activities can be designed to accommodate each child.

In what different ways do individuals learn?

Considerable research has been conducted to identify and explain styles of learning, but the result has been to categorize learning as a complex assortment of more than a dozen different learning styles. In more recent years, multicultural educators have been attracted to the work of Gardner (1993), whose theory explains diversity in learning. Gardner defines intelligence as the ability to process information and to generate solutions or products of value within a particular context. Gardner originally identified seven distinct ways that people demonstrate intelligence and then added an eighth category (Gardner, 1999). Each individual has the potential to engage in all eight means of processing information, although an individual is likely to be more competent in certain dimensions based on personal idiosyncrasies or the influence of culture.

Gardner's eight intelligences include some abilities already recognized in schools, such as *logical-mathematical, linguistic, musical,* and *interpersonal* skills, but he also identifies *bodily-kinesthetic* (mastering physical tasks), *spatial* (understanding spatial relationships), *intrapersonal* (ability to self-analyze), and *natural* (discerning differences in plants and animals). This theory rejects the educational practice of rewarding primarily two intelligences: logical-mathematical and linguistic. Gardner's theory describes a more complete means of understanding intelligence and identifying intellectual abilities. The challenge for teachers is to create instructional strategies and assessment procedures that accommodate more than one kind of intelligence. If teachers can meet this challenge, more students will have successful learning experiences, which will promote self-confidence.

Why is self-confidence necessary for learning?

Scholars have known for some time now that if students think they cannot learn something, they aren't likely to learn it. Combs (1979) claimed, "People behave in terms of what they believe about themselves. Whether we feel adequate or inadequate greatly affects how we approach a task" (p. 108). Al-Hebaish (2012) also found a significant correlation between self-confidence and academic achievement. Briggs (2014) has written that: "Decades of research support the notion that believing in your ability to do something enhances your ability to do it" (n/a). Research studies have also confirmed that attitudes of teachers can positively or negatively affect student self-confidence. Although teachers should not have unrealistic expectations, they should express high expectations for students to facilitate learning.

Video Example 13.1

In this video, Gayle Gregory talks about strategies for teaching that utilize multiple intelligences theory. Think about the ways in which multicultural education is described in Chapter 13. How do the strategies in this video support multicultural education? How might these strategies also promote students' self-confidence?

What must teachers do to implement a multicultural education approach?

Educators must determine which multicultural education approach they will implement. Sleeter and Grant (2003) identified five distinct approaches, two of which also satisfy the criteria included in Nieto's description: multicultural education and education that is multicultural *and* social reconstructionist (see Table 13.1). For purposes of clarity, the latter is referred to here as the *social reconstructionist approach.*

Principles underlying a multicultural education approach are reflected in an early and influential statement provided by the Commission on Multicultural Education entitled "No One Model American" (Hunter, 1974):

> Multicultural education values cultural pluralism . . . (and) rejects the view that schools should seek to melt away cultural differences or the view that schools should merely tolerate cultural pluralism. Instead, multicultural education affirms that schools should be oriented toward the cultural enrichment of all children and youth through programs rooted to the preservation and extension of cultural diversity as a fact of life in American society. (p. 21)

Table 13.1 Approaches to Multicultural Education

Teaching the Exceptional and the Culturally Different

GOALS: To help low-achieving students succeed within traditional education by building bridges between them and the curriculum, and providing special assistance.

CURRICULUM: Based on the traditional curriculum but incorporates students' experiences (especially those who are culturally different). Uses classroom materials that include meaningful contexts for the students.

INSTRUCTION: Implements English as a Second Language or transitional bilingual education for language minority students and culturally relevant teaching for culturally different students; provides remedial classes including special education placement for temporary but intensive remediation; displays images relevant to students on wall posters and bulletin boards.

Human Relations

GOALS: To maintain traditional educational assumptions but with an emphasis on reducing prejudice, developing positive student self-concepts, and promoting acceptance of individual diversity.

CURRICULUM: Based on the traditional curriculum but including content on prejudice and stereotypes, similarities and differences among groups and individuals, and societal contributions from members of diverse groups in society, especially those groups represented by the students in the school.

INSTRUCTION: Uses strategies that build student-student relationships such as conflict mediation, role playing, simulations that address interpersonal relationships, and cooperative learning; displays student work on walls and bulletin boards.

Single Group Studies

GOALS: To provide knowledge about a particular group (Women's Studies, Chicano Studies, etc.) including an examination of structural inequalities affecting members of this group and encouraging students to work for social change.

CURRICULUM: Provides information (for a unit or course) about cultural characteristics and historical experiences of a group with emphasis on perspectives of group members and how this group has been and still is oppressed.

INSTRUCTION: Responds to learning style differences of the group with accommodations for individual learning styles; incorporates media, music, performances, and guest speakers to address aspects of the culture or issues related to the group; wall displays and bulletin boards emphasize societal contributions from individual members of the group.

Multicultural Education

GOALS: To promote cultural pluralism by emphasizing respect for human differences, including individual lifestyles, equal opportunity for all in school and society, and the need for power equity among diverse groups in society.

CURRICULUM: Provides content on diverse groups and their contributions to society with emphasis on perspectives from members of each group; incorporates student experiences to enhance curriculum relevance, and emphasizes the need to be aware of and understand alternative perspectives on issues; addresses "hidden curriculum" by including diversity in special events, holidays, school menus, etc.

INSTRUCTION: Responds to student learning styles and skill levels with emphasis on an analysis of curriculum content and critical thinking activities; promotes respect for and use of other languages and dialects while learning standard English; displays wall posters and bulletin boards that reflect human diversity represented by race, ethnicity, gender, disability, religion, and other diverse groups, as well as issues reflecting individual student interests.

Education That Is Multicultural and Social Reconstructionist

GOALS: To promote cultural pluralism and structural equality for diverse groups in our society, to prepare students to be active participants in our democratic society by understanding structural inequalities and promoting equal opportunity.

CURRICULUM: Provides content on current social issues of oppression and structural inequalities for diverse groups using perspectives of members of those groups and perspectives of students and community members; emphasizes historic and contemporary life experiences for self-reflection, analyzing oppression, and understanding alternative perspectives; addresses "hidden curriculum" by including diversity in special events, holidays, school menus, etc.

INSTRUCTION: Responds to student learning styles and skill levels with emphasis on active student involvement in democratic decision making in the school; engages students in critical thinking and in problem solving to promote the development of social action skills that empower students; employs cooperative learning and group projects, especially those involving the community; avoids testing and tracking procedures that represent narrow views of student learning that label some students as failures; displays wall posters and bulletin boards that reflect cultural diversity, social action themes, and student interests.

SOURCE: Sleeter, C. E., & Grant, C. A. (2003). Used with the approval of the authors.

A *multicultural education approach* insists that a diverse society can achieve unity through diversity; it need not eliminate cultural differences. Although some advocates of this approach focus on racial and ethnic groups, most promote an inclusive view of diversity that provides information on women, LGBTQ people, low-income families, and people with disabilities.

Multicultural education advocates support integration, inclusion, and "de-tracking" to create heterogeneous classrooms emphasizing skill development to gain knowledge and a better understanding of diverse groups in America. Further, a multicultural education approach calls for curricular reform to correct omissions and distortions in textbooks concerning diverse groups, and provides multiple perspectives on important historical or contemporary events. Advocates have criticized visual images in textbooks for not representing diversity in American society adequately and for continuing to depict certain groups in stereotypical ways. They urge teachers to use bulletin boards and media to provide accurate representations of diverse groups.

Advocates for the multicultural education approach challenge teachers to be sensitive to language that is derogatory toward any group and to model the use of inclusive language. Teachers must explore and understand diverse ways of learning to be able to design or modify lessons to accommodate individual differences. In addition to having high expectations for students, multicultural teachers encourage cooperation between students in the classroom through group activities. Teachers should not treat all students the same; rather, they should address students equitably with responses based on their diverse needs.

A *social reconstructionist approach* shares many principles and practices with a multicultural education approach. Four major differences include: (1) attention to structural inequalities in America; (2) emphasis on democratic decision-making in the classroom; (3) development of social action skills to empower students; and (4) use of an activist curriculum with student projects addressing problems in schools and communities.

Social reconstructionism has roots in the Progressive Education movement and in Dewey's 1920 book *Reconstruction in Philosophy*, which inspired the term. In the early 1930s, Counts and Rugg, leaders of a group called "Frontier Thinkers," were concerned about inequities in American society and urged that schools play a more active role in creating a more equitable society (Kneller, 1971). In his 1956 book, *Toward a Reconstructed Philosophy of Education*, Brameld became an influential advocate for reconstructionism, suggesting that schools create a new social order by fostering democratic principles and demanding more citizen control over major institutions and resources.

A social reconstructionist approach to multicultural education focuses less on simply teaching about cultural diversity and more on the struggles of diverse groups against oppression. The curriculum includes examples of both a group's successful resistance to oppression and actions by allies from the dominant group against injustice. This approach emphasizes specific classroom practices to develop student decision-making skills and to encourage social action projects.

What specific instructional strategies are recommended for teachers?

Sleeter (1996) insisted that implementing multicultural education effectively requires that teaching not be regarded as merely experimenting with a variety of classroom strategies; instead she described the importance of "listening to oppressed people, including scholars, with the aim of learning to hear and understand what is being said" (p. 134). By listening to students and their parents, teachers will develop an appreciation for and an understanding of their students, and will genuinely project high regard and high expectations for all students. Nieto (2012) argued that before one can become a multicultural teacher, he or she must first become a "multicultural person." She goes on to say that becoming a multicultural person means knowing about human differences and desiring to learn more; examining personal attitudes for biases, stereotypes, and prejudices; and understanding the need to look at issues from more than one perspective.

Advocates for either of the two multicultural education approaches just described agree that to implement a multicultural curriculum, teachers must employ **critical pedagogy**. Nieto (2012) describes critical pedagogy as a liberating experience that "encourages students to take risks, to be curious, and to question. Rather than expecting students to repeat teachers' words, it expects them to seek their own answers" (p. 56). Critical pedagogy is also illustrated by Sleeter's (1996) description of *Why? Papers*: In this activity students are assigned the task of asking a question about some issue involving race, social class, or gender. In doing research and writing their responses to the questions, students are asked to take the perspective of the oppressed group identified in the question. Examples of "Why?" questions include:

- Why are Mexican American children frequently absent from school?
- Why do Native American students drop out of school?
- Why are many African American males in prison? (p. 120)

Sleeter reports that taking the minority perspective has been effective because students talk with members of oppressed groups as they search for answers; this provides them with unique insights on a group's past experiences along with their perspectives

Application Exercise 13.1

In this video, two teachers plan lessons to align with standards. Consider the ways in which their planning follows a multicultural model. Review the video and complete the activity.

"Teachers not only teach, but they also learn."

—NATIVE AMERICAN (SAUK) PROVERB

on the problems being addressed. As they write their papers, students are influenced by these multiple insights and perspectives, both in their analysis and in their conclusions.

Dover (2013) argues that the *critical pedagogy* approach rejects the assumption that the educational process is or should be politically neutral; instead, it assists students in an analysis of curriculum content, the objectives of pedagogical strategies, and the basic goals of the education process. Using activities emphasizing problem posing and dialogue, this approach encourages student development of a sociopolitical consciousness. Sleeter (2011) cited a study of a class of Black and White elementary school students whose teachers infused content into their lessons concerning Black historical figures, historical examples of racism, and successful challenges to racism. All students, but especially White students, gained a greater understanding of racism, and the experience seemed to have a positive effect on their racial attitudes. Although it appears that critical pedagogy has primarily been used in social science and humanities classes, Dover (2013) has observed an increasing use of a critical pedagogy approach in math classes where students are given such tasks as analyzing "racial and socioeconomic trends in traffic stops, food distribution, and urban revitalization/gentrification" (p. 5).

In addition to promoting critical pedagogy, multicultural educators have also worked to eliminate tracking practices because they have tended to diminish diversity in classrooms and adversely affect student academic achievement. Multicultural educators encourage the use of learning centers or cooperative groups as effective strategies for heterogeneous classrooms. Tiedt and Tiedt (2009) describe a learning center as a part of the classroom set aside for the study of a specific topic or for the purpose of developing a particular set of skills; it may be devoted to studying the issue of prejudice or filled with exercises requiring critical thinking. Before using a learning center, students are given directions concerning the center's activities and instructions for using equipment or materials. Students involved in learning center activities can proceed as individuals learning at their own pace or they can be organized into teams.

Multicultural educators advocate for increased content on diversity and issues of oppression in the curriculum, but critics insist that this will foster hostile attitudes toward the dominant group and will disrupt students' academic learning. The evidence appears to favor the multicultural advocates. Sleeter (2011) reviewed three studies involving middle school students that reported increased levels of student engagement when curricula included authors from the students' ethnic group, and a study evaluating five literacy curricula integrating ethnic content into the lessons that found students increased their academic achievements and their literacy skills. Another study that infused diversity content into math and science lessons reported that students tended to make significant gains in academic achievement.

Some multicultural educators are considering digital learning to explore social justice issues. For example, an ABC *20/20* program upset Lakota youth on the Rosebud Reservation because it depicted youth on their reservations as alcoholic, living in dysfunctional families, and mired in poverty. With teacher assistance, Lakota students in two high school English classes produced a video debunking such stereotypes that was viewed by 70,000 people on YouTube. In 2013, a more dramatic example occurred when undocumented high school students organized a sit-in at the headquarters of Immigration and Customs Enforcement in Los Angeles to protest deportation of undocumented youth and Congress's refusal to pass the Dream Act. The students announced their protest on Twitter and Facebook, and when the sit-in occurred, 300 people who had pledged to come and support them surrounded the protesting students. When the Los Angeles police arrived, 4000 Americans watched on streaming video as police officers arrested students. Then protest organizers texted, blogged, and sent out further information on Twitter and Facebook, including a link to a national support network that ended up receiving numerous donations and signed petitions in support of the undocumented students (Van Galen, 2013). To critics of such activities, multicultural educators respond that if schools are engaged in education relevant to students' lives,

> "One who learns but does not think is lost. One who thinks but does not learn is in great danger."
>
> —CONFUCIUS (551–479 BCE)

this kind of activity is a logical outcome as students use what they have learned in school to participate peacefully in the democratic process.

Finally, cooperative learning strategies are especially attractive to advocates of multicultural education because they involve students of mixed abilities in learning tasks that have clearly defined responsibilities for each group member. Each individual must complete his or her task in order for the group to complete the project. In reviewing research on cooperative learning, Kagan (2006) cites studies documenting that young children in schools with diverse student populations initially interact with others and choose their friends without regard to race, but by the end of their second grade year, self-segregation by race has begun and is dramatically apparent by the end of elementary school. Yet research studies have also found that in classrooms that have implemented cooperative learning strategies, self-segregation was virtually eliminated. Further, Paluck and Green (2009) reviewed meta-analyses of the outcomes of cooperative learning for classrooms of students with racial, ethnic, and disability differences; they found that students had consistently experienced a positive outcome in terms of peer relationships. Based on his review of four decades of research, Kagan (2006) concluded: "Cooperative learning, when it includes heterogeneous teams and team-building, is the single most powerful tool this nation has for improving race relations" (p. 53).

How can multicultural education help to reduce student prejudice?

Reducing prejudice and developing conflict resolution skills are important objectives in multicultural education, but prejudice is not simply a Black and White issue. Sheets (2005) described a study of a school with diverse students in which African American children expressed negative attitudes toward children who were Asian American or Hispanic American. Koyama (2014) reports that most of the participants in over 400 student leaders workshops said they heard degrading language, slurs, and offensive jokes at school multiple times a day. Further, the comments were not just based on race but also on gender, religion, and sexual orientation. Another societal prejudice that appears in schools is the stigma associated with mental illness. Elias (2013) cited a study finding that almost two thirds of high school students diagnosed with a mental illness felt they had been stigmatized by their peers; another study of middle school students found that only half of the students were willing to sit next to a classmate known to have a mental illness. Such rejection does not have to be inevitable. Some teachers have had students complete and discuss surveys that asked questions about mental health issues such as depression to illustrate that many mental health conditions are commonly experienced. A study by the Adolescent Communication Institute concluded that giving teenagers better information about mental illness, especially that appropriate treatment has helped people cope successfully with mental disorders, has proven to be effective: "You have to give kids facts that counter their stereotypes, and then many are open to change" (Elias, 2013, p. 50).

According to Wells, Fox, and Cordova-Corbo (2016), multiple studies have found that being presented with various perspectives when discussing issues in a classroom appears to stimulate critical thinking. Further, a body of research on K–12 schools, largely ignored, reports that when students learn cooperatively in a classroom with diverse students, all students benefit. These classrooms produce more creativity, and better critical thinking and problem solving skills. White students seem to especially benefit from diversity because the presence of students of color appears to cause White students to approach discussions of issues from a more complex perspective that includes divergent points of view. A longitudinal study found that students graduating from K–12 schools with a diverse student population tended to have more positive racial attitudes and were able to function more effectively on college campuses with diverse populations (Wells, Fox, & Cordova-Corbo, 2016). In addition, Gay (2010)

"Prejudices, it is well known, are most difficult to eradicate from the heart whose soil has never been loosened or fertilized by education; they grow there, firm as weeds among stones."

—CHARLOTTE BRONTE (1816–1855)

argues that another way to reduce prejudice is for teachers to work with students in ways that take into account the students' diverse cultures. This approach is called "culturally responsive teaching."

 Self-Check 13.3 Complete this self-check quiz to check your understanding of the assumptions, beliefs, and pedagogical practices that are promoted by advocates for multicultural education.

Multicultural Education as a Context for Culturally Responsive Teaching

Multicultural education incorporates the idea that all students—regardless of their gender, social class, ethnic, racial, or cultural differences—should have an equal opportunity to learn in school. However, the public school system in the United States is plagued with inequalities; on virtually every measure, students of color and students from lower economic classes achieve below the level of their White and middle-class counterparts. This disparity is called "the achievement gap." A recent report assessing efforts over the past 50 years to close the achievement gap between Black and White students in K–12 schools found that the gap has barely narrowed. If improvements continue at this slow pace, it will take over a century to close the reading gap and over two centuries to close the math gap (Camera, 2016). The gap also persists for those living in poverty. Although recent data suggest that achievement gaps between low-income students and their high-income peers has narrowed over the past 10 years, it is still twice as large as the gap between Black and White students (Sacks, 2016). Mainstream explanations tend to blame the achievement gap on uninformed assumptions about families and communities (i.e., "they just don't value education"), but when scholars examine the ways schools are structured, there is evidence that institutional characteristics of schools systematically deny some students equal educational opportunities (Kuznia, 2009). Students in high-poverty, high-minority schools are routinely provided fewer resources, fewer qualified teachers, fewer advanced level courses, and higher levels of policing in their schools than their more affluent White peers. As a result, they experience lower academic achievement, lower rates of high school graduation, and more interaction with the criminal justice system, creating what has been called the *school-to-prison pipeline* (Editors of *Rethinking Schools*, 2011–2012). Many multicultural educators advocate culturally responsive teaching as a key strategy to reduce the achievement gap.

How does culturally responsive teaching address multicultural education goals?

Like multicultural education, culturally responsive teaching has its roots in teacher preparation programs, but its emphasis has been on teachers exploring their cultural identity and that of their students, and implementing culturally responsive activities in their classrooms to improve student achievement. Culturally responsive teachers want to create classrooms that are inclusive of the cultures of all students. They are also challenged to deepen their awareness of inequities due to race, class, and other social categories in their school and in society, and to help students explore and respond to these inequities (Dover, 2013).

Culturally responsive teaching addresses multicultural education's goal of changing school practices that marginalize nontraditional students. It is grounded in the perception of schooling as linked to social forces in society. Schooling is a primary site of socialization, so schools play a key role in sorting students into predetermined places within a society that is hierarchical and socially stratified. Schools prepare students to occupy roles that have unequal value in society—vocational training versus college preparation or special education versus honors courses; therefore, schools become a site of social reproduction. All aspects of schooling are inherently political because knowledge is never neutral; it is infused with the implicit cultural assumptions, frames of reference, biases, and interests of those who hold the power to determine which aspects of knowledge are valid and how they will be measured. Yet schools present the cultural norms, styles, and perspectives of dominant social groups as objective, and they reward those who fit these norms and penalize those who don't.

Other aspects of schooling that contribute to the achievement gap include standardized testing, culturally biased curriculum, tracking, unequal funding between urban and suburban schools, low expectations for students of color, and zero tolerance policies that criminalize minority students and channel them from school into the prison system (Amurao, 2013). From the beginning, as it was being developed and promoted, the concept of culturally responsive teaching was meant to interrupt these inequitable aspects of schooling (Gay, 2000; Ladson-Billings, 1995). While challenging these structural inequities will take time and society-wide effort, multicultural education advocates argue that individual teachers can make an immediate difference in their classrooms by infusing culturally responsive teaching. (See Figure 13.2.)

Gay (2000) defines culturally responsive teaching as using the cultural knowledge, prior experiences, and performance styles of diverse students to make learning more appropriate and effective for them. Rather than viewing these students as deficient, culturally responsive pedagogy teaches to their specific strengths. According to Gay (2000), culturally responsive teaching has the following characteristics:

- It acknowledges the legitimacy of the cultural heritages of different ethnic groups, both as legacies that affect students' dispositions, attitudes, and approaches to learning and as worthy content to be taught in the formal curriculum.

- It builds bridges of meaningfulness between home and school experiences as well as between academic abstractions and lived sociocultural realities.

- It uses a wide variety of instructional strategies that are connected to different learning styles.

- It teaches students to know and praise their own and each other's cultural heritages.

- It incorporates multicultural information, resources, and materials in all the subjects and skills routinely taught in schools (p. 29).

Video Example 13.2

In this video, Dr. Irma Olmedo talks about the "funds of knowledge" that students have and bring to school. How does the concept of "funds of knowledge" relate to Gay (2000)'s notion of culturally responsive teaching characteristics? What might be some examples of funds of knowledge that students bring? How might teachers nurture these funds of knowledge through culturally responsive pedagogy?

Figure 13.2 Computers Can Enhance Culturally Responsive Teaching

With computers and access to the Internet in classrooms, teachers have an effective tool for students to gather current information on diverse groups and social justice issues.

SOURCE: *Monkey Business Images/Shutterstock*

The Council for the Accreditation of Educator Preparation (CAEP) believes culturally competent teachers will be more likely to improve the academic achievement of students from diverse backgrounds; therefore, CAEP expects teacher preparation programs to incorporate multicultural concepts and information related to all aspects of the content being taught (Chiu, Sayman, & Carrero, 2017). Gay (2010) has argued that to learn how to be culturally responsive in their classrooms, pre-service teachers need to develop lesson plans based on realistic issues, on situations and conflicts that have actually occurred and that have affected students from diverse communities.

What are some current issues that make culturally responsive teaching difficult?

Despite the common belief that racial segregation is a practice of the past, our schools are more segregated than ever before (Bouie, 2014). Most students of color and lower-income students are concentrated in urban areas, whereas most middle-class and White students attend largely homogeneous suburban schools. Yet the numbers of students of color are steadily increasing; by 2021 they are expected to constitute 52 percent of all K–12 students (King & Butler, 2015). Yet about 80 percent of America's teachers are White women (Taie & Goldring, 2017), a figure unlikely to change since mainstream teacher education programs continue to attract primarily White women, and 88 percent of teacher education professors are White (DiAngelo, 2012). Almost 18 percent of men and over half of African Americans and other ethnic minorities become licensed teachers through alternative certification programs (King & Butler, 2015). In addition to being White, the vast majority of teachers tend to come from segregated schools and neighborhoods. Studies suggest that unless they have had the experience of creating lessons for a multicultural classroom, these teachers are likely to take a traditional, mono-cultural approach that will continue to result in low academic achievement for students of color (King & Butler, 2015).

Although urban schools may indeed be located in cities and composed predominantly of low-income students and students of color, "urban" does not necessarily indicate location. In more affluent cities such as Seattle, San Francisco, and Boston, schools located inside the city limits that are primarily White are not labeled "urban"; the term *urban* is used as the dominant culture's code for indicating the existence of a percentage of students of color that is "too high" for White families to feel comfortable with. Roda and Wells (2013) found that White parents justified their choice of school as simply wanting a "good" school for their children, but their selection was often a school populated primarily by children from White, advantaged families. When schools are perceived as "not good" because of the presence of a percentage of students of color, and such schools are then labeled "urban" (or "inner-city"), then these parental choices contribute to the re-segregation of America's schools. When White families abandon these schools, the result is often unequal funding and resources, perpetuating the problem (Roda & Wells, 2013). These factors complicate the efforts of teachers to engage in culturally responsive teaching, but they also provide reasons for engaging in such practices to help students.

Which students benefit from culturally responsive teaching?

Research on ethnic studies classes supports the assumption that students of color benefit from being taught information about their group. Sleeter (2011) reviewed research employing different methodologies in different regions of the nation with participants ranging from middle school through higher education and found that students consistently reported a relationship between having a positive attitude toward their own racial group and their individual academic achievement. But students of color are not the only beneficiaries. Since race appears to be a key issue in decisions White people make when choosing schools and neighborhoods, one could easily argue that all students and all teachers could benefit from culturally responsive teaching, regardless of the overall racial demographics of their schools or neighborhoods. Multicultural educators insist that White children attending segregated schools need to be prepared, perhaps more so than any other group, to interact in a culturally diverse society. In her review of ethnic studies research, Sleeter (2011) found that White students felt they benefited from exposure to curricula emphasizing diversity and examining racism, and studies in higher education reported that courses on diversity issues had even more impact on White students than on students of color. Culturally responsive teaching emphasizes the inclusion of multiple perspectives, and numerous studies have found that when students are given diverse perspectives, it has stimulated them to think critically about their own perspective and to become more tolerant for different perspectives that attempt to make sense of the issues (Wells, Fox, & Cordova-Corbo, 2016).

"It is what we think we know already that often prevents us from learning."

—CLAUDE BERNARD (1813–1878)

All of these studies support the claim by multicultural educators that culturally responsive teaching can build a foundation for all students to engage in the critical tasks of empathetic and equitable engagement with a diversity that is so often lacking in their immediate world because of pervasive segregation in schools and neighborhoods. Since any educational approach has to be done well to be effective, the most significant concern is being clear about what is required for an individual teacher to successfully implement this approach.

What characteristics are necessary to be a culturally responsive teacher?

Culturally responsive pedagogy requires teachers to respond to the cultures represented in their classrooms. Teachers must consciously connect new information with the knowledge students bring into the classroom and teach in ways that are consistent with the ways their students learn.

As many advocates of culturally responsive pedagogy have argued, this approach validates the experiences of diverse students. By connecting new information with their existing knowledge, students not only feel capable of learning but also are more likely to demonstrate their capabilities. Richly and Graves (2012) have identified four characteristics that are required for teachers to implement culturally responsive teaching successfully in their classrooms:

- *Caring and empathetic:* This does not simply advocate being "nice"; it means having a strong belief that students can learn and being committed to their success in learning.

- *Reflective about their attitudes and beliefs concerning other cultures:* Since many teachers have grown up in our society and have been exposed to the racist beliefs and attitudes that are so prevalent, it is highly likely that they have internalized at least some stereotypes and false assumptions about diverse cultural groups. Teachers must be reflective, honestly examining their preconceptions about groups represented in their classrooms, and sensitive to language that presents a negative image of a group such as "culturally deprived."

- *Reflective about their own cultural frames of reference:* Teachers need to become conscious of how they view the world and how that view shapes their choices in the classroom. Their worldview will be reflected in images and symbols, awards and celebrations, and other cultural representations on their bulletin boards and in their curricula. If the diverse cultures of their students are not reflected in these cultural artifacts, these students can feel marginalized, which would likely become a factor contributing to their lack of success in school.

- *Knowledgeable about other cultures:* In order to connect new information to students' background knowledge, teachers must be knowledgeable about the cultural perspectives and practices of groups that are represented in the classroom. Such knowledge will be reflected in the teacher's choice of classroom strategies such as cooperative activities or individual problem solving, gender roles, and adult behavioral expectations regarding children. For example, conventional teaching encourages students to view learning as a personal achievement, but other cultures emphasize doing what is best for the entire community, not just what is good for one member of that community. Understanding this should lead to more effective pedagogical strategies for those students. Teachers must also strike a balance between recognizing distinct cultural practices of a particular group and yet not stereotyping students according to such practices. They must always regard each student is an individual who is affected by other influences.

Video Example 13.3

In this video, a teacher, Ms. Adimoolah, discusses why she feels culturally relevant teaching is important. Compare and contrast why she feels culturally relevant teaching is important with how culturally responsive teaching is discussed in Chapter 13.

The characteristics involve ongoing education and self-awareness, particularly for those who have not grown up in environments that offered consistent opportunities to build relationships with people different from themselves in key social areas, such as race and class. Because culturally responsive teaching challenges our conventional worldviews and our sense of self in relation to others, it develops over a lifetime and is not achieved in the short term. At the same time, educators can't grow into culturally responsive teachers without practice, trial and error, and risk taking. Although a school-wide commitment is required for any education reform to achieve authentic transformation in schools, individual teachers may still choose to infuse culturally responsive teaching into their classroom practice.

What actual classroom experiences illustrate culturally responsive teaching?

Learning activities and teacher resources are available to support educators who want to implement culturally responsive teaching (Chiu, Sayman, & Carrero, 2017), but some of the best resources are the lessons developed and implemented by experienced teachers. In the 1990s, Latino performance poetry exploring such issues as inequality, poverty, and racism became popular in southern California and was integrated into English classes in many urban high schools. Several studies found that by engaging in performance poetry, urban students strengthened their skills not only in language but also in critical thinking, and some studies reported that students were using their skills to become activists in their communities. Based on their review of this research, Ramirez and Jimenez-Silva (2015) incorporated performance poetry into their lessons, describing how their Latino students developed stronger analytical skills from writing and performing this poetry and from the rich discussions students had about inequality and social justice issues. In addition to student poetry, poets in their community were invited to read their poetry and participate in classroom discussions. These students strengthened their interpretive skills, and they engaged in questioning, reflection, and higher-order thinking as they identified and analyzed barriers impacting Latinos and other marginalized groups in their community.

A Filipino American educator developed and implemented a curriculum on the history and culture of the Philippines and the experiences of Filipino Americans that included a problem-posing pedagogy and multiple perspectives to encourage critical thinking. Ten years later a survey was taken of the original group of 35 students (30 Filipino Americans and 5 Euro-Americans) who had engaged with this curriculum. All of the students had completed college, and in response to a question about the lasting value of this class, all of them tended to describe "a deeper love and appreciation of ethnic history, culture, identity, and community" (Sleeter, 2011, p. 14). The course stimulated a lifetime commitment to diversity and the value of multicultural perspectives, with some of the Euro-American students choosing to be allies for people of color.

It is commonly assumed that culturally responsive teaching is relevant to only some subjects, such as social studies or reading, but not applicable to others such as science and math. This assumption rests on a belief that the sciences are objective. But no subject is objective or value free; the sciences are as laden with cultural assumptions as any other field. Indeed, much of the early rationale for racist practices in the United States was founded in what is termed "scientific racism"—using racially biased questions, methods, and interpretations of data to justify the lower social and institutional positions of people of color.

A science teacher used a senior level class to teach students about the infamous Tuskegee syphilis study, lasting from 1932 until the 1970s. Medical staff observed African American men who had been diagnosed with syphilis but did not provide them with the normal treatments (e.g., penicillin) that would have helped them, and the men were told that they were not allowed to seek treatment elsewhere. One of the doctors who advised the team conducting the study concluded: "Perhaps here, in conjunction with tuberculosis, will be the end of the Negro problem. Disease will accomplish what man cannot (Kraig-Turner, 2016–2017, p. 31). To understand the moral and medical implications of this study, the teacher provided students with information such as how syphilis progresses and recommended treatments. Each student was given a role to play such as a participant in the study, a widow of a participant, a public health official, or a journalist. Students quickly recognized the barbarity of treating human beings like guinea pigs and compared the Tuskegee study to those conducted by the Nazis at Auschwitz. After students had time to absorb the role assigned to them, they played that role as they walked around the room talking to one another. They completed writing assignments based on what they learned from being the individual they role-played and other roles. The students were provided with information about other questionable medical practices involving vulnerable populations and at the conclusion wrote a code for engaging in bioethical research on human beings (Kraig-Turner, (2016–2017).

Some of the ways we see bias in math and science today are through the corporate interests behind which research gets funded, the questions being asked, the interpretations being made, the cultural assumptions and biases in story problems, the biased assumptions about which students will succeed in math and science, and the homogenous representations of historical and current leaders in the fields. In sum, no field of study—including math and science—is objective and value free because humans are not objective and value free. Not acknowledging the cultural biases that inform individual perspectives keeps them hidden and intact, making it more likely that the dominant perspective is presented as neutral and universal, and that dominant interests will continue to be reinforced. By engaging in culturally responsive practices, we actually expand our view rather than limit it. Thus it is imperative to integrate culturally responsive perspectives and practices throughout the entire curriculum.

Dean (2007) has demonstrated how a math teacher can incorporate culturally responsive teaching. She teaches a math lesson by using typical wages in her students' community to build a bridge between algebra and her students' lives. Her students calculate and graph daily and monthly incomes in service sector jobs, using a day's wages and a month's wages for four full-time service industry occupations that many in their community hold—for example, a retail clerk at Walmart, a security guard, a fast-food restaurant cook, and a home nursing aide. Her students graph four linear relationships on the same coordinate grid and write equations for each. Along the way, they discuss questions such as: "What is a minimum wage, and who gets to set it?" She says, "Following an example that I had prepared in advance, students worked together to draw an x- and y-axis on 11-by-17–inch graph paper. I told them that they would be graphing one day's wages, or eight hours, and that the size of one's paycheck depends on the number of hours worked; therefore, money—the dependent variable—belongs on the y-axis. The independent variable, however, will be the same for everyone: You are all going to work an eight-hour day."

After students complete the graphs, she introduces the variables x and y. In this case, y represents the paycheck and x stands for the number of hours worked. Ms. Dean also challenges her students to write an equation for each line that would show the relationship between time and earnings, and they arrive at equations to represent the lines on their graphs. She then asks her students to respond in writing to the following prompt: "How does the rate of pay affect the shape and steepness of the lines on your coordinate grid? Describe the shape of a graph for the wage of a job at $20 per hour. Describe the shape of a graph for the wage of a job at the federal minimum of $5.15 per hour." The prompt leads students to observe that the steeper the line, the higher the wage, and that each situation produces a straight line. Both observations pave the way for introducing the term "slope," meaning the rate of increase, and "linear," meaning a relationship that graphs as a straight line. This prompt also serves to identify the coefficient of x or the number that multiplies x as the value that determines the steepness of the line. Once students recognize linear relationships, Ms. Dean introduces the concept of y-intercept by having students make a table showing pay minus expenses for the first 10 hours of work. This gives students a real-world context for operating with negative numbers. Other dimensions of her "living algebra" lesson include calculating the cost of housing and other expenses, comparing state and national minimum wages, and learning about the activism and organizing effort behind her state's high minimum wage (Dean, 2007). The pedagogy shaping this lesson is culturally relevant and avoids the problems that teachers have sometimes encountered in implementing culturally responsive teaching.

What problems do teachers encounter when they attempt to implement culturally responsive teaching?

As the examples above illustrate, culturally responsive teaching has the potential to be an effective pedagogical approach, but it is also a challenging one. Sleeter (2010) identified four problems that teachers are likely to encounter and how they can be resolved:

1. The tendency to define students in terms of their membership in sociocultural groups and to engage in practices and activities with students associated with these groups. The best way to avoid this problem is for teachers to learn about their students and their communities.
2. The assumption that culturally responsive teaching simply means teaching culturally diverse students about their respective cultures. Culturally responsive teachers regard students as a cultural resource and enlist students' cultural knowledge to help them apply what they already know to new academic knowledge.
3. The "silver bullet" fallacy—believing there is only one approach that will improve student learning. Teachers must explore alternative approaches, innovative strategies, and new uses of traditional approaches, resulting in a combination of pedagogical strategies. Successful teachers are lifelong learners who keep searching for what works best for their students.
4. The perception that culturally responsive teaching is only necessary when teaching students of color—an especially harmful perception because it transforms students into "the other." Culturally responsive teaching should transform teachers by requiring a rigorous self-examination of how they have been influenced by their culture and how they teach and interact with their students.

Sleeter (2010) argues that culturally responsive teaching is a "starting point" for productive dialogues between teachers and students, teachers and parents, and teachers with other teachers. Although culturally responsive teaching requires extra effort and may even seem daunting, it is no more difficult than any other strategy promoting successful classroom practices that are effective with diverse students. Good teaching is

Video Example 13.4
In this video, three teachers talk about the role of noise in teacher Ms. Williams's classroom. In what ways do her classroom strategies exhibit culturally responsive teaching? And what are some of the challenges of her strategies?

never easy, but in the history of education, there have always been effective teachers, so we know it's not impossible. This should be the response to critics who say that culturally responsive teaching is too idealistic to work in the "real world" of challenges inherent in the everyday task of classroom teaching. Any educational reform will face obstacles, but educators continue to engage in new reform efforts.

What other educational reforms are being implemented?

The most ambitious reform in recent years has been the effort to create a core curriculum to be implemented in every state. Because the Common Core State Standards (CCSS) initiative is the largest attempt in the United States to develop and implement a unified set of standards of knowledge and skills in education, it was inevitable that controversies would emerge. The diverse responses to CCSS as it was being implemented (Fall, 2014) illustrate the complexities involved in a major reform effort, given the current social and political climate. To understand the controversy requires a brief review of the context in which the CCSS was first proposed.

In 2001, the No Child Left Behind Act (NCLB) mandated that all states develop rigorous standards and that students in grades 3–12 had to complete annual tests to assess proficiency. Ten years after it was implemented, more than half of U.S. schools were listed as "failing" (Editors of *Rethinking Schools*, 2013). The goal of the CCSS initiative was to define what students in kindergarten through twelfth grade should know and be able to do in mathematics and English language arts in order to graduate high school prepared to succeed in "entry-level careers, freshman-level college courses, and workforce training programs" (Common Core State Standards Initiative, 2014, n.p.). With a common core of educational standards, it was hoped that clearer comparisons could be made across states in their assessments of student learning, and that there would be consistency for students as they moved from school to school or from state to state (O'Connor, 2014).

Critics of CCSS included conservative groups who view the standards as a federal intrusion on states' rights, teacher unions who say dissenting teachers have been punished for opposing implementation (Bidwell, 2014; Rich, 2014), and early childhood educators who cite mismatches between standards and question their appropriateness in early childhood education (Strauss, 2013). Advocates for CCSS insist that the standards promote a rigorous curriculum while emphasizing student-centered activity utilizing collaboration and reflective learning. One desired outcome of CCSS that is of particular interest to multicultural educators was to improve education for low-income students, giving them the skills to graduate from high school and attend college (Bleiberg & West, 2014). Critics say that CCSS does not address this problem because its emphasis on testing and punitive measures will continue to reproduce inequity in low-income children who face greater obstacles in meeting grade-level proficiencies (Bleiberg & West, 2014; Editors of *Rethinking Schools*, 2013). A further complication is that President Trump has asserted repeatedly that he wants to get rid of CCSS because he thinks it usurps the power of local communities to be in control of their schools (Resmovits, 2017). The president will not be able to keep this promise because CCSS is not a federal law or initiative, so it remains up to the states to opt into or out of implementing these standards. As of 2016, 35 states and the District of Columbia had adopted CCSS (Ujifusa, 2016), but it will take several years to fully measure the impact of this reform.

Another recent reform effort is based on the concept of Restorative Justice. Restorative justice views a school as a community where everyone is connected in a complex web of relationships. When one individual behaves badly toward another, the web is damaged, affecting everyone. In response to conflicts, restorative justice requires practices that address harm done to an individual and to the community. These practices often represent a preventative rather than a reactionary approach; they offer strategies for teachers to foster positive relationships in a school community, not only among students but also between students, teachers, and staff. In response to conflict, restorative justice practices provide students with the opportunity to engage in discussions of the problem that are intended to identify who was harmed, how the individual was affected, and what actions are most likely to resolve the problem (Kline, 2016). Restorative justice advocates argue that it also addresses broader issues of injustice in schools. For example, the U. S. Department of Justice has reported that three times as many Black students are suspended or expelled from school as White students, and the number of suspensions or expulsions increases when Black children are labeled "special needs" students. Receiving a school suspension is the most significant factor to predict which students will drop out of school (Kline, 2016). Further, as disproportionate numbers of Black students are suspended or expelled, educators may perceive them as "discipline problems," reinforcing negative attitudes and stereotypes. When suspended students return to school, they may feel frustrated and stigmatized, leading to further misbehavior and more suspensions. This can result in a cycle that only ends when the student drops out of school.

Instead of emphasizing punishment, restorative practices provide educators with responses to conflicts that are respectful of all students and promote an inclusive attitude emphasizing self-worth, self-efficacy, and community. Individuals learn more easily in an environment that seems safe and when they are part of a community where they feel they belong. Being part of a community means having positive relationships and being able to depend on one another. When conflicts occur, all students are involved to repair the damage, strengthen relationships, and restore the bonds of community. To achieve these goals, educators engage students in strategies such as conferencing, employing *victim offender mediation*, and using restorative justice circles. Victim offender mediation (VOM) has offenders talk with their victims. One school reported that adolescents participating in VOM began to see it as a learning opportunity. As they listened to a victim's perspective concerning an incident, the young people changed their view of their own behavior, often expressing empathy for their victims. Studies appear to show a connection between empathy and remorse, a feeling that typically encourages individuals to alter their attitudes and behaviors (Kline, 2016). One student said restorative justice practices helped him view his behavior through a different lens. In the past he struck out physically against others because: "I didn't know how to express emotions with my mouth . . . . I feel I can go to someone now (n.p.)" (Brown, 2013).

The strategy of restorative justice circles requires all students impacted by the misbehavior to meet in a circle where the emphasis is on equality, connectedness, and shared leadership. The circle symbolizes a "safe space" to have an honest dialogue in order to find a resolution through group consensus. This approach requires forgiveness of the individual who misbehaved, because only by such forgiveness can the individual be invited back into community and as a consequence restore his or her sense of membership in it (Kline, 2016). Restorative justice has become a global education strategy. Researchers conducted a two-year study of 18 Scottish schools employing restorative justice practices. They reported that all 18 schools made progress in achieving their goals, but 14 schools made significant progress. For example, all schools experienced a decrease of discipline referrals within the school and student suspensions, but the 14 schools provided evidence of a change in the school culture that included students focused more on learning than on behavior, increased positive relationships among students, increased development of student skills in conflict resolution, and a reduction of discipline incidents (Kline, 2016).

 Self-Check 13.4 Complete this self-check quiz to check your understanding of the pedagogical approach called *culturally responsive teaching* and how it addresses the goals of multicultural education.

Afterword

Teaching is the second largest profession in the United States, exceeded only by the people engaged in health care. During each academic year, teachers are responsible for the education of over 50 million students (Hollins, 2016). The challenge confronting educators is how to become multicultural individuals. In the teaching profession, that question will be answered primarily by White middle-class people—primarily women. As our schools increasingly consist of students from diverse groups—students of color, students from low-income families, children and youth who are not Christian, gay and lesbian youth, learners with disabilities—teachers continue to enter the profession from the dominant societal group. In 2013, America's public K–12 schools achieved demographic predictions that 50 percent of the children and youth would be students of color, with the largest increase coming from Latinos (Chiu, Sayman, & Carrero, 2017). By contrast, Taie and Goldring (2017) report that 80 percent of teachers are White (see Table 13.2). In addition, some of the largest increases among K–12 students are from low-income families and in programs for English Language Learners (Chiu, Sayman, & Carrero, 2017).

With the diversity among America's K–12 students predicted to continue increasing over the coming decades, there will be more pressure on the nation's K–12 educators to do a better job of meeting the needs of these diverse students. Multicultural education and especially culturally responsive teaching are being promoted as an effective way to accomplish this goal. According to a study by the Schott Foundation, the consequences are significant. If students continue to receive an inadequate education, there will be more workers who are underemployed, more people who face health risks, less civic participation, and higher rates of incarceration. The Schott study projected that students today may end up with $82.2 billion in lost wages over their lifetimes, and taxpayers may have to pay as much as $59.2 billion to address issues stemming from economic inequity (Richly & Graves, 2012).

Over 35 states have enacted programs to increase the numbers of teachers of color, and they have had some success. According to a University of Pennsylvania study, the numbers of teachers of color nearly doubled from 1988 to 2008 to reach a total of 642,000,

> "The role of the teacher remains the highest calling of a free people. To the teacher, America entrusts her most precious resource, her children; and asks that they be prepared, in all their glorious diversity, to face the rigors of individual participation in a democratic society."
>
> —SHIRLEY HUFSTEDLER (1925–)

Table 13.2 U.S. Public School Teachers

Category	Percentage
Gender	
Female	77
Male	23
Race	
White	80
Black	7
Hispanic	9
Other	2
Highest Degree	
Bachelor's	41
Master's	47
Years of Experience	
Less than 10	38.2
10–14	19.4
More than 14	42.3

SOURCE: Data from Taie, S., and Goldring, R. (2017). Characteristics of Public Elementary and Secondary School Principals in the United States: Results From the 2015–16 National Teacher and Principal Survey First Look (NCES 2017-070). U.S. Department of Education. Washington, DC: National Center for Education Statistics. Retrieved [date] from https://nces.ed.gov/pubsearch/pubsinfo.asp?pubid=2017070

and their growth rate was nearly twice the rate for White teachers (Micklos, 2013). Despite this growth, at the national level studies find that the ratio of teachers of color to students of color has not increased. In part this is because the percentage of students of color in our schools keeps increasing, but there is also a retention problem as many people of color who were recruited to become teachers only stay in the profession for a few years and then leave. In one academic year, 47,600 new teachers of color joined the teaching profession, but at the end of that year 56,000 teachers of color left the profession; 30,000 chose to enter another profession (Micklos, 2013). These data make it clear that teacher education programs will need to increase their efforts to enroll people of color in response to the growing numbers of students of color in our K–12 schools.

Summary

- *Diversity*, *pluralism*, and *multicultural* are terms often used synonymously, but knowing the differences between them is essential to understand and describe the educational reform called *multicultural education*.

- *Essentialism* is the traditional approach taken in American schools, but its assumptions about curriculum, learning, and teaching limit the ability of students to learn.

- Multicultural education is based on honoring diverse cultures that students bring to school, requiring significant changes to curricula, learning activities, and teaching strategies to promote the academic achievement of all students.

- Many educators view the pedagogical approach called *culturally responsive teaching* as an especially effective strategy to achieve the goals of multicultural education.

Terms and Definitions

Critical pedagogy Providing opportunities for students to analyze perspectives and use their analysis to understand and act on perceived inconsistencies

Diversity The presence of human beings with perceived or actual differences based on a variety of human characteristics

Global (or international) education Teaching about the cultures of nations around the world

Hidden curriculum Indirect means by which schools teach the norms and values of a society

Multicultural Any society composed of a number of subordinate groups based on race, ethnicity, religion, language, nationality, income, gender, sexual orientation, and degree of physical, mental, or emotional ability

Multicultural education A process of comprehensive school reform that rejects discrimination in schools and society and accepts and affirms pluralism

Multiethnic education Integrating issues and information about race and ethnicity into school curricula

Pluralism The equal coexistence of diverse cultures, institutions, and individuals within a mutually supportive relationship within the boundaries of one nation

Retention The ability of students to recall information they have been taught

Transfer The ability of students to apply retained knowledge to situations occurring inside and outside the classroom

Discussion Exercises

Exercise #1 The Hidden Curriculum: American Indians

Directions: Might children and youth be learning lessons that we aren't aware they are being taught? Through misunderstanding or lack of adequate knowledge of facts, curriculums may be teaching American children to be biased or to stereotype others. The statements below were originally developed as an elementary punctuation exercise (which is why they have no punctuation marks at the end of each statement).

- Explain in what way each phrase or sentence is biased. Underline the word or words that you judge need replacement.
- Other than learning correct punctuation, what else might children completing this exercise have learned that wasn't intended?

1. Indians lived in our country many years before the White man
2. Have you ever seen an Indian
3. Indians belong to the red race
4. Their skin is of a copper color
5. Most of the men are called warriors
6. The women are called squaws
7. Do they live in wigwams and tepees
8. The red man's name for corn was maize
9. Were bows and arrows used for hunting by the Indians
10. A group of Indians living together is called a "tribe"
11. Do little Indian girls and boys play games
12. The squaws carried their babies on their backs
13. What does each Indian tribe call its "leader"
14. The leader of each tribe is called a "chief"
15. A few Indian tribes still live in the western part of our country

Exercise #2 Whom Would You Hire? Selecting Elementary Teachers

Introduction: Being fair to schoolchildren and youth involves providing the best teachers to help them. Imagine that you are a committee member with responsibility for hiring new teachers. You have four positions open in grades 1 to 3 and eight applicants from whom to choose. You have interviewed all eight, and each has impressed you favorably.

Directions: Read the brief descriptions below, and select the four you would hire.

Candidate 1: Forty-year-old woman, single, lives alone, with 18 years of outstanding experience; highly successful with typically unsuccessful children. Possibly in a lesbian relationship.

Candidate 2: Twenty-four-year-old man, single, two years of experience in a inner-city school. A near genius, he brings outstanding recommendations. Leader of local Black power group; his students use African names and openly reject "slave" names.

Candidate 3: Thirty-five-year-old man, married, father of six. Community minded, interested in Cub Scouts. Known for having very well-organized planned lessons and classes. Ten years of experience. Native American heritage.

Candidate 4: Forty-year-old man, single, living with older adult parents. The candidate has extensive experience from being a local business entrepreneur before returning to college for credentials. Just completed requirements and received a $20,000 grant to work with junior high school students in distributive education. Native of India; practicing Catholic.

Candidate 5: Twenty-six-year-old woman, divorced, supports self and three small children. Highly creative; three years of experience; outstanding recommendations on professional capability. Native of Puerto Rico.

Candidate 6: Fifty-eight-year-old man, highly respected former Episcopal minister who left pulpit to work full time with children. Has just completed teaching credentials.

Candidate 7: Forty-eight-year-old woman, widowed. Twenty-five years of experience, including three years in the Infants School of England. Wants to incorporate Infant School concepts here. Independently wealthy through both her own and her spouse's families.

Candidate 8: Twenty-two-year-old woman, single, a year of experience, excellent recommendations. Voluntarily tutored all four years in college, including full time in summers. Living openly in the community with a man of another race.

Follow-up: Discuss the qualifications of each committee member. When your group has selected four teacher candidates for the jobs, post your selections and compare your choices with those of other groups.

Chapter 14
Pluralism in Society: Creating Unity in a Diverse America

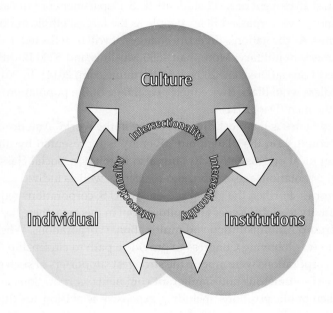

 ## Learning Outcomes

After reading this chapter you will know and be able to:

14.1 Describe and respond to some of the major arguments from both advocates and opponents of affirmative action.

14.2 Explain some reasons why leaders in higher education believe that a diverse student population on a college campus benefits all students.

14.3 Explain the rationale for businesses and corporations to hire employees in order to create a diverse population at the worksite.

14.4 Provide examples of the lack of people of color in conventional mass media, distortions in how they are portrayed in the media, and digital media projects that address diversity issues.

14.5 Describe steps the military has taken in response to diversity among its ranks, and explain what diversity issues still remain for the military to address.

> "How many goodly creatures are there here! How beauteous mankind is! O brave new world, That has such people in't."
>
> — WILLIAM SHAKESPEARE (1564–1616)

All around us, a brave new world is taking shape in America. Despite a wealth of **diversity**, America has not yet become a pluralistic society. **Pluralism** perceives human differences as enriching, and values that diversity. Yet Americans are still wary of one another, and fearful when conflicts occur between groups. Nevertheless, changes are taking place that encourage us to be more accepting of others and more pluralistic. Students in K–12 schools and colleges today will shape our society in the future; yet too many Americans don't realize that nearly 50 percent of today's K–12 children and youth are students of color (Chiu, Sayman, & Carrero, 2017). Children of immigrants constitute almost 18 percent of K–12 students (U.S. Department of Education, 2014). In addition, Latinos have surpassed Black people as the largest ethnic minority group in the United States. As the nation's diversity changes, it will be reflected in organizations such as the American military: More than 4500 Muslims and 5200 Buddhists serve in the U.S. Armed Forces (Dreazen, 2009; WorldTribune.com, 2014). In 2011, 31 percent of women soldiers were Black (twice their percentage of the population) compared to 16 percent of the men (Dao, 2011).

The United States is the most diverse society in the world. Americans come from almost every country on the planet; our diversity is represented by differences not only in geographical origins (ethnicity) but also in religion, social class, disabilities, gender, sexual orientation, age, region, and dialect, as well as individuals who fit into multiple categories. Further, the global presence of U.S. corporations requires that we cultivate sensitivity to global issues and cultures, but in this area, there has been conflict between the Trump Administration and multinational corporations. When the Obama Administration was lobbying Congress to provide a path to citizenship for unauthorized workers, corporations were among the strongest supporters of such efforts. Given President Trump's numerous anti-immigrant comments, corporations both large and small have taken public positions, including expensive television ads during the 2017 Super Bowl, praising immigrant contributions to our nation (Kuttner, 2017).

In support of diversity, corporations have challenged President Trump on other issues as well, such as Planned Parenthood. During the campaign, Trump repeatedly insisted that he agreed with the critics of Planned Parenthood and was prepared to defund it, but since the election there has been stiff opposition to this proposal, including the objections of 41 large corporations who have sent contributions directly to Planned Parenthood as a show of support. This does not appear to be an issue polarized around "liberal" or "conservative" views since many of these corporations are not viewed as politically liberal, including Ford, Nike, American Express, Pepsi, and Coca-Cola. Some national department stores have responded to the president's threat to defund Planned Parenthood by refusing to carry Trump products (Kuttner, 2017). Despite corporate opposition, in April 2017, President Trump signed a bill allowing states to withhold federal money from any organization providing abortion services. Perhaps because of corporate support for Planned Parenthood, no media were invited to the signing ceremony (Merica, 2017).

Some corporations have made transparency about their diversity a high priority. All major U.S. employers are required to submit an affirmative action report to the Equal Employment Opportunity Commission, but they do not have to inform the public about the results. Google went public with its analysis of 44,000 people in its workforce, and the Associated Press (2014) reported that only 2 percent of Google's employees were Black, 3 percent were Hispanic, about 33 percent were Asian American, while 62 percent were White. As for gender, the women to men ratio is about 30 to 70. Another example is Hewlett-Packard, which has been publishing its employment data since 2001.

According to its 2012 report, of 331,800 employees, 7.7 percent were Black, 6.7 percent were Hispanic, 14.6 percent were Asian American, 0.3 percent were Native American, and 64.8 percent were White. The women to men employee ratio was 33 to 67 (Associated Press, 2014). Facebook released its employee numbers with the admission that the company is not yet where it wants to be. In the United States, the number of Latino employees went from 4 percent to 5 percent, and Black employees went from 2 percent to 3 percent. The United States has done better with women employees. With a global workforce of over 2 billion people, the number of women globally rose to 35 percent, the women in technology positions has risen to 19 percent, and women constitute 27 percent of new hires in engineering (Williams, 2017). The emphasis on diversity has its roots in the federal affirmative action initiative, and it is worthwhile to briefly review that history before discussing what is happening in four major societal areas—higher education, business, mass media, and the military.

Origin and Evolution of Affirmative Action

> "For each age is a dream that is dying. Or one that is coming to birth."
> — ARTHUR O'SHAUGHNESSY (1844–1881)

President John F. Kennedy first used the phrase **affirmative action** when he issued Executive Order 10025 mandating that the federal government aggressively recruit and hire African Americans. Title VII of the 1964 Civil Rights Act expanded this concept to include people of color and women being employed by private companies contracted to do work for the federal government. Companies had to file affirmative action plans with hiring goals and timetables for those goals. By mandating affirmative action, the federal government began a major initiative to promote pluralism by reducing acts of discrimination and providing opportunity for women and people of color. Title VII stated that if a finding of discrimination is justified, a court might order an employer "to take such affirmative action as may be appropriate." A 1972 Title VII amendment added "or any other equitable relief as the courts deem appropriate" (Greene, 1989, p. 15). Ever since the Civil Rights Act became law, Title VII has been controversial, keeping the issue of equal opportunity for all Americans in the public eye.

According to the Civil Rights Act, affirmative action plans represent voluntary programs unless a court issues an order that an affirmative action plan be designed and implemented. Determining the need for an affirmative action plan begins by analyzing the diversity of employees at a business or agency or the student population at a university. If population variation is similar to that of available applicants, there is said to be no equity problem. If disparities exist, however, each phase of the application and selection process is evaluated for bias that may advantage some applicants and disadvantage others.

What are some of the major arguments in the affirmative action debate?

Debate concerning affirmative action has resonated from the public square to the U.S. Supreme Court. The crux of the debate concerns whether affirmative action was intended only to redress victims of intentional discrimination or if it mandates that programs create a more just distribution of women and minorities in the workforce and in higher education. In the business community, the principal emphasis has been on compensating victims of discrimination, while in institutions of higher education, admissions policies have been implemented to increase the numbers of women and minorities.

Affirmative action advocates argue that aggressive action is required to address inequities in hiring and college admissions. Proponents insist our society must guarantee equal opportunity to every citizen to address the ample evidence documenting our failure to achieve this goal. Since a college degree is required to qualify for certain jobs, policies and practices of college admission are scrutinized, just as businesses and corporations are monitored to ensure that women and minorities have the same opportunity as White men to be hired and promoted. Advocates explain that monitoring is not intended to be punitive but is designed to achieve the broader goal of strengthening our society by creating racial, gender, and ethnic unity. Arguing for the need to maintain race-based affirmative action programs, advocates note the ongoing racial disparities in unemployment, poverty rates, and wealth accumulation between people of color and White people as well as racial profiling and other inequities in the justice system (Higginbotham, 2014).

Affirmative action opponents counter that equal opportunity programs have created greater American disunity. They denounce affirmative action plans as racist for establishing racial quotas to be achieved by what they call "preferential treatment." Opponents also claim that businesses and schools have often been forced to accept women and minorities who are less qualified than the White men who were rejected. They say it is ironic that affirmative action—with a goal of reducing discrimination—is engaging in "reverse discrimination," decreasing opportunity for qualified White men. Some advocates suggest the compromise of basing action plans on income and not race. They argue that it will result in increased admissions of first-generation college students as well as students of color. Their argument is supported by a 2012 report of 10 leading public universities that implemented an income-based strategy instead of a race-based one; 7 of the 10 maintained or even increased the percent of African American and Latino students in their schools (Kahlenberg & Potter, 2014).

What limitations have the courts placed on affirmative action programs?

Quality and competence were the focus of the *Griggs v. Duke Power* case heard by the U.S. Supreme Court in 1971. Job applicants at the Duke Power Company were required to have a high school diploma or passing scores on a specific standardized test. Lawyers argued that the requirement excluded a higher percentage of Black people than White people because unequal educational opportunities and other inequities prevented more Black than White youth from earning high school diplomas. The U.S. Supreme Court ruled that any hiring practice that was intended to select the most qualified candidates was legitimate. Companies could not be held accountable for past discrimination that adversely affected individuals in the present. As long as job requirements were related to work performance, they could not be labeled discriminatory, even if they did advantage some job applicants.

In 1986, the U.S. Supreme Court used the same concept to uphold the seniority system to determine layoffs during economic downturns in *Wygant v. Jackson Board of Education*. Because of past discrimination against women and minorities, adhering to **seniority system** priorities required employers to lay off people with least seniority: "last hired, first fired." Although the procedure seemed race neutral, lawyers provided evidence that women and minority employees were the most likely to have low seniority and to be dismissed. Supreme Court justices acknowledged the problem but still perceived the seniority system as constitutional because it does not represent intentional discrimination.

Have the courts approved the use of quotas in affirmative action plans?

Whenever **racial quotas** have been employed, the U.S. Supreme Court has always ruled against them, declaring that Title VII never mandated racial (or other) quotas.

Indeed, the justices are correct. There is no mention of quotas in Title VII, nor anything to suggest that employers must hire unqualified applicants; as Greene (1989) noted, section 703 (j) of Title VII states:

> Nothing contained in this title shall be interpreted to require any employer, employment agency, labor organization, or joint labor-management committee subject to this title to grant preferential treatment to any individual or group. (p. 60)

One of the clearest judgments against racial quotas was the Supreme Court's ruling in the case of *Regents of California v. Bakke*. In 1970, 80 percent of the 800 students of color attending medical school in the United States were enrolled in programs at two historically Black universities. Because minorities never comprised more than 3 percent of students at the University of California–Davis Medical School, the university decided to reserve eight of their admissions placements (16 percent) for minority applicants. For two consecutive years, Alan Bakke was rejected by UC–Davis despite having a grade-point average and Medical College Admissions Test scores higher than those of several minority applicants who were admitted. Bakke's lawyers argued relentlessly against the concept of racial quotas while UC–Davis lawyers argued that the university only accepted academically qualified applicants to their medical school and that preferential treatment of minorities was necessary to increase the numbers of minorities in professions "from which minorities were long excluded because of generations of pervasive racial discrimination" (Ball, 2000, p. 92).

The 1978 decision on *Bakke* fragmented the Court. Four justices approved the UC–Davis affirmative action plan, and four justices rejected it, arguing that race should play no role in admission decisions. Justice Powell cast the deciding vote. In his written opinion, Powell said that racial quotas were an unconstitutional strategy for achieving affirmative action goals, but race could be used as one factor among others in considering college applicants.

What was the "set aside" strategy for minority-owned businesses?

Another affirmative action strategy rejected by the courts was the practice of setting aside a certain percentage of tax-funded projects for minority-owned businesses. In 1983, the city of Richmond, Virginia, was 50 percent African American, but in the previous five years, less than 1 percent of funds spent on city projects had been paid to minority-owned businesses. The Richmond city council approved an affirmative action plan to require recipients of city construction projects to subcontract at least 30 percent of the dollar value of these projects to minority-owned businesses. When J.A. Croson Company insisted it could not find any suitable minority-owned businesses and asked for a waiver of the subcontracting requirement, the city refused and informed the company that it would resubmit their part of the project for new bids. The company brought the case to federal court, and the Supreme Court ruled on it in 1989.

Writing for the majority in the *City of Richmond v. J.A. Croson Co.*, Sandra Day O'Connor criticized Richmond's **set-aside program** for its apparently arbitrary determination of the 30 percent figure and for not providing evidence demonstrating that previous contractors had intentionally discriminated against minority-owned businesses. O'Connor said the Richmond City Council could have implemented effective, race-neutral strategies rather than establishing set-aside quotas. The court affirmed the right to remedy past discrimination but again rejected racial quotas as a legitimate constitutional strategy (Crosby & VanDeVeer, 2000).

Should affirmative action programs be eliminated?

By the mid-1990s, retiring Supreme Court Justice Harold Blackmun questioned whether the majority of White Americans believed that discrimination against non-White people

"One who gains strength by overcoming obstacles possesses the only strength which can overcome adversity."

— ALBERT SCHWEITZER (1875–1965)

Video Example 14.1
This video explores an affirmative action ruling in Michigan. What different perspectives on affirmative action from Chapter 14 are discussed in the video? What have the effects of the ruling been on underrepresented populations in higher education?

https://www.youtube.com/watch?v=wgcYjbEfBbA

still existed. Because of ongoing criticism of affirmative action, in 2000, President Clinton appointed a task force to review all federal affirmative action programs. Although some changes were recommended, the task force concluded that the programs reviewed did not include quotas or mandate preferences for unqualified individuals and did not engage in reverse discrimination. Instead, the programs were designed to remedy past discrimination and to provide for equal opportunity (Ball, 2000). Today the evidence reveals that racial disparities still exist: Twice as many Black people as White people are unemployed, living in poverty or homeless, and the disparities are similar for Latinos (Higginbotham, 2014). Yet the Trump Administration has asked the Department of Justice to use its resources to investigate and possibly bring lawsuits against universities whose admissions policies appear to use race to discriminate against White applicants.

✓ Self-Check 14.1 Complete this self-check quiz to check your understanding of the major arguments from both advocates and opponents of affirmative action.

Higher Education and Diversity

Since the 1960s, colleges and universities have implemented affirmative action plans to increase the numbers of students of color on their campuses. Although many administrators initially viewed affirmative action as unnecessary interference, they eventually took a more pluralistic attitude, arguing that having diverse students on campus benefits the entire student population. Administrators, faculty, and student leaders on college campuses have consistently supported setting diversity goals. Musil (1996) summarized their shared perspective in the 1990s:

> To invite that diversity onto campus is not simply an act of charity. It is an act of raw self-interest . . . . it will make higher education better than it is. It expands our notion of learning. It widens what we study and how we study it. It improves our pedagogy. It adds to our resources in human capital. (p. 225)

What are some criticisms of diversity goals in higher education?

Affirmative action plans in higher education and the increased diversity they have helped produce have been the subject of much criticism. Even some people of color say affirmative action has stigmatized students of color because their academic ability is questioned by White people who believe that students of color are admitted through lower standards. Some faculty blame affirmative action for a decline in academic standards and for promoting a multicultural curriculum that has diminished the rigor of a traditional college education.

Faculty who are attempting to create a more inclusive curriculum are accused by critics of promoting a "political agenda" rather than having purely academic objectives. However, it would seem equally appropriate to accuse advocates for the preservation of a curriculum that emphasizes White people of having a political agenda as well. It is true that many traditional college classes based on a Eurocentric curriculum have been replaced by courses with a more inclusive and objective content (Kiley, 2011), but problems persist. Sleeter (2011) reported that students of color in college courses still encounter minimal information written by or about their groups, and often the information provided misrepresents or distorts the group being described. Advocates for diversity argue that exposure to alternative perspectives in course content and class discussions benefits all college students, even White students. Studies report that White students are more cognitively stimulated in such classes than they are in traditional, racially homogenous classes (Wells, Fox, & Cordova-Corbo, 2016). When colleges are inclusive in terms of course content, instructional faculty, and students, everyone benefits.

What are the benefits of increasing diversity among college faculty and in course content?

In addition to the omission of people of color in curriculum, the lack of faculty of color means that college students tend to be taught from the perspective of White men. The National Center for Education Statistics (2015) reported that people of color constitute about 16 percent of full-time higher education faculty, and that the majority had non-tenured positions as lecturers, instructors, or assistant professors. Berner (2012) quotes educational theorist Charles Glenn, who asserts that education "presents pictures or maps of reality that reflect, unavoidably, particular choices about . . . what is significant and what unworthy of notice. No aspect of schooling can be truly neutral" (n.p.). For that reason, courses taught by faculty of color would benefit all students, including White students, by presenting perspectives they are not likely to have encountered. What Reddy (2002) observed over a decade ago is still true today:

> Students—especially but not exclusively white students—arrive in our college classrooms with predictable baggage. Prepared by virtually every element of the society in which we live, they come ready to accept white authority, intelligence and rightness while discounting the views and experiences of people of color. (p. 54)

Because of Reddy's "predictable baggage," it is not inevitable that positive outcomes will occur if White students and students of color are brought together on a college campus; they may or may not enjoy one another or learn from one another. (See Figure 14.1.) To ensure productive interactions between members of diverse groups, colleges must sponsor diversity workshops, require all students to take at least one course on diversity, encourage relevant academic departments to include at least one course with significant content on diversity issues in their majors and minors, and encourage faculty to integrate content about diversity issues into their courses.

Since the 1960s, professors in institutions of higher education have created scholarly courses focusing on one or more diverse groups. As these professors grappled with

> "The surest way to corrupt a youth is to instruct him to hold in higher esteem those who think alike than those who think differently."
>
> — FRIEDRICH NIETZSCHE (1844–1900)

Figure 14.1 Political Correctness?

SOURCE: Courtesy of *The Daily Cardinal*, University of Wisconsin.

diversity issues, their efforts have been learning experiences for themselves as well as their students. Musil (1996) provided this critique of those early efforts:

> Black studies were typically about only men. Women's studies were typically only about white women. Gay and lesbian studies had no practicing Christians or Jews. And none of the three paid much attention to those in the group who were old, working class or disabled. Today it is largely commonplace in the most influential texts . . . in these kinds of courses to recognize the reality of our multiple identities. (p. 228)

Unfortunately, enrollment figures indicate that few White students take ethnic studies courses, and few men enroll in women's studies courses. Although research on college courses is sparse, there is a growing body of research on high school students that has documented the benefits for students who have taken ethnic studies classes, including being more likely to graduate from high school, better school attendance, and improved academic performance. Also, several studies have found that ethnic studies classes helped to reduce the achievement gap between White students and Black or Latino students (Anderson, 2015; Donald, 2016; Lee, 2017). Further, Greenberg (2016) has identified several ways that White students could benefit from participating in ethnic studies classes such as learning a more accurate version of American history, gaining a better understanding of inequality issues, and strengthening their commitment to the shared American values that are at the core of ethnic studies classes.

Feminists and faculty of color continue to challenge the lack of relevance and inclusiveness in college curricula, and corporate America appears to support them. An amicus brief filed by almost half of the Fortune 100 companies supporting affirmative action policies in higher education argued that to be successful in our global economy, corporations must have employees with a broad range of knowledge and experiences with culture, race, religion, and other forms of diversity. Corporations need employees who can demonstrate cross-cultural skills and be able to bring different perspectives and creative approaches to problem-solving rather than being limited to linear, conventional thinking (Wells, Fox, & Cordova-Corbo, 2016). Starting in the late 1980s, colleges and universities began to establish requirements for ethnic studies or other kinds of diversity courses. By the start of the twenty-first century, Humphreys (2000) reported that 63 percent of colleges and universities either had at least one diversity course as a graduation requirement or they were developing such a course; 42 percent required more than one course; and 25 percent had had such a requirement in place for more than 10 years. By 2014, a report on higher education found that nearly every campus included in this national study had some kind of diversity requirement for graduation (Kabbany, 2014).

What have diversity advocates achieved and what issues persist?

As diversity courses have developed over the years, they have not only provided a greater understanding of divergent groups but also helped students appreciate the benefits of diversity in terms of engaging in interactions with different groups of people, learning new perspectives, and gaining a greater understanding of our multicultural society. In a society as diverse and democratic as the United States, colleges and universities must facilitate better understanding between all groups. Ball (2000) noted, "For democracy to flourish, college students have to be able to interact with other students who are different from them" (p. 13). Although critics of pluralism fear it will bring division and disunity, advocates like Berner (2012) insist: "Pluralism is not only more honest about the formational nature of education . . . but the institutions it generates are more democratic than our present system" (n.p.).

Diversity does not just refer to obvious differences of race, ethnicity, gender, or disabilities. Diversity includes other changes taking place in students attending college

"Democracy is a way of life . . . a vibrant, living sweep of hope and progress which constantly strives for the fulfillment of its objective in life—the search for truth, justice, and human dignity."

— SAUL ALINSKY (1909–1972)

today: About 40 percent of all college students are over 24 years old (Nelson, 2014), and 50 percent are the first in their family to attend college (Lynch, 2013); in addition, the enrollment of students with learning disabilities is steadily increasing. Individuals admitted to college today may require modifications of and accommodations within traditional policies and practices on campuses. Yet as demographic developments and affirmative action plans change the face of our campuses, opponents struggle to maintain the status quo. White students filed suit against both graduate and undergraduate admissions programs at the University of Michigan for including race in their admissions procedures. In 2003, the Supreme Court's ruling on this case maintained its consistent position of allowing race to be used as a factor in admissions procedures while rejecting approaches that appear to establish racial quotas.

In response to the accusation that less qualified minority students were being admitted to the University of Michigan law school, a study was conducted of Michigan's law school graduates in terms of their job status, salaries, awards, and community contributions. The study found that minority graduates were just as successful on these measures as their White peers (Johnson, 2011). In writing the majority decision upholding the right for universities to use race as a factor in recruiting students, Sandra Day O'Connor noted: "numerous studies and reports (show) that such diversity promotes learning outcomes and prepares students for an increasingly diverse workforce" (Sue, 2015). She went on to address amicus briefs filed by corporations explaining their need for culturally competent employees to function effectively in the global marketplace. Yet in 2014, the Supreme Court also upheld a constitutional amendment passed by Michigan voters banning the use of affirmative action in determining admission to the state's public universities. In a passionate dissent, Justice Sonia Sotomayor said that the Constitution did not "give the majority free rein to erect selective barriers against racial minorities" (Liptak, 2014, n.p.). This remains a contentious issue, and it is likely that there will be further court decisions in the years ahead.

Video Example 14.2

In this video, a parent discusses how more students in his child's school district are now getting the opportunity to, and choosing to, go to college. How do this parent's responses relate to Chapter 14's discussion of diversity in higher education? What barriers might the students in his district have previously faced when making the decision to go to college?

 Self-Check 14.2 Complete this self-check quiz to check your understanding of why leaders in higher education believe that a diverse student population on a college campus benefits all students.

Corporate, Small Business, and a Diverse Workforce

It surprised opponents of affirmative action to discover that several Fortune 500 corporations filed amicus briefs in support of the admissions policies at Michigan's law school; for the past two decades, the private sector has supported affirmative action. In the early 1980s, many corporations opposed the Reagan Administration's efforts to reduce the demand for contractor compliance on federal projects. According to responses from chief executive officers (CEOs), 122 of 128 major corporations would "retain their affirmative action plans [even] if the Federal government ended [required] affirmative action" (Reskin, 2000, p. 111). CEOs tend to believe that affirmative action has improved hiring, marketing, and productivity.

For that reason, American business executives have become more attentive to diversity, especially in recent years. They have to be. From 2001–2015, Asian and Latino workers experienced the fastest job growth, and it has been spread over a variety of occupations. Women hold 49 percent of all jobs, the highest peacetime percentage yet recorded, and workers 55 and older increased by 40 percent, while the number of employed teenagers dropped by 33 percent (Pizzo, 2015). This is part of the change predicted for our evolving global economy. Over a decade ago, Hymowitz (2005) predicted in a *Wall Street Journal* article: "If companies are going to sell products and services globally, they will need a rich mix of employees with varied perspectives and experiences" (p. R1). By 2030, people of color will represent over half of the American workforce, and Latinos alone will constitute about one third of it (Vuong, 2013). Business leaders understand that responding positively to diversity by implementing pluralistic policies and practices is necessary because it is not only the workforce that is becoming more diverse but also the consumers in the American economy.

Demographers have documented the growing numbers of women and people of color in the workforce and in the population. Experts are predicting that the population of the United States will increase from about 315 million to over 400 million by 2060 with the largest increases occurring in communities of color (Colby & Ortman, 2015). Latinos are getting more attention because they are the fastest growing ethnic group. From 2007 to 2012, Latinos started new businesses at a rate 60 times higher than non-Latinos, and from 2007 to 2016, Latina businesses increased by 137 percent, a rate that was faster than any other group of minority women. These businesses employed about 2.5 million workers, making Latino businesses a major factor in the growth of the U.S. economy (Berenson, 2016). Further, people with money to spend command attention from American businesses. According to recent data, people of color represent slightly more than $3 trillion of purchasing power (see Table 14.1), and women have at least $7 trillion of purchasing power (Cloud, 2016). That figure is certainly an underestimate because women often choose clothes for men and recommend other items that men purchase—but their influence would not be reflected in data on women's purchases. Yet Walter (2012) points out that women make decisions on 85 percent of all purchases; 75 percent of women claim to be the primary shoppers in their households; and women are responsible for almost 60 percent of all online spending. Similarly, experts say that people with a disability influence purchases of their families, so their purchasing power is probably higher than the estimated $408 billion indicated in Table 14.1.

What has been the impact of discrimination lawsuits against corporations?

A Black woman at CNN was tired of hearing her colleagues making racist comments such as complaints about how hard it was to manage Black people or wondering if Black slaves in the 1900s were of more value than if Black people were slaves today. Believing that her seven years of work for CNN should have given her credibility, she complained to the Human Relations office. Five days later she was fired. When she filed a discrimination complaint against CNN, 175 other Black CNN employees joined her in alleging various problems such as being underpaid in comparison to White colleagues and denied promotions to top management positions (Davis, 2017). When corporations lose such cases, the fines can be millions of dollars, and that's a major factor behind corporations today making sure that their policies and practices are bias-free, and many are

Table 14.1 Diversity and Purchasing Power Among U.S. Consumers

Group	Population Numbers	Purchasing Power	
LGBTQ people	(10–20 million)	$830 billion	
People with disabilities	63 million	$408 billion	
African Americans	45 million	$1.2 trillion	
Asian Americans	20 million	$770 billion	
Hispanic Americans	55 million	$1.3 trillion	
Women	161 million	$7 trillion	

SOURCE: Race/ethnic groups from (Love, 2016; Nielsen, 2015; Berenson, 2016); for people with disabilities from Imparato, Houtenville, & Shaffert (2010); for women from Cloud (2016); population data from the Census Bureau.

taking a higher profile in denouncing cases of discrimination. For example, a number of corporations have boycotted North Carolina for passing voter ID laws that have been shown to suppress the votes of people of color in the state. Another conflict began when President Trump issued an executive order repealing former President Obama's guidelines on how transgender students should access bathrooms, causing several of America's largest corporations (e.g., Apple and Google) to defend transgender people on that issue as well as others. Corporations, including sports organizations, have denounced North Carolina for its negative practices regarding transgender citizens and have moved their events and conventions to other states (Kuttner, 2017). Yet some corporations are still slow to embrace diversity.

In 2011, a Muslim woman from California was fired for insisting on wearing her headscarf (hijab) at work. She brought discrimination charges against the parent company, Abercrombie & Fitch, which is no stranger to allegations of discrimination. In 2004, the company paid $50 million in a settlement regarding allegations of discrimination against women and minorities. The Muslim woman was told in her job interview that she could wear her headscarf as long as it contained the company colors. After four months on the job, she was told not to wear the headscarf, and when she questioned the decision, she was suspended and then fired. One of her lawyers was confident they would win the case because the company's actions were "egregious" as well as illegal (May, 2011): "For an employer to, point-blank, require an employee to relinquish their religious practice is a violation of our cherished civil rights laws" (n.p.). In June 2015, the U.S. Supreme Court handed down an eight to one decision against Abercrombie & Fitch, mandating that employers provide religious accommodations for employees (Liptak, 2015). The problems at CNN and Abercrombie & Fitch were not isolated incidents. According to the Equal Employment Opportunity Commission (2014), it collected fines in excess of $372 million on discrimination complaints in 2013, the highest monetary recovery in its history.

What have corporations done to increase their diversity and create a positive work environment?

Most businesses do not address diversity issues in response to legal action but because they recognize the advantages in promoting workplace diversity. Target's website discusses its programs to nurture young Hispanic corporate executive, its leadership program for Asian/Pacific Island employees to develop their leadership skills, and its work with GLSEN to promote "safe and affirming" K–12 schools for LGBTQ students. The website for Darden's Restaurants emphasizes its workforce—52 percent women and 48 percent people of color, 37 percent of its U.S. managers are women, its Supplier Diversity Initiative, and that *Latina Style Magazine* named Darden's as one of the 50 Best Companies for Latinas. The top 10 of DiversityInc (2017) best companies for diversity included AT&T, Johnson & Johnson, PwC, Sodexo, and Marriott International. Hunt, Layton, and Prince (2015) cite a recent study finding that companies in the top 25 percent in terms of gender or racial/ethnic diversity are more likely to have profits exceeding the median for their industry nationwide and that companies in the bottom 25 percent with regard to diversity are more likely to be below the median. The study goes on to say that diversity is a difference that will continue to have a positive impact over time.

Having a positive work environment to accommodate diversity improves productivity and reduces turnover costs. Depending on whether the job is low wage or high wage, the cost in the private sector of hiring a new employee is an average of $4000 for employees in all job categories and $7000 for managerial and professional employees (Greenwood, 2014). By implementing employee-friendly policies, one grocery store chain reduced its full-time worker turnover rate to 4 percent, realizing a significant savings (Lucas, 2012). One corporate consulting firm estimated that for just reducing

"This country will not be a permanently good place for any of us to live in unless we make it a reasonably good place for all of us to live in."
— THEODORE ROOSEVELT (1858–1919)

turnover by 1 percent a year, companies could save between $200,000 and $2 million (Nobscot Corporation, 2014).

In one study of contrasting workplace environments, when color blindness was emphasized, it resulted in an affirmation of the majority group's dominance while minority group members felt marginalized. Minority group employees had lower morale and lower productivity, but in workplaces promoting a multicultural approach, meaning that group differences were viewed as positive and affirmed, White employees engaged in more inclusive behaviors, there was increased interaction between members of different groups, and people of color reported a reduction in feelings of marginalization. Other studies have reported similar outcomes, concluding that workplaces emphasizing a color-blind attitude tend to result in perceptions of bias by employees of color, but workplaces affirming group differences resulted in people of color perceiving less bias at work (Sue, 2015). Some businesses have expanded their view of diversity issues to include the difficulty for single parents and dual career couples to find quality childcare, and they have established day-care centers at the worksite.

PwC is an accounting firm in Dallas ranked in the top 10 in the nation on diversity issues according to DiversityInc. PwC employees were reeling from the Baton Rouge and Dallas shootings, so CEO Tim Ryan called for town hall meetings to share their feelings. As they talked, employees developed a better understanding of one another even though they also became aware of how much they did not know about one another. For example, White employees had no idea that their Black colleagues taught their children explicit strategies so they would not get pulled over by the police. Ryan wanted to bring other CEOs together to share what they learned from the town halls (Hurst, 2015). By 2017, over 150 chief executives had signed up for CEO Action for Diversity and Inclusion, representing over 50 industries in all 50 states with millions of workers. Participation required corporate commitment to making its workplace a welcoming place and a safe place to discuss diversity issues and to developing training programs for employees that addressed problems created by unconscious biases (Business Wire, 2017).

How effective are diversity training programs?

Diversity training is not new, but older programs were considered largely ineffective because they tended to use one of two approaches: sensitivity training, which appeared to have little practical value, or a confrontational approach that antagonized White men. Current diversity training covers a broader range of topics, has a pragmatic business rationale for promoting diversity, and develops specific skills in communication and management. Many businesses are implementing diversity training programs not only to improve work relations between diverse employees and managers but also to ensure that employees will interact effectively with diverse customers. Some programs include **diversity pairing**, in which people from diverse backgrounds are paired to provide them with opportunities to interact and become better acquainted. Such pairs may be combined with mentoring, as when a White male manager is paired with an employee of color or a woman. Many businesses create multicultural teams to improve problem solving, and these teams allow workers to learn more about their colleagues. (See Figure 14.2.)

University Alliance (2014) described diversity training programs at Sodexo and Hewitt Associates. Sodexo is a food and facilities management service. Although it originated in France, it is now one of the largest employers in the United States. Diversity training at Sodexo does not consist of an occasional workshop but is ongoing, engaging employees at all levels of the organization in activities that include community service and mentoring. Sodexo believes that its diversity training is a major factor in both its increased productivity and its retention of women and minorities, and a recent study of the effectiveness of its diversity training programs concluded that its return on investment (ROI) was $19 for every dollar it spent.

Figure 14.2 Diversity at Work

The cartoon illustrates why many corporations and businesses believe it is necessary to engage in diversity training for employees.

Hewitt Associates, a consulting and human resources firm, is a contrasting example. Its leaders believed their "organizational culture" was not conducive to a diversity training program. They spent two years discussing the issue internally and preparing for the implementation. In their training, executives came together with employees for theater-based training that offered new perspectives with insights on how people from diverse backgrounds might react to working at Hewitt. After a year of training, executives were paired with an associate who was culturally different in a program called Cross-Cultural Learning Partners. Partners met for two hours each month, completing a monthly assignment that might include reading, watching a movie, or reflecting on workplace situations. At the end of the second year, an evaluation showed that leaders had embraced the goals of the program, and even quantitative measures found that there had been significant learning (University Alliance, 2014).

Some U.S. corporations have been especially aggressive in their commitment to diversity. In 1995, the CEO at International Business Machines (IBM) was concerned that his senior executive team had minimal diversity, despite IBM's affirmative action efforts. He implemented a new diversity initiative, which over a 10-year period resulted in an increase of five times the number of female senior executives and tripled the number of those who were U.S.-born minorities. In 2000, IBM had no women as country managers for its overseas operations, but by 2005, the company had hired nine women general managers for such countries as France, Spain, Thailand, New Zealand, and Peru. IBM's website (IBM, 2015) notes that 29 percent of its employees are women, as are 25 percent of its managers, 23 percent of its executive managers, and three senior vice presidents. In addition, IBM's current CEO is a woman—Virginia Rometty.

What diversity problems persist?

Diversity problems still arise in the business community. Salary data document that women and minorities still earn substantially less money than White men and that minorities continue to be underrepresented in management. African Americans and Hispanics constitute 36 percent of the U.S. population, but they represent only 18.4 percent of managers—9.1 percent and 9.3 percent, respectively (U.S. Bureau of Labor Statistics, 2017). An EEOC report on racial discrimination identified problems such as employers' unconscious biases, lack of professional networks and mentors, and poor enforcement of regulations (Muhammad, 2013). Racial discrimination lawsuits have been filed against such major employers as Walmart and General Electric (GE). In 2005, a lawsuit against GE alleged that Black managers were being paid less than White managers and were denied promotions; in addition, Black employees encountered racial slurs at work. In 2010, 60 African American employees filed another discrimination lawsuit against GE, which was the parent company of their employer, accusing their supervisor of denying them appropriate medical attention, using racial slurs, and firing Black workers. Further, they alleged that GE executives were aware of the supervisor's inappropriate behavior but took no action (Nittle, 2014).

> "Man cannot degrade women without himself falling into degradation."
>
> — SARAH LEWIS (1739–1848)

Women hold 41.4 percent of managerial positions (U.S. Bureau of Labor Statistics, 2017) and appear to be fairly represented, but the **glass ceiling** prevents them from rising as high as their abilities should permit. Cassidy (2014) describes a 15-year study reporting that only 1.3 percent of CEOs were women, a "scandalously" small number. Further, gender discrimination remains a problem, whether the companies are established or new. A female marketing vice president charged matchmaking mobile app Tinder with sexual harassment and discrimination. Her lawsuit included text messages from her chief marketing officer, documenting his verbal harassment such as calling her a "whore" and threatening to fire her (Sullivan, 2014). Two former Goldman Sachs employees filed a lawsuit in 2010, which was expanded in 2014 to include detailed accounts of sexism and harassment. Women traders were not invited to company-sponsored golf trips and visits to strip clubs, they were asked to do administrative tasks that male traders were never asked to do, and they earned 21 percent less than their male peers. The lawsuit says women were also passed over for promotion, citing the case of a female vice president who earned $9.5 million for Goldman (an increase of $3.5 million from the previous year), only to see a male colleague who had generated less money for the investment bank be awarded the promotion to managing director that she had sought (Sullivan, 2014).

Discrimination at the workplace exists for other groups as well. In a 2014 lawsuit against the Library of Congress, a gay employee claimed he was denied promotions and subjected to a hostile work environment because of his sexual orientation (Thomaston, 2014). A part-time clerk for Walmart who had cerebral palsy brought a doctor's note suggesting that her employer provide her with brief breaks so she could periodically be off her feet, but her manager refused. The EEOC ruled that this was an easy accommodation, and had the supervisors at Walmart examined the situation more carefully, they would have seen that this accommodation was only temporary, not a long-term problem. Walmart paid a $50,000 settlement when the accommodation would have cost them nothing (Greenwald, 2012). There are many good reasons for corporations to create workplaces that are receptive to diversity, and no good reasons not to.

 Self-Check 14.3 Complete this self-check quiz to check your understanding of the rationale for businesses and corporations to hire employees in order to create a diverse population at the worksite.

Mass Media

Kawamoto (2003) has written that traditional definitions of mass media have addressed various means of sending information to a mass audience, and these definitions have traditionally focused on such vehicles as books, newspapers, magazines, radio, and television—what some scholars now refer to as "legacy media." The continuing growth of digital media has challenged these traditional definitions of mass media along with many of the conventional assumptions about how messages and images are created and delivered. This section will begin by addressing conventional forms of mass media in terms of how diversity is represented and how people from diverse groups are involved, and it will conclude by examining digital media.

How diverse is the workforce in mass media?

In conventional mass media, the best evidence of the acceptance of diversity and the promotion of the concept of pluralism is the increasing numbers of women and people of color entering media-related professions. An annual survey of journalism and mass communication graduates reports that women are almost two thirds of students enrolled in programs at both the bachelor's and master's levels, and that people of color comprise more than 25 percent of those enrolled in bachelor's degree programs and over 20 percent of those enrolled in master's degree programs (Becker, Vlad, & Simpson, 2013); further, experts predict that students of color will increase to 40 percent by 2035. The question is, will they find jobs? In 2015, the percentage of women journalists working at daily newspapers in the United States was 30.5 percent, and minority journalists represented slightly less than 13 percent and had been at or near that percentage since 2010. The data get slightly better if you broaden the scope—women journalists working in all forms of news media constituted 37.3 percent of the total, and of those employed in television news, 20 percent were Black or Latino (Statista, 2017). Mass media is still reeling from the effects of the last recession, when journalists experienced an unprecedented decline in employment. Since then, two thirds of journalism students receiving a bachelor's degree have only been able to find jobs writing or editing for Internet outlets.

A racial disparity is reflected in job distributions in mass media organizations. If the percentage of people of color in the U.S. population were reflected in newsrooms, they would represent over 30 percent of the journalists, but according to the 2014 annual survey by the American Association of News Editors, only 13.4 percent are journalists of color—a statistic that has wavered between 12 percent and 14 percent for over a decade (Becker, Vlad, & Simpson, 2013). Many journalists of color have an interest in being sports reporters, yet a 2012 study found that only 14 percent of sports reporters were people of color and 14 percent were women. White men comprised 90 percent of sports editors and well over 80 percent of assistant sports editors and columnists (Waldron, 2013). Journalism jobs have continued to decline. In 2005, there was a 20 to 1 ratio of newspaper journalists to digital-only journalists, but so many newspaper journalists were laid off that by 2015 that ratio had declined to 4 to 1 (Williams, 2016).

Although more women and people of color are appearing on television news and entertainment programs, in the majority of jobs behind the camera—writers, producers, camera operators, and technicians—the numbers of women and people of color are low. A media survey found that people of color were only 20.5 percent of those employed in the field of television, and they were only 7.1 percent of radio employees (Chideya, 2013). According to the Writer's Guild of America report (2015), women constituted about 29 percent of writers, and people of color represented 13.7 percent; further, there were declines in the numbers of executive producers from the previous year to 15.1 percent for women and 5.5 percent for people of color. The report admitted that Black television writers were historically limited to Black-themed shows. This historical disparity suggests a racist belief that Black writers could not write scripts for White actors even though White writers have written for Black actors for many years.

How is diversity portrayed in mass media?

Donaldson (2015) discussed a recent study of media portrayals of Black people that found numerous distortions such as an underrepresentation of Black professionals with expertise or appearing in print ads for luxury items. Instead, the report identified evidence of exaggerated associations of Black people with unemployment, poverty, and crime, especially drug-related crime. According to the report's executive summary: "The idle black male on the street corner is not the 'true face' of poverty in America, but it is the dominant one . . . depicted by the media" (Donaldson, 2015, n.p.). People of color are portrayed in a positive way primarily for their success in sports and entertainment fields. The study concluded that the stereotypes and negative media representations contributed to a pervasive sense of antagonism toward Black people in our society, especially Black men. In a longitudinal study, images of poverty featured in major American newsmagazines were analyzed over almost two decades, and Black people were overrepresented, appearing in over half of the images even though they only constituted about 25 percent of people living in poverty (Donaldson, 2015). In addition to the impact that negative portrayals may have on how others view Black people, it can be argued that these images have an even greater impact on Black youth since they may be internalizing such images of their group as they develop their own sense of identity.

> "Men, in general, seem to employ their reason to justify prejudices . . . rather than to root them out."
>
> — MARY WOLLSTONECRAFT (1759–1797)

Another media controversy concerns the criticism that White criminal suspects are treated more positively than Black victims of crimes. In Florida, an unarmed Black youth named Trayvon Martin was killed by a neighborhood watchman, George Zimmerman. Before long, news articles appeared saying that Martin had been suspended from school for having a baggie that appeared to contain marijuana residue. Although no substance was found and no arrest was made, many news media outlets carried this story. That same year, a White man who killed a dozen people and injured 70 others in an Aurora, Colorado, movie theater was described as "amiable" but "shy" and a "brilliant science student." Two years later, an unarmed Black youth in Missouri named Michael Brown was shot and killed by a White police officer. In the days following the incident, news media reported Brown's history of petty theft and drug use, and the *New York Times* said Brown was "no angel." That same year, a White teenager in Oregon who used an assault gun to kill one student and wound a teacher before killing himself was described as a "straight-arrow kid" and a devoted Mormon. There are many more examples of this media pattern of demonizing Black victims while showing compassion for White murderers (Wing, 2014).

Media has the power to provide positive images of people and to promote social change. In 1984, Levi's aired the first advertisement providing a positive portrayal of an individual with a disability. The energetic wheelchair user "popped a wheelie" to demonstrate his enthusiasm for Levi's jeans. The positive response to this advertisement caused a few more businesses to use people with disabilities in their advertisements. Although their presence remains minimal, people with disabilities are no longer completely absent from television. Heasley (2013) observed the recent increase in portrayals of people with a disability on television programs—twice as many as the previous year. The characters had disabilities ranging from Parkinson's disease, Asperger's syndrome, prosthetic legs, a blind father, and wheelchair users, and it is especially encouraging that half of these characters are portrayed by performers with a disability. But conventional media is no longer the only game in town; digital media also offers an opportunity for all minority group members to express themselves in a variety of ways.

What impact has digital media had on mass media?

At the beginning of the twenty-first century, over half of American households had personal computers, and 72 percent said computers had improved their lives (Kawamoto, 2003). Although men were initially the dominant users of digital media, by 2000, more women than men were going online. One of the first demonstrations of the power of digital media came in 1999 when the World Trade Organization (WTO) met in Seattle in late November. People worldwide had become critical about the policies and practices of the WTO, and for almost a year before the Seattle meeting, activists had been planning for a protest in Seattle. Using digital media, these organizers formed coalitions and alliances, and created a website to disseminate information to an international audience. Protestors planning to come to Seattle were linked to Seattle residents who were willing to provide lodging. When the protests began, conventional media largely ignored the activities and continued to show little interest even as police used tear gas and pepper spray on the crowds and arrested hundreds of protestors. Because so many people in the United States and across the globe who wanted to know more about the protests were compelled to use Internet sources to get information, conventional media finally began providing coverage of the protest activities (Kawamoto, 2003). The Seattle protest demonstrated the observation from Everett (2012) that digital media "have enabled media consumers and political activists to become savvy media producers as well as informed consumers, which has made bloggers and vloggers major competitors for traditional media companies and powers" (p. 147).

Another example of the impact of digital media was its role during Barack Obama's presidential campaigns in 2008 and 2012. Much of the credit given to Obama's campaign staff concerned their effective use of digital media. Everett (2012) described how the campaign used digital media to engage in fundraising, connect supporters, disseminate campaign themes, and respond to "attack ads." On the other hand, digital media was also used against Obama. Conservative blogger Andrew Breitbart edited a video of a speech by Shirley Sherrod, a Black woman in the Obama Administration, that made her appear to be making racist comments. When people looked at the unedited video of Sherrod's speech, they discovered that she was talking about how to overcome racism, both individually and as a nation (Everett, 2012). Media critics argue that people can avoid information they don't want by selectively going only to websites like Breitbart's that affirm their view of reality—a technological illustration of the *confirmation bias* and another factor contributing to the increasing political polarization in the United States. Whether it is put to good or bad uses, the Internet has had a major impact on American society, especially among youth. Instead of being inundated with images and messages from conventional corporate-controlled media, young people today are increasingly likely to be viewing user-generated content on venues such as YouTube or Facebook. According to a study by Luttig and Cohen (2016), young people of all races spent similar (and minimal) amounts of time reading newspapers or watching television news programs, with only young people from higher income homes expressing an interest in traditional news sources. Two-thirds of African Americans said they regularly went to websites that people of color had created. Hispanic Americans and Asian Americans also tended to be active in using social media to get information, especially political information. The study concluded that American youth of all races and ethnicities tended to bypass traditional news sources and use digital media to mobilize their efforts for political engagement and social change.

Another Pew Center study reported that 70 percent of American homes had broadband Internet (Crawford, 2013), but this raises the question of the extent and nature of diversity among Internet users. Some cities charge fees to use the Internet, but cities such as Philadelphia and Boston provide all citizens with access to high-speed wireless Internet for free. Philadelphia's mayor argued that free access was necessary to connect low-income families to the Internet so their children would not fall behind children from middle- and upper-income families. Because of efforts made in the 1990s, most American youth have some access to networked computers at school or in public libraries, but such minimal access cannot compare with what can be done by a user with unfettered Internet access, high bandwidth, and continuous connectivity while sitting in front of a computer at home. Not only are these middle- or upper-class children becoming more adept in their use of technology, but it also likely increases their self-confidence at school.

Becoming a skilled user of technology is not only a concern for children from low-income families but also for racial minorities as well. According to a 2015 Pew Research study, 79 percent of White people owned laptop computers compared to

63 percent of Latinos and 45 percent of Black people. A college graduate was three times more likely to own a laptop than a high school dropout. Also, almost half of Americans owned tablet computers, 10 times as many as in 2010, but 47 percent of White people had them compared to 38 percent of Black people and 35 percent of Latinos. Finally, racial parity can be seen in cell phones, as slightly more than 90 percent of Black, Latino, and White people owned one, as did 86 percent of high school dropouts (Anderson, 2015).

Students also need to gain access to instruction about technology. According to a Gallup poll, almost 60 percent of White and Latino students in grades 7–12 can enroll in computer science classes in their school compared to less than 50 percent of Black students. Rather than receiving computer science instruction at school, Black students are more likely than White students to receive instruction in a group or club at school or outside school at a camp or summer program. Yet Black and Latino students are more likely than their White peers to be aware of specific websites offering computer science instruction. Finally, 68 percent of White students report using a computer at home most days every week, but this is true for only 58 percent of Black students and 50 percent of Latino students (Royal & Swift, 2016). Overall, White students have an advantage over their classmates of color in learning about computer science and becoming more skilled at using technology.

A footnote is necessary to clarify Internet access for American Indians—on most reservations, estimates of Internet access drops to well below 10 percent. The main exceptions are those reservations connected to the Tribal Digital Village (TDV), a solar wireless Internet distribution network in Southern California. Funded by a grant from Hewlett Packard, 100 percent of households on TDV reservations have broadband Internet. Residents report that they use it daily. Their growing competency has occurred largely because of their cultural value of cooperation. The people living on these reservations willingly ask for and receive assistance and advice from their neighbors on how to use their computers. These reservations are now proposing to establish a digital record of their history and culture, including old photographs, songs, stories, and the spoken language, as well as creating Web-based tools for teaching languages (Luther, Lepre, & Clark, 2012).

Digital learning is becoming more prevalent in American schools. Four states have put laws in place mandating that all high school students enroll in at least one online course before they graduate (Van Galen, 2013), but a corporate vision of digital learning is being promoted in many state legislatures, largely consisting of Web-based tutorials, learning games, videos, and quizzes that include remediation activities if student performance is below expectations. Lobbyists for such digital learning emphasize that students are able to move through (corporate-created) content at their own pace. By defining teaching as simply content delivery, this form of digital learning promises higher achievement scores for less money. In one school deemed a model for digital learning, most of the students' time is spent learning content provided by their computer programs, and the student to teacher ratio is 68 to 1. A school in Colorado eliminated three teaching positions in the foreign language faculty by offering online foreign language classes (Van Galen, 2013).

This essentialist approach to digital learning is not the only model, especially for educators committed to teaching for social justice. There is ample evidence of a far more compelling academic experience available to students who engage in digital learning. Media scholar Henry Jenkins has described how digital learning can be used to develop what he calls a *participatory culture*. Participatory culture involves having minimal barriers to artistic expression and engaging in social causes as well as providing support for sharing creations and affirming social connections between media users. In such a culture, digital learning has a profound impact on the way people use information and how they interact with one another because the norms of a participatory culture involve sharing, support, and mentoring people who have not mastered digital tools

(Jenkins, 2006). Using digital tools to create a participatory culture results in people forming social relationships and engaging in social activities.

According to Van Galen (2013), there are three unique approaches that can be taken to engage in meaningful digital learning: (1) engaging with cultural diversity, (2) affirming identity, voice, and audience, and (3) engaging in political activism. An example of the first approach took place in Oakland, California, where groups of low-income students built a transcontinental social networking site connecting with students from New York City; then they expanded it to an international site connecting to students in Australia, Norway, South Africa, and Taiwan. In communicating with each other, these students created a global classroom with enormous learning opportunities. One story posted by a girl in India describing her family's delight in getting a new stove (a single burner on a kitchen floor) was met with considerable response as her peers around the world discussed the role of materialism in gaining satisfaction in life. It prompted Oakland youth to tell their own stories about events in their neighborhood, anticipating questions that their global peers might ask (Van Galen, 2013).

Two examples of a digital learning approach emphasizing identity, voice, and audience were given in the previous chapter with regard to the Lakota high school students and the undocumented student protest in Los Angeles. Another example happened in the San Francisco Bay area where LGBTQ students living in foster homes created videos refuting stereotypes about them and describing their lives; these videos were incorporated into a program to train social workers (Van Galen, 2013).

Finally, the political activism approach attempts to empower students to be politically engaged and to pursue social justice activities. In Philadelphia, young people have used digital media to promote issues like equitable funding for schools; they produce Web radio programs and videos and support a comprehensive website while still engaging in traditional activities such as speaking up at public meetings and contributing to written forums. In Los Angeles, South Central youth disseminate information based on the data they have gathered on air quality as well as their analysis of the effect of pollution on everyday life in their communities (Van Galen, 2013). Teachers as well as community activists need to work with our youth to nurture their efforts to gain digital knowledge and skills to engage in participatory activities that connect and collaborate with their peers and others.

> "We are now at the point where we must decide whether we are to honor the concept of a plural society which gains strength through diversity or whether we are to have bitter fragmentation that will result in perpetual tension and strife."
>
> — JUSTICE EARL WARREN (1891–1974)

Application Exercise 14.1
In this video, three teachers discuss cultural competence, diversity, and school culture in relationship to representation. Pay attention to the first speaker discuss the lack of representation of women of color in the school. And take note of how the second teacher responds about representation in terms of clubs and awards. Think about the ways in which this discussion relates to Chapter 14 and diversity on mass media. Review the video and complete the activity.

 Self-Check 14.4 Complete this self-check quiz to check your understanding of the lack of people of color in conventional mass media, distortions in how they are portrayed in the media, and digital media projects that address diversity issues.

Military Services and Diversity

Diversity in the armed forces of the United States is not a new issue; it is only the nature of the diversity that has changed. Although the military kept no records in its earliest years, there is anecdotal evidence that ethnic diversity in society was reflected in its military: We know of at least one woman—Deborah Sampson—who disguised herself as a man and engaged in combat during the Revolutionary War (Craft-Fairchild, 1997).

Starting in 1856, records exist showing a significant percentage of ethnic immigrants serving in the army—a shortcut to being granted citizenship—but they also reveal problems. During the Mexican-American War, many Irish Catholic soldiers were reluctant to kill Mexican Catholics, and a number of them deserted to avoid doing so (Johnson, 1999). Nevertheless, diversity continued to exist in the U.S. Army. According to Buckley (2001), at the end of the Civil War there were 140 Black regiments with over 100,000 soldiers, and the army continued to recruit Black people and immigrants. Johnson (1999) cited an 1896 army report documenting that 7 percent of that year's recruits were Black and 33 percent were ethnic immigrants.

Significant issues in the twentieth century concerning diversity in the military involved the need for racial desegregation, inclusion of women, and exclusive reliance on volunteers. Each issue created unique problems for military leadership, but they were similar to the problems in the larger society that were based on race and gender. Yet by the 1990s, sociologists Moskos and Butler (1996) reported that even though diversity problems still existed, the U.S. military had made more substantial progress than had occurred in the larger society.

What is the history behind the desegregation of the military?

Desegregation in the military began with a research project during World War II. Black army platoons were integrated into White infantry companies, and the social experiment was carefully monitored. The research team reported that no unusual problems occurred and that all soldiers functioned effectively. Because of this positive result, President Truman issued an executive order mandating military racial desegregation, but military leaders continued to resist the call for change. The executive order was not fulfilled until the Korean War, when desegregation became necessary for the sake of efficiency.

Dansby, Stewart, and Webb (2001) described problems with desegregation that came to the forefront during the Vietnam War. African Americans protesting against unequal treatment rioted at Fort Dix, Fort Bragg, on two aircraft carriers, and at Travis Air Force base. As the Vietnam War was ending in the early 1970s, General Creighton Abrams testified that poor race relations had had a negative impact on combat effectiveness. Complicating matters further, in 1973, Congress ended the draft and established an all-volunteer army. Recruiting and retaining quality soldiers would be affected by how the army addressed issues of race relations.

The army's response was to create a Defense Race Relations Institute charged with the responsibility of creating a race relations training program. The initial program lasted for six weeks; it was later expanded to include sexual harassment and discrimination, and now has become one of the army's most ambitious and, some would argue, most successful program. Forsling (2015) noted that when members of a military unit have varied backgrounds, they perform better, especially when it comes to generating ideas and producing innovative approaches to solve problems. Gender also provides more possibilities. For example, in Iraq, female Marines were sent into local communities to conduct searches and collect information from the women. The military's diversity also makes it more likely that at least one or more members of a military unit is familiar with the culture and fluent with the language in the area where they are deployed. These soldiers can have a more positive relationship with the local population and possibly get actionable intelligence from them.

What problems had to be addressed because of the military's decision to integrate?

Despite the highly regarded DEOMI training program, some of the recruits are not accepting of other races, and their participation in the military has less to do with fighting for their country than learning how to make bombs and become skilled at other military activities they believe they will need in the future to resist government efforts to take away their freedom. The army has been aware of soldiers with such extreme views for quite some time. In the past, military policy merely insisted that these soldiers not participate in extremist activities. Although their numbers have remained small, the Pentagon was concerned enough to revise its policy in 2009 to state that soldiers are not permitted to advocate for extremist causes or for ideologies such as White supremacy, and they cannot promote or participate in activities intended to deprive

"There can be no beauty if it is paid for by human injustice, nor truth that passes over injustice in silence, nor moral virtue that condones it."

— TADEUSZ BOROWSKI (1922–1951)

some Americans of their civil rights. Specific activities of extremist groups that soldiers are forbidden to engage in include recruiting, fundraising, distributing supremacist material (print or online), training new members, and participating in rallies sponsored by an extremist group (Gunter, 2012). This problem had to be addressed because military leaders understood they had to confront any issue that interfered with accomplishing their mission. In a diverse military, racism will interfere.

Sexism interferes as well. Prior to the establishment of the all-volunteer army, fewer than 2 percent of recruits were women, with 90 percent of them receiving medical or administrative assignments (Katzenstein & Reppy, 1999); to maintain recruitment standards, however, the pool of candidates was expanded (see Figure 14.3). By the 1990s, Peterson (1999) reported that female recruits tended to be better educated, had higher scores on aptitude tests, and were less likely to cause disciplinary problems. According to a recent report from Department of Defense (2015), over 200,000 women are on active-duty in the military, representing 14.8 percent of enlisted personnel and 16.7 percent of officers. Although the numbers of women have increased dramatically, this success has been tainted by ongoing problems related to sexual harassment and sexual assault. Women in the military have reported sexual harassment for years but have been ignored or encouraged by male superiors to drop their complaints. In 1999, Kier reported that no action was taken for 56 percent of all sexual harassment complaints (Kier, 1999). At the Air Force Academy (AFA), almost half of female AFA cadets reported that they had personally experienced sexual harassment (Zeigler & Gunderson, 2005). Military leaders took what they considered appropriate actions, but sexist attitudes among military personnel persisted.

Figure 14.3 A Coast Guard Poster to Recruit Women

SOURCE: US Coast Guard

This Coast Guard rescue swimmer saved a drowning fisherman 35 miles at sea.

(Her boyfriend just stopped by to bring her lunch.)

In 2017, a scandal erupted when male Marines posted nude photos of women marines without their consent on a "Marines United" website. The Marine Corps veteran who reported the photos to Marine Corps officials immediately began receiving death threats. Some tried to excuse the behavior as an expression of sexual feelings, but critics say the Marines involved in this scandal were reinforcing a military culture that exploits female peers to build stronger connections between the men, illustrating what feminists have argued for years—that sexual harassment is not about sex but about expressing power. These Marines could have shared numerous available pornographic images, but they chose to target female Marines, violating their privacy and transforming them from a comrade to a sex object. What these Marines did was equivalent to adolescent boys creating "slut pages" on social media consisting of nude photos of female classmates (Cauterucci, 2017). The military has been criticized in the past for glossing over accusations of sexual harassment, but this time both the Navy and Marine Corps announced immediate policy changes clearly stating a ban on the distribution of explicit images without the consent of the individual depicted.

What gender issues have required military leaders to consider new policies?

Opponents to having women in the military argue that there is a double standard that allows women to perform at lower levels of competence. The army's response has been that levels are adjusted to take account of physiological differences for men as well as for women. The army regularly checks to see if male and female soldiers are maintaining an appropriate body weight and fat percentage for their height and age to assure the maximum physical performance and to prevent injuries during training or deployments. All soldiers are assessed at least twice yearly in terms of meeting army standards for weight and fitness (Smith, 2017). Further, female soldiers have developed a tradition of excellent marksmanship, winning the army's highest awards and participating on marksmanship teams at the Olympics (McCall, 2013). The question of a double standard for male and female soldiers has been raised once again now that the army allows women to serve in combat.

During the 1970s and 1980s, the U.S. Army employed a **risk rule** that measured how close certain roles would bring a participant to battle and didn't assign women to roles that might bring them into combat. The risk rule could not be enforced during the 1989 Panama invasion; women soldiers engaged in battle while working in support units. Women driving convoy trucks and flying helicopters to transport wounded men to safety were fired on, as were women in military police units who assisted with cordoning off neighborhoods in search of guerrillas. Some women would have earned medals if their assignments had officially listed them as combatants.

In 1991, Operation Desert Storm made the "risk rule" irrelevant because everyone assigned to the operation was at risk, whether they were infantry or support staff. The military decided to revise the risk rule in a way that opened up more military jobs on or near the front lines to women but still expressly prohibited women from engaging in direct combat. The new definition said that "Women were prohibited from serving in units or missions where the risk of exposure to direct combat, hostile fire, or capture was equal to or greater than the risk in the combat units they supported" (Kasinov, 2013, p. 19). As a result, more women than ever before were given military assignments that were likely to expose them periodically to combat activity.

In 2001, American troops were sent to Afghanistan. After 10 years of fighting, the Department of Defense (DOD) released a report that recommended lifting the ban on women in combat. In 2012, the DOD announced that it was opening more than 14,000 positions to women in combat units that they had historically been denied. Some said the DOD was finally acknowledging the sacrifice of the 149 women who had been killed in Afghanistan while performing their military duties. In January 2013, the DOD announced it would no longer prohibit women from being given combat assignments; the wider range of roles include being assigned to the infantry, artillery, or Special Forces. All branches of the American military have until 2016 to determine how they will integrate and employ women in these new roles (Kasinov, 2013). The majority of women soldiers support the elimination of the ban on combat assignments because they feel that women are already in circumstances that place them at risk, and they want the public to regard women veterans returning from war zones with the same respect given to male veterans.

With new opportunities come new consequences; many women (like male combat veterans) have returned to the United States from Iran or Afghanistan with symptoms of post-traumatic stress disorder (PTSD). Ever since the American Psychological Association (APA) included PTSD in its list of mental health disorders, the majority diagnosed with this disorder have been men. In addition to typical causes of stress in combat, military women have also experienced harassment, assault, and rape by fellow soldiers or even by commanding officers. Although some women report forming positive relationships with other male and female soldiers, many women deployed in combat zones report feeling alienated and marginalized, and at times threatened by the men who are supposed to be their comrades in arms. Although the DOD has developed the term *military sexual trauma* (MST) to identify these experiences, the DOD has yet to address the problem effectively. About 20 percent of women using the military's health care services report being sexually assaulted, abused, or raped during their military service, and some researchers say the number could be as high as 30 percent (Kasinov, 2013).

Having studied demographic predictions, military leaders expect the percentage of women and minorities in the armed forces to increase; they anticipate more recruiting from the growing pool of Hispanic Americans and Asian Americans. Although there

Video Example 14.3

This video explores the role of women in the military today. What kinds of roles do women play in combat and leadership? Based on what you have read in Chapter 14 about women in the military, what questions might you pose to the military women interviewed in the video?

https://www.youtube.com/watch?v=anMq2ZnuOCQ

will be twice as many African Americans in the candidate pool by 2050, about half of the population growth from 2000 to 2050 will occur among Latinos, with a smaller yet significant growth of Southeast Asians. A major concern for Latino recruits is the high school dropout rate: Army policy requires that 90 percent of all recruits must have high school diplomas. Although the Hispanic dropout rate has declined significantly, at 9.2 percent it is still higher than the rate for all other racial or ethnic groups (National Center for Education Statistics, 2017).

How has the military dealt with other forms of diversity such as religion and sexual orientation?

Racial, ethnic, and gender diversity is only the beginning. The American military also has procedures for accommodating religious differences. The military accepts recruits of all faiths, including more obscure faiths such as Wicca. As for sexual orientation, gay Americans have always fought in this country's wars, but their sexual orientation was not an issue until World War I, when military regulations excluded openly gay men from military service. Yet there were closeted gay men in uniform when World War II began, including gay sergeants responsible for training the massive numbers of new soldiers enlisted after the attack on Pearl Harbor (Estes, 2007). Psychiatrists involved in screening procedures during the war rejected fewer than 5000 recruits for being gay, but it is estimated that as many as 650,000 of the 16 million American troops were gay men (Estes, 2007). With the repeal of the "Don't Ask, Don't Tell" (DADT) policy in 2010, the armed forces are now recruiting openly gay men and lesbians into the military.

The history of lesbians entering the military is different since women have always been segregated. The formation of the Women's Army Corps (WACs), the Women Accepted for Volunteer Emergency Service (WAVES), and the admission of women into the Marines in 1943 brought lesbians as well as straight women into military service. The presence of lesbians was well known to military leaders, who waited until the war was over before purging lesbians from the ranks by giving them dishonorable discharges. Female soldiers continued to play traditional support roles in the military until the early 1970s when Congress ended the draft. Military leaders recognized that there were many roles that women could play, so they recruited women as well as men. Some men initially expressed their reluctance to serve with women soldiers, but attitudes have changed as both lesbians and straight women have proven their abilities.

The same outcome has occurred as a consequence of the repeal of the DADT policy. Critics predicted that by forcing heterosexuals to serve with fellow soldiers who were now openly gay or lesbian, unit cohesion and military preparedness would suffer. One year later, an academic research center released a study finding that the transition was a smooth one with no negative impact. This should not be especially surprising since a survey done before the repeal of DADT found that the vast majority of soldiers said they were already serving with someone they knew to be gay or lesbian. Further, the academic study said that repealing DADT enhanced national security because the army no longer had to worry about losing soldiers who happened to be gay men or lesbians who had critical skills such as engineering or fluency in languages (e.g., Arabic), and gay men and lesbians did not have the stress of being in the closet and fearful of being identified. The study reported that there had been no widespread increase in resignations or any decrease in morale; there had been no increase in harassment or anti-gay or anti-lesbian violence and no negative impact on recruitment (Burns & Rothman, 2012). The smooth transition of openly gay and lesbian soldiers serving in the military was regarded as a positive sign that the estimated 15,500 transgender soldiers could be similarly accommodated. The Pentagon reviewed policies from allies that accept transgender soldiers (Smith, 2014). In 2016, Defense Secretary Carter ended the ban on transgender soldiers and initiated a one-year review period to develop an orderly process for implementing this change. The Defense Department commissioned a study that reported "minimal impact" from transgender soldiers serving openly in the military. In July 2017, President Trump decided to reinstate the ban on transgender soldiers. Since then, two federal courts ruled the transgender ban unconstitutional, and one judge ordered that transgender individuals should be allowed to enlist by January. After further review, military leaders announced that they would start recruiting transgender soldiers as of January 1, 2018. The military's decision is largely viewed as a pragmatic response to the increasing legal pressure to accept transgender soldiers serving openly in the military.

Is there diversity among military leaders?

As military recruiters pursue an increasingly diverse pool of candidates, they must offer evidence that advancement is possible. It has been important to assure women and people of color that representatives from their groups could be found at all levels in the military organizational structure, providing soldiers who are women or people of color with proof of genuine opportunity for advancement in the military—rather than a glass ceiling. The numbers show that the military is moving toward achieving this goal. According to a report by the Department of Defense (2015), people of color constitute 33.2 percent of active duty enlisted personnel in all of the military services, and 22.8 percent of all officers are men and women of color. The report also identified the percentage of officers of color in the different branches of the military: Army (26.5 percent), Navy (21 percent), Air Force (19.8 percent), and Marine Corps (19.2 percent).

Although the military services have been successful recruiting people of color, Brook (2014) argues that they need to do more to increase the numbers of officers of color. But the military is currently engaging in downsizing its troops to 450,000 by 2018, and that exacerbates the problem. In 2015, the effort to reduce troops down to 490,000 resulted in the elimination of 550 majors with almost 10 percent of eligible Black majors being dismissed compared to 5.6 percent of White majors. A significant factor in this disparity is that many recruits of color have chosen to enroll in non-combat programs where their training will translate into good jobs when they leave the military. As one military sociologist explained, "That has often meant driving a truck, not a tank" (Brook, 2014, n.p.). This choice has also meant a lack of officers of color in combat roles, a necessity for promotion. Once the directive to downsize the forces has been achieved, it is likely that the U.S. military will once again have to engage in a review of its affirmative action plans and revise them to address this leadership issue.

 Self-Check 14.5 Complete this self-check quiz to check your understanding of the steps the military has taken in response to diversity among its ranks, and explain what diversity issues still remain for the military to address.

Afterword

Although the military has successfully integrated its ranks, Bouie (2014) reports that our schools are more segregated than ever, a concern that multicultural education advocates have expressed for several years. With so many of our children being kept apart from those who are racially, ethnically, or economically different from them, it is critical for teachers to address diversity issues with their students at all levels. Some teachers even use segregation as an excuse for not addressing diversity because there are no—or few—students of color in their schools! But diversity is about more than race or ethnicity; diversity includes religion, class, gender, disability, sexual orientation, and more. Every school has diversity, and the less diversity a school has should be viewed as an even more compelling reason to address diversity issues.

If White students rarely encounter people of color, it is essential that teachers provide accurate information about history, contributions, and issues affecting communities of color in this country both historically and today. Further, this is not just a need for White students: African American students may know little about cultures or experiences of Native Americans; Native American students may only know about the "model minority" and have little knowledge of the past oppression, achievements, and current barriers of Asian Americans. Latino students may not understand why Somali students are in their school, and Somali students may have learned negative stereotypes about Latinos. Middle-class students need to understand the realities for low-income families; students without disabilities must confront misperceptions about people with disabilities; heterosexual students can unlearn myths they have been taught about LGTBQ students. In a diverse society, everyone needs to learn more about the diverse groups of people calling themselves Americans.

During the debate over ratifying the U.S. Constitution, some state leaders focused on the many differences dividing the states and argued that they could never be melded into a single union but should instead remain independent states. Alexander Hamilton rejected the argument, insisting that a unified nation encompassing those diverse cultures had already formed, and the Constitution would simply reflect the shared values and vision of that union (Chernow, 2004).

Today, people living in our 50 states are not defined as much by the state where they live as by their membership in social groups determined by race, gender, disability, social class, and sexual orientation; yet we are all Americans. We live in a nation that adopted the motto "E Pluribus Unum" in 1782, originally meaning "from many states, one nation." Americans today are the descendants of the indigenous people or the immigrants who came here, all of them wanting to live in a nation where they had freedom to work, worship, and live as they pleased in a society promising equal rights and equal opportunities.

> "When we dream alone, we are merely dreaming; but when we dream together, that's the beginning of reality."
> — BRAZILIAN PROVERB

That American dream has always been an ideal. Some groups were granted this ideal more readily than others, but all have sought it. America's history is a history of that struggle. We are farther along than ever today, yet we still have much to do to bring the dream closer to reality for all Americans. Pluralism represents a vehicle to move us forward. Committing ourselves to being pluralistic represents a commitment to the American dream, a commitment to make our nation's motto—"out of the many, one"—a description of the nation we are becoming. That is a dream worth dreaming.

Summary

- Affirmative action opponents complain of preferential treatment and racial quotas, whereas advocates point out that affirmative action does not require an employer to hire an unqualified worker, and courts have consistently struck down racial quotas.

- Leaders at colleges and universities have defended affirmative action in admissions policies, arguing that a diverse student population on a campus means all students will be introduced to diverse perspectives and have a richer educational experience.

- As the workforce becomes more diverse, it is increasingly necessary for companies to have more diverse employees, and as diverse groups in American society become larger and increase their purchasing power, businesses need to respond to their needs.

- Although people of color are a significant portion of mass media majors, they still are underrepresented in media workplaces and still omitted or stereotyped in conventional mass media, but students using digital media have created a variety of projects promoting intercultural exchanges, social justice causes, and self-advocacy.

- With the advent of a completely volunteer army, diversity among recruits has increased for all minority groups, and although the military has effectively addressed racism and now accepts openly LGTBQ soldiers, problems remain for women soldiers.

Terms and Definitions

Affirmative action A written plan required of businesses and institutions of higher education to reduce discrimination in hiring, public contracting, and college admissions

Diversity The presence of human beings with perceived or actual differences based on a variety of human characteristics

Diversity pairing A diversity training strategy in which two people from diverse backgrounds are paired to provide them with opportunities to interact and become better acquainted

Diversity training Programs designed by businesses to promote a positive environment for diverse employees and managers at the worksite

Glass ceiling An informal upper limit that keeps women and minorities from being promoted to positions of greatest responsibility in work organizations

Pluralism The equal coexistence of diverse cultures in a mutually supportive relationship within the boundaries of one nation

Racial quota Designation of a specific number of applicants to be hired or admitted based on their race

Risk rule An army practice of measuring how close certain roles would bring a participant to combat and not assigning women to any role that would bring them too close

Seniority system Requires employees with least seniority to be laid off work if the employer needs to release a certain number of employees

Set-aside program Requiring contractors to hire a certain percentage of minority subcontractors if they are awarded a project funded by tax dollars

Sexual harassment Deliberate and repeated behavior that has a sexual basis and is not welcomed, requested, or returned

Discussion Exercises

Exercise #1 Enhancing Unity in America Discussion: What Should We Do Next?

Directions: America today demonstrates its diversity in our military, marketplace, and manufacturing, in our media, and in federal, state, and local governments. The following questions ask for your speculation to resolve current issues for our future well-being.

1. Should our federal government eliminate, or modify, the current affirmative action program?

   - If you believe it should be eliminated, explain why.
   - If you believe it should be modified, explain how and why.

2. Do you agree that increased diversity among students on a college campus strengthens the education of all students?

   - How many—or what type—of diversity-related courses should all students be required to take?
   - What should be the outcome of any study of American cultural, racial, and societal human differences?

3. Assume that you have majored and matriculated in some aspect of business; following graduation, you receive two job offers: one with a company that has a good reputation for having a positive environment for diversity; the other, which offers a higher salary with better benefits, has little or no record of giving attention to attracting a diverse workforce.

   - Which one would you choose, and why?
   - How can a diverse workforce create unity in America?

4. Now that women are approximately half of all managers, why are women still being excluded from a proportional share of top management positions?

   - What will it take to eliminate this glass ceiling?
   - How might business and industry change if women were adequately represented in leadership roles?

5. If the predictions are correct and 20 years from now print and broadcast media employ significantly greater numbers of women and people of color, how will it make a difference in the following areas:

- Which news stories are covered by print and broadcast journalists

- How new stories are covered

- Which stories are presented by news programs (e.g., *20/20* and *Dateline*)

- Which images and text are presented in advertisements

- What content and diversity of characters are available in prime-time programming

6. Simply requiring that American societal institutions establish policies against sexual harassment has not been effective.

   - What must the military services do to eliminate the problem of sexual harassment?

   - Business and manufacturing?

   - Nonprofit and religious institutions?

Exercise #2 Creating a More Just Society for the 99 percent

Directions: Below are 10 recommendations to make the United States a more just society for all of its citizens. Discuss each one in terms of whether or not you would like to see it enacted, and present your reasons for supporting or rejecting it.

1. Eliminate for-profit schools that have saddled college students with huge debts and have failed to provide jobs to most of their graduates. Increase funds to make low-interest loans available to college students, especially those students from low-income homes.

2. Pass legislation to make banking practices (e.g., credit card charges to both consumers and merchants) more transparent; the federal government must discontinue underwriting questionable financial practices by banks (e.g., derivative transactions).

3. Establish government programs that encourage low-income and middle-income Americans to open savings accounts. Government incentives could include matching grants or an expansion of current programs that assist first-time homeowners.

4. Reduce corporate welfare by eliminating the loopholes, exceptions, and exemptions in the tax code that provide hidden subsidies for corporations.

5. Establish election day as a federal holiday and make voting a requirement for all American citizens (including fines for failing to vote). This has been done successfully in other nations such as Australia, where the percentage of people voting in elections exceeds 90 percent.

6. Establish incentives for American corporations to locate within the United States, keeping jobs in this country rather than exporting them overseas.

7. Strengthen affirmative action legislation to provide better enforcement in order to ensure that workers with comparable qualifications from diverse minority groups (e.g., women, people of color, people with a disability) are receiving fair treatment in terms of hiring and promotion decisions.

8. Increase federal government investment in infrastructure, education, and technology based on the studies reporting that these investments were the basis for much of the financial success experienced in the twentieth century.

9. Reaffirm the estate taxes collected from people inheriting $5 million or more so that inheritances do not create a class of wealthy people who can exercise enormous power over the rest of society from one generation to the next.

10. Eliminate practices such as gerrymandering and the filibuster that are used primarily to manipulate the political system for the benefit of a political party rather than for the good of the nation as a whole.

Source: Adapted from: United for a Fair Economy (www.faireconomy.org) and Stiglitz, J. E. (2012). *The Price of Inequality.* New York, NY: W. W. Norton & Co.

References

Chapter 1

Andrzejewski, J. (Ed.). (1996). Definitions for understanding oppression and social justice. *Oppression and social justice: Critical frameworks.* Boston, MA: Pearson Custom Publishing.

Aronson, E. (2012). *The social animal* (11th ed.). New York, NY: Worth Publishers.

Banks, J. A. (1994). The complex nature of ethnic groups in modern society. In *Multiethnic education: Theory and practice* (3rd ed.). Boston, MA: Allyn & Bacon.

Banks, J. A. (2006). Multicultural education: Characteristics and goals. In J. A. Banks & C. A. McGee Banks (Eds.), *Multicultural education: Issues and perspectives* (6th ed.). New York, NY: Wiley.

Barzun, J. (1965). *Race: A study in superstition* (rev. ed.). New York, NY: Harper & Row.

Bellah, R., Madsen, R., Sullivan, W., Swidler, A., & Tipton, S. (1991). *The good society.* New York, NY: Vintage.

Bellini, S., Pereda, V. Cordero, N., & Suarez-Morales, L. (2016). Developing multicultural awareness in preschool children: A pilot intervention. *Open Journal of Social Sciences.* Retrieved from http://file.scirp.org/pdf/JSS_2016072711440632.pdf

Botkin, B. A. (1957). *A treasury of American anecdotes.* New York, NY: Bonanza Books.

Brown, L. (2016). Ableism/Language. *Autistic Hoya.* Retrieved from http://www.autistichoya.com/p/ableist-words-and-terms-to-avoid.html

Charlton, J. I. (1998). *Nothing about us without us.* Berkeley, CA: University of California Press.

Chavers, D. (1997). Doing away with the "S" word. *Indian Country Today, 16*(37), 5.

Clark, M. (2014, June 11). Celebrity justice: Prison lifestyles of the rich and famous. *Prison Legal News.* Retrieved from https://www.prisonlegalnews.org/news/2010/jul/15/celebrity-justice-prison-lifestyles-of-the-rich-and-famous

Dalton, H. (2008). Failing to see. In P. Rothenberg (Ed.), *White privilege: Essential readings on the other side of racism* (3rd ed.). New York, NY: Worth.

Fawcett, K. (2015). How mental illness is misrepresented in the media. *U. S. News & World Report.* Retrieved from http://health.usnews.com/health-news/health-wellness/articles/2015/04/16/how-mental-illness-is-misrepresented-in-the-media

Feagin, J., & Feagin, C. (2010). Basic concepts in the study of racial and ethnic relations. In *Racial and ethnic relations* (9th ed.). Upper Saddle River, NJ: Prentice Hall.

Ford, D. (2014, Feb. 6). Judge orders Texas teen Ethan Couch to rehab for driving drunk, killing 4, *CNN U.S.* Retrieved from http://www.cnn.com/2014/02/05/us/texas-affluenza-teen

Franklin, K. (2000). Anti-gay behaviors among young adults. *Journal of Interpersonal Violence, 15,* 339–363.

Friedman, R. A. (2008, July/August). Media and madness. *The American Prospect, 19*(7), A2–A4.

Gamber, F. (2007, March/April). Stars come out for NAACP Image Awards. *The Crisis, 114*(2), 36–37.

Gosset, T. F. (1997). *Race: The history of an idea in America.* Dallas, TX: Southern Methodist University Press.

Gould, S. J. (2002). The geometer of race. In *I have landed: The end of a beginning in natural history* (pp. 356–366). New York, NY: Harmony Books.

Green, R. (1975). The Pocahontas perplex: Images of Indian women in American cultures. *Massachusetts Review, 16,* 698–714.

Haag, P. (2000). *Voices of a generation: Teenage girls report about their lives today.* New York, NY: Marlow.

Haley, A. (1976). *Roots.* Garden City, NY: Doubleday.

Hamachek, D. (1999). Effective teachers: What they do, how they do it, and the importance of self knowledge. In R.P. Lipka and T.M. Brinthaupt (Eds.), *The role of self in teacher development* (pp. 189–224). Albany, NY: SUNY Press.

Herbst, P. (1997). Ethnic epithets in society. In *The color of words: An encyclopedic dictionary of ethnic bias in the United States* (pp. 255–259). Yarmouth, ME: Intercultural Press.

Herdt, G. (1997). *Same sex, different cultures: Exploring gay and lesbian lives.* Boulder, CO: Westview.

Highwater, J. (1997). *The mythology of transgression: Homosexuality as metaphor.* New York, NY: Oxford University Press.

Hoffer, E. (1968). *The passionate state of mind and other aphorisms.* New York, NY: Harper Perennial Library.

James, S. D. (2013). Gay man says millennial term "queer" is like the "N" word." *ABC news.* Retrieved from: abcnews.go.com/Health/gay-man-millennial-term-queer-word/story?id=20855582

Jones, J. (1997). *Prejudice and racism* (2nd ed.). New York, NY: McGraw-Hill.

Kennedy, R. (2002). *Nigger: The strange career of a troublesome word.* New York, NY: Pantheon Books.

Kilborn, P. T. (2005). The five-bedroom, six-figure rootless life. In *Class matters* (correspondents of the *New York Times*) (pp. 146–165). New York, NY: Times Books.

Kilbourne, J. (1999). *Deadly persuasion: Why women and girls must fight the addictive power of advertising.* New York, NY: The Free Press.

Kniker, C. R. (1977). *You and values education.* Columbus, OH: Charles E. Merrill.

Kolbert, E. (2017). Why facts don't change our minds. *The New Yorker.* http://www.newyorker.com/magazine/2017/02/27/why-facts-dont-change-our-minds

Lappe, F. M. (1989). *Rediscovering America's values.* New York, NY: Ballantine.

LeBon, G. (1968). The mind of crowds. In R. Evans (Ed.), *Readings in collective behavior* (pp. 10–21). Chicago, IL: Rand McNally.

Lefkowitz, B. (1997). *Our guys: The Glen Ridge rape and the secret life of the perfect suburb.* Berkeley, CA: University of California Press.

Levin, J., & Levin, W. (1982). *The functions of discrimination and prejudice* (2nd ed.). New York, NY: Harper & Row.

Linton, S. (1998). Reassigning meaning. In *Claiming disability: Knowledge and identity* (pp. 8–33). New York, NY: New York University Press.

Macedo, D., & Bartolome, L.I. (2001). *Dancing with bigotry: Beyond the politics of tolerance.* New York, NY: Palgrave.

McGinty, E., Kennedy-Hendricks, A., Choksy, S., & Barry, C. (2015). Trends in news media coverage of mental illness in the United States: 1995–2014. *Health Affairs.* Retrieved from http://namimass.org/wp-content/uploads/Health-Affairs-Media-Article-2016-McGinty-1121-9.pdf

Mead, C. (1985). *Champion: Joe Louis—black hero in white America.* New York, NY: Charles Scribner.

Metzl, J. M., & MacLeish, K. T. (2015). Mental illness, mass shootings, and the politics of American firearms. *American Journal of Public Health.* Retrieved from https://www.ncbi.nlm.nih.gov/pmc/articles/PMC4318286

Miller, C., & Swift, K. (2000). *Words and women.* San Jose, CA: iUniverse.

Mlodinow, L. (2008). *The drunkard's walk: How randomness rules our lives.* New York, NY: Vintage Books.

Myrdal, G. (1944). *An American dilemma: The Negro problem and modern democracy.* New York, NY: Harper & Row.

Newberg, A., & Waldman, M.R. (2006). *Why we believe what we believe: Uncovering our biological needs for meaning, spirituality, and truth.* New York, NY: Free Press.

Olson, S. (2002). *Mapping human history: Discovering the past through our genes.* Boston, MA: Houghton Mifflin.

Pagels, E. (2006). *The Gnostic gospels.* London, UK: Phoenix.

Raths, L., Harmin, M., & Simon, S. (1978). *Values and teaching: Working with values in the classroom* (2nd ed.). Columbus, OH: Charles E. Merrill.

Risberg, D. F. (1978, June 18). *Framework and foundations: Setting the stage and establishing norms.* Paper presented at the first annual National Conference on Human Relations, Minneapolis, MN.

Ryan, W. (1976). *Blaming the victim* (2nd ed.). New York, NY: Vintage.

Schaefer, R. T. (2015). *Racial and ethnic groups* (14th ed.). Upper Saddle River, NJ: Pearson.

Sheinin, D., & Thompson, K. (2014). Redefining the word: Examining a racial slur entrenched in American vernacular that is more prevalent than ever. *The Washington Post.* Retrieved from http://www.washingtonpost.com/sf/national/2014/11/09/the-n-word-an-entrenched-racial-slur-now-more-prevalent-than-ever/?utm_term=.1969e79ae258

Simpson, G. E., & Yinger, J. M. (1985). *Racial and cultural minorities: An analysis of prejudice and discrimination* (5th ed.). New York, NY: Plenum.

Stephan, W. (1999). *Reducing prejudice and stereotyping in schools.* New York, NY: Teachers College Press.

Terry, D., Hogg, M., & Duck, J. (1999). Group membership, social identity, and attitudes. In D. Abrams & M. Hogg (Eds.), *Social identity and social cognition* (pp. 280–314). Malden, MA: Blackwell.

von Humboldt, Alexander, quoted in de Terra, H. (1955). *The life and times of Alexander von Humboldt.* New York, NY: Knopf.

Wade, N. (2006). *Before the dawn: Recovering the lost history of our ancestors.* New York, NY: The Penguin Press.

Wessler, S. L. (2001, January). Sticks and stones. *Educational Leadership, 58*(4), 28–33.

Wright, M. A. (1998). *I'm chocolate, you're vanilla: Raising healthy black and biracial children in a race-conscious world.* San Francisco, CA: Jossey-Bass.

Wodtke, G. T. (2012). The impact of education on intergroup attitudes: A multiracial analysis. National Institute of Health. Retrieved from https://www.ncbi.nlm.nih.gov/pmc/articles/PMC3883053/

Zimbardo, P. (2007). *The Lucifer effect: Understanding how good people turn evil.* New York, NY: Random House.

Zinn, H. (1990). *Declarations of independence: Cross-examining American ideology.* New York, NY: HarperCollins.

Chapter 2

Abdo, G. (2006). *Mecca and Main Street: Muslim life in America after 9/11.* Oxford, UK: Oxford University Press.

Alba, R. (2016). The likely persistence of a white majority. *The American Prospect. 27*(1), 67-71.

Allport, G. (1979). *The nature of prejudice.* Reading, MA: Addison-Wesley.

Amy, J. (2015). Man gets maximum prison term in rundown death of black man. *ABCNews.* Retrieved from http://abcnews.go.com/US/wireStory/men-sentenced-killing-mississippi-black-man-30694267

Anderson, M. (1960). Interview with *Jet* magazine, 19(1).

Ansari, Z. I. (2004). Islam among African Americans: An overview. In Z.H. Buhhari, S.S. Nyang, M. Ahmad, & J.C. Esposito (Eds.), *Muslims' place in the American public square* (pp. 222–267). Walnut Creek, CA: Altamira Press.

Archibold, R. C. (2010, April 23). Arizona enacts stringent law on immigration. *The New York Times.*

Ariely, D. (2008). *Predictably irrational: The hidden forces that shape our decisions.* New York, NY: HarperCollins.

Aronson, E. (2012). *The social animal* (11th ed.). New York, NY: Worth Publishers.

Aronson, E. (2008). *The social animal* (10th ed.). New York, NY: Worth Publishers.

Astor, C. (1997, August). Gallup poll: Progress in black/white relations, but race is still an issue. USIA electronic journal, *U.S. Society & Values, 2*(3), 19–21.

Baker, R. (1981). "Pricks" and "chicks": A plea for persons. In M. Vetterling-Braggin (Ed.), *Sexist language: A modern philosophical analysis* (pp. 161–182). Lanham, MD: Littlefield, Adams.

Ballentine, C. (2017). Why is media portrayal of Muslims so negative? Journalists weigh in. Retrieved from http://www.dukechronicle.com/article/2017/03/why-is-media-portrayal-of-muslims-so-negative-journalists-weight-in

Bell, D. (2002). *Ethical ambition: Living a life of meaning and worth*. New York, NY: Bloomsbury.

Bredin, J. (2008). *The affair: The case of Alfred Dreyfus*. Bethesda, MD: Gryphon Editions.

Burns, C., Barton, K., & Kerby, S. (2012) The state of diversity in today's workforce. Center for American Progress. Retrieved from http://americanprogress.org/issues/labor/report/2012/07/12/11938/the-state-of-diversity-in-todays-workforce

Carroll, J. (2001). *Constantine's sword: The church and the Jews, a history*. Boston, MA: Houghton Mifflin.

Center for American Progress. (2016). Unjust: How the broken criminal justice system fails LGBT people of color. Retrieved from http://www.lgbtmap.org/file/lgbt-criminal-justice-poc.pdf

Chalabi, M. (2015). How anti-Muslim are Americans? Data points to extent of Islamophobia. *The Guardian*. Retrieved from https://www.theguardian.com/us-news/2015/dec/08/muslims-us-islam-islamophobia-data-polls

Chisholm quote source: Rangel, C. (2015). Medal of Freedom Honoree Shirley Chisholm never stood on the sidelines of life. *Black Star News*. Retrieved from www.blackstarnews.com/us-politics/justice/medal-of-freedom-honoree-shirley-chisholm-never-stood-on-the

Coleman, L. M. (2007). Stigma. In L. Davis (Ed.), *The disability studies reader* (2nd ed., pp. 216–233). New York, NY: Routledge.

Costello, M. B. (2016, summer). Minority children suffer from hate rhetoric in presidential campaign, *SPLC Report*, 46(2). (For the full report, go to the following link: https://www.splcenter.org/sites/default/files/splc_the_trump_effect.pdf)

Donald, B. (2013). Stanford study: Participation in a cultural activity may reduce prejudice. *Stanford News*. Retrieved from http://news.stanford.edu/news/2013/august/prejudice-cultural-activity-082213.html

Duckitt, J., & Sibley, C. G. (2007). Right wing authoritarianism, social dominance orientation and the dimensions of generalized prejudice. *European Journal of Personality*, 21(2), 113–130.

Editors of *Rethinking Schools*. (2016-2017). In our hands. *Rethinking Schools*, 31(2), 4-6.

Farley, J. (2005). *Majority-minority relations* (5th ed.). Upper Saddle River, NJ: Prentice Hall.

Feagin, J., & Feagin, C. (1986). *Discrimination American style* (2nd ed.). Malabar, FL: Krieger.

Feagin, J., & Feagin, C. B. (2008). Glossary. *Racial and ethnic relations* (8th ed.). Upper Saddle River, NJ: Prentice Hall.

Fowler, D. (2012). Study: Residential segregation still a problem in the U. S. American Sociological Association. Retrieved from http://www.asanet.org/sites/default/files/savvy/documents/press/pdfs/ASR_June_2012_Kyle_Crowder_News_Release.pdf

Fryer Jr., R. G., Pager, D., & Spenkuch, J.L. (2014). Statistics that hurt. Kellogg School of Management at Northwestern University. Retrieved from http://insight.kellogg.northwestern.edu/article/statistics_that_hurt

Gioseffi, D. (Ed.). (1993). *On prejudice: A global perspective*. New York, NY: Anchor.

Goldhagen, D. J. (2002). *Hitler's willing executioners: Ordinary Germans and the Holocaust* (2nd ed.) New York, NY: Knopf.

Grossfeld, J. (2017). It will take more than single-payer to make Baltimore healthy. *The American Prospect*. 28(4), 13-17.

Hauser, M. D. (2006). *Moral minds: The nature of right and wrong*. New York, NY: Ecco.

Howard, G. R. (2006). *We can't teach what we don't know: White teachers, multiracial schools* (2nd ed.) New York, NY: Teachers College Press.

Jones, J. (1997). *Prejudice and racism* (2nd ed.). New York, NY: McGraw Hill.

Koppelman, K. (1994). *Race and gender equity in urban America: The efforts of six cities to define the issues and provide solutions*. Paper presented at the national conference of the Renaissance Group in San Antonio on October 15, 1994.

Krogstad, J. M. (2015). What Americans, Europeans think of immigrants. Pew Research Center. Retrieved from http://www.pewresearch.org/fact-tank/2015/09/24/what-americans-europeans-think-of-immigrants/

Law, A. O. (2017). This is how Trump's deportation orders differ from Obama's. The Washington Post. Retrieved from: https://www.washingtonpost.com/news/monkey-cage/wp/2017/05/03/this-is-how-trumps-deportations-differ-from-obamas/?utm_term=.c4a9dae3897e

Levin, J., & Levin, W. (1982). *The functions of discrimination and prejudice* (2nd ed., p. 202). New York, NY: Harper & Row.

Lipka, M. (2017). Muslims and Islam: Key findings in the U. S. and around the world. Pew Research Center. Retrieved from http://www.pewresearch.org/fact-tank/2017/05/26/muslims-and-islam-key-findings-in-the-u-s-and-around-the-world/

Marcotte, A. (2013). New research shows that men feel insecure when their partners succeed, but women don't. *Slate*. Retrieved from http://www.slate.com/blogs/xx_factor/2013/08/30/gender_differences_and_self_esteem_new_research_shows_that_men_feel_insecure.html

Martinez, R., & Dukes, R.L. (1991, March). Ethnic and gender differences in self-esteem. *Youth & Society*, 22(3), 318–339.

Michie, G. (2017). Unfolding hope in a Chicago school. *Rethinking Schools*, 31(3), 28-31.

Miller, C., & Swift, K. (2000). *Words and women*. San Jose, CA: iUniverse.

Mogahed, D., & Chouhoud, Y. (2017). American Muslim poll 2017: Muslims at the crossroads. Institute for Social Policy and Understanding. Retrieved from http://www.ispu.org/wp-content/uploads/2017/03/American-Muslim-Poll-2017-Report.pdf

Moore, R. B. (2006). Racism in the English language. In K. Rosenblum & T. Travis (Eds.), *The meaning of difference: American constructions of race, sex and gender, social class, and sexual orientation* (4th ed., pp. 451–459). Boston, MA: McGraw-Hill.

Murrow, E. R. (1955, December 31). Television broadcast (Wikiquote).

Newberg, A., & Waldman, M.R. (2006). *Why we believe what we believe: Uncovering our biological needs for meaning, spirituality, and truth.* New York, NY: Free Press.

Niebuhr, G. (2008). *Beyond tolerance: Searching for interfaith understanding in America.* New York, NY: Viking.

Pearson, A. R., Dovidio, J. F., & Gaertner, S. L. (2009). The nature of contemporary prejudice: Insights from aversive racism. Retrieved from http://www.yale.edu/intergroup/PearsonDovidioGaertner.pdf

Pew Research Center. (2013). *After Boston, little change in views of Islam and violence.* Retrieved from http://www.people-press.org/2013/05/07/after-boston-little-change-in-views-of-islam-and-violence/

Ryan, W. (1976). *Blaming the victim* (2nd ed.). New York, NY: Vintage Books.

Sadker, D., & Sadker, M. (1994). *Failing at fairness: How America's schools cheat girls.* New York, NY: Charles Scribner.

Sartre, J. P. (1995). *Anti-Semite and Jew.* New York, NY: Schocken.

Schaefer, R.T. (2008). *Racial and ethnic groups* (11th ed.). Upper Saddle River, NJ: Pearson.

Siddiqui, S. (2014). Americans' attitudes toward Muslims and Arabs are getting worse. *Huffington Post.* Retrieved from http://www.huffingtonpost.com/2014/07/29/arab-muslim-poll_n_5628919.html

Skuttnab-Kangas, T. (2000). *Linguistic genocide in education—or worldwide diversity and human rights?* Mahwah, NJ: Erlbaum.

Sliwa, J. (2017). Self-Esteem gender gap more pronounced in western countries. American Psychological Association. Retrieved from http://www.apa.org/news/press/releases/2016/01/self-esteem-gender.aspx

Stalcup, M., & Craze, J. (2011, March/April). How we train our cops to fear Islam. *Washington Monthly, 43*(3/4), 20–28.

Steinback, R. (2011, Summer). The jihad against Islam. *Intelligence Report, 142,* 15–20.

Stephan, W. (1999). *Reducing prejudice and stereotyping in schools.* New York, NY: Teachers College Press.

Sue, D. W. (2015). *Race talk and the conspiracy of silence.* Hoboken, NJ: John Wiley & Sons.

Tolev, M. (2010, May 12). Poll: Americans back Arizona's illegal immigrants law. *McClatchy Newspapers* (http://www.mcclatchydc.com/94050/most-Americans-approve-of-Arizonas.html)

U.S. Bureau of the Census. (2008). Statistical abstract of the United States. Retrieved from http://www.census.gov/compendia/statab

U.S. Bureau of Labor Statistics. (2015). Labor force statistics from the current population survey. Retrieved from www.bls.gov/cps/cpsaat37.htm

U.S. Bureau of Labor Statistics. (2013). U.S. Department of Labor, *The Economics Daily,* Women's earnings, 1979–2012. Retrieved from http://www.bls.gov/opub/ted/2013/ted_20131104.htm

Vega, F. (1978). *The effect of human and intergroup relations education on the race/sex attitudes of education majors.* Unpublished doctoral dissertation, University of Minnesota, Minneapolis.

Wessler, S. L. (2001). Sticks and stones. *Educational Leadership, 58*(4), 28–33.

Wolfe, M. (2017). Muslim business entrepreneurs and the American economy. *The Huffington Post.* Retrieved from http://www.huffingtonpost.com/michael-wolfe/muslim-biz-entrepreneurs-_b_9548540.html

Woodruff, M. (2013). The income gap between blacsks and whites has only gotten worse since the 1960s. *Business Insider.* Retrieved from http://www.businessinsider.com/the-income-gap-between-blacks-and-whites-2013-8

Chapter 3

Belenky, M. F., Clinchy, B. M., Goldberger, N. R., & Tarulle, J. M. (1997). *Women's ways of knowing: The development of self, voice, and mind.* New York, NY: Basic Books.

Berne, E. (2004). *Games people play: The psychology of human relationships.* New York, NY: Ballantine. (Originally published in 1964)

Brown, P. L. (2013). Opening up, students transform a vicious cycle. *New York Times.* Retrieved from www.nytimes.com/2013/04/04/education/restorative-justice-programs-take-root-in-schools.html?pagewanted=all

Brownstein, R. (2009). Pushed out. *Teaching Tolerance,* Issue 36, pp. 58–61.

Burgoon, J. K. (2002). Nonverbal signals. In M. Knapp & G. Miller (Eds.), *Handbook of interpersonal communication* (3rd ed., pp. 344–390). Beverly Hills, CA: Sage.

Coleman, P. T., & Fisher-Yokida, B. (2008). Conflict resolution can be taught at all educational levels. In *Conflict resolution: Opposing viewpoints* (pp. 22–32). Detroit, MI: Greenhaven Press.

Deutsch, M. (2006). Cooperation and competition. In M. Deutsch, P. Coleman, & E.C. Marcus (Eds.), *The handbook of conflict resolution* (2nd ed., pp. 21–40). San Francisco, CA: Jossey-Bass.

Dow, B. J., & Wood, J. T. (2006). *The SAGE handbook of gender and communication.* Thousand Oaks, CA: Sage Publications.

Ekman, P. (2003). *Emotions revealed: Recognizing faces and feelings to improve communication and emotional life.* New York, NY: Times Books. [In Figure 3.1 the picture on the left was anger; on the right, contempt.]

Fitzgerald, F. S. (1945). *The crack-up.* New York: New Directions Publishing.

Foster, H. L. (1986). *Ribbin', jivin', and playin' the dozens* (2nd ed.). Cambridge, MA: Ballinger.

Freire, P. (2000). *Pedagogy of the oppressed.* New York, NY: Continuum. (Originally published in 1970)

Garbis, N. (2015). What's next: Future global trends affecting your organization. Retrieved from http://futurehrtrends.eiu.com/report-2015/cultural-differences-inevitability-in-a-global-economy/

Goman, C. K. (2016). Is your communication style dictated by your gender? *Forbes.* Retrieved from https://www.forbes.com/sites/carolkinseygoman/2016/03/31/is-your-communication-style-dictated-by-your-gender/#3eef8889eb9d

Gordon, T. (2000). *Parent effectiveness training: The proven program for raising responsible children.* New York, NY: Crown.

Grumet, G. W. (2008). Eye contact: The core of interpersonal relatedness. In J. DeVito & M. Hecht (Eds.), *The nonverbal communication reader* (3rd ed., pp. 126–139). Long Grove, IL: Waveland.

Hall, M. (2013). Perry's scheme: Understanding the intellectual development of college-age students. John Hopkins University. Retrieved from http://ii.library.jhu.edu/2013/12/13/perrys-scheme-understanding-the-intellectual-development-of-college-age-students/

Harris, T. (2004). *I'm OK—you're OK.* New York, NY: Morrow/Avon.

Hauser, M. D. (2006). *Moral minds: The nature of right and wrong.* New York, NY: Ecco.

Heath, S. B. (2006). *Ways with words.* Cambridge, UK: Cambridge University Press.

Hecht, M. L., & DeVito, J. A. (Eds.). (2008). Perspectives on defining and understanding nonverbal communication: Classic and contemporary readings. In *The nonverbal communication reader* (3rd ed., pp. 3–17). Long Grove, IL: Waveland.

Ismail, N. (2001, September). *Communicating across cultures.* Victoria, BC: Pertinent Information. Available at http://pertinent.com/pertinfo/business/yaticom.html

Jandt, F. E. (1985). *Win-win negotiating: Turning conflict into agreement.* New York, NY: Wiley.

Jandt, F. E. (2003). *Intercultural communication: An introduction* (3rd ed.). Thousand Oaks, CA: Sage.

Johnson, D. W., Johnson, R. T., & Tjosvold, D. (2006). Constructive controversy: The value of intellectual opposition. In M. Deutsch, P. Coleman, & E. C. Marcus (Eds.), *The handbook of conflict resolution* (2nd ed., pp. 65–85). San Francisco, CA: Jossey-Bass.

Kimmel, P. R. (2006). Culture and conflict. In M. Deutsch, P. Coleman, & E. C. Marcus (Eds.), *The handbook of conflict resolution* (2nd ed., pp. 453–474). San Francisco, CA: Jossey-Bass.

King, P. M., & Kitchener, K. S. (1994). *Developing reflective judgment: Understanding and promoting intellectual growth and critical thinking in adolescents and adults.* San Francisco, CA: Jossey-Bass.

Kochman, T. (1981). *Black and white: Styles in conflict.* Chicago, IL: University of Chicago Press.

Kougl, K. (1997). *Communicating in the classroom.* Prospect Heights, IL: Waveland.

Lau, E. (2014). Preschooler gender-typed play behaviors as a function of gender of parents, siblings, and playmates. Retrieved from http://steinhardt.nyu.edu/appsych/opus/issues/2014/fall/lau

McCorkle, S., & Mills, J.L. (1992). Rowboat in a hurricane: Metaphors of interpersonal conflict management. *Communication Reports 5*(2), 57–67.

Meltzoff, N. (2007, Spring). Use another word. *Rethinking Schools 21*(3), 46–48.

Moon, J. (2017). Bullying and the bottom line. *Teaching Tolerance, 57*, 27-29.

Narula, U. (2006). *Handbook of communication models, perspectives and strategies.* New Delhi, India: Atlantic.

Nation, M. (2007). Empowering the victim: Interventions for children victimized by bullies. In J. E. Zins, M. J. Elias, and C. A. Maher (Eds.), *Bullying, victimization, and peer harassment: A handbook of prevention and intervention* (pp. 239–255). New York, NY: The Haworth Press.

Newberg, A., & Waldman, M. R. (2006). *Why we believe what we believe: Uncovering our biological needs for meaning, spirituality, and truth.* New York, NY: Free Press.

Perry Jr., W. G. (1999). *Forms of intellectual and ethical development in the college years: A scheme.* San Francisco, CA: Jossey-Bass, Inc.

Postman, N., & Weingartner, C. (1987). *Teaching as a subversive activity.* New York, NY: Dell Publishing. (Originally published in 1969)

Prince, D. W. (2004). *Communicating across cultures.* Greensboro, NC: Center for Creative Leadership.

Robers, S., Kemp, J., Truman, J., & Snyder, T. (2013). Indicators of school crime and safety: 2012. *Bureau of Justice Statistics/National Center for Educational Statistics.* Retrieved from http://nces.ed.gov/pubs2013/2013036.pdf

Robbins, C. G. (2008). *Expelling hope.* Albany, NY: SUNY Press.

Rogers, C. (1995). *A way of being.* New York, NY: Mariner Books. (Originally published in 1980)

Rychly, L., & Graves, E. (2012). Teacher characteristics for culturally responsive pedagogy. *Multicultural Perspectives, 14*(1), pp. 44–49.

Skuttnab-Kangas, T. (2000). *Linguistic genocide in education—or worldwide diversity and human rights?* Mahwah, NJ: Erlbaum.

Spitzberg, B. H. (2008). Perspectives on nonverbal communication skills. In J. DeVito & M. Hecht (Eds.), *The nonverbal communication reader* (3rd ed., pp. 18–22). Prospect Heights, IL: Waveland.

Stone, G., Singletary, M., & Richmond, V.P. (1999). *Clarifying communication theories: A hands-on approach.* Ames, IA: Iowa State University Press.

Stucki, B. W. (2014). Rethinking zero tolerance. *The American Prospect, 25*(3), pp. 7–11.

Sue, D. W. (2015). *Race talk and the conspiracy of silence.* Hoboken, NJ: John Wiley & Sons.

Tannen, D. (1994). *Gender and discourse.* New York, NY: Oxford University Press.

Tannen, D. (2007). *You just don't understand: Women and men in conversation.* New York, NY: Harper Collins. (Originally published in 1990)

Varner, I., & Beamer, L. (2010). *Intercultural communication in the global workplace.* (5th ed.). New York, NY: McGraw Hill/Irwin.

Waley, A. (Ed.). (1938). *The analects of Confucius.* New York, NY: Vintage.

Chapter 4

Andrzejewski, J. (1996). Definitions for understanding oppression and social justice. In J. Andrzejewski (Ed.), *Oppression and social justice: Critical frameworks* (5th ed., pp. 52–59). Needham, MA: Simon & Schuster.

Aronson, B., & Amatullah, T. (2016). Culturally relevant education: Extending the conversation to religion. *Multicultural Perspectives, 18*(3), 140–149.

Associated Press. (2014). *Officials overwhelmed by influx of children crossing Mexican border into U.S. on their own.* Retrieved from http://www.theblaze.com/stories/2014/06/07/officials-overwhelmed-by-influx-of-children-crossing-mexican-border-into-u-s-on-their-own

Bale, J. (2015). English-Only to the core. *Rethinking Schools,* 30(1), 20-27.

Baron, D. (2000). English in a multicultural America. In K. E. Rosenblum & T. C. Travis (Eds.), *The meaning of difference: American constructions of race, sex and gender, social class, and sexual orientation* (pp. 445–451). Boston, MA: McGraw-Hill.

Barrett, J. R., & Roediger, D. (2002). How white people became white. In P. Rothenberg (Ed.), *White privilege: Essential readings on the other side of racism* (pp. 29–34). New York, NY: Worth.

Becerra, H. (2014). *Immigration court backlog adds to border crisis.* Retrieved from http://www.latimes.com/nation/la-na-immigration-court-20140710-story.html#page=1

Blake, A. (2014). *Anti-immigrant sentiment is down in the United States.* Retrieved from http://www.washingtonpost.com/blogs/the-fix/wp/2014/06/27/americans-were-for-immigration-before-they-were-against-it

Bloomekatz, A. (2017). *Curtis Acosta on the Tucson ethnic studies victory. Rethinking Schools,* 32(1), 8.

Brands, H. W. (2000). *The first American: The life and times of Benjamin Franklin.* New York, NY: Doubleday.

Brodkin, K. (2002). How Jews became white folks. In P. Rothenberg (Ed.), *White privilege: Essential readings on the other side of racism* (pp. 35–48). New York, NY: Worth.

Browne, C. (2014). *The employee turnover for the border patrol.* Retrieved from http://work.chron.com/employee-turnover-border-patrol-19955.html

Carjuzaa, J., Baldwin, A. E., & Munson, M. (2015). Making the dream real: Montana's Indian education for all initiative thrives in a national climate of anti-ethnic studies. *Multicultural Perspectives,* 17(4), 198–206.

Chavez, L. (2009). The realities of immigration. In W. Dvorak (Ed.), *Immigration in the United States* (pp. 40–49). New York, NY: The H. W. Wilson Company.

Cohn, J. (2015). Why public silence greets government success. *The American Prospect,* 26(2), 22–25.

Cooper, J. J. (2010, May 11). Arizona ethnic studies law signed by Governor Brewer, condemned by UN human rights experts. *Huffington Post.* Retrieved from http://www.huffingtonpost.com/2010/05/12/arizona-ethnic-studies-la_n-572864

Costello, M. B. (2016). Minority children suffer from hate rhetoric in presidential campaign, SPLC Report, 46(2). (Full report can be accessed at: https://www.splcenter.org/sites/default/files/splc_the_trump;_effect.pdf)

Crawford, J. (2000). *At war with diversity: US language policy in an age of anxiety.* Clevedon, UK: Multilingual Matters LTD.

Daniels, R. (2002). *Coming to America: A history of immigration and ethnicity in American life* (2nd ed.) New York, NY: Perennial (HarperCollins).

Davis, J. H. Sanger, D. E., & Haberman, M. (2017). Trump to order Mexican border wall and curtain immigration.

New York Times. Retrieved from https://www.nytimes.com/2017/01/24/us/politics/wall-border-trump.html

Delgado, R. (1997). Citizenship. In J.F. Perea (Ed.), *Immigrants out!: The new nativism and the anti-immigrant impulse in the United States* (pp. 318–323). New York, NY: New York University Press.

DeParle, J. (2011). The anti-immigrant crusader. *New York Times.* Retrieved from http://www.nytimes.com/2011/04/17/us/17immig.html?pagewanted=all&_r=0

DeSilver, D. (2017, March 6). Immigrants don't make up a majority of workers in any U. S. industry. Retrieved from http://www.pewresearch.org/fact-tank/2017/03/16/immigrants-dont-make-up-a-majority-of-workers-in-any-u-s-industry

Dubose, L. (2013). Immigration nation. *The Washington Spectator,* 39(4), 8.

Eck, D. L. (2001). *A new religious America: How a "Christian Country" has become the world's most religiously diverse nation.* New York, NY: HarperCollins.

Feagin, J. (1997). Old poison in new bottles: The deep roots of modern nativism. In J. F. Perea (Ed.), *Immigrants out!: The new nativism and the anti-immigrant impulse in the United States* (pp. 13–43). New York, NY: New York University Press.

Feagin, J., & Feagin, C. (1996). Basic concepts in the study of racial and ethnic relations. In *Racial and ethnic relations* (5th ed., pp. 6–26). Upper Saddle River, NJ: Prentice Hall.

Fitz, M., Wolgin, P. E., & Oakford, P. (2013). Immigrants are makers, not takers. *Center for American Progress.* https://www.americanprogress.org/issues/immigration/news/2013/02/08/52377/immigrants-are-makers-not-takers

Fuchs, L. H. (1990). *The American kaleidoscope: Race, ethnicity and the civic culture.* Hanover, NH: University Press of New England.

Goldenberg, C. (2008, Summer). Teaching English Language Learners. *American Educator,* 32(1), 8–23, 42–43.

Gort, M. (2005). Bilingual education: Good for U.S.? In T. Osborn (Ed.), *Language and cultural diversity in U.S. schools: Democratic principles in action* (pp. 25–37). Westport, CT: Praeger.

Grant, M. (1970). *The passing of the great race, or the racial basis of European history* (Rev. ed.). New York, NY: Arno Press. (Original work published 1916)

Grosjean, F. (2012). Life as a bilingual. *Psychology Today.* Retrieved from http://www.psychologytoday.com/blog/life-bilingual/201205/bilinguals-in-the-united-states

Haglage, A. (2014). *Hate crime victimization statistics show rise in anti-Hispanic crime.* Retrieved from http://www.thedailybeast.com/articles/2014/02/20/hate-crime-victimization-statistics-show-rise-in-anti-hispanic-crime.html

Hanes, S. (2013). Immigration: Assimilation and the measure of an American. *The Christian Science Monitor.* Retrieved from http://www.csmonitor.com/USA/Society/2013/0707/Immigration-Assimilation-and-the-measure-of-an-American

Henderson, T. J. (2011). *Beyond borders: A history of Mexican migration to the United States.* Chichester, U.K.: Wiley-Blackwell.

Hennesey, J. (1985). *American Catholics: A history of the Roman Catholic community in the United States.* New York, NY: Oxford University Press.

Higham, J. (1955). *Strangers in the land: Patterns of American nativism, 1865–1925.* New Brunswick, NJ: Rutgers University Press.

Ji, Q., & Batlalova, J. (2013). College educated immigrants in the United States. *Migration Policy Institute.* Retrieved from http://www.migrationpolicy.org/article/college-educated-immigrants-united-states

Kariel, H. (1961). *The decline of American pluralism.* Redwood City, CA: Stanford University Press.

Kammen, M. (1972). *People of paradox: An inquiry concerning the origins of American civilization.* New York, NY: Vintage.

Kenny, C. (2015, August 3-9). Immigrants to the rescue. *Bloomberg/Businessweek,* 10-11.

KryssTal. (2010). *The 30 most spoken languages in the world.* Retrieved from http://www.krysstal.com/spoken.html

Kugler, A., & Oakford, P. (2013). Immigration helps American workers' wages and job opportunities. *Center for American Progress.* Retrieved from http://www.americanprogress.org/issues/immigration/news/2013/08/29/73203/immigration-helps-american-workers-wages-and-job-opportunities

Lee, E. Y. (2017). Majority of Americans oppose funding Trump's border wall. *Think Progress.* Retrieved from https://thinkprogress.org/americans-dont-want-border-wall-c14b729fbdbc

Lynn, R. (2001). *Eugenics: A reassessment.* Westport, CT: Prager.

Lind, D. (2014). *13 facts that help explain America's child-migrant crisis.* Retrieved from http://www.vox.com/2014/6/16/5813406/explain-child-migrant-crisis-central-america-unaccompanied-children-immigrants-daca

Liou, Daniel D. (2016). Fostering college-going expectations of immigrant students through the sympathetic touch of school leadership. *Multicultural Perspectives,* 18(2), 82–90.

Meacham, J. (2009). Who are we now. In W. Dvorak (Ed.), *Immigration in the United States* (pp. 171–175). New York, NY: The H. W. Wilson Company.

Mejina, B., & Carcamo, C. (2016). As more Latino kids speak only English, parents worry about chatting with grandma. *The Los Angeles Times.* Retrieved from http://www.latimes.com/local/california/la-me-latino-immigrants-english-fluency-20160422-story.html

Myers, G. (1960). *History of bigotry in the United States.* New York, NY: Capricorn.

Navarro, L. (2011, April). The melting pot. *The American Prospect,* 22(3), A18–A20.

Nevins, J. (2010). *Operation gatekeeper and beyond.* New York, NY: Routledge.

Olivera, M. (2012). *Bilingual mania: Parents are taking a second look at raising bilingual children.* Retrieved from http://nbclatino.com/2012/10/04/bilingual-mania-parents-are-taking-a-second-look-at-raising-bilingual-children

Ozimek, A. (2012). *Is the U.S. the most immigrant friendly country in the world?* Retrieved from http://www.forbes.com/sites/modeledbehavior/2012/11/18/is-the-u-s-the-most-immigrant-friendly-country-in-the-world

Pabst, G. (2011, March 31). Report: Hispanic workforce growing. Retrieved from the *Milwaukee Journal Sentinel* at http://www.jsonline.com/business/119034319

Pai, Y., & Adler, S. (2006). Schooling as Americanization: 1600s–1970s. In *Cultural foundations of education* (4th ed., pp. 55–91). Upper Saddle River, NJ: Merrill Prentice Hall.

Papademetriou, D. G. (2013). The fundamentals of immigration reform. *The American Prospect* 24(2), 16–24.

Partnership for a New American Economy. (2013). *Better business: How Hispanic entrepreneurs are beating expectations and bolstering the U.S. economy.* Retrieved from http://www.renewoureconomy.org/research/better-business

Peterson, B. (2017). The struggle for bilingual education. *Rethinking Schools,* 32(1), 45-49.

Pipher, M. (2002). *The middle of everywhere: The world's refugees come to our town.* New York, NY: Harcourt.

Potok, M. (2011, Spring). Murder of Ecuadoran man dismissed with a shrug. *Intelligence Report,* Issue 141, pp. 10–11.

Ramos, J. (2002). *The other face of America.* New York, NY: Rayo.

Rendall, S. (2014). At elite media, "scientific" racists fit in fine. *Extra!* 27(8), 12–13.

Robbins, L. & Dickerson, C. (2018). What does the latest court ruling on DACA mean? Here are some answers. The New York Times. Retrieved from https://www.nytimes.com/2018/01/23/us/daca-dreamers-shutdown.html.

Roberts, D. (1997). Who may give birth to citizens: Reproduction, eugenics, and immigration. In J. F. Perea (Ed.), *Immigrants out!: The new nativism and the anti-immigrant impulse in the United States* (pp. 205–219). New York, NY: New York University Press.

Rodriguez, C. Y. (2013). Fewer Latinos will speak Spanish, more non-Latinos will, report says. CNN. Retrieved from http://www.cnn.com/2013/09/20/us/spanish-declining-among-hispanics/index.html

Ryan, C. (2013). *Language use in the United States: 2011.* Retrieved from http://www.census.gov/prod/2013pubs/acs-22.pdf

Salas, K. D. (2006). Defending bilingual education. *Rethinking Schools,* 20(3), 33–37.

Sampson, R. J. (2015). Immigration and America's urban revival. *The American Prospect,* 26(3), 20–24.

Sanchez, R. (2017). *After ICE arrests, fear spreads among undocumented immigrants.* CNN. Retrieved from http://www.cnn.com/2017/02/11/politics/immigration-roundus-community-fear/index.html

Scherer, M. (2005). Scrimmage on the border. *Mother Jones,* 30(2), 50–57.

Scherr, S. (2008, Fall). Legionnaires' Disease. *Intelligence Report,* 131, 28–35.

Schuck, P. H. (2014). *Why government fails so often and how it can do better.* Princeton, NJ: Princeton University Press.

Selden, S. (1999). *Inheriting shame: The story of eugenics and racism in America.* New York, NY: Teachers College Press.

Seminara, D. (2013). *New Pew report confirms visa overstays are driving increased illegal immigration.* Retrieved from http://www.cis.org/seminara/new-pew-report-confirms-visa-overstays-are-driving-increased-illegal-immigration

Shorris, E. (2001). *Latinos: A biography of the people.* New York, NY: W.W. Norton.

Skutnabb-Kangas, T. (2000). *Linguistic genocide in education—or worldwide diversity and human rights?* Mahwah, NJ: Lawrence Erlbaum Associates.

Soergel, A. (2016). "Undocumented" immigrants pay billions in taxes. U. S. News and World Report. Retrieved from https://www.usnews.com/news/articles/2016-03-01/study-undocumented-immigrants-pay-billions-in-taxes

Steinbeck, J. (1966). *America and Americans.* New York, NY: Viking Press.

Stubblefield, A. (2007, Spring). "Beyond the pale": Tainted whiteness, cognitive disability, and eugenic sterilization. *Hypatia, 22*(2), 162–180.

Tse, L. (2001). *"Why don't they learn English?": Separating fact from fallacy in the U.S. language debate.* New York, NY: Teachers College Press.

US English. (2014). Retrieved from http://www.us-english.org

U.S. Immigration and Customs Enforcement. (2014). *ICE immigration removals.* Retrieved from https://www.ice.gov/removal-statistics

Wilson, D. L. (2008, October). The illusion of immigrant criminality. *Extra! 21*(5), 21–22.

Chapter 5

Baker, P., & Davenport, C. (2017). Trump revives Keystone pipeline rejected by Obama. Retrieved from https://www.nytimes.com/2017/01/24/us/politics/keystone-dakota-pipeline-trump.html?_r=0

Banks, J. A. (2009). *Teaching strategies for ethnic studies* (8th ed.). Boston, MA: Allyn & Bacon.

Berkhofer Jr., R., (2004). *The white man's Indian: Images of the American Indian from Columbus to the present.* New York, NY: Vintage Books.

Bixler, M. T. (1992). *Winds of freedom: The story of the Navajo code talkers of World War II.* Darien, CT: Two Bytes Publishing Company.

Cárdenas, V., & Kerby, S. (2012). *The state of Latinos in the United States.* Retrieved from http://www.americanprogress.org/issues/race/report/2012/08/08/11984/the-state-of-latinos-in-the-united-states/

Carjuzaa, J, Baldwin, A. E., & Munson, M. (2015). Making the dream real: Montana's Indian education for all initiative thrives in a national climate of anti-ethnic studies. *Multicultural Perspectives, 17*(4), 198-206.

Chernow, R. (2004). *Alexander Hamilton.* New York, NY: Penguin Books.

Connolly, M. R. (2000, September/October). What's in a name?: A historical look at Native American-related nicknames and symbols at three U.S. universities. *Journal of Higher Education, 17*(5), 515–548.

Cornelius, J. D. (2000). Literacy, slavery, and religion. In J. Birnbaum & C. Taylor (Eds.), *Civil rights since 1787: A reader on the black struggle* (pp. 85–89). New York, NY: New York University Press.

Cox, G. (2015). *Sociology of the American Indian.* Lewiston, NY: The Edwin Mellen Press.

Deloria, P. (2001). Sovereignty. In B. Ballantine & I. Ballantine (Eds.), *The Native Americans: An illustrated history.* North Dighton, MA: J. G. Press.

Duignan, P. J., & Gann, L. H. (1998). *The Spanish speakers in the United States: A history.* Lanham, MD: University Press of America.

East-West Center. (2012). *Asia matters for Americans.* Retrieved from http://www.asiamattersforamerica.org/asia/data/population/states

Editors of *Rethinking Schools.* (2016–2017). Water is life. *Rethinking Schools, 31*(2), 7-9.

Feagin, J., & Feagin, C. B. (2008). *Racial and ethnic relations* (8th ed.). Upper Saddle River, NJ: Pearson Prentice Hall.

Fitzgerald, F. S. (2005). Early success. In J. L. West (Ed.), *My lost city: Personal essays, 1920–1940* (pp. 184–192). Cambridge, UK: Cambridge University Press.

Fitzpatrick, J. P. (1971). *Puerto Rican Americans: The meaning of migration to the mainland.* Englewood Cliffs, NJ: Prentice Hall.

Fong, T. P. (2000). A brief history of Asians in America. In T. P. Fong & L. H. Shinagawa (Eds.), *Asian Americans: Experiences and perspectives* (pp. 13–30). Upper Saddle River, NJ: Prentice Hall.

Fong, T. P., & Shinagawa, L. H. (2000). Employment and occupation. In T. P. Fong & L. H. Shinagawa (Eds.), *Asian Americans: Experiences and perspectives* (pp. 191–192). Upper Saddle River, NJ: Prentice Hall.

Franklin, J. H., & Moss Jr., A. A. (2000). *From slavery to freedom: A history of African Americans.* New York, NY: Alfred A. Knopf.

Freeman, A. L. (2013). *All-American sweatshops.* Retrieved from http://garmentworkercenter.org/all-american-sweatshops

Friedman, T. L., & Mandelbaum, M. (2011). *That used to be us: How America fell behind in the world it invented and how we can come back.* New York, NY: Farrar, Straus and Giroux.

Gandhi, M. K. (1922). Statement before Mr. C. N. Broomfield, I. C. S., district and sessions judge, Ahmedabad. Retrieved from http://www.consciencelaws.org/ethics/ethics052.aspx

Gedicks, A. (1993). *The new resource wars: Native and environmental struggles against multinational corporations.* Boston, MA: South End Press

Gell-Mann, M. (1994). *The quark and the jaguar: Adventures in the simple and the complex.* New York, NY: W.H. Freeman.

Glenn, E. N., & Yap, S. G. H. (2000). Chinese American families. In T.P. Fong & L.H. Shinagawa (Eds.), *Asian Americans: Experiences and perspectives* (pp. 277–292). Upper Saddle River, NJ: Prentice Hall.

Goldstone, L. (2011). *Inherently unequal: The betrayal of equal rights by the Supreme Court, 1865–1903.* New York, NY: Walker and Company.

Hamilton, D., Cottom, T. M., Darity Jr., W., Aja, A. A., & Ash, C. (2015) Still we rise. *The American Prospect, 26*(4), 54-61.

Hansen, K. N., & Skopek, T. A. (2011). Introduction: The rise of the first nation in state politics (pp. 1–24), and Afterword: The death of Indian gaming and tribal sovereignty (pp. 209–216). In K. N. Hansen & T. A. Skopek (Eds.), *The new politics of Indian gaming: The rise of reservation interest groups.* Reno, NV: University of Nevada Press.

Hughes, L. (1994). Let America be America again. In A. Rampersad & D. Roellel (Eds.), *The collected poems of Langston Hughes* (pp. 189–191). New York, NY: Alfred A. Knopf.

Josephy Jr., A. (2005). *500 nations: An illustrated history of North American Indians.* London: Pimlico.

Kar, S. B., Campbell, K., Jiminez, A., & Gupta, S.R. (2000). Invisible Americans: An exploration of Indo American quality of life. In T. P. Fong & E. H. Shinagawa (Eds.), *Asian Americans: Experiences and perspectives* (pp. 303–319). Upper Saddle River, NJ: Prentice Hall.

Kazin, M. (2011). *American dreamers: How the left changed a nation.* New York, NY: Alfred Knopf.

Koppelman, K. (2001). Was Orwell wrong? In *Values in the key of life: Making harmony in the human community* (pp. 57–63). Amityville, NY: Baywood.

Lajimodiere, D. K. (2013). American Indian females and stereotypes: Warriors, leaders, healers, feminists; not drudges, princesses, prostitutes. *Multicultural Perspectives, 15*(2), 104–109.

Le May, J. L. (Ed.). (1987). *Benjamin Franklin: Writings* (pp. 442–446). New York, NY: Library of America.

Lesser, G., & Batalova J. (2017). Central American immigrants in the United States. Migration Policy Institute. Retrieved from http://www.migrationpolicy.org/article/central-american-immigrants-united-states

Lewis, D. L. (1993). *W.E.B. Du Bois: Biography of a race, 1868–1919.* New York, NY: Henry Holt.

Lewis, D. L. (2000). *W.E.B. Du Bois: The fight for equality and the American century, 1919–1963.* New York, NY: Henry Holt.

Loewen, J. (2008). *Lies my teacher told me: Everything your American history textbook got wrong.* New York, NY: The New Press.

Lomax, L. E. (1963). *The Negro revolt.* New York, NY: Signet Books.

Louie, M. C. (2000). Immigrant Asian women in Bay Area garment sweatshops: "After sewing, laundry, cleaning and cooking, I have no breath left to sing." In T. P. Fong & L. H. Shinagawa (Eds.), *Asian Americans: Experiences and perspectives* (pp. 226–242). Upper Saddle River, NJ: Prentice Hall.

Lowe, L. (2000). Heterogeneity, hybridity, multiplicity: Marking Asian American difference. In T. P. Fong & L. H. Shinagawa (Eds.), *Asian Americans: Experiences and perspectives* (pp. 412–421). Upper Saddle River, NJ: Prentice Hall.

Lui, M. (2004). Doubly divided: The racial wealth gap. In C. Collins, A. Gluckman, M. Lui, B. L. Wright, & A. Scharf (Eds.), *The wealth inequality reader* (pp. 42–49). Cambridge, MA: Dollars & Sense.

Lopez, G., & Patten E. (2015). Hispanics of Puerto Rican origin in the United States, 2013. Pew Research Center. Retrieved from http://www.pewhispanic.org/2015/09/15/hispanics-of-puerto-rican-origin-in-the-united-states-2013/

Malcolm X. (2000). The ballot or the bullet. In J. Birnbaum & C. Taylor (Eds.), *Civil rights since 1787: A reader on the black struggle* (pp. 589–603). New York, NY: New York University Press.

Mintz, S. (2004). *Huck's raft: A history of American childhood.* Cambridge, MA: Belknap Press of Harvard University Press.

Painter, N. I. (2005). *Creating Black Americans: African-American history and its meaning, 1619 to the present.* Oxford, UK: Oxford University Press.

Painter, N. I. (2010). *The history of white people.* New York, NY: W. W. Norton.

Pember, M. A. (2015). Intergenerational trauma: Understanding native's inherited pain. Retrieved from https://indiancountrymedianetwork.com/free-reports/intergenerational-trauma-understanding-natives-inherited-pain

Persio, S. L. (2017). New U. S. Cuba policy is unpopular, just like President Trump. *Newsweek.* Retrieved from http://www.newsweek.com/new-us-cuba-policy-unpopular-just-president-trump-627867

Pipher, M. (2002). *The middle of everywhere: The world's refugees come to our town.* New York, NY: Harcourt.

Portes, A., & Bach, R. L. (1985). *Latin journey: Cuban and Mexican immigrants in the United States.* Berkeley, CA: University of California Press.

Raboteau, A. (2000). Slave religion, rebellion and docility. In J. Birnbaum & C. Taylor (Eds.), *Civil rights since 1787: A reader on the black struggle* (pp. 29–34). New York, NY: New York University Press.

Reiss, O. (1997). *Blacks in colonial America.* Jefferson, NC: McFarland.

Sanchez, A., & Hagopian, J. (2017). What we don't learn about the Black Panther party – but should. *Rethinking Schools, 37*(1), 26-33.

Schuck, P. H. (2014). *Why government fails so often and how it can do better.* Princeton, NJ: Princeton University Press.

Shorris, E. (2001). *Latinos: A biography of the people.* New York, NY: W.W. Norton.

Smith, V. (2001). Cleanliness. In P. Sterns (Ed.), *Encyclopedia of European social history: From 1350 to 2000* (Vol. 4, pp. 343–353). New York, NY: Scribner.

Spivey, D. (2003). *Fire from the soul: A history of the African-American struggle.* Durham, NC: Carolina Academic Press.

Spring, J. (2001). *Deculturalization and the struggle for equality: A brief history of the education of dominated cultures in the United States* (3rd ed.). Boston, MA: McGraw-Hill.

Suzuki, D., & Knudtson, P. (1992). *Wisdom of the elders: Honoring sacred native visions of nature.* New York, NY: Bantam Books.

Takaki, R. (1993). *A different mirror: A history of multicultural America.* Boston, MA: Little, Brown.

U.S. Census Bureau. (2016). Facts for features: Hispanic heritage month. Retrieved from https://www.census.gov/newsroom/facts-for-features/2016/cb16-ff16.html

Vargas, Z. (2000). Citizen, immigrant, and foreign wage workers: The Chicana/o labor refrain in U.S. labor historiography. In R. I. Rochin & D. N. Valdes (Eds.), *Voices of a new Chicana/o history* (pp. 153–165). East Lansing, MI: Michigan State University Press.

Vento, A. C. (1998). *Mestizo: The history, culture and politics of the Mexican and the Chicano.* Lanham, MD: University Press of America.

Wallace, A. (1993). *The long, bitter trail: Andrew Jackson and the Indians.* New York, NY: Hill & Wang.

Weatherford, J. (1988). *Indian givers: How the Indians of the Americas transformed the world.* New York, NY: Fawcett.

White, R. (2001). Expansion and exodus. In B. Ballantine & I. Ballantine (Eds.), *The native Americans: An illustrated history.* North Dighton, MA: J. G. Press.

Williams, J. (1987). *Eyes on the prize: America's civil rights years, 1954–1965.* New York, NY: Viking.

Williams, W. C. (1954). *The American background. Selected essays of William Carlos Williams* (pp. 134–161). New York, NY: Random House.

Wilson, J. (1998). *The earth shall weep: A history of native America.* New York, NY: Atlantic Monthly Press.

Wolfe-Rocca, U. (2017). Standing with Standing Rock. *Rethinking Schools, 31*(3), 14-20.

Woodward, C. V. (1966). *The strange case of Jim Crow.* Oxford, UK: Oxford University Press.

Wu, C. (Ed.). (1972). *"Chink!" A documentary history of anti-Chinese prejudice in America.* New York, NY: World Publishing.

Zia, H. (2000). *Asian American dreams: The emergence of an American people.* New York, NY: Farrar, Straus and Giroux.

Zinn, H. (2003). *A people's history of the United States.* New York, NY: HarperCollins.

Chapter 6

Abdo, G. (2006). *Mecca and Main Street: Muslim life in America after 9/11.* Oxford, UK: Oxford University Press.

al-Hibri, A. Y. (2001). Standing at the precipice: Faith in the age of science and technology. In A. al-Hibri, J. B. Elshtain, & C. C. Haynes (Eds.), *Religion in American public life: Living with our deepest differences.* New York, NY: W.W. Norton.

Allen, R. S. (1996). *Without a prayer: Religious expression in public schools.* Amherst, NY: Prometheus.

American Academy of Religion. (2010). *Guidelines for teaching about religion in K–12 public schools in the United States.* Retrieved from https://www.aarweb.org/sites/default/files/pdfs/Publications/epublications/AARK-12CurriculumGuidelines.pdf

Aronson, B., & Amatullah, T. (2016). Culturally relevant education: Extending the conversation to religion. *Multicultural Perspectives, 18*(3), 140-149.

Associated Press. (2015, Dec. 10). Who are US Muslims? *La Crosse Tribune,* p. A3.

Bagby, I. (2012). *The American mosque 2011.* http://www.hartfordinstitute.org/The-American-Mosque-Report-2.pdf

Barrett, P. M. (2007). *American Islam: The struggle for the soul of a religion.* New York, NY: Farrar, Straus and Giroux.

Berlet, C. (2012). Islamophobia, antisemitism and the demonized "other." *Extra! 25*(8), 13–15.

Burns, A. (2017). 2 federal judges rule against Trump's latest travel ban. New York Times. Retrieved from https://www.nytimes.com/2017/03/15/us/politics/trump-travel-ban.html

Carroll, J. (2001). *Constantine's Sword: The church and the Jews, a history.* Boston, MA: Houghton Mifflin.

Chalabi, M. (2015). How anti-Muslim are Americans? Data points to extent of Islamophobia. *The Guardian.* Retrieved from https://www.theguardian.com/us-news/2015/dec/08/muslims-us-islam-islamophobia-data-polls

Chernow, R. (2004). *Alexander Hamilton.* New York, NY: Penguin Books.

Clark, C., Vargas, M. B., Schlosser, L., & Allmo, C. (2002, Winter). It's Not Just "Secret Santa" in December: Addressing educational and workplace climate issues linked to Christian privilege. *Multicultural Education,* 53–58.

Dinnerstein, L. (1994). *Anti-Semitism in America.* New York, NY: Oxford.

Domonoske, C. (2017). 4th circuit court ruling keeps Trump's travel ban on hold. Retrieved from http://www.npr.org/sections/thetwo-way/2017/05/25/530051807/4th-circuit-court-ruling-keeps-trumps-travel-ban-on-hold

Douglass, S. (2002). Teaching about religion. *Educational Leadership, 60*(2), 32–36.

Eck, D. L. (2001). *A new religious America: How a "Christian Country" has become the world's most religiously diverse nation.* New York, NY: HarperCollins.

El-Atwani, K. (2015). Envisioning multicultural education development in U.S. Islamic schools in light of reviewed literature, *Multicultural Perspectives, 17*(3), 145-151.

Fasciano, M. (2015). Extreme prejudice. *Teaching Tolerance,* Issue 51, 26-28.

Fraser, J. W. (1999). *Between church and state: Religion and public education in a multicultural America.* New York, NY: St. Martin's.

Gallup Poll. (2010). *In U.S., religious prejudice stronger against Muslims.* Retrieved from http://www.gallup.com/poll/125312/Religious-Prejudice-Stronger-Against-Muslims.aspx

Gaustad, E., & Schmidt, L. (2002). *The religious history of America: The heart of the American story from colonial times to today.* New York, NY: HarperCollins.

Goodavage, M. (2013). Hundreds of voucher schools teach creationism in science classes. *PBS.* Retrieved from http://www.pbs.org/independentlens/blog/hundreds-of-voucher-schools-teach-creationism-in-science-classes

Goodrich, F., & Hackett, A. (1956). *The diary of Anne Frank.* New York, NY: Random House.

Hanania, R. (2014). *American Arab and Muslim groups denounce ISIS beheadings.* Retrieved from http://thearabdailynews.com/2014/09/03/american-arab-muslim-groups-denounce-isis-beheadings

Hendry, J. (2003). Mining the sacred mountain: The clash between the Western dualistic framework and Native American religions. *Multicultural Perspectives, 5*(1), 3–10.

Herberg, W. (1955). *Protestant-Catholic-Jew: An essay in American religious sociology.* Garden City, NY: Doubleday.

Hudson, W. S. (1973). *Religion in America: An historical account of the development of American religious life* (2nd ed.). New York, NY: Charles Scribner.

Intelligence Report. (2010, Winter). Intelligence briefs: Ground zero battle may be stoking anti-Muslim violence. Issue 140, 3–5.

Jacoby, S. (2005). Original intent. *Mother Jones, 30*(7), 29–31, 74.

Kosmin, B. A., & Lachman, S. P. (1993). *One nation under God: Religion in contemporary American society.* New York, NY: Crown.

Lee, E. (2004). American gate keeping: Race and immigration law in the twentieth century. In N. Foner & G. M. Frederickson (Eds.), *Not just black and white: Historical and contemporary perspectives on immigration, race and ethnicity in the United States* (pp. 119–144). New York, NY: Russell Sage Foundation.

Lim, V. (2011, Fall). The unaffiliated unite. *Teaching Tolerance,* Issue 40, 33–35.

Lindberg, M. (2015). Religions vs. equality: A social studies dilemma. *Teaching Tolerance,* Issue 51, 36-39.

Lipka, M. (2015). *Muslims expected to surpass Jews as second-largest U.S. religious group.* Retrieved from http://www.pewresearch.org/fact-tank/2015/04/14/muslims-expected-to-surpass-jews-as-second-largest-u-s-religious-group

Lippy, C. H. (1994). *Being religious, American style: A history of popular religiosity in the United States.* Westport, CT: Praeger.

Manning, J. E. (2017). Membership of the 115th Congress: A profile. Retrieved from https://fas.org/sgp/crs/misc/R44762.pdf

Markoe, L. (2015). *Anti-Semitism in U.S. spikes after nearly a decade in decline.* Retrieved from http://www.religionnews.com/2015/03/31/anti-semitism-us-spikes-decade-decline

McCloud, A. B. (2006). *Transnational Muslims in American society.* Gainesville, FL: University of Florida Press.

McMillan, R. C. (1984). *Religion in the public schools: An introduction.* Macon, GA: Mercer University Press.

Miller, G. T. (1976). *Religious liberty in America: History and prospects.* Philadelphia, PA: Westminster.

Myers, G. (1960). *History of bigotry in the United States* (rev. ed.), G. Christman (Ed.). New York, NY: Capricorn.

Naureckas, J. (2015). Non-Muslim terrorists a surprise—to consumers of corporate media. *Extra!* 28(7), p. 2.

Niebuhr, G. (2008). *Beyond tolerance: Searching for interfaith understanding in America.* New York, NY: Viking.

Nimer, M. (2004). Muslims in the American body politic. In Z. H. Buhhari, S. S. Nyang, M. Ahmad, & J. C. Esposito (Eds.), *Muslims' place in the American public square* (pp. 145–164). Walnut Creek, CA: Altamira Press.

Nord, W. A. (1995). *Religion and American education: Rethinking a national dilemma.* Chapel Hill, NC: University of North Carolina Press.

Painter, N. I. (2010). *The history of white people.* New York, NY: W. W. Norton

Pauken, P. (2003, January). *I Pledge Allegiance to the Curriculum: The establishment clause and the legal balance between educational authority and individual rights.* Presented at the Hawai'i International Conference on Education, Honolulu.

Paulson, M. (2014). *Americans claim to attend church more than they do.* Retrieved from http://www.nytimes.com/2014/05/18/upshot/americans-claim-to-attend-church-much-more-than-they-do.html?-r=0&abt=0002&abg=0

Pew Research Center. (2012). *The rise of Asian Americans.* Retrieved from http://www.pewsocialtrends.org/2012/06/19/the-rise-of-asian-americans

Pew Research Center. (2013). *The religious affiliation of U.S. immigrants: Majority Christian, rising share of other faiths.* Retrieved from http://www.pewforum.org/2013/05/17/the-religious-affiliation-of-us-immigrants/#affiliation

Potok, M. (2015). Living while Muslim. *Intelligence Report,* Issue 158, 19-20.

Ravitch, F. S. (1999). *School prayer and discrimination: The civil rights of religious minorities and dissenters.* Boston, MA: Northeastern University Press.

Rendall, S. (2012, November). Why do they hate us back? *Extra! 25*(11), 10–11.

Rendall, S., & McCloskey, S. (2013). A media microscope on Islam-linked violence. *Extra! 26*(8), 8–9.

Ribuffo, L. P. (1997). Henry Ford and the international Jew. In J. Sarna (Ed.), *The American Jewish experience* (2nd ed., pp. 201–218). New York, NY: Holmes & Meier.

Schrobsdorff, S. (2016). My life as a "None" and other tales from the ranks of the unaffiliated and the agnostic. *Time,* 188(12), 63.

Secular Student Alliance. (2012). *The unstoppable secular students.* Retrieved from https://www.secularstudents.org/unstoppable-secular-students

Taggar, S. V. (2006). Headscarves in the headlines! What does this mean for educators? *Multicultural Perspectives 8*(3), 3–10.

Waldman, S. (2006). The framers and the faithful. *Washington Monthly, 38*(4), 33–38.

Wegner, G. P. (2002). *Anti-Semitism and schooling under the Third Reich.* New York, NY: Routledge Falmer.

Chapter 7

Adams, D. W. (1995). *Education for extinction: American Indians and the boarding school experience, 1875–1928.* Lawrence, KS: University Press of Kansas.

Appleton, N. (1983). *Cultural pluralism in education: Theoretical foundations.* New York, NY: Longman.

Aronson, E. (1999). *The social animal* (8th ed.). New York, NY: W. H. Freeman.

Barrett, J. R., & Roediger, D. (2002). How white people became white. In P. Rothenberg (Ed.), *White privilege: Essential readings on the other side of racism* (pp. 29–34). New York, NY: Worth.

Bonilla-Silva, E. (2001). *White supremacy and racism in the post-civil rights era.* Boulder, CO: Lynne Rienner.

Bouie, J. (2012). The democrats' demographic dreams. *The American Prospect, 23*(6), 6–11.

Brooks, R. L. (1996). *Integration or separation?: A strategy for racial equality.* Cambridge, MA: Harvard University Press.

Chua, A. (2007). *Day of empire: How hyperpowers rise to global dominance—and why they fall.* New York, NY: Doubleday.

Claiborne, R. (1983). *Our marvelous native tongue: The life and times of the English language.* New York, NY: Times Books.

Cole, S. G., & Cole, M. W. (1954). *Minorities and American promise.* New York, NY: Harper Brothers.

Cronon, E. D. (1955). *The story of Marcus Garvey and the universal Negro Improvement Association.* Madison, WI: University of Wisconsin Press.

Dewey, J. quoted in Gates, H. L. (1992). *Loose Canons.* New York, NY: Oxford University Press.

Dickens, S. (2011). U.S. immigrants and the dilemma of Anglo conformity. *Socialism and Democracy Online.* Retrieved from http://sdonline.org/48/us-immigrants-and-the-dilemma-of-anglo-conformity

Eck, D. L. (2001). *A new religious America: How a "Christian Country" has become the world's most religiously diverse nation.* New York, NY: HarperCollins.

Foner, E. (2000). Affirmative action and history. In J. Birnbaum & C. Taylor (Eds.), *Civil rights since 1787: A reader on the black struggle* (pp. 697–699). New York, NY: New York University Press.

Fuchs, L. H. (1990). *The American kaleidoscope: Race, ethnicity and the civic culture.* Hanover, NH: University Press of New England.

Gladwell, M. (2005). *Blink: The power of thinking without thinking.* New York, NY: Little, Brown.

Gordon, M. (1964). *Assimilation in America: The role of race, religion, and national origins.* New York, NY: Oxford University Press.

Greeley, A. (1975, summer). On ethnicity and cultural pluralism, *Change,* pp. 38–44.

Guerrero, R. (1974). *Tapestry* (a film). Retrieved from http://www.texasarchive.org/library/index.php?title=Tapestry_%281974%29

Holmes, J. H. (1927). *Wisdom in small doses.* Lincoln, NE: The University Publishing Company.

Infact Canada. (2009). *Nestle Boycott.* Retrieved from http://www.infactcanada.ca.

Jones, J. (1997). *Prejudice and racism* (2nd ed.). New York, NY: McGraw Hill.

Jones, G. R., & George, J. M. (2003). Managing diverse employees in a diverse environment. In *Contemporary management* (3rd ed., pp. 112–149). New York, NY: McGraw-Hill.

Kazin, M. (2011). *American dreamers: How the left changed a nation.* New York, NY: Alfred A. Knopf.

Lame Deer, J. (1972). *Lame Deer: Seeker of visions.* New York, NY: Washington Square Press.

Laosa, L. (1974). Toward a research model of multicultural competency-based education. In W. A. Hunter (Ed.), *Multicultural education through competency-based education* (pp. 135–145). Washington, DC: American Association of Colleges for Teacher Education.

Locke, A. (1989). *The philosophy of Alain Locke: Harlem renaissance and beyond,* L. Harris (Ed.). Philadelphia, PA: Temple University Press.

Maciag, M. (2015). A state-by-state look at growing minority populations. Retrieved from http://www.governing.com/topics/urban/gov-majority-minority-populations-in-states.html

Martin Jr., W. (1984). *The mind of Frederick Douglass.* Chapel Hill, NC: University of North Carolina Press.

Menand, L. (2001). *The metaphysical club.* New York, NY: Farrar, Straus, & Giroux.

Naisbitt, J. (1982). *Megatrends: Ten new directions transforming our lives.* New York, NY: Warner Books.

Naisbitt, J., & Aburdene, P. (1990). Global lifestyles and cultural nationalism. In *Megatrends 2000* (pp. 118–153). New York, NY: William Morrow.

Nieto, S. (2011). *Affirming diversity: The sociopolitical context of multicultural education* (6th ed.). Boston, MA: Pearson.

Pai, Y., & Adler, S. (1997). *Cultural foundations of education* (2nd ed.). Upper Saddle River, NJ: Merrill/ Prentice Hall.

Painter, N. I. (2010). *The history of white people.* New York, NY: W.W. Norton.

Pipher, M. (2002). *The middle of everywhere: The world's refugees come to our town.* New York, NY: Harcourt.

Pew Research Center. (2015). Chapter 5: U. S. foreign-born population trends. Retrieved from http://www.pewhispanic.org/2015/09/28/chapter-5-u-s-foreign-born-population-trends

Schlesinger Jr., A. (1991). *The disuniting of America: Reflections on a multicultural society.* Knoxville, TN: Whittle Books.

Schuck, P. H. (2014). *Why government fails so often and how it can do better.* Princeton, NJ: Princeton University Press.

Seldon, H. (1996). On being color-blind. In J. Andrzejewski (Ed.), *Oppression and social justice: Critical frameworks* (5th ed., pp. 297–298). Needham, MA: Simon & Schuster.

Simpson, E. (Ed.). (1967). Meditation 17. *John Donne: Selected prose* (pp. 100–101). London: Oxford University Press.

Sleeter, C. (1993). How white teachers construct race. In C. McCarthy & W. Crichlow (Eds.), *Race identity and representation in education* (pp. 157–191). New York, NY: Routledge.

Sue, D. W. (2015). *Race talk and the conspiracy of silence.* Hoboken, NJ: John Wiley & Sons.

Stewart, M. (2014). Ferguson businesses try to rebuild after protests. *The Huffington Post.* Retrieved from http://www.huffingtonpost.com/2014/12/12/ferguson-businesses-protests_n_6309616.html

Stolberg, S. G. (2015). Crowds scatter as Baltimore curfew takes hold. *The New York Times.* Retrieved from http://www.nytimes.com/2015/04/29/us/baltimore-riots.html?_r=0

Tatum, B. D. (1997). *"Why are all the black kids sitting together in the cafeteria?" and other conversations about race.* New York, NY: Basic Books.

Teixeira, R., & Halpin, J. (2013, October). Building an all-in nation: A view from the American public. *Center for American Progress.* Retrieved from http://americanprogress.org/issues/race/report/2013/10/22/77665/building-an-all-in-nation

Terry, R. W. (1975). *For whites only* (2nd ed.). Grand Rapids, MI: William B. Eerdmans.

Terry, R. W. (1993). *Authentic leadership: Courage in action.* San Francisco, CA: Jossey-Bass.

Thomas, G. S. (2012). Minorities form racial majority in 106 U. S. cities. Retrieved from https://www.amren.com/news/2012/03/minorities-form-racial-majority-in-106-u-s-cities

U.S. Department of Labor. (2009). *Education pays.* Retrieved from http://www.bls.gov/emp/emptab7.htm

Williams, C. (2003). Managing individuals and a diverse work force. In *Management* (2nd ed., pp. 343–371). Versailles, KY: Thomson Southwestern.

Williams, J. (1987). *Eyes on the prize: America's civil rights years, 1954–1965.* New York, NY: Viking Penguin.

Yen, H. (2012). Census: White population will lose majority in U.S. by 2043. *Huffington Post.* Retrieved from http://www.huffingtonpost.com/2012/12/12/census-hispanics-and-black-unseat-whites-as-majority-in-united-states-population_n_2286105.html

Zangwill, I. (1915). *The melting pot.* New York, NY: Macmillan.

Zeldin, T. (1994). *An intimate history of humanity.* New York, NY: HarperCollins.

Chapter 8

Alexander, M. (2010). *The new Jim Crow: Mass incarceration in the age of colorblindness.* New York, NY: The New Press.

Allport, G. (early 1950s) *The Language of Prejudice.* Retrieved from http://teacherweb.com/CA/NewburyParkHighSchool/bond/LanguageofPrejudice-GAllport.pdf

Andrzejewski, J. (1996). Definitions for understanding oppression and social justice. In J. Andrzejewski (Ed.), *Oppression and social justice: Critical frameworks* (5th ed., pp. 52–58). Needham, MA: Simon & Schuster.

Arendt, H. (1978). Thinking. *The life of the mind.* New York, NY: Harcourt, Inc.

Arielly, D. (2008). *Predictably irrational: The hidden forces that shape our decisions.* New York, NY: HarperCollins.

Aronson, E. (2008). *The social animal* (10th ed.). New York, NY: Worth Publishers.

Ashkenas, J., & Park, H. (2014). The race gap in America's police departments. *New York Times.* Retrieved from http://www.nytimes.com/interactive/2014/09/03/us/the-race-gap-in-americas-police-departments.html?emc=eta1

Associated Press. (2010, June 19). Vote system that elected NY Hispanic could expand. *La Crosse Tribune*, p. A5.

Associated Press. (2012, October 29. Racial Attitudes Survey. Retrieved from http://surveys.ap.org/data%5CGfK%5CAP_Racial_Attitudes_Topline_09182012.pdf

Boas, F. (1962). *Anthropology and modern life.* New York, NY: Norton.

Bohonos, J. (2013). *Can the concept of "fit" facilitate discrimination in the hiring process?* Retrieved from http://www.blackperspective.com/index.php/blog/latest-entries/307-can-the-concept-of-fit-facilitate-discrimination-in-the-hiring-process

Bonilla-Silva, E. (1999). The new racism: Racial structure in the United States, 1960s–1990s. In P. Wong (Ed.), *Race, ethnicity, and nationality in the United States: Toward the twenty-first century* (pp. 55–101). Boulder, CO: Westview.

Bonilla-Silva, E. (2001). *White supremacy and racism in the post-civil rights era.* Boulder, CO: Lynne Rienner.

Bonilla-Silva, E. (2009). *Racism without racists: Color-blind racism and the persistence of racial inequality in America.* Lanham, MD: Rowman & Littlefield.

Bouie, J. (2012). The other glass ceiling. *The American Prospect* 23(3), 6–11.

Buckley, G. (2001). *American patriots: The story of blacks in the military from the Revolution to Desert Storm.* New York, NY: Random House.

Citation: Bureau of Labor Statistics (2015). Table 27. Retrieved from https://www.bls.gov/opub/gp/pdf/gp14_27.pdf

Burnett III, J. H. (2012). Racism learned. Boston Globe. Retrieved from https://www.bostonglobe.com/business/2012/06/09/harvard-researcher-says-children-learn-racism-quickly/gWuN1ZG3M40WihER2kAfdK/story.html

Callahan, R. M. (2005, Summer). Tracking and high school English learners: Limiting opportunity to learn. *American Educational Research Journal*, 42(2), 305–328.

Carjuzaa, J, Baldwin, A. E., & Munson, M. (2015). Making the dream real: Montana's Indian education for all initiative thrives in a national climate of anti-ethnic studies. *Multicultural Perspectives*, 17(4), 198-206.

Carnevale, A. P., & Strohl, J. (2013). *Separate and unequal.* Georgetown University. Retrieved from cew.georgetown.edu/separateandunequal.

Center for American Progress. (2016). Unjust: How the broken criminal justice system fails LGBT people of color. Retrieved from http://www.lgbtmap.org/file/lgbt-criminal-justice-poc.pdf

Cobb, J. (2016). The matter of black lives. The New Yorker, retrieved from: https://www.newyorker.com/magazine/2016/03/14/where-is-black-lives-matter-headed

Cohen, R. M. (2016). School closures: A blunt instrument. *The American Prospect*, 27(2), 48–53.

Cox, W. (2016). Suburbs (continue to) dominate jobs and job growth. New Geography. Retrieved from http://www.newgeography.com/content/005264-suburbs-continue-dominate-jobs-and-job-growth

Davis, M. (2009, March/April). Editorial: Obama at Manassas. *New Left Review*, 56, 5–40.

Diamond, J. (2015). New Obamacare numbers: 16.4 million covered. *CNN*. Retrieved from http://www.cnn.com/2015/03/16/politics/obamacare-numbers-16-million-insured-rate

DiAngelo, R. (2006). My class didn't trump my race: Using oppression to face privilege. *Multicultural Perspectives*, 8(1), 51–56.

DiAngelo, R. (2012). *What does it mean to be white? Developing white racial literacy.* New York, NY: Peter Lang.

DiJulio, B., Norton, M., Jackson, S., & Brodie, M. (2015). Survey of Americans on race. Retrieved from http://www.kff.org/report-section/survey-of-americans-on-race-section-1-racial-discrimination-bias-and-privilege

Du Bois, W. E. B. (1994). *The souls of black folk.* New York, NY: Dover.

Editors of *Rethinking Schools*. (2016). Racism, xenophobia, and the election. *Rethinking Schools*, 31(1), 5–7.

Editors of *Rethinking Schools*. (2015). Black students' lives matter. *Rethinking Schools*, 29(3), 4–7.

Edwards, H. S. (2016, March 14). You only think you're covered. *Time*, 187(9), 44-47.

Epperly, J. (2014). *UCLA report finds changing U.S. demographics transform school segregation landscape 60 years after* Brown v. Board of Education. Retrieved from http://civilrightsproject.ucla.edu/news/press-releases/2014-press-releases/ucla-report-finds-changing-u.s.-demographics-transform-school-segregation-landscape-60-years-after-brown-v-board-of-education/National-report-press-release-draft-3.pdf

Farley, J. (2010). *Majority-minority relations* (6th ed.). Upper Saddle River, NJ: Prentice-Hall.

Feagin, J., & Feagin, C. (1986). *Discrimination American style* (2nd ed.). Malabar, FL: Krieger.

Freire, P. (1985). *The politics of education.* Westport, CT: Bergin & Garvey Publishers.

Furman, J. (2014). *Six economic benefits of the Affordable Care Act.* Retrieved from https://www.whitehouse.gov/blog/2014/02/06/six-economic-benefits-affordable-care-act

Ghilarducci, T. (2015). Senior class: America's unequal retirement. *The American Prospect*, 26(2), 46–49.

Goodman, J. D. (2013, Dec. 27). More diversity in New York City's police department, but blacks lag. Retrieved from http://www.nytimes.com/2013/12/27/nyregion/more-diversity-in-new-york-citys-police-but-blacks-lag.html?pagewanted=all

Hamilton, D., Cottom, T. M., Darity Jr., W., Aja, A. A., & Ash, C. (2015) Still we rise. *The American Prospect*, 26(4), 54–61.

Hattie, J. (2009). *Visible learning: A synthesis of over 800 meta-analyses relating to achievement*. New York; NY: Routledge.

Hilliard, A. (1992). *Racism: Its origins and how it works.* Paper presented at the meeting of the Mid-West Association for the Education of Young Children, Madison, WI.

Hodson, G., Dovido, J., & Gaertner, S. (2004). The aversive form of racism. In J. L. Chin (Ed.), *The psychology of prejudice and discrimination (Race and Ethnicity in Psychology)* (Vol. 1, pp. 119–136). Westport, CT: Praeger.

Howard, G. R. (2006). *We can't teach what we don't know: White teachers, multiracial schools.* New York, NY: Teachers College Press.

Jackson, J. (2013). Dreaming away the reality of racism. *Extra! 26*(10), 6–7.

Jenkins, A. (2007, May). Inequality, race and remedy. *The American Prospect*, 18(5), A8–A11.

Jenkins, A. (2009). Recovering opportunity. *The American Prospect*, 20(7), A4–A7.

Jones, J. (1997). *Prejudice and racism* (2nd ed.). New York, NY: McGraw Hill.

Kirp, D. L. (1991, Summer). Textbooks and tribalism in California. *Public Interest*, 104, 20–37.

Kivel, P. (2002). *Uprooting racism: How white people can work for racial justice* (Rev. ed.). Gabriola Island, BC: New Society Publishers.

Kline, D. M. S. (2016). Can restorative practices help to reduce disparities in school discipline data? A review of the literature. *Multicultural Perspectives*, 18(2), 97-102.

Kozol, J. (1988). Quoted in P. Galloway's *Poverty's Scribe*. Retrieved from http://articles.chicagotribune.com/1988-02-15/features/8803300660_1_homelessness-jonathan-kozol-shelter/3

Levine, M. (2010). *Research update: The crisis deepens: Black male joblessness in Milwaukee 2009*. Retrieved from http://www.uwm.edu/ced/publications.cfm

Lipsitz, G. (2008). The possessive investment in whiteness. In P. Rothenberg (Ed.), *White privilege: Essential readings on the other side of racism* (pp. 61–84). New York, NY: Worth.

Loewen, J. (1995). *Lies my teacher told me: Everything your American history textbook got wrong.* New York, NY: The New Press.

Losen, D. J. (2011). *Discipline policies, successful schools, and racial justice.* Boulder, CO: National Education Policy Center. Retrieved from http://nepc.colorado.edu/publication/discipline-policies

Manning, J. E. (2017). *Membership of the 174th Congress: A profile.* Retrieved from http://fas.org/sgp/crs/misc/R44762.pdf

Massey, D. S. (2001). Residential segregation and neighborhood conditions in U.S. metropolitan areas. In N. Smelser, W. Wilson, & F. Mitchell (Eds.), *America becoming: Racial trends and their consequences.* East Lansing, MI: National Center for Research on Teacher Learning. (ERIC Document Reproduction Service No. ED449286)

Massey, D. S. (2003). The race case. *The American Prospect*, 14(3), 22.

McIntosh, P. (2001). White privilege: Unpacking the invisible knapsack. In P. Rothenberg (Ed.), *Race, class, and gender in the United States: An integrated study* (5th ed., pp. 163–168). New York, NY: Worth.

Meizhu, L., Robles, B., & Leondar-Wright, B. (2006). *The color of wealth: The story behind the U.S. racial wealth divide.* New York, NY: The New Press.

Miah, M. (2010). Race and class: Blacks still taking the hit. Retrieved from http://www.solidarity-us.org/site/node/2604

National Fair Housing Alliance. (2017) The case for fair housing. Retrieved from http://nationalfairhousing.org/wp-content/uploads/2017/04/TRENDS-REPORT-4-19-17-FINAL-2.pdf

Oakes, J. (2005). *Keeping track: How schools structure inequality.* New Haven, CT: Yale University Press.

Oakes, J., Quartz, K. H., Ryan, S., & Lipton, M. (2000). *Becoming good American schools: The struggle for civic virtue in school reform.* San Francisco, CA: Jossey-Bass.

Oliver, M. L., & Shapiro, T. M. (2008, October). Sub-prime as a black catastrophe. *The American Prospect*, 19(10), A9–A11.

Packer, Z. (2005). Sorry, not buying. *The American Prospect*, 16(12), 46–48.

Picca, L., & Feagin, J. (2007). *Two-faced racism: Whites in the backstage and frontstage.* New York, NY: Routledge.

Pitts, L. (2001). Sept. 12, 2001: We'll go forward from this moment. *Miami Herald*. http://www.miamiherald.com/2001/09/12/v-print/374188/sept-12-2001-well-go-forward-from.html

Potok, M. (2013, Spring). The year in hate and extremism. *Intelligence Report*, 153, 41–44.

Quinlan, C. (2016). How racial bias affects the quality of black students' education. Think Progress. Retrieved from https://thinkprogress.org/how-racial-bias-affects-the-quality-of-black-students-education-642f4721fc84

Quintana, S. M. (2008). Racial perspective taking ability: Developmental, theoretical, and empirical trends. In S. M. Quintana & C. McKown (Eds.), *Handbook of race, racism, and the developing child* (pp. 1–15). Hoboken, NJ: John Wiley & Sons, Inc.

Reaves, B. A., & Hickman, M. J. (2002). *Police departments in large cities, 1990–2000.* U.S. Department of Justice. Retrieved from http://www.ojp.usdoj.gov/bjs

Reed, S. (2011). *The diversity index.* New York, NY: AMACOM.

Rehmeyer, J. J. (2007). Separate is never equal. *Science News*. Retrieved from http://www.sciencenews.org/view/generic/id/8907/title/Math_Trek_Separate_Is_Never_Equal

Rothstein, R. (2017). *A forgotten history of how our government segregated America.* New York, NY: Liveright Publishing Corporation

Rothstein, R. (2014). The colorblind bind. *The American Prospect*, 25(4), 70–77.

Sargent, J. F. (2012). Videogame bigotry and the illusion of freedom. *Extra! 25*(11), 14–15.

Schaefer, R. T. (2008). Prejudice. In *Racial and ethnic groups* (11th ed., pp. 37–65). Upper Saddle River, NJ: Pearson Education.

Schuck, P. H. (2014). *Why government fails so often and how it can do better*. Princeton, NJ: Princeton University Press.

Sensoy, Ö., & DiAngelo, R. (2012). *Is everyone really equal? Key concepts in critical social justice education*. New York, NY: Teachers College Press.

Shorris, E. (2001). *Latinos: A biography of the people*. New York, NY: W.W. Norton.

Stainback, K. (2013). Storytelling and the myth of reverse discrimination. Retrieved from http://workinprogress.oowsection.org/2013/05/22/storytelling-and-the-myth-of-reverse-discrimination/

Steinzor, R. (2016). Dangerous bedfellows. *The American Prospect*, 27(2), 72-57.

Stiglitz, J. E. (2012). *The price of inequality: How today's divided society endangers our future*. New York: W.W. Norton & Company.

Sue, D. W. (2015). *Race talk and the conspiracy of silence*. Hoboken, NJ: John Wiley & Sons.

Sullivan, E., & Gillum, J. (2014). AP exclusive: Police short on Hispanic officers. Retrieved from http://bigstory.ap.org/article/ap-exclusive-police-short-hispanic-officers

Thompson, H. A. (1999). Rethinking the politics of white flight in the postwar city. *Journal of Urban History*, 25(2), 163–199.

Tobin, G. A., & Ybarra, D. R. (2008). Chapter one: Textbooks are in trouble. *The trouble with textbooks: Distorting history and religion*. Lanham, MD: Lexington Books.

U.S. Bureau of Labor Statistics. (2011, September). *Employment situation summary*. Retrieved from http://www.bls.gov/news.release/empsit.nr0.htm

U.S. Bureau of Labor Statistics. (2014). *Economic news release*. Retrieved from http://www.bls.gov/news.release/empsit.t02.htm; and Labor force statistics from the current population survey. Retrieved from http://www.bls.gov/web/empsit/cpsee_e16.htm

U.S. Department of Education. (2014). *Data snapshot: School discipline*. Retrieved from http://www2.ed.gov/about/offices/list/ocr/docs/crdc-discipline-snapshot.pdf

Vick, K. (2015, August 24). What is it like being a cop now? *Time*, 186(7), 32-41.

Wellman, D. (1977). *Portraits of white racism*. New York, NY: Cambridge University Press.

White House Report. (2013). Trends in health care cost growth and the role of the affordable care act. Retrieved from http://www.whitehouse.gov/sites/default/files/docs/healthcostreport_final_noembargo_v2.pdf

Williams, C. (2013). Managing individuals and a diverse workforce. In *Management* (7th ed., pp. 484–525). Mason, OH: South-Western.

Wilson, W. J. (1996). *When work disappears: The world of the new urban poor*. New York, NY: Knopf.

Wise, T. (2005). *Affirmative action: Racial preference in black and white*. Berkeley, CA: Soft Skull.

Chapter 9

Abramsky, S. (2012). Creating a countercyclical welfare system. *The American Prospect*, 23(6), 62–64.

American Federation of Labor. (2011). CEO pay: Feeding the 1%. *Executive Paywatch*. Retrieved from http://www.aflcio.org/corporatewatch/paywatch

Anderson, J. (2017). Myths and stereotypes of aging. Retrieved from http://www.aplaceformom.com/blog/14-18-4-aging-myths-dispelled/

Arana, G. (2013). Log cabins and lost souls. *The American Prospect*, 24(4), 7–10.

Arvedlund, E. (2017, July 9). When boomerang kids move home, boomers' health and wallets suffer. *La Crosse Tribune*. H1–H2.

Austin, A. (2013). Children of color in the persistent downturn. *The American Prospect*, 24(3), 71–72.

Badger, E. (2015). Redlining: Still a thing. *The Washington Post*. Retrieved from https://www.washingtonpost.com/news/wonk/wp/2015/05/28/evidence-that-banks-still-deny-black-borrowers-just-as-they-did-50-years-ago/?utm_term=.d35762c88cbe

Badger, E. (2014). How small changes to federal housing policy could make a big difference for poor kids. *The Washington Post*. Retrieved from http://www.washingtonpost.com/blogs/wonkblog/wp/2014/10/15/how-small-changes-to-federal-housing-policy-could-make-a-big-difference-for-poor-kids

Barber, E. (2014, March 3). *Forbes'* richest people: Number of billionaires up significantly. *The Christian Science Monitor*. Retrieved from http://www.csmonitor.com/USA/USA-Update/2014/0303/Forbes-richest-people-number-of-billionaires-up-significantly-video

Barber, S. J., & Mather, M. (2014). Stereotype threat in older adults: When and why does it occur, and who is most affected? In P. Verhaeghen & C. Hertzog (Eds.), *The Oxford handbook of emotion, social cognition, and problem solving during adulthood* (pp. 302–320). Oxford, UK: Oxford University Press.

Bensman, D. (2015). Security for a precarious workforce. *The American Prospect*, 26(4), 95-97.

Berliner, D. C. (2005, August). Our impoverished view of educational reform. *TCRecord*. Retrieved from http://www.tcrecord.org

Bernhardt, A., Milkman, R., & Theodore, N. (2009). Broken laws, unprotected workers. *The American Prospect*, 20(8), A3.

Billionaires Mailing List. (2017). Our World of Wealth. Retrieved from https://www.billionairemailinglist.com/billionaires-list.html

Brown, E., Strauss, V., & Douglas-Gabriel, D. (2017). Trump's first full education budget: Deep cuts to public school programs in pursuit of school choice. *The Washington Post*. Retrieved from https://www.washingtonpost.com/local/education/trumps-first-full-education-budget-deep-cuts-to-public-school-programs-in-pursuit-of-school-choice/2017/05/17/2a25a2cc-3a41-11e7-8854-21f359183e8c_story.html?utm_term=.7d760d753732

Butler, R. (2008). *The longevity revolution: The benefits and challenges of living a long life*. New York, NY: Public Affairs.

Bytheway, B. (2005). Ageism. In M. L. Johnson (Ed.), *The Cambridge handbook of age and aging* (pp. 338–345). Cambridge, UK: Cambridge University Press.

Caplinger, D. (2014). Social Security benefits: The striking gap between men and women. Retrieved from https://www.fool.com/retirement/general/2014/09/21/social-security-benefits-the-striking-gap-between.aspx

Carey, K. (2012). The assets between your ears. *Washington Monthly, 44*(7/8), 33–34.

Carroll, C. (2014). Better academic performance – is nutrition the missing link? *Today's Dietitian,* 16(4), p. 64-69.

Child Trends. (2013). *Child recipients of welfare (AFDC/TANF).* Retrieved from http://www.childtrends.org/?indicators=child-recipients-of-welfareafdctanf

Children's Defense Fund. (2014). *The state of America's children.* Retrieved from http://www.childrensdefense.org/child-research-data-publications/state-of-americas-children

Children's Defense Fund (2017). Ending Child Poverty. Retrieved from http://www.childrensdefense.org/library/PovertyReport/EndingChildPovertyNow.html

Collins, C. (2013). The politics of inherited advantage. *The American Prospect, 24*(3), 64–68.

Common Core State Standards Initiative. (2014). *Common Core State Standards Initiative: Preparing America's students for college & career.* Retrieved from http://www.corestandards.org

Connell, T. (2011). *Make work pay for us—CEO pay vs. the rest of us.* Retrieved from http://blog.aflcio.org/2011/10104

Cooper, D., & Hall, D. (2013). *Raising the federal minimum wage to $10.10 would give working families, and the overall economy, a much-needed boost.* Retrieved from http://www.epi.org/publication/bp357-federal-minimum-wage-increase

Cooper, M. (2015). The downsizing of the American dream. The Atlantic. Retrieved from https://www.theatlantic.com/business/archive/2015/10/american-dreams/408535/

Couch, R. (2014). *Think welfare recipients abuse the system? You should see this chart.* Retrieved from http://www.huffingtonpost.com/2014/05/09/welfare-abuse-america_n_5289997.html

Cramer, R. (2012). The asset agenda. *Washington Monthly, 44*(7/8), 44–45.

D'Alessio, M. (2014). *Will Common Core make college a reality for more low-income students?* Retrieved from https://www.uschamber.com/blog/will-common-core-make-college-reality-more-low-income-students

deMause, N. (2014). Flunking the revised SATs, *Extra! 27*(15), 7–8.

Draut, T. (2013). Intergenerational injustice. *The American Prospect, 24*(3), 73–76.

Dreier, P. (2004). *Reagan's legacy: Homelessness in America. National Housing Institute.* Retrieved from www.nhi.org/online/issues/135/reagan

Edelman, M. W. (2001). Introduction. *A Children's Defense Fund report: The state of America's children.* Boston, MA: Beacon.

Eichelberger, E. (2014). Ten poverty myths, busted. *Mother Jones.* Retrieved from http://www.motherjones.com/politics/2014/03/10-poverty-myths-busted

Extra! (2011). MisEducation Nation. *Extra!, 24*(11), 13–15.

Falk, G. (2016). The temporary assistance for needy families (TANF) block grant: Responses to frequently asked questions. *Congressional Research Service.* Retrieved from https://fas.org/sgp/crs/misc/RL32760.pdf

Feagin, J., & Feagin, C.B. (1986). *Discrimination American style* (2nd ed.). Malabar, FL: Robert E. Krieger.

Federal Deposit Insurance Corporation. (2015). FDIC national survey of unbanked and underbanked households. Retrieved from https://www.fdic.gov/householdsurvey/2015/2015execsumm.pdf

Feeney, L. (2015). Living on $2 a day: Exploring extreme poverty in America. Retrieved from http://www.pbs.org/newshour/updates/poverty

Feyman, Y. (2014). *No inversion is not unpatriotic. Yes we need corporate tax reform.* Retrieved from http://www.forbes.com/sites/theapothecary/2014/08/25/no-inversion-is-not-unpatriotic-yes-we-need-corporate-tax-reform

Friedman, T. L., & Mandelbaum, M. (2011). *That used to be us: How America fell behind in the world it invented and how we can come back.* New York, NY: Farrar, Straus and Giroux.

Garces, M., & Rendall, S. (2012). Media not very concerned about the very poor. *Extra! 25* (9), 5–6.

Gavett, G. (2012). Who isn't graduating from high school? *PBS.* Retrieved from http://www.pbs.org/wgbh/pages/frontline/education/dropout-nation/who-isnt-graduating-from-high-school

Geewax, M. (2015). The tipping point: Most Americans no longer are middle class. Retrieved from http://www.npr.org/sections/thetwo-way/2015/12/09/459087477/the-tipping-point-most-americans-no-longer-are-middle-class

Ghilarducci, T. (2015). Senior class: America's unequal retirement. *The American Prospect, 26*(2), 46-49.

Gillespie, P. (2014). Over 48 million Americans live in poverty. CNN. Retrieved from http://money.cnn.com/2014/10/16/news/economy/48-million-americans-poverty-census-bureau/index.html

Goldstein D. (2012). The "assets effect." *Washington Monthly, 44*(7/8), 31–32.

Graham, C. (2013). *Pursuing happiness: Social mobility and well-being.* Retrieved from http://www.brookings.edu/blogs/social-mobility-memos/posts/2013/10/24-american-dream-pursuit-of-happiness-graham

Gullette, M. M. (2011). *Agewise: Fighting the new ageism in America.* Chicago, IL: The University of Chicago Press.

Gurley, G. (2017). Taking a scalpel to Medicaid. *The American Prospect, 28*(2), 68-71.

Hanauer, N. (2016). Confronting the parasite economy. *The American Prospect, 27*(3), 35-40.

Harris, D., & Shaefer, L. (2017). Fighting child poverty with a universal child allowance. *The American Prospect, 28*(2), 18-19.

Haycock, K. (2001). Closing the achievement gap. *Educational Leadership, 58*(6), 6–11.

Hicken, M. (2014). Why many retired women live in poverty. CNN. Retrieved from http://money.cnn.com/2014/05/13/retirement/retirement-women/index.html

Hightower, J. (2013). One in three Americans are now poor, sapping our nation's social, economic, and moral strength. *The Hightower Lowdown, 15*(6), 1–4.

Hinden, S. (2017). Women and social security benefits. AARP. Retrieved from http://www.aarp.org/work/social-security/info-2014/women-and-social-security-benefits.html

Hirschfeld, P. (2015). Rent-to-own a raw deal for poor people, lawmakers say. Retrieved from http://digital.vpr.net/post/rent-own-raw-deal-poor-people-lawmakers-say#stream/0

Holzer, H. J. (2012). Upgrading skills, upgrading opportunity. *The American Prospect*, 23(6), 26–28.

Howell, D. R. (2016). Reframing the minimum wage debate. *The American Prospect*, 27(3), 48-52.

Hudson, M. (2011). *The costly "banks" that welcome the poor*. Retrieved from http://aliciapatterson.org/stories/costly-banks-welcome-poor

Jairrels, V. (2008). *African Americans and standardized tests: The real reason for low test scores*. Sauk Village, IL: African American Images.

Johnson, D. (2011, February 14). *Nine pictures of the extreme income/wealth gap*. Retrieved from www.truth-out.org/nine-pictures-of-the-extreme-incomewealth-gap67743

Johnston, D. C. (2014). The legacy of Carl Levin. *The American Prospect*. 25(5), 80-85.

Kahlenberg, R. (2016). Acting education secretary champions economic, racial integration. *The American Prospect*. Retrieved from http://prospect.org/article/acting-education-secretary-champions-economic-racial-integration

Karp, S. (2006). Band-Aids or bulldozers: What's next for NCLB? *Rethinking Schools*, 20(3), 10–13.

Katz, M. B. (1986). *In the shadow of the poorhouse: A social history of welfare in America*. New York, NY: Basic Books.

Kirp, D. L. (2007, December). Nature, nurture, and destiny. *The American Prospect* 18(12), A19–A21.

Kirp, D. L. (2015). It's all about the money. *The American Prospect*, 26(2), 119-121.

Kivel, P. (2002). *Uprooting racism: How white people can work for racial justice* (rev. ed.). Gabriola Island, BC: New Society Publishers.

Klein, A. (2017). Trump issues executive order calling for local control of K-12. Education Week Retrieved from http://blogs.edweek.org/edweek/campaign-k-12/2017/04/trump_executive_order_local_control_education.html

Komisar, L. (1977). *Down and out in the USA: A history of public welfare* (rev. ed.). New York, NY: New Viewpoints.

Kuttner, R. (2012). Greedy geezers reconsidered. *The American Prospect*, 23(8), 56–59.

Lamont, R. A., Swift, H. J., & Abrams, D. (2015). A review and meta-analysis of age-based stereotype threat: Negative stereotypes, not facts do the damage. *Psychology and Aging*. pp. 1–14. ISSN 0882-7974

Laws.com. (2013). *Knowing the tax evasion statistics*. Retrieved from http://fraud.laws.com/tax-fraud/tax-evasion/tax-evasion-statistics

Lawson, A. (2015). We need to expand the most effective anti-poverty program in America. Retrieved from http://billmoyers.com/2015/01/22/need-expand-effective-anti-poverty-program-america

Lee, J. (2006). *Tracking achievement gaps and assessing the impact of NCLB on the gaps: An in-depth look into national and state reading and math outcomes*. Cambridge, MA: The Civil Rights Project at Harvard University.

Lerner, S. (2012). Pre-K on the range. *The American Prospect*, 23(8), 60–67.

Levinson, M. (2012). Mismeasuring—and its consequences. *The American Prospect*, 23(6), 42–43.

Levy, B., & Banaji, M. (2002). Implicit ageism. In T. Nelson (Ed.), *Ageism*. London, UK: MIT Press.

Longley, R. (2014). *Who is in the middle class?* Retrieved from http://usgovinfo.about.com/od/incometaxandtheirs/a/Who-Is-In-The-Middle-Class.htm

Longman, P. (2012). How to save our kids from poverty in old age. *Washington Monthly*, 44 (7/8), 24–26.

Macnicol, J. (2006). *Age discrimination: An historical and contemporary analysis*. Cambridge, UK: Cambridge University Press.

Mandela, N. (2010). *Conversations with myself*. New York, NY: Farrar, Straus and Giroux.

Mills, C. W. (1951). *White collar: The American middle classes*. London, UK: Oxford University Press.

Meyerson, H. (2016). The first post-middle-class election. *The American Prospect*, 27(3), 24-27.

Miners, Z. (2009). *Charter schools might not be better*. Retrieved from www.usnews.com/education/blogs/on-education/2009/06/17/charter-schools-might-not-be-better

National Center on Family Homelessness. (2014). *America's youngest outcasts: A report card on child homelessness*. Retrieved from http://www.homelesschildrenamerica.org/mediadocs/282.pdf

National Coalition for the Homeless. (2006). *McKinney-Vento act*. Retrieved from http://www.nationalhomeless.org/publications/facts/Mckinney.pdf

Nelson, T. D. (2009). Ageism. In T. D. Nelson (Ed.), *Handbook of prejudice, stereotyping, and discrimination* (pp. 431–440). New York, NY: Psychology Press.

Noah, T. (2014). *Sorry conservatives—America's mobility problem is real*. Retrieved from http://www.msnbc.com/msnbc/us-social-mobility-problem

Office of Family Assistance. (2012). *Characteristics and financial circumstances of TANF recipients, fiscal year 2010*. Retrieved from http://www.acf.hhs.gov/programs/ofa/resource/character/fy2010/fy2010-chap10-ys-final

Phillips, K. (1990). Wealth and favoritism. In *The politics of rich and poor: Wealth and the American electorate in the Reagan aftermath*. New York, NY: Random House.

Piketty, T. (2014). *Capital in the twenty-first century*. Cambridge, MA: The Belknap Press of Harvard University Press.

Pipher, M. (2002). *The middle of everywhere: The world's refugees come to our town*. New York, NY: Harcourt.

Porter, A., McMaken, J., Hwang, J., & Yang, R. (2011). Common core standards: The new U.S. intended curriculum. *Educational Researcher*, 40(3), 103–116.

Porter, E. (2015). Education gap between rich and poor is growing wider. New York Times. Retrieved from https://www.

nytimes.com/2015/09/23/business/economy/education-gap-between-rich-and-poor-is-growing-wider.html

Potts, M. (2013). Homeless families in the suburbs. *The American Prospect, 24*(2), 64–73.

Pyke, A. (2013). *Huge spike in poverty among elderly women catches analysts by surprise.* Retrieved from http://thinkprogress.org/economy/2013/09/27/2695071/huge-spike-in-poverty-among-elderly-women-catches-analysts-by-surprise

Quigley, B. (2014). Ten examples of welfare for the rich and corporations. *The Huffington Post.* Retrieved from http://www.huffingtonpost.com/bill-quigley/ten-examples-of-welfare-for-the-rich-and-corporations_b_4589188.html

Ratcliffe, J. (2009). A bridge to somewhere. *The American Prospect, 20*(6), A4–A6.

Rethinking Schools. (2013). The trouble with the Common Core. *Rethinking Schools, 27*(4). Retrieved from http://www.rethinkingschools.org/archive/27_04/edit274.shtml

Rosenbaum, S. (2017). Weakening Medicaid from within. *The American Prospect, 28*(4), 17–19.

Rothstein, R. (2009). Equalizing opportunity. *American Educator, 33*(2), 4–7, 45–46.

Rowe, C. (2014). How much do high school drop outs cost us? The real numbers behind pay now or pay later. *Seattle Times.* Retrieved from http://blogs.seattletimes.com/educationlab/2014/01/03/how-much-do-dropouts-cost-us-the-real-numbers-behind-pay-now-or-pay-later/

Savage, G. C., O'Connor, K., & Brass, J. (2014). Common Core State Standards: Implications for curriculum, equality and policy. *Journal of Curriculum and Pedagogy, 11*(1), 18–20.

Scheve, T., & Venzon, C. (2017). 10 stereotypes about aging (that just aren't true). Retrieved from http://health.howstuffworks.com/wellness/aging/aging-process/5-stereotypes-about-aging.htm

Schmidt, F. (2011). *Top 20 stereotypes of older people.* Retrieved from http://the-senior-citizen-times.com/2011/11/23/top-20-stereotypes-of-older-people/

Schuck, P. H. (2014). *Why government fails so often and how it can do better.* Princeton, NJ: Princeton University Press.

Schwartz-Nobel, L. (2002). *Growing up empty: The hunger epidemic in America.* New York, NY: HarperCollins.

Schwarz, J. (2000). *Fighting poverty with virtue: Moral reform and America's urban poor, 1825–2000.* Bloomington, IN: Indiana University Press.

Shepard, D. S., Setren, E., & Cooper, D. (2011). Hunger in America: Suffering we all pay for. *Center for American Progress.* Retrieved from http://www.americanprogress.org/issues/2011/10/hunger

Shorris, E. (2001). *Latinos: A biography of the people.* New York, NY: W.W. Norton.

Skinner, C. (2013). Child poverty by the numbers. *The American Prospect, 24*(3), 62–63.

Smith, K. (2013). *Report: More seniors are living in poverty.* Retrieved from http://www.politico.com/story/2013/05/report-more-seniors-are-living-in-poverty-91631.html

Springer, A. (2013). *Six ways to tell if you're middle class.* Retrieved from http://abcnews.go.com/blogs/politics/2013/07/6-ways-to-tell-if-youre-middle-class

Steinzor, R. (2017). The banks are even worse. *The American Prospect, 28*(1), 104-105.

Stiglitz, J. E. (2012). *The price of inequality: How today's divided society endangers our future.* New York, NY: W.W. Norton & Company.

Stucki, B. (2013). Welfare row. *The American Prospect, 24*(5), 12–13.

Tavernise, S. (2011, Sept. 13). Soaring poverty casts spotlight on "lost decade." *New York Times.* Retrieved from www.nytimes.com/2011/09/14/us/14census.html

Teachout, Z. (2017). Goodbye to all that democracy. *The American Prospect, 28*(3), 93-95.

Tillman, L. (2013). What does it take for traumatized kids to thrive? *Pacific Standard, 6*(3), 60–67.

U.S. Census Bureau. (2014). *Poverty thresholds.* Retrieved from https://www.census.gov/hhes/www/poverty/data/threshld

U.S. Department of Education. (2008). *Questions and answers on special education and homelessness.* Office of Special Education and Rehabilitative Services. Retrieved from www.doe.sd.gov/oess/documents/SPED_IEP_Homeless.pdf

U.S. Department of Health and Human Services. (2011). *A profile of older Americans: 2011.* Retrieved from http://www.aoa.gov/aoaroot/aging_statistics/Profile/2011/docs/2011profile.pdf

Vick, K. (2017). Where did America's summer jobs go? *Time, 190*(2/3), 52–59.

Washington Post/ABC News. (2014). *Midterm elections poll.* Retrieved from http://www.washingtonpost.com/politics/polling/americans-generally-economic-wealthy/2015/04/24/e5e93c3e-5e8f-11e4-827b-2d813561bdfd_page.html

Webley, K. (2011, Oct. 10). The preschool wars. *Time, 178*(14), 47–49.

White, D. (2011). *Profile of Race to the Top.* Retrieved from http://usliberals.about.com/od/education/a/RacetotheTop.htm

Whitman, D., & Purcell, P. (2007). Topics in aging: Income and poverty among older Americans in 2004. In L. O. Randal (Ed.), *Aging and the elderly: Psychology, sociology and health* (pp. 177–196). New York, NY: Nova Science Publishers.

Wilson, D. M. (2012). Struggling in suburbia. *Teaching Tolerance, 42*, 40–43.

Wolfe, A. (1998). *One nation, after all: What middle-class Americans really think about God, country, family, racism, welfare, immigration, homosexuality, work, the right, the left, and each other.* New York, NY: Viking Penguin.

Wong, V. (2014). *Top CEOs make 331 times the average worker. Does anyone care?* Retrieved from http://www.businessweek.com/articles/2014-04-18/top-ceos-make-331-times-the-average-worker-dot-does-anyone-care

Zinn, H. (2003). *A people's history of the United States.* New York, NY: HarperCollins.

Chapter 10

Alter, C. (2016, June 27). Seeing sexism from both sides: What trans men experience. *Time, 187*(24), 24–25.

American Association of University Women. (1993). *Hostile hallways: The AAUW survey on sexual harassment in America's schools.* Washington, DC: Author.

American Association of University Women. (2011). *Crossing the line: Sexual harassment at school.* Washington, DC. Retrieved from www.aauw.org

American Association of University Women. (2016). The gender pay gay by state and congressional district. Retrieved from http://www.aauw.org/resource/gender-pay-gap-by-state-and-congressional-district/

American Bar Association. (2017). *A current glance at women in the law.* Retrieved from http://www.americanbar.org/content/dam/aba/marketing/women/current_glance_statistics_january2013.authcheckdam.pdf

Andrzejewski, J. (1996). Definitions for understanding oppression and social justice. In J. Andrzejewski (Ed.), *Oppression and social justice: Critical frameworks* (5th ed., pp. 52–58). Needham, MA: Simon & Schuster.

Arliss, L. P. (1991). *Gender communication.* Englewood Cliffs, NJ: Prentice Hall.

Association of American Medical Colleges. (2016). *Number of medical school enrollees reaches 10-year high.* Retrieved from https://news.aamc.org/press-releases/article/applicant-enrollment-2016

Boschma, J. (2017). Why women don't run for office. *Politico.* Retrieved from: http://www.politico.com/interactives/2017/women-rule-politics-graphic

Branch, T. (1998). *Pillar of fire: America in the King years 1963–65.* New York, NY: Simon & Schuster.

Brooke-Marciniak, B. (2016) Here's why women who play sports are more successful. *Fortune.* Retrieved from http://fortune.com/2016/02/04/women-sports-successful

Burgat, C. (2017) Among House staff, women are well represented. Just not in the senior positions. *The Washington Post.* Retrieved from https://www.washingtonpost.com/news/monkey-cage/wp/2017/06/20/among-house-staff-women-are-well-represented-just-not-in-the-senior-positions/?utm_term=.894fb2bf5ce9

Camera, L. (2016). Boys bear the brunt of school discipline. *U.S. News & World Report.* Retrieved from https://www.usnews.com/news/articles/2016-06-22/boys-bear-the-brunt-of-school-discipline

Catalano, S. (2012). *Stalking victims in the United States—revised.* Retrieved from http://www.bjs.gov/content/pub/pdf/svus_rev.pdf

Center for American Women and Politics. (2017) Retrieved from http://www.cawp.rutgers.edu/women-us-congress-2017

Centers for Disease Control. (2012). *Sexual violence.* Retrieved from http://www.cdc.gov/violenceprevention/pdf/sv-datasheet-a.pdf

Close, K. (2016). More than half of low-wage workers in the U. S. are women. *Fortune.* Retrieved from fortune.com/2016/12/28/gender-gap-low-wage-work

Collins, G. (2003). *America's women: 400 years of dolls, drudges, helpmates, and heroines.* New York, NY: Harper Collins.

Coontz, S. (2016). Can the working family work in America?. *The American Prospect, 27*(2), 95-99.

Department of Justice. (2013). Office of Justice Programs, Bureau of Justice Statistics, Female Victims of Sexual Violence, 1994-2010. Retrieved from http://www.bjs.gov/content/pub/pdf/fvsv9410.pdf

Downey, A. (2016). Will millennials ever get married? *Science Daily.* Retrieved from https://www.sciencedaily.com/releases/2016/10/161017124248.htm

Dusenbery, M,. & Lee, J. (2012). Charts: The state of women's athletics, 40 years after Title IX. *Mother Jones.* Retrieved from http://www.motherjones.com/politics/2012/06/charts-womens-athletics-title-nine-ncaa

Edwards, H. S. (2015). The next social security crisis. *Time, 186*(5), 48–52.

Edwards, S., Bradshaw, K., & Hinsz, V. (2014) Denying Rape but endorsing forceful intercourse: Exploring differences among responders. *Violence and Gender, 1*(4): 188–193.

Entmacher, J., Robbins, K. G., & Frohlich, L. (2014). Six new facts on why we must raise the minimum wage and advance equal pay. *National Women's Law Center.* Retrieved from http://www.nwlc.org/our-blog/six-new-facts-why-we-must-raise-minimum-wage-and-advance-equal-pay

Equal Employment Opportunity Commission. (2016). *Charges alleging sexual harassment.* Retrieved from http://www.eeoc.gov/eeoc/statistics/enforcement/sexual_harassment_new.cfm

Evans, S. (1989). *Born for liberty: A history of women in America.* New York, NY: The Free Press.

Faludi, S. (2006). *Backlash: The undeclared war against American women.* New York, NY: Three Rivers Press.

Feuer, A. (2017). Date rape comments by Brooklyn police captain are condemned. *New York Times.* Retrieved from: https://www.nytimes.com/2017/01/10/nyregion/Brooklyn-police-peter-rose-date-rape-comments.html

FBI. (2012, January 6). *Attorney General Eric Holder announces revisions to the Uniform Crime Report's definition of rape.* Press release retrieved from http://www.fbi.gov/news/pressrel/press-releases

Gonnerman, J. (2005). The unforgiven. *Mother Jones, 30*(4), 38–43.

Goshe, B. (2016). Cybergullying among young adults: Effects on mental and physical health. Retrieved from http://digitalcommons.uconn.edu/cgi/viewcontent.cgi?article=2012&context=gs_theses

Gould, S. J. (1983). Big fish, little fish. In *Hen's teeth and horses toes* (pp. 21–31). New York, NY: W.W. Norton.

Grall, T. (2016). Custodial mothers and fathers and their child support. Retrieved from https://www.census.gov/content/dam/Census/library/publications/2016/demo/P60-255.pdf

Grogan, S. (2008). *Body image: Understanding body dissatisfaction in men, women, and children.* (2nd ed.). New York, NY: Routledge.

Gurian, M. (2010). Boys and girls learn differently! San Francisco, CA: Jossey-Bass.

Hall, K., & Spurlock, C. (2013). *Paid parental leave: U.S. vs. the world.* Retrieved from http://www.huffingtonpost.com/2013/02/04/maternity-leave-paid-parental-leave-_n_2617284.html

Holland, G. (2016). A systematic review of the impact of the use of social networking sites on body image and disordered eating outcomes. *Body Image, 17,* 100110.

Inter-Parliamentary Union. (2017). Women in national parliaments. Retrieved from http://www.ipu.org/wmn-e/classif.htm

Javier, S. J., Abrams, J. A., Maxwell, M. L., & Belgrave, F. Z. (2013). Determining beauty: Body dissatisfaction among African Americans, Asian Americans and Latina women. In L. B. Sams & J. A. Keels (Eds.) *Handbook on body images: Gender different, sociocultural influences and healthy implications* (pp. 139–167). New York, NY: Nova Publishers.

Kabat-Farr, D., & Cortina, L. M. (2012). Selective incivility: Gender, race, and the discriminatory workplace. In S. Fox & T. R. Lituchy (Eds.), *Gender and the dysfunctional workplace* (pp. 120–134). Northampton, MA: Edward Elgar Publishing, Inc.

Kilman, C. (2012). Title IX at 40: Beyond the playing field. *Teaching Tolerance*. Issue 42, 30–33.

Kimmel, P. R. (2006). Culture and conflict. In M. Deutsch & P. Coleman (Eds.), *The handbook of conflict resolution*. San Francisco, CA: Jossey-Bass.

Kitchin, P. (2010). Crossing the line: The ninth circuit's guidelines for flirting at work. Retrieved from http://www.hirecentrix.com/crossing-the-line-the-ninth-circuits-guide-lines-for-flirting-at-work.html

Knapp, D. (2016). Sexual harassment and the real "north country": Revelations of an expert witness. *Employee Responsibilities and Rights Journal*, 28(1), 1-22.

Knapton, S. (2015) Marriage is more beneficial for men than women, study shows. *The Telegraph*. Retrieved from http://www.telegrap.co.uk/science/2016/03/14/marriage-is-more-beneficial-for-men-than-women-study-shows

Levine, M. P., & Chapman, K. (2011). Media influence on body image. In T. F. Cash & L. Smolak (Eds.), *Body image: A handbook of science, practice and prevention* (2nd ed., pp. 101–109). New York, NY: The Guilford Press.

MacKinnon, C. A. (1987). A rally against rape. In *Feminism unmodified: Discourses on life and law* (pp. 81–84). Cambridge, MA: Harvard University Press.

Manning, J. (2017). Membership of the 115th Congress: A profile. Retrieved from https://fas.org/sgp/crs/misc/R44762.pdf

McKinley, N. M. (2011). Feminist perspectives on body image. In T. F. Cash & L. Smolak (Eds.), *Body image: A handbook of science, practice and prevention* (2nd ed., pp. 48–55). New York, NY: The Guilford Press.

Meyer, E. J. (2014). New solutions for bullying and harassment: A post-structural, feminist approach. (pp. 209-330). In R. M. Schott & D. M. Sondergaard, (Eds.). *School bullying: New theories in context*. Cambridge, NY: Cambridge University Press.

Meyer, E. J. (2009). *Gender, bullying and harassment: Strategies to end sexism and homophobia in schools*. New York, NY: Teachers College Press.

Miller, K. (2017). *AAUW Report: The Simple Truth*. Retrieved from http://www.aauw.org/aauw_check/pdf_kownload/show_pdf.php?file=The-Simple-Truth

Nathman, A. (2017) Leah Juliett is standing up for revenge porn victims. *Teen Vogue*. Retrieved from: http://www.teenvogue.com/story/leah-juliett-stands-up-for-revenge-porn-victims

National Center for Educational Statistics. (2013). *Digest of education statistics*. Retrieved from http://nces.ed.gov/programs/digest/d13/tables/dt13_318.30.asp

National Women's Law Center. (2014). *Fair pay for women requires increasing the minimum wage and tipped minimum wage*. Retrieved from http://www.nwlc.org/resource/fair-pay-women-requires-increasing-minimum-wage-and-tipped-minimum-wage

Nilsen, A. P. (1977a). Sexism as shown through the English vocabulary. In A. P. Nilsen, H. Bosmajian, H. L. Gershuny, & J. P. Stanley (Eds.), *Sexism and language* (pp. 27–41). Urbana, IL: National Council of Teachers of English.

Nilsen, A. P. (1977b). Sexism in the language of marriage. In A. P. Nilsen, H. Bosmajian, H. L. Gershuny, & J. P. Stanley (Eds.), *Sexism and language* (pp. 131–140). Urbana, IL: National Council of Teachers of English.

O'Neill. J. (2017). Commish pledges NYPD commitment to investigating rape in wake of precinct captain's 'insensitive' comments. *NY Daily News*. Retrieved from http://www.nydailynews.com/new-york/nypd-vows-rape-precinct-captain-commens-article-1.2941931

Parker, P. (2015) The Historical Role of Women in Higher Education. *Administrative Issues Journal*. Retrieved from http://files.eric.ed.gov/fulltext/EJ1062478.pdf

Partridge, E. (2009). *Origins: A short etymological dictionary of modern English* (p. 92). New York, NY: Routledge.

Piercy, M. (1982). *Circles in the water*. New York, NY: Alfred A. Knopf.

RAINN. (2014). *Rape, Abuse, and Incest National Network*. Retrieved from http://www.rainn.org

Reuben, E. (2014) How stereotypes impair women's careers in science. *Proceedings of the National Academy of Sciences*, 111(12), 4403–4408.

Riley, G. (1986). *Inventing the American woman: A perspective on women's history, 1607–1877: Vol. 1.* Arlington Heights, IL: Harlan Davidson.

Sadker, D., & Sadker, M. (1994). *Failing at fairness: How America's schools cheat girls*. New York, NY: Charles Scribner.

Santa Cruz, J. (2014) Body-image pressure increasingly affects boys. *The Atlantic*. Retrieved from https://www.theatlantic.com/health/archive/2014/body-image-pressure-increasingly-affects-boys/283897

Shapiro, M. (2012). Dreaming big: What's gender got to do with it? *CGO Insights, Briefing Note #35*. Retrieved from http://www.simmons.edu/som/docs/insights_35_v2_%282%29.pdf

Showalter, A. & Wilson, W. (2016, March 14). How the pay gap hurts women's financial security. *Time*, 187(9), 14.

Stalking Resource Center. (2014). *The use of technology to stalk*. Retrieved from http://www.victimsofcrime.org/our-programs/stalking-resource-center

Storrs, C. (2011). Does love benefit men's or women's health more? *The Huffington Post*. Retrieved from http://www.huffingtonpost.com/2011/03/03/loves-health–benefits-_n_830455.html#s248099&title=Depression

Strauss, S., & Espeland, P. (1992). *Sexual harassment and teens: A program for positive change*. Minneapolis, MN: Free Spirit.

Tavris, C. (1999). *The mismeasure of woman*. New York, NY: Peter Smith.

Tiggemann, M. (2011). Sociocultural perspectives on human appearance and body image. In T. F. Cash & L. Smolak (Eds.), *Body image: A handbook of science, practice and prevention* (2nd ed., pp. 12–19). New York, NY: The Guilford Press.

U.S. Bureau of the Census. (2012). Mean earnings by highest degree earned. Retrieved from http://www.census.gov/compendia/statab/2012/tables/12s0232.xls

U.S. Bureau of Labor Statistics. (2013a). *Household data, 2013.* Retrieved from http://www.bls.gov/cps/cpsaat11.pdf

U.S. Bureau of Labor Statistics. (2013b). *Highlights of women's earnings in 2012.* Report 1045. Retrieved from http://www.bls.gov/cps/cpswom2012.pdf

U.S. Bureau of Labor Statistics. (2017). Retrieved from https://www.bls.gov/cps/cpsaat11.htm

U.S. Department of Education. (2012). *Gender equity in education.* Retrieved from http://www2.ed.gov/about/offices/list/ocr/docs/gender-equity-in-education.pdf

Wakeman, J. (2016) Life After Sexual Assault. *Rolling Stone.* Retrieved from http://www.rollingstone.com/culture/features/life-after-sexual-assault-inside-doc-audrie-daisy-w441794

Webb, S. (2000). *Step forward: Sexual harassment in the workplace* (2nd ed.). New York, NY: Mastermedia.

Wetzel, R., & Brown, N. W. (2000). *Student-generated sexual harassment in secondary schools.* Westport, CT: Bergin & Garvey.

Wilson, A. (2017). NCAA Report: 45 years of Title IX. Retrieved from http://www.ncaapublications.com/productdownloads/TitleIX-45.pdf

Women in National Parliaments. (2014). Retrieved from http://www.ipu.org/wmn-e/classif.htm

Women's Sports Foundation. (2016). Retrieved from https://www.womenssportsfoundation.org/support-us/do-you-know-the-factors-influencing-girls-participation-in-sports

Zimbalist, A. (2016) The N.C.A.A.'s Women Problem. *New York Times.* Retrieved

Zumbrun, J. (2014). Is the gender pay gap closing or has progress stalled? *The Wall Street Journal.* Retrieved from http://blogs.wsj.com/economics/2014/04/11/is-the-gender-pay-gap-closing-or-has-progress-stalled

Chapter 11

Anti-Defamation League. (2009). *What you need to know: The new federal hate crime law.* Retrieved from http://www.adl.org/combating_hate

Bailey, J. M. (2016). What scientists know – and don't know – about sexual orientation. Association for Psychological Science. Retrieved from https://www.psychologicalscience.org/news/releases/what-scientists-know-and-dont-know-about-sexual-orientation.html

Bérbubé, A. (1989). Marching to a different drummer: Lesbian and gay GIs in World War II. In M. Duberman, M. Vicinus, & G. Chauncey, Jr. (Eds.), *Hidden from history: Reclaiming the gay and lesbian past* (pp. 456–476). New York, NY: Meridian.

Boswell, J. (1994). *Same-sex unions in pre-modern Europe.* New York, NY: Villard.

Bumiller, E. (2011). Obama ends "don't ask, don't tell" policy. *New York Times.* Retrieved from www.nytimescom/2011/07/23/us/23military.html

Burns, C. (2012). *Report: Unions are key to securing LGBT workplace equality.* Retrieved from http://thinkprogress.org/lgbt/2012/09/07/813181/report-unions-are-key-to-securing-lgbt-workplace-equality

Burns, C., & Krehely, J. (2011). *Gay and transgender people face high rates of workplace discrimination and harassment.* Retrieved from http://www.americanprogress.org/issues/lgbt/news/2011/06/02/9872/gay-and-transgender-people-face-high-rates-of-workplace-discrimination-and-harassment

Burns, C., & Rothman, A. (2012). *The repeal of don't ask, don't tell—1 year later.* Retrieved from http://www.americanprogress.org/issues/lgbt/report/2012/09/20/38764/the-repeal-of-dont-ask-dont-tell-1-year-later

Carmon, I. (2015). Here are the wildest arguments against marriage equality. MSNBC News. Retrieved from http://www.msnbc.com/msnbc/the-wildest-arguments-against-marriage-equality

Center for American Progress. (2016). Unjust: How the broken criminal justice system fails LGBT people of color. Retrieved from http://www.lgbtmap.org/file/lgbt-criminal-justice-poc.pdf

Chauncey, G., Jr. (1989). Christian brotherhood or sexual perversion? Homosexual identities and the construction of sexual boundaries in the World War I era. In M. Duberman, M. Vicinus, & G. Chauncey, Jr. (Eds.), *Hidden from history: Reclaiming the gay and lesbian past* (pp. 456–476). New York, NY: Meridian.

Chaves, M. (2014). *American congregations at the beginning of the 21st Century.* Duke University National Congregations Study. Retrieved from http://www.soc.duke.edu/natcong/Docs/NCSII_report_final.pdf

Chiariello, P. (2013). *A global historical survey: Does accepting homosexuality lead to civilizational ruin?* Retrieved from http://appliedsentience.com/2013/07/19/a-global-historical-survey-does-accepting-homosexuality-lead-to-civilizational-ruin

Child Molestation Research and Prevention Institute. (2014). *Early diagnosis and effective treatment.* Retrieved from http://www.childmolestationprevention.org/pages/tell_others_the_facts.html

Coffin Jr., W.S. Quoted in J.C. Lang. (2008). *William Sloane Coffin, Jr.: Preacher to America's conscience.* Ann Arbor, MI: UMI Microform, ProQuest LLC.

Crompton, L. (1998). *Byron and Greek love: Homophobia in 19th century England.* Swaffham, U.K.: Gay Men's Press.

Cushner, K., McClelland, A., & Safford, P. (2008). Education in a changing society. In *Human diversity in education: An integrative approach* (6th ed.). New York, NY: McGraw-Hill.

D'Emilio, J. (1989). Gay politics and community in San Francisco since World War II. In M. Duberman, M. Vicinus, & G. Chauncey, Jr. (Eds.), *Hidden from history: Reclaiming the gay and lesbian past* (pp. 456–476). New York, NY: Meridian.

Doupe, G.E. (2001). True to our tradition. In W. Blumenfeld (Ed.), *Homophobia: How we all pay the price* (pp. 187–204). Boston, MA: Beacon.

Duberman, M., Vicinus, M., & Chauncey, G. Jr. (Eds.). (1989). *Hidden from history: Reclaiming the gay and lesbian past.* New York, NY: Meridian.

Duggan, L. (2004). Making it perfectly queer. In D. Carlin & J. DiGrazia (Eds.), *Queer cultures* (pp. 51–67). Upper Saddle River, NJ: Pearson Prentice Hall.

Eidelson, J. (2014). *Most Americans think it's illegal to fire someone for being gay. They're wrong.* Retrieved from http://www.businessweek.com/articles/2014-06-23/discrimination-at-work-is-it-legal-to-fire-someone-for-being-gay

Ellerton, P. (2011). *1,500 animal species practice homosexuality.* Retrieved from http://pactiss.org/2011/11/17/1500-animal-species-practice-homosexuality

Equal Rights Center. (2014). *Federal contractors show anti-LGBT hiring bias.* Retrieved from http://www.equalrightscenter.org/site/DocServer/Freedom_to_Work_6.16.14.pdf?docID=2481

Franklin, K. (2013). Masculinity, status and power: Implicit messages in western media discourse on high-profile cases of multiple perpetrator rape. In M. Horvath & J. Woodhams (Eds.), *Handbook on the study of multiple perpetrator rape* (pp. 37–66). New York, NY: Routledge.

Fuller, R.B. (1981). *Critical path.* New York, NY: Macmillan.

Gaille, B. (2017). 39 shocking LGBT discrimination statistics. Retrieved from http://brandongaille.com/37-shocking-lgbt-discrimination-statistics/

Gates, G.J. (2013). *LGBT parenting in the United States.* Retrieved from http://williamsinstitute.law.ucla.edu/wp-content/uploads/LGBT-Parenting.pdf

GLSEN. (2015). 2015 National school climate survey. Retrieved from https://www.glsen.org/article/2015-national-school-climate-survey

Goodman, J. (2013). *Preparing for a generation that comes out younger.* Retrieved from http://www.huffingtonpost.com/josh-a-goodman/preparing-for-a-generation-that-comes-out-younger_b_2556346.html

Gould, S.J. (1983). How the zebra gets its stripes. In *Hen's teeth and horse's toes* (pp. 366–375). New York, NY: W.W. Norton.

Hogenboom, M. (2015). Are there any homosexual animals? British Broadcasting Corporation. Retrieved from http://www.bbc.com/earth/story/20150206-are-there-any-homosexual-animals

Human Rights Campaign. (2017). State maps of laws and policies. Retrieved from http://www.hrc.org/state-maps/employment

Human Rights Campaign. (2014). *The cost of the closet and the rewards of inclusion.* Retrieved from http://hrc-assets.s3-website-us-east-1.amazonaws.com//files/assets/resources/Cost_of_the_Closet_May2014.pdf

Human Rights Campaign. (2009). *Issue: Hate Crimes Prevention Act.* Retrieved from www.hrc.org/issues/pages/hate-crimes-prevention-act

Kann, L., Olsen, E. O., McManus, T. et al. (2016). Sexual identity, sex of sexual contacts, and health-related behaviors among students in grades 9-12, United States and selected sites, 2015. Retrieved from http://www.cdc.gov/mmwr/volumes/65/ss/ss6509a1.htm

Katz, J. (1985). *Gay American history: Lesbians and gay men in the U.S.A.* New York, NY: Harper Colophon.

Kinsey, A.C., Pomeroy, W.B., & Martin, C.E. (1948). *Sexual behavior in the human male.* Philadelphia, PA: W.B. Saunders.

Lawrimore, J. (2014). *7 reasons why it's time to come out to your co-workers.* Retrieved from http://lgbtqblog.dallasnews.com/tag/workplace

Liebman, J. (1946). *Peace of mind.* New York, NY: Simon and Schuster.

Marcus, E. (1992). *Making history: The struggle for gay and lesbian equal rights, 1945–1990.* New York, NY: HarperCollins.

Mitchum, P. (2013). 4 years later: Examining bias-motivated crimes against LGBT people after the Shepard-Byrd act. *Center for American Progress.* Retrieved from http://www.americanprogress.org/issues/lgbt/news/2013/10/31/78518/4-years-later-examining-bias-motivated-crimes-against-lgbt-people-after-the-shepard-byrd-act

Morales, L. (2011). *U.S. adults estimate that 25% of Americans are gay or lesbian.* Retrieved from http://www.gallup.com/poll/147824/adults-estimate-americans-gay-lesbian.aspx

Obama quote source: Hensch, M. (1916). Obama: LGBT rights are human rights. *The Hill.* Retrieved from http://thehill.com/blogs/blog-briefing-room/news/280140-obama-lgbt-rights-are-human-rights

Park, H. and Mykhyalyshyn, I. (2016). LGBT people are more likely to be targets of hate crimes than any other minority group. The New York Times. Retrieved from https://www.nytimes.com/interactive/2016/06/16/us/hate-crimes-against-lgbt.html

Pauwels, M. (2012). *Bisexuals endure worst mental health problems.* Retrieved from http://www.gaystarnews.com/article/bisexuals-endure-worst-mental-health-problems

Perrin, E.C., & Siegel, B.S. (2013). Promoting the well-being of children whose parents are gay or lesbian. *The American Academy of Pediatrics.* Retrieved from pediatrics.aappublications.org/content/early/2013/03/18/peds/2013-0377

Pew Research Center. (2017). Gay marriage around the world. Retrieved from http://www.pewforum.org/2017/08/08/gay-marriage-around-the-world-2013/

Pew Research Center. (2013a). *Gay marriage: Key data points from Pew research.* Retrieved from http://www.pewresearch.org/key-data-points/gay-marriage-key-data-points-from-pew-research

Pew Research Center. (2013b). *In gay marriage debate, both supporters and opponents see legal recognition as "inevitable."* Retrieved from http://www.people-press.org/2013/06/06/in-gay-marriage-debate-both-supporters-and-opponents-see-legal-recognition-as-inevitable/

Philpott, T. (2013). Gay, lesbian spouses to gain full military benefits. *Stars and Stripes.* Retrieved from http://www.stripes.com/news/us/gay-lesbian-spouses-to-gain-full-military-benefits-1.227956

Pillard, R.C. (1997). The search for a genetic influence on sexual orientation. In V. Rosario (Ed.), *Science and homosexualities* (pp. 226–241). New York, NY: Routledge.

Rankin, S.R. (2005, Fall). Campus climates for sexual minorities. In R. Sanlo (Ed.), *Gender identity and sexual orientation: Research, policy and personal perspectives,* No. 111 (pp. 17–23). San Francisco, CA: Jossey-Bass.

Rogers, C. (1995). *On becoming a person*. New York, NY: Houghton Mifflin Harcourt.

Rowse, A.L. (1977). *Homosexuals in history: A study of ambivalence in society, literature and the arts*. New York, NY: Dorset.

Sample, I. (2014). *Male sexual orientation influenced by genes, study shows*. Retrieved from http://www.theguardian.com/science/2014/feb/14/genes-influence-male-sexual-orientation-study

Schlatter, E., & Steinback, R. (2010, Winter). 10 myths. *Intelligence Report, 140*, 31–35.

Schwartzapfel, B. (2013). Little boxes. *The American Prospect, 24*(2), 36–47.

Sears, J.T. (1992). Educators, homosexuality, and homosexual students: Are personal feelings related to professional beliefs? In K. Harbeck, *Coming out of the classroom closet: Gay and lesbian students, teachers and curricula* (pp. 28–79). Binghamton, NY: Harrington Park Press.

Shilts, R. (1987). *And the band played on: Politics, people and the AIDS epidemic*. New York, NY: St. Martin's Press.

SLDF. (2010). *About "don't ask, don't tell."* Servicemembers Legal Defense Fund. Retrieved from www.sldn.org/pages/about-dadt

Sontag, S. (1989). *AIDS and its metaphors*. New York, NY: Farrar, Straus, and Giroux.

Stanton, G. (2015). What is the actual US divorce rate and risk? The Witherspoon Institute. Retrieved from http://www.thepublicdiscourse.com/2015/12/15983/

Steakley, J.D. (1989). Iconography of a scandal: Political cartoons and the Eulenberg affair in Wilhelmine Germany. In M. Duberman, M. Vicinus, & G. Chauncey, Jr. (Eds.), *Hidden from history: Reclaiming the gay and lesbian past* (pp. 233–263). New York, NY: Meridian.

Steinmetz, K. (2017, March 27). Infinite identities. *Time*, 189(11), p. 48-54.

Steinmetz, K. (2014). America's transition. *Time 183*(22), 38–46.

Storrs, C. (2016). Bisexuality on the rise, says new survey. CNN. Retrieved from http://www.cnn.com/2016/01/07/health/bisexuality-on-the-rise/index.html

Sullivan, N. (2003). *A critical introduction to queer theory*. Washington Square, NY: New York University Press.

Terry, D. (2015). In the crosshairs. *Intelligence Report*, Issue 158, 27-35.

Volokh, E. (2014). *What percentage of the U.S. population is gay, lesbian or bisexual?* Retrieved from http://www.washingtonpost.com/news/volokh-conspiracy/wp/2014/07/15/what-percentage-of-the-u-s-population-is-gay-lesbian-or-bisexual/

Williams, W.L. (2001). Benefits for non-homophobic societies: An anthropological perspective. In W. Blumenfeld (Ed.), *Homophobia: How we all pay the price* (pp. 258–274). Boston, MA: Beacon.

Williams, W.L. (2010). *The "two-spirit" people of indigenous North Americans*. Retrieved from http://www.theguardian.com/music/2010/oct/11/two-spirit-people-north-america

Wolpert, S. (2016). Why people oppose same-sex marriage. UCLA Newsroom. Retrieved from http://newsroom.ucla.edu/releases/why-people-oppose-same-sex-marriage

Young, S. (2004). Dichotomies and displacement: Bisexuality in queer theory and politics. In D. Carlin & J. DiGrazia (Eds.), *Queer cultures* (pp. 83–98). Upper Saddle River, NJ: Pearson Prentice Hall.

Zeldin, T. (1994). *An intimate history of humanity*. New York, NY: HarperCollins.

Chapter 12

Adelman, H.S. (1996). The classification problem. In W. Stainback & S. Stainback (Eds.), *Controversial issues confronting special education: Divergent perspectives* (pp. 29–44). Boston, MA: Allyn & Bacon.

API Healthline. (2012). *The pros and cons of full inclusion of disabled students*. Retrieved from http://api-healthline.net/2012/10/the-pros-and-cons-of-full-inclusion-of-disabled-students.html

Barnett, J. C. & Vornovitsky, M. S. (2016). Health insurance coverage in the United States: 2015. Retrieved from https://www.census.gov/content/dam/Census/library/publications/2016/demo/p60-257.pdf

Barzun, J. (2000). *From dawn to decadence: 500 years of Western cultural life (1500 to the present)*. New York, NY: HarperCollins.

Batavia, A. (2001). The new paternalism: Portraying people with disabilities as an oppressed minority. *Journal of Disability Policy Studies, 12*(2), 107–113.

Batavia, A. (2002). Consumer direction, consumer choice, and the future of long-term care. In L. Powers (Ed.), *Journal of Disability Policy Studies, 13*(2), 67–73.

Bernell, S. (2003). Theoretical and applied issues in defining disability in labor market research. *Journal of Disability Policy Studies, 14*(1), 36–45.

Block, L. (2014). *Stereotypes about people with disabilities*. Disability History Museum. Retrieved from http://www.disabilitymuseum.org/dhm/edu/essay.html?id=24

Brault, M. (2012). Americans with disabilities: 2010. *Current Population reports*. Washington, D.C.: U.S. Census Bureau, 70–131.

Brown, S.E. (2011). *Disability culture: Beginnings*. Retrieved from http://www.instituteondisabilityculture.org/disability-culture-beginnings-a-fact-sheet.html

Cardichon, J. (2014). How to address the over-representation of students of color in special education. Retrieved from https://all4ed.org/how-to-address-the-over-representation-of-students-of-color-in-special-education/

Castro, J. (2014). *Disability rights in housing*. Retrieved from http://portal.hud.gov/hudportal/HUD?src=/program_offices/fair_housing_equal_opp/disabilities/inhousing

Charlton, J.I. (1998). *Nothing about us without us*. Berkeley, CA: University of California Press.

Coleman, L.M. (2006). Stigma. In L. Davis (Ed.), *The disability studies reader* (pp. 216–233). New York, NY: Routledge.

Colker, R. (2013) Disabled education. *Rethinking Schools, 28*(1), 20–27.

Coutinho, M.J., & Oswald, D.P. (2010). *Disproportionate representation of culturally and linguistically diverse students in special education: Measuring the problem*. Retrieved from http://www.ldonline.org/article/5603

DeNavas-Walt, C. & Proctor, B. D. (2014). Income, poverty and health insurance coverage in the United States. U. S. Census Bureau. Retrieved from https://poverty.ucdavis.edu/faq/how-poverty-status-related-disability

deMause, N. (2013). Disabled are new target for charges of cheating. *Extra! 26*(6), 11–13.

DeRose, R. (2012). *People with disabilities still suffer discrimination in hiring*. Retrieved from http://blog.nj.com/njv_guest_blog/2012/07/people_with_disabilities_still.html

Diament, M. (2016). Graduation rates lagging for students with disabilities. Retrieved from https://www.disabilityscoop.com/2016/01/22/graduation-rates-lagging/21815/

Diament, M. (2014a). *Congress passes bill limiting sheltered workshop eligibility*. Retrieved from http://www.disabilityscoop.com/2014/07/10/congress-sheltered-eligibility/19500/

Diament, M. (2014b). *Obama signs ABLE act*. Retrieved from: http://www.disabilityscoop.com/2014/12/22/obama-signs-able-act/19935/

Dollar, E. P. (2014). Yes, we can change cultural assumptions about disabilities. Here's how. Retrieved from http://www.patheos.com/blogs/ellenpainterdollar/2014/04/yes-we-can-change-cultural-assumptions-about-disabilities-heres-how/

EEOC. (2014). *Americans with Disabilities Act of 1990 (ADA) Charges*. Retrieved from http://www.eeoc.gov/eeoc/statistics/enforcement/ada-charges.cfm

Ellin, A. (2012). *Judge rules in favor of fired employee with bipolar disorder*. Retrieved from http://abcnews.go.com/Business/judge-rules-favor-fired-employee-bipolar-disorder/story?id=16079631&singlePage=true#.T37f13mnfd4

Ellis, J. (2016). The difficult decision we shouldn't have to make: Employment or life. Retrieved from http://www.rudermanfoundation.org/blog/article/the-difficult-decision-we-shouldnt-have-to-make-employment-or-life

Ervelles, N. (2001). In search of the disabled subject. In J.C. Wilson & C. Lewicki-Wilson (Eds.), *Embodied rhetorics: Disability in language and culture* (pp. 92–111). Carbondale, IL: Southern Illinois University Press.

Fiedler, C. (2008). *Making a difference: Advocacy competencies for special education professionals*. Austin, TX: Pro Ed.

Fiedler, C., & Rylance, B. (Eds.). (2001, Fall). *Journal of Disability Policy Studies, 12*(2).

Fiedler, L. (1993). *Freaks: Myths and images of the secret self*. New York, NY: Anchor Books.

Filler, D. (2017). CFP: Beyond disadvantage – disability, law and bioethics. Retrieved from http://www.thefacultylounge.org/2017/08/cfp-beyond-disadvantage-disability-law-and-bioethics.html

Fine, M., & Asch, A. (2000). Disability beyond stigma: Social interaction, discrimination, and activism. In M. Adams, W.J. Blumenfeld, R. Castaneda, H.W. Hackman, M.L. Peters, & X. Zuniga (Eds.), *Readings for diversity and social justice* (pp. 330–339). New York, NY: Routledge.

Finkelstein, Victor, quoted in Deborah A. Stone. (1984). *The Disabled State*. Philadelphia, PA: Temple University Press.

Fifield, J. (2016). What happens to developmentally disabled as parents age, die? PBS Newshour. Retrieved from http://www.pbs.org/newshour/rundown/happens-developmentally-disabled-parents-age-die/

Foucault, M. (1989). *Madness and civilization: A history of insanity in the age of reason*. London, UK: Routledge.

Garrett History Brief. (2001). *Journal of Disability Policy Studies, 12*(2), 70–78.

Gill, C.J. (1994). Questioning continuum. In B. Shaw (Ed.), *The ragged edge: The disability experience from the pages of the first fifteen years of "The Disability Rag"* (pp. 42–49). Louisville, KY: The Advocado Press.

Gluck, S. (2016). Mild, moderate, severe intellectual disability differences. Retrieved from https://www.healthyplace.com/neurodevelopmental-disorders/intellectual-disability/mild-moderate-severe-intellectual-disability-differences/

Greenwald, J. (2012). *Jury returns $3.5M verdict against Rite Aid in disability discrimination case*. Retrieved from http://www.businessinsurance.com/article/20120725/NEWS07/120729937/1250

Gregory, S. (2013, February 11). Sports: Disabled kids get in the game *Time, 181*(5), 56.

Haddix, J. (2014). State association offer athletic opportunities for students with disabilities. Retrieved from http://www.nfhs.org/articles/state-associations-offer-athletic-opportunities-for-students-with-disabilities/

Hahn, H. (1994). The minority group model of disability: Implications for medical sociology. *Research in the Sociology of Health Care, 11*, 3–24.

Hehir, T. (2005). *New directions in special education*. Cambridge, MA: Harvard Education Press.

Hines, R.A. (2001). *Inclusion in middle schools*. (Report No. EDO-PS-01-13). Champaign, IL: ERIC Clearinghouse on Elementary and Early Childhood Education, Children's Research Center, University of Illinois. (ERIC Document Reproduction Service No. 459000)

Horn, C. (2012). Disability and pity. *Bethesda Institute*. Retrieved from http://bethesdablog.wordpress.com/2012/08/28/disability-and-pity

Institute on Disability. (2014). *Annual disability statistics compendium*. Retrieved from http://disabilitycompendium.org/compendium-statistics/medicaid-and-medicare

Kardish, C. (2015). Hidden or unemployed: America's failure to get disabled people jobs. Retrieved from http://www.governing.com/topics/mgmt/gov-american-disabilities-act-compliance.html

Kessler Foundation. (2015). National employment and disability survey. Retrieved from http://kesslerfoundation.org/sites/default/files/filepicker/5/KFSurvey2015_ExecutiveSummary.pdf

Klepper, D. (2017). Case of maggots in throat offers rare look at neglect probes. Retrieved from https://finance.yahoo.com/news/ap-exclusive-maggot-case-gives-051123707.html

Kliewer, C., & Biklin, D. (1996). Labeling: Who wants to be called retarded? In J. Stainbeck & S. Stainbeck (Eds.), *Controversial issues confronting special education: Divergent perspectives* (pp. 83–95). Baltimore, MD: Brookes.

Kochhar, C.A., West, L.L., & Taymans, J.M. (2000). *Successful inclusion: Practical strategies for a shared responsibility.* Upper Saddle River, NJ: Prentice-Hall.

Krahn, G., Walker, D., and Correa-De-Araujo, R. (2015). Persons with disabilities as an unrecognized health disparity population. Retrieved from https://www.ncbi.nlm.nih.gov/pmc/articles/PMC4355692/

Kraus, L. (2017). 2016 disability statistics annual report. Durham, NH: University of New Hampshire.

Krupa, K. (2014). *City council OKs "visitability" rules; all new homes must be wheelchair accessible.* Retrieved from http://kut.org/post/city-council-oks-visitability-rules-all-new-homes-must-be-wheelchair-accessible

Langtree, I. (2017). Disability pride: Definitions and awareness information. Retrieved from https://www.disabled-world.com/definitions/disability-pride.php

Leys, T. (2017). "Stubborn" Iowa hangs on to state institutions for disabled people. The Des Moines Register. Retrieved from http://www.desmoinesregister.com/story/news/health/2017/02/23/stubborn-iowa-hangs-state-institutions-disabled-people/98060824/

Linton, S. (1998). *Claiming disability: Knowledge and identity.* New York, NY: New York University Press.

Longmore, P.K. (2003). *Why I burned my book and other essays on disability.* Philadelphia, PA: Temple University Press.

Mihail, T. (2014). *Myths and facts about supported inclusive education.* Retrieved from http://www.tommihail.net/inclusion_myths.html

Myers, C., & Bersani H., Jr. (2008–2009). Ten quick ways to analyze children's books for ableism. *Rethinking Schools,* 23(2), 52–54.

National Council on Disability. (2012). *Deinstitutionalization: Unfinished business.* Retrieved from http://www.ncd.gov/publications/2012/Sept192012

National Institutes of Health. (2013). Cerebral Palsy: Hope through research. Retrieved from https://www.ninds.nih.gov/Disorders/Patient-Caregiver-Education/Hope-Through-Research/Cerebral-Palsy-Hope-Through-Research#3104_11

Ne'eman, A. (2017). The GOP health care plan could force Americans with disabilities back into institutions. Retrieved from https://www.vox.com/the-big-idea/2017/3/22/15026856/ahca-plan-medicaid-cut-hurts-disabled-institutions

Nelson, K. L. (2017). Is it "segregation" if people with disabilities work with their peers? Agencies, government at odds. USA Today. Retrieved from http://www.knoxnews.com/story/news/local/tennessee/2017/05/31/sheltered-workshops-safe-space-isolating-developmentally-disabled/345462001/

Orkis, K. (2010). *The ADA, 20 years later. A Harris interactive poll sponsored by the Kessler Foundation/National Organization on Disability.* Retrieved from http://kesslerfoundation.org/researchcenter/sci/files/surveyresults_sad.pdf

Osgood, R.L. (2005). *The history of inclusion in the United States.* Washington, DC: Gallaudet University Press.

Padden, C., & Humphries, T. (1998). *Deaf in America: Voices from a culture.* Cambridge, MA: Harvard University Press.

Pai, Y., & Adler, S. (1997). *Cultural foundations of education.* Upper Saddle River, NJ: Merrill/Prentice Hall.

Peacock, G. Iezzoni, L. & Harkin, T. (2015). Health care for Americans with disabilities – 25 years after the ADA. The New England Journal of Medicine. Retrieved from http://www.nejm.org/doi/full/10.1056/NEJMp1508854?af=R&rss=currentIssue&

Pollack H. and Bagenstos, S. (2015). We don't need "modern asylums." *The American Prospect,* 26(3), 18-19.

Posner, B. (1979). Israel: A tale of two people. *Disabled USA,* 2(8), 16–17.

Putnam, M. (2005). Conceptualizing disability. *Journal of Disability Policy Studies,* 16(3), 188–198.

Reagan, T. (2005). A case study in cultural and linguistic difference: The DEAF-WORLD. In T. Osborn (Ed.), *Language and cultural diversity in U.S. schools* (pp. 53–64). Westport, CT: Praeger.

Repa, B. K. (2017). Your right to a reasonable accommodation under the Americans with Disabilities Act. Retrieved from http://www.nolo.com/legal-encyclopedia/free-books/employee-rights-book/chapter7-8.html

Ribton-Turner, C.J. (1972). *A history of vagrants and vagrancy.* Montclair, NJ: Patterson Smith.

Rogers, H. (2015). A decent living for home caregivers – and their clients. *The American Prospect,* 26(3), 52-55. (*article also saved under Ageism*)

Rudowitz, R. (2016). Medicaid financing: The basics. Retrieved from http://www.kff.org/report-section/medicaid-financing-the-basics-issue-brief/

Scan Foundation. (2013). *Who pays for long-term care in the U.S.?* Retrieved from http://www.thescanfoundation.org/sites/default/files/who_pays_for_ltc_us_jan_2013_fs.pdf

Schroeder, F. K. (2015). People with disabilities: The orphan minority. Retrieved from https://nfb.org/images/nfb/publications/bm/bm15/bm1506/bm150605.htm

Schur, L. (2013). *Reducing obstacles to voting for people with disabilities.* Retrieved from https://www.supportthevoter.gov/files/2013/08/Disability-and-Voting-White-Paper-for-Presidential-Commission-Schur.docx_.pdf

Seligson, S. (2011). *Should the deaf be considered an ethnic group?* Retrieved from http://www.bu.edu/today/2011/should-the-deaf-be-considered-an-ethnic-group

Simon, C.C. (2013). Disability studies: A new normal. *The New York Times.* Retrieved from http://www.nytimes.com/2013/11/03/education/edlife/disability-studies-a-new-normal.html?pagewanted=all&_r=0

Sinnott-Armstrong, W. & Miller, F. (2012). What makes killing wrong? Retrieved from http://jme.bmj.com/content/early/2012/01/19/medethics-2011-100351.full

Smith, A. (2014). Employees with disabilities can boost success. Retrieved from http://www.businessnewsdaily.com/7599-hiring-people-with-disabilities.html

Stone, M. (2014). *GOP candidate claims disabled children are God's punishment for abortion.* Retrieved from http://www.patheos.com/blogs/progressivesecularhumanist/2014/04/gop-candidate-claims-disabled-children-are-gods-punishment-for-abortion/

Taylor, H., Krane, D., & Orkis, K. (2010). *The ADA, 20 years later.* Retrieved from http://www.2010disabilitysurveys.org

Tirrell-Corbin, C. (2017). How to teach children about cultural awareness and diversity. Retrieved from http://

www.pbs.org/parents/expert-tips-advice/2015/08/teach-children-cultural-awareness-diversity/

U.S. Department of Education. (2014). *Data snapshot: School discipline.* Retrieved from http://www2.ed.gov/about/offices/list/ocr/docs/crdc-discipline-snapshot.pdf

U.S. Department of Labor. (2014). *Employers and the ADA: Myths and facts.* Retrieved from http://www.dol.gov/odep/pubs/fact/ada.htm

U.S. Supreme Court (1988). *Honig v. Doe,* et al. Retrieved from www.wrightslaw.com/case/caselaw/ussupct/honig.doe.htm

Vallas, R. (2013). The real story is it's incredibly hard to qualify. *Extra! 26*(12), 9–10.

Vallas, R., & Fremstad, S. (2014). *Disability is a cause and consequence of poverty.* Retrieved from http://talkpoverty.org/2014/09/19/disability-cause-consequence-poverty

Wehmeyer, M. (2000, Summer). Riding the third wave. *Focus on Autism & Other Developmental Disabilities, 15*(2), 106–116.

Whitted, B.R., Cleary, L.A., & Takiff, N.E. (2011). *Educational mandates for children with disabilities: School policies, case law, and the school social worker.* Retrieved from www.wct-law.com/CM/Publications/publications17.asp

Wilson, J.C., & Lewicki-Wilson, C. (2001). Disability, rhetoric, and the body. In J.C. Wilson & C. Lewicki-Wilson (Eds.), *Embodied rhetorics: Disability in language and culture* (pp. 1–24). Carbondale: Southern Illinois University Press.

Winzer, M.A. (1997). Disability and society before the eighteenth century: Dread and despair. In L. Davis (Ed.), *The disability studies reader* (pp. 75–109). London, UK: Routledge.

Wolfensberger, W. (1970). *The principle of normalization in human services.* Toronto: National Institute on Mental Retardation.

Yang, K. L. & Tan, H. E. (2016). Disability statistics. Cornell University. Retrieved from http://disabilitystatistics.org/reports/acs.cfm?statistic=1

Chapter 13

Agee, J. (1940). *Let us now praise famous men.* New York, NY: Ballantine Books. (With photographs by Walker Evans.)

Aintablian, X. W. (2014). The importance of teaching global education in the classroom. Retrieved from https://www.thoughtco.com/importance-of-teaching-global-education-1435626

Al-Hebaish, S.M. (2012). The correlation between general self-confidence and academic achievement. *Theory and Practice in Language Studies, 2*(1), 60–65.

Amurao, C. (2013). Fact sheet: How bad is the school-to-prison pipeline? PBS. Retrieved from http://www.pbs.org/wnet/tavissmiley/tsr/education-under-arrest/school-to-prison-pipeline-fact-sheet/

Appleton, N. (1983). *Cultural pluralism in education: Theoretical foundations.* New York, NY: Longman.

Banks, J.A. (2004). Multicultural education: Characteristics and goals. In J.A. Banks & C.M. Banks, (Eds.), *Multicultural education: Issues & perspectives* (5th ed., pp. 3–27). New York, NY: John Wiley & Sons.

Banks, J.A. (2006). *Cultural diversity and education: Foundations, curriculum and teaching* (5th ed.). Boston, MA: Allyn & Bacon.

Banks, J. (2014). *An Introduction to Multicultural Education* (5th ed.). Boston, MA: Pearson Education.

Bidwell, A. (July 15, 2014). Common Core in flux as states debate standards, tests. *US News & World Report.* Retrieved from http://www.usnews.com/news/articles/2014/07/15/common-core-status-in-flux-as-states-debate-standards-tests

Bleiberg, J., & West, D. (2014, March). In defense of the Common Core Standards. *Center for Technology at Brookings, 1-15.* Retrieved from http://www.brookings.edu/~/media/research/files/papers/2014/03/common%20core%20state%20standards/bleiberg_west_common%20core%20state%20standards.pdf.

Bouie, J. (2014). *Still separate and unequal.* Retrieved from http://www.slate.com/articles/news_and_politics/politics/2014/05/brown_v_board_of_education_60th_anniversary_america_s_schools_are_segregating.html

Brameld, T.B.H. (1956). *Toward a reconstructed philosophy of education.* New York, NY: Dryden Press.

Briggs, S. (2014). Why self-esteem hurts learning but self-confidence does the opposite. Retrieved from http://www.opencolleges.edu.au/informed/features/self-efficacy-and-learning/

Brown, P. L. (2013). Opening up, students transform a vicious cycle. *The New York Times.* Retrieved from http://www.nytimes.com/2013/04/04/education/restorative-justice-programs-take-root-in-schools.html

Camera, L. (2016). Achievement gap between white and black students still gaping. US News & World Report. Retrieved from https://www.usnews.com/news/blogs/data-mine/2016/01/13/achievement-gap-between-white-and-black-students-still-gaping

Carse, J. (1986). *Finite and infinite games: A vision of life as play and possibility.* New York, NY: Free Press.

Chiu, C. L., Sayman, D. and Carrero, K. M. (2017). Developing culturally competent preschool teachers. *Multicultural Perspectives, 19*(1), 47-52.

Combs, A.W. (1979). *Myths in education: Beliefs that hinder progress and their alternatives.* Boston, MA: Allyn & Bacon.

Common Core State Standards Initiative. (2014). What parents should know. *Common Core State Standards Initiative: Preparing America's students for college & career.* Retrieved from http://www/corestandards.org/what-parents-should-know

CREDO. (2013). *National charter school study.* Retrieved from http://credo.stanford.edu/documents/NCSS%202013%20Final%20Draft.pdf

Dean, J. (2007). Living algebra, living wage. *Rethinking Schools, 21*(4), 31–35.

DiAngelo, R. (2012). *What does it mean to be white? Developing white racial literacy.* New York, NY: Peter Lang.

Dornoo, M. (2015). Teaching mathematics education with cultural competency. *Multicultural Perspectives, 17*(2), 81-86.

Dover, A.G. (2013). Teaching for social justice: From conceptual frameworks to classroom practices. *Multicultural Perspectives, 15*(1), 3–11.

Editors of *Rethinking Schools.* (2011–2012). Stop the school-to-prison pipeline. *Rethinking Schools. 26*(2), 3–5.

Editors of *Rethinking Schools.* (2013, Summer). The trouble with the Common Core. *Rethinking Schools, 27*(4). Retrieved from http://www.rethinkingschools.org/archive/27_04/edit274.shtml.

Elias, M. (2013). The shame game. *Teaching Tolerance, 45,* 49–52.

Gardner, H. (1993). *Multiple intelligences: The theory in practice.* New York, NY: Basic Books.

Gardner, H. (1999). *Intelligence reframed: Multiple intelligences for the 21st century.* New York, NY: Basic Books.

Gay, G. (1977). Curriculum design for multicultural education. In C.A. Grant (Ed.), *Multicultural education: Commitments, issues, and applications* (pp. 94–104). Washington, DC: Association for Supervision and Curriculum Development.

Gay, G. (2000). *Culturally responsive teaching: Theory, research, & practice.* New York, NY: Teachers College Press.

Gay, G. (2010). *Culturally responsive teaching: Theory, research, and practice.* New York, NY: Teachers College Press.

Gayle-Evans, G., & Michael, D. (2006). A study of pre-service teachers' awareness of multicultural issues. *Multicultural Perspectives, 8*(1), 44–50.

Gollnick, D. M. & Chinn, P. C. (2013). *Multicultural education in a pluralistic society.* (9th ed.). Boston, MA: Pearson Education.

Gurley, G. (2016). The great diversion. *The American Prospect, 27*(2), 54-57.

Hattie, J. (2009). *Visible learning: A synthesis of over 800 meta-analyses relating to achievement.* New York; NY: Routledge.

Hilliard, A. (1974). Restructuring teacher education for multicultural imperatives. In W.A. Hunter (Ed.), *Multicultural education through competency-based teacher education* (pp. 40–55). Washington, DC: American Association of Colleges for Teacher Education.

Hines, M.B. (2007). Ways of reading, ways of seeing: Social justice inquiry in the literature classroom. In K. Kumashiro & B. Ngo (Eds.), *Six lenses for anti-oppressive education* (125–140). New York, NY: Peter Lang.

Hoffman, S. (2014). Why students forget what they've learned and how to increase learning retention. Retrieved from http://www.readinghorizons.com/blog/review-%E2%80%93-is-it-worth-it

Hollins, E. (2016). Achieving equity and excellence in urban schools: What it takes. *Annual Conference of the National Association for Multicultural Education,* Nov. 10.

Hunter, W.A. (1974). Antecedents to development of and emphasis on multicultural education. In W.A. Hunter (Ed.), *Multicultural education through competency-based teacher education* (pp. 11–31). Washington, DC: American Association of Colleges for Teacher Education.

Kagan, S. (2006, Fall). The power to transform race relations. *Teaching Tolerance, 30,* 53.

King, E. & Butler, B. R. (2015). Who cares about diversity? A preliminary investigation of diversity exposure in teacher preparation programs. Multiple Perspectives, 17(1), 46-52.

Kline, Dana M. S. (2016). Can restorative practices help to reduce disparities in school discipline data? A review of the literature. *Multicultural Perspectives,* 18(2), 97-102.

Kneller, G.F. (1971). *Introduction to the philosophy of education* (2nd ed.). New York, NY: Macmillan.

Kraig-Turner, G. (2016-2017). Medical apartheid: Teaching the Tuskegee syphilis study. *Rethinking Schools,* 31(2), 28-33.

Koyama, J. (2014). *Racism 101: Let's talk about diversity and prejudice in America's public schools.* Retrieved from http://www.psmag.com/navigation/books-and-culture/donald-sterling-need-talk-racism-americas-public-schools-81162/

Kumashiro, K. (2010, November). *When race, gender, and sexuality turn queer: Troubling frames by the right to undo public education.* NAME Conference, Las Vegas.

Kuznia, R. (2009). *Racism in schools: Unintentional but no less damaging.* Retrieved from http://www.psmag.com/navigation/books-and-culture/racism-in-schools-unintentional-3821

Ladson-Billings, G. (1995). Toward a theory of culturally relevant pedagogy. *American Educational Research Journal, 32*(3), 465–491.

Micklos Jr., J. (2013). You belong here. *Teaching Tolerance, 45,* 46–48.

Moreno, I., Fenn, L. & Melia, M. (2017, December 14). Charter schools put growing numbers in isolation. *La Crosse Tribune,* A1, A2).

Myrdal, G. (1944). *An American dilemma: The Negro problem and modern democracy.* New York, NY: Harper & Row.

Nieto, S. (2012). Affirming diversity: The sociopolitical context of multicultural education. (6th ed.). Boston, MA: Pearson Education.

Nieto, S. (2008). *Affirming diversity: The sociopolitical context of multicultural education* (5th ed.). Boston, MA: Pearson Allyn & Bacon.

Oakes, J. (2005). *Keeping track: How schools structure inequality* (2nd ed.). New Haven, CT: Yale University Press.

Oakes, J., Quartz, K.H., Ryan, S., & Lipton, M. (2000). *Becoming good American schools: The struggle for civic virtue in school reform.* San Francisco, CA: Jossey-Bass.

O'Connor, J. (2014, February 10). Core questions: How does Common Core address poverty? *State Impact: A reporting project of NPR reporting stations.* Retrieved from http://stateimpact.npr.org.florida.2014/02/10/core-questions-how-does-common-core-address-poverty

Pai, Y., & Adler, S. (1997). *Cultural foundations of education* (2nd ed.). Upper Saddle River, NJ: Merrill Prentice Hall.

Paluck, E.L., & Green, D.P. (2009). Prejudice reduction: What works? A review and assessment of research and practice. *Annual Review of Psychology, 60,* 339–367.

Partridge, E. (1983). *Origins: A short etymological dictionary of modern English* (p. 92). New York, NY: Greenwich.

Piaget, J. (1974). *The language and thought of the child* (Rev. ed.). New York, NY: New American Library.

Ramirez, P. C., & Jimenez-Silva, M. (2015). The intersectionality of culturally responsive teacher and performance poetry: Validating secondary Latino youth and their community. *Multicultural Perspectives, 17*(2), 87-92.

Rich, M. (2014, August 18). Fight on Common Core is dividing Louisiana. *New York Times.* Retrieved from http://www.nytimes.com/2014/08/19/us/fight-on-common-core-id-dividing-louisiana.html?r=0

Richly, L., & Graves, E. (2012). Teacher characteristics for culturally responsive pedagogy. *Multicultural Perspectives, 14*(1), 44–49.

Resmovits, J. (2017). Trump reiterates a common core promise he can't keep and gives L.A. schools a shoutout. *Los Angeles Times*. Retrieved from http://www.latimes.com/local/education/la-essential-education-updates-southern-trump-reiterates-a-common-core-promise-1491330603-htmlstory.html

Roda, A., & Wells, A.S. (2013). School choice policies and racial segregation: Where white parents' good intentions, anxiety, and privilege collide. *American Journal of Education*. *119*(2), 261–293.

Sacks, V. H. (2016). The other achievement gap: Poverty and academic success. Retrieved from https://www.childtrends.org/the-other-achievement-gap-poverty-and-academic-success/

Sheets, R.H. (2005). *Diversity pedagogy: Examining the role of culture in the teaching-learning process*. Boston, MA: Pearson Education.

Sleeter, C.E. (1996). *Multicultural education as social activism*. Albany, NY: State University of New York Press.

Sleeter, C.E. (2010). Culturally responsive teaching: A reflection. *Journal of Praxis in Multicultural Education*, *5*(1), 116–119.

Sleeter, C.E. (2011). *The academic and social value of ethnic studies: A research review*. Washington, DC: National Education Association.

Sleeter, C.E., & Grant, C.A. (2003). *Making choices for multicultural education: Five approaches to race, class, and gender* (4th ed.). New York, NY: John Wiley.

Stanton, C. R. (2015). Beyond the margins: Evaluating the support for multicultural education within teachers' edition of U. S. history textbooks. *Multicultural Perspectives*, *17*(4), 180-189.

Strauss, V. (2013, January 29). A tough critique of Common Core on early childhood education. *The Washington Post*. Retrieved from http://www.washingtonpost.com/blogs/answer-sheet/wp/2013/01/29/a-tough-critique-of-common-core-on-early-childhood-education

Taie, S. & Goldring, R. (2017). Characteristics of public elementary and secondary school teachers in the United States: Results from the 2015-2016 national teacher and principal survey. National Center for Education Statistics. Retrieved from https://nces.ed.gov/pubs2017/2017072.pdf

Tiedt, P.L., & Tiedt, I.M. (2009). *Multicultural teaching: A handbook of activities, information, and resources* (6th ed.). Boston, MA: Pearson.

Toppo, G. (2013). More teachers are grouping kids by ability. USA Today. Retrieved from https://www.usatoday.com/story/news/nation/2013/03/18/elementary-teachers-grouping-reading-ability/1990917/

Ujifusa, A. (2016). Map: Tracking the common core state standards. Education Week. Retrieved from http://www.edweek.org/ew/section/multimedia/map-states-academic-standards-common-core-or.html

Van Galen, J.A. (2013) Learning in the digital age: Control or connection? *Rethinking Schools*, *27*(2), 47–51.

Wells, A. S., Fox, L. & Cordova-Corbo, D. (2016). How racially diverse schools and classrooms can benefit all students. Retrieved from https://tcf.org/content/report/how-racially-diverse-schools-and-classrooms-can-benefit-all-students/

Chapter 14

Alinsky, S. (1969). *Reveille for radicals*. New York, NY: Vintage Books.

Anderson, Melinda. (2015). The value of ethnic studies – for all students, Teaching Tolerance. Retrieved from https://www.tolerance.org/magazine/the-value-of-ethnic-studiesfor-all-students

Anderson, Monica. (2015). The demographics of device ownership. *Pew Research Center*. Retrieved from http://www.pewinternet.org/2015/10/29/the-demographics-of-device-ownership/

Associated Press. (2014, May 30). Google workforce mostly white, male. *La Crosse Tribune*, C8.

Ball, H. (2000). *The Bakke case: Race, education, and affirmative action*. Lawrence, KS: University Press of Kansas.

Becker, L.B., Vlad, T., & Simpson, H.A. (2013). *Annual survey of journalism and mass communication graduates*. Retrieved from http://www.grady.uga.edu/annualsurveys/Enrollment_Survey/Enrollment_2013/2013EnrollCombined.pdf

Berner, A.R. (2012). *The case for educational pluralism*. Retrieved from http://www.firstthings.com/article/2012/12/the-case-for-educational-pluralism

Borowski, T. (1976). This way to the gas, ladies and gentlemen. New York, NY: Penguin Books.

Bouie, J. (2014). *Still separate and unequal*. Retrieved from http://www.slate.com/articles/news_and_politics/politics/2014/05/brown_v_board_of_education_60th_anniversary_america_s_schools_are_segregating.html

Brook, T.V. (2014). Army commanders: White men lead a diverse force. *USA Today*. Retrieved from http://www.usatoday.com/story/news/nation/2014/09/11/army-officer-corps-dominated-by-white-men/14987977

Buckley, G. (2001). *American patriots: The story of blacks in the military from the Revolution to Desert Storm*. New York, NY: Random House.

Burns, C., & Rothman, A. (2012). *The repeal of don't ask, don't tell—1 year later*. Retrieved from http://www.americanprogress.org/issues/lgbt/report/2012/09/20/38764/the-repeal-of-dont-ask-dont-tell-1-year-later

Business Wire. (2017). Exelon joins 150 corporations in an unprecedented commitment to advance diversity and inclusion in the workplace. Retrieved from http://www.cbs8.com/story/35642469/exelon-joins-150-corporations-in-an-unprecedented-commitment-to-advance-diversity-and-inclusion-in-the-workplace

Cassidy, J. (2014). *The hole in the glass ceiling is getting bigger*. Retrieved from http://www.newyorker.com/news/john-cassidy/hole-glass-ceiling-getting-bigger

Cauterucci, C. (2017). Marine's secret trove of nonconsensual nude photos is about power, not sex. Retrieved from http://www.slate.com/blogs/xx_factor/2017/03/06/the_marines_secret_trove_of_nonconsensual_nude_photos_is_about_power_not.html

Chernow, R. (2004). *Alexander Hamilton*. New York, NY: Penguin.

Chideya, F. (2013). *How to fix journalism's class and color crisis*. Retrieved from http://www.thenation.com/article/174351/how-fix-journalisms-class-and-color-crisis#

Chiu, C. L., Sayman, D. and Carrero, K. M. (2017). Developing culturally competent preschool teachers. *Multicultural Perspectives*, 19(1), 47-52.

Colby, S. L. & Ortman, J. M. (2015). Projections of the size and composition of the U. S. population: 2014 to 2060. Retrieved from https://www.census.gov/content/dam/Census/library/publications/2015/demo/p25-1143.pdf

Craft-Fairchild, C. (1997, Fall). Women warriors in the 18th century. *St. Thomas*, 32–35.

Crawford, S. (2013). *Latest Pew study shows 70 percent of U.S. has broadband. But access is still unequal.* Retrieved from http://www.wired.com/2013/08/latest-pew-results-show-digital-divide-and-mobile-paradox-for-u-s-broadband/

Crosby, F.J., & VanDeVeer, C. (Eds.). (2000). *City of Richmond v. J.A. Croson Co.* In *Sex, race, and merit: Debating affirmative action in education and employment* (pp. 280–293). Ann Arbor, MI: University of Michigan Press.

Dansby, M.R., Stewart, J.B., & Webb, S.C. (Eds.). (2001). Overview. In *Managing diversity in the military: Research perspectives from the Defense Equal Opportunity Management Institute* (pp. xvii–xxxii). New Brunswick, NJ: Transaction.

Dao, J. (2011). Black women enlisting at higher rates in U.S. military. *New York Times*. Retrieved from www.nytimes.com/2011/12/23/us/black-women-enlist-at-higher-rates-in-us-military.html

Davis, J. (2017). 175 cases cited in racial discrimination lawsuit against CNN. Retrieved from http://www.westernjournalism.com/175-cases-cited-racial-discrimination-lawsuit-cnn/

Department of Defense. (2015) 2015 demographics: Profile of the military community. http://download.militaryonesource.mil/12038/MOS/Reports/2015-Demographics-Report.pdf

Diamond, J. (2017). Trump to reinstate US military ban on transgender people. CNN. Retrieved from http://www.cnn.com/2017/07/26/politics/trump-military-transgender/index.html

DiversityInc. (2017). The 2017 DiversityInc top 50 companies for diversity. Retrieved from http://www.diversityinc.com/the-diversityinc-top-50-companies-for-diversity-2017/

Donald, B. (2016). Stanford study suggests academic benefits to ethnic studies courses. Retrieved from http://news.stanford.edu/2016/01/12/ethnic-studies-benefits-011216/

Donaldson, L. (2015). When the media misrepresents black men, the effects are felt in the real world. The Guardian. Retrieved from https://www.theguardian.com/commentisfree/2015/aug/12/media-misrepresents-black-men-effects-felt-real-world

Dreazen, Y. (2009). Muslim population in the military raises difficult issues. *Wall Street Journal*. Retrieved from wsj.com/article/SB125755853525335343.html

Equal Opportunity Employment Commission. (2014). *EEOC releases FY 2013 enforcement and litigation data.* Retrieved from http://www.eeoc.gov/eeoc/newsroom/release/2-5-14.cfm

Estes, S. (2007). *Ask & tell: Gay and lesbian veterans speak out.* Chapel Hill, NC: The University of North Carolina Press.

Everett, A. (2012). Have we become postracial yet? Race and media technology in the age of President Obama. In L.

Nakamura & P.A. Chow-White (Eds.), *Race after the Internet* (pp. 146–167). New York, NY: Routledge.

Forsling, C. (2015). Why the military needs diversity. Retrieved from http://taskandpurpose.com/why-the-military-needs-diversity/

Greenberg, J. (2016). 6 reasons I want my white child to take ethnic studies. Retrieved from http://everydayfeminism.com/2016/03/white-child-ethnic-studies/

Greene, K.W. (1989). *Affirmative action and principles of justice.* New York, NY: Greenwood.

Greenwald, J. (2012). *Wal-Mart settles employee's EEOC disability discrimination lawsuit for $50,000.* Retrieved from http://www.workforce.com/articles/wal-mart-settles-employee-s-eeoc-disability-discrimination-lawsuit-for-50-000

Greenwood, B. (2014). *The average cost to hire a new employee.* Retrieved from http://work.chron.com/average-cost-hire-new-employee-13262.html

Gunter, B. (2012). Extremists in the military. *Intelligence Report*, 148, 30–31.

Higginbotham, F.M. (2014). Race-based affirmative action is still needed. *The New York Times.* Retrieved from http://www.nytimes.com/roomfordebate/2014/04/27/should-affirmative-action-be-based-on-income/race-based-affirmative-action-is-still-needed

Humphreys, D. (Ed.). (2000, Fall). National survey finds diversity requirements common around the country, *Diversity Digest*, 1–2.

Hunt, D.M. (2007). Whose stories are we telling? *Writers Guild of America.* Retrieved from http://www.wga.org/uploadedFiles/who_we_are/HWR07.pdf

Hunt, H. Layton, D., and Prince, S. (2015) Why diversity matters. Retrieved from http://www.mckinsey.com/business-functions/organization/our-insights/why-diversity-matters

Hurst, A. (2015). How PwC's Tim Ryan creates trust-based leadership. Fast Company. Retrieved from https://www.fastcompany.com/40417229/how-pwcs-tim-ryan-creates-trust-based-leadership

Hymowitz, C. (2005, November 14). The new diversity. *Wall Street Journal*, R1, R3.

IBM. (2015). *Workforce diversity*. Retrieved from http://www-07.ibm.com/ibm/au/corporateresponsibility/pdfs/GL_9833_diversity_nocov.08.pdf

Imparato, A.J., Houtenville, A.J., & Shaffert, R.L. (2010). *Increasing the employment rate of people with disabilities.* Retrieved from http://www.google.com/search?q=Increasing+the+employment+rate+of+people+with+disabilities&ie=utf-8&oe=utf-8&aq=t&rls=org.mozilla:en-US:official&client=firefox-a

Jenkins, H. (2006, October 16). White Paper—Confronting the challenges of participatory culture: Media education for the 21st Century. *The MacArthur Foundation.* Retrieved from www.digitallearning.macfound.org

Johnson, D. (1999). The U.S. Army and ethnic diversity: A historical overview. In L.J. Matthews & T. Pavri (Eds.), *Population diversity and the U.S. Army* (pp. 45–56). Carlisle, PA: Strategic Studies Institute.

Johnson, M.T. (2011). *The diversity code*. New York, NY: AMACOM.

Kabbany, J. (2014). *Study: Most colleges don't require history, economics—yet mandate diversity lessons*. Retrieved from http://www.thecollegefix.com/post/19736

Kahlenberg, R.D., & Potter, H. (2014). Class-based affirmative action works. *New York Times*. Retrieved from http://www.nytimes.com/roomfordebate/2014/04/27/should-affirmative-action-be-based-on-income/class-based-affirmative-action-works

Kasinov, L. (2013). Women, war and PTSD. *Washington Monthly*, 45(11/12), 18–23.

Katzenstein, M.F., & Reppy, J. (Eds.). (1999). Introduction: Rethinking military culture. In *Beyond zero tolerance: Discrimination in military culture* (pp. 1–21). Lanham, MD: Rowman & Littlefield.

Kawamoto, K. (2003). *Media and society in the digital age*. Boston, MA: Allyn & Bacon.

Kier, E. (1999). Discrimination and military cohesion: An organizational perspective. In M.F. Katzenstein & J. Reppy (Eds.), *Beyond zero tolerance: Discrimination in military culture* (pp. 25–32). Lanham, MD: Rowman & Littlefield.

Kiley, K. (2011). *Decline of "Western Civ"?* Retrieved from https://www.insidehighered.com/news/2011/05/19/national_association_of_scholars_report_finds_no_mandatory_western_civilization_courses_at_top_universities

Kuttner, R. (2017). Corporate America and Donald Trump. *The American Prospect*, 28(2), 9-12.

Lee, E. (2017). Can ethnic studies education change academic outcomes for minority students? Retrieved from https://psmag.com/news/can-ethnic-studies-education-change-academic-outcomes-for-minority-students

Liptak, A. (2014). Court backs Michigan on affirmative action. *The New York Times*. Retrieved from http://www.nytimes.com/2014/04/23/us/supreme-court-michigan-affirmative-action-ban.html

Liptak, A. (2015). Muslim woman denied job over head scarf wins in Supreme Court. *New York Times*. Retrieved from http://www.nytimes.com/2015/06/02/us/supreme-court-rules-in-samantha-elauf-abercrombie-fitch-case.html

Lucas, S. (2012). *How much does it cost companies to lose employees?* Retrieved from http://www.cbsnews.com/news/how-much-does-it-cost-companies-to-lose-employees

Luther, C.A., Lepre, C.R., & Clark, N. (2012). *Diversity in U.S. mass media*. Malden, MA: Wiley-Blackwell.

Luttig, M. D. and Cohen, C. J. (2016). How social media helps young people – especially minorities and the poor – get politically engaged. The Washington Post. Retrieved from https://www.washingtonpost.com/news/monkey-cage/wp/2016/09/09/how-social-media-helps-young-people-especially-minorities-and-the-poor-get-politically-engaged/?utm_term=.f6443932ed60

Lynch, M. (2013). *It's tough to trailblaze: Challenges of first-generation college students*. Retrieved from http://diverseeducation.com/article/50898

May, C. (2011). *Abercrombie & Fitch faces another diversity lawsuit*. Retrieved from http://dailycaller.com/2011/06/27/abercrombie-fitch-faces-another-diversity-lawsuit

McCall, A. (2013). *U.S. Army marksmanship unit—the best of the best*. Retrieved from http://armylive.dodlive.mil/index.php/2013/01/u-s-army-marksmanship-unit-the-best-of-the-best

Merica, D. (2017). Trump privately signs anti-Planned Parenthood law. CNN. Retrieved from http://www.cnn.com/2017/04/13/politics/donald-trump-planned-parenthood-money/index.html

Moskos, C.C., & Butler, J.S. (1996). *All that we can be: Black leadership and racial integration in the army*. New York, NY: Basic Books.

Muhammad, D. (2013). *Workplace discrimination*. Retrieved from http://www.huffingtonpost.com/dedrick-muhammad/workplace-discrimination_b_3459315.html

Musil, C.M. (1996, November/December). The maturing diversity initiatives on American campuses. *American Behavioral Scientist*, 40(2), 222–232.

National Center for Education Statistics. (2015). Fast Facts. Retrieved from https://nces.ed.gov/fastfacts/display.asp?id=61

National Center for Education Statistics (2017). The condition of education, 2017 (NCES 2017-144), Status dropout rates. Retrieved from https://nces.ed.gov/fastfacts/display.asp?id=16

Nelson, L. (2014) https://www.vox.com/2014/4/4/5579150/youre-imagining-the-typical-college-student-wrong

New York Times. (2012, June 4). Women in combat. A24.

Nittle, N.K. (2014). *Top companies hit with racial discrimination suits*. Retrieved from http://racerelations.about.com/od/theworkplace/tp/Top-Companies-Hit-With-Racial-Discrimination-Suits.htm

Nobscott Corporation. (2014). *Potential savings for reducing employee turnover*. Retrieved from http://www.nobscot.com/library/co_stats.cfm

Patten, E., & Parker, K. (2011). *Women in the U.S military: Growing share, distinctive profile*. Retrieved from www.pewsocialtrends.org/2011/12/222/women-in-th-u-s-military-growing-share-distinctive-profile/2/#active-duty-women

Peterson, M.J. (1999). Women in the U.S. military. In L.J. Matthews & T. Pavri (Eds.), *Population diversity and the U.S. Army* (pp. 99–106). Carlisle, PA: Strategic Studies Institute.

Pizzo, L. (2015). Uncovering surprises in the labor market's gender, age, and race composition. Retrieved from http://www.economicmodeling.com/2015/03/31/uncovering-surprises-in-the-labor-markets-gender-age-and-race-composition/

Reddy, M.T. (2002). Smashing the rules of racial standing. In B. Tusmith & M.T. Reddy (Eds.), *Race in the college classroom: Pedagogy and politics* (pp. 51–61). New Brunswick, NJ: Rutgers University Press.

Reskin, B.F. (2000). The realities of affirmative action in employment. In F.J. Crosby & C. VanDeVeer (Eds.), *Sex, race, and merit: Debating affirmative action in education and employment* (pp. 103–113). Ann Arbor: University of Michigan Press.

Roush, P.E. (1999). A tangled Webb the Navy can't afford. In M.F. Katzenstein & J. Reppy (Eds.), *Beyond zero tolerance: Discrimination in military culture* (pp. 81–100). Lanham, MD: Rowman & Littlefield.

Royal, D. and Swift, A. (2016). U. S. minority students less exposed to computer science. *Gallup*. Retrieved from http://www.gallup.com/poll/196307/minority-students-less-exposed-computer-science.aspx

Sleeter, C. (2011). *The academic and social value of ethnic studies: A research review*. Washington, DC: National Education Association.

Smith, S. (2017). U. S. Army weight charts. Retrieved from https://www.thebalance.com/weight-charts-3344603

Smith, S.E. (2014). *The Pentagon takes on transgender troops*. Retrieved from http://www.care2.com/causes/the-pentagon-takes-on-transgender-troops.html

Statista. (2017). Journalism: Statistics and facts. Retrieved from https://www.statista.com/topics/2096/journalism/

Sue, D. W. (2015). *Race talk and the conspiracy of silence*. Hoboken, NJ: John Wiley & Sons.

Sullivan, G. (2014). *Goldman Sachs, Tinder slapped with sex discrimination lawsuits*. Retrieved from http://www.washingtonpost.com/news/morning-mix/wp/2014/07/02/goldman-sachs-tinder-slapped-with-sex-discrimination-lawsuits

Thomaston, S. (2014). *Gay employee's discrimination lawsuit can proceed, judge rules*. Retrieved from http://equalityontrial.com/2014/04/03/gay-employees-discrimination-lawsuit-can-proceed-judge-rules/

University Alliance. (2014). *The value of diversity training*. Retrieved from http://www.notredameonline.com/resources/intercultural-management/the-value-of-diversity-training/#.VElXeefmaM4

U.S. Bureau of Labor Statistics. (2017). Labor force statistics from current population survey. Retrieved from https://www.bls.gov/cps/cpsaat11.htm

U.S. Department of Defense. (2010). *Population representation in the military services*. Retrieved from http://prhome.defense.gov/RFM/MPP/ACCESSIONPOLICY/PopRep2010/contents/contents.html

U.S. Department of Labor. (2014). *Accommodations*. Retrieved from: http://www.dol.gov/odep/topics/Accommodations.htm

Van Galen, J.A. (2013) Learning in the digital age: Control or connection? *Rethinking Schools*, 27(2), 47–51.

Vuong, A. (2013). *The role of people of color in the future workforce*. Retrieved from http://www.americanprogress.org/issues/immigration/news/2013/10/25/77924/the-role-of-people-of-color-in-the-future-workforce/

Waldron, T. (2013). *The leading driver of diversity in sports journalism? It's ESPN*. Retrieved from http://thinkprogress.org/alyssa/2013/02/26/1643281/diversity-sports-journalism-espn

Walter, E. (2012). *The top 30 stats you need to know when marketing to women*. Retrieved from http://thenextweb.com/socialmedia/2012/01/24/the-top-30-stats-you-need-to-know-when-marketing-to-women

Wells, A. S., Fox, L. & Cordova-Corbo, D. (2016). How racially diverse schools and classrooms can benefit all students. Retrieved from https://tcf.org/content/report/how-racially-diverse-schools-and-classrooms-can-benefit-all-students/

Williams, A. T. (2016). Employment picture darkens for journalists at digital outlets. Retrieved from https://www.cjr.org/business_of_news/journalism_jobs_digital_decline.php

Williams, M. (2017). Facebook diversity update: Building a more diverse inclusive workforce. Retrieved from https://newsroom.fb.com/news/2017/08/facebook-diversity-update-building-a-more-diverse-inclusive-workforce/

Wing, N. (2014). *When the media treats white suspects and killers better than black victims*. Retrieved from http://www.huffingtonpost.com/2014/08/14/media-black-victims_n_5673291.html

WorldTribune.com. (2014). *Obama administration tracking Muslim candidates for military positions*. Retrieved from http://www.worldtribune.com/2014/07/09/obama-looking-muslim-candidates-military-pentagon-positions/

Writer's Guild of America (2015). WGAW 2015 TV staffing brief. Retrieved from http://www.wga.org/uploadedFiles/who_we_are/tvstaffingbrief2015.pdf

Zeigler, S.L., & Gunderson, G.G. (2005). *Moving beyond G. I. Jane: Women and the U.S. military*. Lanham, MD: University Press of America.

Index

A

AAUW (American Association of University Women), 257

Abbott v. Burke, 233

Abercrombie & Fitch, 349

ABLE (Achieving a Better Life Experience) Act, 303

Ableism
cultural, 289–292
defined, 288
disability rights, 289
individual, 294–297
institutional, 297–310

Abrams, Creighton, 358

Abuse
of people with disabilities, 300
of women, 248–250. *See also* Rape

ACA (Affordable Care Act), 195, 225, 300

Academic achievement
adoption and, 213
in charter schools, 318
disparity in, 327
gender economic disparity and, 253
gender equity issues and, 258–260
individual, emphasis on, 325, 329
poverty and, 213–214
research on, 214
school closures and, 192
self-confidence and, 321

Accessibility, for people with disabilities, 304–306

ACE (Averse Childhood Experiences), 213

Achievement gap, 327, 328. *See also* Academic achievement

Achieving a Better Life Experience (ABLE) Act, 303

Acquired immunodeficiency syndrome (AIDS), 170, 268–269

ADA (Americans with Disabilities Act), 288, 304, 305

Adams, John, 2, 70, 173

ADC (Aid to Dependent Children), 224

Addams, Jane, 74

Adequate Yearly Progress (AYP) benchmarks, 214

ADHD (Attention Deficit Hyperactivity Disorder), 296

Adoption, 206
academic achievement and, 213

AFA (Air Force Academy), 359

AFDC (Aid to Families with Dependent Children), 224 *See also* TANF (Transitional Assistance for Needy Families)

Affirmative action programs
in business, 343, 347–352
federal government and, 341–344
future, 343–344
in higher education, 342–344
judicial limitations on, 342–343
for minority-owned businesses, 343
quotas and, 342–343
race and, 185, 188, 196–197

"Affluenza," 4

Affordable Care Act (ACA), 195, 225, 300

Affordable housing, 234

AFL (American Federation of Labor), 124

African Americans, 106–116
affirmative action programs and, 185, 188, 196–197
after World War I, 113–114
after World War II, 114–115
"black" identity and, 14–15
body image and, 246
Civil Rights Movement and, 115–116
digital media and, 355–356
as indentured servants, 107
intellectual disability diagnosis among, 296
Internet use by, 356
migrating to northern cities, 111–112
neighborhood segregation and, 191–192
and New Deal programs, 113–114
as New World explorers, 106
politics and, 193–194
portrayal in media, 353–354
purchasing power, 348
racial profiling, 36
as Revolutionary War soldiers, 108
separatism and, 166
as slaves, 107–108
white beliefs about, 185–186
during the World Wars, 113, 114

AGE (Americans for Generational Equity), 226

Agee, James, 319

Ageism, 225–228
defined, 226
economic consequences, 229–230

institutionalization, 228
manifestations, 226–228
women and, 230, 246

Agnosticism, 145

Aid to Dependent Children (ADC), 224

Aid to Families with Dependent Children (AFDC), 224 *See also* Transitional Assistance for Needy Families (TANF)

AIDS (acquired immunodeficiency syndrome), 170, 268–269

Air Force Academy (AFA), 359

Al-Baghdadi, 152

Albany Plan, 98

Alcohol abuse, poverty and, 207

Alexander the Great, 281, 267

Alexei, Sherman, 99

Alien Land Laws (1913, 1920), 119

Alinsky, Saul, 346

Allport, Gordon, 190

Alvarado, Pedro, 106

AMA (American Medical Association), homosexuality and, 265–266

American Academy of Pediatrics, 280

American Association of University Women (AAUW), 257

American culture, values defining, 3–4

American Federation of Labor (AFL), 124

American Medical Association (AMA), homosexuality and, 265–266

American Party, 72

American Psychological Association (APA)
homosexuality and, 265
mental retardation and, 296
nonsexist language recommended by, 244
PTSD and, 360

American Sign Language (ASL), 293

Americanization
of immigrants, 73
of Native Americans, 163–164
of religion, 145, 148

Americans for Generational Equity (AGE), 226

Americans with Disabilities Act (ADA), 288, 304, 305

AmeriCorps, 209

Anabaptists, 136